lonely planet

Taiwan

THIS EDITION WRITTEN AND RESEARCHED BY

Robert Kelly
Chung Wah Chow

PLAN YOUR TRIP

ON THE ROAD

MOSON KUO/GETTY IMAGES ©

YUNLIN COUNTY, P227

CRAIG FERGUSON/GETTY IMAGES ©

NIGHT MARKET, P46

RICHARD I'ANSON/GETTY IMAGES ©

Contents

BAO'AN TEMPLE (P65), TAIPEI

ON THE ROAD

CRAIG FERGUSON/GETTY IMAGES ©

TAIPEI, P52

CHENG JUNG KUO/GETTY IMAGES ©

SIKA DEER

Contents

UNDERSTAND

SURVIVAL GUIDE

SPECIAL FEATURES

Welcome to Taiwan

With its all-round adventure landscape, heritage-rich capital, diverse folk traditions and feted night market scene, Taiwan offers a continent-sized travel list for one green island.

The Beautiful Isle

Famed for centuries as Ilha Formosa (Beautiful Isle), this is a land with more faces than the 11-headed Guanyin. Towering sea cliffs, marble-walled gorges and tropical forests are just the start of your journey, which could take you as far as Yushan, Taiwan's 3952m alpine roof.

In Taiwan you can criss-cross mountains on colonial-era hiking trails or cycle a lone highway with the blue Pacific on one side and green volcanic arcs on the other. And if you simply want a classic landscape to enjoy, you'll find them around every corner.

Have You Eaten?

The words are used as a greeting here, and the answer is always 'yes', as there's just too much nibbling to do. Taiwan offers the gamut of Chinese cuisines, as well as the best Japanese outside Tokyo, and a full-house of local specialities from Hakka stir-fries and Taipei beef noodles to aboriginal-style barbecued wild boar. Night markets around the island serve endless feasts of snacks including stinky tofu, steamed dumplings, oyster omelettes, shrimp rolls and shaved ice. And when you're thirsty you can look forward to fresh local juices, outstanding Taiwan teas and, in a surprising twist, Asia's best gourmet coffee.

Asian Values on Their Terms

Defying those who said it wasn't in their DNA, the Taiwanese have created Asia's most vibrant democracy, and liberal society, with a raucous free press, gender equality and respect for human rights and increasingly animal rights as well. The ancestors are still worshipped, and mum and dad still get their dues, but woe befall the politician who thinks it's the people who must pander, and not him. If you want to catch a glimpse of the people's passion for protest, check out Taipei Main Station on most weekends, or just follow the local news.

The Tao of Today

Taiwan is heir to the entire Chinese tradition of Buddhism, Taoism, Confucianism and that amorphous collection of deities and demons worshipped as folk faith. But over the centuries the people have blended their way to a unique and tolerant religious culture that's often as ritual-heavy as Catholicism and as wild as Santeria.

Taiwanese temples (all 15,000) combine worship hall, festival venue and art house under one roof. Watch a plague boat burn at Donglong Temple, go on a pilgrimage with the Empress of Heaven, study a rooftop three-dimensional mosaic, and learn why a flag and ball have come to represent prayer.

Why I Love Taiwan

By Robert Kelly, Author

I have been living in Taiwan for the past 17 years and when I wake up in the morning I still wonder how I can possibly find time for all the new passions I've developed here: go cycling or hike in the lush mountains in my Taipei neighbourhood? Visit a traditional temple and study historical allusions in yet another sculptured masterpiece? Try a new strain of organic tea or single-origin coffee? Improve my Mandarin? Or just catch the latest mass rally downtown of locals trying to make this a better place? I love that Taiwan gives me the freedom to go anywhere, do anything, and that no matter what I delve into, I'm always rewarded for going deeper.

For more about our authors, see page 400

Above: Xingtian Temple (p69), Taipei

Taiwan

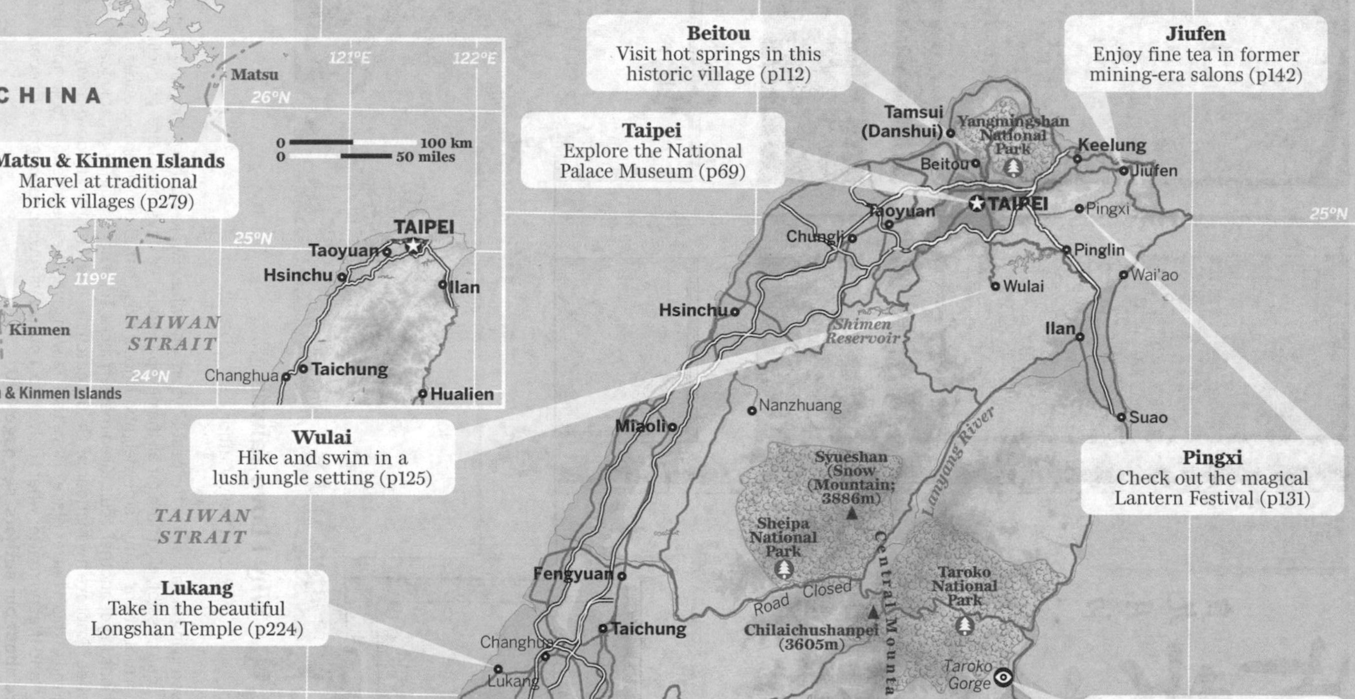

0 50 km
0 25 miles
121°E
122°E
25°N
24°N
Beitou
Visit hot springs in this historic village (p112)
Jiufen
Enjoy fine tea in former mining-era salons (p142)
Taipei
Explore the National Palace Museum (p69)
Matsu & Kinmen Islands
Marvel at traditional brick villages (p279)
Wulai
Hike and swim in a lush jungle setting (p125)
Pingxi
Check out the magical Lantern Festival (p131)
Lukang
Take in the beautiful Longshan Temple (p224)
Taroko Gorge
Don't miss this marble-walled top draw (p179)
Sun Moon Lake
Do the lake circuit on a bike (p229)
CHINA
Matsu
Kinmen
26°N
119°E
0 100 km
0 50 miles
TAIWAN STRAIT
Matsu & Kinmen Islands
TAIPEI
Taoyuan
Hsinchu
Ilan
Changhua
Taichung
Hualien
Tamsui (Danshui)
Yangmingshan National Park
Beitou
Keelung
Jiufen
Pingxi
Pinglin
Wai'ao
Wulai
Chungli
Shimen Reservoir
Nanzhuang
Miaoli
Suao
Lanyang River
Syueshan (Snow Mountain; 3886m)
Sheipa National Park
Central Mountain Range
Taroko National Park
Road Closed
Fengyuan
Chilaichushanpei (3605m)
Taroko Gorge
Lukang
Caotun
Puli
Nenggaoshan (3349m)
Sun Moon Lake
Shuili

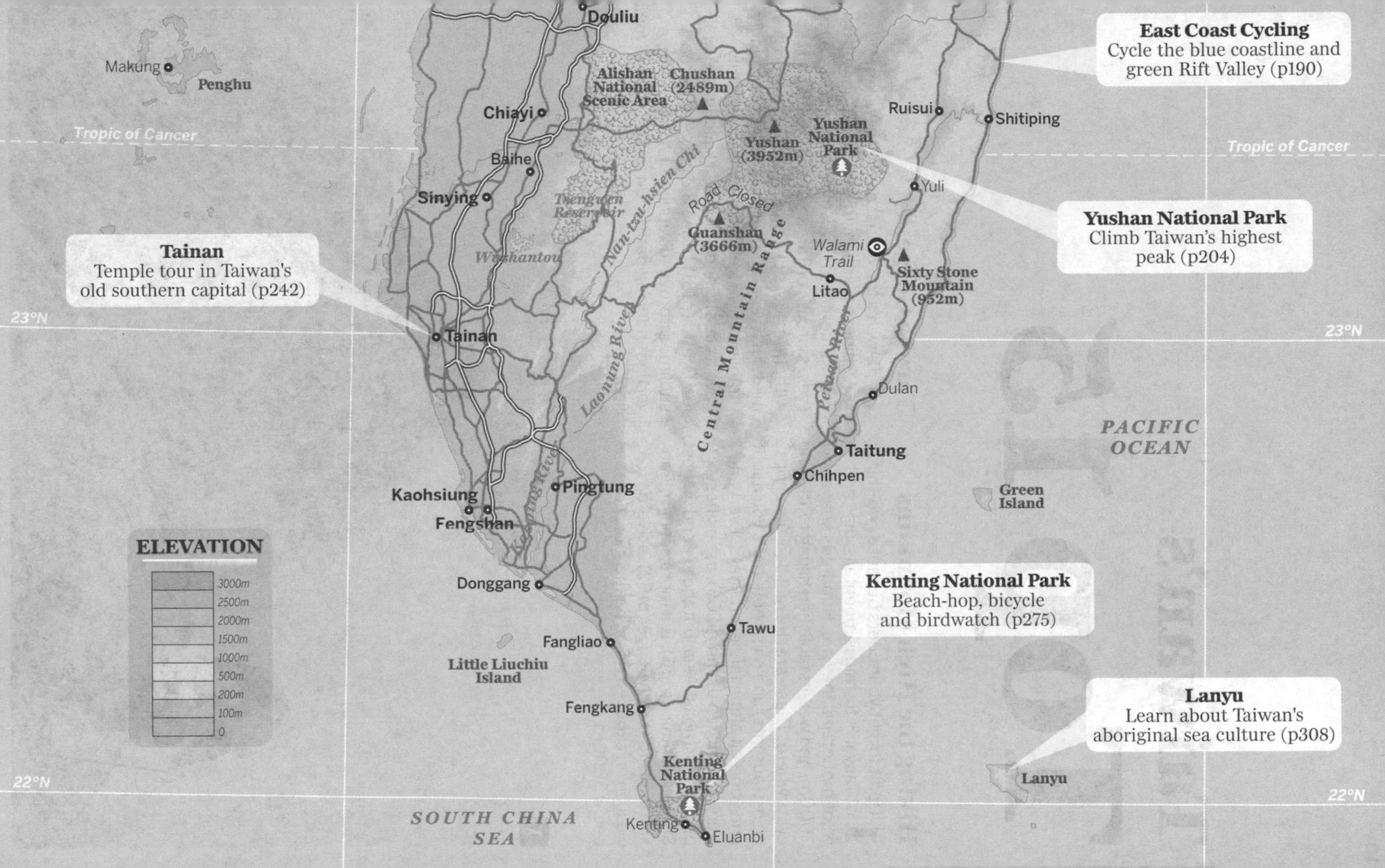
East Coast Cycling
Cycle the blue coastline and green Rift Valley (p190)
Yushan National Park
Climb Taiwan's highest peak (p204)
Tainan
Temple tour in Taiwan's old southern capital (p242)
Kenting National Park
Beach-hop, bicycle and birdwatch (p275)
Lanyu
Learn about Taiwan's aboriginal sea culture (p308)
Makung
Penghu
Tropic of Cancer
Douliu
Chiayi
Baihe
Sinying
Tainan
Kaohsiung
Fengshan
Pingtung
Donggang
Fangliao
Fengkang
Kenting
Eluanbi
Kenting National Park
Little Liuchiu Island
Alishan National Scenic Area
Chushan (2489m)
Yushan (3952m)
Yushan National Park
Ruisui
Shitiping
Yuli
Road Closed
Guanshan (3666m)
Nan-tzu-hsien Chi
Laonung River
Central Mountain Range
Walami Trail
Litao
Sixty Stone Mountain (952m)
Dulan
Taitung
Chihpen
Tawu
Green Island
Lanyu
PACIFIC OCEAN
SOUTH CHINA SEA
23°N
22°N
ELEVATION
3000m
2500m
2000m
1500m
1000m
500m
200m
100m
0

Taiwan's Top 15

Hiking the High Mountains

1 Don't forget your boots because two-thirds of Taiwan's terrain is mountainous – and what mountains they are. Hundreds soar above 3000m, and well-established hiking routes run everywhere. These are the real deal (no shops, no restaurants) and on remote trails you might find yourself alone for several days. Everyone wants to tackle Yushan (p205), the highest peak in Northeast Asia, but the second highest, Snow Mountain (p156), is a more scenic climb and leads to O'Holy Ridge (p157), a five-day walk on an exposed ridgeline that never drops below 3000m. Below: Hiking on O'Holy Ridge

Taroko Gorge

2 Taiwan's top tourist draw is a walk-in Chinese painting. Rising above the froth of the blue-green Liwu River, the marble walls (yes, marble!) of Taroko Gorge (p179) swirl with the colours of a master's palette. Add grey mist, lush vegetation and waterfalls seemingly tumbling down from heaven, and you truly have a classic landscape. Walk along the Swallow Grotto (p181) to see the gorge at its most sublime or brave the Jhuilu Old Trail (p181), a vertigo-inducing path 500m above the canyon floor.

1

2

National Palace Museum

3 By a pure accident of history, Taiwan houses the greatest collection of Chinese art in the world. With ancient pottery, bronzes and jade, Ming vases, Song landscape paintings and calligraphy even a foreign eye can appreciate, Taipei's National Palace Museum (p69) isn't merely a must-visit, it's a must-repeat-visit. Why? Out of the nearly 700,000 pieces in the museum's collection – pieces spanning every Chinese dynasty – only a tiny fraction is ever on display at the one time.

Cycling the East Coast

4 Cycling fever has taken over the island, and the unspoiled and sparsely populated east coast has emerged as the top destination for multiday trips. Like the sea? Then ride Highway 11 (p185), with its stunning coastline, beaches, fishing harbours and funky art villages. Love the mountains? Try the Rift Valley (p190), bounded on each side by lush green ranges. On both routes there are enough roadside cafes, campgrounds, homestays and hot springs to ensure your cycling trip won't be an exercise in logistics.

3

IMAGEMORE CO, LTD./GETTY IMAGES ©

4

5

6

Temple Treasures

5 There are 15,000 official temples in Taiwan, three times the number of 30 years ago. Still the focus of local culture, temples play the role of community centres as much as houses of worship. Both Tainan and Lukang boast a wealth of old buildings, from understated Confucius temples to Matsu temples rich in examples of southern folk decorative arts. But if you can only visit one temple in Taiwan, head to Bao'an Temple (p65) in Taipei, a showcase of traditional design, rites and festivities. Top: Longshan Temple, Lukang (p224)

Sun Moon Lake National Scenic Area

6 Sun Moon Lake is the largest body of water in Taiwan and boasts a watercolour-like background that's ever changing with season and light. The area is packed with tour groups but it's easy to escape the crowds on the trails, cycling paths and village cafes. For diverse fun, loop down to the old train depot at Checheng (p235) or visit the Chung Tai Chan monastery (p232) in nearby Puli. No matter what, don't miss the region's high-mountain oolong tea: it's some of the finest in the world.

PHILIP GAME/GETTY IMAGES ©

The Teas of Taiwan

7 Boasting good soil, humid conditions and sunny weather, Taiwan is a prime tea-growing area. High-mountain oolongs will blow your taste buds away with their creamy texture and honey flavour (and that's without milk or sugar, of course). The fruity aroma of Oriental Beauty tea might just convince you to make it your new 'coffee'. Whether you brew it old-man style or in Song dynasty bowls, you'll find a teahouse to your tastes in scenic areas such as Maokong (p117) or the old gold-mining town of Jiufen (p140).

Jungle Treks & River Swims

8 Taiwan is 50% forested and the urban jungle gives way to the real thing quickly. In the mountainous Wulai township (p124), 30 minutes from Taipei, old aboriginal hunting trails cut through tropical forests. Monkeys chatter in the trees, lizards peek out from the underbrush and a host of native birds and butterflies flutter about. Take a break from your trek to enjoy crystal-clear streams and deep swimming pools. Paradise? You bet, and you can repeat this experience all over the island. Above right: Hiking on Walami Trail (p195)

The Birds & the Butterflies

9 Taiwan is a special place for winged creatures (p227). More than 500 species of birds and an almost equal number of butterflies live here, with a very high percentage of them found nowhere else. Habitats are well preserved and you don't need to trek into the jungle for a glimpse. Indigenous species like the long-tailed blue magpie can be spotted on the edge of Taipei; raptor migrations can be seen from parking lots in Kenting National Park; and in this Kingdom of Butterflies, the Lepidoptera will probably find you first. Above right: Red-base Jezebel

9

The Magic Lights of Lantern Festival

10 One of the oldest of the lunar events, the Lantern Festival celebrates the end of the New Year's festivities. The focus, of course, is light, and everywhere streets and riversides are lined with glowing lanterns, while giant neon and laser displays fill public squares. Making the mundane surreal and the commonplace magical, the little mountain village of Pingxi (p131) takes simple paper lanterns and releases them en masse into the night sky. There are few sights more mesmerising.

CRAIG FERGUSON/GETTY IMAGES ©

A Stationary Feast: Night Markets

11 Taiwan's night markets are as numerous as they are varied. Fulfilling the need for food, entertainment and socialising, the markets bring happy crowds almost every night of the week to gorge on a bewildering array of snacks and dishes. Check out the Miaokou Night Market (p139) in Keelung, in many ways the granddaddy of them all, for the quintessential experience of food and people-watching. The night market snacks in Tainan are copied everywhere but best enjoyed on their home turf.

The Matsu Pilgrimage

12 This mother of all walks across Taiwan is, appropriately enough, dedicated to Matsu ('old granny'), the maternal patron deity of the island. For nine days and 350km, hundreds of thousands of the faithful follow a revered statue of Matsu across Taiwan (p212), while several million more participate in local events. This is Taiwan's folk culture at its most exuberant and festive, with crowds, wild displays of devotion, theatrical performances and a whole lot of fireworks.

11

12

Aboriginal Taiwan

13 Though long suppressed, tribal culture and pride has made a remarkable turnaround in the past decade. Gain an understanding at the Shung Ye Museum of Formosan Aborigines (p71) in Taipei, then check into a homestay run by Yami islanders on Lanyu during the Flying Fish Season. Or visit the communally run Smangus, a high-mountain centre of Atayal culture and language. In the summer, head to the east coast for exuberant festivals celebrating harvests, coming of age and a deep love of live music. Above: Aboriginal musicians

Hot Springs: Wild & Tamed

14 Formed by the collision of two major tectonic plates, Taiwan's surface has plenty of fissures and an abundance of hot springs. The waters are considered effective for everything from soothing muscles to conceiving male offspring (we can only vouch for the former). Nature lovers heading to hot springs in Beitou (p111) and Taian (p165) will find them a double happiness: stone, wood and marble are in these days, as are mountain views. And if you're willing to walk in, many pristine wild springs still lie deep in the valleys, such as Lisong Hot Spring (p201).

The Cold War Frontiers: Matsu & Kinmen Islands

15 Close enough to see China even on a hazy day, Matsu and Kinmen Islands were long the front lines in the propaganda (and occasional real) wars between the nationalists and communists. These days, with the military presence scaling down, travellers are discovering islands whose rich history is not limited to recent times – Matsu (p290) and Kinmen (p281) are treasure troves of preserved old villages. Visitors will also find some fine cycling and birdwatching among the varied landscapes. Above: Cinbi Village, Matsu (p296)

Need to Know

For more information, see Survival Guide (p367)

Currency

New Taiwanese dollar (NT$)

Language

Mandarin and Taiwanese

Money

ATMs and banks widely available. Credit cards accepted in most mid- to top-range hotels (but few B&Bs) and better restaurants.

Visas

Generally not required for stays of up to 90 days (see p377).

Mobile Phones

Local SIM cards can be used in mobile phones from most countries. Purchase local SIM cards at the airport. Cheap mobile-phone rentals are also available at the airport.

Time

Taiwan is GMT plus eight hours, the same as Hong Kong and Singapore.

When to Go

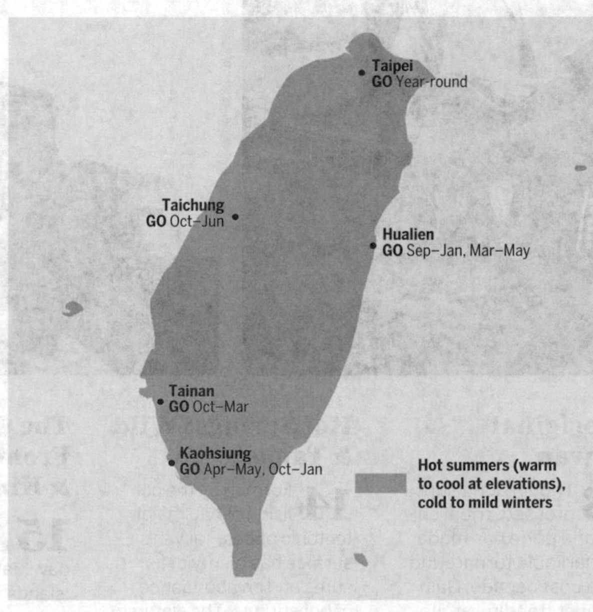

High Season

(Jul & Aug)

- Accommodation costs increase 30% to 50% in tourist areas.
- Saturday nights (year-round) and Chinese New Year also see increases.

Shoulder

(Sep & Oct, Apr–Jun)

- Good discounts on accommodation midweek.
- Crowds at major sights on weekends.
- Best time to visit outer islands.
- Peak time for Chinese tour groups from March to May.

Low Season

(Nov–Mar)

- Few crowds except during January and Chinese New Year.
- Best discounts on accommodation at major tourist sights (up to 50%).
- Saturday-night rates may still be high-season prices.
- High season for hot spring hotels.

Websites

Forumosa (www.forumosa.com) Expat community site.

Information for Foreigners (http://iff.immigration.gov.tw) Visa regulations and daily life matters.

Lonely Planet (www.lonelyplanet.com) Visit the Thorn Tree forum for updates from fellow Lonely Planet readers.

Taiwanease (www.taiwanease.com) Expat community site, covering family-related matters, restaurants and nightlife.

The View from Taiwan (http://michaelturton.blogspot.com) Local political and cultural coverage, plus weekly bike trips.

Important Numbers

When calling local long-distance numbers, the '0' in the area codes is used. When dialling from overseas it's dropped.

Emergency	☎119
Country code	☎886
International access code	☎002
Taipei area code	☎02
24-hour tourism hot line	☎0800-011 765

Exchange Rates

Australia	A$1	NT$28.37
Europe	€1	NT$40.19
Japan	¥100	NT$29.68
Malaysia	MYR1	NT$9.24
Singapore	SGD1	NT$23.68
UK	UK£1	NT$47.41
US	US$1	NT$29.91

For current exchange rates see www.xe.com.

Daily Costs

Budget: NT$1800–2500

- ➡ Dorm bed: NT$400–700
- ➡ Tourism Shuttle Buses: day pass NT$50–100
- ➡ MRT: average ride NT$30
- ➡ Decent coffee: per cup NT$30–60
- ➡ Multiday bike rental: per day NT$300–400
- ➡ Steamer of dumplings: NT$80–120
- ➡ Taiwan beer can from convenience store: NT$40
- ➡ Admission to temples: free

Midrange: NT$2500–5000

- ➡ Double room in a hotel or B&B: NT$1400–2600
- ➡ Lunch or dinner at a decent local restaurant: NT$250–500
- ➡ Scooter/car rental: per day NT$300–600/1800–2400
- ➡ Short taxi trip: NT$140
- ➡ Gourmet coffee: per cup NT$180–260
- ➡ Soak in a private hot-spring room: per 90 minutes NT$1000–1400
- ➡ Good bowl of beef noodles: NT$180
- ➡ Beer at a decent pub or bar: NT$120–220

Top End: More than NT$5000

- ➡ Double room at four-star hotel: NT$4000–6000
- ➡ Hotel restaurant meals: NT$500–1200
- ➡ Ecotour guide: per day NT$4000–6000
- ➡ Well-made tea pot: NT$3000–8000
- ➡ Cocktail at a good bar: NT$280–350

Opening Hours

Banks 9am-3.30pm Monday to Friday

Night markets 6pm-midnight

Cafes 11am-9pm

Bars & clubs 10pm-4am; many bars open earlier for dinner

Restaurants 11.30am-2pm and 5-9pm

Shops 10am-9pm

Arriving in Taiwan

Taiwan Taoyuan International Airport (p378) Buses run every 15 minutes to the city (NT$115–150) from 4.30am to 12.20am. A taxi (40 to 60 minutes) to the city costs NT$1200 to NT$1400.

Kaohsiung International Airport (www.kia.gov.tw) MRT trains leave every six minutes from 6am to midnight (NT$35). A taxi costs NT$350 to downtown.

Getting Around

Transport is reasonably priced and covers most of the country. In mountain areas and outer islands your own transport is best.

Train Trains service the north and both coasts; High Speed Rail down the west serves the main cities. Four small tourism branch lines extend into the interior.

Scooter & Car Useful for touring at your own pace, staying at B&Bs, and exploring national parks and Taiwan's scenic backcountry. Rentals widely available. Drive on the right.

Bus Routes connect most north, south and west coast towns, cities and major tourist sights. Fewer routes on the east coast.

Tourism Shuttle Buses (www.taiwantrip.com.tw) cover hard to get to sites and regions.

For much more on **getting around**, see p379

If You Like...

Outdoor Activities

Hiking is outstanding and scenic cycling routes are endless. As for water sports, there's scuba diving, river tracing, surfing and one gusty archipelago for world-class windsurfing.

Wulai Just a short ride from Taipei, this expanse of sub-tropical forest and wild rivers is one of the north's top spots for hiking, cycling and river tracing. (p125)

Yushan National Park 1050 sq km of high mountains and deep valleys crossed by hiking trails. (p204)

Highway 11 This coastal highway backed by steep, green mountains is Taiwan's premier biking destination. (p185)

Penghu One of the windiest places in the world in autumn, Penghu offers Asia's finest windsurfing. (p306)

Lanyu Unspoiled reefs, an abundance of fish life and a unique island culture make this a mecca for scuba and snorkelling fans. (p310)

Hot Springs

Taiwan has over 100 hot springs ranging from common sulphur springs to rare seawater springs on an offshore volcanic isle. There's even a cold spring or two for the summer heat. Facilities are equally diverse, with Japanese and Western designs, and many left as nature intended them.

Taian A favourite with Japanese police on R&R in the 1920s, Taian's new stylish modern spas overlook rugged wilderness. (p165)

Beitou In the wooded mountains surrounding Taipei, these springs are reachable by a quick MRT ride. (p111)

Guguan Think outdoor pools with a mist-shrouded mountain backdrop. (p218)

Green Island Indulge yourself with a swim in an exceptional seawater hot spring by the ocean. (p314)

Lisong This wild spring deep in a remote river valley sprays down on you from a multi-coloured cliff face. (p201)

Beaches

Taiwan's beaches vary from short crescents with tropical blue waters to long stretches of black sand to some exceptionally fine coral-sand beaches on the outer islands. What's more, most are free and not overrun with resorts.

Shanshui Swim, surf, snorkel or just hang out at this superb beach next to a pretty village. (p306)

Baishawan Clear blue tropical waters, coconut palms and a white-crescent beach make this the south's top beach. (p138)

Nanao This wide-crescent bay has a black-sand beach and looks down a stunning coastline of high, steep cliffs. (p148)

Chipei Sand Tail The finest white-sand beach in Taiwan, with an ever-changing shape. (p307)

Taimali There's no swimming, but camping and bonfires are encouraged. (p199)

Wai'ao A long black-sand beach with the north's most happening surf scene. (p145)

IF YOU LIKE... CHALLENGING YOUR TASTE BUDS

Try stinky tofu (see boxed text p87) – think of it as Taiwanese blue cheese – or aboriginal food like fried bees, rice and mushrooms steamed in bamboo and barbecued wild boar (p128). Yum.

(Top) Hiking through Yushan National Park (p204)
(Bottom) Stinky tofu (p87)

Temples

With 15,000 and counting, there is a temple for every god and occasion. Storehouses of history, display rooms for decorative arts and, of course, vibrant houses of worship, temples are a quintessential part of Taiwan's living folk culture.

Bao'an Temple This Unesco heritage award winner is a top example of southern temple art and architecture. (p65)

Tzushr Temple The temple's post-WWII reconstruction was overseen by an art professor – and it shows. (p135)

Lukang Longshan This walled temple is a treasure house of woodcarving and design. (p224)

Tainan Confucius Temple Taiwan's first Confucius temple and a model of graceful design and dignified atmosphere. (p242)

Chung Tai Chan Monastery Designed by the same architect as Taipei 101, the rocket-ship-meets-mosque exterior belies an interior filled with traditional decorative arts. (p232)

Traditional Festivals

Rising living standards and economic prosperity haven't killed folk culture in Taiwan: it just means there is more money than ever to hold extravagant and sometimes outlandish festivals.

Matsu Pilgrimage Taiwan's largest religious festival is a nine-day 350km walk around the island for Matsu believers – which is almost everyone. (p212)

Burning of the Wang Yeh Boats A sublime weeklong religious festival that concludes with the torching of a 'plague ship' on a beach. (p267)

Lantern Festival High-tech lantern shows are held in every city, but the most riveting spectacles are Pingxi's sky lantern release (p131) and **Bombing Master Handan** (p200) in Taitung

Yenshui Fireworks Festival Like Spain's Running of the Bulls, only they let fireworks loose here and you're not supposed to run from them. Loads of fun and games and sometimes people do lose an eye. (p258)

Night Markets

Taiwan's reputation as a culinary hot spot is spreading; even street food–obsessed Singaporeans and Malaysians are beating a fast path here to sample the nightly goodies.

Raohe Street The cognoscenti's night market, Raohe is Taipei's oldest, and unrivalled in snacking opportunities. (p93)

Miaokou Nightly offerings from the bounty of the sea at Taiwan's most famous snacking destination. Afterwards pray at the temple that gives the market its name to atone for your gluttony. (p139)

Liuhe Every night 100 stalls line the market road, offering everything from squid-on-a-stick to fresh chicken wraps. (p260)

Fengjia (p210) Make a pilgrimage to this frenetic market, the birthplace of many quirky yet popular snacks in Taiwan.

Tainan It seems half the city and every temple square is a night market – the unique local snacks like coffin cakes and shrimp rolls are well worth the trip down south.

Unique Wildlife

Taiwan has a rate of endemism far higher than the world average, which means there are lots of critters and plants you won't find anywhere else. Birds and butterflies are easiest to spot, but with conservation efforts, even larger mammals such as deer are making a comeback. See p361 for more.

Birds Taiwan's range of habitats supports over 600 species, of which at least 24 are endemic and 59 are endemic subspecies.

Butterflies Taiwan isn't known as the 'Kingdom of Butterflies' for nothing. Over 400 species (56 endemic), numerous reproductive valleys and yearly mass migrations are a few highlights.

Fish Check out the Formosan salmon; it never leaves the rivers of its birth.

Mammals Seventeen endemic species are here, including the Formosan rock monkey and the giant flying squirrel – one of the world's largest.

Mountain Retreats

With the land over two-thirds mountainous, there's lots of space to get away from the crowds and the heat in summer. Small villages dot the foothills of major mountain ranges, forest reserves and national parks. A few even offer splashy hot-spring facilities.

Taipingshan This mist-shrouded, high-mountain reserve features a small village with outstanding views over the Snow Mountains, and hot springs are nearby. (p154)

Nanzhuang Village In the stunning foothills of the Snow Mountains, the villages here are a mix of Hakka, Taiwanese and aboriginal people. (p163)

Dasyueshan In the heart of Taiwan's pine-and-hemlock belt, this high-mountain reserve is a prime birding venue. (p211)

Mingchih On the remote North Cross-Island Highway, Mingchih lies near wild hot springs and two forests of ancient cedars. (p152)

Alishan National Scenic Area Lures travellers with its aboriginal culture, rare alpine railway, ancient cedars and phenomenal sea of clouds. (p219)

Tea

Taiwan has ideal conditions for growing tea, and not surprisingly, it has the goods to satisfy the novice looking for a flavourful brew as well as the connoisseur willing to pay thousands of dollars for a few ounces of dry leaves – *if* they are of high-enough quality.

High Mountain Oolongs Grown above 1000m in moist but sunny conditions, these teas have a creamy texture and a bouquet of flavours that must be experienced to be believed.

Bao Chung A national favourite with a slightly floral fragrance; a good tea to start your explorations. (p132)

Oriental Beauty Unique to Taiwan, this reddish-coloured sweet tea has a fruity aroma and lacks all astringency. (p162)

Lei cha A field-worker's drink; rich and hearty with puffed rice and pounded nuts added. (p166)

Black tea Sun Moon Lake black-tea growers spent a decade reviving their industry. Drink this tea straight without sugar or milk. (p228)

Month by Month

TOP EVENTS

Matsu Pilgrimage April

Lantern Festival January or February

Spring Scream April

Aboriginal Festivals July and August

Kaohsiung Lion Dance Competition December

January

Generally wet and cool in the north, dry and sunny in the south. There are few people other than students travelling, unless the week of Chinese New Year (CNY) falls in this month.

Southern Beaches

If you want to swim in the winter months, head south to Kenting National Park. Beaches in the north, the east and on Penghu will be closed and the waters choppy and chilly.

Chinese New Year

Held in January or February depending on the lunar calendar, CNY is mostly a family affair in Taiwan until the very end, when several spectacular Lantern Festival activities are held.

February

Generally very wet and cool in the north, dry and sunny in the south. Possibility of cold fronts and sand storms. Travel during the week of CNY is difficult but usually easy before and after.

Lantern Festival

One of the most popular traditional festivals, with concerts and light shows across Taiwan. However, the simplest of all, the Pingxi sky lantern release (p131), is the most spectacular. On the same day, Yenshui holds a massive fireworks festival (p258), and Taitung has its Bombing Master Handan (p200).

Mayasvi

This dramatic Tsou aboriginal festival (p221) thanks gods and ancestral spirits for their protection. It's held on 15 February in Tsou villages in Alishan.

April

Usually very wet and warm in the north, wet and hot in the south. Generally low season for individual travel but peak time for Chinese tour groups.

Spring Scream

Taiwan's largest and longest-running outdoor music event (p276) is held in the bright sunshine of Kenting National Park.

Bao'an Folk Arts Festival

Bao'an Temple won a Unesco heritage award for reviving traditional temple fair, and this is your chance to see lion dancing, god parades, folk opera, fire walking and god birthday celebrations. The festival runs from early April to early June.

Matsu Pilgrimage

This annual religious pilgrimage (p212) is Taiwan's premier folk event. Hundreds of thousands of believers follow a revered Matsu statue on a nine-day, 350km journey, with a million more participating in local events (www.dajia-mazu.org.tw).

Youtong Flowers

The tall branching youtong tree is found all over the north. In spring its large white flowers make entire mountainsides look as if they are dusted with snow. Check them out at Sansia, Sanyi, Taian Hot Springs and Sun Moon Lake.

May

Start of plum rain; expect heavy afternoon showers. Travel picks up across the island and on outer islands.

Start of Mango Season

Taiwan's mangoes are rated number one in Japan for good reason: they are sweet, succulent, fleshy and nearly sublime. Prices vary each year depending on the rains. The season ends around September.

Welcoming the City God

A smaller-scale pilgrimage (p283) than the Matsu, but with unique and colourful parades across the charming landscape of Kinmen.

June

Warming up everywhere. Heavy showers possible. Major destinations are crowded on weekends.

Dragon Boat Festival

Honouring the sacrifice of the poet-official Qu Yuan, the Dragon Boat Festival is celebrated all over Taiwan with flashy boat races on the local rivers and tasty sticky-rice dumplings.

Taipei Film Festival

One of the highest-profile international cultural events (p78) in Taipei, with 160 film showings from 40 countries. Venues include Huashan 1914 Creative Park and Zhongshan Hall. Held in June and July.

(Above) A performer dressed for a religious ceremony
(Below) Red lanterns are often displayed during festivals

Taiwan International Balloon Fiesta

Held in Taitung County's Gaotai plateau (Luye), this recently established two-month festival (p197) is becoming one of the summer's biggest draws.

July

Hot and humid across the island. Heavy afternoon showers in the north but not in the south or east. Possibility of typhoons which can disrupt travel. Major destinations busy, especially on weekends.

Aboriginal Festivals

Every July and August a number of traditional aboriginal festivals (p195) are held along the east coast. Themes include coming of age, ancestor worship, courting, harvest and good old-fashioned displays of martial and hunting skills.

August

Hot and humid but generally drier than July. High possibility of typhoons. Many student and family groups travelling. Major destinations very busy especially on weekends.

Day Lily Season

Orange day lilies are grown for food in the mountains of the east coast, and their blooming in late August and early September in places such as Sixty Stone Mountain (p196) is an enchanting sight that attracts flower lovers from all over the island.

Ghost Festival

One of the most important traditional festivals in Taiwan. Events include the opening of the gates of hell, offerings to wandering spirits, and a water-lantern release. Biggest celebrations held in Keelung (p139).

September

The weather is cooling but still hot during the day. High possibility of typhoons but conditions generally dry and windy. Local travel dropping. Autumn is a great time to cycle.

Confucius' Birthday

Held on 28 September with elaborate early-morning celebrations at Confucius Temples across Taiwan. Those at Taipei's Confucius Temple (p66) are the most impressive.

Sun Moon Lake International Swimming Carnival

The world's largest mass open-water swim (p230) takes place every September in Taiwan's largest body of water. The 3.3km swim is not meant to be challenging, but fun. Expect tens of thousands of swimmers.

October

The most stable weather across the island if there's no typhoon – dry, warm and windy. Best time of year in the north. Few travellers except for tour groups.

Boat-Burning Festival

Held for one week every three years (autumn 2015, 2018 etc), this spectacular display of folk faith concludes with a 14m-long wooden boat being burned to the ground on the beach (p267). Attended by tens of thousands, it's both a celebration and a solemn ritual.

December

Cooling in the north but still warm to hot during the day. In the south it's usually dry with temperatures in the high 20s. Travel generally low except for tour groups to major destinations.

Kaohsiung Lion Dance Competition

Teams from Taiwan, China, Malaysia, Singapore and around the world compete in various traditional temple dance routines. This lively and colourful contest (p259) is held in Kaohsiung Arena and sells out fast.

Purple Butterfly Overwintering

Mass overwintering of purple butterflies in the valleys stretching across southern Taiwan. Can be seen in Maolin Recreation Area (p265) from December to March during the morning hours.

Hot Springs

You can, of course, visit hot springs year-round but the days are cooling, especially in the mountains where many springs are located. It's a good chance to avoid the big crowds in January and February at outdoor pools.

Itineraries

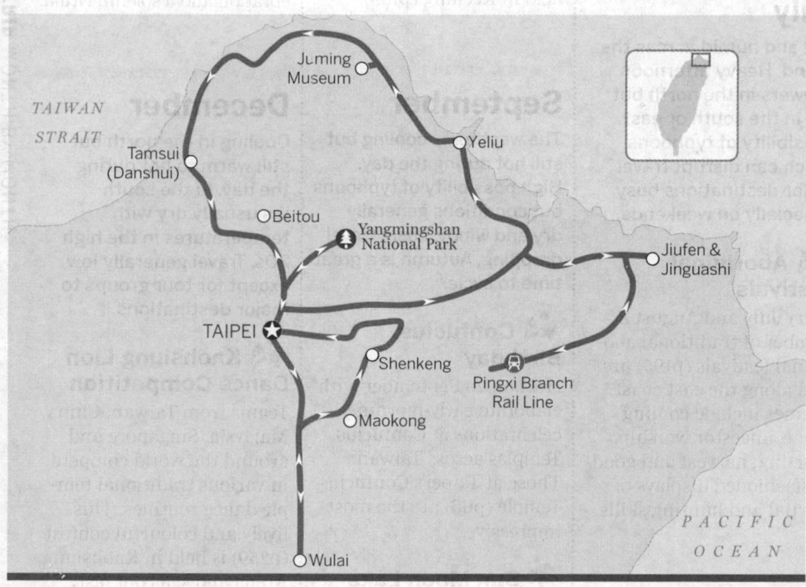

Taipei & the North

Start with four days in **Taipei** being awestruck by the National Palace Museum collection, sensory-overloaded at Longshan and Bao'an Temples, over-caffeinated at gourmet cafes, as well as shopping and snacking at night markets and local design shops.

Activities abound. If you like tea, take the gondola to mountainous **Maokong** and its traditional teahouses. For hot springs, historic **Beitou** is just an MRT ride away. For fun, go on a stinky tofu tour along the restored old street of **Shenkeng**. To burn off calories, rent a bike and ride along the river paths in Taipei or hike the trails in **Yangmingshan National Park** or **Wulai**, a mountainous district with pristine jungles and natural swimming pools.

On day five, bus further afield to the old mining towns of **Jiufen** and **Jinguashi**, used for historic movie settings and music videos. The next day head to nearby Ruifang and catch the **Pingxi Branch Rail Line** down an 18km wooded gorge to photograph the old frontier villages, and hike paths cut into steep crags.

On day seven round off the trip, head back up the coast, stopping at the bizarre rocks of **Yeliu** and renowned sculptures at **Juming Museum**. From **Tamsui**, a seaside town with beautiful colonial houses, the MRT takes you back to Taipei.

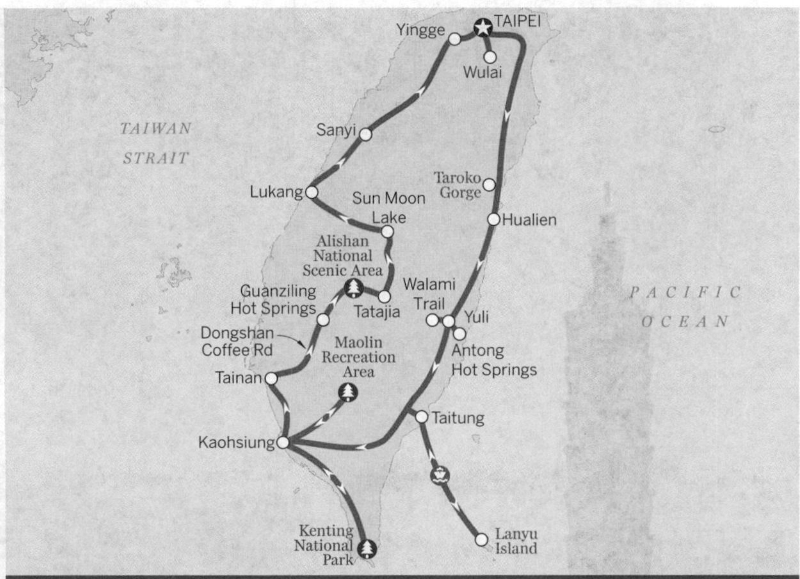

Ultimate Taiwan

Start with a few days in **Taipei** to see the sights and catch the groove of this dynamic Asian capital. It has the best Chinese art collection in the world, a thriving street food and coffee scene, a living folk-art heritage, and some world-class cycling and hiking in **Wulai** and other on-the-doorstep locations.

Then hop a train to **Hualien** and spend two days wandering the bedazzling marble-walled **Taroko Gorge**. More scenic delights await down Hwy 9, which runs through the lush Rift Valley. Take a train to **Yuli** and hike the nearby **Walami Trail**, an old patrol route running deep into subtropical rainforest, then recuperate at **Antong Hot Springs**. Next, head to **Taitung** and catch a flight or ferry to **Lanyu**, an enchanting tropical island with pristine coral reefs and a unique indigenous culture.

Back on the mainland, another train ride – across Taiwan's fertile southern tip – takes you to **Kaohsiung**, Taiwan's buzzing second-largest city. For beaches or scootering along beautiful coastline, head down to **Kenting National Park**. In winter take a two-day side trip to **Maolin Recreation Area**, home of Rukai aborigines and where millions of purple butterflies await spring.

Continue by train up the coast to the old capital of **Tainan** for a couple of days of temple touring and snacking on local delicacies. Rent a car or scooter for the drive up the winding **Dongshan Coffee Road** then spend the evening in rare mud hot springs in **Guanziling**. The following day continue up into the wild expanse of mountain ranges in the **Alishan National Scenic Area**. Check out sunset and sunrise, then hike around **Tatajia** in the shadow of Yushan, Taiwan's highest mountain.

The drive from Yushan to **Sun Moon Lake** the following morning passes some sublime high-mountain scenery and should be taken slowly. At the lake, stop to sample oolong tea and maybe catch a boat tour. Heading north, fans of traditional arts and crafts will enjoy the following day's stops in **Lukang**, home to master lantern, fan and tin craftsmen; **Sanyi**, Taiwan's woodcarving capital; and **Yingge**, a town devoted to ceramics.

SUPERSTOCK/GETTY IMAGES ©

Top: Taipei 101 (p75) as seen from Elephant Mountain (p77)
Bottom: Tea leaf picker, Alishan (p213)

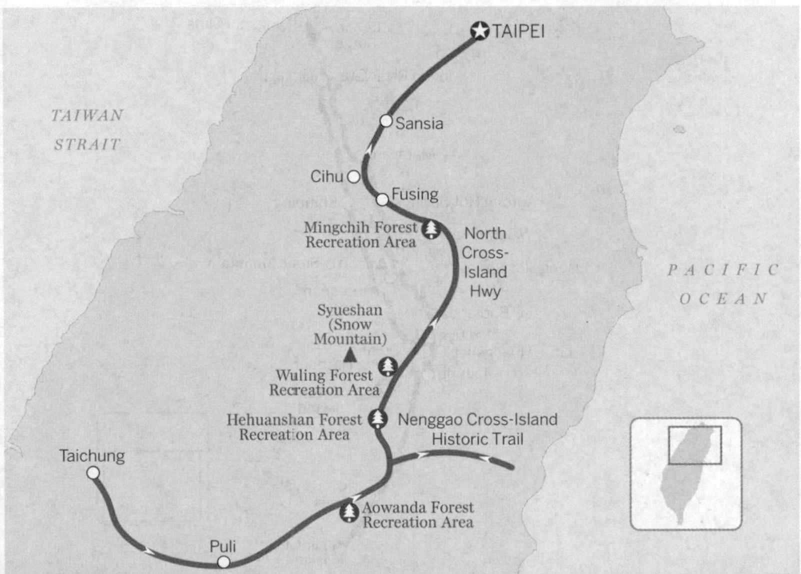

A Cross-Island Tour

After **Taichung** your first stop is the Chung Tai Chan Temple in **Puli**, an amazing centre of Buddhist art and research. After Puli the highway rises into the Central Mountains, where one gorgeous landscape after another begs to be photographed. For a side trip head to **Aowanda Forest Recreation Area**, a top birdwatching venue, and spend a night in little cabins among cherry and plum trees.

Returning to Hwy 14, continue to the end to find the **Nenggao Cross-Island Historic Trail**. You can walk the whole thing or just hike in and spend a night in the cabin before heading north up Hwy 14甲. Prepare for an endless windy road and numerous washouts – and a stunning landscape of receding blue-tinged mountain ranges.

After Wuling Pass (3275m), the highest bit of road in Northeast Asia, stop in **Hehuanshan Forest Recreation Area** to photograph (and maybe stroll over) the treeless hills of Yushan cane. Then head up Hwy 8 to Hwy 7甲 and follow this north to **Wuling Forest Recreation Area**, an area of thick forests, high waterfalls and cool mountain streams, some of which are home to the endangered Formosan landlocked salmon. If you have a few days to spare, climb **Snow Mountain**, Taiwan's second-highest mountain.

Past Wuling the road winds down the mountains past aboriginal villages, with their trademark churches and steeples, to the Lanyang River plains and one very large cabbage patch. From here it's a seamless connection with the **North Cross-Island Hwy**. First stop: **Mingchih Forest Recreation Area** and its nearby forest of ancient trees. More ancient trees can be found a couple of hours later at Lalashan, or you can continue on to enjoy stunning views of high forested mountains and rugged canyons. Stop for lunch at **Fusing** and then explore Chiang Kai-shek's legacy at nearby **Cihu**. At Daxi head north towards **Sansia** and stop to look at the masterful Tzushr Temple before connecting with National Fwy 3 to **Taipei**.

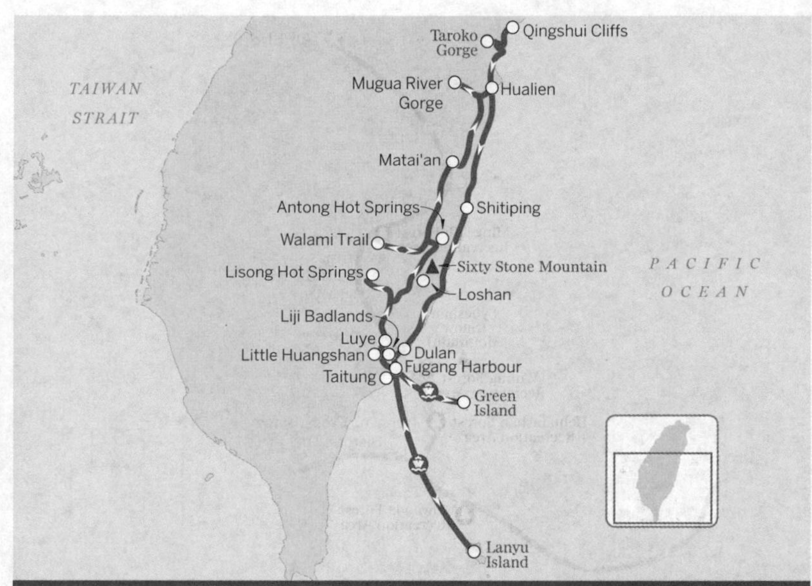

The East Coast Loop

From **Hualien**, a low-key coastal town with good eating and seaside parks, it's a quick hop to **Taroko Gorge**, Taiwan's premier natural attraction. After a couple of days hiking, biking and marvelling at the marble walls, head up Hwy 11 to the **Qingshui Cliffs**, among the world's highest.

Return to Hualien and take Hwy 11 to Taitung. It's three days on a bike alongside some of Taiwan's best coastal scenery; otherwise rent a car or scooter. Plan to stop often, but in particular at **Shitiping** for seafood and jaw-dropping views, and **Dulan**, Taiwan's funkiest town, for an art scene centred around a reclaimed sugar factory. From Taitung, catch a ferry or flight to **Green Island** and/or **Lanyu** for a few days of snorkelling, hot springs and exploring the island culture of the aboriginal Tao.

To head back north, take Hwy 11乙 west and connect with 東45 and later County Rd 197 for a scenic drive up the Beinan River Valley, with the crumbling **Liji Badlands** on one side and the jagged cliffs of **Little Huangshan** on the other.

The 197 drops you off on Hwy 9, near **Luye**, a bucolic pineapple- and tea-growing region with a stunning plateau. Just north, connect with the **South Cross-Island Hwy** for some yodel-inducing high-mountain scenery, and the chance to hike to **Lisong**, a wild hot spring that cascades down a multicoloured cliff face.

For more scenic eye-candy, stop at the organic rice fields of **Loshan** and the flower fields of **Sixty Stone Mountain**. Spend the night at **Antong Hot Springs** so you are fully rested for a cycle the next day out to historic **Walami Trail**, a Japanese-era patrol route.

Opportunities to indulge in local foods are numerous along this route, but don't miss aboriginal **Matai'an**, a wetland area with some unique dishes. You'll be well fed for the final stretch back to Hualien, which you should do along quiet County Rd 193. For one last adventure, veer off before Hualien and ride up the wild **Mugua River Gorge** for a dip in a marble-walled natural swimming hole.

Plan Your Trip

Taiwan Outdoors

With its rugged mountainous spine, dense forest cover over half the island, vast backcountry road network that includes the highest pass in Northeast Asia, and 1566km of shoreline, Taiwan abounds with venues for hiking, cycling and water sports. Get to know Ilha Formosa at the pace it deserves.

Hiking

Taiwan's landscape is striking, and with multiple bio-geographical zones ranging from tropical to alpine, the flora and fauna is ever changing. It's possible to hike year-round on a well-developed trail network from sea level to 3952m. You don't need a guide for most hikes, and it's possible to go for days without seeing others. National park trails feature inexpensive cabins with water and bedding (but usually no food).

National Parks & Other Hiking Venues

Over 50% of Taiwan is mountainous and heavily forested, and about 20% is protected land divided between national parks, forest recreation areas, reserves and various state forests.

National parks and forest recreation areas (FRAs) have excellent quality trails. Within the boundaries of each you'll find a visitor information centre and often a small village with basic accommodation and food. Paved trails lead to scenic spots, while unspoiled areas with natural paths may be further in the park. Forestry reserves may have good trails but usually offer few facilities for hikers.

Many trails are also maintained at the regional level and offer excellent day and sometimes overnight hikes. They are usually sign-posted in English and Chinese.

Taiwan's Best

Hiking

There are hundreds of well-maintained natural trails in Taiwan. Some of the best low-altitude trails are within an hour of Taipei. The best high-mountain trails are in Yushan and Sheipa National Parks. In most cases, you don't need a guide.

Cycling

Taiwan has good roads with wide shoulders in popular biking areas. There are also hundreds of kilometres of bike-only routes around cities. Bikes are allowed on Mass Rapid Transit (MRT), trains and some buses, and day and multiday rental programs are widely available.

Hot Springs

Springs are located all over the island. The most accessible are in Beitou, reachable by Taipei MRT. Don't miss Taian Hot Springs in Miaoli County.

Water Sports

The offshore islands are top spots for diving. Hundreds of clean mountain streams make the island an ideal river-tracing destination. There is beginner to advanced surfing around northern Taiwan, the east coast and Kenting National Park. In winter, head to Penghu for world-class windsurfing.

Planning Your Hike

You can hike year-round, but the best weather is from September to December and March to May. Midweek is best for popular trails but many are never busy. July to August are also good months for high-altitude hikes if the weather cooperates (the sun can be fierce), as there are fewer hikers about. Winter hiking above the snowline is possible, though Yushan National Park requires that a team leader be certified for winter hiking. Sheipa National Park simply asks to see that hikers are adequately prepared (such as having crampons and an ice pick).

Weather

Afternoon fogs are common year-round, as are thunderstorms in summer. Typhoons affect the island from early summer to late autumn, while monsoon rains batter the island in May and June. Obviously do not go out hiking during storms or typhoons, but also avoid going to the mountains in the few days after as landslides, swollen rivers and streams can wash out roads and trails.

Always be prepared for a change of weather and for the weather in the mountains to be different from the city.

Natural Disasters

Earthquakes are common all over the island and are especially strong along the east coast – don't hike for a few days after a big earthquake. Taiwan is also prone to massive landslides (it has been called the landslide capital of the world) and huge sections of trail are often washed out after earthquakes and typhoons. Trails can be closed for months or even years (sometimes forever) – don't attempt trails that have been closed.

Plants & Animals

Māo yào rén (貓咬人; cat bite people) Taiwan's version of poison ivy. Grows at mid-elevations.

Snakes Most are harmless but Taiwan has its share of deadly venomous snakes, which often have triangular-shaped heads, very distinctive patterns, thin necks and tapered tails. Large, fat python-like snakes are usually harmless rodent eaters. You won't find snakes at higher elevations. For more check out www.snakesoftaiwan.com.

Ticks A possible problem at lower altitudes, even around cities. Be careful in summer and always check yourself after hiking.

Wasps Most active in autumn, these dangerous insects kill and put people in the hospital every year. In danger areas you will often see warning signs. Avoid wearing perfumes and bright clothing.

Rabies In 2013 Taiwan had its first rabies outbreak in 50 years. At the time of writing, the disease was limited to ferret-badgers and house shrews.

Getting Lost

It's easy to get lost hiking in Taiwan if you are not on a well-made trail. The forest is extremely thick in places, and trails are sometimes little more than foot-wide cuts across a steep mountainside with many unmarked branches. Trails also quickly become overgrown (some need teams to come in every year with machetes just to make them passable). Never leave a trail, or attempt to make your own. If you hike alone let someone know.

PRACTICAL TIPS

➡ Don't be tempted to head to the summit of a mountain in light clothing and with limited supplies simply because the weather looks good. Always be prepared with wet- and cold-weather gear and plenty of food and water. Deaths are not uncommon on Taiwan's high mountains and they are often related to hikers being unprepared for fast-changing conditions.

➡ When it comes to a good night's sleep in a cabin, snoring can be a terrible nuisance, as can Taiwanese hikers' habit of getting up at 3am so they can catch the sunrise on the peak. Bring earplugs!

➡ Ribbons are placed on trails by hiking clubs to indicate the correct path to take on a complicated or easily overgrown system. If you aren't sure where to go, following the ribbons is usually sound advice.

Emergency Numbers

Even in high mountains it's often possible to get mobile-phone reception, but remember that phones lose power quickly in the cold and in areas with low signals. Hiking maps highlight good reception areas. If you can't communicate by voice, try texting.

- Basic emergency numbers ☎119 or ☎112
- ☎112 connects you to available signals even if your mobile phone doesn't have a SIM card
- National Rescue Command Centre ☎0800-077 795
- Ministry of Defence Rescue Centre ☎02-2737 3395
- Emergency radio frequencies: 145MHz, 149.25MHz, 148.74MHz or 148.77MHz

Books

Good titles to whet your appetite for the north's great hikes include *Taipei Escapes 1* and *2* and *Yangmingshan, the Guide,* both by Richard Saunders. *Taiwan Forest Vacation Guide,* published by the Forestry Bureau, covers 21 forest recreation areas around Taiwan.

Maps

For northern Taiwan maps, **Taiwan Jiaotong Press** (台北縣市近郊山圖) publishes a series of 14 maps at a scale of 1:25,000 that covers the north from Sansia/Wulai up. These are available at mountain-equipment stores around the Taipei Main Station. These stores will also carry variously scaled topographic maps of most of the 100 Top Peaks and other popular hiking trails. Itineraries are included in Chinese.

National park maps are available at park visitor centres or mountain-equipment shops. Most national park websites have basic maps (in English) of the climbing routes. Topographical maps may be available at national park bookstores.

Clubs

Richard Saunders (richard0428@yahoo.com), author of *Taipei Escapes 1* and *2,* runs a free weekend hiking club. 523 Mountaineering Association (p78) runs a couple of free day hikes each month, as well as reasonably priced longer hikes.

Hiking Companies & Guides

523 Mountaineering Association (Map p62; http://523.org.tw) Nonprofit organisation with a good reputation. Mix of locals and foreigners. Also offers free day hikes around Taipei.

Barking Deer (www.barking-deer.com) Foreign-run company that provides full hiking packages. Can also arrange permit and transport-only packages. Its website has a wealth of information on how to apply for national park and mountain permits.

Cloud Leopard Hiking Association (雲豹登山隊; ☎04-9299 5034; 5217783@gmail.com) Bunun cooperative focusing on portering and guiding services. Japanese and Chinese language services.

Taiwan Adventures (www.taiwan-adventures.com) Day and overnight hiking trips around Taiwan, as well as some free hikes. Also offers a set of mobile apps filled with inspiring photos.

Websites & Blogs

Forest Recreation Areas (www.forest.gov.tw)

Hiking Taiwan (http://hikingtaiwan.blogspot.com)

National Trail System (www.forest.gov.tw) Old website but still useful information on trail histories, terrain, and flora and fauna.

Off the Beaten Track (http://taiwandiscovery.wordpress.com)

Pashan (http://hikingintaiwan.blogspot.com)

Lower-Altitude Trails (Under 3000m)

There are low-altitude trails all over Taiwan. Trails run through subtropical and tropical jungles, broadleaf forests, temperate woodlands and along coastal bluffs. Some are just a few hours' long while others go on for days. All three major cities – Taipei, Kaohsiung and Taichung – have mountains and trails either within the city limits or just outside.

Permits are not needed for most low-altitude hikes, except for areas that restrict the number of hikers who can enter per day. For these areas you may need to register at a police checkpoint on the way into the area – this is a simple process but you'll need a passport.

Some great places to hike include Wulai, Maokong, the Pingxi Branch Rail Line,

Taiwan Outdoors

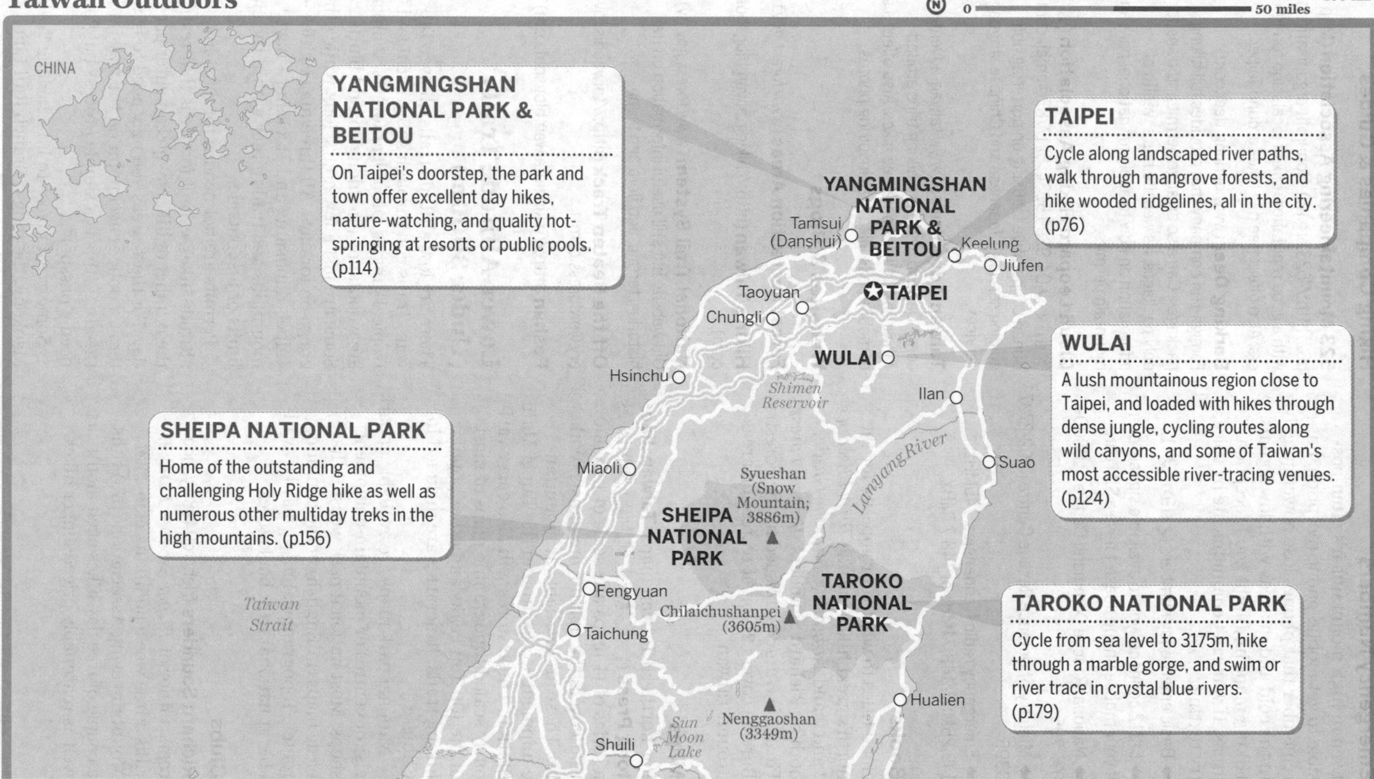

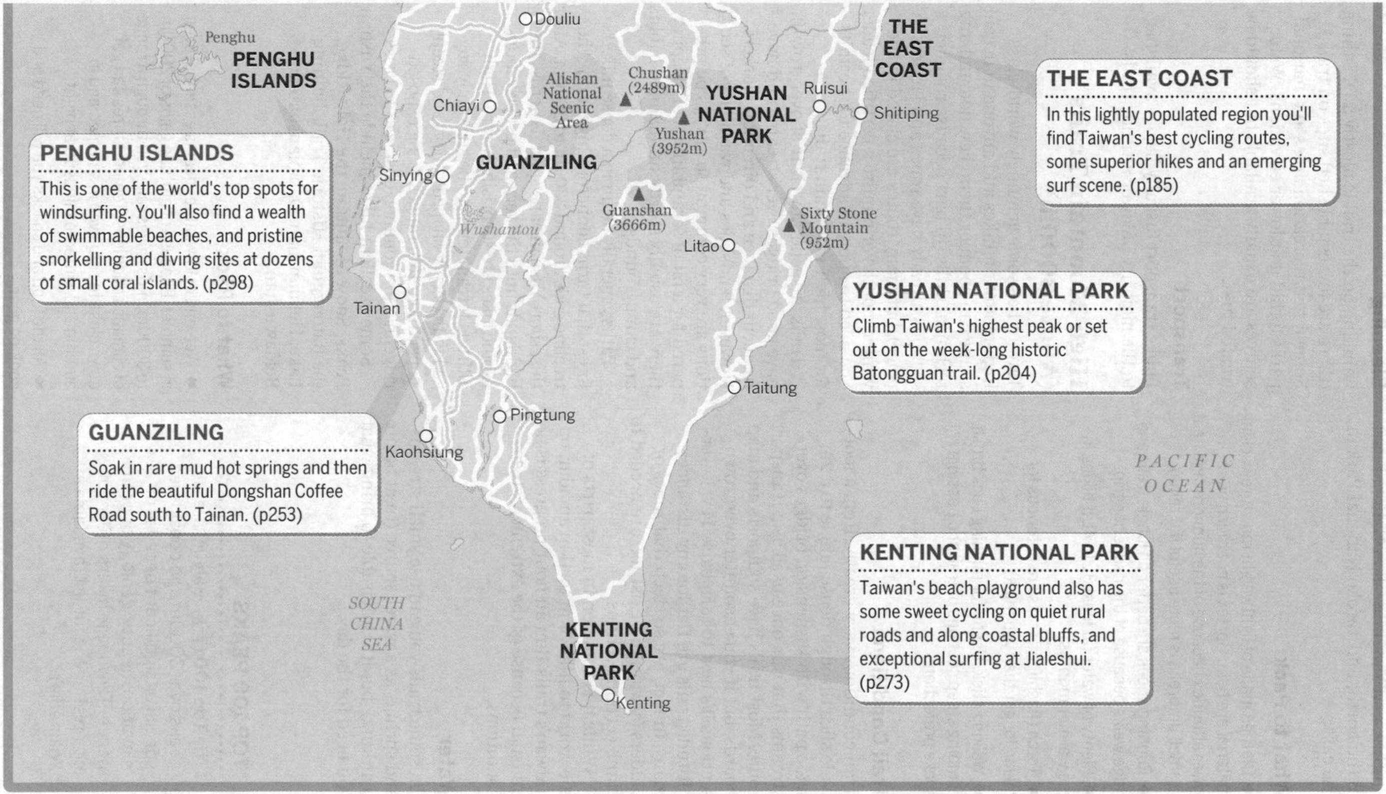

Penghu
PENGHU ISLANDS
Douliu
Chiayi
Alishan National Scenic Area
Chushan (2489m)
Yushan (3952m)
YUSHAN NATIONAL PARK
Ruisui
Shitiping
THE EAST COAST
Sinying
GUANZILING
Wushantou
Guanshan (3666m)
Sixty Stone Mountain (952m)
Litao
Tainan
Taitung
Pingtung
Kaohsiung
PACIFIC OCEAN
SOUTH CHINA SEA
KENTING NATIONAL PARK
Kenting

PENGHU ISLANDS

This is one of the world's top spots for windsurfing. You'll also find a wealth of swimmable beaches, and pristine snorkelling and diving sites at dozens of small coral islands. (p298)

GUANZILING

Soak in rare mud hot springs and then ride the beautiful Dongshan Coffee Road south to Tainan. (p253)

THE EAST COAST

In this lightly populated region you'll find Taiwan's best cycling routes, some superior hikes and an emerging surf scene. (p185)

YUSHAN NATIONAL PARK

Climb Taiwan's highest peak or set out on the week-long historic Batongguan trail. (p204)

KENTING NATIONAL PARK

Taiwan's beach playground also has some sweet cycling on quiet rural roads and along coastal bluffs, and exceptional surfing at Jialeshui. (p273)

Shiting, and Yangmingshan National Park in the north; and Taroko National Park in the east.

What to Pack

- Clothes made of lightweight moisture-wicking material are best. Gortex is not much use at lower altitudes because of the humidity and heat (a small umbrella is more useful if it rains).
- Running shoes are better on jungle trails and ridge walks because of their superior grip.
- Plenty of water (at least 3L to 4L if hiking in the warmer months).
- Torch (flashlight; trails are notorious for taking longer than you think).
- Walking stick. Useful for pushing back brush, climbing steep sections of trail and possible snake protection.

Trail Conditions

Trail conditions vary greatly, from a foot-wide slice through dense jungle to a 2m-wide path with suspension bridges over streams that was once used as a transport route. Most trails have signposts and map boards, but if you encounter overgrown sections it's best to turn back. Few lower-altitude trails are flat for any distance: many, in fact, are so steep that ropes or ladders (always pre-existing) are needed to climb certain sections.

While it is common in most parts of the world to hike 3km to 4km an hour, on Taiwan's trails 1km an hour progress is not unusual because of the extremely steep conditions.

Water

On some trails you can use small streams and springs as a water source (treat before drinking), but it is advisable to bring what you need for the day.

> **TOP 100 PEAKS**
>
> The **Top 100** (百岳, Bǎiyuè) are all peaks over 3000m and considered special or significant because of elevation, beauty, geology or prominence. Taiwanese hikers dream of completing the full list (available at Wikipedia).

Sleeping

Camping on the trail is mostly a DIY thing (there are few established sites on trails). Some forest recreation areas and national parks forbid it at lower elevations. Water sources are usually available but should be treated first.

Transport

Public transport (usually bus) is available to the majority of lower-altitude trails.

High-Mountain Trails (Above 3000m)

Taiwan has some genuinely world-class high-mountain hikes and anyone in decent shape can conquer them. Few demand any technical skills (in part because rougher sections already have ropes and ladders in place), but many routes are closed in the winter months or require a certified leader. You need to apply in advance for permits for most high-mountain trails.

Trails are generally clear of overgrowth, have good bridges over streams and have frequent distance and direction markers. However, landslides and washouts of sections are very common so always be prepared for a bit of scrambling. For sleeping there are usually sturdy un-manned cabins and campgrounds.

Paths generally begin in a dense mixed forest that turns coniferous higher up. The treeline ends around 3300m to 3600m. After this, short Yushan cane spreads across the highlands until the very highest elevations. Alpine lakes are surprisingly rare. High-altitude terrain tends to be strikingly rugged with deep V-shaped valleys and steeply sloped mountain ranges. Long exposed ridgelines are common obstacles to cross.

Some excellent hikes include the Yushan Peaks, Snow Mountain, the Holy Ridge, the Batongguan Historic Trail, Jiaming Lake, Hehuanshan, Dabajianshan and Beidawushan.

What to Pack

- Wet- and cold-weather gear is essential even in summer. Because of altitude gains of 2000m to 3000m, most hikes take you through a range of climatic conditions. Temperatures can get down close to zero even in summer, and in autumn and winter to minus 10 at night.
- All the food and snacks you will need and cooking gear.

HIGH-MOUNTAIN PERMITS

Permits are largely a holdover from martial-law days, but they do prevent overcrowding on the trails, and let authorities know who is in the mountains in case of an emergency (such as an approaching typhoon). Restrictions have eased in recent years (for example, you no longer need a guide and solo hikers can apply), but if you are caught without a permit you will be fined. If a rescue is required you will have to pay the full costs. Note that everything mentioned here is subject to change.

First off, permits are required to hike the high mountains. Anyone can apply (foreigners, locals, groups or individuals) but the process is complicated and many people pay to have the permits done for them. Permits are nontransferable and valid only for the date you apply for. If a typhoon cancels your hike, permits cannot be changed to another date (you have to reapply). Note that Taroko National Park only allows Taiwanese to apply for permits (though foreigners can join a local hiking group).

There are two kinds of permits depending on where you hike: **National park permits** (入園, *rù yuán*) for entering restricted areas in a national park and **Police permits** (入山, *rù shān*) for entering a restricted high-mountain area. Hiking in national parks requires both kinds of permits.

National park permits must be applied for at least seven days in advance (for the Yushan main route, at least a month in advance). It is best to apply online, but you'll need a valid Republic of China (ROC) ID number. Passport and Alien Resident Card (ARC) numbers do not work online. Online forms are in Chinese but English forms can be printed and mailed to the national park. National parks will also usually process police permits for you. The **Sheipa National Park** (www.spnp.gov.tw) website has a sample of a completed form in English.

Police permits can be applied for at the **Ministry of the Interior** (www.moi.gov.tw/english; 7 Zhongxiao E Rd, Sec 1, Taipei), at a police station in the same county as the hike, or at the police squad within the national park. You'll need triplicate copies of your itinerary written out, the trail map, a name list of group members (including their dates of birth and emergency contacts) and a national park permit (you must have this before applying for a police permit). Make sure you have ID and/or your passport. Free printable English sample police permits are available online from **Barking Deer Adventures** (http://barkingdeernews.blogspot.com) for almost all major hike itineraries.

Non-national-park hikes usually require only a police permit.

➡ Walking stick. Trails are steep and these help with balance and to spread the weight of a pack.

Trail Conditions

In general, high-mountain trails are well made and clear to follow. Solid metal or wood bridges will be in place where needed. Almost all trails require a great deal of steep uphill climbing, often more than 1000m of elevation gain a day. Many trails require at least some rope or chain climbs (these will be fixed in place and are generally not especially demanding).

Water

Most high-altitude trails will have water sources, which are available from streams or rainwater-collecting tanks at cabins. Maps show water sources, but always ask at the national park headquarters for the latest; sources do sometimes dry up in winter. Water should be filtered or chemically treated.

Sleeping

Cabins and campgrounds are available on most trails. Cabins can range from boxy cement structures to stylish wood A-frames offering bunk beds with thick foam mattresses, solar lighting and ecotoilets. Water sources are usually available at the cabin or nearby. With the exception of Paiyun Cabin on Yushan, cabins are usually unmanned and do not provide sleeping bags, meals or snacks. Campgrounds are flat clearings in forest (sometimes the sites of former police outposts). Water sources are sometimes available.

Transport

There are public buses to Sheipa, Yushan, and Taroko National Parks, as well as Hehuanshan. For most other hiking areas you will need your own vehicle or to arrange transport.

Cycling

Taiwan is one of Asia's top cycling destinations. And don't the locals know it! Cycling fever struck the island around 2005, and all ages and levels of society now participate in the sport. You'll find yourself well treated by fellow cyclists and also passerbys.

Much of the riding focus is on the more sparsely populated east coast, but there are excellent routes everywhere. In addition to world-class road cycling minutes from urban centres such as Taipei, Taiwan has challenging high-mountain and cross-island routes, as well as leisurely paths through rice and tea fields with no end of dramatic mountain and coastal scenery to enjoy.

Planning Your Bike Trip

The best time to cycle in Taiwan is from September to December for generally good weather islandwide. Winter in the south and coastal west sees warm and dry conditions. Riding after a typhoon (assuming there has been no road damage) is usually a good way to ensure clear weather. Other than directly during a typhoon or sand storm, you can ride all year.

Sleeping & Eating

An explosion of B&Bs islandwide means quality (and reasonably priced) accommodation is easy to find everywhere. B&Bs and hotels are used to cyclists and will find a place to store your bike safely. There are also plenty of campgrounds on the east coast. Cheap restaurants are everywhere in rural areas and only on the cross-island highways would you ride more than a few hours without finding food or lodging.

Convenience stores are ubiquitous, again except on cross-island roads. They provide drinks, decent food and washrooms. On popular cycling routes they usually have bicycle pumps and repair kits.

On many popular cycling routes the local police station functions as a rest stop for cyclists. Inside you are welcome to use the bicycle pump, repair kit, water and rest area. Some stations even allow camping out back.

Bikes on Public Transport

You can take a bagged folding bike on practically any form of transport.

The government-run Kuo Kuang Bus Company (p379), and most county bus companies, will usually take a full-sized bagged bike as luggage (for half fare).

Train policy on full-sized bikes is confusing and inconsistent. For longer distances, it's still best to ship the bike (remove anything that might break or fall off and bag the bike or secure it with cardboard) to your destination train station one day before. You only need to give your phone number, ID number, value of the bike and the destination in Chinese. You cannot ship from Taipei Main Station – go to Wanhua or Songshan.

The baggage room is called *xínglǐ fáng* (行李房). Tell the attendant *Wǒ yào tuōyùn jiǎotàchē* (我要托運腳踏車; 'I want to ship a bike').

You can take a non-bagged bike on designated slow local trains, and a bagged (full-sized) bike on any local train. Some fast Tze-chiang trains have a 12th car with bike storage so you can ride on the same train as your bike. Visit www.railway.gov.tw and look for the bike symbol next to the schedule (note that the English website is not as comprehensive as the Chinese).

The High Speed Rail (HSR) network allows you to take bagged bikes on as luggage.

Renting Bikes

City bike-rental programs are available in Taipei (p105) and Kaohsiung (p259), while day rentals are available in many towns down the east coast, the outer islands, and in rural tourist areas.

For multiday rentals, **Giant Bicycles** (www.giantcyclingworld.com) has the best program: three days for NT$1200 and NT$200 for each additional day. These are good quality road bikes and include saddle bags and repair kits. We list where these are available in individual chapters, but as it's best to reserve in advance, you need

WHERE TO CYCLE

Taiwan has three types of cycling venues: bike-only paths, roads and mountain-biking trails. Mountain biking seems a lot quieter than years ago, but there are still popular routes around Taipei. Bike-only paths are concentrated in Taipei, Kaohsiung and down the east coast. To date there are about 1000km of such paths and the network is growing as the government works on a round-the-island path. Roads in Taiwan are generally in good condition, with wide shoulders (often marked as exclusively for bikes and scooters) on many popular routes.

LOCATION	CYCLING OPPORTUNITIES	DESCRIPTION	CYCLING ROUTES
Northern Taiwan	plenty	Road cycling either along steep mountain or flat coastal routes; hundreds of kilometres of riverside paths in Taipei; some mountain-biking trails	North Cross-Island Highway, Wulai, Hwy 9, Hwy 2, Taipei, Hsinchu
Western Taiwan	plenty	Mostly road cycling on mountain routes in the interior; challenging grade in many areas	Sun Moon Lake circuit, Hwy 21, Daxueshan FRA Rd
Eastern Taiwan	plenty	Range of routes along the coast, inland valleys and up rugged gorges; some exceptionally challenging rides up to the high mountains	Hwy 11, Hwy 9, Taroko Gorge, Hwy 14 (Mugua River Gorge), County Rds 193 and 197
Southern Taiwan	plenty	Mostly gentle road riding on quiet country routes; some coastal riding and mountain biking on old trails	County Rd 199, Dongshan Coffee Road
Taiwan's Islands	fair	Mostly flat coastal ring roads; often windy conditions; difficult to transport bike to islands but some have free rentals	See individual islands

someone to call first in Chinese (try asking for help at a tourist information centre).

For mountain bikes rentals (and weekend rides) around Taipei check out Alan's Mountain Bike (p77).

Tours

Most cycling companies are used to local customers only, so tours may not appeal to Western travellers. Routes are also often chosen for convenience and speed and may not be particularly scenic. If a tour involves much riding on Provincial Hwy 1, avoid it.

In Motion Asia (www.inmotionasia.com) is a foreign-run company focusing on small group mountain- and road-biking tours into remote areas. **Giant Adventure** (www.giantcyclingworld.com/web/travel_en.php) also runs a program of round the island trips with full backup.

Websites & Blogs

Rank (http://rank.blogspot.com) Great information on long and more obscure routes.

Taiwan in Cycles (http://taiwanincycles.blogspot.tw) A serious rider with interesting commentary.

Biking in Taiwan (www.bikingintaiwan.com) Detailed writing and pics on routes around Taiwan.

The View from Taiwan (http://michaelturton.blogspot.com) Politics during the week and cycling on the weekend.

Dangers & Annoyances

Feral dogs are common in the mountains. The best approach if they run after you is simply to stop, place your bike in front of you, and remain calm or indifferent. Dogs may snarl and bark but they will quickly grow tired if you don't give them any reason to get excited. Throwing rocks or squirting dogs with water is counterproductive. More extreme measures can result in a fine and/or Facebook shaming.

Drivers are used to scooters so you won't encounter aggression for being a two-wheeled vehicle on the road. However, general driving skills are poor and vehicles cutting across lanes when rounding bends, passing on the outside lane on blind corners and driving too fast and carelessly are all common and potential hazards for cyclists.

Water Sports

Water sports have boomed in the past 10 years. The Japanese influence has spawned interest in river tracing and surfing. Scuba diving, snorkelling and windsurfing are less popular but top notch.

General dangers to be aware of include the fact that Taiwan has no continental shelf. The deep blue sea is just offshore and dangerous currents and riptides flow around the island. Do not swim at a beach unless you know for certain it is safe.

Hot Springs

Taiwan is ranked among the world's top 15 hot-spring sites and harbours a great variety of springs including sulphur springs, cold springs, mud springs and even seabed hot springs. Hot springing was first popularised under the Japanese and many of the most famous resort areas were developed in the early 20th century. In the late 1990s and early 21st century hot-spring fever struck Taiwan a second time and most of the hotels and resorts you'll find today are of recent vintage.

Before entering public hot springs, shower thoroughly using soap and shampoo. Mixed pools require a bathing suit (there are no nude mixed pools in Taiwan). Bathing caps must be worn in all public pools.

Random health checks show overuse at many hot-spring areas with hotels and resorts often diluting natural hot-spring water, and even recycling water between bathers. This is common around the world, even in Japan, and if you want to avoid it, remember that in general the less developed the area, the purer the water quality. In popular spots go midweek when there are fewer bathers.

What's in the Water?

Water bubbling up from underground picks up a variety of minerals that offer a veritable bouquet of health benefits (some more believable than others) according to aficionados.

WATER TYPE	BENEFICIAL FOR	WHERE TO FIND
alkaloid carbonic	nervousness, improving skin tone	Taian
sodium bicarbonate	general feelings of malaise, broken bones	Jiaoxi
alkaline	making good coffee	Antong
sodium carbonate	skin tone	Wulai
ferrous	conceiving a male child	Ruisui
sulphurous	arthritis, sore muscles	Beitou
mud spring	improving skin tone	Guanziling

Hotels & Resorts

The best developed springs are set in forested valleys, meadows or overlooking the ocean. Private rooms and public spas in these areas are usually both available. Private rooms featuring wood or stone tubs can be basic or very luxurious and are rented out by the hour (average NT$600 to NT$1200). Rooms with beds can also be rented for the night (average NT$2500 to NT$8000). Public spas (indoors and outdoors) are sometimes just a few stone-lined pools, but some are a whole bathing complex, with multiple pools, jets and showers. The average cost for unlimited time at a public spa is NT$300 to NT$800.

Hot springs worth checking out are in Beitou, Yangmingshan National Park, Wulai, Jiaoxi, Taian, Antong, Green Island and Guanziling.

Wild Springs

There are still probably one hundred or more wild springs deep in the mountains. Some can be hiked into relatively easily while others require several days. Wild springs worth checking out are Wenshan (p182) in Taroko Gorge, Sileng (p153) on the North Cross-Island Highway, and Lisong on the South Cross-Island Highway.

River Tracing

River tracing (*sùoxī*) is the sport of walking and climbing up a riverbed. At the beginning stages it involves merely walking on slippery rocks. At advanced stages it can involve climbing up and down waterfalls. Taiwan has hundreds of fast clean streams and rivers, some just minutes from the cities. There are no dangerous animals in the water and the landscape is exotic.

The general season for tracing is June to September. On the hottest days of summer many people simply trace up to deep waterfall-fed pools for swimming. Be aware that afternoon thundershowers in summer are common in the north and central mountains and water levels can rise fast.

River-tracing sites worth checking out include Wulai, which is one of the best venues for amateurs (it has deep river pools for swimming, endless waterfalls and a jungle landscape), and various locations in Hualien, including the Golden Canyon, a full-day trip into a beautiful gorge. Contact Hualien Outdoors (p173) for guided tours.

Equipment required for river tracing includes a life jacket, helmet, ropes or climbing slings, and a waterproof bag. Felt-bottomed rubber shoes are necessary for gripping the slippery rock – you can pick up a pair for NT$300 to NT$400 at a mountain-equipment store. Neoprene can be useful even in summer as it can get chilly in higher mountain streams, especially when you've been in the water all day.

Diving & Snorkelling

Taiwan has an excellent range of venues for scuba diving and snorkelling, with good visibility and warm waters year-round in the south. There are well-preserved deep- and shallow-water coral reefs off Lanyu, Green Island, Kenting and the east coast. Green Island alone has 200 types of soft and hard corals and plenty of tropical reef fish. It also has a yearly hammerhead shark migration during the winter months (for advanced divers only).

In the north there's good diving from Yeliu down to Ilan, including off Turtle Island. With the Kuroshio Current (north-flowing ocean current) running close to shore, you'll find an intriguing mix of tropical and temperate sea life, including some gorgeous soft coral patches.

In Taiwan currents are strong and have been known to sweep divers out to sea. Exits on shore can be hard. The biggest problem, though, is usually sunburn, so wear a shirt with SPF protection even when snorkelling. Sharks and jellyfish are not usually a problem but caution is advised.

The best time to dive is during the shoulder season, which runs before and after summer. Winter is also a good time to escape the crowds, with visibility in the south and the east still very good (20m).

John Boo (p275) has a good reputation among divers for his skill and knowledge. For serious dives, such as going out to watch the hammerhead shark migration, contact Andy Gray at **Taiwan Dive** (www.taiwandive.com). Green Island Adventures (p381) is a foreign-run dive company, specialising in tours in the east.

Windsurfing

Taiwan has two main windsurfing venues: Penghu and the west coast of Hsinchu (p161) and Miaoli Counties. Penghu is Asia's top-rated windsurfing destination and the windiest place in the northern hemisphere during autumn. The unique topography of the archipelago keeps the waves down and advanced windsurfers can reach some impressive speeds.

Plan Your Trip
Eat & Drink Like a Local

The Taiwanese are a force to be reckoned with when it comes to round-the-clock eating. There's a lot to love about Taiwanese food, and a lot of it to love. Follow the sound of lips smacking and let the food extravaganza begin.

The Year in Food

Spring (Mar–May)

Lanyu's Flying Fish Festival (April/May), a traditional coming-of-age ceremony for the island's young men, is the only time of the year that flying fish can be eaten.

Summer (Jun–Aug)

Try refreshing drinks made from local favourites like winter melon, lotus root, pickled plums and mesona (a type of mint). Alternatively, down a few bowls of shaved-ice desserts with colourful sweet toppings.

Autumn (Sep–Nov)

Grapefruit, persimmons, dragon fruit, star fruit and pears are all in season in autumn. Crabs, too.

Winter (Dec–Feb)

This season is dedicated to the Taiwanese love of Chinese medicinal ingredients, chiefly *dāngguī* (當歸, female ginseng), in their cooking. The two classic winter dishes, cooked with ginseng and rice wine, are a soothing mutton stew (羊肉爐, Yángròu lú) and a ginger-heavy duck stew (薑母鴨, Jiāngmǔ yā).

Taiwanese Food Experiences

Meals Not to Miss

➡ **James Kitchen** (p90; Taipei) Taiwanese homestyle cooking brought to a higher, fresher level.

➡ **Yongkang Beef Noodles** (p90; Taipei) One of Taipei's best beef noodle restaurants in the *hóngshāo* (red spicy broth) variety.

➡ **Addiction Aquatic Development** (p95; Taipei) Fresh seafood in a chic environment. Opposite the Taipei Fish Market.

➡ **Dou Sang** (p176; Hualien) Homestyle Taiwanese cooking (made with no concern for your waistline) in a rustic, Japanese-style house.

➡ **Cifadahan Cafe** (p192; Matai'an) Gourmet aboriginal food such as 18-vegetable salads, mountain boar, and hot pot on heated stones.

➡ **Daybreak 18 Teahouse** (p250; Tainan) Tea art in a 1930s Japanese-style wooden structure.

➡ **By the Sea** (p269; Donggang) Unusual seafood galore, such as sea grapes and mullet roe.

Cheap Treats

➡ **Night market** (p46) Visit any in Taiwan for a filling meal that's light on your wallet.

➡ **Steamed pork sandwich** (刈包, *guā bāo*) Lan Jia (p89) in Taipei sets the standard.

- **A-gei** (阿給, *Ā gěi*) Fist-sized pouches of fried tofu filled with crystal noodles and served in hot broth.
- **Sweet peanut soup** (花生湯, *huāshēng tāng*) A speciality of Ningxia Night Market (p91) in Taipei.
- **Taiwan bubble tea** Sweet, milky tea with giant tapioca balls, available widely throughout the country.
- **Danzai noodles** Ever-reliable noodle snack, served with pork in shrimp stock in Tainan.
- **Beef soup** A Tainan speciality, served mostly between 4am and 9am, when the meat is at its freshest.

Dare to Try

- **Stinky tofu** (p87; 臭豆腐, *chòu dòufu*) The classic Taiwanese snack that – figuratively speaking – separates the men from the boys.
- **Ice cream** (鐵蛋, *Tiě dàn*) Taipei's Snow King (p88) has over a hundred flavours, including pig's knuckle, curry and Kaoliang (sorghum wine).
- **Medicinal drinks** Try Herb Alley (p96) in Taipei for Chinese traditional medicinal drinks – the bitter tea is quite horrific.
- **Iron eggs** Braised and dried eggs with a black rubbery consistency.
- **Coffin cake** (棺材板, *guāncái bǎn*) Tainan's fat, deep-fried-in-egg toast planks, hollowed out and filled with a thick chowder of seafood and vegetables.
- **Jiāng sī chǎo dàcháng** (薑絲炒大腸) Hakka-style stir-fried pig intestines with ginger.
- **Fried sandworms** (炒沙蟲, *chǎo shāchóng*) A speciality of Kinmen; best served hot.

Local Specialities

Taiwanese cuisine can be divided into several styles of cooking, though the boundaries are often blurred. You'd be hard-pressed to find some of Taiwan's more emblematic dishes (stinky tofu, for example) anywhere in China outside of restaurants specialising in Taiwanese cuisine, though you'll find much food of close comparison in Fujian province. Straddling both sides of the straits, Hakka food is distinct enough to warrant its own category, though the Hakka cuisine you'll find on Taiwan will be more seafood-heavy than what's found in China's inland regions. And of course, any cuisine you can find on the mainland – Cantonese, Sichuanese, Beijing, Shanghainese and so forth – you'll also find in Taiwan.

Taiwanese

Taiwanese cooking has a long, storied and complex history, with influences ranging from all over China mixed with a rather unique aboriginal/Polynesian base. In general, food that you see people enjoying at roadside markets and restaurants tends to emphasise local recipes and ingredients – seafood, sweet potatoes, taro root and green vegetables cooked very simply are at the heart of most Taiwanese meals. *Xiǎoyú huāshēng* (小魚花生; fish stir-fry with peanuts and pickled vegetables) is one example of a Taiwanese favourite.

Chicken rates second in popularity to seafood, followed by pork and beef. *Kézǎi* (蚵仔, oysters) are popular, and *kézǎi tāng* (蚵仔湯; clear oyster soup with ginger) is an excellent hangover cure and overall stomach soother.

Hakka

Hakka dishes are very rich and hearty, sensible for a people who historically made their living as farmers and needed plenty of energy to work the fields. Dishes are often salty and vinegary, with strong flavours. Pork, a favourite of the Hakka, is often cut up into large pieces, fried and then stewed in a marinade. Our favourite Hakka dish is *kèjiā xiǎo chǎo* (客家小炒; stir-fried cuttlefish with leeks, tofu and pork).

Hakka cuisine is also known for its tasty snacks, including *zhà shūcài bǐng* (fried, salty balls made from local mushrooms and flour), *kèjiāguǒ* (客家粿; turnip cakes with shrimp and pork) and *kèjiā máshǔ* (客家麻糬; sticky rice dipped in sugar or peanut powder).

Fujianese

Much of Taiwanese cuisine has Fujianese roots, as the earliest wave of Han Chinese immigration to the island in the 18th century comprised primarily Fujian mainlanders. Fujianese cuisine particularly abounds on the Taiwan Strait islands of Matsu and Kinmen (both of which are a stone's throw away from Fujian province), but you'll find Fujianese cuisine all over Taiwan.

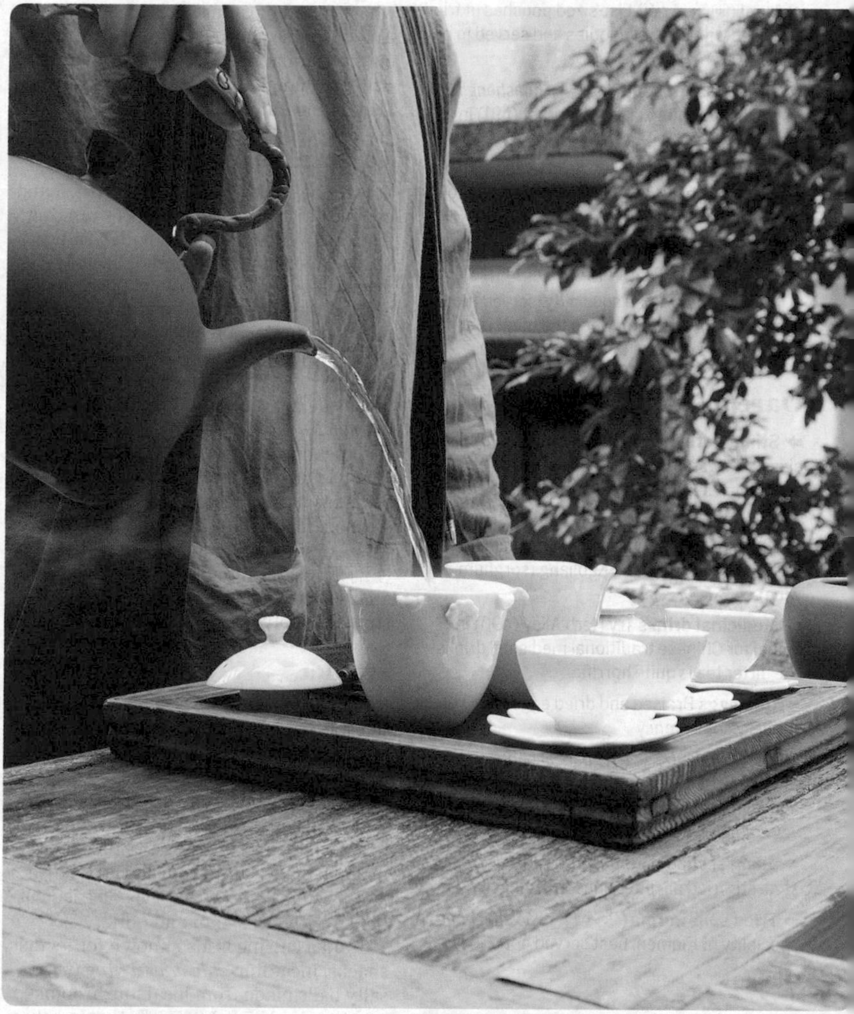

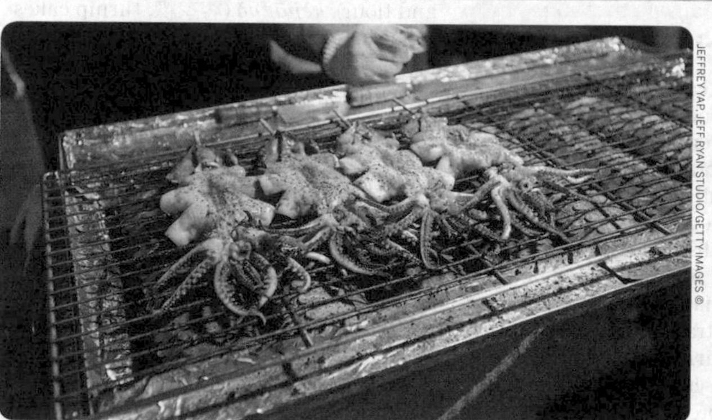

Top: Jiufen Teahouse (p142)

Bottom: Grilled cuttlefish

JEFFREY YAP; JEFF RYAN STUDIO/GETTY IMAGES ©

One of the most popular dishes is *fó tiào qiáng* (佛跳牆, 'Buddha Jumps Over the Wall'), a stew of seafood, chicken, duck and pork simmered in a jar of rice wine. Allegedly the dish is so tasty that even the Buddha – a vegetarian, of course – would hop over a wall to get a taste.

Cantonese

This is what non-Chinese consider 'Chinese' food, largely because most émigré restaurateurs in other countries originate from Guangdong (Canton) or Hong Kong. Cantonese flavours are generally more subtle than other Chinese styles – almost sweet, with very few spicy dishes. Cantonese cooking emphasises the use of fresh ingredients, which is why so many restaurants are lined with tanks full of live fish and seafood.

Cantonese *diǎnxīn* (點心, dim sum) snacks are famous and can be found in restaurants around Taiwan's bigger cities. As well as *chāshāobāo* (叉燒包, barbecued pork buns), you'll find *chūnjuǎn* (春卷, spring rolls), *zhōu* (粥, rice porridge) and, of course, *jī jiǎo* (雞腳, chicken feet) – an acquired taste.

Aboriginal

Travellers who visit Taiwan without sampling the dishes of the tribal peoples who called the island home millennia before the first Han sailor ever laid eyes on Ilha Formosa are definitely missing out. The product of hunters, gatherers and fishing people, aboriginal dishes tend to be heavy in wild game and mountain vegetables, as well as a variety of seafood.

One must-try dish is *tiěbǎn shānzhūròu* (鐵板山豬肉, fatty wild boar grilled, sliced, and grilled again with onions and wild greens). A staple that's easy to carry and an excellent source of calories to bring along on a hike is *zhútǒng fàn* (竹筒飯, steamed rice – with and without meat – stuffed into a bamboo stalk); these bamboo-inspired energy bars are a speciality of the Tsou aboriginal tribe in Alishan, who are also known for their love of bird's nest fern, tree tomatoes and millet wine.

Over in Sandimen, millet is the staple of the Rukai diet, while *qínàbù* (奇那步), or taro and meat dumplings, and grilled wild boar with papaya (木瓜拌山豬肉, *Mùguā bàn shānzhūròu*) can also be tasted in many Rukai villages. The Baiyi in Cingjing, who originally came from Yunnan, infuse their mushroom and meat dishes with herbs such as mint, chillies and stinging 'flower peppers'.

Vegetarian

Taiwanese vegetarian cuisine has plenty to offer any traveller, vegetarian or not. The country's Buddhist roots run deep, and while only a small (but still sizeable) percentage of Taiwanese are vegetarian, a fair chunk of the population abstains from meat for spiritual or health reasons every now and again, even if only for a day or a week.

Buddhist vegetarian restaurants are easy to find. Just look for the gigantic *savastika* (an ancient Buddhist symbol that looks like a reverse swastika) hanging in front of the restaurant. Every neighbourhood and town will generally have at least one vegetarian buffet. The Taiwanese are masters at adding variety to vegetarian cooking, as well as creating 'mock meat' dishes made of tofu or gluten on which veritable miracles have been performed.

Drinks

Tea

Tea is a fundamental part of Chinese life. In fact, an old Chinese saying identifies tea as one of the seven basic necessities of life (along with fuel, oil, rice, salt, soy sauce and vinegar). Taiwan's long growing season and hilly terrain are perfectly suited for producing excellent tea, especially high-mountain oolong, which is prized among tea connoisseurs the world over (and makes a great gift for the folks back home).

There are two types of teashops in Taiwan. The first are traditional teashops (more commonly called teahouses) where customers brew their own tea in a traditional clay pot, choosing from several types of high-quality leaves, and sit for hours playing cards or Chinese chess. These places can be found tucked away in alleys in almost every urban area, but are best visited up in the mountains. Taipei's Maokong is an excellent place to experience a traditional Taiwanese teahouse.

NOCTURNAL FOOD FUN

One Taiwan experience you can't miss out on is eating at a night market. Though Taipei's night markets are arguably the most famous, all cities in Taiwan have at least a few of their own, and even a medium-sized town will have a street set up with food stalls selling traditional Taiwanese eats late into the night. We've listed our favourite night markets in our city headings, but you're sure to find ones you like all over the island.

So what kind of food can you expect to find on the fly in Taiwan? Some items won't surprise people used to eating Asian food back home. Taiwanese *shuǐjiǎo* (水餃, dumplings) are always a good bet, especially for those looking to fill up on the cheap. Stuffed with meat, spring onion and greens, *shuǐjiǎo* can be served by the bowl in a soup, and sometimes dry by weight. For a dipping sauce, locals mix chilli (辛辣, *làjiāo*), vinegar (醋, *cù*) and soy sauce (醬油, *jiàngyóu*) in a bowl according to taste. Other street snacks include *zhà dòufu* (炸豆腐, fried tofu), *lǔ dòufu* (滷味, tofu soaked in soy sauce) and *kǎo fānshǔ* (烤番薯, baked sweet potatoes), which can be bought by weight.

Probably the most recognisable Taiwanese street snack is *chòu dòufu* (stinky fermented tofu). This deep-fried dish is something of an acquired taste, like certain European cheeses: generally speaking, people either love the stuff or they can't stand it. Another strange food to look out for is *pídàn* (皮蛋, 'thousand year eggs'), duck eggs that are covered in straw and stored underground for six months – the yolk turns green and the white becomes like jelly. Other interesting snacks available at markets include *jī jiǎo* (chicken feet), *zhū ěrduo* (豬耳朵, pig ears) and even *zhū jiǎo* (豬腳, pig feet).

The second are the stands found on every street corner. These specialise in bubble tea – a mixture of tea, milk, flavouring, sugar and giant black tapioca balls. Also called pearl tea, the sweet drink is popular with students, who gather at tea stands after school to socialise and relax, much in the way that the older generation gathers at traditional teahouses.

Coffee

Coffee, once hard to come by, is now widely consumed all over Taiwan (p96). A world-class coffee culture – certainly the best in Asia – is fast laying roots here. Not only is Taiwan big on coffee consumption – good quality coffee can be easily found in big cities like Taipei, Tainan and Kaohsiung – but the island is experimenting with growing the stuff as well.

In the past few years a number of coffee plantations in southern Taiwan have begun producing coffee for domestic consumption and export. Key coffee-growing regions include Dongshan Coffee Road in Tainan, Dewen in Sandimen and Gukeng near Chiayi.

Juices

Fresh-fruit stands selling juices and smoothies are all over Taiwan – these drinks make wonderful thirst quenchers on a hot summer day. All you have to do is point at the fruits you want (some shops have cut fruit ready-mixed in a cup) and the person standing behind the counter will whiz them up in a blender for you after adding water or milk. Especially good are iced-papaya milkshakes.

Popular juices include *hāmìguā* (哈密瓜, honeydew melon), *xīguā* (西瓜, watermelon), *píngguǒ* (蘋果, apple) and *gānzhè* (甘蔗, sugarcane). Sugarcane juice is usually sold at speciality stands selling raw sugarcane rather than ordinary fruit stands.

Harder Stuff

The Taiwanese tend to be fairly moderate drinkers (with some exceptions, such as banquets, being a time when much drinking occurs), but Taiwan does have a number of locally produced inebriants well worth trying. The most famous of these is *gāoliáng jiǔ* (高粱酒, Kaoliang liquor). Made from fermented sorghum, Kaoliang is produced on Kinmen and Matsu, the islands closest to mainland China. Another local favourite is *wéishìbǐ* (維士比, Whisbih), an energy drink with a fine mixture of *dānguī* (當歸, a medicinal herb), ginseng, taurine, various B vitamins and caffeine – and some ethyl alcohol to give it a kick.

How to Eat & Drink

When & Where

Most breakfast places open at about 7am and close midmorning. A traditional breakfast in Taiwan usually consists of watery rice porridge (鹹粥, *xián zhōu*), baked layered flatbread (燒餅, *shāobǐng*) and steamed buns (饅頭, *mántóu*), served plain or with fillings; the meal is generally washed down with plain or sweetened hot soybean milk (豆漿, *dòujiāng*). Other popular breakfast foods include rolled omelettes (蛋餅, *dàn bǐng*), egg sandwiches (雞蛋三明治, *jīdàn sānmíngzhì*) and turnip cakes (蘿蔔糕, *luóbo gāo*).

The Taiwanese generally eat lunch between 11.30am and 2pm, many taking their midday meal from any number of small eateries on the streets. *Zìzhù cāntīng* (自助餐廳, self-serve cafeterias) are a good option, offering plenty of meat and vegetable dishes to choose from.

Dinner in Taiwan is usually eaten from 5pm to 11pm, though some restaurants and food stalls in bigger cities stay open 24 hours. Taiwan's cities – especially the larger ones – all have a fair-to-excellent selection of international restaurants. Don't be surprised to run into a small Indonesian, Indian or even Mexican eatery on a back alley.

The most important thing to remember in Taiwan when it comes to food is that some of the best eats are found on the street – gourmands know that some of Asia's best street eats are found in night markets in and around Taiwan's cities.

Bars often keep long hours in Taiwan, opening in the afternoon and closing late at night. Most bars offer a limited menu, while some offer full-course meals. Expect to pay around NT$150 or more for a beer.

For a list of menu items, see p385.

Etiquette for Dining Out

➡ In restaurants, every customer gets an individual bowl of rice or a small soup bowl. It is quite acceptable to hold the bowl close to your lips and shovel the contents into your mouth with your chopsticks. If the food contains bones, just place them on the tablecloth (it's changed after each meal), or into a separate bowl if one is provided.

➡ Remember to fill your neighbours' teacups when they are empty, as yours will be filled by them. You can thank the pourer by tapping your middle finger on the table gently. On no account should you serve yourself tea without serving others first. When your teapot needs a refill, signal this to the wait staff by taking the lid off the pot.

➡ Taiwanese toothpick etiquette is similar to that of neighbouring Asian countries: one hand wields the toothpick while the other shields the mouth from prying eyes.

➡ Probably the most important piece of etiquette comes with the bill: although you are expected to try to pay, you shouldn't argue too hard, as the one who extended the invitation will inevitably foot the bill. While splitting the cost of the meal is fashionable among the younger generation, as a guest you'll probably be treated most of the time.

Regions at a Glance

Taipei is surrounded by forested hills and heritage towns that make the best day trips. Within the city limits there are world-class museums, historic temples, and never-ending opportunities for snacking and shopping. Heading out towards the coast or the mountains puts the traveller in northern Taiwan, with its hot springs, surf spots, and many cycling and hiking routes. The dusty plains of western Taiwan hold some of the best temple towns, while heading east the unspoiled Central Mountains rise quickly to over 3000m. Over the mountains lies eastern Taiwan, the least developed region of the country, with a landscape that's pure eye candy. In tropical southern Taiwan, ecotourists brush against culture vultures taking in traditional festivals and night markets. Finally, scattered on both sides of the mainland are Taiwan's islands, boasting a Cold War legacy, timeless seaside villages and a top windsurfing destination.

Taipei

Food
History
Shopping

Eating

With hundreds of restaurants incorporating culinary influences from every corner of China, some of the best Japanese outside Japan, hands-down Asia's best coffee, and a night market scene loaded with unique local snacks, Taipei definitely has it all foodwise.

History

Co-existing with Taipei's flashy modernity, you'll find temples and markets dating back centuries, as well as neighbourhoods and parks from the Japanese colonial era now being revived as culture and entertainment centres.

Shopping

Taipei shines in locally designed products such as ceramics, glassware, clothing, tea sets, jade, home furnishings and knickknacks. You'll also find a host of enticing agricultural products, from designer desserts to organic teas.

p52

Northern Taiwan

Outdoor Activities
Hot Springs
Museums

Hiking & Cycling

The north's network of trails cross landscapes that vary from tropical jungles to alpine meadows above 3000m. The roads offer some first-class cycling, with day and multiday options along coastal routes, riverside paths and cross-island highways.

Hot Springs

With dozens of hot springs dotting the north, there's always a place for a dip somewhere close by. And with facilities ranging from five-star resorts to natural pools deep in the mountains, there's something for every taste and style.

Museums

Once a centre for traditional cottage industries such as tea, pottery and woodcarving, as well as gold and coal mining, the north boasts a rich, little collection of museums highlighting them all. Master carver Juming and his internationally acclaimed works have their own outdoor park.

p122

Taroko National Park & the East Coast

Landscapes
Cycling
Culture

Gorges, the Coast & the Rift Valley

Much of the east has hardly changed its face for modern times. It's still a land of 1000m seaside cliffs, marble gorges, subtropical forests and vast yellow rice fields nestled between blue-tinged mountain ranges.

Cycling

The scenery that makes the east a draw for nature lovers is best viewed at cycling speeds. The premier challenge is an 86km route from sea level to 3275m through Taroko Gorge, but most opt for all or part of the 400km loop down the coastline and back through the Rift Valley.

Aboriginal Festivals & Art

Hunting, fishing and coming-of-age festivals dot the summer calendar. Woodcarvers operate small studios up and down the driftwood-rich coastline, while Dulan's weekly bash at a former sugar factory is keeping the music alive.

p170

Yushan National Park & Western Taiwan

Mountains
Culture
Wildlife

Hiking & Landscapes

The 3000m plus spine of Taiwan runs through the west, with three ranges competing for scenic supremacy. Yushan (3952m), the highest mountain in Taiwan, is just one of many worthy hiking opportunities.

Temples & Traditional Festivals

As one of the first areas settled by Chinese immigrants, the west is home to some of Taiwan's oldest temples. Exuberant yearly festivals such as the week-long Matsu Pilgrimage honour a pantheon of traditional folk gods.

Bird- & Butterfly-Watching

With its wealth of protected reserves and national parks, the west is a haven for endemic species such as the Mikado pheasant and several hundred butterfly species. Vast numbers of purple milkweed butterflies pass through each year.

p202

Southern Taiwan

Culture
Wildlife
Food

Temples & Traditional Festivals

Early immigrants to Taiwan faced a hostile environment. In the south, the legacy of the faith that sustained them is evident in a wealth of old temples and the spectacular boat-burning festival in Donggang.

Bird- & Butterfly-Watching

The warm, sheltered valleys of the south provide a safe winter haven for millions of butterflies. The ponds, forests, grasslands and lakes of Kenting National Park support hundreds of species of birds year-round, making the region one of Taiwan's top twitching venues.

Night Markets & Traditional Snacks

Tainan's traditional snacks are famous throughout Taiwan: slack season noodles and coffin cake are just a couple of quirky, mouth-watering highlights. Kaohsiung's night markets serve everything, but specialise in fresh-off-the-boat seafood.

p240

Taiwan's Islands

Landscapes
Activities
History

Beaches & Coastal Scenery

Penghu's beaches are Taiwan's finest, and the traditional villages are a nice backdrop. The volcanic origins of Lanyu, Green Island and Penghu have left coastal formations such as towering basalt columns. Kinmen's landscape includes lakes, mudflats and fine beaches.

Windsurfing & Snorkelling

As the windiest place in the northern hemisphere in late autumn, Penghu attracts windsurfers from all over the world. For snorkellers, the easily accessed coral reefs off Lanyu and Green Island burst with marine life and colour year-round.

History

Former frontiers of the civil war, Matsu and Kinmen have a rich legacy of old military tunnels, memorials and museums. More interesting to many are the traditional villages, wonderfully preserved because of their frontier status.

p279

On the Road

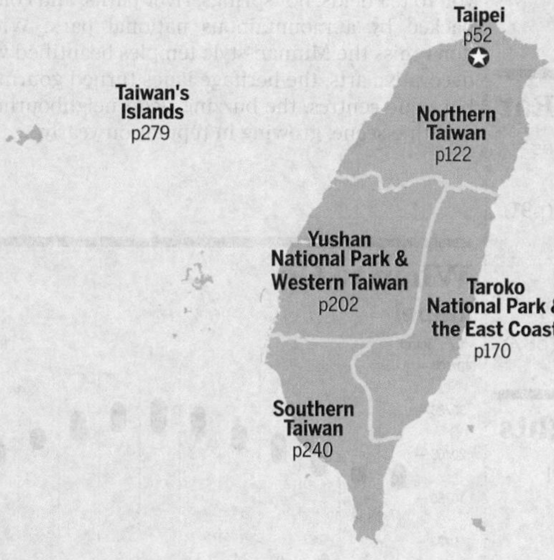

Taipei
p52

Taiwan's Islands
p279

Northern Taiwan
p122

Yushan National Park & Western Taiwan
p202

Taroko National Park & the East Coast
p170

Southern Taiwan
p240

Taipei

☎02 / POP 2.6 MILLION

Includes ➡

Best Places to Eat

- ➡ Yongkang Beef Noodles (p90)
- ➡ Ningxia Night Market (p91)
- ➡ Addiction Aquatic Development (p95)
- ➡ Drunken Monkey (p89)
- ➡ Shenkeng Old Street (p87)

Best Small Sights

- ➡ Miniatures Museum of Taiwan (p73)
- ➡ Treasure Hill (p65)
- ➡ Land Bank Exhibition Hall (p59)
- ➡ National Museum of History (p64)
- ➡ Formosa Vintage Cafe (p63)

Why Go?

For a 300-year-old city, Taipei is having a very late coming-of-age party. But then again, this unhurried but vibrant capital has taken a while to become comfortable in its own skin. With Chinese, Japanese and Western influences in its food, culture, folk arts and architecture, Taipei has finally decided that it's a mix, and all the better for it.

As with the multifarious street food, the traveller is advised to go for the *xiao chi* (little snacks) in everything. Day trips are particularly delicious, and a quick MRT ride takes you to tea fields, hot springs, river parks, and colonial towns backed by a mountainous national park. Within Taipei don't miss the Minnan-style temples beautified with unique decorative arts, the heritage lanes turned gourmet cafe and boutique centres, the buzzing neon neighbourhoods or the nightlife scene, growing in reputation yearly.

When to Go

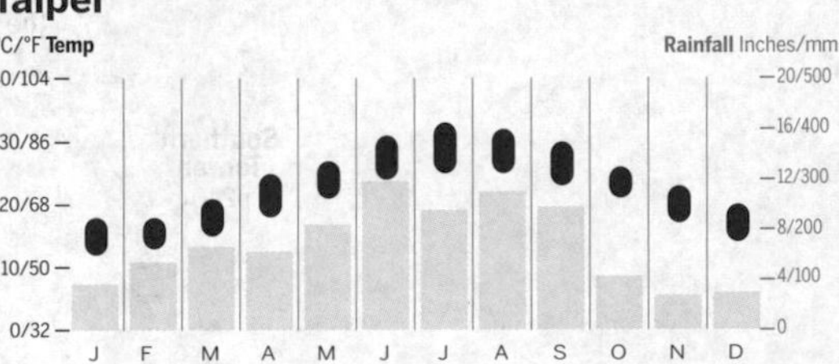

Jan & Feb The weeks before and after the Lunar New Year are a great time to visit.

Jun–Sep Fresh, luscious tropical fruits are readily available.

Oct–Dec The hot summer is gone but the winter chill yet to begin: the perfect time to explore Taipei.

Taipei Highlights

❶ See an art legacy spanning millennia at the **National Palace Museum** (p69).

❷ Be charmed by the historic district of **Tamsui** (p106).

❸ Explore the spiritual and artistic legacy of temples such as **Bao'an** (p65).

❹ **Cycle** urban riding lanes and riverside paths (p76).

❺ Shop, snack and people-watch in **Ximending** (p60).

❻ Hike and hot spring in **Yangmingshan National Park** (p114).

❼ Sip gourmet coffee along historic **Dihua Street** (p67).

❽ Feast at night markets such as **Ningxia Night Market** (p91), currently Taipei's best.

❾ Touch the sky from the top of Asia's tallest building, **Taipei 101** (p75).

Greater Taipei

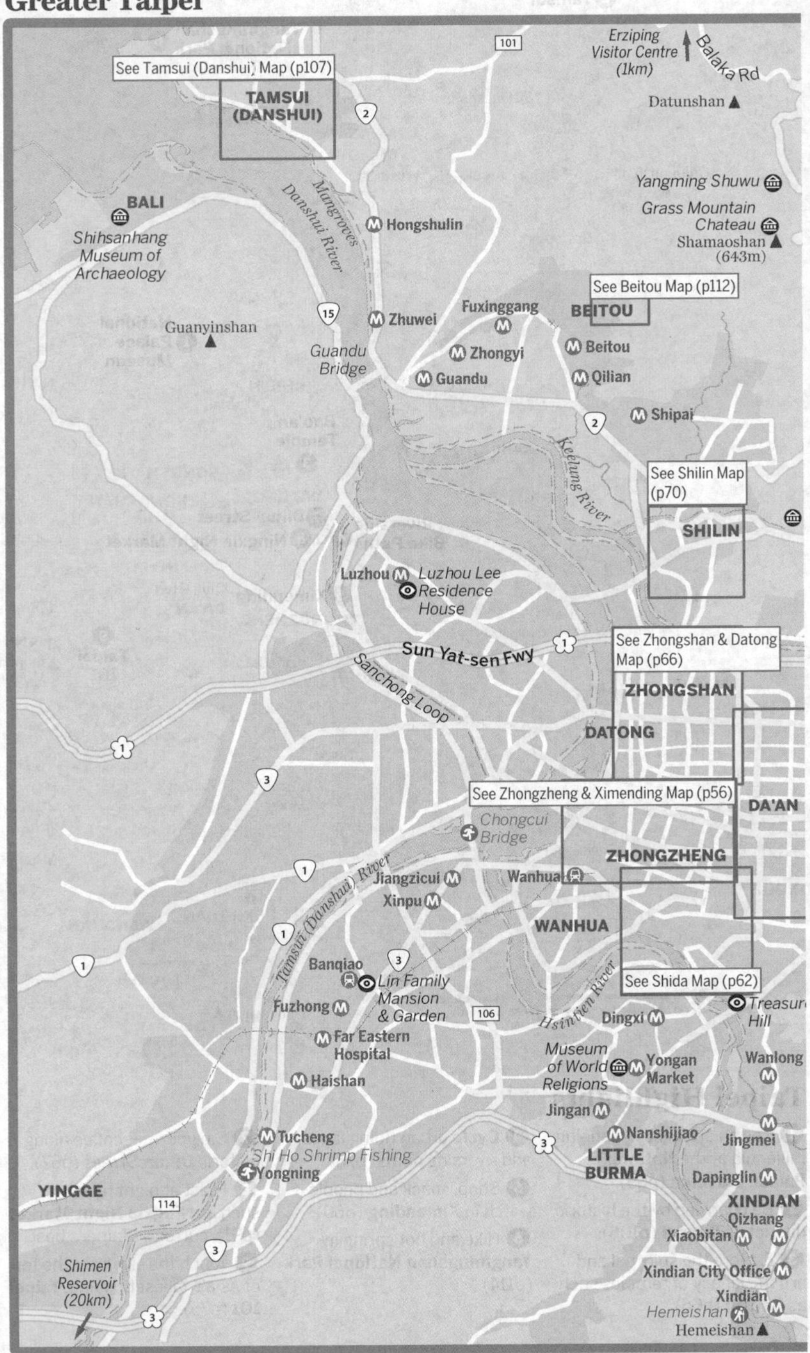

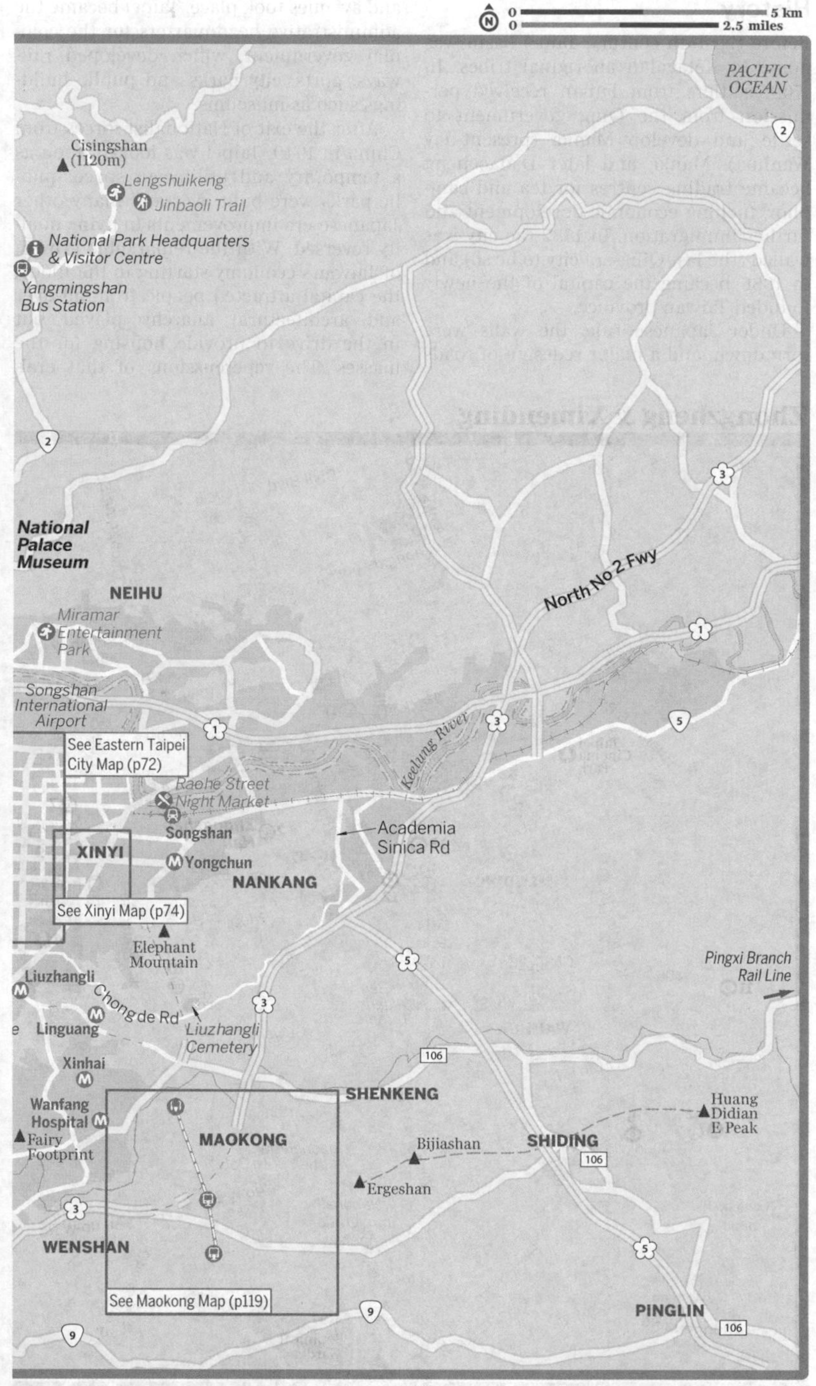

0 5 km
0 2.5 miles
PACIFIC OCEAN
Cisingshan (1120m)
Lengshuikeng
Jinbaoli Trail
National Park Headquarters & Visitor Centre
Yangmingshan Bus Station
National Palace Museum
NEIHU
Miramar Entertainment Park
Songshan International Airport
See Eastern Taipei City Map (p72)
Raohe Street Night Market
Songshan
XINYI
Yongchun
NANKANG
See Xinyi Map (p74)
Elephant Mountain
Liuzhangli
Chongde Rd
Linguang
Liuzhangli Cemetery
Xinhai
Wanfang Hospital
Fairy Footprint
MAOKONG
WENSHAN
See Maokong Map (p119)
Keelung River
Academia Sinica Rd
North No 2 Fwy
Pingxi Branch Rail Line
SHENKENG
Huang Didian E Peak
Bijiashan
SHIDING
Ergeshan
PINGLIN

History

Before the 18th century, Taipei basin was home to Ketagalan aboriginal tribes. In 1709, settlers from Fujian received permission from the Qing government to settle and develop Manka (present-day Wanhua). Manka and later Dadaocheng became trading centres for tea and camphor, fuelling economic development and further immigration. In 1882 the city was walled (the last Qing-era city to be so) and in 1886 became the capital of the newly founded Taiwan province.

Under Japanese rule, the walls were torn down, and a major redesign of roads and avenues took place. Taipei became the administrative headquarters for the colonial government, which developed railways, ports, city parks and public buildings such as museums.

After the exit of Nationalist forces from China in 1949, Taipei was looked upon as a temporary and utilitarian space: public parks were built over and many other Japanese-era improvements in living quality reversed. With the remarkable growth of Taiwan's economy starting in the 1960s, the capital attracted people from all over and architectural anarchy played out in the drive to provide housing for the masses. The repercussions of that era's

Zhongzheng & Ximending

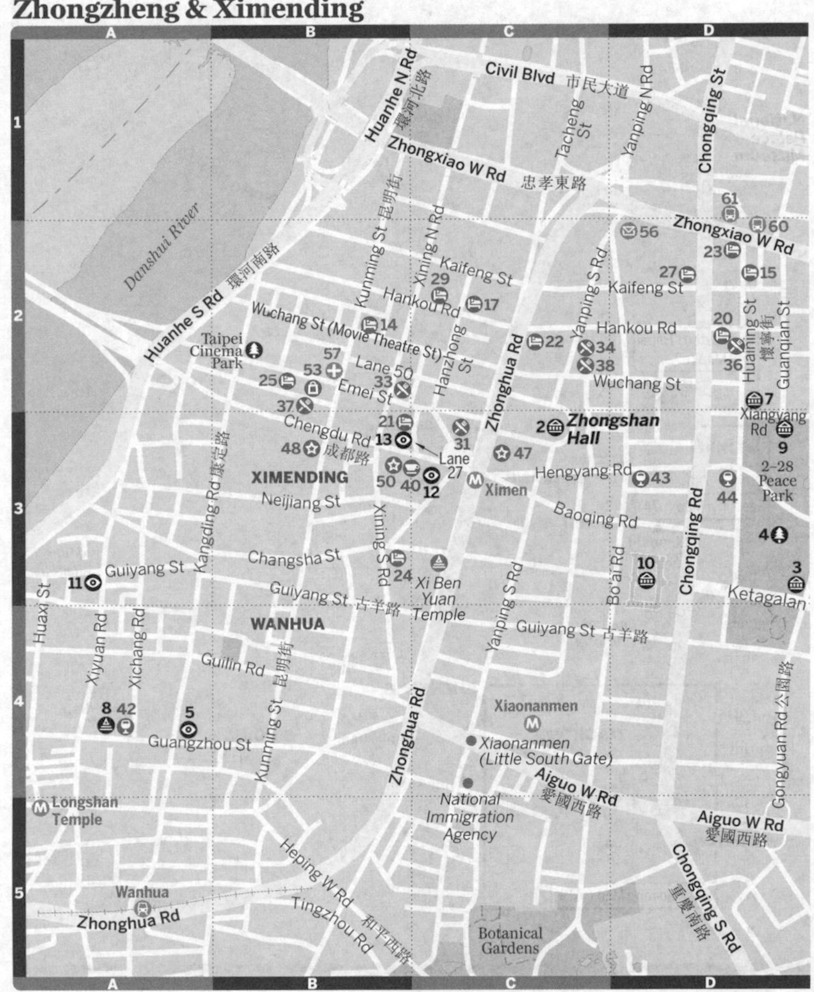

lack of planning played no small part in winning Taipei the reputation as the 'Ugly Duckling' of Asia.

Since the late 1990s, however, beginning with the mayorship of Chen Shui-bian, the city has made a remarkable transformation into one of the most liveable and vibrant cities in Asia. Current mayor Hau Lung-bin ran on a platform of making the city beautiful and, while he still has some way to go, Taipei is cleaner, greener, has more visible heritage and is more visitor-friendly than ever.

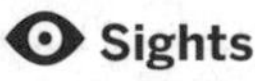

Sights

Zhongzheng 中正

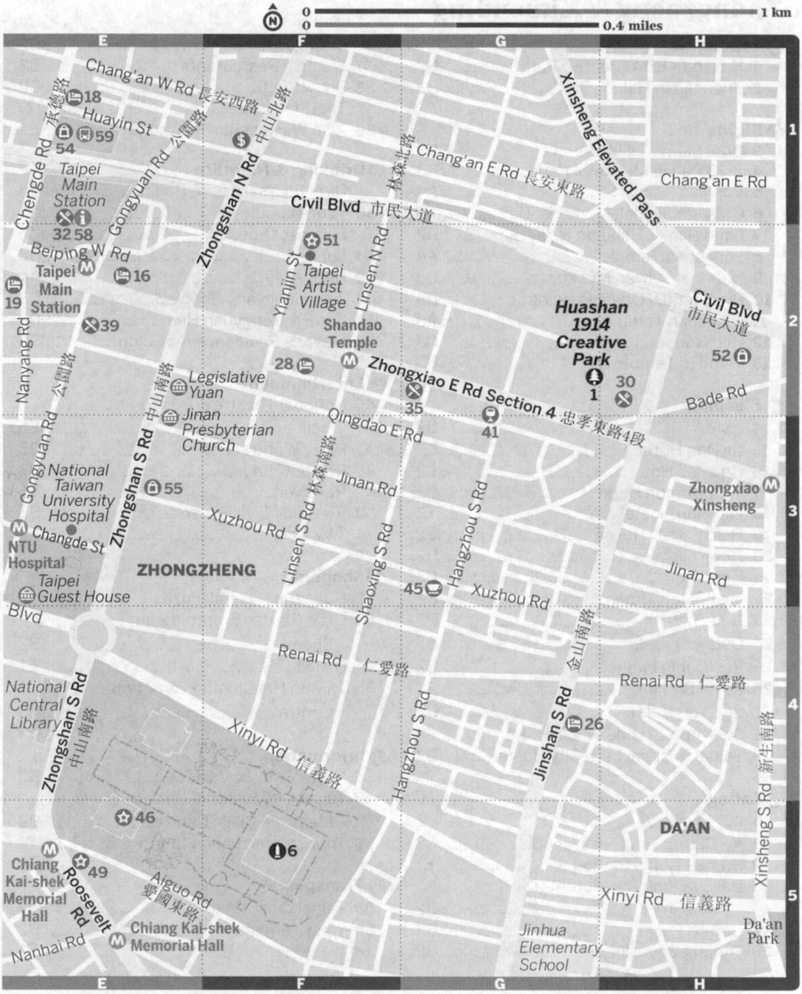

Named after Chiang Kai-shek, this central district includes most of the government offices in Taipei, as well as museums, parks, historical sites and Taipei Main Station (for trains, High Speed Rail, MRT and buses). Zhongzheng (Zhōngzhèng) covers the old Qing-era walled city, in addition to the areas planned under the Japanese. As such you'll find the Main Station area has narrow streets and arcade walkways, while south and west the roads are wide tree-lined boulevards.

★Huashan 1914 Creative Park CULTURE PARK

(華山1914; Map p56; www.huashan1914.com; ⌚24hr, shops & restaurants vary; 📶; Ⓜ Zhongxiao Xinsheng) Borrowing from Western urban regeneration models, this early 20th-century wine factory has been restored into Taipei's most retro-chic venue. Remodelled warehouses now hold live music performances, shops sell innovative Taiwan-designed products, and a host of stylish restaurants, cafes and bars will have you nodding to the ambience as much as the food.

The factory opened in 1916 as a private wine-making facility, and was finally shuttered in 1987. The area would probably be just another block of overpriced city apartments today if not for arts groups, which discovered, in 1997, that the old factory provided a perfect venue for performances, workshops and installations (the warehouses are spacious, have high ceilings and are flooded with natural light).

In 2003, after years of pressure, the city gave management of Huashan to the Council for Cultural Affairs. After a multiyear resto-

Zhongzheng & Ximending

Top Sights

1 Huashan 1914 Creative Park G2
2 Zhongshan Hall C3

Sights

3 2-28 Memorial Museum D3
4 2-28 Peace Memorial Park D3
5 Bopiliao A4
6 Chiang Kai-shek Memorial Hall F5
7 Land Bank Exhibition Hall D2
8 Longshan Temple A4
9 National Taiwan Museum D3
10 Presidential Office Building D3
11 Qingshan Temple A3
12 Red House C3
13 Tien-Ho Temple B3

Sleeping

14 AMBA B2
15 CityInn Hotel D2
16 Cosmos Hotel E2
17 East Dragon Hotel C2
18 Flip Flop Hostel E1
19 Holo Family House E2
20 Hotel Flowers D2
21 Hotel Puri B3
22 Just Sleep Ximen C2
23 New Stay Inn D2
24 Qstay B3
25 Red Cabin Inn B2
26 Royal Biz Hotel G4
27 See You Hotel D2
28 Sheraton Grande Taipei Hotel F2
29 Taipei Backpackers-City Hostel C2

Eating

30 Alleycat's H2
31 Ay-Chung Flour Rice Noodle C3
32 Breeze Taipei Station E1
33 Dai Sya Rinn Restaurant (Da Che Lun) B2
34 Dongyi Paigu C2
35 Fuhang Soy Milk G2
36 Loving Hut D2
37 Sichuan Restaurants B2
38 Snow King C2
Thai Flavors .... (see 12)
39 Xiao Wei Sichuan Restaurant E2

Drinking & Nightlife

Director Tsai's Café Galerie .... (see 2)
40 Fong Da Coffee C3
Fortress Cafe .... (see 2)
41 Funky G2
42 Herb Alley A4
43 Jolly Hengyang Shop D3
44 Lao Pai Gongyuan Hao D3
45 Mayor's Residence Art Salon G3

Entertainment

46 National Theatre & Concert Hall E5
47 Party World C3
48 Rainbow Sauna B3
49 Revolver E5
50 Riverside Live House B3
51 TAV Cafe F2

Shopping

52 Guanghua Digital Plaza H2
53 Little Garden Embroidered Shoes B2
54 Q Mall E1
55 Taiwan Handicraft Promotion Centre E3

Information

56 North Gate Post Office D2
57 Taipei City Hospital Chinese Medicine Clinic Centre B2
58 Tourist Information Booth E1

Transport

59 Taipei Bus Station E1
60 West Terminal A D2
61 West Terminal B D1

ration Huashan emerged as a popular gathering spot for families and hipsters alike, a source of urban pride, and a venue for both the promotion and dissemination of new ideas about both art and urban living.

The factory grounds are open 24/7 but individual shops, restaurants and performance venues vary. There's an information centre near the front as you face the grounds off Bade Rd.

Land Bank Exhibition Hall MUSEUM
(土銀分館, Tǔyín Fēnguǎn; Map p56; 25 Xiangyang Rd; admission $20; ⏲9.30am-5pm; Ⓜ NTU Hospital) Evolution is the theme at this museum, set in a 1930s former bank: evolution of life, evolution of money and banking, and evolution of the bank from the Japanese colonial era to modern Taipei. It's an odd juxtaposition but the displays at each level, from soaring sauropod fossils to the open bank vault, are well presented and rich in details.

The original building opened in 1933 as the Kangyo Bank, and is a mix of Western and Japanese styles. The 1st-floor exhibit takes you into the old bank vault for a look at money, lending facilities and bank machinery. The fossil display area includes full replicas of a tyrannosaurus, triceratops, sauropod and fossil elephants from Penghu that you can examine from toes to nose from the staircase that winds round the atrium.

2-28 Peace Memorial Park PARK
(二二八和平紀念公園, Èrèrbā Hépíng pinyin Gōngyuán; Map p56; Ⓜ NTU Hospital) Established in 1908, this was the first urban public park in Taiwan built on European models. Known as Taihoku (Taipei) Park under the Japanese, then Taipei New Park under the Kuomintang (KMT), its present name hails from 1996 in recognition that one of the pivotal events in Taiwanese modern history began here: the massacre known as the 2-28 Incident. The incident (p330) involved an uprising in which Taiwanese protested against the post-WWII Chinese government set in place by Chiang Kai-shek. In the months following, tens of thousands of people were killed.

In the centre of the park stands a memorial to 2-28 and in the southern end of the park a museum dedicated to the event. But otherwise this lovely little area of old trees, pond, pavilions, pathways, bandstands, shrines and historical relics is used just as its founders intended: as a meeting place, a hangout and a general refuge from the city.

2-28 Memorial Museum MUSEUM
(二二八紀念館, Èrèrbā Jìniànguǎn; Map p56; admission $20; ⏲10am-5pm Tue-Sun; Ⓜ NTU Hospital) Located inside the 2-28 Park, the 2-28 Memorial Museum offers an explanation of the events of the 28 February 1947 massacre and the repercussions that followed. Acknowledgement of the 2-28 incident was a pivotal part of Taiwan's transformation from dictatorship to democracy.

Though there is little in the way of English signage in the museum, a very good multilingual walking tour device is available. In addition to the 2-28 Incident itself, displays cover the drive for self-rule in Taiwan in the 1920s and '30s, and the role radio played in society at the time. The museum building itself was once the Taiwan Radio Station, and it was from here that KMT officials tried to calm the masses as panic swept the island (for more, see p330).

Chiang Kai-shek Memorial Hall MONUMENT, MUSEUM
(中正紀念堂, Zhōngzhèng Jìniàn Táng; Map p56; 21 Zhongshan S Rd; ⏲9am-6pm; 📶; Ⓜ Chiang Kai-shek Memorial Hall) FREE This grandiose monument to authoritarian leader Chiang Kai-shek is a popular attraction, but don't let anyone convince you it's a great piece of architecture. Mocked for politically correct bad taste, the hall is a prime example of the so-called palace, or neo-classical, style favoured by CKS as a counterpoint to the Cultural Revolution's destruction of real classical culture in China.

Entrance to the main hall is made via a series of 88 steps (the age of Chiang when he died). Inside the cavernous hall is an artefact museum with Chiang's two Cadillacs, various documents and articles from daily life. The hourly changing of the honour guard is probably the most popular sight with most visitors.

In 2007, the park was renamed 'Liberty Square' in honour of Taiwan's long road to democracy, and for a time it was conceivable that the memorial itself would be renamed and the Chiang sculpture itself removed. That didn't happen, and the reasons (which will vary depending on who you ask) pretty much summarise where modern Taiwan is at both politically and socially.

Presidential Office Building HISTORIC BUILDING
(總統府, Zǒngtǒng Fǔ; Map p56; www.president.gov.tw; 122 Chongqing S Rd, Sec 1; with passport free; ⏲9-11.30am Mon-Fri; Ⓜ NTU Hospital) FREE

Built in 1919 as the seat of the Japanese Governor-General of Taiwan, this striking building has housed the offices of the Republic of China (ROC) president since 1949. Its classical European-fusion style includes many Japanese cultural elements, such as a sunrise facing front, and a shape in the form of the character 日, part of 日本 (Japan), as seen from the air.

National Taiwan Museum MUSEUM

(國立台灣博物館, Guólì Táiwān Bówùguǎn; Map p56; www.ntm.gov.tw; 2 Xiangyang Rd; admission NT$20; ⏲9.30am-5pm Tue-Sun; 📶; Ⓜ NTU Hospital) Established in 1908 as Taiwan's first public museum, the present location in 2-28 Park hails from 1915. Unless there is a special exhibit happening (they are frequent and often excellent), give this place a miss as the permanent natural history and prehistory displays aren't particularly interesting and have little accompanying English write-up.

Ximending & Wanhua

When the port of Tamsui was forced open after the Second Opium War (1856–60), northern Taiwan began to pass the south as the island's political and economic centre. Manka, the first part of the city to develop, grew rich with the trading of tea, coal and camphor. Over time the area lost its importance, however, and is now mostly thought of as an ageing if not decaying community. Of all the areas of Taipei, you'll probably find this the most run-down, though it's generally as safe as anywhere else.

Ximending is technically part of Wanhua District but we treat this ultraconsumerist heart of Taipei's mainstream youth culture as its own little world. In the Japanese era it was the entertainment centre for Wanhua and today, like Tokyo's Ginza, this eight-branched intersection (largely pedestrianised) is chock-full of cosplay (costume play) dressers, fast food, and shops selling novelties, cosmetics and select designs. There's an entire street (Wuchang) devoted to movie theatres and a lane to tattooing and nail art (Lane 50 Hanzhong). If it's young and trendy it's here, but there are also some historic structures, and visitors of any age will enjoy the great range of food available.

Longshan Temple BUDDHIST TEMPLE

(龍山寺, Lóngshān Sì; Map p56; 211 Guangzhou St; ⏲6am-10pm; Ⓜ Longshan Temple) Founded in 1738 by Han immigrants from Fujian, this temple has served, in addition to being a house of worship, as a municipal, guild and self-defence centre. These days it is one of the city's top religious sites, and a prime venue for exploring both Taiwan's vibrant folk faith (p345) and its unique temple arts and architecture (p347).

Longshan is dedicated to the bodhisattva of mercy, Guanyin, though in true Taiwanese style there are over 100 other gods and goddesses worshipped in the rear and side halls. Matsu, goddess of the sea, is enshrined in the back centre; Wenchang Dijun, the god of literature, to the far right (come during exam period to see how important he is); red-faced Guan Gong, the god of war and patron of police and gangsters, enshrined to the far left; and in front of that, the Old Man under the Moon, known as the Matchmaker or the Chinese cupid.

As with most temples in Taiwan, Longshan has been rebuilt multiple times after destruction by earthquakes, typhoons and even bombing in the last days of WWII. The present structure (with elements from the masterful 1920s and post-WWII reconstructions) doesn't have the same flow and elegance as Bao'an Temple, but it is still an impressive structure with sweeping swallowtail eaves, colourful *jiǎnniàn* (mosaic-like temple decoration) figures on the roof, and elaborate stone and woodcarvings.

Check out the two-of-their-kind bronze pillars outside the front hall and the incense holders outside the main hall. The handles depict a common temple motif: 'the fool holding up the sky'. The Western-style appearance of the 'fools' is no coincidence. They are said to represent the Dutch (or sometimes Dutch slaves), who occupied Taiwan in the 17th century.

The best times to visit Longshan are around 6am, 8am and 5pm, when crowds of worshippers gather and engage in hypnotic chanting. Or try Guanyin's birthday on Lunar 19 February, or the weeks before and during Chinese New Year.

★Zhongshan Hall HISTORIC BUILDING

(中山堂, Zhōngshān Táng; Map p56; http://english.zsh.taipei.gov.tw; 98 Yanping S Rd; ⏲9am-9pm; 📶; Ⓜ Ximen) FREE This handsome four-storey building, constructed in 1936 for the coronation of Emperor Hirohito, is where the Japanese surrender ceremony was held in October 1945, and later where Chiang Kai-shek delivered public speeches from the terrace following his four 're-elections'. The 3rd-floor tearoom contains the masterwork *Water Buffalo* by Huang Tu-shui (1895–1930), the first Taiwanese artist to study in Japan.

Zhongshan Hall was one of the most modern buildings in Taiwan at the time it was built, and blends modernist and Western classical styling. Note the filings on the bricks (custom-made by a kiln in Beitou): the design scatters direct sunlight, making the building hard to see by enemy bombers (a worry as Japan had been skirmishing with China since 1931).

The hall is frequently used for performances and you can explore the inside at any time. The terrace of the Fortress Cafe is where Chiang gave his speeches.

Bopiliao STREET

(剝皮寮, Bō Pí Liáo; Map p56; cnr Kangding St & Gui; ⏲9am-6pm Tue-Sun; Ⓜ Longshan Temple) **FREE** One of the best-preserved historic sections of Wanhua, Bopiliao covers both Qing and early Japanese-era architecture. Inside are a number of permanent exhibitions on the history of Taipei, ranging from the establishment of Western medicine to education under the Japanese.

During the Japanese era the narrow Qing-built street and shops became the back alley to a new, wider Guangzhou St. As such the eras neatly divide themselves with Japanese buildings to the south and Qing in the north. The differing styles are easy to spot: Qing-era buildings are commonly red brick and store fronts are set back from arcades. Japanese buildings incorporate Western baroque designs and facades are embellished with flowers and other common motifs.

Bopiliao was the setting for many scenes in the Taiwan gangster flick *Monga*.

Red House CULTURAL CENTRE

(紅樓, Hónglóu; Map p56; www.redhouse.org.tw; 10 Chengdu Rd; admission free, except during events; ⏲11.30am-9.30pm; Ⓜ Ximen) Ximending's most iconic building was built in 1908 to serve as Taipei's first public market. These days it's a multifunctional cultural centre with regular live performances and exhibitions. There's an artist and designer weekend market in the north square (2pm to 9.30pm Saturday and Sunday) and 16 studios selling the works of local designers (2pm to 9.30pm Tuesday to Sunday) behind the main entrance.

In the Japanese era, the Red House came to symbolise the bustling commercialism of the Ximending district. Post-WWII it was an opera house, performance theatre, movie theatre and, finally, derelict building. These days it's once again the centrepiece of the district. Riverside Live House (p99) is at the back of the complex, and in the south court

TAIPEI IN...

Two Days

Admire the art and devotional atmosphere at **Bao'an**, **Longshan**, and **Xiahai Temples**, shop for ceramics on **Dihua St**, and then lunch in **Ximending**. Enjoy a coffee at **Fortress Cafe** before checking out other Japanese-era buildings and small museums around **2-28 Park**. After pondering the meaning of **Chiang Kai-shek Memorial Hall**, dine in retro-chic **Huashan 1914** and end the day with some late-night snacking at **Raohe Street Night Market**.

Start the next day with a coffee at **Haaya's Coffee**, then take the MRT to **Sun Yat-sen Memorial Hall** and ride a Youbike over to **Taipei 101**. Have lunch at **Good Cho's** then head to the **National Palace Museum**, one of the world's best for Chinese art. For dinner try dumplings or beef noodles on **Yongkang St**, followed by a stroll in **Da'an Park** and a nightcap at **Ounce Taipei** or tea at **Wistaria**.

Four Days

Follow the itinerary above and then plan for a full day in historic **Tamsui** with its temples, forts and colonial neighbourhoods. Begin with a stroll through the mangrove forests at **Hongshulin**.

The next morning hike through **Yangmingshan National Park**, have lunch at **Grass Mountain Chateau** and then catch a quick bus down to Beitou's **Taiwan Folk Arts Museum**. From here wander down past hot springs, temples and museums. Head back to Taipei for snacking at **Ningxia Night Market**.

are a dozen or so restaurants and bars, many catering to the city's gay crowd.

Qingshan Temple DAOIST TEMPLE
(青山宮, Qīngshān Gōng; Map p56; Guiyang St; ⌚5.30am-9pm; Ⓜ Longshan) Along with Longshan and Qingshui, this elegant temple is one of Wanhua's top houses of worship. First built in 1856, there is an abundance of top-quality wood, stone and decorative artwork to see here and the **god's birthday festival** is one of Taipei liveliest religious events.

Qingshan's resident god (Qingshan Wang, 青山王) is credited with saving the people

Shida

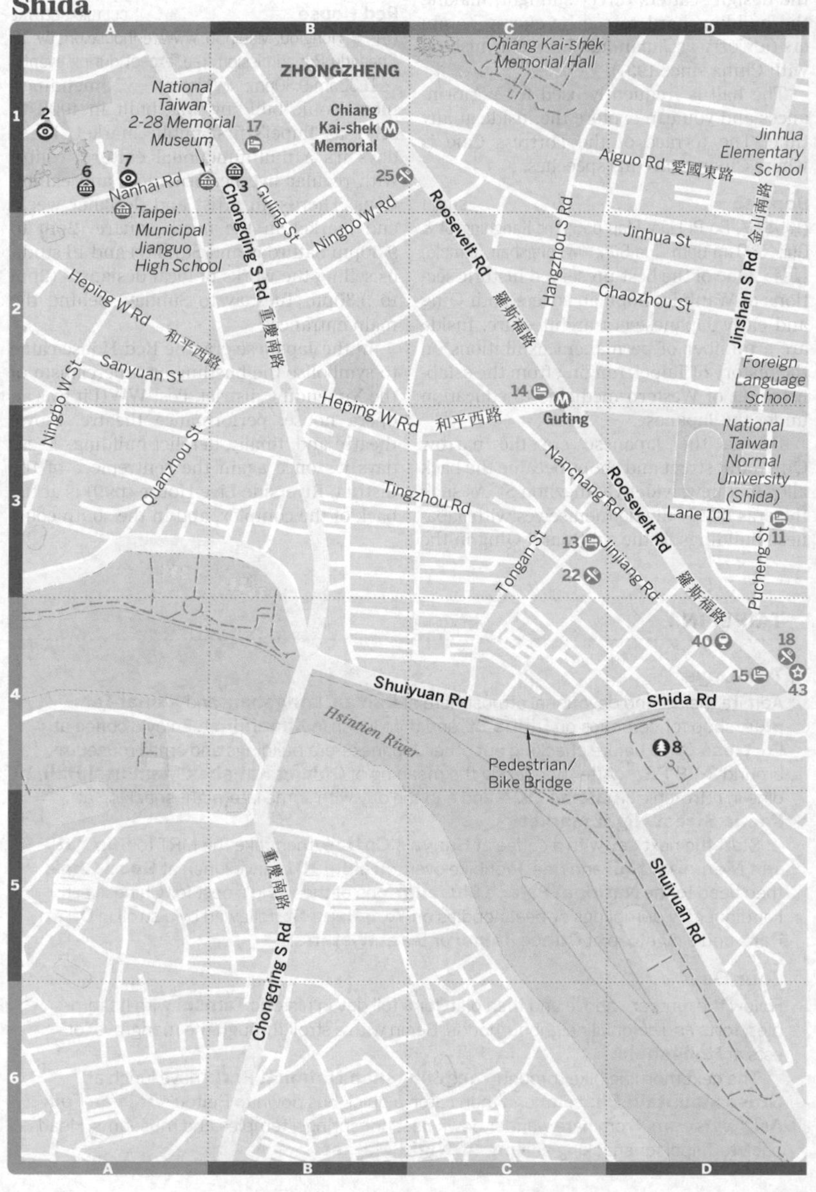

of Wanhua from a deadly plague. During the days of his birthday celebrations he sets out on a pilgrimage to expel evil from the neighbourhood. There are fireworks, gongs, lanterns and a colourful parade of people dressed up as gods, giant Infernal Generals, and other Taoist and folk figures. What makes this pilgrimage particularly dramatic and worth attending is that it takes place at night. Called the **Night Patrol** (夜間出巡, Yèjiān Chūxún), the parade takes place from 5pm to 9pm over two nights (the 20th and 21st days of the Lunar 10th month – around the end of November or early December).

The temple is worth a visit anytime to examine the stone work in the main hall, the octagonal plafond ceilings (built without nails), the lively cochin (brightly coloured, glazed ceramic) figures on either side of the worship hall, and the striking multicoloured *jiǎnniàn* (mosaic-like decoration) work on the roof, which you can admire up close by climbing the stairs at the back of the temple.

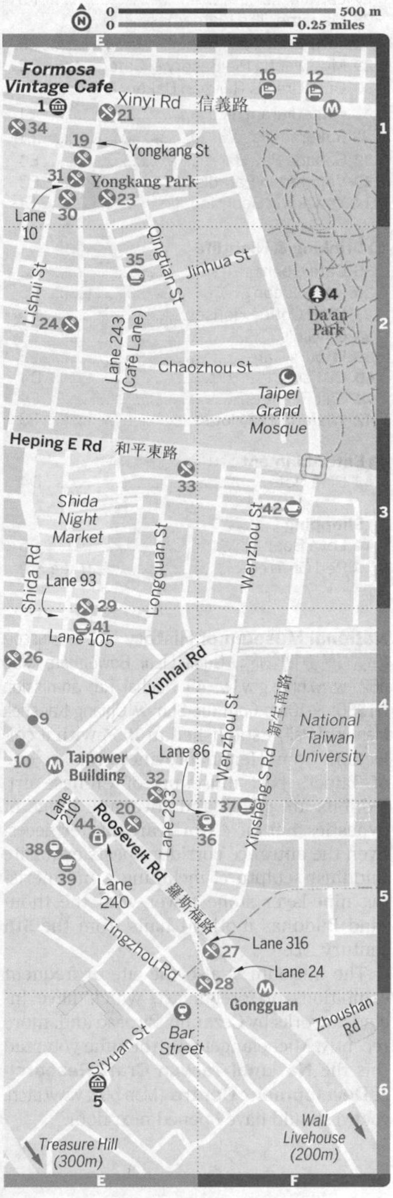

Tien-Ho Temple DAOIST TEMPLE

(天后宮, Tiānhòu Gōng; Map p56; 51 Chengdu Rd, Ximending; 6am-10pm; Ximen) This small but atmospheric temple appears from the outside as a narrow, but elaborate, storefront in the Ximending area. But walk through the gate and you'll find one of Taipei's most intriguing temples, a place where Japanese and Chinese worship patterns existed, and still exist, side by side.

The original Tien-ho Temple (devoted to the goddess Matsu, also known as Tienho, or the Empress of Heaven) was built in 1746, and demolished during the last years of Japanese rule to make way for a roadway. The current structure was erected in 1948 on the grounds of a former Japanese temple devoted to Hong Fa Da Shi. As you face the exit you can see a statue of Hong Fa Da Shi to the right, while on the left is a group of Jizō (the Ksitigarbha Bodhisattva) statues. Even today many local worshippers will pray to the Japanese deities as they make their way round the temple.

Shida & Da'an 師大區、大安區

Da'an is an important commercial and residential area (property prices are among the highest in the city) with several major universities. You'll find some of Taipei's ritziest shopping areas here, but also leafy Da'an Park and the laid-back Shida neighbourhood surrounding National Taiwan Normal University.

★ **Formosa Vintage Cafe** MUSEUM

(秋惠文庫, Qiū Huì Wénkù; Map p62; 3rd fl, 178 Xinyi Rd, Sec 2; 11am-7pm Tue-Sun; ; Dongmen) FREE Documenting Taiwan's hybrid

Shida

Top Sights
1 Formosa Vintage Cafe ... E1

Sights
2 Botanical Gardens ... A1
3 Chunghwa Postal Museum ... B1
4 Da'an Park ... F2
5 Museum of Drinking Water ... E6
6 National Museum of History ... A1
7 National Taiwan Craft Research & Development Centre ... A1
8 Taipei City Hakka Cultural Theme Park ... D4

Activities, Courses & Tours
9 523 Mountaineering Association ... E4
10 523 Mountaineering Association ... E4

Sleeping
11 Chocolate Box Backpackers ... D3
12 Dandy Hotel ... F1
13 Eight Elephants Hostel ... C3
14 Friends Hotel ... C2
15 Li-Yuan Hotel ... D4
16 Rido Waikoloa Hotel ... F1
17 Taipei Teacher's Hostel ... B1

Eating
18 Beijing Lou ... D4
19 Chi Fan Shi Tang ... E1
20 Cotton Land Organic Health Store ... E5
21 Din Tai Fung ... E1
22 Drunken Monkey ... C3
23 Hui Liu ... E1
24 James Kitchen ... E2
25 Jinfeng Braised Meat Rice ... B1
26 KGB ... E4
27 Lan Jia ... F5
28 Madame Jill's Vietnamese Cuisine ... F5
29 My Sweetie Pie Bakery & Cafe ... E3
30 Oma Ursel's German Bakery & Restaurant ... E1
31 Rakumenya ... E1
32 Sababa Pita Bar ... E4
33 Vegetarian Paradise ... E3
34 Yongkang Beef Noodles ... E1

Drinking & Nightlife
35 Cafe Libero ... E2
36 Cafe Odeon ... F5
37 Drop Coffee House ... F5
38 GinGin's ... E5
39 H*ours Cafe ... E5
40 Ol' Farts ... D4
41 Salt Peanuts ... E4
42 Wistaria Tea House ... F3

Entertainment
43 Blue Note ... D4

Shopping
44 Love Boat ... E5
Red On Tree ... (see 35)

social and cultural history is this delightful private collection of Lin Yu-fang, a former dentist turned curator. Pieces range from Japanese-era commercial posters to shell figurines, musical instruments, temple implements and decorative carvings saved from the wrecking ball. The oldest piece hails from the Dutch occupation of Taiwan.

Mr Lin's collection counts over 10,000 pieces, only a portion of which are on display at any time. You'll still see a lot on any visit, though, as almost every space in the cafe is utilised. Juxtapositions can be amusingly jarring, such as when you turn from examining a wooden torch used in Beiguan musical performances to playful statues of the patron god of prostitutes or a propaganda leaflet that urges children to 'eat mooncakes and kill communist bandits'.

The museum is free but stay for a coffee, best enjoyed on one of the old marble-topped round tables.

National Museum of History MUSEUM
(國立歷史博物館, Guólì Lìshǐ Bówùguǎn; Map p62; www.nmh.gov.tw; 49 Nanhai Rd; admission NT$30; 10am-6pm Tue-Sun; M Chiang Kai-shek Memorial Hall) Established in 1955 with a collection from Henan province, this is one of Taipei's best museums of Chinese art. Exhibits are small, and cover the range of dynasties, but most works are masterpieces. Even the entrance corridor boasts exquisite Buddhist sculpture, including a mesmerising nine-layer stone tower with the thousand Buddhas motif. It hails from the 5th century AD.

The museum is also the site of frequent exhibitions of foreign art, which have included works by Cezanne, Picasso and, more recently, Michelangelo. By the time you read this the **National Taiwan Craft Research & Development Centre** (Map p62; www.ntcri.gov.tw) should have opened next door.

Botanical Gardens GARDENS
(植物園, Zhíwùyuán; Map p62; 53 Nanhai Rd; 4am-10pm; M Xiaonanmen) FREE An oasis in the city, this 8-hectare park has well-stocked greenhouses, literature- and Chinese-zodiac-themed gardens, a lotus pond and myriad lanes where you can lose yourself in quiet contemplation. The gardens were established by the Japanese in 1921 and are part of a larger neighbourhood that maintains an old Taipei feel.

Within the park itself look for the **Qing administrative office** (built 1888) and a **herbarium** (from 1924). On Nanhai Rd check out the **Taipei Municipal Jianguo High School** (Map p62; built 1909), the **National Taiwan 228 Memorial Museum** (Map p62; 1931), and the buildings associated with the National Museum of History and the adjacent Nanhai Academy.

Da'an Park PARK
(大安公園, Dàān Gōngyuán; Map p62; M Da'an Park) This is Taipei's central park, where the city comes to play. And play it does, from kids rollerblading and playing tag to teens playing basketball and ultimate Frisbee to old men engaged in *xiàngqí* (Chinese chess). The park is a great place to hang out after a meal on nearby Yongkang St.

In the early mornings, you'll see folks practising taichi, and in the evenings, ballroom dancing. On big holidays, especially Christmas, New Year and Chinese New Year, the amphitheatre hosts free stage shows featuring some of the biggest names in Taiwanese entertainment.

Museum of Drinking Water MUSEUM, WATER PARK
(自來水園區, Zìláishuǐ Yuán Qū; Map p62; http://waterpark.twd.gov.tw/english/index_e.htm; adult/child NT$80/50; 9am-6pm Sep-Jun, to 8pm Jul-Aug; M Gongguan) Located within a water park (open in summer only), this museum covers the history of water treatment in Taipei and is set in a rather beautiful former pump station built in baroque style in 1908.

Treasure Hill VILLAGE
(寶藏巖, Bǎozàng Yán; M Gongguan) Head down to the river from the Museum of Drinking Water, turn left and you'll soon come across this ramshackle village founded in the late 1940s by soldiers who fled to Taiwan with Chiang Kai-shek.

While praised for its 'living memories' and off-the-grid community lifestyle (villagers 'borrowed' electricity, set up organic farms by the river, built homes out of discarded materials and recycled grey water), the village underwent a makeover in 2010 and is now largely an artist village. Still, it's a very photogenic place, very dreamy to explore at night, and architects, activists and anarchists are likely to find it fascinating.

Taipei City Hakka Cultural Theme Park PARK
(客家文化主題公園, Kèjiā Wénhuà Zhǔtí Gōngyuán; Map p62; 9am-6pm Tue-Sun; M Taipower Building) FREE This 4-hectare park is richly informative of the Hakka (descendants of immigrants from Guandong province) across Taiwan, though largely in the form of video and posters. The best time to visit is during a traditional event, such as the **Yimin Festival** (18th to 20th of the seventh lunar month).

The park connects via a very cool bike bridge to the riverside. If you are coming from Treasure Hill, head north until you see the bridge going over the dike walls.

Chunghwa Postal Museum MUSEUM
(郵政博物館, Yóuzhèng Bówùguǎn; Map p62; 45 Chongqing S Rd, Sec 2; admission NT$5; 9am-5pm Tue-Sun; M Chiang Kai-shek Memorial Hall) Stamps, uniforms, machinery, history and so much more for a token admission price.

Zhongshan & Datong

Dadaocheng or Datong (大同) is one of the oldest areas of the city, and much of it feels like it's seen better days. But there's a new vibe to the Dihua St area, which still retains its Qing- and Japanese-era mansions and shops, and you don't want to miss the temples in this district (they are Taipei's finest). Zhongshan (中山區) was once a centre for finance and international business and today is still loaded with hotels and near endless eateries (especially Japanese). There are also numerous small but excellent museums and the always changing Taipei Expo Park.

★ **Bao'an Temple** TAOIST TEMPLE
(保安宮, Bǎoān Gōng; Map p66; www.baoan.org.tw/english; 61 Hami St; 7am-10pm; M Yuanshan) FREE Recipient of a Unesco Asia-Pacific Heritage Award for both its restoration and revival of temple rites and festivities, the Bao'an Temple is a must-visit when in Taipei. This exquisite structure is loaded with prime examples of the traditional decorative arts, and the yearly folk arts festival is a showcase of traditional performance arts.

Zhongshan & Datong

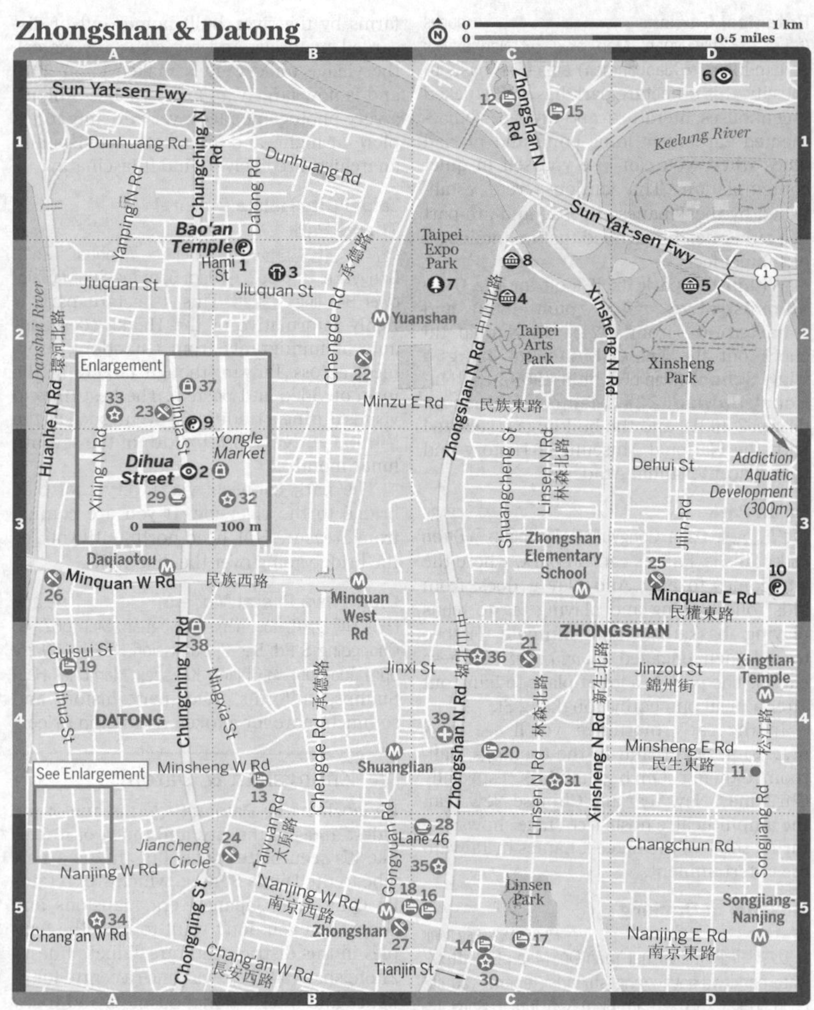

The temple was founded in 1760 by immigrants from Quanzhou, Fujian province, and its modern size and design began to take shape in 1805. The main resident god is Baosheng Dadi, an historical figure revered for his medical skills. The rear shrine is dedicated to Shengnong, the god of agriculture.

From 1995 to 2002, the temple underwent its largest renovation project. Under sound management (the board of directors are all university professors), skilled artisans were employed and top-quality materials used. In addition, the temple began holding an annual **folk arts festival** from March to June which includes the Five Day Completion Rituals to Thank Gods (essentially to transform the temple from an everyday to a sacred space), the gods' birthday celebrations, lion dances, parades, Taiwanese opera performances and even free Chinese medicine clinics. See the temple website or the Taipei City Government (www.taipei.gov.tw) website for event dates, all of which are free. For a DIY extended walk through the temple, see p350.

Confucius Temple CONFUCIAN TEMPLE

(孔廟, Kǒng Miào; Map p66; 275 Dalong Rd ⌚8.30am-9pm Tue-Sat, to 5pm Sun; Ⓜ Yuanshan)

Zhongshan & Datong

Top Sights
1 Bao'an Temple ... B2
2 Dihua Street ... A3

Sights
3 Confucius Temple ... B2
4 Fine Arts Museum ... C2
5 Lin Antai Historic House ... D2
6 National Revolutionary Martyrs' Shrine ... D1
7 Taipei Expo Park ... C2
8 Taipei Story House ... C2
9 Xiahai (Hsiahai) City God Temple ... A2
10 Xingtian Temple ... D3

Activities, Courses & Tours
11 Edison Tours ... D4

Sleeping
12 Chientan Youth Activity Centre ... C1
13 CU Hotel ... B4
14 Dandy Hotel ... C5
15 Grand Hotel ... C1
16 Royal Inn Taipei ... C5
17 Taipei International Hotel ... C5
18 Tango ... B5
19 Vintage Travel & Hostel ... A4
20 Yomi Hotel ... C4

Eating
21 #21 Goose & Seafood ... C4
22 21 Worker House ... B2
23 Fleisch ... A2
24 Ningxia Night Market ... B5
25 Paris 1930 ... D3
26 Qing Tian Xia ... A3
27 Shin Yeh ... B5

Drinking & Nightlife
28 Dance Cafe ... C5
Le Zinc ... (see 37)
29 Lugou Cafe ... A3

Entertainment
30 @Matt Bar ... C5
31 ANIKi Club ... C4
32 Dadaocheng Theatre ... B3
33 Lin Liu-Hsin Puppet Theatre Museum ... A2
34 Office Sauna ... A5
35 SPOT – Taipei Film House ... C5
36 Taipei Eye ... C4

Shopping
37 Hakka Blue ... A2
38 Lin Mao Sen Tea Co ... A4
Ming Xing Dao ... (see 26)

Information
39 Mackay Memorial Hospital ... C4

FREE Constructed by the famous Fujian craftsman Wang Yi-shun in the late 1920s, this temple is a beautiful example of Minnan (southern) style architecture and of Taiwan's delightful local decorative arts. Throughout the temple there are informative displays (in English) on the history of Confucius, the temple and the Six Confucian Arts (such as archery and riding).

When you walk through the first gate (Lingxing Gate) across from the pond, head to the far back left and look up for a delightful ceramic relief of a boy holding a lantern: the lantern actually dangles out from the panel! Other gorgeous panels of vases with blooming flowers are across the courtyard on the Yi Gate. Inside the main hall (Dacheng Hall) look for a magnificent plafond ceiling.

Confucius' birthday is celebrated on 28 September with a ceremony (starting at 6am) presided over by the mayor of Taipei. It's a colourful event and tickets, which go on sale at the temple about five days in advance, always sell out.

★ Dihua Street — HISTORIC STREET

(迪化街, Díhuà Jiē; Map p66; Ⓜ Zhongshan, Daqiaotou) This former 'Centre Street' has long been known for its Chinese medicine shops, fabric market and lively Lunar New Year sundry market. After a decade of restoration, the street has also become a magnet for young entrepreneurs eager to breathe new life into the neighbourhood with cafes, restaurants, art studios and antique shops.

Díhuà Jiē was constructed in the 1850s after merchants on the losing side of an ethnic feud (all too common in Taiwan's history over different groups' ancestor origins) in the Wanhua area fled to Dadaocheng (now Datong). The merchants prospered here (and some might say got their revenge) as the Wanhua port, further downstream, eventually silted up.

After Taiwan's ports were opened following the Second Opium War (1856–60), Western tea merchants flooded into the area and built handsome mansions and trading stores. Later, during the Japanese era, baroque and modernist architectural and decorative touches were added to many shops, making Dihua Taipei's most historically diverse street. The **first house/shop** on the street is at 156 Dihua St, Sec 1. Notice its low profile and narrow arcades. Further up the street, near Minquan W Rd, are typical shops from the late 19th century with arched windows and wide arcades. Closer to Yongle Market are the Western-style merchant houses and shops renovated during Japanese times.

On the 8th and 9th floors of **Yongle Market** is Dadaocheng Theatre (p100), a popular venue for traditional performances.

Xiahai (Hsiahai) City God Temple TAOIST TEMPLE

(霞海城隍廟, Xiáhǎi Chénghuáng Miào; Map p66; www.tpecitygod.org; 61 Dihua St, Sec 1; Ⓜ Zhongshan) This lively and well-loved temple on Dihua St was built in 1856 to house the City God statue that the losers in the Wanhua feud took as they fled upstream. Little-changed since those days, the temple is a terrific spot to witness folk worship rituals as well as admire some gorgeous pieces of traditional arts and crafts.

The temple management deserves kudos for the clear English signs about the temple introducing the City God, the City God's Wife and the Matchmaker (said to have brought together 6000 couples), as well as some of the temple's outstanding decorative pieces. Two of the most interesting are clay sculptures in the main hall just before the altar that demonstrate the Chinese talent for using homonyms in art. The sculpture on the left, for example, shows a man on an elephant holding a pike and chime. Since the Chinese for pike is *ji* and chime is *qing* together these form the homonym *jiqing* meaning 'auspicious' (note that different characters would represent the different meanings, but the sounds are the same).

The other sculpture shows a man riding a lion while holding a flag and ball. Flag is *qi* and ball is *qiu* which sound like *qiqiu*, or to 'pray for'.

On the **City God's Birthday**, (the 14th day of the fifth Lunar month) dozens of temples around Taipei send teams here to entertain the City God. The procession stretches over a kilometre and performances include lion dances, god dances and martial arts displays. Things get going around 2pm to 3pm and the entire festivities last five days. See Xiahai's English website for more.

Taipei Expo Park PARK

(化博公園, Huàbó Gōngyuán; Map p66; Ⓜ Yuanshan) The site of Taipei's wildly popular 2010 floral exposition, this expansive park covers three distinct sections, all linked up so you can enjoy a long stroll exploring them and the various sights within.

First off is Yuanshan Park, where you'll find gardens, a lively **outdoor food court** and the **Eco Ark** (a giant structure made of recycled bottles). Across Zhongshan N Rd you'll find the **Fine Arts Museum** and further west **Xinsheng Park** with its innovative pavilions from the flora expo (some of which may still be open when you arrive) and **Lin Antai Historic House**. North of here the park merges with the **Dajia Riverside Park** for biking and views of the Grand Hotel.

➡ Fine Arts Museum

Constructed in the 1980s, this airy, four-storey **museum** (市立美術館, Shìlì Měishùguǎn; Map p66; 181 Zhongshan N Rd, Sec 3; admission NT$30; ⏲9.30am-5.30pm Tue-Sun; 📶; Ⓜ Yuanshan) of marble, glass and concrete showcases contemporary art, with a particular focus on Taiwanese artists. These include pieces by Taiwanese painters and sculptors from the Japanese period to the present.

➡ Taipei Story House

This **house** (台北故事館, Táiběi Gùshìguǎn; Map p66; Zhongshan N Rd, Sec 3; adult/child NT$50/free; ⏲10am-5.30pm Tue-Sun; Ⓜ Yuanshan) was built in 1914 by a tea trader said to have been inspired by a building he saw at the 1900 Paris Expo. Today it's a space for Taipei nostalgia and history, and past exhibitions (which change often) have included topics such as Chinese sweets, toys, matchboxes and comic books.

➡ Lin Antai Historic House

This Fujian-style 30-room **house** (林安泰古厝, Lín Āntài Gǔ Cuò; Map p66; ⏲9am-5pm Tue-Sun; Ⓜ Yuanshan) FREE, Taipei's oldest residential building, was first erected between 1783 and 1787, near what is now Dunhua S Rd. As was typical in those times, the house expanded as the family grew in number and wealth, reaching its present size in 1823.

In the 1970s, the heyday of the Taiwan 'economic miracle', the home was set to be demolished for the great purpose of road widening. Thankfully, public opinion saved the day and the house was painstakingly dismantled and, in 1983, rebuilt on this field in Xinsheng Park. Today the historic house is notable for its central courtyard, swallowtail roof and period furniture.

Xingtian Temple TAOIST TEMPLE

(行天宮, Xíngtiān Gōng; Map p66; 109 Minquan E Rd, Sec 2; ⏲5am-11pm; Ⓜ Xingtian Temple) Although it was only established in 1967, Xingtian Temple is considered especially efficacious as temples go, and has emerged as one of the city's top centres of folk worship. While a progressive moral system is taught here, with a de-emphasis on the literal meaning of ritual, you'll find all manner of fortune telling, including a subterranean 'Street of Fortune Telling' under Minquan E Rd.

National Revolutionary Martyrs' Shrine SHRINE

(國民革命忠烈祠, Guómín Gémìng Zhōngliè Cí; Map p66; 139 Bei'an Rd; ⏲9am-5pm; Ⓜ Jiantan) FREE This large shrine marks the memory of almost 400,000 soldiers who have died for the ROC (mostly within China). The bulky complex, which was built in 1969, is typical of the northern 'palace style' architecture that was popularised during Chiang Kai-shek's reign. The hourly changing of the guards is a popular tourist attraction.

Shilin 士林區

North of the city centre, Shilin (Shìlín) is an affluent residential area sitting at the base of Yangmingshan National Park. It's home to some of Taipei's best-known cultural attractions, including the National Palace Museum. In 2015 look for the opening of the heady **Taipei Performing Arts Centre** directly across from Zhishan MRT.

★**National Palace Museum** MUSEUM

(故宮博物院, Gùgōng Bówùyuàn; admission NT$160; ⏲8.30am-6.30pm Sun-Thu, to 9pm Fri & Sat; 📶; Ⓜ Shilin) Home to the world's largest and arguably finest collection of Chinese art, this vast collection covers treasures in painting, calligraphy, statuary, bronzes, laquerware, ceramics, jade and religious objects. Some of the most popular items, such as the famous jade cabbage, are always on display but, given the size of the museum's collection, much is on rotation.

The historical range at this museum is truly outstanding. Even within a single category, such as ceramics, pieces range over multiple dynasties, and even back to Neolithic times.

THE NATIONAL PALACE MUSEUM: AN ART ODYSSEY

The National Palace Museum traces its origins back thousands of years. As early as the Western Han Dynasty (206 BC–AD 9) emperors sent teams of servants to confiscate all manner of paintings, sculptures, calligraphy, bronzes and anything else of value. Many of those items eventually found a home in the Forbidden City in Beijing (established in the 1400s), a place that truly lived up to its name: unauthorised visitors could be executed. The viewing public at the time was, shall we say, rather limited.

The Chinese revolution of 1911 forever changed the fate of this collection, though it was not until 1925, a year after the Emperor Puyi finally left the Forbidden City, that ordinary Chinese citizens could see the art for themselves.

With the Japanese invasion of Manchuria in 1931 foreshadowing greater trouble, the museum's contents were moved for safekeeping. The priceless treasures spent the war years shuttling across KMT-held strongholds in southern China. Despite China suffering heavy bombing attacks and fierce battles for nearly a decade, virtually the entire collection survived and a public exhibition was held in Nanjing in 1947.

In 1949, near the end of the civil war between the KMT and the Chinese Communist Party (CCP), the collection was moved to the Taiwan port of Keelung. When it became clear that a retaking of the mainland would not happen soon, plans were made for a new venue to showcase the art. In 1965, the National Palace Museum in Shilin was officially opened.

For decades the collection remained a bone of contention between the CCP and the KMT, with Chinese leaders accusing the Nationalists of stealing the country's treasures (as they had the gold reserve). These days, however, with Chinese tourists making up the bulk of daily visitors to the museum, such talk seems passe. More current is the challenge from the Taiwanese side: you can have your treasures back in exchange for recognising our independence.

Chances are the very colourful history of this superb collection is still far from told.

Shilin

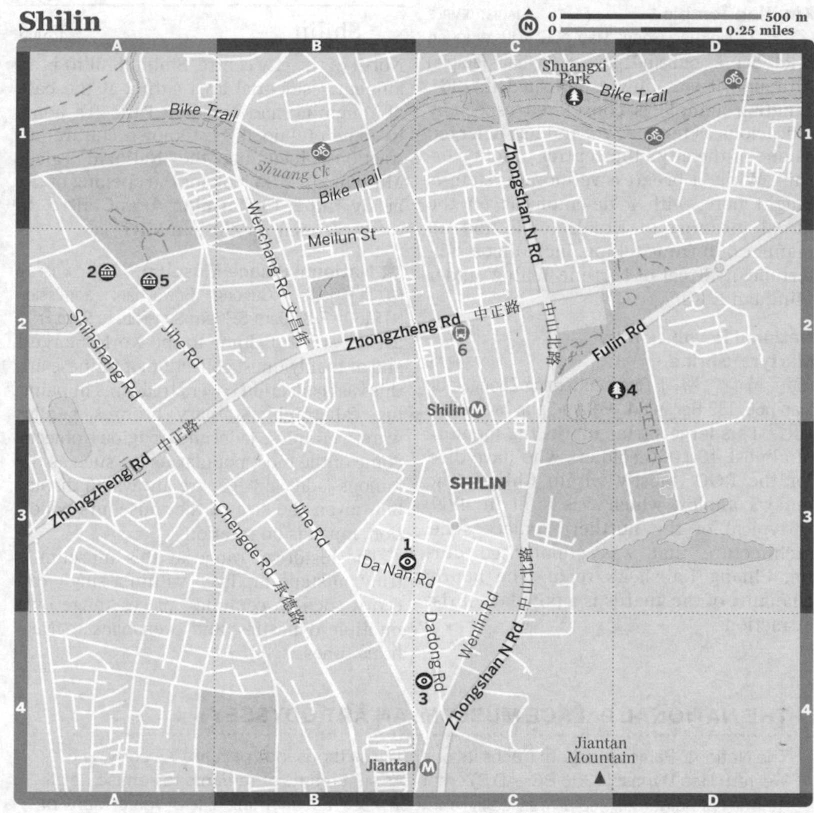

Shilin

Sights
1 Cixian Temple............B3
2 National Taiwan Science Education Centre............A2
3 Shilin Night Market............C4
4 Shilin Official Residence............D2
5 Taipei Astronomical Museum............A2

Transport
6 Buses to National Palace Museum............C2

Level 1 includes rare books, special exhibits, Qing and Ming dynasty furniture, religious sculptures, and a great orientation gallery to give you an overview of dynasties.

Level 2 includes painting, calligraphy, a history of Chinese ceramics with abundant examples, and an interactive area with videos and a virtual tour of 20 famous paintings.

Level 3 contains bronzes, weapons and ritual vessels, and Ming and Qing dynasty carvings. There is also the stunning jade collection, covering weapons, teapots, jewellery, ritual objects and the jade cabbage.

Level 4 contains the **Sanxitang Teahouse**, which offers tea, dim sum and a good vegetarian selection. There's also an eating area in the museum annex with the classy **Silks Palace** restaurant on the ground level, and the **Taiwanese Food Court** on B1.

The museum offers free **guided tours** in English at 10am and 3pm. If you prefer to move about at your own pace, there's an English **headphone guide** (NT$100).

An annex at the front of the museum (to the left as you head up the stairs) holds regular special exhibitions, which cost extra to attend.

To reach the museum from Shilin MRT station, head out Exit 1 to Zhongzheng Rd and catch R30 (red 30), minibus 18 or 19, or buses 255, 304 or 815. It's about 15 minutes to the museum. From Dazhi MRT station take bus B13 (brown 13).

Shung Ye Museum of Formosan Aborigines MUSEUM

(順益台灣原住民博物館, Shùnyì Táiwān Yuánzhùmín Bówùguǎn; www.museum.org.tw; 282 Jishan Rd, Sec 2; admission NT$150; ⌚9am-5pm Tue-Sun, closed 20 Jan-20 Feb; Ⓜ Shilin) There are currently 14 recognised indigenous tribes in Taiwan, and the exhibits at this museum cover the belief systems, festivals, geographic divisions, agriculture and art of them all. Fine examples of aboriginal handicrafts can be seen on each level, and videos relate the tribes' histories and other aspects of tribal life.

The museum is across the road and up a short distance from the entrance to the National Palace Museum.

Shilin Official Residence PARK, GARDENS

(士林官邸, Shìlín Guāndǐ; Map p70; 60 Fulin Rd; gardens free, house NT$100; ⌚8am-5pm Mon-Fri, to 7pm Sat & Sun; Ⓜ Shilin) For 26 years, this two-storey mansion and its elaborate Chinese- and Western-style gardens were once part of the official residence of Chiang Kaishek and his wife, Soong Mei-ling. Today the entire estate is a lovely public park and even the house itself is open, though it merely displays the rather humdrum domestic life, and middlebrow tastes, of the Chiangs.

Shilin Night Market MARKET

(士林夜市, Shìlín Yèshì; Map p70; Ⓜ Jiantan) Locals have mostly abandoned this market as a place to eat, but it's still hugely popular with travellers, who come to enjoy the carnival of streetside snacking, shopping, games and people-watching. It's best to avoid the basement food court area across from Jiantan MRT station, however, as the amount of smoke and grease in the indoor venue can be unpleasant.

Cixian Temple DAOIST TEMPLE

(慈誠宮, Cíchéng gōng; Map p70; 84 Da Nan Rd; Ⓜ Jiantan) Dedicated to the worship of Matsu, this 1927 reconstruction of the original 1864 design sits at ground central for Shilin Night Market. It's worth a visit even if you aren't in the area to snack in order to examine the masterful cochin ceramic panels above the arched doors in the main hall, as well as the exquisite stone and woodcarvings throughout.

> **FAR FROM THE MADDING MUSEUM CROWD**
>
> Let's face it, touring a world-class museum is not enjoyable if you literally have to battle the masses to see anything worthwhile. And since Taiwan opened to Chinese tourism in 2008, the National Palace Museum has become unbearable at times. Fortunately, if you can schedule your visit for Friday or Saturday evening after 6pm (tour groups leave then for dinner and do not return), you will find the museum the vessel of quietude and fine art it once was.

You can reach the temple most easily by heading up Jihe St from Jiantan MRT and turning right at Da Nan St.

National Taiwan Science Education Centre MUSEUM

(國立台灣科學教育中心, Guólì Táiwān Kēxué Jiàoyù Zhōngxīn; Map p70; http://ntsec.gov.tw; 189 Shihshang Rd; adult/child NT$100/70; ⌚9am-5pm Tue-Fri, to 6pm Sat & Sun; Ⓜ Shilin) Interactive exhibits at this children's museum cover the gamut of scientific knowledge, from anatomy (a walk-through digestive tract!) to zoology (a cat-head-shaped helmet that gives the wearer feline hearing powers) to chemistry, life science and physics. There's good English translations at every point. The 3D theater and special exhibits are not covered by the general admission ticket.

Taipei Astronomical Museum MUSEUM

(天文科學教育館, Tiānwén Kēxué Jiàoyùguǎn; Map p70; www.tam.gov.tw; 363 Jihe Rd; adult/child NT$40/20; ⌚8.50am-5pm Tue-Fri & Sun, 9am-8pm Sat; Ⓜ Shilin) This children's museum houses four floors of constellations, ancient astronomy, space science and technology, telescopes and observatories. Though a good place to while away an hour, there is a dearth of English content. More English-friendly attractions (at an extra charge) are at the IMAX theatre, 3D theatre and the 'Cosmic Adventure', an amusement-park ride through 'outer space'.

Eastern Taipei 東台北市

With rivers and established subcities to the north and west, and mountains to the south, Taipei could only expand in direction: east.

Eastern Taipei City

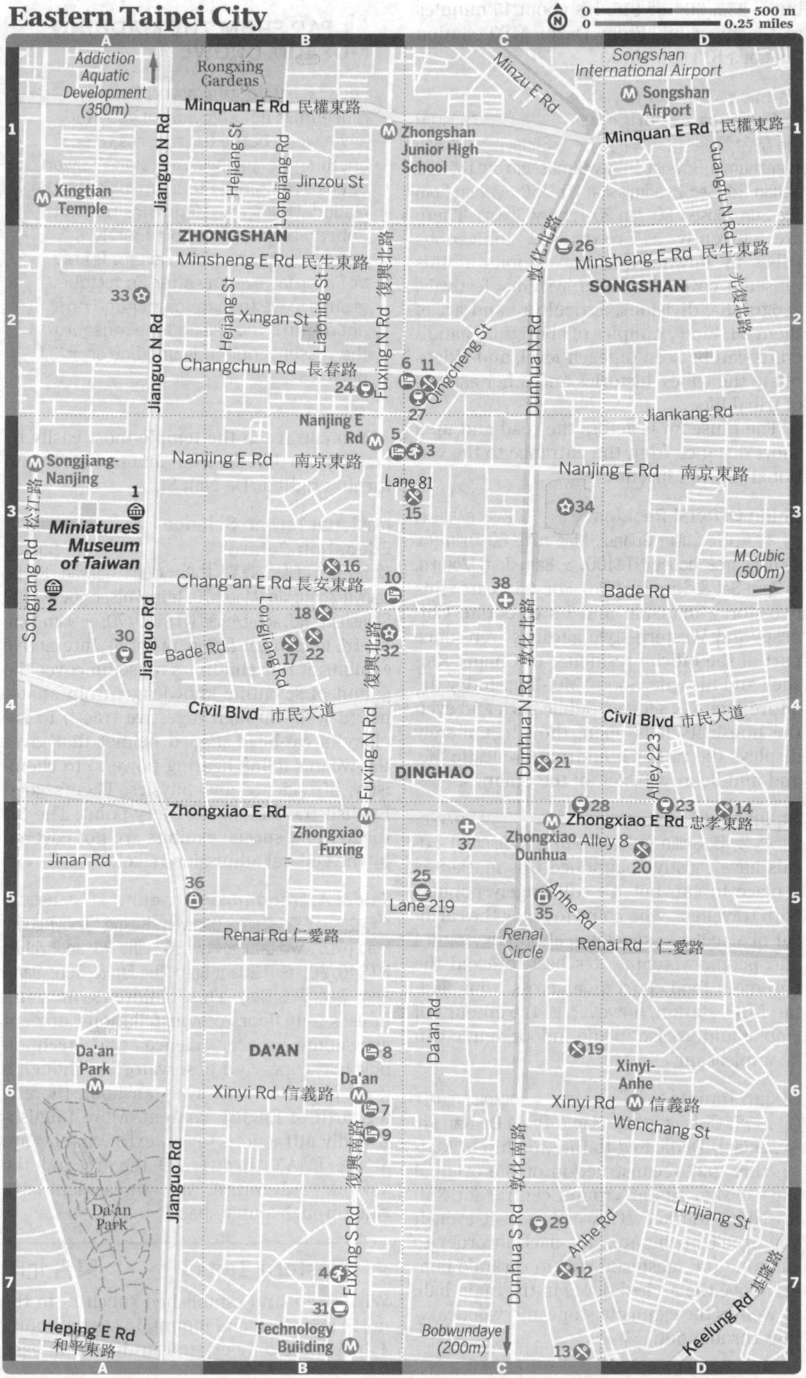

0 500 m
0 0.25 miles
A
B
C
D
1
2
3
4
5
6
7
Addiction Aquatic Development (350m)
Rongxing Gardens
Minquan E Rd 民權東路
Minzu E Rd
Songshan International Airport
Songshan Airport
Zhongshan Junior High School
Minquan E Rd 民權東路
Jianguo N Rd
Hejiang St
Longjiang Rd
Jinzou St
Guangfu N Rd
Xingtian Temple
ZHONGSHAN
敦化北路
26
Minsheng E Rd 民生東路
Minsheng E Rd 民生東路
SONGSHAN
光復北路
33
Hejiang St
Liaoning St
Xingan St
復興北路
Fuxing N Rd
Qingcheng St
Dunhua N Rd
Changchun Rd 長春路
6
11
24
27
Jiankang Rd
Nanjing E Rd
5
3
Songjiang-Nanjing
Nanjing E Rd 南京東路
Nanjing E Rd 南京東路
Lane 81
15
1
松江路
Miniatures Museum of Taiwan
34
M Cubic (500m)
16
Chang'an E Rd 長安東路
10
38
Bade Rd
Songjiang Rd
2
Longjiang Rd
18
復興北路
32
30
Bade Rd
17
22
Jianguo Rd
敦化北路
Civil Blvd 市民大道
Civil Blvd 市民大道
Fuxing N Rd
Dunhua N Rd
21
DINGHAO
Alley 223
28
23
14
Zhongxiao E Rd
Zhongxiao E Rd 忠孝東路
37
Zhongxiao Fuxing
Zhongxiao Dunhua
Alley 8
20
Jinan Rd
36
25
Lane 219
35
Anhe Rd
Renai Rd 仁愛路
Renai Circle
Renai Rd 仁愛路
Da'an Rd
19
Da'an Park
DA'AN
8
Xinyi-Anhe
Da'an
Xinyi Rd 信義路
Xinyi Rd 信義路
7
Wenchang St
9
復興南路
敦化南路
Jianguo Rd
Da'an Park
Linjiang St
Fuxing S Rd
29
Anhe Rd
基隆路
4
12
Dunhua S Rd
31
Heping E Rd 和平東路
Technology Building
Bobwundaye (200m)
13
Keelung Rd

Eastern Taipei City

Top Sights
1 Miniatures Museum of Taiwan A3

Sights
2 Su Ho Paper Museum A3

Activities, Courses & Tours
3 Giant C3
4 Wild Bird Society of Taipei B7

Sleeping
5 Brother Hotel B3
6 Delight Hotel C2
7 Fu Hau Hotel B6
8 Hope City Fushing Hotel B6
9 Taipei Fullerton 41 Hotel B6
10 Taipei Hotel B B3

Eating
11 Ankor Wat Snacks C2
12 Dressed C7
13 Duome C7
14 Ice Monster D5
15 Kunming Islamic Restaurant C3
16 Liaoning Street Night Market B3
17 Lin Dong Sen Beef Noodles B4
18 Matsu Noodles B4
19 NOMURA C6
Plum Blossom Room .... (see 5)
20 Slack Season Tan Tsu Noodles D5
21 Toasteria Cafe C4
22 Yangzhou Guan Tangbao B4

Drinking & Nightlife
23 AQ Cava D5
24 Brass Monkey B2
25 Cha Cha Thé C5
26 Haaya's Coffee C2
27 Jolly Brewery & Restaurant C2
28 Luxy C5
29 Ounce Taipei C7
30 Taipei Brewery A4
31 Water Moon Tea House B7

Entertainment
32 Ambassador Theatre B4
33 Taboo A2
34 Taipei Arena C3

Shopping
35 Eslite C5
36 Jianguo Weekend Holiday Jade Market A5

Information
37 Dr Simon Chan Clinic C5
38 Taiwan Adventist Hospital C3

Encompassing Songshan, Da'an, Xinyi and pretty much everything east of Jianguo Rd, Eastern Taipei is a mix of typical narrow-laned neighbourhoods and spiffy new high-rise blocks.

★ Miniatures Museum of Taiwan MUSEUM
(袖珍博物館, Xiù Zhēn Bówùguǎn; Map p72; 96 Jianguo N Rd, Sec 1; adult/child NT$180/100; ⏲10am-6pm Tue-Sun; Ⓜ Songjiang-Nanjing) Whimsical, wondrous and oh so fantastically detailed are the creative works at this delightful private museum. On display are dozens of dollhouse-sized replications of Western and Eastern houses, castles, chalets, palaces and villages as well as scenes from classic children's stories such as *Pinocchio* and *Alice in Wonderland*.

Give yourself plenty of time to enjoy this place for within each structure is a whole world of tiny figures in costume and surrounded by their respective daily furnishings. The peeks into the living rooms and backstreets of 19th-century London are worth admission alone, as is the outstanding Japanese village, complete with blooming cherry blossoms.

Su Ho Paper Museum MUSEUM
(樹火紀念紙博物館, Shùhuǒ Jìniàn Zhǐ Bówùguǎn; Map p72; ☎2507 5539; www.suhopaper.org.tw; 68 Chang'an E Rd, Sec 2; admission NT$100, with paper-making session NT$180; ⏲9.30am-4.30pm Mon-Sat; Ⓜ Songjiang-Nanjing) Fulfilling the lifelong dream of Taiwanese paper-maker Chen Su Ho, this stylish four-storey museum displays a working traditional paper mill, temporary exhibits (with a focus on paper sculpture or installation art), as well as good overviews of paper making around the world and in Taiwan. For a DIY experience, join the daily paper-making classes at 10am, 11am, 2pm and 3pm.

At the museum shop you can purchase cards, posters and other elegant designs constructed from handmade paper. And before you leave the building, check out the bathrooms. You'll never feel so grateful to be alive in modern times.

Xinyi

Taipei's financial and city government district, this is the bright-lights, big city part of town, with the tallest buildings, the swankiest malls and the hottest nightclubs. And

Xinyi

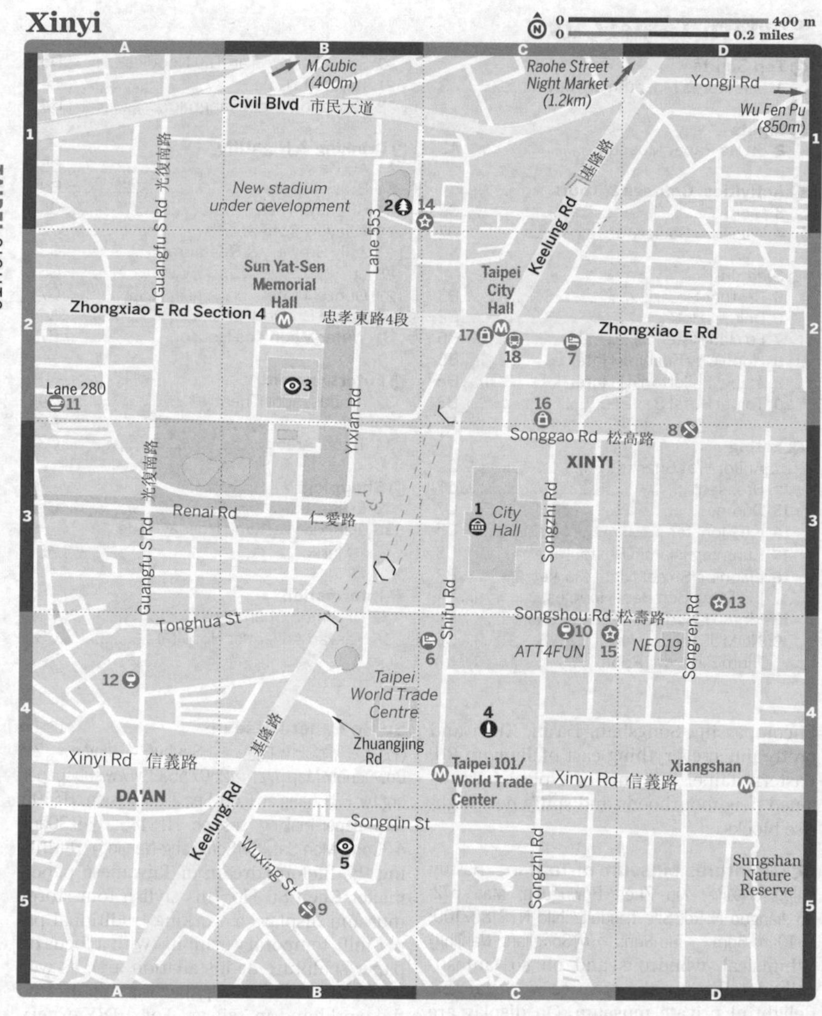

yet, nicely, it is also a casual place, a sporting place even, with hiking trails to Elephant Mountain starting a stone's throw from Taipei 101, and wide sidewalks circulating through the area where cyclists plod along on city Youbikes.

Village 44 (Xingyi Assembly Hall) VILLAGE

(信義公民會館, Xìnyì Gōngmín Huìguǎn; Map p74; cnr Zhuangjing & Songqin Sts; Ⓜ Taipei 101) FREE When the Nationalist army decamped to Taiwan in 1949, one million soldiers (and their eventual families) had to be rehoused. Thus arose military dependants villages, which once were scattered across Taiwan. Village 44, in the shadow of Taipei 101, was Taipei's first.

For decades these villages formed their own highly organised social systems, based on a shared embrace of anti-communist beliefs, a desire to retake the mainland, and also fear of the local Taiwanese. (One of Taiwan's biggest criminal gangs, in fact, was first hatched by young men from these villages, who organised themselves for protection.) As time went on, however, and as many of the soldiers retired and entered

Xinyi

civilian life (and also married Taiwanese women), relationships between the ethnic groups mellowed.

Rarely well built, the villages naturally succumbed to the wrecking ball as Taipei and other cities developed. These days, however, there is a recognition that they form an important part of Taiwan's modern history and a few have been preserved as heritage sites. Treasure Hill (p65) is probably the most famous.

There isn't a lot to see at Village 44: a few old buildings and sometimes a photographic display in the main hall, but it is a pleasant park-like setting where you can sit and contemplate the tides of history. Inside the village is an excellent cafe/art centre called Good Cho's (p92).

Songshan Culture & Creative Park — CULTURE PARK

(松山文創園區, Sōngshān Wén Chuàng Yuánqū; Map p74; www.songshanculturalpark.org/en; Guangfu S Rd; 9am-6pm; ; M Sun Yat-sen Memorial Hall) FREE Set in a former tobacco factory (or more accurately an industrial village) from the 1930s, the culture park opened to the public in 2011 with a well-attended design expo. That's not a coincidence as the government hopes to turn this appealing warren of warehouses, courtyards, housing blocks and offices into a center for creative design and arts education.

At the time of writing you could stroll through the grounds, explore the buildings, catch the occasional exhibit and visit the **Taiwan Design Museum** (台灣設計館; www.tdm.org.tw; admission NT$50; 9.30am-5.30pm; M Sun Yat-sen Memorial Hall), which highlights industrial and commercial design from around Taiwan and the world. Expect more from this museum, and the culture park in general, as the years go on. The outdoor areas of the park are opened from 8.30am to 10pm.

Taipei 101 — TOWER

(台北101, Táiběi Yīlíngyī; Map p74; www.taipei-101.com.tw; adult/child NT$500/450; 9am-10pm, last ticket sale 9.15pm; M Taipei 101) Towering above the city like the gigantic bamboo stalk it was designed to resemble, Taipei 101 is impossible to miss. At 508m, Taipei 101 held the title of 'world's tallest building' for a number of years, though it now must be content with the world's tallest green building (as in eco-friendly, not envious).

Ticket sales are on the 5th floor of the Taipei 101 Shopping Mall. The pressure-controlled lift up is quite a rush; at 1010m per minute it takes a mere 40 seconds to get from ground level to the 89th-floor observation deck. Observation decks are on the 88th and 89th floors, with an outdoor deck on the 91st floor opened on some occasions, weather permitting. Don't miss the massive gold-coloured iron wind damper that keeps the tower stable through typhoons and earthquakes.

In the basement is a decent food court, and the first five floors are taken up by one of Taipei's swankiest malls. By the time you read this, the Taipei 101/World Trade Centre MRT station should have opened. Otherwise get off at Taipei City Hall and walk.

For views of Taipei 101, climb Elephant Mountain or head to WOOBAR at the W Hotel.

Miniatures Museum of Taiwan MUSEUM
(台北探索館, Táiběi Tànsuǒ Guǎn; Map p74; www.discovery.taipei.gov.tw; 1 Shifu Rd, Taipei City Hall; ⏲9am-5pm Tue-Sun; 📶; Ⓜ Taipei City Hall) FREE This is a great place to get your bearings on the city and its history. Maps and models show Taipei's evolution from a walled, gated city in 1882 to the bustling metropolis it is today. There are also exhibits on geography, topography, commerce, famous residents and natural resources.

Sun Yat-sen Memorial Hall CULTURE CENTRE
(國父紀念館, Guófù Jìniànguǎn; Map p74; ⏲9am-6pm; Ⓜ Sun Yat-sen Memorial Hall) FREE The hall and its surrounding gardens occupy an entire city block. The latter are well used by picnickers, kite flyers, break dancers and the early morning taichi crowd, while the cavernous interior serves as a cultural centre with regular exhibitions and performances. There's a large, though sparsely informative, museum on the life of SYS, the founder of modern China.

Though designed in a similar palace style as the Chiang Kai-shek Memorial Hall, this hall (finished earlier in 1972) is largely considered a decent piece of architecture, blending modernity with tradition without a fetish for 'classical' decorative features.

Activities

Cycling

Taipei is almost certainly the best major metropolis for cycling in Asia. In recent years the sport has transformed from a fringe activity to a genuine craze that affects all income and age levels.

The most popular biking venues are the **riverside lanes**, which are exclusive to walkers and cyclists, and form a linked network hundreds of kilometres long. Lanes run through landscapes parks or along wild sections of the river, and offer scenic landscapes as varied as volcanic peaks, mangrove swamps and grassy soccer fields. Among the best sections are between Guandu and Tamsui; Wanhua to Xindian (on either side); the Sanchong loop; and the round-Taipei path, which takes about five hours and includes a section through the massive Liuzhangli Cemetery.

Sunny summer weekend afternoons can see the paths become very congested, but weekdays, and especially winter weekdays, they are wonderfully open. The paths are lit at night and it's common to see groups out past midnight (a perfectly safe thing to do in this city).

There are 10 **rental stations** within Taipei and another seven in New Taipei City, including at Gongguan, Bali, Guandu, Datong, Bitan, Tamsui and Taipei Zoo. Pick up a map of routes and stations at any visitor centre.

TWO GREAT TAIPEI RIDES

Road riding around Taipei is world class, and we cover several routes that you can start from the capital in the Northern Taipei chapter. Here are two within the city limits to whet your appetite. See the Greater Taipei map for general directions.

Balaka Road

A classic ride into beautiful Yangmingshan National Park, the Balaka has many variations. A short version is covered here (www.bikingintaiwan.com/2010/09/balaka_road) and starts at Hongshulin MRT: you can take the MRT on weekends with your bike or ride up along the river paths. From the MRT station, you quickly head into the hills on Hwy 2 and eventually link with the grueling 101甲, aka Balaka Road. Later, when you connect with Hwy 2甲 you can either fly down to Taipei or head east to Jinshan and the coast. This route is best done in the early morning and on weekdays.

Graveyard Ride

This well-known and very steep ride goes through a massive cemetery followed by a fast descent to Taipei Zoo and the flat riverpaths. It starts on Chongde Rd near Liuzhangli MRT (see http://rank.blogspot.tw for directions) and quickly ascends into the cemetery. The first section is the Muslim Cemetery, with famous resident General Bai Chongxi, while further up is the White Terror Memorial (dedicated to those who died during Martial Law; see p332). At the junction with Academia Sinica Rd (Yanjiuyuan Rd) you can go left to Nangang (this is part of the round-Taipei bike route) or right to Taipei Zoo.

Rates are NT$250 to NT$350 per day, or NT$25 to NT$60 per hour (depending on the quality of bike). It's another NT$80 to drop the bike off at another station. Some people are also starting to use the shared bicycle program Youbike (p105).

For quality road bikes and multiday rentals visit **Giant** (捷安特南京店; Map p72; ☎8771 4045; http://tw.myblog.yahoo.com/giant-nanjing; 278 Nanjing E Rd, Sec 3; 3-day rental NT$1200; ⏲11am-10pm Fri-Wed; Ⓜ Nanjing E Rd).

Being surrounded by mountains, Taipei also has some good spots for **mountain biking**. **Alan's Mountain Bike** (☎2933 4319; www.alansmountainbike.com.tw; 38 Roosevelt Rd, Sec 5; ⏲noon-9pm Mon-Sat; Ⓜ Gongguan) rents good-quality bikes for NT$1000 per day, and organises free weekend rides.

Bicycles are allowed on all MRT lines except the Brown (Muzha to Neihu). Taipei Main, Tamsui and Dongmen stations also prohibit bikes; MRT maps show which stations can be used. There is a NT$80 charge (which also covers the passenger) for taking a bike on the MRT. Folding bicycles are allowed on any train at any time free of charge; they must be fully disassembled and placed in a bag.

Hiking & Walking

First-time visitors are usually astounded by just how thin the line between Taipei's urban jungle and jungle-jungle can be. Throughout the city you'll find a range of hikes in genuine wooded hills, to say nothing of long pleasant riverside walks that are available from the exits of many MRT stations.

In addition to those listed below, see the hikes in Bitan (p120), Yangmingshan (p115), Maokong (p118) and also the Northern Taiwan chapter for more nearby hikes.

Some excellent **walks** include the riverpaths at Bitan (across from Xindian MRT), Taipei Zoo MRT, and north and south of Bali, across from Tamsui by a quick ferry. For a great one-hour walk between MRT stations, head out of Gongguan MRT down to the river, turn right at the paths and walk to an obvious pedestrian overpass which takes you to the Hakka Cultural Theme Park (p65) near Taipower MRT.

A local favourite is the walk from Hongshulin MRT to Tamsui, which runs alongside and even through a dense mangrove forest with views of the emerald, volcanic-shaped Guanyinshan rising up across the river.

Elephant Mountain HIKING
(象山) This mountain actually has its own MRT station (Xiangshan, which means Elephant Mountain). Just exit and follow the signs about five minutes to the trailhead. Elephant Mountain is the vantage point of all the classic shots of Taipei 101 so expect a steep trail up. Weekends it gets crowded especially around sunset.

Fairy Footprint HIKING
(仙跡岩) Just a few minutes' walk from the Jingmei MRT station (Exit 2), this hike takes you up to a short wooded ridge that extends into Taipei from the surrounding hills. There are excellent views of Taipei 101 from the top.

Jiantan Mountain HIKING
(劍潭山) The mountain rises up behind the Grand Hotel and has great views over the Keelung River basin and city. To access the trailhead, cross Zhongshan N Rd from Jiantan MRT and take a short walk south.

Birdwatching

The riverside parks and the Guandu Nature Park are great places to watch herons, cranes, egrets, kingfishers, drongos and so on. The Botanical Gardens and most large city parks are good places to spot the Malaysian night heron. On the edge of the city, in wooded hills around Neihu, Maokong, Xindian and Yangmingshan National Park it's easy to spot indigenous birds such as the Formosan blue magpie, Taiwan barbet and Taiwan whistling thrush.

The **Wild Bird Society of Taipei** (台北市野鳥學會, Táiběi Shì Yěniǎo Xuéhuì; Map p72; ☎2325 9190; www.wbst.org.tw; 3 Lane 160, Fuxing S Rd, Sec 2; Ⓜ Technology Building) arranges birdwatching tours around Taipei and Taiwan. **Taiwan Ecotours** (www.taiwanbirding.com) also offers short- and long-term birding tours around Taiwan with an English-speaking guide. For guidebooks check out the link to 'Books from Taiwan' on its website.

Tours

Various travel agencies offer short- and long-term tours.

Edison Tours TOUR
(Map p66; www.edison.com.tw; 190 Songjiang Rd) Edison Tours offers three-hour city tours (adult/child NT$900/700) with an English guide that take in the Martyrs' Shrine, National Palace Museum, Chiang Kai-shek Memorial Hall, a temple visit and some

shopping. Other options include a Taipei-by-night tour, and trips around Taipei to places such as Yangmingshan and the northeast coast. Edison also works with Tribe Asia (p382) for custom tours to aboriginal areas.

523 Mountaineering Association HIKING
(523 Dēngshān Huì; Map p62; www.523.org.tw; 7th fl, 189 Roosevelt Rd, Sec 3; Ⓜ Taipower Building) A government-approved, non-profit organisation since 1999, 523 organises frequent hikes (with English-speaking guides) to the high mountains, as well as free lower-altitude trails around the north. The office is sporadically staffed, so contact 523 via email.

Festivals & Events

Chinese New Year in Taipei is mostly a family event and many shops, restaurants and museums close during this period. The best **Lantern Festival** events (p131) happen outside the city. There are, however, dozens of vibrant, visually rich **temple fairs** each year, including those at Xiahai City God Temple, Qingshui Temple, Confucius Temple and Bao'an Temple; the latter has a two-month-long folk arts festival every spring.

Bitan, the riverside park beside Xindian MRT station, has frequent weekend activities in summer and autumn, which can include free music performances, acrobatics, food fairs and so on.

For the dates of current and upcoming events visit Taipei City's (www.taipeitravel.net) website and the Taipei Cultural Centre (www.tmseh.taipei.gov.tw) website.

Sokran Festival NEW YEAR
Taipei has a large Burmese and Thai community and their annual water festival to celebrate the New Year is a popular event for locals and visitors. The event happens in April in the suburb of Zhonghe, near the Nanshijiao MRT.

Urban Nomad Film Festival FILM
(http://urbannomaden.blogspot.tw) Held in May, the Urban Nomad Film Festival highlights creativity and energy in documentary film making at SPOT Huashan Cinema.

Taipei Film Festival FILM
(http://eng.taipeiff.org.tw/Index.aspx) This influential festival showcases over 200 local and international films from the end of June through July. Venues include SPOT Huashan Cinema and Zhongshan Hall.

City Walk
Through Qing- & Japanese-era Taipei

START LONGSHAN TEMPLE
END HUASHAN 1914 CREATIVE PARK
LENGTH 5KM; FOUR HOURS

The tour begins at ❶ **Longshan Temple** (p60) in Wanhua, the oldest district of Taipei. Restored numerous times over the centuries, Longshan remains the spiritual heart of this district as when Fujian immigrants first established it in 1738.

From Longshan head to ❷ **Bopiliao** (p61), a former thriving commercial area with excellent examples of both late-Qing and Japanese-era shops. The red-brick arcades here are popular spots for photos.

Returning to Longshan, head north, staying on the left to enjoy the row of shops selling Buddhist statuary. At Guiyang St check out the exquisite Qing-era stone pillars, hanging lanterns and ceramic figures at ❸ **Qingshan Temple** (p62), built in 1856.

Head to ❹ **Qingshui Temple**, founded in 1787. Note the fine Qing-era temple design: single-storey halls and sweeping swallowtail roof. Both the outer dragon pillars and dragon and tiger side carvings hail from the 18th and early 19th centuries.

Cut up to Changsha St and follow to the remains of the ❺ **Xi Ben Yuan Temple**, once the largest Japanese Buddhist monastery in Taiwan.

Retrace your steps and head down Hanzhong St, followed by Neijiang St. At No 25 turn right into the back of the ❻ **Red House** (p61), an octagonal structure built in 1908 as Taipei's first public market. The area you are now in is called Ximending, a reference to the former west gate *(ximen)* of the former Qing-era city walls.

Now cross the road (note how the streets have widened) to ❼ **Zhongshan Hall** (p60), built in 1936 at a time when architectural tastes were changing from Western classical hybrids to more modernist designs. The hall is a mix of both.

Continue up Yanping S Rd to ❽ **Taipei Futai Street Mansion**. The two-storey former office, built in 1910 in a Western style, is the only surviving building on Futai

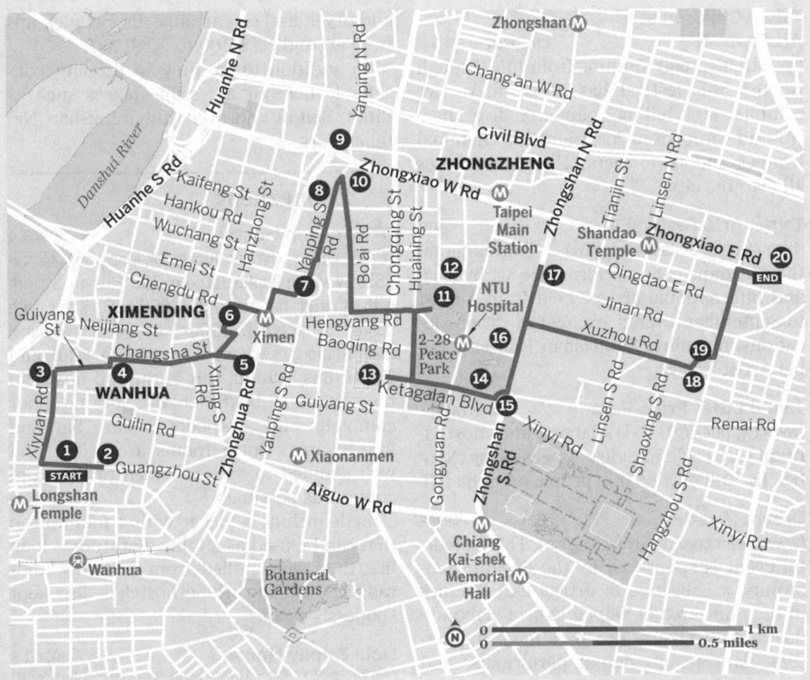

St from that era. Just up from here is the 9 **North Gate** (the only remaining Qing-era gate that has its original appearance) and the 10 **Taipei Beimen Post Office**, built in 1930.

Head back down Bo'ai Rd and then along Hengyang St, noting the Japanese-era shops and the pleasant arcades (covered walkways, a traditional Taiwanese design).

At 2-28 Park check out the 11 **National Taiwan Museum** (p60). Built in 1915, it was the first major public building under Japanese colonial rule. The 12 **Land Bank Exhibition Hall** (p59) across the way was the most architecturally advanced structure in Taiwan when completed in 1933, yet it still incorporated traditional arcades into the outer structure.

Next is the 13 **Presidential Office Building** (p59), completed in 1919 and restored in 1947. Originally the office of the Japanese colonial governor, the building faces east to the rising sun, and the design (as seen from the air) also forms the character 日 (sun), part of 日本 (Riben, Japan).

Now head to 14 **Taipei Guest House**, built at the turn of the 19th century and widely considered the most beautiful baroque-style building from the Japanese era. Note again how wide the boulevards are in this area: this is Taipei as the Japanese wanted it to be, modelled on Paris of the 1890s.

Head up to the 15 **East Gate** and then turn in to the old 16 **National Taiwan University Hospital**, built in 1912. The next few blocks along Zhongshan North Rd have a wealth of beautiful Japanese-era buildings, including the 17 **Jinan Presbyterian Church**, built in 1916 and an unusual example of Gothic architecture in Taipei.

Retrace your steps to Xuzhou St and stop in at the 18 **Mayor's Residence Art Salon** (p97), one of the best-preserved wooden Japanese houses in Taiwan. Then cut through the 19 **College of Social Sciences National Taiwan University**. These buildings, completed in 1919, are a good example of how the Japanese often blended Eastern and Western elements: the buildings are largely classical in style, with Grecian pillars and semicircular arches, but have roofs in traditional Japanese black tiles. The pond and gardens (both originals) are also Japanese in style.

End your journey at 20 **Huashan 1914 Creative Park** (p58), a restored wine factory from the 1920s that now houses chic restaurants, cafes, whisky bars, performance halls and excellent gift shops.

Taipei Children's Art Festival CHILDREN'S FESTIVAL
(www.taipeicaf.org) Running from July through August, this festival has films, interactive exhibits, storytelling, puppetry, live theatre and more from local and international troupes and performers. There are venues all over the city.

Taipei Arts Festival ART
(http://eng.taipeifestival.org.tw) Experimental theatre, dance and performance art by local and international artists, held from August to September. Events are held in various locations, including Zhongshan Hall and Taipei Artist Village.

Taipei LGBT Pride Parade GAY, PARADE
(www.twpride.org) Asia's largest and most vibrant Gay Pride parade happens every October. In 2012 over 65,000 people participated.

Dream Parade PARADE
(www.dreamcommunity.tw/english) This colourful event is sponsored by the Dream Community, a collective of artists and families in the Shijr area of Taipei. Expect elaborate floats, stiltwalkers, fire breathers, puppeteers, dancers, aboriginal performers, and lots of great costumes and painted faces. The 2013 parade had 6000 participants, including 600 drummers. The event kicks off in October at Chiang Kai-shek Memorial Hall.

Taipei Golden Horse Film Festival FILM
(www.goldenhorse.org.tw) Part of the Chinese-speaking world's biggest film awards event, this month-long film festival is held in November. See the website for venues.

Sleeping

Taipei has more and more hostels, but many are cramped, humid places so we've been judicious in our selection. Note that as almost all hostels are technically illegal due to antiquated regulations, they may not have signs outside and may not be open to drop-ins. Booking online is best.

YHA card holders can receive discounts at many regular hotels. See www.yh.org.tw/en for the complete list.

Rates below are high-season rack rates. Most hotels offer daily reductions of 20% to 50% off these rates (these are given without asking) except during Chinese New Year.

It's worth noting that most hotels now feature a laundry room with a free washer and dryer, and can arrange airport pick-ups from around NT$1100 to NT$1500.

In addition to sleeping in the city, consider leafier but accessible places such as Bitan, Beitou and even Yangmingshan National Park.

Zhongzheng

★Flip Flop Hostel HOSTEL $
(夾腳拖的家, Jiā Jiǎo Tuō de Jiā; Map p56; ☎2558 3553; www.flipflophostel.com; 103 Huayin St; dm with shared bathroom NT$600-650, s/tw with shared bathroom NT$900/1400; @ 📶; M Taipei Main Station) Across from the Q Mall and Taipei Bus Station, this is the top hostel in town, with a bistro-looking ground floor complete with a wooden square bar and lounge area. Dorm rooms are bright and well planned to offer as much privacy and comfort as possible.

Beds include a locker with a fold-up top that can be used as a table. Bathrooms look like they were pulled from a trendy midrange hotel. The whole hostel is also kept spotlessly clean.

Holo Family House HOSTEL $
(阿羅國際旅館, Āluó Guójì Lǚguǎn; Map p56; ☎2331 7272; www.holo-family-hostel.com; 22nd fl, 50 Zhongxiao W Rd, Sec 1; dm/s/d with shared bath NT$690/890/1200, s/d NT$1400/1580; @ 📶; M Taipei Main Station) Directly south of Taipei Main Station, atop a shopping mall, this well-run (if slightly institutional in feel) hostel has brightly painted and clean six-bed dorms and private rooms. The common areas are lively, and feature computers, books, maps and posters, and everything you'd need to plan your trip around Taiwan.

CityInn Hotel HOTEL $$
(新驛旅店, Xīnyì Lǚdiàn; Map p56; ☎2314 8008; www.gocityinn.com; 7 Huaining St; d/tw from NT$2600/3200; 📶; M Taipei Main Station) One of five CityInns around the city centre, this branch offers much the same fresh, trendy appeal of the others. Rooms are on the small side but make up for it with cheerful colours and lighting. There are 30% discounts on weekdays and YHA card holders get a special rate. Staff speak decent English.

Taipei Teacher's Hostel HOTEL $$
(台北教師會館, Táiběi Jiàoshī Huìguǎn; Map p62; ☎2341 9161; www.tth.url.tw; 15 Nanhai Rd; d/tw NT$1800/2400; @ 📶; M Chiang Kai-shek Memorial Hall) Not a hostel but a tidy lower-end midrange hotel just a minute away from the

Botanical Gardens and a short walk to Chiang Kai-shek Memorial Hall (and the MRT). The broader neighbourhood has many historic buildings from the Japanese era.

New Stay Inn HOTEL **$$**
(新站旅店, Xīn Zhàn Lǚdiàn; Map p56; ☎2370 2888; www.newstayinn.com; 5th fl, 72 Zhongxiao W Rd, Sec 1; d/tw NT$2300/2500; @ 📶; M Taipei Main Station) The exterior is not promising, but this new 5th-floor business hotel is a solid midrange option with friendly English-speaking staff and a welcoming sunlit foyer. Rooms are somewhat utilitarian, though splashed with a bit of funky wallpaper. New Stay is just west of Taipei Main Station. Take Exit Z6.

See You Hotel HOTEL **$$**
(喜苑旅店, Xǐ Yuàn Lǚdiàn; Map p56; ☎2388 7269; www.taipeiseeyouhotel.com.tw; 18 Chongqing S Rd, Sec 1; r from NT$2280, weekday discount 10%; @ 📶; M Taipei Main Station) A tower of fresh, modern rooms close to the train station. Rooms have Jacuzzis and are spacious at the NT$3200 level. The location is close to both Taipei Main Station and Ximending.

Hotel Flowers HOTEL **$$**
(華華大飯店, Huáhuá Dàfàndiàn; Map p56; ☎2312 3811; 36 Hankou Rd, Sec 1; r incl breakfast from NT$2400; 📶; M Taipei Main Station) Flowers is ageing a bit style-wise with its heavy woven quilts and lacquered furniture, but it's still a decent midrange with weekday discounts of 30%. The hotel is right off a busy downtown street, so road-facing rooms can be a bit noisy. The upside is you won't have to walk far for a snack.

Cosmos Hotel HOTEL **$$$**
(天成大飯店, Tiānchéng Dàfàndiàn; Map p56; ☎2311 8901; www.cosmos-hotel.com.tw; 43 Zhongxiao W Rd, Sec 1; d/tw from NT$4000/4500, 30% weekday discounts; @ 📶; M Taipei Main Station) Hovering somewhere between a midrange and a superior business hotel, the

GAY & LESBIAN TAIPEI

Foreign-born gay and lesbian travellers will find Taipei friendly and exciting. An open-minded city, Taipei hosts Asia's finest Gay Pride parades every autumn. The centre of gay nightlife is the bar and restaurant area around Red House in Ximending.

Check out www.fridae.com and **Utopia** (www.utopia-asia.com/tipstaiw.htm) for more.

Men's Saunas

Rainbow Sauna (彩虹會館; Map p56; http://rainbow-sauna.com; 2nd fl, 142 Kunming St; M Ximen) is popular with the younger, cute type. **Office Sauna** (公司會館; Map p66; ☎2550-7766; 265 Changan W Rd; M Zhongshan) is for the bears, while **ANIKi Club** (Map p66; www.aniki.com.tw; 20 Lane 353, Linsen N Rd; M Shuanglian) is currently one of the most popular saunas with younger men. These places are open 24/7.

LGBT Venues

Taboo (Map p72; www.taboo.com.tw; 90 Jianguo N Rd, Sec 2; ⏱7pm-1am Wed & Thu, 10pm-4am Fri & Sat; M Xingtian Temple) Mostly a lesbian venue. Friday and Saturday are usually the biggest nights. There's a dance floor and DJ. Taboo often has theme parties: those who dress up get in cheaper. Be sure to bring your ID!

@Matt Bar (Map p66; www.facebook.com/mattbar.club; 11 Lane 121, Zhongshan N Rd, Sec 1; ⏱9pm-3am Tue-Thu, to 5am Fri & Sat, to 3am Sun; M Zhongshan) A Japanese-style KTV (karaoke) bar for older gay men.

Funky (Map p56; www.funky.club.tw; B1-10 Hangzhou S Rd, Sec 1; ⏱9.30pm-late; M Shandao Temple) Opened since 1991, this is still one of the most popular gay clubs in the city.

M Cubic (www.facebook.com/mcubic2013; 12th fl, 138 Bade Rd, Sec 4, Core Pacific City Mall; ⏱10pm-4am Fri & Sat; M Sun Yat-sen Memorial Hall) New lesbian club opened in 2013.

GinGin's (晶晶書庫; Map p62; www.ginginbooks.com; 8 Alley 8, Lane 210, Roosevelt Rd, Sec 3, Shida; ⏱1.30-9.30pm Wed-Mon; M Taipower Building) Gay and lesbian bookshop and cafe.

Love Boat (愛之船拉拉時尚概念館; Map p62; www.lesloveboat.com; 11 Lane 240, Roosevelt Rd, Sec 3, Shida; ⏱2-10pm Tue-Sun; M Taipower Building) A shop for the LGTB community with both in-store and online sales.

Cosmos offers tight service, a flashy lobby, rooftop gym, and somewhat mismatched decor in its generously sized rooms. If Cosmos were any closer to Taipei Main Station it would be inside – as it is the hotel gets its own sign on Exit 3!

Sheraton Grande Taipei Hotel HOTEL $$$
(台北喜來登大飯店, Táiběi Xǐláidēng Dàfàndiàn; Map p56; ☎2321 5511; www.sheraton-taipei.com; 12 Zhongxiao E Rd, Sec 1; r from NT$12,000, discounts up to 40%; @ 🛜 🏊; Ⓜ Shandao Temple) Smack in the centre of Taipei's government district, the Sheraton is a well-run, well-designed five-star blending Chinese and Western aesthetics. There's top-notch service and a range of eating and drinking options (including Chinese, Japanese and Western). There are two dedicated smoking rooms.

Ximending & Wanhua

Taipei Backpackers-City Hostel HOSTEL $
(Map p56; ☎2311 9559; www.twhostel.com; 41 Hankou St, Sec 2; dm/s/d with shared bath NT$520/900/1300, d from NT$1300; @ 🛜; Ⓜ Ximen) Just on the outside of the Ximending pedestrian area, this neat little hostel has mixed and female-only dorms, and small private rooms. The check-in lobby on Hankou St looks a bit like a faux heritage gift shop. Rooms are in buildings nearby.

Red Cabin Inn HOTEL $
(紅菱閣旅店, Hóng Líng Gé Lǚdiàn; Map p56; ☎2361 9696; www.redcabininn.com.tw; 80 Emei St; r from NT$1180; 🛜; Ⓜ Ximen) Close to Taipei Cinema Park and the pedestrian areas of Ximending, this is your no-frills, rock-bottom-priced hotel if you want to avoid hostels. Rooms start at NT$980 on weekdays.

Hotel Puri HOTEL $$
(璞麗商務旅館, Púlì Shāngwù Lǚguǎn; Map p56; ☎2371 8616; www.hotel-puri.com; 6 Lane 27, Chengdu Rd; r from NT$3500, daily discounts 30-40%; Ⓜ Ximen) Renovated in 2012, Puri sports a fresh, trendy look that matches the youthful vibe of Ximending. In fact, it's located down a well-known alley lined with speciality clothing shops. There's plenty to do and see just outside the front door.

Qstay HOTEL $$$
(Map p56; ☎2331 4506; www.qstay.com.tw; 42 Changsha St, Sec 2; r NT$2280; @ 🛜; Ⓜ Ximen) Taipei's first gay-owned hotel is just a stone's throw from the bars and clubs at Red House. Rooms are a bit small, but there's a rooftop garden, and the kitchen/mini-bar has free snacks all day. Staff speak English and welcome all travellers.

East Dragon Hotel HOTEL $$
(東龍大飯店, Dōnglóng Dàfàndiàn; Map p56; ☎2311 6969; www.east-dragon.com.tw; 23 Hankou St, Sec 2; d/tw incl breakfast NT$2100/2800; @ 🛜; Ⓜ Ximen) This comfortable 70-room hotel just outside the Ximending pedestrian plaza is popular with tourists from around Asia. Rooms are a bit small and dated, but there are daily 20% to 25% discounts.

AMBA BOUTIQUE HOTEL $$$
(Map p56; ☎2375 5111; www.amba-hotels.com; 5th fl, 77 Wuchang St; d/tw incl breakfast NT$6600/7600; @ 🛜; Ⓜ Ximen) Opened in 2012 within Ximending's pedestrian plaza, AMBA (run by the Ambassador Hotel) is clearly aimed at young, savvy 'lifestyle' travellers. The interior sports an industrial-chic design matched with fun colours and posters, and there are nods to organic living and environmental consciousness (the front lobby desk, for example, is made from recycled plastic bottles, and toiletries are all natural).

As you walk down Wuchang St (the movie theatre street) look for the stylish Eslite Mall. The entrance to AMBA is beside the MAC shop down the back of an outdoor cafe.

Just Sleep Ximen BOUTIQUE HOTEL $$$
(Map p56; ☎2370 9000; www.justsleep.com.tw; 41 Zhonghua Rd, Sec 1; r incl breakfast from NT$5000; @ 🛜; Ⓜ Ximen) Just Sleep is one of several boutique hotels that have recently opened in Ximending and are both riding the wave of the district's newfound popularity and vitality, and helping to define it. Owned by Silks Palace Hotel (p183), Just Sleep features 150 stylish, technologically sophisticated and pampering rooms. Even the pillow menu gives you five selections. Discounts of 20% usually apply.

Shida & Da'an

Chocolate Box Backpackers HOSTEL $
(Map p62; ☎2364 5848; www.chocolatebox-backpackers.com; 2nd fl, 11-1 Pucheng St; dm NT$500-550, d NT$1300; @ 🛜; Ⓜ Guting) A solid, friendly backpackers hostel down a quiet street behind Shida University. The neighbourhood is filled with places to eat and drink (there's a good cafe right downstairs) and the MRT is just a couple minutes' walk away. To get here head out Exit 3, turn left on Lane 101, and follow it one block to Pucheng St.

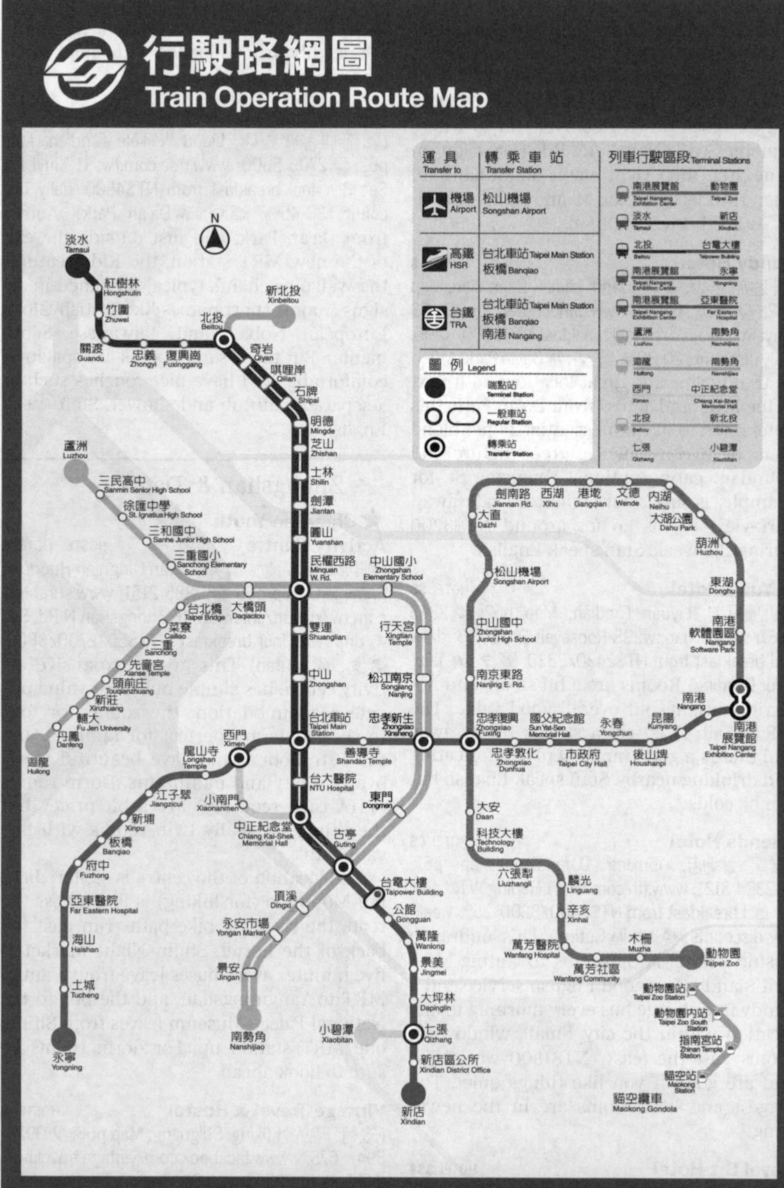

Eight Elephants Hostel HOSTEL $
(八隻大象青年之家, Bāzhīdàxiàng Qīngniánzhījiā; Map p62; ☎2360 0301; www.eehostel.com; 1st fl, 6 Alley 4, Lane 48, Jin-Jiang St, 晉江街48巷4弄6號1樓; dm/s/tw 550/1130/1560; @ 📶; Ⓜ Guting)

Set in a quiet neighbourhood of twisting alleys that lead unexpectedly to ornate temples and old houses, this clean and serene hostel has a basement entertainment spot with stereo, TV and public computers.

Toilets and showers are separated, minimising waiting time, and there's a communal kitchen fully stocked with stove, microwave, fridge and other appliances.

To get here take Guting MRT Exit 2 and walk a block down Roosevelt Rd to where it merges with Nanchang Rd. Turn right on Lane 202, then right again on Jinjiang St. Then turn left on Lane 48 and right onto Alley 4. The hostel is 50m up.

Dandy Hotel HOTEL **$$**
(丹迪旅店-大安店, Dāndí Lǚdiàn-Dàān diàn; Map p62; ☎2707 6899; www.dandyhotel.com.tw; 33 Xinyi Rd, Sec 3; d/tw incl breakfast NT$3600/4200, daily discounts 20-30%; @ Wi-Fi; M Da'an Park) With its trendy vibe and great location, both next to the MRT and across from Da'an Park, this hotel offers that quintessential Taipei blend of modern convenience, green nature and abundant eating options: Yongkang St, for example, is just a few minutes' walk away. Park-view rooms go for around NT$3200 during the week. Staff speak English.

Li-Yuan Hotel HOTEL **$$**
(儷園飯店, Lìyuán Fàndiàn; Map p62; ☎2365 7367; www.liyuan.tw; 98 Roosevelt Rd, Sec 3; d/tw incl breakfast from NT$2430/3830; @ Wi-Fi; M Taipower Building) Rooms are a bit small, and not terribly bright, but overall good value. The MRT (Exit 4) is just a stone's throw away and there's a good range of places for eating and drinking nearby. Staff speak English but can be cold.

Friends Hotel HOTEL **$$**
(友星大飯店, Yǒuxīng Dàfàndiàn; Map p62; ☎2394 3121; www.ffh.com.tw; 11 Heping W Rd, Sec 1; r incl breakfast from NT$2400/3200, 25% weekday discounts; @ Wi-Fi; M Guting) This midrange business hotel is right next to Guting MRT Exit 8 and offers good English service and a handy free shuttle bus every morning to any location within the city. Small, windowless rooms cost the least (NT$1800 weekdays) and are good if you like things quiet. The biggest and best rooms are in the newer wing.

Royal Biz Hotel HOTEL **$$$**
(金來商旅, Jīnlái Shānglǚ; Map p56; ☎2397 9399; www.royalbiz.com.tw; 71 Jinshan St, Sec 1; d/tw incl breakfast from NT$6000/6500, daily discounts 30-40%; @ Wi-Fi; M Dongmen) This 48-room business hotel has a reputation for warm service (and staff speak good English), spacious rooms and a good breakfast buffet. Just up from Dongmen MRT, just down from Huashan 1914, and also close to Da'an Park, the hotel is conveniently located and the neighbourhood loaded with small eateries and boutique shops.

Rido Waikoloa Hotel BOUTIQUE HOTEL **$$$**
(麗都唯客樂飯店, Lìdōu Wéikèlè Fàndiàn; Map p62; ☎2706 5600; www.rido.com.tw; 11 Xinyi Rd, Sec 3; r incl breakfast from NT$4500, daily discounts 30-45%; @ Wi-Fi; M Da'an Park) Across from Da'an Park, and just outside the exit of the new MRT station, the Rido features the Waikoloa chain's typical over-the-top designs (rooms sport names like British Glory, European Nobles and Taiwanese Sentiments). But those same rooms are spacious, comfortable and have nice touches such as a separate bathtub and shower. Staff speak English.

Zhongshan & Datong

★Chientan Youth Activity Centre HOSTEL, HOTEL **$**
(劍潭青年活動中心, Jiàntán Qīngnián Huódòng Zhōngxīn; Map p66; ☎2885 2151; www.surehigh.com.tw/xiayun/chientan; 16 Zhongshan N Rd, Sec 4; dm/tw/q incl breakfast NT$850/2700/3800; @ Wi-Fi; M Jiantan) This green, expansive activity centre has simple but great value private accommodation: the rooms for four to six people are perfect for families, and the 10th-floor twins have beautiful views over the city and mountains. Dorm rooms (YHA card required) are a bit pricey but then they are really twin rooms with private baths.

The location of the centre is stellar: Jiantan Mountain (for hiking) is just across the road, the riverside bike paths run past the back of the hostel, Shilin Night Market is five minutes away, buses leave from Jiantan MRT to Yangmingshan, and the bus to the National Palace Museum leaves from Shilin, one MRT station up. For dorm rooms be sure to book ahead.

Vintage Travel & Hostel HOSTEL **$**
(旅行, 時光, Lǚxíng, Shíguāng; Map p66; ☎0929-894 675; www.facebook.com/vintage.travel.hostel; 2nd fl, 222 Guisui St; dm weekday/weekend NT$650/850; @ Wi-Fi; M Daqiaotou) Just a short walk from historic Dihua St is this sweet little 2nd-floor hostel kitted out with furnishings and knick-knacks from the 1950s and '60s. There are only nine beds, including the popular if tight Harry Potter room (the cupboard under the staircase), and you have

use of the kitchen, laundry and a cosy living area.

Alex, your host, grew up in the area and is a wealth of information on the history, sights and shopping. Email for reservations.

CU Hotel HOSTEL $$
(西悠飯店, Xiyōu Fàndiàn; Map p66; ☎2558 5500; www.toongmao.com.tw; 198 Minsheng W Rd; dm/d NT$600/2750; M Shuanglian) Billed as the city government's first hostel, CU is actually just a few dorm rooms inside a spiffy new midrange hotel sitting above the newly refurbished Shuanglien Market. It's a nice place, don't get us wrong, and at just 50m from Ningxia Night Market and close to historic Dihua St, it's well located.

Hostel rooms fit two to four people, and are windowless but clean and tidy. NT$150 gets you a buffet breakfast.

Dandy Hotel HOTEL $$
(丹迪旅店, Dāndí Lǚdiàn; Map p66; ☎2541 5788; www.dandyhotel.com.tw 70 Tianjin St; r from NT$3800, 20-30% daily discounts; @ ; M Zhongshan) Just on the edge of the somewhat sleazy Linsen District, the fresh and colourful Dandy is popular with young Asian travellers. The neighbourhood is filled with good restaurants and many interesting boutique shops. Staff speak English.

Royal Inn Taipei HOTEL $$
(老爺商務會館, lǎoyé Shāngwù huìguǎn; Map p66; ☎2351 6171; www.royal-inn-taipei.com.tw; 8th-11th fl, 1 Nanjing W Rd; r incl breakfast from NT$3400; @ ; M Zhongshan) This inn-cum-business-hotel takes up the 8th to 11th floors of a building in a lively shopping district. Rooms are small and not terribly bright, but the comfortable lounge area off reception overlooks the street. Take Exit 4 of the MRT. Staff speak English and there are small discounts for booking online.

Yomi Hotel HOTEL $$$
(優美飯店, Yōuměi Fàndiàn; Map p66; ☎2525 5678; www.yomihotel.com.tw; 28 Minsheng E Rd, Sec 1; r from NT$4950, daily discounts 40-50%; @ ; M Shuanglian) This popular business hotel is just a few minutes' walk from the MRT on busy Minsheng Rd. Rooms are spacious and neatly arranged (the decor is a little dated) and deluxe rooms feature inset bathtubs and saunas for just a few hundred NT$ more. Yomi also offers a business centre, gym, free bicycles, afternoon tea and English-speaking staff.

Tango BOUTIQUE HOTEL $$$
(柯旅天閣, Kēlǚ Tiāngé; Map p66; ☎25367 9999; www.tango-hotels.com; 3 Nanjing E Rd; r incl breakfast from NT$6600, daily discounts 30-40%; @ ; M Zhongshan) Just outside Exit 4 of the MRT, on a busy shopping street, the Tango pulls you into its plush, private world as soon as you enter the curtained lobby. Rooms are a bit small and dimy lit but optimally arranged for comfort and convenience, and feature very fast internet, whirlpool baths and warmed toilet seats. Staff speak English.

Grand Hotel HERITAGE HOTEL $$$
(圓山大飯店, Yuánshān Dàfàndiàn; Map p66; ☎2886 8888; www.grand-hotel.org; 1 Zhongshan N Rd, Sec 4; r from NT$5700, daily discounts for foreign travellers 40%; @ ; M Yuanshan) This landmark Taipei hotel is a pleasant if kitchsy place to stay, with excellent English service, a range of top-notch restaurants, and dreamy views over the Keelung River (the hotel rests on the side of Jiantan Mountain). Just don't take the claims of traditional architectural grandeur too seriously. This is Old China about as much as General Tso's Chicken.

The hotel was established in 1952 as Chiang Kai-shek felt Taipei had no proper hotels for hosting foreign dignitaries. The main building was completed in 1973 on the grounds of the former Taipei Grand Shrine, though it underwent major renovations after a fire in 1995. Today there are three main sections, including the Golden Dragon (the newest and where most foreign guests are put) and the Chi Lin (older and smoky but offering the best views over the river). Interior rooms in the main building are small, ageing and have no windows.

Eastern Taipei

Taipei Hotel B HOTEL $$
(台北碧瑤飯店, Táiběi Bìyáo Fàndiàn; Map p72; ☎2781 3121; www.hotelb.com.tw; 367 Bade Rd, Sec 2; d/tw incl breakfast NT$4300/4900, 40% discounts usual; @ ; M Nanjing E Rd) The rooms here are small but updated and those that face the street gets lots of natural light. The location is also excellent for food (the Liaoning Night Market is a few minutes' walk away), shopping and travel around the city by MRT. Facilities include a small gym and business centre. YHA cardholders get a discount here and staff speak good English.

Fu Hau Hotel HOTEL $$

(富濠飯店, Fù Háo Fàndiàn; Map p72; ☎2325 0722; www.fuhauhotel.com.tw; 9 Fuxing S Rd, Sec 2; r incl breakfast from NT$3800, weekday discounts 30%; @ 🛜; M Da'an) Just south of the MRT, the intimate and modern Fu Hau is perfectly situated for travel around the city in any direction, especially with the new Xinyi Line to Taipei 101 opening. A row of tiny quirky eateries sits just outside the front door, but there are vastly more choices nearby, and good shopping too.

Delight Hotel HOTEL $$

(大來飯店, Dàlái Fàndiàn; Map p72; ☎2716 0011; www.delighthotel.com.tw; 432 Changchun Rd; d/tw incl breakfast from NT$3800/4380; @ 🛜; M Nanjing E Rd) Rooms are larger than most in this price range, though the decor is in line with basic notions of modern midrange comfort. There's a good breakfast buffet, a small gym and business centre, and staff speak decent English. Weekday discounts bring the starting price of a double down to NT$2520.

Hope City Fushing Hotel HOTEL $$$

(豪城大飯店, Háochéng Dàfàndiàn; Map p72; ☎2703 9999; www.city-hotel.com.tw; 275 Fuxing S Rd, Sec 1; r incl beakfast from NT$4200; @ 🛜; M Da'an) This mid-priced business hotel keeps you on the Fuxing main drag, close to restaurants, cafes, bars and the MRT for maximum travel convenience. Rooms are discounted 20% to 50% daily (weekday rates can be as low as NT$2100 if you book online) and staff speak English.

Taipei Fullerton 41 Hotel BOUTIQUE HOTEL $$$

(台北馥敦飯店-復南館, Táiběi Fùdūn Fàndiàn-Fùnán Guǎn; Map p72; ☎2703 1234; www.taipeifullerton.com.tw; 41 Fuxing S Rd, Sec 2; r incl breakfast from NT$5600; @ 🛜; M Da'an) One of Taipei's first boutique hotels, the Fullerton 41 still features an elegant, contemporary design, great service and amenities such as a business centre, sauna, gym and inner garden. The location is excellent for restaurants and quick travel around Taipei on the MRT. Book online for discounts of up to 40%.

Taipei International Hotel HOTEL $$$

(台北國際飯店, Táiběi Guójì Fàndiàn; Map p66; ☎2562 7569; www.htl.tw; 66 Nanjing E Rd, Sec 1; r incl breakfast from NT$7200; @ 🛜; M Zhongshan) Eurasian in feel and well located at the corner of Linsen N Rd for eating and drinking, the International has English-speaking staff, a slick ground-floor cafe, and standard business-style rooms: think white cotton spreads, upholstered chairs, neutral carpeting. There's also a small gym. Book online for discounts of up to 40%.

Brother Hotel HOTEL $$$

(兄弟大飯店, Xiōngdì Dàfàndiàn; Map p72; ☎2712 3456; www.brotherhotel.com.tw; 255 Nanjing E Rd, Sec 3; r incl breakfast from NT$4730, weekday discounts 30%; @ 🛜; M Nanjing E Rd) Well situated on the corner of Nanjing and Fuxing Rds, this midsized business hotel gets plenty of light and is close to bars and a host of good eateries (including the hotel's own popular dim sum). The hotel is literally adjacent to the MRT exit.

Xinyi

★ **W Hotel** HOTEL $$$

(Map p74; ☎7703 8890; www.wtaipei.com; 10 Zhongxiao E Rd, Sec 5; r from NT$9300; @ 🛜 🏊; M Taipei City Hall) The W gets Taipei. It gets the naive, fun, technology-intoxicated vibe of this city that's also surrounded by lush nature. So expect lots of wood, stone and cutting-edge light installations (and a touch of Asian cutesiness). Also expect cityscape views that are just as stunning as those of nearby hills gleaming with greeness on a sunny day.

Service is a bit odd here, though, and the black-garbed staff seem not always sure if they are working in a hotel or a hot nightclub. But you will be indulged with whatever request they haven't anticipated. The hotel's WOOBAR (p98) is now one of the city's trendiest spots, and the 10th-floor outdoor pool is Taipei's best for views and design.

Grand Hyatt Hotel HOTEL $$$

(台北君悅大飯店, Táiběi Jūnyuè Dàfàndiàn; Map p74; ☎2720 1234; www.taipei.grand.hyatt.com; 2 Songshou Rd; r from NT$7800; @ 🛜 🏊; M Taipei 101) If you need a five-star in the Xinyi District and the W is booked, the Grand Hyatt is a good option. Rooms are large, bright and have views of either the city or the nearby mountains. Check online for weekend packages and other deals.

Eating

Though well known within Asia, Taipei's food scene is increasingly attracting the attention of Western food journalists, celebrities, bloggers and even chefs eager to introduce a new trend. Why? Because when you combine a food-obsessed people, a history involving colonisation and immigration, and a fertile landscape that can grow or provide nearly anything fresh, it's hard not to create something special. And Taipei has.

It doesn't matter if you're a Southeast Asian looking to compare Taipei's street food with your own, a Japanese looking for the comforts of home, or a Western traveller curious about how the stinky tofu and *guā bāo* (steamed pork sandwich) compare to back home, you'll find Taipei consistently delivers on quality, variety, flavour and pure culinary adventure.

Check out A Hungry Girl's Guide to Taipei (http://hungryintaipei.blogspot.com) and Taipei 534 (http://taipei543.com/category/food) for more.

Zhongzheng

In addition to upscale food courts in Main Station, the warren of roads stretching southwest to Ximending has scores of cafes, cheap noodle and dumpling joints, and midpriced restaurants. In the Huashan 1914 area you'll find half a dozen retro-chic places for a meal, including a Japanese whiskey bar, a sushi bar and the best pizza in town.

Jinfeng Braised Meat Rice TAIWANESE $
(金峰魯肉飯, Jīnfēng Lǔròu Fàn; Map p62; 10 Roosevelt Rd; dishes NT$25-60; ⏲8am-1am; Ⓜ Chiang Kai-shek Memorial Hall) This long-running place serves Taiwanese comfort food quick

A STINKY TOFU TOUR

Along with beef noodles, stinky tofu is one of those dishes that nearly defines Taiwanese street food. So it's not surprising there's an entire street devoted to this blue cheese (or stinky socks) of tofu and all its varieties: braised, barbecued, steamed, skewered, stewed and deep-fried.

Shenkeng Old Street (老街) is in the town of Shenkeng (深坑), about a 10-minute drive east from the Taipei Zoo. Once a prominent market and administrative area during the Japanese era, the street's handsome arcades and Western-style mansions were restored in 2012. Even if you have no interest in tofu, the historical blocks are pleasant to stroll along, open to beautiful mountain views in the back, and there are plenty of other dishes to sample as well.

Here are a few recommended places to indulge in the stinky stuff. Shops generally open from 11am to 7pm, and dishes are inexpensive.

Jin Da Ding (金大鼎; Shenkeng St) At the start of the street is this stall that's said to have been in business since the first stinky tofu vendors moved into the area in the 1950s. The tofu here is actually 'fragrant' and not stinky. Try the *yuánwèi kǒuwèi* (原味口味; original recipe barbecued skewers). There are pleasing contrasts between the nutty smooth centre and the spongy outer skin.

Gu Zao Cuo (古早厝; 140 Shenkeng St) Look for the row of hanging yellow chickens outside a mansion filled with movie posters, then go in and try the signature dish of *yā xuè chòu dòufu* (鴨血臭豆腐; stewed stinky tofu with spicy duck's blood) or *hóngshāo dòufu* (紅燒豆腐; braised tofu) in a light broth. Both are pleasantly stinky and offer interesting contrasts in texture. The creamy braised tofu yields in the mouth like a ripe peach.

Wang Shui Cheng (王水成; 144 Shenkeng St) For something uniquely Taiwanese, try the *málà dòufu* (麻辣豆腐; tofu in an oily spicy sauce) at the shop that invented the dish. The tofu here looks like a baked abode brick and is topped with pickled mustard leaves and red chillies.

Shenkeng Zhenwei (深坑臻味; Shenkeng St) This stall outside Jishun Temple (about halfway up the street on the right) is another 1950s original, but serves the stinky version of the barbecued skewers.

Finally, to top off the feast, head to the end of the street for a cone or bowl of soft tofu ice-cream (it's not stinky).

Getting There & Away

Catch bus 666 (NT$15, frequent) across from Muzha MRT station and get off at the head of the old street near a large spreading banyan tree. A taxi from the station (or from the Taipei Zoo) will cost less than NT$150.

and cheap without fuss or atmosphere. Try the *lǔròu fàn* (魯肉飯; rice and meat strips); *kōng ròu fàn* (焢肉飯; slow braised pork belly and rice) or *fènglí kǔguā jī* (鳳梨苦瓜雞; bitter melon pineapple chicken).

Fuhang Soy Milk BREAKFAST $
(阜杭豆漿, Fùháng Dòujiāng; Map p56; 2nd fl, 108 Zhongxiao E Rd, Sec 1; 5.30am-12.30pm Tue-Sun; M Shandao Temple, Exit 5) A popular shop in the Huashan Market for a traditional Taiwanese breakfast such as *dòujiāng* (豆漿; soybean milk), *yóutiáo* (油條; fried bread stick), *dàn bǐng* (蛋餅; spring onion–filled crepes and egg) and *shāobǐng* (燒餅; stuffed layered flat bread).

Dongyi Paigu PORK RICE $
(東一排骨總店, Dōngyī Páigǔ Zǒngdiàn; Map p56; 2nd fl, 61 Yanping S Rd; rice dishes NT$130-160; 9am-8.30pm Tue-Sun, 2-8.30pm Mon; M Ximen) Disco lives, or at least glitter balls, mirrored walls and stained-glass ceilings at this flashy but friendly place specialising in simple but well-prepared *páigǔ fàn* (pork with rice). There's no English menu, but the wall pictures are enough. While pork is the house speciality, we found the breading a bit thick and preferred the chicken leg.

★ **Snow King** ICE CREAM $
(雪王, Xuě Wáng; Map p56; www.snowking.com.tw; 65 Wuchang St; per cup NT$55-125; noon-10pm; ; M Ximen) Taipei's most renowned ice-cream shop (running since 1947) offers 73 flavours, including a number of daredevil options such as curry, pig's knuckle, Kaoliang liquor (one bowl packs a punch), basil and bitter melon. Most flavours are standard, however, such as chocolate, mint, strawberry and other fruits.

Loving Hut VEGETARIAN $
(愛家國際餐館, Ài Jiā Guójì Cānguǎn; Map p56; www.lovinghut.com/tw; 44 Huaining Rd; dishes NT$45-90; 11am-8.30pm, closed 1st Sunday each month; ; M Taipei Main Station) Though part of a worldwide chain of over 200 restaurants, each Loving Hut is allowed to create its own menu and here in Taipei you'll find offerings of wontons, dumplings, and various noodle and tofu concoctions. The flower and fruit drinks (NT$75) make a nice dessert. There's a picture menu available.

Breeze Taipei Station FOOD COURT $
(Map p56; 2nd fl, Taipei Main Station; 10am-10pm; ; M Taipei Main Station) A branch of the food court of a top-end mall, this location on the 2nd floor above the ticket purchase area at Main Station boasts cafes, restaurants and stalls serving Shanghainese dumplings, beef noodles (there's an entire sub-section devoted to them), Japanese box sets, ramen, teppanyaki, traditional Taiwanese (again its own sub-section), Indian, sandwiches and local fast food.

Xiao Wei Sichuan Restaurant SICHUAN $$
(小魏川菜餐廳, Xiǎo Wèi Chuāncài Cāntīng; Map p56; 3rd fl, 13 Gongyuan Rd; dishes NT$120-360; 11am-2pm & 5-9pm; ; M Taipei Main Station) With decor last updated during martial law and its somewhat indifferent service, Xiao Wei could easily be a must-not visit, except for the food, which is among the best Sichuan in the city. Try their classic kung pao chicken or shrimp (宮保雞丁, 宮保蝦仁), stir-fried string beans (乾扁四季豆) or spare ribs steamed in lotus leaves (荷葉排骨).

Alleycat's PIZZERIA $$
(Map p56; www.alleycatspizza.com; Huashan 1914 Culture Park, 1 Bade Rd, Sec 1; 10" pizza NT$280-470; 11am-11pm Sun-Thu, to 1am Fri & Sat; ; M Shandao Temple) With its rustic-chic setting inside a former brick warehouse, and perfected stone-oven recipes, this is one of the top spots for pizza in Taipei. You can sit indoors under a soaring vaulted ceiling, or outdoors in a garden zone. Calzones, panini and appetisers are available, as is a good selection of beer on tap. Salads are poor value.

Ximending & Wanhua

This area is loaded with restaurants and food stalls on the pedestrian streets. If you are looking for **Sichuan** (Map p56; Lane 25, Kanding St), there is an entire lane devoted to it. Enter off Kunming St.

Ay-Chung Flour Rice Noodle NOODLES $
(阿宗麵線, Ā Zōng Miànxiàn; Map p56; 8-1 Emei St; noodles NT$45-60; 10am-10.30pm Mon-Sat; ; M Ximen) Every visiting Hong Kong traveller has to sample (and blog about, it seems) a bowl of rice noodles from this Ximending stalwart. Though the slurpalicious, salty noodles are very appealing on a cool Taipei evening, much of the fanfare comes from the fact you get to eat streetside (just don't forget to return your bowl when finished).

Thai Flavors THAI $$
(泰風味, Tài Fēngwèi; Map p56; 25 Lane 10, Chengdu Rd; dishes NT$80-180; 2-10pm Tue-Sun; ; M Ximen) Ximending's Red House

boasts a dozen or so restaurants and bars in the south courtyard but don't overlook this unassuming place in the far corner. Run by Thai immigrants, Thai Flavors serves some of the most authentic and delicious curries, soups and salads in Taipei and at rock-bottom prices. Three types of Thai beer (NT$80) are also on offer.

Dai Sya Rinn Restaurant (Da Che Lun) JAPANESE $$$
(大車輪餐飲企業, Dà Chēlún Cānyǐn Qǐyè; Map p56; www.dsr.tw; 53 Emei St; dishes from $180; ⏲11am-9.30pm; Ⓜ Ximen) Plates of raw fish and assorted sushi are pulled past customers by tiny trains and Taiwanese pop music from the '50s fills the air in this fun throwback to a time when Emei Street was a major commercial centre. Taipei's first conveyor-belt sushi joint, Da Che Lun still serves first-rate seafood in this narrow, near-subterranean hideout.

Ordering here is a little different from most sushi bars as most of what you see chugging past on the friends of Thomas is for display only. In general if it's wrapped, order a fresh copy from a waitress. Otherwise it's OK to just pull the plate off as you would at any other sushi bar.

Shida & Da'an

The Shida (National Taiwan Normal University) area is loaded with cafeterias, small eateries, funky cafes, fast-food outlets and a few excellent Western restaurants. In 2012 and 2013, the night-market area became the target of a zealous community organisation. After their initial success in closing shops down the narrowest lanes, the group began pushing to rid the area of bars, music venues, and anything else they didn't like. The area may be very changed by the time you get there.

Further south, around Gongguan MRT (across from National Taiwan University), however, you'll find another warren of cheap eat streets. Just west of Da'an Park are the quintessential Taipei eating streets: Yongkang and Lishui Streets.

There are eat streets and then there are these streets, and their bustling side alleys, which practically define Taipei's food scene as the joyful and near superlative experience it is. Some of the best dumplings, beef noodles, Taiwanese and Japanese restaurants can be found here, in addition to places serving shaved ice, Vietnamese and vegetarian dishes. Stylish cafes with private decks and patios dot the blocks south of Yongkang Park, the small centrepiece of the neighbourhood. Dongmen MRT station Exit 5 literally drops you off at the top of Yongkang Street.

> **AFTER-HOURS EATS**
>
> Between Technology Building and Da'an MRT stations you'll find restaurants serving stomach-soothing Taiwanese items such as *wēn dòujiāng* (温豆漿; warm soy milk) and *qīngzhoù* (thin rice porridge served with chunks of sweet potato). Some are open very late, and are popular with the post-libation bar crowd. Other places for a late-night fill include 21 Goose & Seafood (p92), Lin Dong Sen Beef Noodles (p94) and Matsu Noodles (p94).

Shida Night Market MARKET $
(師大路夜市, Shīdà Lù Yèshì) Though the market has been reduced in scale, at the time of writing it was still a lively place for a cheap feed of traditional snacks, for shopping, or for just hanging out in any number of small restaurants and cafes.

★Lan Jia TAIWANESE $
(藍家, Lán Jiā; Map p62; 4 Alley 8, Lane 316, Roosevelt Rd, Sec 3; ⏲11am-midnight; Ⓜ Gongguan) Lan Jia is widely regarded as having the best *guā bāo* (刮包) in Taiwan. What's *guā bāo*? Think of a savoury slow-braised pork hamburger with pickled mustard and ground peanuts stuffed inside a steamed bun. Yep, delicious, and it's starting to take the West by storm, with shops and trucks offering it now in London, Berlin and across the US. To get here take the MRT Exit 4 and turn left at the second lane (Lane 316).

★Drunken Monkey TAIWANESE $
(醉悟空格鬥熱炒, Zuì Wù Kòng Gédòu Rèchǎo; Map p62; 227 Tingzhou Rd, Sec 2; dishes NT$100-120; ⏲6-10pm; 📶 📋; Ⓜ Guting) Quick-fry dishes are a Taiwanese tradition and this friendly, almost intimate two-storey place has loads of them (the English menu features 88 dishes). Recommended are the fried oysters, three-cups chicken and the kung pao chicken.

Sababa Pita Bar MIDDLE EASTERN $
(Map p62; www.sababapita.com; 17 Lane 283, Roosevelt Rd, Sec 3, 羅斯福路三段283巷17號; dishes NT$120-250; ⏲11.30am-10pm; 📶 📋; Ⓜ Taipower

POT LUCK IN THE PARK

Since 2008, a merry mix of musicians and friends, both foreigners and Taiwanese, have gathered on the first Sunday of each month in Da'an Park to 'jam, drum, dance, juggle, play Frisbee, share food, make new friends and music, and share thoughts'. It is a community and environmentally conscious crowd aiming to create a fun haven for foreign/local interaction.

Anyone is welcome (including kids). Bring a friendly attitude, vegetarian-only food to share, your own bowl and utensils, and any musical instruments you have. The meeting time is between 3pm and 9pm at the second pavilion north of the Heping andJianguo Rd Intersection.

Check out the group's Facebook (www.facebook.com/groups/taipeipotluck) page for the next get-together.

Building) This Israeli-American venture has been serving delicious, healthy, authentic Middle Eastern staples such as stuffed pitas and hummus for years now, and they never miss a beat. Sababa is in a funky neighbourhood of other worthwhile eateries and cafes but we keep going back here. Try the Pita Beirut, with falafel and chicken.

Vegetarian Paradise VEGETARIAN, BUFFET $
(素食天地, Sùshí Tiāndì; Map p62; 182 Heping E Rd; meals from NT$100; ⏲11am-2pm & 5-8pm; Ⓜ Tai-power Building) Because of its location (right across from Shida University), this is usually the first vegetarian buffet many newly arrived students visit. The owners haven't let success go to their heads, though, and they still serve the same sublime vegetarian cuisine as always. Price is by weight.

My Sweetie Pie Bakery & Cafe DESSERT $
(Map p62; 3 Lane 93, Shida Rd; cakes from NT$80; ⏲noon-midnight Mon-Fri, 11am-midnight Sat & Sun; Wi-Fi; menu; Ⓜ Taipower Building) This popular nook for Western pies and cakes (also coffee, milkshakes and light meals) is on a quiet alley across from Grandma Nitti's (which runs Sweetie Pie), a long-running Western breakfast and lunch venue.

★ James Kitchen TAIWANESE $$
(大隱酒食; Map p62; ☎2343 5355/ 2343 2275; 65 Yongkang St; dishes NT$150-395; ⏲11am-2pm & 5.30pm-midnight Tue-Sun; menu) This is Taipei's top spot for Taiwanese food. Though James Kitchen has a warm down-home setting, the presentation and freshness of each dish is anything but commonplace. Try the oysters with bread sticks, the bamboo shoots, the bean curd mushroom rolls, or pretty much anything that catches your eye. It's best to make a reservation.

There is a second eating area at 42-5 Yongkang St (just around the corner) if you find the main restaurant closed.

★ Yongkang Beef Noodles NOODLES $$
(永康牛肉麵, Yǒngkāng Niúròu Miàn; Map p62; 17 Lane 31, Jinshan S Rd ; large/small beef noodle NT$180/200; ⏲11am-9.30pm; menu; Ⓜ Dongmen) Opened since 1963, this is one of Taipei's top spots for beef noodles, especially of the *hóngshāo* (red spicy broth) variety. Beef portions are generous and melt in your mouth. Other worthwhile dishes include steamed ribs. Expect-line ups at lunch and dinner.

KGB BURGERS $$
(Map p62; ☎2363 6015; www.kgbburgers.com; 5 Lane 114, Shida Rd, 師大路114巷5號; burgers NT$145-195; ⏲noon-11pm, last order 10pm; Wi-Fi menu; Ⓜ Taipower Building) Opened in 2007 by a gregarious New Zealander, KGB (short for Kiwi Gourmet Burger) has developed a near cult following among locals and expats alike, both because of its chilled-out atmosphere and amazing burgers (including a number of vegetarian selections). KGB is located down a tiny alley off the north side of Shida Rd. Take MRT Exit 3.

Madame Jill's Vietnamese Cuisine VIETNAMESE $$
(翠薪越南餐廳, Cuì Xīn Yuènán Cāntīng; Map p62; 11 Lane 24, Roosevelt Rd, Sec 4; dishes NT$100-160; ⏲11am-2.30pm & 5-9pm; menu; Ⓜ Gongguan) Opened by overseas Chinese fleeing the Vietnamese War in 1974, Madame Jill's was Taipei's first Vietnamese restaurant and is still one of the best. Though there are a few sops to local tastes (such as the choice of Taiwanese or Vietnamese spring rolls), flavours are mostly authentic, and with a six-page menu there is plenty to choose from. Take Exit 4 of Gongguan MRT and turn left on Lane 24.

Din Tai Fung DUMPLINGS $$
(鼎泰豐, Dǐngtàifēng; Map p62; ☎2321 8928; www.dintaifung.com.tw; 194 Xinyi Rd, Sec 2; dishes NT$90-260; ⏲10am-9pm; menu; Ⓜ Dongmen, Exit 5) Taipei's most celebrated Shanghai-style dumpling shop (the *New York Times* once

called it one of the 10 best restaurants in the world) is now a worldwide franchise. This is the place that started it all and daily mealtime line-ups attest to an enduring popularity. Try the classic *xiǎolóng bāo* (steamed pork dumplings), done to perfection every time.

There are branches in the Taipei 101 food court, and the SOGO food court under Zhongxiao-Fuxing MRT.

Chi Fan Shi Tang TAIWANESE **$$**
(喫飯食堂, Chīfàn Shítáng; Map p62; www.sit-fun.com.tw; 5 Lane 8, Yongkang St; dishes NT$120-180; ⏲11.30am-2pm & 5-9.30pm; 📋; Ⓜ Dongmen) Taking homestyle Taiwanese cooking to a higher level of freshness and presentation is this popular eatery off Yongkang Park. Chi Fan's dim lighting and grey slate-and-wood interior complements the modern approach, though the boisterous clientele keep the atmosphere down to earth. Try the cold chicken plate, the superb pumpkin and tofu (南瓜豆腐) or the oysters in garlic sauce (蒜泥蚵).

Hui Liu VEGETARIAN **$$**
(回留, Huíliú; Map p62; 9 Lane 31, Yongkang St; dishes NT$90-200, set meals from NT$400; ⏲11.30am-10pm; 📋; Ⓜ Dongmen) On the far side of Yongkang Park, Hui Liu serves vegetarian fare such as dumplings, quiche and hand-pulled sesame noodles marked by freshness and a Zen-like presentation on unglazed dishes. The atmosphere is a mix of rustic teahouse and ceramic studio, and is meant to appeal to urban professionals. High-quality organic teas and ceramic pieces are on sale.

Rakumenya RAMEN **$$**
(麵屋日式拉麵, Miàn Wū Rìshì Lāmiàn; Map p62; 7 Lane 10, Yongkang St; ramen NT$180-220; ⏲11.30am-10pm; 📋; Ⓜ Dongmen) Japanese ramen joints are popping up all over Taipei. This authentic and ever-crowded eatery asks you to choose both your broth flavour and thickness as well as noodle thickness and texture. Extra noodles are provided free at any time as long as you have broth left. Plenty of excellent cold dishes are also available.

Oma Ursel's German Bakery & Restaurant GERMAN **$$**
(歐嬤烏蘇拉, Ōumā Wūsūlā; Map p62; 8 Lane 10, Yongkang St; set lunch/dinner from NT$280/350; ⏲11.30am-2pm & 5.30-9pm; 📋; Ⓜ Dongmen) With its two-storey cottage design, including a pleasant brick terrace, this is a charming place to enjoy classic German fare such as sausages, pig knuckle or meatloaf. Oma is renowned for its desserts, especially cakes, and also its selection of breads, many of which can be purchased at the front bakery for takeaway. There's also a good wine and beer selection.

Beijing Lou PEKING DUCK **$$$**
(北京樓, Běijīng Lóu; Map p62; 157 Roosevelt Rd, Sec 3; half duck NT$850, dishes NT$188-588; ⏲11am-2pm & 4.30-9pm; 📋; Ⓜ Taipower Building) One of the best Beijing duck restaurants in town, with a cosy old-school decor and ageing but attentive waitresses. The half duck is sufficient for two or three people.

Zhongshan & Datong

Linsen Road and the surrounding alleyways are popular among Japanese businessmen and tourists, so if you've got a hankering for sipping sake or trying teppanyaki, Kobe beef or *tekka maki* (raw tuna sushi roll), you'll find it there. The heritage shops along Dihua St are now seeing a second life as hip restaurants, cafes and wine bars.

Ningxia Night Market MARKET **$**
(寧夏夜市, Níngxià Yèshì; Map p66; cnr Ningxia & Nanjing W Rd; Ⓜ Zhongshan) This is an excellent venue for sampling traditional snacks, not least because the street is not cramped and most stalls have tables. The food here is very fresh and dishes to try

ORGANIC EATS

Need something to balance out the night markets' assorted artery-clogging goodness? Taipei has a number of places to get organic fruits, vegetables and other healthy products.

Cotton Land Organic Health Store (棉花田生機園地, Miánhuā Tián Shēngjī Yuándì; Map p62; www.sun-organism.com.tw; 273 Roosevelt Rd, Sec 3; Ⓜ Taipower Building) is a well-regarded chain (45 branches across the city) that also has light meals and fresh juices. Try a *jing li tang* (精力湯), a delicious veggie shake with enough greens packed in to last a week.

Santa Cruz (聖德科斯天然有機, Shèng Dékēsī Tiānrán Yǒujī; www.santacruz.com.tw) is another organic chain, with branches all over the city.

include fish soup, oyster omelette, satay beef, *huāshēng tāng* (花生湯; sweet peanut soup) and *yùbǐng* (芋餅; fried taro cake). If you are feeling brave try the *kǔchá* (苦茶; bitter tea).

21 Worker House NOODLES $

(21 工房, 21 Gōngfáng; Map p66; 25 Lane 10, Jiuquan St; noodles NT$50-100; ⌚10am-9pm; Ⓜ Yuanshan) Just a minute south of the Yuanshan MRT is this casual shop taking chilled sesame noodles to a higher, fresher level (the way a chic bistro would with a plain ham sandwich). Try the pork sausage and sesame noodles. There's a picture menu to help you order.

Fleisch CAFE $$

(Map p66; 76 Dihua St; set meals NT$350; ⌚11.30am-8pm; 📶; Ⓜ Zhongshan) In a historic building on Dihua St, this stylish cafe has good lunch options, including fresh sandwiches on homemade bread. On the 3rd floor is Speakeasy, a private function restaurant for small groups. On the 4th floor is a stylish lingerie shop.

#21 Goose & Seafood TAIWANESE $$

(21號鵝肉海鮮, 21 Hào Éròu Hǎixiān; Map p66; 21 Jinzou St; dishes from NT$120; ⌚5pm-4.30am; Ⓜ Zhongshan Elementary School) Loud, rustic and fun, 21 offers great food in a genuine Taiwanese environment (you sit on little bamboo benches in an open shop facing street side). The place gets its name from its two specialities: roasted goose meat and an assortment of fried and stewed fish dishes.

Get here early as seats fill up fast with locals and Japanese tourists. There's a picture menu to help you order (and a reported English menu) or just point at what looks good around you. The kung pao chicken (宮保雞丁, *gōngbǎo jī dīng*) here is some of the best around.

Shin Yeh TAIWANESE $$

(欣葉台菜, Xīnyè Tái Cài; Map p66; www.shinyeh.com.tw; 8th fl, 2 Nanjing W Rd; dishes NT$240-340; ⌚11am-9pm; 🗐; Ⓜ Zhongshan) This well-regarded chain serves traditional Taiwanese food in an upscale environment. Try the fried tofu, stewed pork or fried oysters. To get here take Exit 3 of the MRT and look for the elevator.

★ Qing Tian Xia GUIZHOU $$$

(黔天下, Qián Tiānxià; Map p66; http://tw.myblog.yahoo.com/ufodavid2004; 358-2 Dihua St; dishes NT$170-350; ⌚11.30am-2.30pm & 5.30-9.30pm Tue-Sun; 🗐; Ⓜ Daqiaotou) At the nothern end of historic Dihua St is Taipei's only Guizhou restaurant. The interior is upscale but relaxed, and dishes are authentic and well presented. Just ask the manager and he'll be happy to introduce the history behind any particular item.

Guizhou cuisine, like that of nearby Sichuan province, is noted for its spice, but dishes generally have a greater range and more delicate flavours. The restaurant's blog has a good introduction in English to Guizhou cuisine though the link is in Chinese. Use Google Translate to read it.

The restaurant is in a courtyard off the main street, just south of Minquan W Rd.

Paris 1930 FRENCH $$$

(巴黎廳, Bālítīng; Map p66; ☎2597 1234; http://taipei.landishotelsresorts.com; 2nd fl, 41 Minquan E Rd, Sec 2; average meal NT$2000-4000; ⌚6-10pm daily & 11.30am-2pm Sat & Sun; 🗐; Ⓜ Zhongshan Elementary School) This restaurant in the Landis Hotel is consistently rated as having the best French food in town. In 2012, the hotel underwent its first renovation in 33 years, though it retained its signature art-deco touches. In addition, the menu was altered to allow for lighter dining (three or four courses as opposed to the standard eight). Reservations are recommended.

Xinyi

If you like wandering about a nice neighbourhood and choosing where to eat, then take Exit 2 at SYS Memorial Hall MRT. The back area, and especially Lanes 240 to 280, is filled with cafes and restaurants serving Sichuan, hot pots, vegetarian, Russian, Mexican, burgers and so on. Many have open decks and patios.

Around Taipei 101 there are more high-end malls than seems sustainable, but they all do a roaring business in their food courts and restaurants.

★ Good Cho's CAFE $

(好丘, Hǎo Qiū; Map p74; 54 Songqin St; dishes NT$150; ⌚10am-9.30pm Tue-Fri, 8am-6pm Sat & Sun; 📶🗐; Ⓜ Taipei 101) 🌿 Inside former military dependent Village 44 is this subdued cafe/performance space/lifestyle shop with marble floors, retro lighting and great acoustics. With its emphasis on history, community and local products, Good Cho's is a welcome break from the flash and consumerism of the Xinyi District.

WORTH A TRIP

EATING LARGE IN LITTLE BURMA

In the western suburb of Zhonghe, near the Nanshijiao MRT station (see the Greater Taipei map, p54), is a small but vibrant community of immigrants from Thailand and Myanmar (Burma). Huaxin Street (華新街) is the centre of this community and, not surprisingly, a great place to go for food.

To get here take Exit 4 of the MRT and go right. In about five minutes you'll reach Huaxin Street. There are at least a dozen restaurants and canteens to choose from here (and a score of small grocery shops with Southeast Asian food staples and oddities such as durian-filled Oreos), with dishes averaging NT$60 to NT$100. Don't expect any English menus, but almost everyone has a picture menu on the wall.

If you need a recommendation try **Burmese Flavors** (南國風味, Nánguó Fēngwèi ; Lane 1, 43 Zhongxiao Jie , 忠孝街1巷43號; dishes NT$80-150; ⏲9am-3pm & 5-9pm Fri-Wed). It's the first shop on an alley on the left about 400m down Huaxin Street. Try its *sānjiǎo* (三角; samosas), *jiāo má jī* (椒麻雞; fried chicken on shredded cabbage), *gālí* (咖喱; curry) or *liǎng bàn jiāng sī* (兩辦薑絲; ginger salad).

Light dishes such as bagels and quiche are available and are freshly made daily and served with local spreads such as delicious mulberry jam. Access to Good Cho's is off Zhuangjing St.

Wuxing Street MARKET $
(吳興街; Map p74; Ⓜ Taipei 101) In the shadow of Taipei 101 is this eating street and night market that arose to satisfy the tastes of mainlanders at nearby military Village 44. Look for steamed dumplings, beef noodles, pork rice, as well as tea shops and modern cafes. The eating area extends from Keelung Rd down to Songzhi Rd.

Bella Vita Gourmet Food Hall FOOD COURT $$$
(Map p74; www.bellavita.com.tw; 28 Songren Rd; ⏲11am-10pm; 📶📋; Ⓜ Taipei City Hall) In the basement of Taipei's newest and most opulent European-styled mall, this food court (ahem, sorry, gourmet food hall) offers an oyster bar and patisserie, in addition to Japanese, Italian, Thai, Chinese and more. If you go with friends, try the We Share Everything service; you order from separate venues and the food is delivered to your table.

Eastern Taipei

Taipei city east of Fuxing Rd is vast and offers a plethora of flavours. Anhe Road is a playground for young professionals with Japanese whisky bars and upscale restaurants for brunch and dinner. The alleys around Zhongxiao-Fuxing MRT station are loaded with small eateries. Dunhua S Rd Lane 160 (running west) is half a kilometre of Japanese restaurants: from brightly lit sushi bars to dark wood and smoky barbecue joints, to cheerful lunchbox outlets. Many places have decks that spill out onto the alley.

★ **Raohe Street Night Market** MARKET $
(饒河街觀光夜市, Ráohéjiē Guānguāng Yèshì; Ⓜ Yongchun) Taipei's oldest night market, Raohe Street is a single pedestrian lane stretching between two ornate gates. In between you'll find a great assortment of Taiwanese eats, treats and sometimes even seats. Look for pork ribs in herbal broth, vermicelli and oysters, spicy stinky tofu and steamed buns.

At the eastern end of Raohe St sits the multistorey **Ciyou Temple** (慈祐宮, Cíyòu Gōng), dedicated to the Goddess Matsu. The rooftop *jiannian* (mosaic-like decoration) is delightfully vibrant. To get here, head out of Exit 5 at Yongchun MRT, turn left on Songshan Rd and follow it for about 10 minutes.

Ankor Wat Snacks CAMBODIAN $
(吳哥窟小吃, Wú Gē Kū Xiǎochī; Map p72; 454-2 Changchun Rd; dishes NT$70-100; ⏲11.30am-8.30pm Tue-Sun; Ⓜ Nanjing E Rd) In recent years, Taipei has started to get a number of tiny family-run restaurants serving excellent ethnic cuisine at rock-bottom prices. Ankor Wat is one of these. Try the *jiāo má jī* (椒麻雞, fried chicken on shredded cabbage) or Cambodian curry (柬式咖哩) with pho noodles (河粉), rice noodles (米粉) or French bread. There's a picture menu to help you decide.

To get here exit Nanjing MRT station and head up the back road (Qingcheng St) a couple of blocks to Changchun Rd and turn left.

WORTH A TRIP

ANGLING FOR SHRIMP

Looking for an offbeat Taiwanese eating experience? Love shrimp? Then get serious and take the blue line to the last stop west. About 100m right from Yongning MRT Exit 1 you'll find **Shi Ho Shrimp Fishing** (溪湖釣蝦場, Qīhú Diàoxiāchǎng; ☎2269 4933; 134 Zhongyang Rd, Sec 3, Tucheng City, 土城市中央路三段134號; ⏱noon-3am; Ⓜ Yongning), a stark place that looks like a warehouse with several large cement pools built into the floor.

Here's how it works: the ponds are filled with big tasty shrimp. Customers rent special shrimping poles (NT$250 to NT$300 per hour depending on the pool you want to fish at) and commence shrimping. The attached restaurant will cook your catch in a variety of tantalising ways.

With its warehouse atmosphere, shrimp fishing is definitely not for everyone, but it's a social experience, and there are some real characters about.

Lin Dong Sen Beef Noodles NOODLES $
(林東芳牛肉麵, Líndōngfāng Niúròu Miàn; Map p72; 274 Bade Rd, Sec 2; small/large bowl NT$130/160; ⏱11am-5am; Ⓜ Nanjing E Road) You can't miss this place for the open, streetside kitchen displaying vats of roiling beef noodle broth. Nor should you as the *hóngshāo*-style (red spicy broth) beef noodles here are renowned. Expect line-ups and to eat standing.

Liaoning Street Night Market MARKET $
(遼寧街夜市, Liáoníng Jiē Yèshì; Map p72; Liaoning St; Ⓜ Nanjing E Rd) Heading north from Chang'an E Rd is this small but well-regarded night market. On the left, stalls serve traditional Taiwanese dishes such as *gòngwán* (貢丸, meatballs), *ô-á-chian* (蚵仔煎, oyster omelette) and *dànzǎi miàn* (擔仔麵, tangy noodles). On the right are classic quick-fry places serving all manner of salty dishes and cheap mugs of Taiwan beer.

Matsu Noodles NOODLES $
(馬祖麵食館, Mǎzǔ Miàn Shíguǎn; Map p72; 7 Liaoning St; noodles NT$35-55; ⏱24hr; 📋; Ⓜ Nanjing E Rd) Cheap, excellent bowls of sesame paste noodles (麻醬麵, *májiàng miàn*) are served here literally any time of the day or night.

Yangzhou Guan Tangbao DUMPLINGS $
(揚州灌湯包, Yángzhōu Guàn Tāngbāo; Map p72; 284 Bade Rd, Sec 2; dumpling steamer NT$80-100; ⏱11am-9pm Tue-Sun; Ⓜ Nanjing E Rd) An excellent value, family-run restaurant serving some of the city's best *tāng bāo* (湯包), thick dumplings filled with a soupy broth in addition to meat and veggies. A steamer holds eight dumplings. Pair up with some savoury lamb soup (羊肉清湯).

Duōme BRUNCH $$
(多麼, Duōme; Map p72; 16 Alley 217, Anhe Rd, Sec 2; set lunch NT$240-300; ⏱noon-1am Mon-Fri, 10.30am-1am Sat & Sun; 📶📋; Ⓜ Technology Building) With a minimalist design making it look like a cosy woodshed, a diverse Western menu and wi-fi, Duome is a top spot for a long afternoon meal. The German sausage with slow-roasted tomatoes and mushrooms (and eggs done your way) is a favourite.

Duome also makes great coffee and desserts. Italian dishes are on the dinner menu, though this place is mostly known for brunch.

Toasteria Cafe SANDWICHES $$
(Map p72; www.toasteriacafe.com; 3 Lane 169, Dunhua S Rd, Sec 1; sandwiches NT$150-210; ⏱11am-2am Mon-Thu, 9am-2pm Sat, to midnight Sun; 📶📋; Ⓜ Zhongxiao Dunhua) Being defiantly anti–low-fat cheese, diet soda and credit cards seems at least part of what's won Toasteria a loyal enough following that they now have two branches in the city. You can't go wrong with the classic grilled cheese on wholemeal toast, but there's a wide selection of other melts, as well as pastas and Western breakfasts.

Slack Season Tan Tsu Noodles NOODLES $$
(度小月, Dù Xiǎo Yuè; Map p72; 12 Alley 8, Lane 216, Zhongxiao E Rd, Sec 4; dishes NT$150-260; ⏱11.30am-11pm; 📋; Ⓜ Zhongxiao Dunhua) An upscale branch of a famous Tainan-based snack restaurant, Slack Season (which refers to the style of tangy noodles served during the fishing off-season) serves a long menu of southern dishes, including mullet roe, bamboo shoots with pork, outrageously good fried shrimp rolls, and of course the noodles (a mere NT$50 per bowl).

To get here take Exit 3 of the MRT and turn right on Lane 216 and again on Alley 8. The restaurant is just down the alley. Look for the sign reading 'Since 1895'.

Kunming Islamic Restaurant INDIAN **$$**
(昆明園, Kūnmíng Yuán; Map p72; http://kunming-islamic.myweb.hinet.net; 26 Lane 81, Fuxing N Rd; dishes NT$150-300; 11.30am-2pm & 5.30-9.30pm Mon-Fri, 5.30-9.30pm Sat & Sun; ; Nanjing E Rd) This Halal restaurant serves some of the best, if not the best, Indian food in town. Try the lamb vindaloo.

Ice Monster DESSERT **$$**
(Map p72; www.ice-monster.com; 297 Zhongxiao E Rd, Sec 4; dishes NT$160-250; 10.30am-11.30pm; ; Sun Yat-sen Memorial Hall) A super popular shaved-ice joint with a wide menu, including strawberry, kiwi fruit and, most famously, mango.

Dressed SALAD **$$**
(Map p72; www.dressedsalad.com.tw; 169 Anhe Rd, Sec 2; custom salads NT$230; 11am-8pm; ; Xinyi Anhe) We don't know if this specialised salad joint is going to survive, but here's hoping, as Dressed serves great custom salads (choose from rocket to mesclun mix) as well as chef specials, panini, sandwiches and smoothies. The ambience is diner style with funky electronic music playing in the background.

★ **Addiction Aquatic Development** SEAFOOD **$$$**
(上引水產, Shàng Yǐn Shuǐchǎn; www.addiction.com.tw; 18 Alley 2, Lane 410, Minzu E Rd, 民族東路410巷2弄18號; 6am-midnight; Xingtian Temple) Housed across from the Taipei Fish Market under a single roof is this collection of chic eateries serving the freshest seafood imaginable. There's a stand-up sushi bar, a seafood bar (with wine available), hot pot, an outdoor grill, a wholesale area for take-home seafood and a lifestyle boutique. This place is popular and doesn't take reservations.

NOMURA JAPANESE **$$$**
(Map p72; 2755 6587; 34 Alley 78, Anhe Rd, Sec 1, 安和路一段78巷34號; lunch/dinner per person NT$1200/2500; 11.30am-2pm & 5-9pm Tue-Sun; Xinyi Anhe) It's widely believed that outside of Japan, Taipei is the best place in the world for Japanese food. Several Edomae-style sushi (sushi that follows the Tokyo traditions) restaurants have a great reputation for Michelin-level quality of food and presentation. Among these is Nomura, named after the Japanese chief who founded the restaurant in 2011.

Nomura is a tiny, discreet place with a simple bamboo interior, making it an ideal place for those who want to sample top-end food without feeling they need to dress to the nines and mind their P's and Q's. Reservations are usually needed, especially for dinner.

Plum Blossom Room DIM SUM **$$$**
(梅花廳, Méihuā Tīng; Map p72; www.brotherhotel.com.tw; 2nd fl, 255 Nanjing E Rd, Sec 3; dishes NT$220-350; 9am-9.30pm; ; Nanjing E Road) Taipei restaurants rarely do dim sum well, with the exception of this classy (but loud and jovial in the usual dim sum way), 2nd-floor place in the Brother Hotel. Dim sum dishes average NT$85 to NT$120.

Drinking & Nightlife

Tea growing and drinking has a venerable tradition in Taiwan and, while most people head to Maokong when they want to enjoy brewing and imbibing, there are a few excellent places within the city as well. In addition to teahouses listed here, try Hui Liu (p91) or Mayor's Residence Art Salon (p97).

If bubble tea is your cuppa, you'll find endless roadside stands and stalls throughout the city selling it hot or cold with ice. Most of these places also offer fruit-flavoured teas such as lemon or passionfruit, and sweetened/unsweetened black and green tea–flavoured drinks.

There's no lack of bars within the city either, though the once popular student-bar scene around Shida is now largely dead. Typically, beers sell for between NT$100 and NT$180, spirits or cocktails NT$250 to NT$300. Most places have happy hours.

A few good outdoor areas for drinking include the Red House (p61) in Ximending (mostly but not exclusively a gay scene), the bar strip along Siyuan Rd, just west of Gongguan MRT, and the riverfront at Bitan.

The Xinyi District is the undisputed capital of the club scene, with the pulsating neon-wonderland streetside good preparation for the flash and sparkle inside the city's trendiest clubs. Wednesday, Friday and Saturday from around 10pm to 5am are club nights with cover charges averaging NT$700 (including two free drinks). Check club Facebook and website pages as some have cheaper admission early and late, drink specials and ladies nights (usually Wednesday).

Check out www.taipeitrends.com.tw and http://taipei543.com for more nightlife listings.

★Herb Alley TRADITIONAL DRINKS

(青草巷, Qīngcǎo Xiàng; Map p56; Lane 224, Xichang Rd; drinks NT$20-40; Ⓜ Longshan Temple) Just around the corner from Longshan Temple is this herb-selling area that dates back to Qing times. It's a great place to sample some of the incredible range of Chinese herbal drinks available, though some may truly curdle your liver.

Try the refreshing roselle (洛神花), the soothing wax gourd tea (冬瓜茶) or the incredibly bitter, bitter tea (苦茶). Herb alley is just to the right of Longshan as you face the entrance (Lane 209, though the official address is Lane 224, Xichang St). Wander through and as you pop onto Xichang St, you'll see the drink stalls.

★Fortress Cafe CAFE

(堡壘咖啡, Bǎolěi Kāfēi; Map p56; www.csh.taipei.gov.tw; 2nd fl, 98 Yanping S Rd; ⏲11am-10pm; ; Ⓜ Ximen) It may be hard to believe, but you can actually enjoy a coffee (or beer or meal) here on the stone terrace of Zhongshan Hall that authoritarian leader Chiang Kai-shek used to stand on to deliver speeches to the people.

★Wistaria Tea House TEAHOUSE

(紫藤廬, Zíténg Lú; Map p62; www.wistariatea-house.com; 1 Lane 16, Xinsheng Rd, Sec 3; ⏲10am-11pm; ; Ⓜ Da'an Park) History, nostalgia and fine tea combine in this charming former Japanese-era wooden dormitory. Wistaria was built in 1920 for naval personnel and later used as a hangout for artists, literati and political dissidents following the 1979 Kaohsiung Incident (which led to the arrest and imprisonment of most of the top democracy advocates in Taiwan; see p334).

It has a fine selection of oolongs, Tie Guanyin (p119), green teas, and some rare pu'er (dark fermented tea) that could set you back thousands in one afternoon of drinking. Light meals and snacks are also served.

★Ounce Taipei BAR

(Map p72; www.ouncetaipei.com; 40 Lane 63, Dunhua S Rd, Sec 2; ⏲7pm-midnight Mon, to 2am Tue-Sat; ; Ⓜ Xinyi Anhe) Taipei's first speakeasy-style bar is everything you'd expect it to be, including being hidden behind a secret door, heavy on the dark hardwood and dim lights, and serving top-rated cocktails. The establishment is fronted by Relax cafe.

Le Zinc WINE BAR

(Map p66; www.facebook.com/lezinclo; 67 Dihua St, Sec 1; ⏲noon-7pm Tue & Wed, to 11pm Thu-Sat, to 7pm Sun; ; Ⓜ Zhongshan) This warm and

ASIA'S COFFEE CAPITAL

In recent years, Taipei has emerged as Asia's great coffee capital. Exactly how all this began is still being explored. It seems the Dutch first planted coffee around the Gukeng area (Yunlin County) in the 17th century, but for centuries the red beans were used only for decorative purposes by aboriginals.

Things really began about 10 years ago as Taiwanese living or studying abroad started bringing back new ideas about how to make proper coffee. As is usual here, they found a ready audience both eager to try new things and also to learn to appreciate the drink at a high level. Today you'll find scores of cafes serving gourmet coffee, often from single-origin beans (some locally grown), roasted on the premises and brewed in a slow, labour-intensive way right in front of you.

Passable fresh brewed coffee is available at any convenience store for NT$30 to NT$40. Some of the best coffee, and ridiculously cheap for the quality, comes from chains such as CAMA, which roast on the premises and cater to take out.

There are high concentrations of cafes on Lane 243 just south of Yongkang Park, the alleys north of Zhongshan MRT Exit 2, and Dihua St Sec 1. Also be sure to check out Frank & Sams Cafe Salon (p111) in Tamsui, which is set in a restored brick warehouse overlooking the river.

While most people understand the English terms it's good to know some Chinese:

Americano – 美式咖啡, *Měishì kāfēi* or 黑咖啡 (*hēi kāfēi*, black coffee)

espresso – 濃縮咖啡, *nóngsuō kāfēi*

latte – 拿鐵, *ná tiě*

stylish cafe/wine bar is set at the far back of one of Dihua St's traditional brick shops (originally a medicine shop built in 1923). Enter via the Hakka Blue, a wonderful ceramic studio, to get a look at how these very long and narrow buildings were constructed to facilitate air flow and natural lighting. If you arrive late, enter from the back alley.

Taipei Brewery BREWERY

(台灣啤酒346倉庫餐廳; Map p72; 85 Bade Rd, Sec 2; ⌚5.30pm-1am; Ⓜ Zhongxiao Xinsheng) Built in 1919 as Taiwan's first brewery, this landmark building has gone through many names, beginning with Takasago Brewery. At the back of the brewery is the large warehouse 346 that serves nightly as a rowdy beer hall, with cheap mugs of draft, quick-fry dishes and frequent live entertainment.

Lao Pai Gongyuan Hao TRADITIONAL DRINKS

(老牌公園號, Lǎopái Gōngyuán Hào; Map p56; 2 Hengyang Rd; drinks NT$25; ⌚10am-8pm; Ⓜ NTU Hospital) Across from 2-28 Park in an old Japanese-era corner shop is this decades-old place selling a refreshing *suan mei tang* (酸梅湯, sour plum juice).

Haaya's Coffee CAFE

(哈亞咖啡, Hāyà Kāfēi; Map p72; 307 Dunhua N Rd, Songshan; ⌚9am-9pm, closed 1st & 3rd Mon of each month; 📶; Ⓜ Songshan Airport) A pioneer in the new coffee culture with an upscale atmosphere and award-winning single-origin beans.

Lugou Cafe CAFE

(爐鍋咖啡, Lúguō Kāfēi; Map p66; 2nd fl, 1 Lane 32, Dihua St, Sec 1; ⌚3.30-10pm Tue-Sun; 📶; Ⓜ Zhongshan) Speciality coffees (including some local choices such as Alishan) in a heritage building on Dihua St. Perfect on both counts.

Mayor's Residence Art Salon CAFE

(市長官邸藝文沙龍, Shìzhǎng Guāndǐ Yìwén Shālóng; Map p56; www.mayorsalon.tw; 46 Xuzhou St; ⌚9am-10pm; 📶; Ⓜ Shandao Temple) Built in 1940, this is one of the best preserved large Japanse-style residences in Taiwan. With its heritage styling, great natural lighting and park-like setting, it's a superb place for a coffee, tea or light meal. Frequent art exhibits are held here.

Cafe Libero CAFE

(Map p62; 1 Lane 243, Jinhua St; ⌚noon-midnight Mon-Fri, to 6pm Sat & Sun; 📶; Ⓜ Dongmen) Set in a house from the 1950s with vintage furniture and a Zelkovia parquet floor, this is the type of hip place you take someone to show them your insider knowledge of the city. Libero is on a street with another half-dozen worthy cafes.

At the back right of the cafe look for the nook occupied by **Red On Tree** (在欉紅, Zài Cóng Hóng; Map p62; www.redontree.com), a speciality dessert shop selling prettily packaged tropical fruit jams and pastries made with high-quality locally sourced organic ingredients.

La Crema CAFE

(克立瑪咖啡店, Kèlìmǎ Kāfēi Diàn; Map p74; 45 Lane 280, Guangfu S Rd, Xinyi; ⌚noon-11pm; 📶; Ⓜ Sun Yat-sen Memorial Hall) Some of the city's best coffee in a relaxed airy space down a lane loaded with good restaurants. Take Exit 2 of the MRT and walk straight to reach Lane 280.

Dance Cafe CAFE

(跳舞咖啡廳, Tiàowǔ Kāfēi Tīng; Map p66; 1 Lane 46, Zhongshan N Rd, Sec 2, 中山北路2段46巷1號; ⌚10am-10pm; 📶; Ⓜ Shuanglian) Elegant, serene and loaded with history, this cafe is located in a former wooden dormitory (with a large deck spilling onto a grassy lawn) built by the Japanese in 1925. It was later used as a studio by Tsai Jui-yueh, a pioneer of modern dance in Taiwan.

Drop Coffee House CAFE

(滴咖啡, Dī Kāfēi; Map p62; 1 Lane 76, Xinsheng S Rd, Sec 3; ⌚10.30am-11pm; 📶; Ⓜ Gongguan) Set in an 80-year-old gutted Japanese-era private residence, and serving single-origin coffee from places such as Rwanda and Brazil, this place looks so inviting you'd stop in even without a recommendation.

Director Tsai's Café Galerie CAFE

(蔡明亮咖啡走廊, Cài Míng-liàng Kāfēi Zǒuláng; Map p56; 4th fl, 98 Yanping S Rd; ⌚10am-9pm; 📶; Ⓜ Ximen) Founded by Taiwanese director Tsai Ming-liang, this cafe is set in a long gallery on the 4th floor of Zhongshan Hall. It's the perfect setting for reading or meeting a friend.

Salt Peanuts CAFE

(鹹花生, Xían Huāshēng; Map p62; 23 Lane 60, Taishun St, Shida, 泰順街60巷23號; 📶; Ⓜ Taipower Building) Very popular cafe and restaurant in the Shida area with dark-wood ambience. Good desserts and a wide selection of beers as well. From Shida Rd turn right on Lane 105 (this turns into Lane 60, Taishun St).

H*ours Cafe CAFE
(Map p62; www.facebook.com/hours.cafe; 12 Alley 8, Lane 210, Roosevelt Rd, Sec 3, Shida; ⏲2-11pm Mon-Fri, noon-11pm Sat & Sun; 📶; Ⓜ Taipower Building) Lovely little gay-owned cafe and bookstore serving food and beverages.

Fong Da Coffee CAFE
(蜂大咖啡, Fēngdà Kāfēi; Map p56; 42 Chengdu Rd; ⏲8am-10pm; Ⓜ Ximen) One of Taipei's original coffee shops, Fong Da dates from 1956 and still uses some of the original equipment. This is the shop that introduced iced drip coffee to Taiwan. It's also a great place to buy whole beans or coffee-brewing devices such as syphons or Italian stovetop espresso makers.

Water Moon Tea House TEAHOUSE
(水月草堂, Shuǐ Yuè Cǎotáng; Map p72; www.teawatermoon.com; 2 Alley 180, Fuxing S Rd, Sec 2; ⏲2-10pm; Ⓜ Technology Building) With some of the city's oldest and finest teas, an elegant design and classes in tea appreciation, this is the place for the serious tea drinker, or someone looking to learn more about the art. Friday nights the teahouse closes early for lectures/meetings (ask if you can join), Saturday afternoons feature Nanguan music, and Sundays see a large foreign crowd.

Cha Cha Thé TEAHOUSE
(采采食茶文化, Cǎi Cǎi Shí Chá Wénhuà; Map p72; www.chachathe.com; 23 Lane 219, Fuxing S Rd, Sec 1; ⏲11.30am-10pm; 📶; Ⓜ Zhongxiao Fuxing) Hyper stylish but genuinely serene teahouse by designer Shiatzy Chen. One wall is made of compressed tea bricks. There's beautifully packaged tea for sale.

Cafe Odeon BAR
(Map p62; www.cafeodeon.com.tw; 11 Lane 86, Xinsheng S Rd, Sec 3; ⏲5pm-1am Mon-Fri, 11am-1.30am Sat & Sun; 📶; Ⓜ Gongguan) A fixture of the National Taiwan University area since 1997, Odeon has one of the largest beer menus in Taiwan, with brews from Belgium, England, Quebec and elsewhere. Drinks are expensive here, so it's more of a place to linger and chat with friends than party.

Jolly Brewery & Restaurant BREWERY
(Map p72; www.jollys.tw; 29 Qingcheng St; ⏲11.30am-2.30pm & 5.30-11pm; 📶; Ⓜ Nanjing E Road) Jolly, one of Taipei's few remaining brew pubs, does a roaring business nightly, which begs the question why more places don't also serve handcrafted stout, pilsner and pale ale. The Qingcheng St branch has outdoor seating, while a new branch just opened on **Hengyang Street** (Map p56; 60 Henyang St, Ximending; Ⓜ Ximen), near the train station in an historic building. Both serve good Thai food.

Speakeasy Bar BAR
(Map p74; 554 Guangfu S Rd, Xinyi; ⏲6pm-2am Sun-Thu, to 4am Fri & Sat; 📶; Ⓜ Sun Yat-sen Memorial Hall) Just outside the bright lights of the Xinyi District is this classic long, dark and friendly Irish bar with a good range of pub grub such as cottage pie. English premier league games are shown on weekends.

Brass Monkey SPORTS BAR
(Map p72; www.brassmonkeytaipei.com; 166 Fuxing N Rd; ⏲5pm-2am; 📶; Ⓜ Nanjing E Rd) This popular sports bar is also known for its Pub Quiz Night (usually Wednesday). Ladies Night is every Thursday.

WOOBAR BAR
(Map p74; www.wtaipei.com; 10th fl, 10 Zhongxiao E Rd, Sec 5, Xinyi; ⏲10am-2am; 📶; Ⓜ Taipei City Hall) Inside the trend-setting W Taipei, WOOBAR is a quiet, natural light–infused lounge in the day and a flashier (literally as the lighting system changes) nightspot after dark.

Ol' Farts BAR
(Map p62; 2nd fl, 38 Roosevelt Rd, Sec 3; ⏲5pm-12.30am Tue-Sun; Ⓜ Taipower Building) A quiet place for a casual drink. Good whisky selection.

AQ Cava BAR
(Map p72; www.aqcava.com; 2nd fl, Alley 223, Zhongxiao E Rd, Sec 4; ⏲5.30pm-1am; Ⓜ Zhongxiao Dunhua, Exit 2) One of four AQ shot bars in the same vicinity, Cava is the most popular, with a large open space and outdoor smoking areas. Shots start at NT$50.

Roxy 99 BAR
(www.roxy.com.tw) Roxy was moving at the time of writing. Check the website for the latest location of this Taipei stalwart on the student party, young workers and rock and roll scene.

Club Myst CLUB
(Map p74; www.facebook.com/myst.taipei; 9th fl, 12 Songshou Rd, Xinyi; Ⓜ Taipei 101) In the aptly named ATT4FUN building, you'll find the city's biggest dance floor and a rather swoon-inducing view of Taipei.

Luxy CLUB

(Map p72; www.luxy-taipei.com; 5th fl, 201 Zhongxiao E Rd, Sec 4; M Zhongxiao Dunhua) Taiwan's largest club, the perennially popular Luxy (an outlier being in the Dinghao rather than Xinyi District) often features international bands and DJs. Check the website for the latest offerings.

Spark 101 CLUB

(Map p74; www.spark101.com.tw/101; B1, 45 Shifu Rd, Xinyi; M Taipei 101) In the basement of Taipei 101, this club is renowned for the pulsating lights of the dance floor and ceiling.

☆ Entertainment

Taipei attracts a full calendar's worth of international performances and concerts, and also has its own home-grown talent to share, such as the renowned **Cloud Gate Dance Theatre of Taiwan** (雲門舞集; www.cloudgate.org.tw) and the dance and drum troupe U-Theatre (p118). The live music scene is more happening than ever, with local and international bands playing in multiple genres nightly.

Check the following websites for dates and times:

➡ **Taipei Travel** (www.taipeitravel.net/en) Lists the dates for current and upcoming festivals and other large events.

➡ **Taipei Cultural Center** (www.tmseh.taipei.gov.tw) For theatre, opera, dance, puppetry, etc.

➡ **Gig Guide** (www.gigguide.tw) For live music.

➡ **ArtsTicket** (www.artsticket.com.tw) For ticket information and times.

Party World KARAOKE

(錢櫃, Qiángui; Map p56; www.cashboxparty.com; 55 Zhonghua Rd, Sec 1; ⏲24hr; M Ximen) This outlet of the popular chain of KTVs (karaoke) with private room rentals is in the Ximending area.

Live Music

Wall Live House LIVE MUSIC

(www.thewall.com.tw; B1, 200 Roosevelt Rd, Sec 4, Shida; ⏲8pm-late; M Gongguan) The cavernous Wall is Taipei's premier venue for independent music, both local and international. Check www.gigguide.tw for an English list of upcoming shows.

Riverside Live House LIVE MUSIC

(河岸留言, Hé'àn Liúyán; Map p56; www.riverside.com.tw; 177 Xining S Rd; M Ximen) One of Taipei's best live music venues, the 800-seat Riverside sits at the back of the historic Red House in Ximending. Acts range from local Mandopop (Mandarin pop music) to jazz and straight-on rock and roll. See www.gigguide.tw for an English list of upcoming events.

Revolver LIVE MUSIC

(Map p56; www.facebook.com/revolver.taipei; 1-2 Roosevelt Rd, Sec 1; ⏲noon-3am Mon-Thu, to 5am Fri & Sat, to 1am Sun; 📶; M Chiang Kai-shek Memorial Hall) One of Taipei's liveliest spots at the time of writing, this British-run bar/pub/dance club (and cafe during the day) is a

TAIPEI FOR CHILDREN

Taipei is probably not on the bucket list for many children, but families will find there is a lot to keep young ones entertained, and certainly well fed. Night markets, in particular, are a favourite with kids, offering endless fried stuff, sugary drinks and downright weird items to sample.

Active families will love the easy access to hikes and cycling routes. Water activity fans should check out the pedal boats at Bitan, the natural river pools at Wulai (p125), the open hot-spring complex at Tienlai (p116), and in summer the water parks at the Museum of Drinking Water (p65) and **Formosa Fun Coast** (www.formosafuncoast.com.tw; adult/child NT$650/550; ⏲9am-5pm Jun & Sep, to 9pm Jul & Aug). Also in summer look for the Taipei Children's Art Festival (p80) and the **Yi-lan International Children's Folklore & Folkgame Festival** (www.yicfff.tw/2013/en; adult/child NT$600/300) in nearby Yilan County. The Ferris wheel at **Miramar Entertainment Park** (www.miramar.com.tw; tickets NT$200; ⏲11am-11pm; m Jiannan Rd) is just across from Jiannan Rd MRT.

The rules for when children get discount tickets vary. Sometimes it is based on height (which also varies from 90cm to 150cm) and sometimes age (under 12).

Also popular with visiting families are Land Bank Exhibition Hall (p59), Lin Liu-Hsin Puppet Theatre Museum (p100), Taipei 101 (p75), Bopiliao (p61), Taipei Expo Park (p68) and National Taiwan Science Education Centre (p71).

great place to catch a live music act, hang out, play pool and drink cheap beer.

TAV Cafe LIVE MUSIC

(藝術村餐坊, Yìshù Cūn Cān Fang; Map p56; www.tavcafe.com; 7 Beiping E Rd; noon-2am Tue-Sun;) For live foreign jazz and folk music most weekends check out this small bar/cafe inside the Taipei Artist Village (TAV). TAV has a surprisingly large garden area out back with lots of trees for shade during the day. Talk to A-Liang if you want the scoop on the local music scene. See the website for upcoming events

Bobwundaye LIVE MUSIC

(無問題, Wú Wèntí; http://bobwundaye.blogspot.tw; 77 Heping E Rd, Sec 3; 7pm-2am Mon-Sat; ; M Liuzhangli) This laid-back, foreign-run neighbourhood bar (the name means 'no problem') features regular live music, both local and international, and sees a similarly mixed crowd. See the website for events.

Blue Note JAZZ

(藍調, Lándiào; Map p62; 4th fl, 171 Roosevelt Rd, Sec 3; 7.30pm-1am; M Taipower Building, Exit 3) Taipei's longest-running jazz club, Blue Note has been in the same location since 1978.

Brown Sugar Live & Restaurant JAZZ

(黑糖; Map p74; www.brownsugarlive.com; 101 Songren Rd, Xinyi; noon-2.30am; ; M Taipei City Hall) A bit hidden off Songren Rd is Taipei's pre-eminent club for R & B and jazz mixes. Brown Sugar hosts local house and guest musicians from around the world. Wednesday is Ladies Night.

Chinese Opera & Theatre Venues

★Lin Liu-Hsin Puppet Theatre Museum PERFORMING ARTS

(林柳新紀念偶戲博物館, Línliǔxīn Jìniàn Ǒuxì Bówùguǎn; Map p66; www.taipeipuppet.com; 78 Xining N Rd; museum adult/child NT$80/50; 10am-5pm Tue-Sun; M Zhongshan) A combination interactive museum, workshop and theatre, this complex is a must-visit for anyone interested in traditional performing arts. For starters, the Asian puppet collection here is the largest in the world. There are also two puppetry troupes who regularly perform both here and internationally. All performances have English subtitles projected on a screen.

At the time of writing a new 90-seat indoor theatre was almost ready to open. See the informative English website for dates and times of shows.

Dadaocheng Theatre OPERA

(大稻埕戲苑, Dàdàochéng Xìyuàn; Map p66; www.facebook.com/dadaochen2011; 8th & 9th fl, 21 Dihua St, Sec 1; 9am-5.30pm Tue-Sun; M Zhongshan) Above the Yongle Market, this theatre regularly holds performances of Taiwanese opera. In May and June they host free shows in the outside square. To find the lifts to the 8th floor, look for the entrance to the right as you face the market.

Taipei Comedy Club COMEDY

(卡米地喜劇俱樂部, Kǎmǐdì Xǐjù Jūlèbù; Map p74; 2764 5529; www.comedy.com.tw; 20 Lane 553, Zhongxiao E Rd, Sec 4, Xinyi; 6pm-1am Wed-Mon; M Sun Yat-sen Memorial Hall) At Taipei's only comedy club, shows are a mixed bag of Chinese and English, funny and not so. But a night here is usually good for a few laughs. Admission is typically NT$250 to NT$400 and includes a free drink. Wednesday is open mike (starts at 8pm, NT$100 minimum purchase).

Taipei Eye PERFORMING ARTS

(台北戲棚, Táiběi Xìpéng; Map p66; 2568 2677; www.taipeieye.com; 113 Zhongshan N Rd, Sec 2; tickets NT$880; M Shuanglian) Taipei Eye showcases Chinese opera together with other rotating performances, including puppet theatre and aboriginal dance. This is a tourist show but is well regarded and booking can be done online in English. There are three to four shows weekly, usually starting around 8pm.

National Theatre & Concert Hall CONCERT VENUE

(國家戲劇院, 國家音樂廳, Guójiā Xìjù Yuàn, Guójiā Yīnyuè Tīng; Map p56; 3393 9888; www.ntch.edu.tw; M Chiang Kai-shek Memorial Hall) Located inside Liberty Plaza, the National Theatre and Concert Hall hosts large-scale concerts and cultural events including dances, musicals, Chinese and Western opera and concerts of Chinese and Western classical and popular music. The halls, completed in 1987, were among the first major performance venues built in Asia.

Taipei Arena PERFORMANCE SPACE

(臺北小巨蛋, Táiběi Xiǎo Jù Dàn; Map p72; www.taipeiarena.com.tw; M Nanjing E Rd) Vast, cavernous and shaped like a flying saucer, the Taipei Arena hosts concerts, sporting events and noteworthy performances. Check out the website for the latest schedule.

Cinemas

Ximending is the place to head for a large variety of movies, where there's a cluster of movie theatres along Wucheng St. Other leading multiplexes are at **Vie Show Cinemas** (威秀影城, Wēi Xiù Yǐng Chéng; Map p74; www.vscinemas.com.tw; 20 Songshou Rd, Xinyi; Ⓜ Taipei City Hall) in Xinyi District and Breeze Centre's **Ambassador Theatre** (國賓影城, Guóbīn Yǐngchéng; Map p72; www.ambassador.com.tw; 39 Fuxing N Rd, Sec 1; Ⓜ Zhongxiao Fuxing).

Taipei's most respected art-house cinema is **SPOT – Taipei Film House** (光點台北, GuāngdǐanTáiběi ; Map p66; ☎ ext 400 2511 7786; www.spot.org.tw; 18 Zhongshan N Rd, Sec 2; movies NT$260; ⏲ 11am-10pm; Ⓜ Zhongshan), an excellent cinema with a bookshop and an indoor/outdoor cafe. The building, a landmark that dates back to 1925, was once the home of the US ambassador. There is also a branch of SPOT at Huashan 1914 Creative Park (p58).

Shopping

With its endless markets, back-alley emporiums, speciality shops and glittering shopping malls, Taipei offers the complete gamut of shops and shopping experiences. Go local and you can't go wrong. Taiwan has a rich tradition of wood, ceramic, metal and glass production and young designers are now pushing the envelope with everything from clothing and stationery to tea sets. Agricultural products, from organic teas and coffees to dark sesame oil, pineapple cakes and tropical fruit jams, are also superb.

For an endless list of places to shop, check out the **One Town One Product** (http://otop.tw) website.

★ Hakka Blue CERAMICS

(客家藍, Kèjiā Lán; Map p66; www.hakka-blue.com; 67 Dihua St; ⏲ 11am-7pm; Ⓜ Zhongshan) In a restored longshop from 1923, this exceptional ceramic studio sells works inspired by the indigo colour of Hakka clothing. Its spice rack set, with individual holders shaped like little *xiǎolóng bāo* (steamed dumplings), is probably the most original gift you can take home from Taiwan.

★ Lin Mao Sen Tea Co DRINK

(林茂森茶行; Map p66; quality_tea@hotmail.com; 195-3 Chongqing N Rd, Sec 2; ⏲ 8am-10pm; Ⓜ Daqiaotou) This is reportedly the oldest tea- selling shop in Taipei, going back some 133 years. The current fourth-generation merchants are more than happy to talk tea and let you sample the wares, which sit in large metal drums about the warehouse. Prices per *jin* (600g) are written clearly on the top of each drum.

Ming Xing Dao ANTIQUES

(名行道, Míng Xíng Dào; Map p66; www.facebook.com/mingxingdao; 358 Dihua St, Sec 1; ⏲ 10am-8pm Tue-Fri, to 5.30pm Sat & Sun; Ⓜ Daqiaotou) One of Taipei's most interesting small antique shops is run by an ordained lama. This is where you go for your Yuan dynasty Islam-influenced double-necked vases or rare Tibetan *thangkas,* but there are also many affordable items and, in any case, the owner doesn't mind browsers. The shop is back from the main road in a courtyard.

VVG Thinking BOUTIQUE

(好樣思維, Hǎo yàng sīwéi; ⏲ noon-9pm; Ⓜ Zhongxiao Xinsheng) In the funky loft space above a fusion restaurant in the Huashan 1914 Creative Park is this quirky boutique bookstore/design shop with a rich collection of art and cook books, vintage collectables and designer products. VVG is in the complex of red-brick buildings to the west of the giant smokestack.

Indigenous Cultural & Economic Centre ABORIGINAL DESIGNS

(Map p74; ⏲ 12.30pm-9pm Tue-Sun; Ⓜ Taipei City Hall) Literally within Taipei City Hall MRT station (head to Exit 4) is this small shop selling a range of exquisite aboriginal designs, including clothing, jewellery, vases and knick-knacks.

Little Garden Embroidered Shoes SHOES

(小花園繡花鞋, Xiǎo Huāyuán Xiùhuāxié; Map p56; http://tw.myblog.yahoo.com/little-garden; 70 Emei St; ⏲ 12.30-6pm; Ⓜ Ximen) This third-generation shop is the last remaining traditional embroidered shoe outlet in Taipei. Most of the dainty little items (with patterns such as auspicious dragons, peonies and phoenixes) are now made with computer-controlled machines, but you can still order completely hand-stitched ones. Shoes start at NT$690.

Eslite BOOKS

(誠品, Chéngpǐn; Map p72; 245 Dunhua S Rd; Ⓜ Zhongxiao Dunhua) This is Taipei's most renowned bookshop, with locations all over town. The flagship Dunhua S Rd location is open 24 hours. The **Xinyi Branch** (誠品信義店; Map p74; 11 Songgao Rd, Xinyi; ⏲ 10am-midnight; Ⓜ Taipei City Hall) is the largest bookstore in Taiwan and the B2 level is dedicated to local designs, including innovative jewellery, bags, shoes, stationery, knick-knacks and home furnishings.

Taiwan Handicraft Promotion Centre GIFTS
(台灣手工業推廣中心; Map p56; www.handicraft.org.tw; 1 Xuzhou Rd; ⏲9am-5.30pm; 📶; Ⓜ NTU Hospital) Four floors of jade, ceramics, tea sets, jewellery, scrolls, Kinmen knifes, Kavalan whisky (www.kavalanwhisky.com/en) and handmade soap are just highlights of the variety on offer here. Colourful **Franz** (www.franzcollection.com) porcelain is featured in a special section.

Jianguo Weekend Holiday Jade Market JADE, JEWELLERY
(建國假日玉市, Jiànguó Jiàrì Yùshì; Map p72; ⏲9am-6pm Sat & Sun; Ⓜ Da'an) This is perhaps the largest market for jade and other semi-precious stones in Asia. It's a good place to buy jewellery, trinkets and religious items, but it lacks appeal if you are just browsing. The market is literally under Jianguo Overpass. Just south is a weekend flower market.

Wu Fen Pu CLOTHING
(五分埔, Wǔ Fēn Pǔ; ⏲noon-late; Ⓜ Yongchun) Easily the largest clothing market in the city, Wu Fen Pu encompasses several square blocks of lanes and alleys. You'll find everything from the latest fashions (most shops cater to women) to T-shirts with comically bad Chinglish slogans. To get here take MRT Exit 5 and then turn left on Songshan Rd.

Guanghua Digital Plaza ELECTRONICS
(光華數位新天地, Guānghuá Shùwèi Xīntiāndì; Map p56; 8 Civic Blvd, Sec 3; ⏲10am-9pm; 📶; Ⓜ Zhongxiao Xinsheng) Six storeys of electronics, software, hardware, laptops, peripherals, mobile phones and gadgets of all kinds. Dozens of smaller shops in the surrounding neighbourhood.

ℹ Orientation

Taipei is divided into 12 districts (區, qū), though most travellers will visit only a few. Major streets run east–west and north–south and are labelled as such (for example, Zhongshan North Rd). They are also numbered by section (Zhongshan N Rd, Sec 1) according to their distance from the city centre (basically where Zhongshan and Zhongxiao Rds intersect). When getting or giving addresses it's very important to know the street direction and section.

Taipei also has numbered 'lanes', which generally run perpendicular to the main streets. A typical address is 5 Lane 114, Shida Rd. On Shida Rd look for where number 114 would be. You'll find the lane instead of a building. The actual building address is 5 on this lane (in this case the restaurant KGB).

Then there are alleys, which are to lanes as lanes are to streets. It sounds complicated but after one or two tries it becomes intuitive.

Surrounding Taipei is New Taipei City (formerly Taipei County) with various municipalities such as Zhonghe, Yonghe, Banqiao and Tamsui arbitrarily divided from Taipei by the river. When sights in these areas are accessible by MRT we cover them in this chapter. Otherwise, see Northern Taiwan for sights within New Taipei City.

ℹ Information

EMERGENCY

Citizen Hotline (☎1999) The most useful number to call for anything from noise and environmental complaints to asking to be connected to the police or fire department. English service.

Police (☎110)

Fire & Ambulance (☎119)

English-language directory assistance (☎106)

INTERNET ACCESS

Nearly all hotels and hostels, libraries and major sights have broadband or wi-fi. Chain cafes usually have paid service only (such as WIFLY) but gourmet cafes will have free wi-fi. Internet cafes where you pay for a computer and internet are getting scarce but are still to be found around university areas.

Taipei has 10,000 free wi-fi hotspots, including every MRT station, as part of its Taipei Free wi-fi program (www.tpe-free.taipei.gov.tw/tpe). Signal strength is generally good. Register at the airport or Taipei Main Station.

For paid wi-fi, you can buy daily or monthly service at 7-Eleven, or online, for the WIFLY system (www.wifly.com.tw/Wifly7/tw), which includes coverage at all 7-Elevens, Starbucks, MOS Burgers and thousands of other spots around Taipei and Taiwan.

INTERNET RESOURCES

Taipei City buses (www.taipeibus.taipei.gov.tw)

Taipei MRT (http://english.trtc.com.tw)

Taiwan Culture Portal (www.culture.tw) For articles on Taiwanese culture and history.

LEFT LUGGAGE

The basement floor of Taipei Main Station has several rows of coin-operated lockers for NT$30/70 per three hours for small/large lockers. There's a six-day limit for small lockers and three for large. Taipei Songshan Airport and Taoyuan International Airport also have lockers and left-luggage service, as do most hotels and hostels.

MEDICAL SERVICES

Almost every hospital in Taipei has English speakers on staff. If you don't have local insurance, rates are still very cheap compared to the West. Once you've registered with a hospital, subsequent appointments can be made online.

Dr Simon Chan Clinic (Map p72; ☎2731-6530; 3rd fl, 126-3 Zhongxiao E Rd, Sec 4; Ⓜ Zhongxiao Dunhua) This private clinic of a fluent English-speaking doctor trained at UCLA is very popular with Taipei's expat population. Call for appointments.

Mackay Memorial Hospital (馬偕紀念醫院, Mǎxié Jìniàn Yīyuàn; Map p66; ☎2543 3535; 92 Zhongshan N Rd, Sec 2; Ⓜ Shuanglian) Well-regarded private Christian hospital. Takes Taiwan's National Health Insurance (NHI).

Taiwan Adventist Hospital (臺安醫院, Táiān Yīyuàn; Map p72; ☎2771 8151; 424 Bade Rd, Sec 2; Ⓜ Zhongxiao Fuxing) Well regarded for its foreigner friendliness. Takes NHI.

Taipei City Hospital Chinese Medicine Clinic Centre (臺北市立聯合醫院中醫門診中心; Map p56; ☎2388 7088; 100 Kunming St; ⏲9am-noon, 1.30-4.30pm & 5.30-8.30pm Mon-Fri, 8.30-noon & 1.30-4.30pm Sat; Ⓜ Ximen) If you're interested in checking out traditional medicine, this hospital has English-speaking doctors. Takes NHI.

MONEY

ATMs abound in Taipei and most are connected to either the Cirrus or Plus network and accept foreign cards from aligned banks. In addition to banks, look for ATMs at 7-Elevens and other convenience stores. ATMs give you the choice of handling the transaction in English or Chinese.

You can exchange money or travellers cheques (US$ denominations are best) at the airport, or most commercial banks in the city, especially any Bank of Taiwan. There is no black market for currency exchange, nor are there currency-exchange kiosks.

POST

North Gate Post Office (台北北門郵局; Map p56; 114 Zhongxiao W Rd, Sec 1; ⏲7.30am-9pm; 📶; Ⓜ Taipei Main Station) Taipei's main post office is in an historic building southwest of Taipei Main Station. There are branch offices throughout the city. Post-office workers can generally understand a bit of English and are overall pretty helpful.

TOURIST INFORMATION

There are visitor information centre booths scattered around the city, all with the usual assortment of maps and pamphlets on Taipei

TAIPEI STREET DECODER

Taipei street, lane and alley signs are all bilingual but most locals can neither read nor write a romanised address. Showing someone that you want to go to 14 Zhongxiao Rd is going to elicit blank stares in most cases. Another problem is that while officially Taipei uses Hanyu Pinyin, you will run into varying romanisations, especially on name cards.

Below are some major streets with their characters, Hanyu Pinyin and possible alternative spelling.

East–West Streets	Pinyin	Possible Alternative
和平路	Heping Rd	Hoping Rd
信義路	Xinyi Rd	Hsinyi Rd
仁愛路	Ren'ai Rd	Jen-ai Rd
忠孝路	Zhongxiao Rd	Chunghsiao Rd
八德路	Bade Rd	Pateh Rd
市民大道	Shimin Blvd	Civil Blvd
North–South Streets		
中華路	Zhonghua Rd	Junghua Rd
延平路	Yanping Rd	Yenping Rd
重慶北路	Chongqing Rd	Chungching Rd
承德路	Chengde Rd	Chengteh Rd
中山路	Zhongshan Rd	Chungshan Rd
建國路	Jianguo Rd	Chienkuo Rd
敦化路	Dunhua Rd	Tunhua Rd

EASY DOES IT

If you're going to spend any length of time in Taipei, buy yourself an EasyCard (aka Yoyo Card), the stored-value card of the Taipei Rapid Transit Association (TRTA). Adult/child EasyCards sell for NT$500/300, of which NT$100 is a deposit. In addition to MRT rides (which the card gives ycu a discount on) the card is valid on buses within Taipei City, New Taipei City, Keelung City, Taichung City (buses here are free with an EasyCard), Yilan County, Matsu Islands and Tainan City. It is also good for local trains in the north, non-reserved HSR rides, some taxis, the Youbike program and purchases at all convenience stores, Starbucks and dozens of other shops. There's also a 10% to 15% discount on Tourism Shuttle Buses when you use the card.

When you're done using your EasyCard, simply take it to an MRT ticket booth, where your deposit plus any remaining value will be refunded. You can add value to the cards at any MRT station or 7-Eleven.

and other parts of Taiwan, and generally helpful English-speaking staff. The most convenient **centre** (Map p56) is on the main floor of Taipei Main Station and open 8am to 10pm.

Several free magazines published in English have loads of Taipei-specific information, including *Discover Taipei*, which has a useful calendar of current events. The city's tourism website (www.taipeitravel.net/en) is also very useful for current and upcoming events.

Getting There & Away

As the nation's capital, Taipei is well connected to the rest of the island, as well as the outer islands, by rail, bus and air.

AIR

Taipei is directly connected to most major cities in Asia, and there are daily flights to North America, Europe and Oceania countries such as Australia. Most international flights leave from Taoyuan International Airport (www.taoyuanairport.gov.tw), 40km from downtown Taipei. Domestic flights as well as direct flights to China, Japan and Korea leave from Taipei Songshan Airport (www.tsa.gov), located in the city itself and accessible by MRT.

You can also book tickets at any ezTravel office, including the one in Taipei Main Station on the ground floor near the TRA ticket counter.

BUS

Taipei city is serviced by four major bus stations.

West Terminal A (台北西站A棟, Táiběi Xī Zhàn A Dòng; Map p56) Directly to the west of Taipei Main Station on Zhongxiao Rd. Has buses to Taoyuan International Airport (see Getting Around), Taoyuan, Chungli, Keelung, Jinshan and other destinations (mostly) in northern Taiwan.

West Terminal B (台北西站B棟, Táiběi Xī Zhàn B Dòng; Map p56) Next to West Terminal A, this station is serviced exclusively by Taiwan's government-run Kuo Kuang Bus Company (p379). Buses run to southern and central destinations like Taichung, Sun Moon Lake, Alishan, Tainan and Kaohsiung.

Taipei Bus Station (台北轉運站, Táiběi Zhuǎnyùn Zhàn; Map p56) Directly to the north of Taipei Main Station, and connected by underground walkways through Q Mall, is this multistorey station which offers a wide variety of luxury buses to destinations including Jiaoxi and Yilan (only with **Kamalan Bus Company** (葛瑪蘭), Hsinchu, Taichung, Chiayi, Tainan and Kaohsiung.

Taipei City Hall Bus Station (市府轉運站; Map p74) In the east part of the city, and connected to Taipei City Hall MRT station, this station serves much the same routes as the others, including Jiaoxi and Yilan (with Capital Bus only).

HIGH SPEED RAIL (HSR)

High Speed Rail (www.thsrc.com.tw) trains run from 6.30am to 11pm. Tickets can be purchased at the HSR counter and automated kiosks at Basement Level 1 of Taipei Main Station, and can also be purchased at at 7-Eleven ibon kiosks (in Chinese only). Booking can also be done via the HSR website. There are discounts of 10% to 35% for booking eight to 28 days in advance, respectively.

DESTINATION	FARE (NT$) STANDARD	DURATION
Chiayi	915	1hr 23min
Hsinchu	290	31min
Taichung	700	1hr
Tainan	1350	1hr 40min
Taoyuan	160	20min
Kaohsiung (Zuoying)	1490	1½-2hr

STANDARD TRAINS (TRA)

Taiwan's trains are clean, convenient and nearly always on schedule. Unlike the HSR, TRA train stations are almost always in the centre of town (Taitung is an exception). You can find schedules and fares in English at the TRA (http://twtraffic.tra.gov.tw/twrail) website.

DESTINATION	FARE (NT$) FAST/SLOW TRAIN	DURATION FAST/SLOW TRAIN
North/East Line		
Hualien	440/340	2½-3½hr
Ilan	218/140	1-2hr
Keelung	41	50min
Taitung	785/605	6-7hr
West Line		
Chiayi	598/461	3½-4½hr
Hsinchu	177/114	1-2hr
Kaohsiung	843/650	5-7hr
Taichung	375/289	2-3hr
Tainan	738/569	4-6hr

 Getting Around

TO/FROM THE AIRPORT

Two airports serve Taipei. Taiwan Taoyuan International Airport is about 40km west of the city centre and Taipei Songshan Airport is just north of the city centre. International flights are handled at the former; domestic and direct international flights to China, Japan and Korea at the latter.

Taipei Songshan Airport

Taipei Songshan Airport has its own MRT station. A **taxi** from the city centre will cost NT$200 to NT$300.

Taoyuan International Airport

A **taxi** to the city centre is NT$1200 to NT$1400. Buses (55 to 70 minutes) cost between NT$115 and NT$150 depending on where you are going in the city.

Bus 1819 (NT$125) runs every 15 to 20 minutes from 4.30am to 12.20am from West Terminal A, just west of Taipei Main Station. There's a special late-night bus to the airport at 1.50am.

Bus 1840 (NT$125) runs every 15 to 20 minutes between Taipei Songshan Airport and Taoyuan International Airport.

Bus 1968 (NT$135) runs every 30 minutes to/from Xindian MRT station (for travellers who want to stay in Bitan).

Other frequent buses run to/from Banqiao MRT station, Nanjing E Rd MRT station, Zhongxiao-Fuxing MRT station, Taipei City Hall Bus station,Grand Hyatt Taipei, the Sheraton Hotel and Minquan W Rd MRT station.

Bus 705 (NT$30) runs every 10 minutes to/from Taoyuan High Speed Rail (HSR) station.

BICYCLE

Within the city, riding conditions are generally good as Taipei is mostly flat, and almost all major roads now have wide sidewalks that can be ridden (riding with Taipei traffic can be dangerous). There are also hundreds of kilometres of riverside paths (p76). The city's excellent **Youbike** (微笑單車, Wéixiào Dānchē; www.youbike.com.tw) shared bicycle program offers thousands of bikes at 62 stations (set to increase to 173 by the end of 2013). Bikes can be rented at one location and dropped off at another. The first 30 minutes are free and then it's NT$10 for every subsequent 30 minutes. Bikes can be rented with an EasyCard (register the card on the Youbike website) or a credit card.

Most Youbike stations are currently outside MRT stations, but new stations are planned at major tourist sites such as outside the Confucius Temple. The smartphone app 'Fun Travel in Taipei' shows the location of all stations or consult the Youbike website.

BUS

City buses are generally clean and comfortable and run frequently, though with the proliferation of new MRT routes and stations it's often easier just to walk the final minutes to your destination than wait for a bus. Bus stops always display the schedule and some have LED screens telling you when the next bus will arrive. Mobile apps with route and real-time schedule information were still a bit hit and miss at the time of writing. The official city bus website (www.e-bus.taipei.gov.tw) is pretty good for searching for routes.

Most city buses have LED displays at the front in Chinese and English and also a screen above the driver announcing stops in Chinese and English. Fares are NT$15 on most routes within the city centre. If the sign over the fare box reads 上車 (*shàngchē*), that means you pay getting on and 下車 (*xiàchē*) means you pay getting off. All buses take EasyCard payments.

CAR

An international driver's licence is required to rent a car. For English-speaking staff try **VIP Car Rental** (☎2713-1111; www.vipcar.com.tw; per day from NT$1800), which has about the lowest rates around. Also good are Easy Rent (p380) and Car Plus (p380).

SUBWAY (MRT)

Clean and safe, MRT trains run from 6am until midnight. Most places in the city centre are within a 20-minute walk of a station. Announcements and signs are in Chinese and English, as are fares and routes at ticket machines. Coins and bills are accepted and change is provided, though it's best to buy day passes or an EasyCard. All stations have clean public toilets which

TAIPEI BUSES

Buses to all major cities run every 20 to 30 minutes from around 6am to 11pm. Buses to Kaohsiung and Tainan run 24/7. There are often discounts midweek and during off-peak hours. The following are full-fare examples with Kuo Kuang Bus Company.

DESTINATION	FARE (NT$)	DURATION	STATION
Hsinchu	150	1hr 40min	Taipei Bus Station, City Hall
Tainan	360	4hr 20min	West Terminal B, Taipei Bus Station, City Hall
Kaohsiung	530	5hr	West Terminal B, Taipei Bus Station, City Hall
Keelung	55	1hr	West Terminal A
Sun Moon Lake	460	4hr	West Terminal B
Taichung	260	2hr 40min	West Terminal B, Taipei Bus Station, City Hall

you can use even if you are not riding the MRT (just ask the booth attendant to let you in).

TAXI

The base fare is NT$70 for the first 1.25km plus NT$5 for each 250m thereafter. From 11pm to 6am there is a surcharge of NT$20 on top of the fare. Two days prior to the Chinese New Year's Eve until the end of the holidays, the nighttime rate applies to all rides plus an extra NT$20. For nighttime travel during Chinese New Year holidays, there is an extra NT$40 charge.

AROUND TAIPEI

Taipei's MRT has made once out-of-the way places a mere 30-minute ride away, which has not led them to becoming tourist traps, but to a rediscovery of their heritage. Any trip to Taipei more than a day long should make time for a visit out of town.

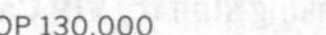

Tamsui (Danshui) 淡水

POP 130,000

This historic town at the mouth of the Danshui River quickly became a popular destination when the MRT line was extended here in 1998. The final leg of the journey runs past mountains and thick mangrove forests making it feel like a trip well out of town. And when you pop out of the station into the wide riverside park with street musicians, bike paths, moored wood junks, and views of an emerald volcanic peak (Guanyinshan) dominating the skyline it all looks very promising – and it is.

For centuries, Tamsui (which means 'fresh water') occupied an important trade and defensive post for the various empires that sought to control Taiwan. Its strategic position, at the mouth of the largest river system in the north where it empties into the Sea of China, and its steep terrain, made it ideal both as a natural port and a location for forts and cannons. In 1629, the town's most famous landmark, Fort San Domingo, was established by the Spanish; it was later controlled by the Dutch, Chinese, British and Japanese.

Other signs of Western influence include a row of late-19th-century mansions and Taiwan's oldest university. All of these were founded by George Leslie MacKay, a 19th-century Canadian doctor and missionary whose name is nearly synonymous with Tamsui.

Mackay came to Taiwan in 1872 and is revered in certain Taiwanese circles for introducing Western techniques of education and medicine. Thanks in no small part to his influence, Presbyterianism is the most popular Christian denomination in Taiwan.

By the 20th century, silting had caused Tamsui to lose its importance as a port and the area reverted to a sleepy fishing and farming community until the recent boom in tourism.

These days work continues on landscaping and beautifying the riverfront as well as restoring historic sights scattered among the narrow lanes winding up the hillsides.

Sights

The following route takes you from the MRT to the forts on the far hillsides overlooking town. Though only a few kilometres long, this route is so packed with history and landscapes it can take a whole morning or afternoon to cover.

Start by walking along the riverside and at the McDonald's literally cut through to Zhongheng Rd. At 112 look for a lane leading up to a colourful wet market in the middle of which lies **Longshan Temple** (龍山寺, Lóngshān Sì), one of five Longshans in Taipei, and as such devoted to the Guanyin Buddha. Built in 1738 and then rebuilt in the 1850s, the temple retains much of its southern architectural roots. The swallowtail roof is particularly elegant.

About 100m further along Zhongzheng Rd is smoky **Fuyou Temple** (福祐宮, Fúyòu Gōng). Built in 1796, this beautiful low-lying structure is the oldest temple in Danshui, and dedicated to Matsu, Goddess of the Sea. Check out the roof truss over the altar; the topmost posts are carved in the motif 'the fool holding up the sky'.

Tamsui (Danshui)

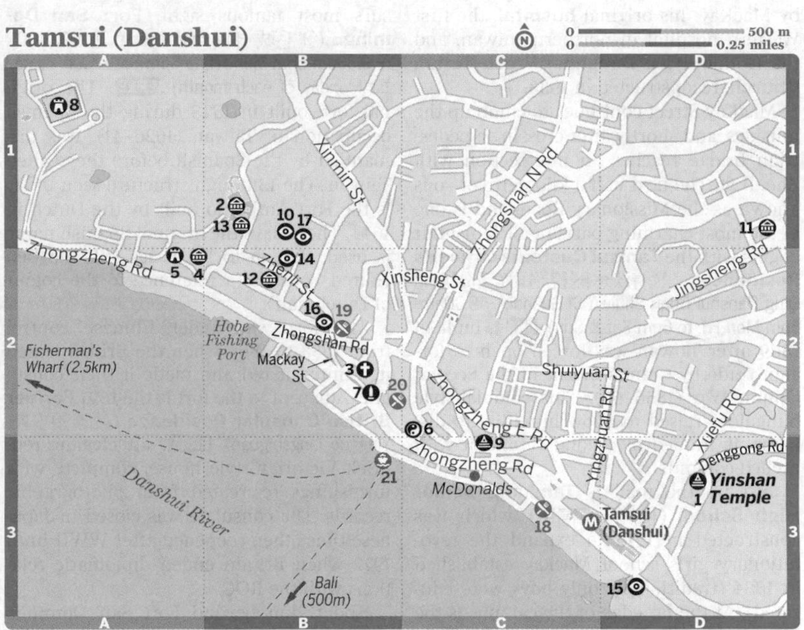

Tamsui (Danshui)

Top Sights
1 Yinshan Temple D3

Sights
2 Alethia University B1
3 Danshuei Presbyterian Church B2
4 Former British Consular Residence A2
5 Fort San Domingo A2
6 Fuyou Temple C2
7 George Mackay Statue B2
8 Hobe (Huwei) Fort A1
9 Longshan Temple C3
10 Mackay Family Cemetery B1
11 Maritime Museum D1
12 Missionary House B2
13 Oxford College B1
14 Tamkang Senior High School B2
15 Tamsui Art & Culture Park D3
16 Tamsui Customs Officer's Residence B2
17 Tamsui Foreign Cemetery B1

Eating
18 Gongming Street C3
19 Laopai Wenhua A-gei B2
20 Red Castle 1899 .... B2
Restaurant .... (see 12)

Drinking & Nightlife
Frank & Sam's Cafe Salon .... (see 15)

Transport
21 Ferry B3

From the temple head up Zhongzheng Rd to Alley 14 and then walk up the 106 narrow granite steps to Red Castle 1899 (p110), a beautiful red-brick heritage building and now the site of a restaurant and cafe.

Back on Zhongzheng Rd, continue to a roundabout with a large **bust of George MacKay** and an astonishing cafe with a staircase winding up the outside edge of the building. Across from this look for the narrow **MacKay Street**. Just up this character-filled lane are two buildings founded by MacKay: his original **hospital**, the first Western hospital in northern Taiwan, and the Gothic-styled **Danshuei Presbyterian Church**, reconstructed in 1933.

MacKay Street continues to climb up the hillsides, and shortly after crossing a pedestrian bridge reaches an intersection with Zhenli St. The next half a kilometre or so is known as the Missionary Road, and is one of the most charming parts of all Tamsui. It begins with the **Tamsui Customs Officer's Residence** (前清淡水關稅務司官邸, Qián Qīng Danshuǐ Guān Shuìwù Sī Guāndǐ; ⏲9.30am-5pm Mon-Fri, to 6pm Sat & Sun) FREE, built in 1869 after Taiwan was forced open to foreign trade by China's defeat in the Second Opium War (1856–60). This colonial-style bungalow, raised to allow humidity to disperse, is framed by a long verandah with arched columns.

Just up the road is **Tamkang Senior High School** (私立淡江高中), which was constructed in 1916 to expand the revolutionary girls school Mackay established in 1884 (traditionally only boys were educated). At the far edge of the campus is the **Mackay Family Cemetery** (馬偕家族墓園, Mǎ Xié Jiāzú Mùyuán), where Mackay himself is buried, and the **Tamsui Foreign Cemetery** (淡水外僑墓園, Dànshuǐ Wàiqiáo Mùyuán), the final resting ground of missionaries, sailors, engineers and many others. Look for a stone building covered in a deep-green algae with a spreading banyan. The graveyards are to the right.

Across from the campus is a row of charming late-19th- and early-20th-century houses with wide lawns overlooking the river. You'll find the white bungalow Mackay lived, married and passed away in, as well as red-brick mansions built for female and male missionaries. Only the yellow-coloured **Missionary House** (教士會館, Jiàoshì Huìguǎn; ⏲10am-5pm Tue-Sun) is open to the public, and has a charming **restaurant** (set meals NT$200-240; ⏲10am-5pm Tue-Sun) and cafe inside, but you can walk along the verandahs and lawns of the others.

At the end of the street is **Alethia University** (真理大學, Zhēnlǐ Dàxué), the first Western university in Taiwan, and of course founded by Mackay. The university's original building, **Oxford College** (牛津學堂, Niújīn Xuétáng), was built in 1882 and fronts a Chinese-style pond and a large, more recent chapel.

Just down the hill to the right sits Tamsui's most famous sight, **Fort San Domingo** (紅毛城, Hóngmáo Chéng; ☎2623 1001; ⏲9.30am-5pm Mon-Fri, to 6pm Sat & Sun, closed 1st Monday of each month) FREE. The original fort, built in 1628 during the Spanish occupation of Taiwan (1626–41), was dismantled by the Spanish before they exited Taiwan. The 13m high structure seen today is the Fort Anthonio built by the Dutch in 1644. These days the original Spanish name is used, though to locals it's still the Red Haired Fortress (a reference to the colour of Dutch hair).

The fort was under Chinese control from 1683 to 1868 when the British leased it, painted it red and made it their consulate. Adjacent to the fort is the 1891 **Former British Consular Residence** (英國領事館, Yīngguó Lǐngshìguǎn) FREE, an elegant red-brick Victorian-style house, complete with furnishings re-created from photographic records. The consulate was closed in Japanese times then reopened after WWII until 1972 when Britain ended diplomatic relations with the ROC.

About 1km beyond Fort San Domingo on Zhongzheng Rd is the turn-off for **Hobe Fort** (滬尾砲台, Hùwěi Pàotái; admission NT$25; ⏲9am-5pm Tue-Sun), built in 1886 when then governor Liu Ming-chuan was attempting to shore up Taiwan's defences to protect it against foreign invaders. If Fort San Domingo is meant to convey authority, Hobe Fort was built for military action. This prime heritage spot (it's suffered almost no reconstruction) has thick earthen walls, massive gates, four batteries and steep steps to its ramparts to deter intruders. While it was used by the Japanese as a base for artillery firing practice, the fort never saw any military action.

Back on Zhongzheng Rd, you can catch a bus or follow the boardwalk back to town. If you go right you'll end up at the sunset-viewing cementland of Fisherman's Wharf,

DON'T MISS

SUBURBAN SPECIALS

Lin Family Mansion & Gardens

In 1778, Lin Ying-yin migrated to Taiwan from Fujian province and his family amassed a great fortune trading rice and salt. Eventually the family settled in what is now Banqiao City and in the mid-19th century built their **mansion** (林本源園邸, Lín Běnyuán Yuándǐ; ☎info 2965 3061; http://en.linfamily.tpc.gov.tw; 9 Ximen St; ⏰9am-5pm, closed 1st Monday of each month; 🚌307, 310 to Beimen St) FREE and expansive gardens in the mid-19th century. Today both are the largest remaining examples from that period left in Taiwan. Beautiful carvings in stone and wood abound, as well as traditional architectural motifs representing luck and fortune: look out in particular for the varied windows in the shape of butterflies, bats, coins, peaches and fans. The garden is designed in the southern Chinese style with abundant viewpoints created in the limited space by narrow maze-like walkways.

You can tour the garden area, which included ponds, pavilions and numerous buildings, on your own, but to visit the **residence** (三落大厝, Sān Luò Dà Cuò) you need to sign up for a tour (also free) at the entrance. At the the time of writing, tour times were at 10am, 11am, 1.30pm, 2.30pm and 3.30pm.

To get here take Fuzhong MRT Exit 3 and follow the English signs (about a 10-minute/700m walk).

Museum of World Religions

Though founded by a Buddhist order, the stated goal of the **museum** (世界宗教博物館, Shìjiè Zōngjiào Bówùguǎn; www.mwr.org.tw; 7th fl, 236 Zhongshan Rd, Sec 1, Yonghe City; admission NT$150; ⏰10am-5pm Tue-Sun; Ⓜ Dingxi, then bus 706, 297 or 243) is not to promote Buddhism, but to build harmony by showing the communality of all religions. Highlights include detailed scale models of the world's great religious holy sites, such as Islam's Dome of the Rock, Sikhism's Golden Temple and Christianity's Chartres Cathedral; remarkably, the insides of these models can be viewed via tiny cameras. The museum also features riveting multimedia presentations, reflection-inducing exhibits such as the Hall of Life's Journey, a meditation room and a Kid's Land. The **cafeteria** (⏰11am-8pm Tue-Sun) serves good vegetarian food.

Signage in English is mostly good and there's a recorded English audio tour available for NT$50. To get to the museum, take Yongan Market MRT Exit B, turn right and go straight. Turn left at Yongzhen Rd, walk to Zhongshan Rd, then turn left here and look for the museum at the edge of a department store.

Luzhou Lee Residence House

This sprawling traditional red-brick *siheyuan* (four-sided) **residence** (蘆洲李宅蹟; www.luchoulee.org.tw; admission NT$60; ⏰9.30am-4pm; Ⓜ Luzhou) has miraculously survived demolition. Take the MRT to Luzhou station, take Exit 1 and cross the street to Zhongzheng Rd. Follow this down half a kilometre to Lane 224, which is marked by a wooden arch. The residence is just down the alley.

now passé even among Taiwanese given the incredible beauty of natural lookouts in Bali or Tamsui.

★Yinshan Temple — BUDDHIST TEMPLE

(鄞山寺, Yínshān Sì; cnr Denggong & Xuefu Rds) This dainty two-hall temple was constructed in 1822 by Hakka immigrants from Dingzhou in Guangdong province. The resident deity, the Dingguang Buddha (the guardian of Dingzhou), is only worshipped by the Hakka and only in this and one other temple in Taiwan.

The temple only has three front doors (fronted by a traditional wooden picket fence). According to Taiwan custom, temples that worship emperors, queens and gods are allowed to have five doors; those built to worship generals, ministers and others are allowed only three doors.

Owing to a dearth of pilgrims over the years, money has been lacking for reconstruction, and Yinshan Temple has largely preserved its original appearance. The swallowtail roof epitomises southern elegance, while the *jiǎnniàn* (mosaic-like temple decoration) figures and the interior woodcarvings demonstrate the refined skills of Qing-era craftsmen. On the front wall look for clay sculptures depicting stories of Dingguang quelling the threat of flood dragons and tigers.

Tamsui Art & Culture Park HISTORIC SITE
(淡水文化園區, Dànshuǐ Wénhuà Yuánqū; ⌚9am-5.30pm Tue-Sun) FREE This handsome and serene collection of old brick warehouses was once the Shell Tamsui Warehouse: as in Royal Dutch Shell, that is. The oil company leased the land in 1897 and held on until the 1990s, when it donated it to the Tamsui Culture Foundation. There's a small display area at the back and a wonderful cafe (p111).

Maritime Museum MUSEUM
(海事博物館, Hǎishì Bówùguǎn; ⌚9am-5pm Mon-Sat) FREE This four-storey museum (shaped like an ocean liner) is anchored by dozens of large model ships from around the world. Expect steamers, frigates, explorers' ships and aircraft carriers as well as information on the Chinese Admiral Zheng He's travels around the world.

The museum is on the Tamkang University campus, in the hills above town. Take a taxi up (NT$150) and walk down.

Bali 八里

Just across the wide mouth of the Danshui River where it pours into the Sea of China is this little waterfront village (Bālǐ) with landscaped parks, boardwalks and bike paths running north and south through one of the most postcard-perfect landscapes in the north.

A 10-minute **ferry** (ticket NT$23; ⌚7am-8pm, every 3-5min weekends, every 15min weekdays) ride connects Tamsui with Bali making it possible to visit both in one day. Consider sailing over in the late afternoon for a few hours of biking after seeing the sights in Tamsui. Heading south, the bike and walking paths run along a landscaped riverside and offer open views of Tamsui framed by Yangmingshan mountains, as well as Bali's own emerald volcanic Guanyinshan.

Heading north, the paths run past a row of food stalls, cafes and restaurants, then a dark-sand beach, more landscaped parks, and the 60-hectare Wazihwei Wetlands (an important habitat for migratory birds). Further along (3.5km from the pier) is the **Shihsanhang Museum of Archaeology** (十三行博物館, Shísānxíng Bówùguǎn; ☎2619 1313; www.sshm.tpc.gov.tw; ⌚9.30am-5pm, closed 1st Mon of each month) FREE, which displays the prehistory of the Bali region, in particular the Shihsanheng Culture, which thrived some 500 to 1800 years ago.

Bicycles can be rented in Bali at varying prices at a number of shops right off the boat dock from Tamsui. Most places rent until 8pm, the time of the last ferry back to Tamsui.

Eating & Drinking

The MRT area is chock-a-block with restaurants and food stalls. Zhenli St, on the way to Fort San Domingo, has some charming little cafes, the Missionary House restaurant, as well as some of the best *a-gei* (阿給, *Ā gěi*) outlets in town. *A-gei* is fist-sized pouches of fried tofu filled with crystal noodles and served in hot broth. Along with 'iron eggs' (铁蛋, tiě dàn; braised and dried eggs that are black and have a rubbery consistency) it is one of Tamsui's signature local snacks.

Along the waterfront are dozens of small outlets, stands and cafes as well as some fancier and more romantic digs further north where the banyan trees slump over the boardwalk. Just north is Hobe Fishing Port (about the size of an Olympic swimming pool), which at the time of writing had a row of tiny, hip river-facing cafes-cum-bars and a small pizza outlet.

There are also numerous places to eat at Bali, including a little night market area around the wharf.

Laopai Wenhua A-gei TAIWANESE SNACK $
(老牌文化啊給, Lǎopái wénhuà a gěi; 6-4 Zhenli St; a-gei bowl NT$35; ⌚6.30am-6.30pm) Tamsui's best *a-gei* (阿給, *Ā gěi*) is in this old shop just before the beginning of Missionary Road.

Gongming Street TAIWANESE SNACK $
This popular market street by the MRT has a number of stalls and shops selling local snacks such as *a-gei* (阿給 *Ā gěi*) and grilled squid, chicken and corn.

Red Castle 1899 CHINESE $$$
(紅樓, Hónglóu; www.rc1899.com.tw; dishes NT$230-600; ⌚noon-2.30pm & 5.30-9pm Mon-Fri, noon-9pm Sat & Sun) This Victorian-style building is an architectural landmark in Tamsui, and was built between 1895 and 1899. Beautifully restored and reborn as a swank eatery, Red Castle serves both West-

ern and Chinese dishes. The third floor cafe/bar called Red 3 Cafe has sublime views over the river from its outdoor deck and is open till at least 11pm.

To find the place, walk along Zhongzheng Rd to Alley 14 and then head up the 106 narrow granite steps.

★Frank & Sam's Cafe Salon CAFE
(霞客咖啡, Xiá Kè Kāfēi; ⏲11am-9pm; 📶) Set at the back of the Tamsui Art & Culture Park in a handsome renovated brick warehouse, this place serves perfect coffee in a perfect setting. The cafe faces the river, Guanyinshan, and a tiny inlet with fishing boats and stilt houses. Single-source beans are available here and brewed with spring water collected in Yangmingshan.

ℹ Orientation

All the sights below are within walking distance of the MRT station. English maps and information abound both around the station and on the streets. Across the river by ferry is the Bali riverside backed by volcanic Guanyinshan.

ℹ Getting There & Around

Tamsui MRT station is the last stop on the red line north. For trips along the northern coast, buses leave just outside the station. See the Northern Taiwan chapter for more information.

Beitou 北投

Hot springs and history form the major attractions in this mountainous suburb, just a 30-minute MRT ride north of Taipei. And there are plenty of both. What is now called Beitou Park was once the largest hot-spring spa in Asia under Japanese rule, attracting visitors from around the world (Sun Yat-sen was one).

The first hot-spring business was started by a German in 1893, but it was the Japanese who really developed the area, initially building army nursing homes, and then opening Beitou Park in 1911. Today's Beitou Park is about a third the size but still a lovely wooded space with old stone bridges, heritage buildings and a hot-spring stream running through the centre.

As an entertainment district, Beitou developing a unique culture based on hot springs, music (called Nakasi and played by itinerant musicians) and tavern food. Though always linked to prostitution, in the 1960s Beitou became notorious as a red light district for American soldiers on leave from the Vietnam War. Prostitution was banned in 1979, and by the '90s, Beitou had became a quiet backwater, with ageing facilities. That all changed with the opening of the Xinbeitou MRT station in 1997 and the start of the modern hot-spring craze that is still going strong.

👁 Sights

Taiwan Folk Arts Museum MUSEUM
(台灣民俗北投文物館, Táiwān Mínsú Běitóu Wénwùguǎn, Beitou Museum; www.beitoumuseum.org.tw; 32 Youya Rd; admission NT$120; ⏲10am-5.30pm Tue-Sun) This museum opened in 2008 in a Japanese-style building that was constructed in 1921 as a high-class hotel. The 1st floor features exhibits of various folk arts, such as cochin pottery, wood and stone carving, and puppetry. The museum's 2nd floor preserves the look of the original tatami-floored banquet and performance hall.

Outside are traditional gardens and decks overlooking the town and mountains. The teahouse offers tea and set meals from NT$450.

Beitou Hot Spring Museum MUSEUM
(北投溫泉博物館, Běitóu Wēnquán Bówùguǎn; 2 Zhongshan Rd; ⏲9am-5pm Tue-Sun) FREE Built in 1913 as the Beitou Public Baths, this handsome building is a copy of the bathhouses in Shizuokaken Idouyama in Japan. It is also a good example of the turn-of-the century fascination among Japanese architects for blending Eastern and Western architecture and esthetics.

The exterior, with its high roof and chimney, was built to resemble a British countryside villa. Upstairs, wooden verandahs surround a tatami room where bathers once took tea and relaxed.

Di-re Valley (Beitou Thermal Valley) SCENIC AREA
(地熱谷, Dirè Gǔ, Hell Valley; ⏲9am-5pm Tue-Sun) FREE Throughout the Japanese era this geothermal valley was considered one of Taiwan's great scenic wonders. The area has been much altered since so it isn't quite that special any more, but the stone-lined basin filled with near 100°C green sulphur waters is still a fascinating sight, especially on cool winter days when a thick and sulphurous-smelling mist can be seen lifting off the waters.

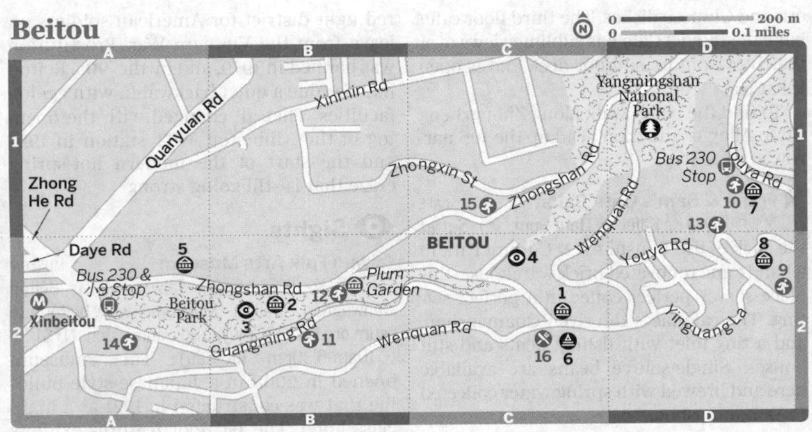

Beitou

Sights

1 Bank of Taiwan Dormitories........C2
2 Beitou Hot Spring Museum........B2
3 Beitou Library........B2
4 Di-re Valley (Beitou Thermal Valley)........C2
5 Ketagalan Culture Centre........A2
6 Puji Temple........C2
7 Taiwan Folk Arts Museum........D1
8 Whispering Pine Inn........D2

Activities, Courses & Tours

9 Asia Pacific Resort........D2
10 Former Residence of Marshal Zhang (Shann Garden)........D1
11 Longnaitang........B2
12 Outdoor Public Bath/Millenium Hot Springs........B2
13 Spring City Resort........D1
14 SweetMe Hot Spring Resort........A2
15 Villa 32........C1

Eating

16 Man Ke Wu Hot Spring Noodles........C2

Ketagalan Culture Centre MUSEUM

(凱達格蘭文化館, Kǎidágélán Wénhuàguǎn; 3-1 Zhongshan Rd; ⏲9am-5pm Tue-Sun) FREE This multistorey centre explores Taiwan's aboriginal culture with exhibits, performances, pictures and artefacts.

Beitou Library LIBRARY

(圖書館北投, Túshūguǎn Běitóu; 251 Guangming Rd; admission free; ⏲8.30am-9pm Tue-Sat, 9am-5pm Sun & Mon; @ 📶) FREE Opened in 2006, this beautiful wooden building was Taiwan's first green construction project. You can go inside and wander about or just hang out on the decks.

Activities

Beitou has three different types of spring water: green sulphur, white sulphur and iron sulphur, all reportedly very good for the skin. Below are just a few options. For high-end luxury and pampering check out **Villa 32** (www.villa32.com) and **Asia Pacific Resort** (www.apresort.com.tw).

Former Residence of Marshal Zhang (Shann Garden) HOT SPRING

(少帥禪園, Shǎo Shuài Chán Yuán; www.sgarden.com.tw; 34 Youya Rd; per hour NT$1200-1500; ⏲10am-10pm) This gorgeous collection of old Japanese buildings was once the Xin Gao Hotel, used to wine and dine kamikaze pilots before their last flight. It's now a hi-end restaurant (set meals NT$1280) and a hot-spring spa with private rooms sporting black-slate tubs, tatami floors and dreamy views over Beitou, all the way to volcanic Guanyinshan.

Marshall Zhang was a famous 20th-century Chinese commander who kidnapped Chiang Kai-shek in 1936 to force him into a united front with the Communists against the Japanese. Never one to hold a grudge, afterwards Chiang held Zhang under house arrest for the next 40 years.

There is a NT$150 admission fee if you just want to go in and see the buildings and grounds. A beautiful teahouse is aso open from 1pm to 6pm. Bus 230 drops you off right outside the residence.

Spring City Resort HOT SPRING
(春天酒店, Chūntiān Jiǔdiàn; www.springresort.com.tw; 18 Youya Rd; unlimted time NT$800; 9am-10pm;) On the road down from the Folk Arts Museum is this styish hotel with one of the few mixed sex (swimsuit required), outdoor hot-spring garden complexes. There are beautiful views over the town and mountains (that's volcanic Guanyinshan in the distance) from the pools. Rates are lower in summer (NT$500) and drop after 7pm.

Outdoor Public Bath/ Millenium Hot Springs HOT SPRING
(公共露天溫泉, Gōnggòng Lùtiān Wēnquán; Zhongshan Rd; unlimited time NT$40; 5.30-10pm) This mixed sex (swimsuit required) public hot spring boasts a number of pools ranging in temperature from comfortably warm to near scalding. It can get unpleasantly crowded here. The pools are closed for cleaning every 1½ hours or so for 30 minutes.

Longnaitang HOT SPRING
(瀧乃湯, Lóng Nǎitāng; 244 Guangming St; unlimited time NT$90; 6.30am-9pm) Built in 1907, this is Taiwan's oldest operating bathhouse. The small nude pools are segregated by sex and the facilities show their age, but the stone is the original and contains hokutolite, a weakly radioactive crystalline substance found only in Beitou and Japan. Bathing here is not an experience for everyone, but many travellers enjoy it very much.

SweetMe Hot Spring Resort HOT SPRING
(水美温泉會館, Shuǐměi Wēnquán Hùiguǎn; www.sweetme.com.tw; 224 Guangming Rd; unlimited time NT$800) An easy walk from Xinbeitou MRT station, SweetMe is a good choice if you want nude segregated bathing in an upscale environment. There are also private rooms for rent (per hour NT$1200).

Sleeping & Eating

Most of Beitou's hot-spring resorts have rooms for overnight stays. Rates start at NT$6000. For midrange accommodation you can also head up to Yangmingshan for the International Hotel, but for budget options you're better off returning to the city.

In addition to the restaurants at Marshal Zhang and the Folk Arts Museum, the area around Thermal Valley has a row of small eateries. Resorts such as SweetMe and Spring City also have their own restaurants that offer a few of Beitou's tavern dishes: try the red skin chicken, deep fried pork ribs or the fried taro balls.

LOCAL KNOWLEDGE

A DAY OF HIKING & HOT SPRINGS

Both Beitou and Yangmingshan National Park can be visited together in one superb day trip. Frequent buses connect the two via scenic mountain roads in 30 minutes. Visit YMS first for a morning hike, lunch at Grass Mountain Chateau (p114), and then bus down to Beitou. From the Chateau, bus 小9 (this is the Taiwan Tourism Shuttle Bus; www.taiwantrip.com.tw) takes you to Beiotu Park. Or from the main bus station at YMS, catch bus 230 down to the Beitou Museum (Folk Arts Museum). After exploring this, and having tea in the Japanese-era teahouses, head down the hill to Beitou Park.

★ **Solo Singer Inn** BOUTIQUE HOTEL $$
(2891 4171; www.thesolosinger.com; 7 Lane 21, Wenquan Rd, 溫泉路21巷7號; r from NT$3850;) During the early post-WWII boom decades, dozens of small family-run inns dotted the winding alleys of Beitou. Solo Singer, the love project of a group of young Taiwanese artists, historians and hotel professionals, is a charming restoration (the owners would say rebirth) of one of these. There's only a handful of rooms here so book ahead.

Man Ke Wu Hot Spring Noodles RAMEN $
(滿客屋溫泉拉麵, Mǎn Kè Wū Wēnquán Lāmiàn; 110 Wenquan Rd; noodles NT$120-200; 11am-2pm & 5-9pm Tue-Sun) This popular restaurant serves fantastic ramen noodles (拉麵) in a miso base prepared with hot-spring water. Try the standard ramen with pork (正油叉燒拉麵), ramen with kimchee (泡菜叉燒拉麵) or the ramen and side of fried pork ribs (排骨拉麵). The soft boiled hot-spring egg with dried seaweed (溫泉蛋; NT$25) is the simplest of dishes but so tasty.

Orientation

There are myriad roads in the area worth exploring but the main attractions start across the street from the MRT. A good way to cover Beitou, however, is to first take bus 230 (every 30 minutes) up to the Folk Arts Museum and then wind your way down (continue on the museum road, not the road the bus took).

It's about 20-minutes' walking to the Di-re Valley area and around 40 minutes to the MRT. Along the way you'll pass, among many modern hot-spring spas, historic **Whispering Pine Inn**, **Puji Temple**, a Japanese-style temple built in 1905 and dedicated to Guanyin, and the **Bank of Taiwan Dormitories**, built between 1919 and 1922, originally as hotels.

Getting There & Around

Beitou is easily reached by MRT in 30 minutes from Taipei Main Station. Take the Tamsui (red) line to Beitou station and transfer to a spur train to Xinbeitou station.

In addition to the buses listed above, and taxis, Beitou has a unique system of **motorcycle taxis**, which hails from the red light district days (with its winding roads it was easier to move prostitutes and musicians around Beitou on two wheels than four). Call ☎ 2894 9669 (Chinese only) for a pick up.

Yangmingshan National Park 陽明山國家公園

How fortunate Taipei is to have this diverse **park** (Yángmíngshān Guójiā Gōngyuán; www.ymsnp.gov.tw) at its doorstep, complete with forested mountains, hot springs, rolling grass hills, and some handsome lodgings and restaurants. The park covers 114.55 sq km, with a top elevation of 1120m, and is easily accessible from the downtown area by frequent buses.

The park was formed by the volcanic action that produced the Datun Mountains (which may still be dormant and not extinct as long thought). This explains the high concentration of hot springs (13 in all), and also the smoking fumaroles one sees at Xiaoyoukeng. During the Qing dynasty, the area was a source of sulphur for the empire, and it is said that the park's iconic grasslands were created by Qing soldiers burning forest cover. In fact, Yangmingshan was originally called Grass Mountain until changed by Chiang Kai-shek in honour of the Ming scholar Wang, Yang-ming. Though it has been a protected area since Japanese times, the national park was officially established in 1985.

You can visit any time of year but in early spring (mid-February to mid-April) note that the annual flower festivals really bring in the crowds. Avoid weekends during this time and any time expect long bus rides down to Taipei at the end of the day. If you are interested in flowers, the first month is dedicated to cherry blossoms and azaleas, while the second is dedicated to the white calla lily.

Sights

The park has a few heritage sights if nature isn't your thing.

Grass Mountain Chateau MUSEUM
(草山行館, Cǎoshān Xíngguǎn; www.grassmountainchateau.com.tw; admission NT$30; ⌚9am-5pm Tue-Sun, meals 11am-9pm) Built in 1920 and visited by Japanese Crown Prince Hirohito, this handsome building became Chiang Kai-shek's first residence in 1949. The chateau is now a museum, exhibition centre and well-regarded **restaurant** (set meals NT$488) with dishes favoured by the Generalissimo such as meatballs, braised spare ribs and lamb. Tourism shuttle bus 小9 runs here from the park's main bus stop on the way to Beitou.

Yangming Shuwu HISTORIC BUILDING
(陽明書屋, Yángmíng Shūwū, Yangming Villa; admission NT$50) The last and largest retreat built for Chiang Kai-shek. Entrance is on a Chinese language tour only at 9am and 1.30pm. Ask at the visitor centre for directions.

Chungshan Hall HISTORIC BUILDING
(中山樓, Zhōngshān Lóu) FREE Built in 1965 to commemorate the centennial birthday of Sun Yat-sen, it's just a minute's walk back down the road from the main bus station. Entrance is on a Chinese language tour only at 8.30am, 10am, 1.30pm and 3pm.

Activities

Hiking & Walking

The park has a wide network of trails, most staired and well marked with English signage. The park website lists them all and includes times, distances and maps. Richard Saunders' *Yangmingshan, The Guide* also outlines hikes both short and long in loving detail.

In addition to the hikes below, consider tackling volcanic Mt Datun (大屯山) in the west side of the park: it's an all-day event if you go from Beitou. Or try the 1.8km trail up from Erziping Visitor Centre. It's wheelchair accessible.

Flatter walking paths run parallel to the main loop road around the park, as well as along the Balaka Rd towards Erziping Visitor Centre. It would take you all day to complete these but you can catch a shuttle bus from various points when you get tired.

★Qixingshan (Mt Qixing) to Xiaoyoukeng HIKING

(七星山 - 小油坑, Qīxīng shān–Xiǎo Yóu Kēng) This route takes you to the top of Yangmingshan's tallest peak (1120m) and ends at one of the park's most iconic landscapes: the smoky, sulphurous fumaroles of Xiaoyoukeng. You can begin the hike directly from the park headquarters. The trail is about 4.9km one way and takes about three to four hours.

To begin head out from the park headquarters on a side road to the **Mt Qixing Hiking Trail** (Miaopu Entrance). It's 2.5km to the summit from here, and about 1.6km to **Qixing Park**, which on a clear day affords great views of the peak and also over Taipei. If you are feeling less than eager to tackle the summit once you arrive here, you can take a 1.7km side route down to Lengshuikeng, the free public hot-spring area.

Assuming you reach the summit, continue on north to **Xiaoyoukeng**. This is a bewitching landscape of smoky pits, emerald hills, suplhur crystals and bubbling hot-spring water. Park shuttle bus 108 stops here which means you can also bus it here from the park headquarters without the hike up Qixingshan.

Jinbaoli Trail HIKING

(魚路古道, Yú Lù Gǔdào, Fisherman's Trail) This historic trail follows a former fish trade route from Shilin to Jinshan. It begins along one of the most enchanting parts of Yangmingshan: the rolling grass hills of Qingtiangang, a lava plateau and former cattle-grazing area that still has a population of wild water buffalo.

The trail begins at the Qingtiangang bus stop, reached by shuttle bus 108 from the park headquarters, or directly from Jiantan MRT on Xiao (小) 15. The trail is 6.6km, takes about four to five hours and finishes at the Tienlai Hot Springs area (see p116). From here you can catch an hourly Royal Bus back to the park headquarters (30 minutes) or on to Jinshan at the coast.

There are plenty of shorter routes in the area to take, including the Qingtiangang Loop Trail, which is only 2.4km and takes about an hour.

Cycling

The park is a popular spot for local riders. See p76 for one of the best routes.

Birdwatching

With 110 bird species, and easy access to a variety of terrain including grasslands, forest and ponds, Yangmingshan is one of northern Taiwan's top twitching destinations. For the casual visitor, be on the lookout for the Formosan blue magpie, an adorable bird with a striped tail nearly twice its body length. It's the national bird of Taiwan.

THE TIGERS OF DATUNSHAN

Most of Taiwan's big cat species have unfortunately become extinct, but one species of the genus *Parantica*, known casually as the chestnut tiger *(Parantica sita niphonica)*, can do something no feline ever could: fly all the way to Japan.

The 'tiger' in question is actually a midsized butterfly that lives in a well-studied colony on Yangmingshan National Park's Datunshan. In 2000, the lepidopterist world was rocked when one member of the colony, marked NTU1032C, was found in southern Japan – 1200km away. At first, researchers thought this was another instance of butterfly migration, but over the past decade only 12 other tigers have been found making that long ocean journey. Most likely dumb luck and strong winds account for the occasional long voyage. But it's still hard not to be impressed with such a feat.

The best time to see the tigers of Datunshan is June mornings when they swarm trailside. The butterflies, which are used to human presence, will often land right on you if you wear bright clothes. To get to the prime viewing areas, take park shuttle bus 108 to **Erziping Visitor Centre** (⌚8.30am-4.30pm) and ask for directions.

In addition to the chestnut tigers, there are around 150 other butterfly species in the park, which can be seen from May to September.

Hot Springs

Tienlai Resort & Spa HOT SPRING
(天籟渡假酒店, Tiānlài Dùjiǎ Jiǔdiàn; www.tienlai.com.tw; hot springs unlimited time NT$800; ⌚7am-midnight) Taiwan's largest outdoor hot-spring area has 14 pools of all shapes and sizes (many scented with essential oils), as well as waterfalls, jet showers, a bubbling spring (that massages you from below), saunas, steam rooms and swimming pools. The sweeping views of green mountains are just icing on the cake.

To get here take a Royal Bus (30 minutes, hourly) from the park headquarters to the resort's own stop. Be sure to check the exact return schedule as buses don't run late.

Lengshuikeng HOT SPRING
(冷水坑, Lěngshuǐkēng; ⌚6am-12.30pm & 2-9pm, closed last Mon of each month) FREE The public bath on the park's eastern side has separate men's and women's indoor baths, although free admission means there can be long queues to enter. Lengshuikeng means 'cold water valley', and compared with other local hot springs it's chilly at 40°C. High iron content makes the waters reddish brown.

Shuttle bus 108 stops here on its clockwise route around the park. You can get here directly from Jiantan MRT on Xiao (小) 15.

Sleeping

International Hotel HOTEL $$
(國際大旅館, Guójì Dàlǔguǎn; ☎2861 7100; www.ihhotel.com.tw; 7 Hushan Rd, Sec 1; d/tw incl breakfast NT$2310/3190; 📶) Built in 1952, the International has maintained its original character with a rustic stone facade and basic rooms. The hotel is close to a hot-spring source and offers both public and in-room hot-spring baths. Three-hour use of rooms (including hot springs) is NT$990. It's a low NT$100 for use of the segregated public pools.

Landis Resort Yangmingshan RESORT $$$
(陽明山中國麗緻大飯店, Yángmíngshān Zhōngguó Lìzhì Dàfàndiàn; ☎2861 6661; www.landisresort.com.tw; 237 Gezhi Rd; r from NT$7700; 📶🏊) With its low-slung profile, slate surfaces and lots of grainy wood, this intimate resort feels inspired by Frank Lloyd Wright. Rooms in the deluxe category and up have hot-spring baths but any guest may use the spa and indoor/outdoor pools. Book online for good deals.

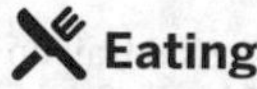

Eating

There are simple eateries, a Starbucks and convenience stores around the main bus station, and snacks are available at visitor centres around the park. Grass Mountain Chateau has a lovely restaurant; the International Hotel has an OK one. In general, if you are going hiking it's best to take food and water with you.

Orientation

You can access the park from the Shilin District, from Beitou (see boxed text p113) and also from Jinshan on the northeast coast. The easiest way for first time visitors is a bus from Jiantan MRT (Shilin District) to Yangmingshan Bus Station (陽明山國家公園公車站).

This is a potentially confusing area as English signs are scant. You can catch the park shuttle bus 108 here, but first head up the side road at the back of the lot, near the bathrooms, where there's a short, well-marked walking path to the National Park Headquarters & Visitor Centre (p116). Here you can get maps, and information in English.

To the northwest of the bus station and park headquarters are Yangming Park and Zhuzihu, sites for the flower festivals in spring.

Park shuttle bus 108 leaves frequently from in front of the park headquarters. See the following Getting There & Around section for details.

Information

There are visitor centres at major tourist sights within the park and most usually have an English speaker on hand. All these centres have simple maps of the park that include basic information and hiking-trail details in English. It's best to pick up the detailed *Map of Yangmingshan National Park* (NT$50) at the cafeteria/bookstore in the **National Park Headquarters & Visitor Centre**, just up from the main bus station. The park website is also a good resource.

Getting There & Around

Red 5 (NT$30, 30 minutes, frequent) From Jiantan station, this bus goes directly to Yangmingshan main bus station from 5.40am-12.40am.

Xiao (小) 15 (NT$30, 40 minutes, every 20 to 60 minutes) From Jiantan station, this bus goes directly to Lengshuikeng and Qingtiangang from 5.40am to 10.30pm

230 (NT15, 30 minutes, every 30 to 60 minutes) Runs between the Yangmingshan main bus station and Beitou MRT (via the Folk Arts Museum).

Park Shuttle Bus 108 Does a clockwise loop around the park every 10 to 20 minutes starting at the main bus station from 7am to 5.30pm. Fares are NT$15 for each ride or NT$60 for a day pass.

Guandu 關渡區

This riverside neighbourhood in the Beitou District has its own MRT stop with a number of excellent attractions nearby. The Guandu Bridge is a Taipei landmark and the start of kilometres of beautiful restored mangrove swamps that extend all the way to Tamsui. The Taipei riverside bike paths pass by here, and you can rent bikes north of Guandu Temple on Zhixing Rd near Guandu Wharf.

Sights & Activities

Guandu Temple TAOIST TEMPLE
(關渡宮, Guāndù Gōng; 360 Zhixing Rd) Dating back to 1661, this gawdy, grand, multistorey temple (one of Taipei's oldest) is built right into the side of a mountain. In fact, a 100m-plus tunnel runs through the mountain itself. Lined with brightly painted deities, the hall leads to a balcony offering a panoramic view of the Tamsui riverscape.

Guandu Temple is a riot of decorative arts, especially rooftop *jiǎnniàn* (mosaic-like temple decoration), and there are Qing-era stone columns in the worship hall. On the riverside sits a food court serving all manner of Taiwanese delicacies. For many visitors, Guandu is a perfect example of the mixed role that most Taiwanese temples play: house of worship, art house, carnival venue and street food market.

Guandu Nature Park PARK
(關渡自然公園, Guāndù Zìrán Gōngyuán; 55 Guandu Rd; adult/child NT$50/30; 9am-5pm Tue-Sun) Ten years in the planning, this 57-hectare nature reserve opened in 2001 under the control of the Wild Bird Society of Taipei. There's a visitor centre, good trails and hides, as well as over 100 species of birds, 150 species of plants and 800 species of animals.

The park, situated at the confluence of the Danshui and Keelung Rivers (and their smaller tributaries), has a wide variety of habitats, including grass, mangroves, saltwater marsh and freshwater ponds. On weekdays it's rather busy with school groups, and on weekends with other tourists.

Tittot Glass Art Museum MUSEUM
(琉園水晶博物館, Liúyuán Shuǐjīng Bówùguǎn; www.tittot.com; 16 Lane 515, Zhong-Yang N Rd, Sec 4; admission NT$100; 9am-5pm Tue-Sun; M Guandu) From the outside, this museum just east of Guandu MRT station looks like a factory. Inside, however, beautiful glassware objects are displayed on two levels as well as detailed explanations of glass-making techniques (such as the lost wax technique).

Glass-blowing demonstrations are held daily, and classes are also given in glass-making. To get here take Exit 1, turn left and walk a minute back alongside the tracks.

Getting There & Around

Take the red line to Guandu MRT station and leave by Exit 1. Both the nature park and temple are about 15 minutes' walk from the station and there are English signs along the way. Visit the nature park first then the temple, as this forms a nice loop. Alternatively, bus 302 from Guandu station terminates at the temple.

Taipei Zoo 木柵動物園

The **Taipei Zoo** (Mùzhà Dòngwùyuán; http://english.zoo.taipei.gov.tw; adult/child NT$60/30; 9am-5pm; M Taipei Zoo) is one of Taiwan's top attractions for locals, and popular with visitors and expat residents with families as well. Its sprawling 165-hectare grounds include a wide variety of simulated geographical regions, including a tropical rainforest zone, a desert and an enclosed 'nocturnal world' section. The koala, panda and penguin houses are popular with the little ones.

The zoo has a minitrain (NT$5) for getting around (though you can certainly walk), and at the back you'll find a gondola station if you want to add a visit to Maokong (recommended). The zoo has its own MRT stop, making it extremely convenient to visit.

Maokong 貓空

The lush hilly region of southern Taipei, known as Maokong (Māokōng), has a long association with tea cultivation. In fact, for a time it was Taiwan's largest tea-growing area. But these days the verdant landscape is not just a place to grow tea; it's also somewhere to enjoy drinking it. There are few activities so quintessentially Taiwanese and in recent years the city has made an extra effort to attract visitors to the region. This includes restoring old trails, landscaping roads, building lookouts and adding public transport options, such as a scenic gondola ride starting from the MRT Zoo station. Cyclists in particular appreciate the low traffic conditions in the hills, and Maokong has emerged as one of the most popular of the many scenic day rides around Taipei.

Sights

★U-Theatre LIVE PERFORMANCE
(優劇場, Yōu Jùchǎng; www.utheatre.org.tw) One of Taiwan's most mesmerising performance groups, U-Theatre combines traditional drumming and music with dance inspired by Taoism, meditation and martial arts. As their website states, 'The U-people believe that the combination of Tao and skill is the goal of their life and artistic creation'.

U-Theatre's unique outdoor nighttime shows are sometimes held in a natural amphitheatre in Maokong. Check the website for the schedule.

Zhinan Temple TEMPLE
(指南宮, Zhǐnán Gōng) The serene and stately Zhinan Temple sits high above Wenshan District in a near feng shui–perfect perch: two rivers converge in the valley below, while lush wooded hills flank its rear halls. First built in 1891, the temple is dedicated to Lu Tung Pin, one of the eight immortals of classic Chinese mythology.

Eleven shrines and three large temples comprise the entire complex. In the far right temple, dedicated to the Sakyamuni Buddha, look for a central Thai-style black Buddha. This was a gift from a Thai prime minister exiled during a coup and later reinstated, it is said, with the help of the Zhinan Temple pantheon.

Zhinan Temple's final claim to fame is the notorious habit of its resident god to split apart unmarried couples (Lu himself was a jilted lover). Many young Taiwanese still avoid the place for this reason.

Activities

Gondola GONDOLA
(纜車, lǎnchē; ride NT$50; ⌚9am-9pm Tue-Thu, to 10pm Fri & Sat) The 4.3km long gondola ride is as much an attraction in its own right as a mode of transport. On clear days or nights the views across Taipei and up the lush Zhinan River valley are enchanting; on foggy days they are dreamy. The gondola has four stations, with stops at the zoo, Zhinan Temple and Maokong itself.

Avoid taking the gondola on weekend mornings or afternoons. Take the bus up instead and catch the gondola down after 9pm. Most visitors are with family and don't linger long after dinner. Note that during heavy rains or thundershowers (common in summer), as well as after major earthquakes, the gondola is temporarily shut down.

Cycling

Maokong is the 'bee's knees' as one local rider described it. One minute you're in the grit and heat of Taipei's streets, the next you're rolling (slowly) up lanes that are virtually traffic-free and lined with spreading camphor trees. There are no easy routes, but if you've gotten used to climbing hills (or want to) you won't find Maokong unmanageable. The loop starting on Lane 34, Zhinan Rd, Sec 3, and finishing down Zhinan Rd, Sec 3, is a classic. To avoid traffic around the university area, head into the campus and follow the university ring road up to the lane marked 'Bike Shortcut'.

Walking & Hiking

With its light traffic conditions Maokong is a pleasant place just to stroll around on the roads. Go left out of the gondola to head up the valley (it gets delightfully remote in feel after a kilometre). Or head straight out along the main road and in about 200m look for a sign on the right that leads to a wide trail running through the tea fields along retaining walls.

Maokong has a range of hiking routes that can be combined for full-day excursions. Trails are in good shape, natural (not staired like Yangmingshan), and many thickly wooded sections feel delightfully remote despite Taipei being just over the ridge. There are trail signs now in English and Chinese, so getting around is pretty safe.

A good two- to three-hour return hike (that intersects with many others to give you an idea of the area's potential) goes to the **Silver Stream Waterfall** (Yínhé Dòng Pùbù), which you can climb behind via a temple carved into the cliff. From Maokong Gondola Station follow the trail beside **San Xuan Temple** up to the ridge, then head straight down. At the bottom head downstream until you reach the falls. (An easier route starts behind Lioujisiang teahouse and is well marked.)

Maokong

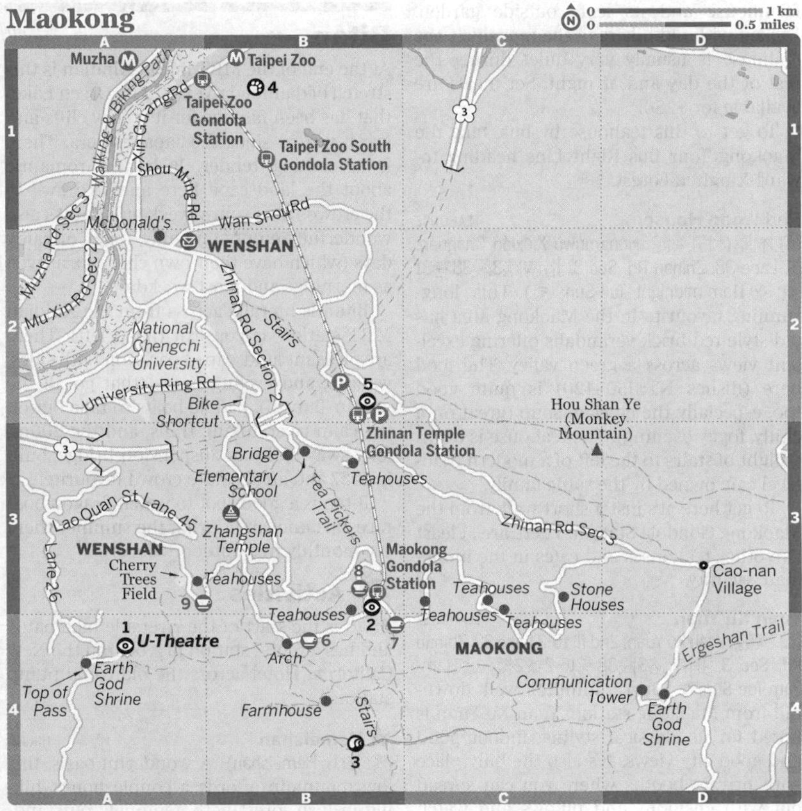

Maokong

Top Sights

1 U-Theatre....A4

Sights

2 San Xuan Temple....B3
3 Silver Stream Waterfall....B4
4 Taipei Zoo....B1
5 Zhinan Temple....B2

Drinking & Nightlife

6 Lioujisiang....B4
7 Red Wood House....B4
8 Yuan Xu Yuan....B3
9 Zi Zai Tian....A3

Drinking & Nightlife

There are dozens of teahouses in Maokong and most are open from around noon to at least 10pm (later on weekends) and are closed on Mondays. Typically you pay for a small packet of tea leaves (NT$300 to NT$800), which is enough for a group of four to enjoy for hours. You also pay a small 'water fee' of NT$100 to NT$150 per person. Many teahouses serve food (and coffee and flower drinks) and it's usually no problem just to have a meal. English menus are common now, as is wi-fi.

Locally grown tea is mostly a type of delightful tightly wound oolong called Tieguanyin (鐵觀音, Tiě Guānyīn, Iron Goddess of Compassion). Originally from Anxi in Fujian province, the tea was introduced to Maokong by Zhang Nai-miao in 1895. The tea is roasted and has a reddish colour when brewed and a smooth nutty flavour. But you can find a wide variety of other teas for sale in every teahouse.

★ Zi Zai Tian TEAHOUSE
(自在田, Zìzài Tián; 27 Lane 45, LaoQuan St, 老泉街45巷27號; ⏲10am-10pm Tue-Sun) This gem is set inside a remodelled traditional stone

farmhouse and its leafy outside garden. Packed with old hikers in the mornings, the teahouse is usually very quiet during the rest of the day and at night. Set meals are available for $280.

To get to this teahouse by bus, take the Maokong Tour Bus Right Line heading toward Xinghua Forest.

Red Wood House TEAHOUSE
(紅木屋休閒茶館, Hóngmùwū Xiūxián Cháguǎn; 31 Lane 38, Zhinan Rd, Sec 3, 指南路3段38巷31號; 11am-midnight Tue-Sun;) This long-running favourite in the Maokong area has old-style red-brick verandahs offering excellent views across a green valley. The food here (dishes NT$150–420) is quite good too, especially the chicken soup (great on a chilly, foggy evening). The teahouse is down a flight of stairs to the left of a modern road-level cafe owned by the same family.

To get here, it's just a short walk from the Maokong Gondola Station. There are at least five other teahouses and cafes in the immediate vicinity.

Yuan Xu Yuan TEAHOUSE
(緣續緣, Yuán Xù Yuán; 2nd fl, 16-2 Lane 38, Zhinan Rd, Sec 3, 指南路3段38巷16-2號2樓; 11am-2am Tue-Sun;) Just a minute's walk downhill from Maokong station, Yuan Xu Yuan is noted for its classical styling, indoor pond and good city views. It's also the only place with private booths where you can spread out with cushions and pillows and watch carp swim beneath the glass flooring. Food is available until 9pm.

Lioujisiang TEAHOUSE
(六季香茶坊, Liùjìxiāng Cháfang; 53 Lane 34, Zhinan Rd, Sec 3, 指南路3段34巷53號; 9am-late) The owners claim they run the oldest tea farm in Maokong. Try their namesake *liùjìxiāng* tea (six-seasons fragrant). Lioujisiang is a 10-minute walk from Maokong Gondola Station. The arch beside the teahouse leads to the network of trails.

Getting There & Around

In addition to the gondola, a bike or your own two feet, the Maokong Tour Bus (NT$15) runs every seven to 15 minutes on weekends and every 15 to 20 minutes on weekdays from 9am to 10.30pm. Stops include the Taipei Zoo MRT station, Zhinan Temple Station and Maokong Gondola Station.

Bitan 碧潭

At the end of the MRT line at Xindian is this stretch of dammed river (Bì Tán, Green Lake) that has been famous for its rocky cliffs and green waters since the Japanese era. There is something tender, lush and romantic about the landscape here and it draws in the crowds on a sunny weekend. But it's also wonderfully empty on chilly, foggy or rainy days (which have their own charms), as well as mornings and most weekdays.

Bitan is literally across from the Xindian MRT station as you exit (head left). There are pleasant landscaped parks on both sides, walking and cycling paths (that go all the way to Tamsui), paddle boats to take out on the calm river, hiking trails, and the 200m-long swaying Bitan Suspension Bridge, built in 1937 and an absolute crowd favourite.

Bitan is a good spot to watch dragon boat races in June, and during the summer there are monthly free outdoor concerts.

Activities

Bitan is the start of the riverside bike paths and has a rental station just behind the New California Hotel across the old canal pump station.

★Hemeishan HIKING
(和美山, Héměishān) A wonderful oasis, this low mountain affords a couple hours' hiking in lush forest with genuinely outstanding views of the higher mountains heading south and across Taipei. This place teems with bird, butterfly, insect and squirrel life, and in April it is a great spot to view fireflies after dusk.

To find the trailhead simply cross the Bitan Suspension Bridge and look for the secret stairs to the left just after the map board.

Sleeping & Eating

With its own MRT station, direct airport buses and half a dozen hotels, Bitan is a great option for travellers to Taipei.

Along the right bank is a stretch of outdoor restaurants with a canopy cover, mist machines and live music in the evenings, but unfortunately they serve sub-par food. The atmosphere and scenery are excellent, though.

On Xindian Rd (which runs parallel to the river; head left as you exit the MRT) there is a small night market. The best stall here is **Athula's Curry House** (Xindian St; rotis NT$55-85; ⌚3-11pm Wed-Sun) run by a resident Sri Lankan whose lamb, chicken and chickpea rotis are loved by many.

New California Hotel HOTEL $
(新加州景觀旅館, Xīn Jiāzhōu Jǐngguān Lǚguǎn; ☎2916-1717; www.new-california.com.tw; 1 Beixin Rd, Sec 1; d/tw NT$2550/3100, weekday discounts 30%; 📶) Directly across from the Xindian MRT station (50m from where the airport bus drops you off) is this refurbished hotel with friendly staff, updated rooms and a good little cafe on the ground floor.

Green Hornet Cafe WESTERN, PUB $
(www.greenhornetcafe.com; 108 Xindian Rd; dishes NT$120-180; ⌚5.30pm-midnight Tue-Sun; 📶📋) A friendly expat-run bar on Xindian Rd serving quality pastas, burritos and nachos for low prices. Also a good bar selection.

Drinking & Nightlife

Bi Ting TEAHOUSE
(碧亭, Bì Tíng; tea per person NT$250; ⌚10am-10pm) Across the Bitan Suspension Bridge on the left is this 50-year-old teahouse built on a rocky cliff overlooking the river and mountains.

Getting There & Around

Bus 1968 from Taoyuan International Airport runs directly to Bitan. Take the bus to the final stop at Xindian MRT.

Northern Taiwan

Includes ➡

Best Hikes

➡ Huangdi Dian

➡ Caoling Historic Trail

➡ Pingxi Crags (p130)

➡ Sandiaoling Waterfall Trail (p130)

➡ Wuliao Jian (p136)

Best Small Museums

➡ Yingge Ceramics Museum (p133)

➡ National Centre of Traditional Arts (p147)

➡ Guqifeng (p159)

➡ Juming Museum (p136)

➡ Jiufen Kite Museum (p141)

Why Go?

For many travellers, heading outside Taipei into the north gives them their first taste of how big this little island is. It's not just that there are mountains reaching 3886m, offering hikes along such enticingly named trails as the Holy Ridge. It's that those mountains, and their valleys and meadows, seem near endless and around every corner is a new hot-spring village, forest reserve, aboriginal hamlet, or a town devoted to a traditional industry such as pottery, glass, tea or woodcarving.

There's generally good transport across the north but if you can manage it, cycling is world class, with routes along coastlines, rivers, through rural townships, and over cross-island highways. But remember: the north is a big place. While the blue magpie can fly those few kilometres in no time, the winding road takes a bit longer.

When to Go

Keelung

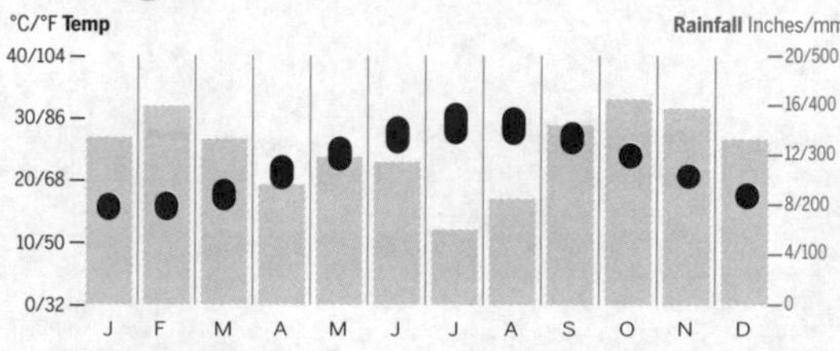

Apr Youtong flowers in bloom.

Sep–Dec Best months for cycling and hiking.

Dec Start of the hot-spring season.

Northern Taiwan Highlights

1. Explore the heritage-rich mining villages of **Jiufen** and **Jinguashi** (p137).
2. Hike, swim and cycle under a jungle canopy in **Wulai** (p124).
3. View the work of Taiwan's master carver at the **Juming Museum** (p136).
4. Cycle routes all over the north, including the **North Cross-Island Highway** (p149).
5. Marvel at the private collection or art and curios at Guqifeng (p159) in **Hsinchu**.
6. Soak in top-quality hot-spring water at Sunrise Hot Spring Hotel (p166) after hiking in **Taian**.
7. Hike for days along **Holy Ridge** (p157) in Sheipa National Park.
8. Revel in the beauty of the Snow Mountain foothills at **Nanzhuang** (p163).
9. Explore frontier villages and endless waterfalls on the **Pingxi Branch Rail Line** (p129).

Climate

The weather in the north is generally warm and dry in autumn and wet and cool in winter, with possible sandstorms in spring. It can be hot and muggy in summer, though cool in the mountains.

National Parks & Forest Recreation Areas

The country's north has more than its fair share of parks and is a hiker's paradise, with trails literally beginning at Taipei's outer edges. Sheipa National Park (approximately 60km south of Taipei) has the second-highest mountain in Taiwan, Snow Mountain, and also the world-class, five-day Holy Ridge trail. There are also more than a dozen forest recreation areas with highlights including hiking trails, ancient forests, waterfalls and birdwatching.

Getting There & Around

There's excellent train and bus transport along the coastlines and between cities. Tourism Shuttle Buses (www.taiwantrip.com.tw) are now making making inland mountainous areas accessible and connecting many popular destinations on one route. If you are driving, traffic is light on weekdays, especially on mountain roads.

Thanks to a mountainous terrain and political patronage (with a heavy emphasis on road building) excellent cycling routes abound. Quality road bikes can be rented in Taipei at Giant (p77).

NEW TAIPEI CITY

It's best to think of this region (新北市, Xīnběi Shì; formerly Taipei County) surrounding Taipei city as the county it once was called. Much of it is still rural or mountainous, and there are some real treats for nature and culture lovers once you get away from the urban sprawl.

See the Travel New Taipei City (http://tour.tpc.gov.tw) website for more information about the region.

Wulai 烏來

02 / POP 7000

This mountainous township 25km directly south of Taipei is a world apart from its urban neighbour. In the thickness of jungle that covers most of the area you'll find spectacular waterfalls, deep river pools for swimming, endless hiking trails and top birdwatching venues. Wulai (Wūlái, which means 'hot-spring water') is a beautiful and largely untamed slice of Taiwan.

The main village in the township, also called Wulai, is a popular place for hot springing. The village area is a bit shabby but the tourist street is fun for sampling aboriginal snacks, and sitting down to a hearty meal after a long day in the wilds.

There's one main road through the township, Provincial Hwy 9甲, which terminates at Fushan (福山), the start of hiking trails running across to Ilan County and Baling on the North Cross-Island Hwy.

Sights

Neidong Forest Recreation Area SCENIC AREA

(内洞森林遊樂區, Nèidòng Sēnlín Yóulè Qū; http://recreate.forest.gov.tw; admission weekday/weekend NT$65/80; 8am-5pm) About 4km past Wulai Waterfall is this forested area popularly known as Wawagu (Valley of the Frogs). With its hiking trails through broadleaf and cedar forests, bird and insect life, river views and rushing waterfalls (especially the three-tiered Hsinhsian Waterfall; Xìnxián Pùbù), this place is worth a dedicated trip. It's particularly enchanting on a misty winter's day.

If you don't have a vehicle you can walk to Neidong from Wulai in about an hour. Take the pedestrian walkway along the river or the minitrain to the end of the line and then make your way to the main road. After you pass through a small tunnel, cross a bridge to the left and follow the road on the other side upstream to Neidong.

Wulai Waterfall WATERFALL

(烏來瀑布, Wūlái Pùbù; gondola per person NT$220, minitrain per person NT$50; gondola 8.30am-10pm) This 80m-high waterfall is a beauty, and the fact that you can float past it on a **gondola** is one more reason to come to Wulai. There's a **minitrain** to the base, or you can walk the pedestrian route beside the train line (about 1.5km) along a pleasant wooded lane with some dramatic mountain scenery.

To get to the minitrain station walk to the end of the pedestrian eating street in Wulai, cross the bridge and head up the wooden stairs. At the end of the line are lookouts and a strip of cafes and restaurants.

Wulai

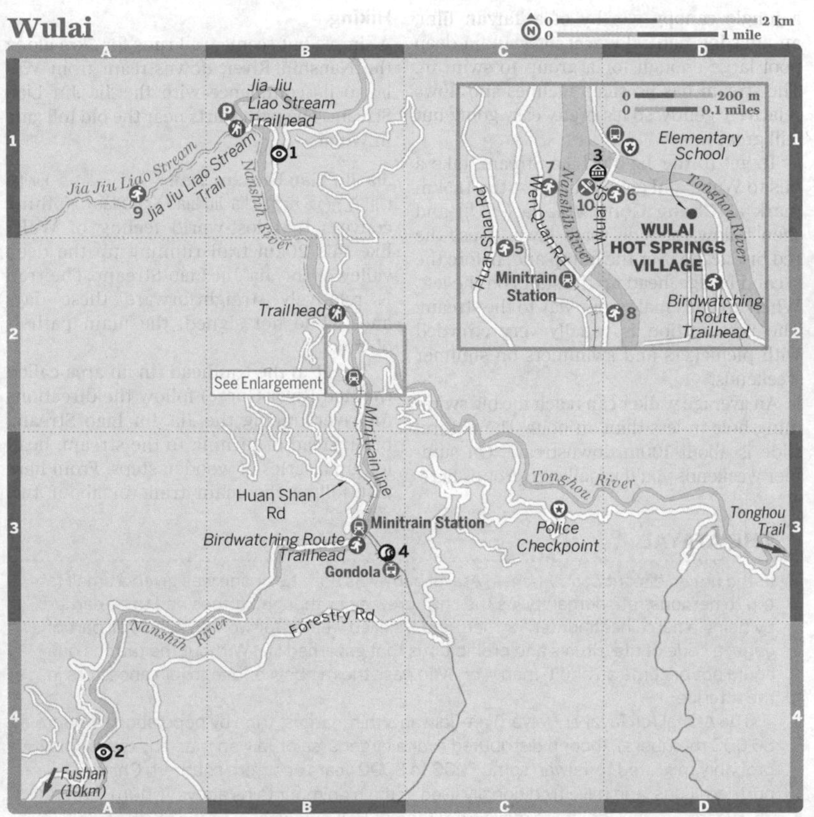

Wulai Atayal Museum MUSEUM

(烏來泰雅民族博物館, Wūlái Tàiyǎ Mínzú Bówùguǎn; Wulai St; ⌚9.30am-5pm Tue-Fri, to 6pm Sat & Sun) FREE The Atayal are the third largest aboriginal tribe in Taiwan, and form a big presence in Wulai (part of their traditional territory). Inside the museum are replicas of traditional bamboo and wood houses, and informative displays on hunting, farming, religious beliefs, musical instruments, facial tattooing and head hunting. For more information about the Atayal, see p126.

Activities

Swimming & River Tracing

Every weekend in the hot summer months, river-tracing clubs or informal groups of friends flock to the rivers and streams around Wulai to practise river tracing, which combines scrambling, swimming and hiking (and true technical climbing and rappelling at higher levels).

Wulai

Sights

1 Cheng Gong Village B1
2 Neidong Forest Recreation Area A4
3 Wulai Atayal Museum C1
4 Wulai Waterfall B3

Activities, Courses & Tours

5 Dashan Hot Springs C2
6 Full Moon Spa D1
7 Outdoor Pools C1
8 Outdoor Pools D2
9 Waterslide A1

Eating

10 Taiya Popo C1

Jia Jiu Liao Stream WATER SPORTS

(加九寮溪, Jiā Jiǔ Liáo Xī) A popular river tracing venue, the Jia Jiu Liao Stream features a jungle canopy worthy of a Tarzan film, an amazing natural **waterslide** and a deep pool large enough for a group to swim in. The stream has no steep inclines and flows relatively gently, so it's pretty easy going but still great fun.

To get to the Jia Jiu Liao Stream, take a bus to Wulai and get off just past the 11.5km mark at **Cheng Gong Village** (成功) and then follow the side road down. Cross the red bridge, go over the hump and, before the second bridge, head up the stairs on the left. When obvious make your way to the stream. The first section is usually very crowded with picnickers and swimmers on summer weekends.

An average walker can reach the big swimming hole in less than an hour. The natural slide is about 100m downstream. On summer weekends you'll usually see groups here.

Hiking

A simple but scenic trail runs for 5km along the Nanshih River, downstream from Wulai to its confluence with the Jia Jiu Liao Stream. The path starts near the old toll gate in Wulai.

Jia Jiu Liao Stream Trail HIKING

(加九寮溪步道, Jiā Jiǔ Liáo Xī Bùdào) Nothing conveys that lost-world feeling of Wulai like this 20km trail running up the deep valley of the Jia Jiu Liao Stream. The trail is relatively straightforward these days and, while not signed, the main path is obvious.

To get to the trailhead (in an area called the Red River Gorge) follow the directions for river tracing the Jia Jiu Liao Stream, but instead of turning to the stream, head left up a series of wooden steps. From here just follow the main trail. In about two

THE ATAYAL

In the not so distant past, when an Atayal baby was born he or she was given a small tattoo to demonstrate humanity. As the child grew older though, tattoos had to be earned: by being a fierce headhunter for men, and a skilled weaver for women. It was all part of *gaga*, a code of rite, rituals and prohibitions that governed life. Without the tattoos one could not become an adult, marry, or even pass the rainbow bridge to join ancestors in the afterlife.

The Atayal (or Tayal or Daiyan) are Taiwan's third-largest tribe by population (around 80,000 members), though distributed over a larger area of Taiwan than any other. They probably migrated to Taiwan some 7000 to 8000 years ago from southern China/northern Laos, and have traditionally lived in the high mountains above 1000m. Around 250 years ago they began to move from today's Ren'ai Township to the north as part of a great migration story that is still central to their identity. Today they can be found from Nantou to Wulai, and also in Ilan and Hualien Counties.

The Atayal had little contact with Taiwanese until the late 19th century (when camphor became a major export) and until the 1920s still lived a mostly self-sufficient life in small villages, growing rice, millet, beans and root crops, supplemented with hunting and fishing. In the following decades, the Japanese began forcing the Atayal to grow rice in paddy fields, banned tattooing and headhunting, and relocated many villages to lowland areas. After 1949, the Kuomintang (KMT) continued much the same policies and until 1987 limited access to the mountains to anthropologists, government officials and missionaries. One result of this was to see 84% of Atayal convert to Christianity.

As with all aboriginal groups in the 20th century, the Atayal lost much more of their cultural traditions than just religious beliefs. But starting in the late '90s, this trend began to reverse. Weaving, for example, is once again a focus of culture and continuity though it is no longer gender specific. Language too has been revived, and in villages such as Smangus it is common to hear Atayal of all ages speaking fluently in their native tongue. Finally, government has also begun to take aboriginal identity more seriously which led to the recognition of the Truku people in 2004 and the Seediq in 2008. Previously both had been classified as Atayal.

Land rights and usage are still a major problem, however, as seen in Wulai where Atayal are now less than half the population in their traditional territory.

To further your understanding of the Atayal, visit the Wulai Atayal Museum (p125), and the villages of Smangus and Qingquan. Also check out Chen Wen-pin's documentary *A Thousand Years of Atayal* (泰雅千年).

hours you'll reach a small cabin, which is a popular place for lunch. If you want to continue to the end, which drops you off just down from Manyueyuan Forest Recreation Area in Sansia, pick up a copy of *Taipei Escapes 2* by Richard Saunders.

Fu-Ba National Trail HIKING

(福巴越嶺古道, Fú-bā Yuèlǐng Gǔdào) This 18km national trail is named after the two villages it connects: Fushan and Upper Baling. Two hundred years ago the Atayal hacked this route up the mountains to facilitate trade and marriage and it's still common to see Atayal hunting or fishing in the area. Hiking up takes eight to 10 hours.

The trail begins in a dense broadleaf jungle, ascends through forests of fir, beech and crepe myrtle, before reaching the mist-shrouded stands of ancient red cypress at Lalashan (2000m), a forest reserve near Upper Baling.

The trailhead is past Fushan Village, just before Km17.5 (the distance from Wulai) on the left. On the trail, there are several good wild campgrounds (with water from nearby streams) or you can spend the night at a B&B in Upper Baling where there are buses to Taoyuan.

Taxis in Wulai can sometimes be persuaded to take you to the Fushan trailhead. Coming back it's possible to hitchhike. Note that on the way to Fushan you need to stop and register at a police checkpoint. Bring your passport.

Tonghou Trail HIKING

(桶後越嶺古道, Tǒnghòu Yuèlǐng Gǔdào) One of several cross-island trails (also a popular mountain bike route) in the region, the Tonghou follows the eponymous river along a wide trail up to a watershed. After running along a grassy ridge for a spell, it then drops down onto dirt roads that eventually turn into pitched farm roads leading all the way to Jiaoxi on the coast.

You need to cycle or drive to the trailhead. From Wulai, head east along the Tonghou River and in a few kilometres register at the police checkpoint (bring your passport). There is a daily limit on vehicles so arrive early.

At the end of the road (20km from Wulai) continue on foot or mountain bike. It takes about three to four hours' hiking to reach the trail end, and another couple of hours down to Jiaoxi. The trail is marked and signposted to the end but after that it can be tricky navigating down via farm roads.

Cycling

With its wild mountain scenery so close to the capital, Wulai is a popular biking destination. To get here, most cyclists ride Provincial Hwy 9 (and then Hwy 9甲) from Bitan to Wulai.

Within Wulai the Tonghou Trail is popular with mountain bikers and the road to Fushan with road cyclists. As the crow flies, Fushan isn't far from Wulai (about 18km), but the landscape takes a noticeable turn to the wild along the road here as the Nanshih River valley narrows, and the sandstone cliffs drip with dark vegetation. Landslides are very common and Fushan is often isolated for months at a time.

Birdwatching

Wulai is renowned for its birdwatching areas. One route follows the road to Neidong Forest Recreation Area (FRA) from the mini-train; the other runs along a narrow road/trail above the Tonghou River, starting past the elementary school.

Among the birds you can see in Wulai are kingfishers, collared scops owls and flocks of grey-chinned minivets. Winter is a particularly good viewing time as many mid-altitude species migrate to the lower river valleys. For more information pick up a copy of *Birdwatcher's Guide to the Taipei Region*.

Hot Springs

Wēnquán (hot-spring) hotels start a few kilometres before the main village as you ride in from Taipei. There are more along the tourist street as well as spreading into the hills around the village. Undoubtedly there are too many visitors competing for a limited resource, so it's best to come midweek.

For cheap but decent options head to the end of the tourist street, cross the bridge and turn left. There are a row of small hot-spring hotels facing the river charging NT$200 to NT$300 for private bathing tubs, and NT$600 to NT$1400 for rooms (including bed, bathroom and hot-spring tub) per two hours.

Down along the river across from the tourist street is a ramshackle complex of free **outdoor pools**. Wash up at the entrance before heading in for a dip.

Dashan Hot Springs HOT SPRING

(大山温泉, Dàshān Wēnquán; public pool unlimited time NT$200; ⏲8am-midnight) High above the main tourist street, Dashan's three small outdoor pools are nothing fancy to look at, which is fine as the surrounding scenery of lush green mountains certainly is. This is a popular place for locals who like to barbecue (NT$260 per person; bring your own food), so it's best to come here with friends.

Dashan is just a short distance from one of the spring sources in Wulai so the water is reputedly quite good here.

Full Moon Spa HOT SPRING
(明月溫泉, Míngyuè Wēnquán; ☎2661 7678; www.fullmoonspa.net; 1 Lane 85, Wulai St; public pools unlimited time NT$600; d incl dinner from NT$3600, 20% weekday discounts;) One of the more stylish hotels along the tourist street, Full Moon has mixed and nude segregated pools with nice views over the Tongshi River. Its private rooms feature wooden tubs and can be rented by the hour (NT$1200 to NT$1500) or for an overnight stay. Go for the lower rooms as the views are surprisingly better than higher up.

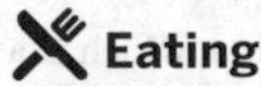

Eating

Aboriginal cuisine is the standard fare in Wulai. A few mouth-watering selections that can be found at any number of shops along Wulai St include mountain vegetables, chicken and boar, *zhútǒng fàn* (竹桶飯; sticky rice steamed and served in bamboo tubes) and freshwater fish.

Snacks and alcoholic drinks made from *xiǎomǐ* (小米; millet) can be found at many shops and stalls in the village.

Taiya Popo ABORIGINAL **$$**
(泰雅婆婆, Tàiyǎ Pópó; www.typp.idv.tw; 14 Wulai St; dishes NT$70-350; 10.30am-10pm;) This long-running restaurant on the tourist street, just past the Atayal Museum, serves some excellent if obscure aboriginal dishes such as bird's nest fern, betel-nut salad, bamboo partridge and fried bees (they taste like popcorn chicken).

THE GOOD-HEARTED MAMAS

Wulai may be a small paradise for hikers, cyclists and birdwatchers, but for dogs it can be a living hell. Remote in feel, but so close to the city, the area's quiet lanes and overgrown dead-ends are, sadly, a favourite dumping ground for Taipei's unwanted pets.

It's not just Wulai though. According to Council of Agriculture statistics, around 50,000 stray dogs are put down each year because of overcrowding in shelters. It's a terribly high number, and this, plus the practice of dumping pets, is something most Taiwanese are ashamed to admit still happens.

But for every action there is an equal reaction. When dumping started to become common (around 30 years ago, as Taiwan became increasingly urbanised), some people, such as Helen Chang, stepped up to help. One of hundreds of women known islandwide as an *Àixīn māmā* (good-hearted mother), she currently takes care of two dozen dogs on her own property, and also goes out every day to nearby parks to feed strays and provide medical care.

'I started helping animals because I couldn't bear to see them suffering,' Helen said. 'I also hoped that I can set an example for other people.'

Thirty years ago in Taiwan, animals were still largely treated as objects, or possessions, a holdover from the attitudes of agricultural society. Women like Helen were looked down upon as foolish, frivolous and sentimental. But the times have changed and dozens, if not hundreds, of animal welfare organisations have sprung up in recent years, including Taiwan's first Society for the Prevention of Cruelty to Animals (SPCA). Wealthy philanthropists, and even pop stars, have also taken up the cause.

After years of lobbying, various municipalities are also starting to turn to alternative measures to deal with strays. Most of Taipei city, for example, now practises catch-neuter-release of stray cats rather than catch and euthanise. New shelters are also being built to replace older, crowded ones and adoption rates are increasing. Also increasing is the courts' willingness to hand down fines and even jail sentences for animal abuse. The feeling among most in the animal welfare world, including Helen, is that in recent years the tide has genuinely turned.

For more information on the current animal welfare situation in Taiwan visit the **Taiwan SPCA** website (www.spca.org.tw) and **Taiwan Animal SOS** (www.facebook.com/TaiwanAnimalSOS).

LOCAL KNOWLEDGE

CYCLING IN THE NORTH OF TAIWAN

Daniel Carruthers initially came to Taiwan to represent New Zealand at the Deaflympics in 2009. In the months that followed he discovered that Taipei and the rest of Taiwan really are a cyclist's paradise.

Best Advice

There is literally world-class riding within minutes of Taipei – if you can manage riding in the Taipei traffic for 15 to 20 minutes, you can find yourself out on beautiful smooth roads that criss-cross the surrounding mountains. The beauty of this area is that you can always find new roads to explore, and many with very little traffic.

Best Rides for Views

Coastal Hwy 2 Brilliant sea views and mountains. Ride from Tamsui to Yangmingshan with a stop for tuna sandwiches and coffee in Jinshan.

Taipei to Yilan via Hwy 9 Stunning scenery: panoramic mountain vistas and rivers, and lush green jungle.

Wulai to Fushan Ride into a stunning gorge, with a sheer drop down to the cascading river.

Most Challenging Ride

Most decent rides in the north are very challenging. If you spend any length of time here, your climbing skills will rapidly improve. If I had to choose the most challenging ride, I would say the **Balaka Rd** from Tamsui up County Rd 101 to the top (over 1000m elevation gain). It finishes with a painful 3km to 4km, 18% grade climb to the peak. Speed demons can enjoy a screaming fast descent back to Taipei – reaching speeds in excess of 80km/h!

For more on Dan's ride both in Taiwan and around the world check out his blog (www.danielcarruthers.com).

Information

DANGERS & ANNOYANCES

If you go river tracing *(suòxī)*, plan to be out of the water by 3pm or 4pm. Afternoon showers are a daily occurrence in late spring and summer, and rivers can become swollen very quickly. Also keep an eye open for snakes and leeches on the more overgrown trails.

Getting There & Away

Bus 849 to Wulai (NT$15, 40 minutes, every 15 to 20 minutes) runs frequently from the taxi stand area at Xindian MRT station in New Taipei City.

Pingxi Branch Rail Line 平溪支線

☎02

Despite Taiwan's heavily urbanised landscape, the north has retained much of its frontier past where a slower pace of life prevails in makeshift-looking villages. Such are the settlements that dot a wild, wooded gorge served by the Pingxi Branch Rail Line (Píngxī Zhīxiàn). Along this picturesque valley, you'll find thrilling hikes, high waterfalls, river pools, a cat town, and the remains of what was once a thriving coal industry. Pingxi town itself is the site of the annual sky lantern release during the Lantern Festival, an event not to be missed.

The line branches off the main east-coast trunk at Ruifang, and extends to Jingtong. The most interesting stops are Houtong, Sandiaoling, Shifen, Pingxi and Jingtong. The entire ride takes about 45 minutes.

At the **Shifen Scenic Administration Office** (☎2495 8409; ⏲8am-6pm), near Shifen station, you can pick up English-language brochures and consult the large maps on the 1st floor.

History

Once a sleepy farming community whose residents grew yams and tea and harvested camphor, Pingxi was blasted into modern times with the discovery of 'black gold' in 1907: coal that is, not oil. By 1921, the Japanese Taiyang Mining Company had constructed the 13km Pingxi branch line from Sandiaoling to Jingtong and there was hardly a moment's rest for the next 60 years. At the height of operations, 18 mines were open, employing over 4000 miners. About 80% of the town's residents made their living directly from the mines.

Conditions were bad, even by the appalling standards of most coal mining. The mine veins ran deep underground, and the narrow pits forced miners to work lying down, often naked because of the oppressive heat and humidity. By the 1970s, cheaper foreign coal was already slowing down operations and by the mid-'80s mining ceased altogether in Pingxi. In 1992 the branch line was declared a scenic tourist line, thus saving it, and nicely the local villages too, from decay and closure.

Sights & Activities

The following are presented in the order you will encounter them on the train starting from Riufang.

Houtong VILLAGE

(侯硐, Hóu Dòng) This former coal mining town is a scenic place to spend a couple of hours, with restored warehouses, stations, pits, dormitories, and most importantly... cats. In recent years, Houtong has become synonymous with its 'Cat Village', a large population of tame wandering strays, who now, thanks to government largesse, even have their own dedicated bridge.

★**Sandiaoling Waterfall Trail** WATERFALL

(三貂嶺瀑布步道, Sāndiāolǐng Pùbù Bùdào) The upstream watersheds of the Keelung River receive more than 6000mm of rain a year and have more waterfalls than any other system in Taiwan. On the wonderful Sandiaoling Waterfall Trail, once part of a trade route between Ilan and Taipei, you can see half a dozen of the biggest, most beautiful falls in the north in their natural glory.

To get to the trailhead, exit Sandiaoling station and follow the tracks south until they split. Cross under and follow the tracks to the right (the Pingxi line). After a few minutes you will see the wooden signpost (in English) for the trailhead. The trail is simple and clear to follow, at least as far as the third fall (about an hour away).

The first waterfall is **Hegu Falls** (合谷瀑布, Hégǔ Pùbù, Joining of the Valleys Falls). The trail runs over the streams that feed this waterfall and you can wade down to sit on top the rocky ledge and look down 40m to the base. Next up are two 30m falls that look almost identical and are in remarkably close succession: **Motian Falls** (摩天瀑布, Mótiān Pùbù) and **Pipa Dong Falls** (枇杷洞瀑布, Pípádòng Pùbù). You can get right in behind Motian via a cave formed by the overhang: it's like something out of *The Last of the Mohicans*.

If you have the afternoon or the whole day, you can continue along trails and sweet back-country roads all the way to Shifen station. There are more falls to see along the way, including the 40m-wide **Shifen Waterfall** (十分瀑布, Shífēn Pùbù), the broadest fall in Taiwan, and a large section of rare **kettle holes** near the end. The holes are formed by small pebbles that are spun around in the river current, wearing circles into the limestone riverbed. See Richard Saunders' *Taipei Escapes 1* for full details.

Shifen VILLAGE

(十分, Shífēn) In little Shifen, the train passes through the village just metres from the two- and three-storey houses running parallel to the tracks. It's the only place left in Taiwan where this occurs, and the quaint scene seems to tug at people's nostalgic heart strings no matter where they come from.

There are plenty of places to eat in the village. Traditional snacks include *mìfānshǔ* (蜜蕃薯; sweet potatoes cooked in wheat sugar) and *zhēngyùtóu* (蒸芋頭; steamed taro).

If you didn't walk to Shifen from Sandiaoling, go take a look at Shifen Waterfall and the kettle holes – about a 15-minute walk from the station. Head back along the tracks (east) towards the visitor centre and follow the signs. At the time of writing a beautiful Japanese-style wooden teahouse was about to open on the edge of town as you head towards the falls.

Pingxi VILLAGE

(平溪, Píngxī) There are two reasons travellers step off the train in Pingxi: to climb the **Pingxi crags** and to release sky lanterns during the Lantern Festival. Around Pingxi Station you'll find the obligatory 'old street' for snacking. You can also walk the remaining distance (1.8km) to Jingtong on the back streets running beside the rail line.

As for the crags, the highest is only 450m or so, but to reach the top you must scramble up metal ladders and steps that are carved into the rock face. No technical skill is required, but it's an adrenalin rush nonetheless.

To reach the trails, walk to the main road from the train station and go right. Just past the spiffy-looking red-brick school you'll see a set of stairs to the left and an English map-board. Head up the stairs, and then after a five-minute walk along the path look for the sign for **Cimu Feng** (慈母峰, Címǔfēng).

Now follow the path as it alternates running atop a ridge and hugging a steep grey limestone cliff. In one to 1½ hours you'll reach a set of cement stairs. You can take these down to Pingxi (essentially completing a loop) or begin the better loop up to the crags, which can take another couple of hours to complete depending on your route. There are signposts everywhere, and while you may get sidetracked, you won't get lost.

Jingtong VILLAGE

(菁桐, Jīngtóng) The village of Jingtong marks the end of the line, and **Jingtong Station** (菁桐站, Jīngtóng zhàn) is one of the best-preserved traditional train stations in Taiwan. With nearby coal carts, train engines, abandoned buildings strangled by roots, Japanese-era wooden houses and hiking trails, it's a fun place to explore and take pictures.

There's also some great hiking in the area. One favourite is up to the pyramid-shaped **Shulong Point** (薯榔尖, Shǔláng Jiān; also Shulangjian Mt Trail; 622m) the highest mountain in the area. To get to the trailhead from the train station, cross the tracks and climb to the first level. Head left and when the road splits turn right and head up the narrow lane through tiny Er Keng Village. There are English signs for the trailhead just past the village.

Eating & Drinking

Palace Restaurant RESTAURANT, TEAHOUSE **$$**

(皇宮咖啡簡餐, Huánggōng Kāfēi Jiǎncān; ☎02-2495 2021; set meals NT$260; ⏲10.30am-6pm Wed-Fri, 10am-8pm Sat & Sun; 📖) Set in a short row of Japanese-era houses, this restaurant has both an old-time wooden interior and good food. Guests can sit on the floor, Japanese style, or at tables. Set meals are available but you can also just enjoy a coffee or brew your own tea.

LANTERN FESTIVAL

Over the past decade the **Lantern Festival** (元宵節, Yuánxiāo Jié) has emerged as one of the most popular holiday events in Taiwan. Of all the ancient Chinese festivals, it has best been re-imagined for the modern age, with spectacular light shows, live concerts and giant glowing mechanical lanterns on show across the island. Yet one of the best spectacles is still the simplest and most traditional: the sky lantern release in Pingxi.

A *tiāndēng* (sky lantern) is a large paper lantern with a combustible element attached to the underside. When the element is lit, hot air rises into the lantern sack and the lantern floats into the sky like a hot-air balloon.

In Pingxi people have been sending sky lanterns into the air for generations. Long ago, the remote mountainous villages were prone to attacks from bandits and marauders. Sky lanterns were used to signal to others, often women and children, to get packing and head into the high hills at the first sign of trouble. But today it's all about the sublime thrill of watching glowing colourful objects float up against a dark sky.

During the festival, which is spread over two weekends (around February, but this varies with the lunar calendar), there are shuttle buses all day to the site. After dark, lanterns are released en masse every 20 minutes.

If you wish to light your own lantern, remember first to write some special wish on it. As it floats away to the heavens repeat your wishes to yourself… and pray your lantern doesn't burn up prematurely and crash down into the crowds, or light a tent on fire, as occasionally happens.

Which gets us to the last point. Over the past two years, the local township has allowed the sale and release of sky lanterns at any time, and anywhere. The surrounding forests are now littered with the ugly shells of spent lanterns and it is only a matter of time before there is a major fire. If you wonder why we endorse the Lantern Festival release, it's because at this time all roads to the area are closed, fire trucks are on hand to deal with any incidents, there are after-festival clean-up crews, and it is also a very wet time of the year (making the risk of a forest fire negligible). During the rest of the year there are zero precautions. Act responsibly if you visit the area.

To reach the restaurant, cross the bridge over the Keelung River and turn right. Palace is 150m down the road. There are signs in Chinese. If you are interested in a homestay in the area enquire at the restaurant.

★Jingtong Crown Prince Chalet TEAHOUSE
(菁桐太子賓館, Jīngtóng Tàizǐ Bīngguǎn; www.hanyappf.com; admission incl drink NT$150; ⊙10.30am-5.30pm Wed-Sun) Built in 1939, with hinoki cedar from the Alishan region, the chalet is actually one of the largest and best-preserved wooden Japanese-style houses in Taiwan. After a multiyear renovation, it's now open as a teahouse/cafe. Choose from one of a dozen small tatami rooms, or one of the larger meeting rooms, to relax in.

The house sits on a picturesque shelf above the river, just below the village. Head to the road from the train station – you can't miss it.

Getting There & Around

BUS

Taiwan Tourism Shuttle Buses (www.taiwantrip.com.tw; NT$45) run from Muzha MRT station (walk to main road and cross for the bus stop) to Shifen Visitor Centre with stops at Jingtong and Pingxi every hour or so on weekdays and every 30 minutes on weekends. Weekday morning buses run at 7.15am, 8.20am and 9.45am, with an 11am bus just to Pingxi. The last return bus leaves Shifen at 8.35pm.

TRAIN

If starting your journey at Houtong or Sandiaoling, catch a direct train (hourly) from Taipei. If going to other stops first, take the train to Ruifang (fast/slow train NT$76/49, 40/50 minutes, every 30 minutes) and then transfer to the Pingxi line on the same platform. All-day passes cost NT$52.

Pinglin 坪林

☎02 / POP 7000

Pinglin (Pínglín), which means 'forest on level ground', is famous nationwide for its honey-flavoured bao chung tea (a type of oolong). Less than an hour from Taipei by bus (about 26km east of Xindian), or a couple of hours by bike, the region is well loved by day trippers for its emerald mountain landscape, picture-perfect tea fields, scenic mountain roads, and clear, swimmable rivers teeming with fish. The town also features a tea museum that's worth visiting if you're in the area.

Sights

Tea Museum MUSEUM
(茶葉博物館, Cháyè Bówùguǎn; ⊙9am-5pm Mon-Fri, to 6pm Sat & Sun, closed first Mon of each month) FREE The two floors of this classically designed museum feature displays, dioramas, charts, equipment and, of course, tea in all its forms. There are sections on the history of tea production in Taiwan and China, the culture of tea drinking, and tea-making methods over the centuries. All exhibits have complete English translations.

Activities

Cycling

Pinglin's 20km bike path is a beautiful ride across tea fields and up the lush Jingualiao River valley. You can rent OK bikes on the main street (per hour NT$100 to NT$150, per subsequent hour NT$50) and pick up a map at the **visitor centre** (⊙9am-5pm), though once you are on the path it is well marked.

Many cyclists now ride to Pinglin from Taipei as a day trip or part of an extended journey to the coast. All the routes are pretty simple to follow.

Bitan to Xiaogetou (& Pinglin) CYCLING
This loop ride starts at Bitan, climbs up Provincial Hwy 9 to **Xiaogetou** (about 15km) and then drops back towards Taipei on the winding 北47 or 北47-1. The latter roads run along steep mountainsides before dropping into Shihting. From there it's a flat ride back to Taipei on the 106乙 via Muzha and the city bike paths.

Instead of turning back at Xiaogetou you can also continue another 11km to Pinglin. It's all downhill just past Helen Coffee and the views over the green-blue Feicui Reservoir are spellbinding.

From Pinglin, riders sometimes continue to Jiaoxi on the coast. This is about 40km further, and consists of a long climb out of Pinglin followed by a long, steep, winding descent to the alluvial plains of Ilan County

Swimming

There are many sweet spots for a dip in the rivers around Pinglin. You can swim just under the bridge across from the Tea Museum or head northeast on County Rd 北42.

Hiking & Walking

In the hills just north of the village, along the rivers and through the tea fields, there are short paths suitable for families and strolling couples. Children usually like watching the 'flashing fish' in the rivers.

If you have your own vehicle (and map) there are numerous more challenging trails in the Pinglin area. Look for the trail signs (in English and Chinese) around town to point you in the right direction.

Sleeping & Eating

There are a couple of campgrounds heading south along the bike path, and also off County Rd 北42. You need your own transport to reach these as they are quite far from the town centre.

For simple, cheap fare there are noodle shops and convenience stores along the main road. The Tea Museum has a good attached **restaurant** (dishes NT$70-350) with tea-flavoured dishes. For something simple go for the *guā bāo* (刮包; braised pork on a tea-flavoured bun) or green tea noodles.

Drinking & Nightlife

Helen Coffee COFFEE

(www.helencoffee.com.tw; coffee NT$80; ⏲morning to dusk) Most cyclists stop here, just past Xiaogetou at the very top of the pass (around 16km from Bitan, or 11km from Pinglin). The coffee shop is unmistakable on the left and has a deck with a half-million-dollar view (there are some power lines) over a big forested valley. The turn-off for 北47 is just a few metres away.

Shopping

Around town there is no end of stores selling tea and products made with tea. While tea jellies, ice lollies and *tǒngzǎi mǐgāo* (筒仔米糕; sticky rice) are inexpensive, a jar of decent *bāo zhǒng chá* (包種茶; bao chung tea), or Oriental Beauty (東方美人; Dōngfāng Měi Rén), can cost between NT$1000 and NT$6000 or more. Both these delicious teas can easily be appreciated by the untrained palate. If you want something nicely packaged, go to the Tea Museum gift shop.

Orientation

Pinglin Village is quite small and easy to navigate. The township, however, is large and encompasses endless mountains, rivers, campgrounds and hiking trails. Pick up a copy of the Sunriver map (see p33) for an overview.

From the final bus stop in Pinglin, head right to reach the main street, left to the 'old street' and the Tea Museum. A nice loop of less than an hour is to follow the main street about three blocks down to the visitor centre and then cross. Look for the suspension bridge, cross that, and head left along the river paths to reach the museum.

Getting There & Away

In Taipei, take the MRT to Xindian station and catch bus 923 to the left when you exit the turnstiles. Buses leave hourly on weekdays (on the half-hour after 7.30am) and every 30 minutes on weekends. The last return bus to Taipei leaves weekdays at 9.10pm, weekends at 8pm.

Yingge 鶯歌

☎02 / POP 87,000

This little town (Yīnggē) in the very southern part of New Taipei City lives by and for the production of high- and low-quality ceramic and pottery objects: everything from cupboard handles to Song-dynasty vases and cutting-edge objets d'art.

Pottery was first introduced to Yingge in 1804, but it remained a cottage industry producing cheap earthenware until the Japanese ramped up production in the 1930s. In addition to daily-life items, the local kilns began to fire ceramic parts for mines and weapons. After WWII, ceramicists from all over Taiwan began to settle in Yingge and by the 1970s the town was the third-largest ceramic production centre in the world.

Mass production moved to China in the '90s, but with the 1999 opening of the NT$6 billion Yingge Ceramics Museum and the creation of the 'Old Street', the town made a very successful leap from manufacturing base to cultural venue. These days, Yingge makes an enjoyable day trip from Taipei and fits in naturally with a stopover at nearby Sanxa with its masterfully restored Tzushr Temple and blocks of heritage buildings. If you have all day, consider renting a bike and riding down the riverside to Daxi.

Sights

Yingge Ceramics Museum MUSEUM

(鶯歌陶瓷博物館, Yīnggē Táocí Bówùguǎn; www.ceramics.ntpc.gov.tw; 200 Wenhua Rd; museum admission free, ceramic studio admission NT$50; ⏲9.30am-5pm Tue-Sun, ceramic studio 2-3pm & 3.40-4.40pm Sat & Sun, book a place 30min earlier) At this stylish and informative museum, exhibits cover everything from 'snake kilns' and woods used in firing, to influences on Taiwanese ceramics from China, Japan and the Netherlands. Special exhibitions show the direction modern Taiwanese ceramics is

WORTH A TRIP

TWO RIDGE WALKS: BIJIA SHAN & HUANGDI DIAN

The little town of **Shihting** (石碇, Shídìng), known for its tofu and mountain chicken, sits in the foothills about 15km east of Taipei Zoo. The valley it sits in cuts a long ridgeline in two, making the village the start of not just one but two of the best ridge walks in Taiwan. There's English signage on both trails now, and ropes and guide poles in the more-dangerous sections, but only go if you have a head for heights. Though not quite knife-edged, in many sections these ridgelines are narrow enough that two people can't pass.

Bijia Shan

The 18km Bijia Shan (筆架山, Bǐjiàshān) trail runs west of Shihting (back to Taipei) along a wooded ridgeline which creates the illusion that you aren't so high or so precariously situated. From the bus stop in Shihting cross the narrow red-brick bridge and head down the street. In 600m, at a junction, you'll see maps and signs for the trail, which climbs up to the ridgeline in about 40 minutes.

The way is obvious for the next three to four hours until you drop into a little saddle at the junction to **Ergeshan** (二格山). Follow the signs down towards Mt Hou-shan-yue and a few minutes later stay left at the sign for **Cao-nan** (草楠). Keep left on this trail all the way down to a road (about a 15-minute walk). Then simply follow that road down past the old banyan in Cao-nan Village until you reach a major road. Buses go by here back to Taipei Zoo or Wanfang Community MRT Station.

Huangdi Dian

Huangdi Dian (皇帝殿, Huángdìdiàn, the Emperor's Throne) runs east of Shihting and is the more sporting of the two hikes and the more dramatically scenic, with views over a range of forested hills and jagged peaks. From the bus stop in Shihting head up the narrow road to the left of a Hi-Life convenience store (as you face it) and take the first left. Follow this road up to the stone steps and map board that start the trail.

After 30 to 40 minutes of climbing stairs you'll reach the ridgetop. Progress is slow from here on with numerous climbs up and down steel ladders and chains, scrambles over boulders and rock faces, and traverses across uneasily narrow and bare sections of ridge. Don't go on a windy day!

The entire hike can take six to eight hours, but if you want to cut it short, a number of side trails lead off the ridge down to roads leading (eventually) back to Shihting. Pick up a copy of Richard Saunders' *Taipei Escapes I* for a full description of this hike and all its possibilities.

To get to Shihting take the bus of the beast, 666 (NT$30, 20 minutes), from Muzha MRT station in Taipei: exit the station, walk to the main road and cross. The bus runs about every hour: the morning schedule is 5.50am, 9.12am, 10.12am, 11.15am and 12.15pm. Useful return buses are at 2.40pm, 3.40pm, 4.40pm and 5.40pm.

taking, and the flashy videos and occasional humorous display help to keep interest high as you move around the three floors. The museum has a DIY ceramic class on weekends. See the website for details.

To get here, exit on the right side of the Yingge train station, cross the street and head through a covered alley (it's obvious). This quickly opens up to a beautiful river landscape. Head down to the park and go right. The museum is a five minute-walk away.

Yingge Old Street STREET

(鶯歌老街, Yīnggē Lǎo Jiē) Although not really old, the street is rather quaint, with its cobbled roads, traditional street lamps, red-brick facades and walk-in kiln. Dozens of pottery shops and stalls, large and small, compete for your business, and you could spend hours just browsing.

Prices start at around NT$20 for a cup or saucer, while quality handmade pieces can cost tens of thousands. A good compromise for the budget shopper (who still wants something nice) are tea sets, coffee mugs, and earthenware jars and vases that can be purchased for NT$1000 to several thousand dollars. Most shops close about 6pm or 7pm.

To get to the Old Street from the museum, turn left as you exit and look for a wooded boardwalk next to a stream. Follow 150m to the end, and take the first alley to the right. Head up and cross the railway tracks on the pedestrian bridge and you are on the street.

Activities

One branch of the Taipei riverside bike path network runs to Yingge. A lazy ride starting near Taipei Main Station would take about three hours.

From Yingge there is also a beautiful ride heading south on the left bank of the Dahan River, which passes a wide reservoir and then long sections hemmed in by tall grass and steep hills that feel delightfully remote. At the handsome **Daxi Bridge** (大溪橋, Dàxī Qiáo), a steel suspension bridge built in 1934, you can cross over to Daxi and check out the Japanese-era baroque-style buildings on Heping Rd. Daxi was once the most inland port in Taiwan, with ships sailing from Wanhua and Dadaocheng until the 1930s (when the river became too silted).

Instead of heading into town, you can also follow the signs across the rice fields to **Li Tengfang's Ancient Residence** (李騰芳古厝, Li Téngfāng Gǔcuò). This Qing-era Hakka residence is typical of the type of structure wealthy clans began to construct in the mid-19th century to show off their wealth.

OK quality **bikes** (per 2hr NT$100; ⌚9am-6pm Fri-Wed) can be rented from a large warehouse/exhibition space across from the museum at the end of the pedestrian overpass.

Eating

On the Old Street there are vendors, small restaurants and cafes to help you line your stomach. Next to the museum there's a street filled with the usual noodle shops. You can also save your appetite for snacking in Sansia.

Getting There & Around

Trains from Taipei Main Station (NT$31, 30 minutes) run about every 30 minutes.

Sansia (Sanxia) 三峽

☎02 / POP 102,000

Across National Hwy 3 from Yingge, this old town (Sānxiá) is most noted for a temple that has been described as an 'Eastern palace of art' and a couple of blocks of perfectly restored Qing- and Japanese-era buildings. In short, Sansia and Yingge go hand in hand, contrasting and complementing each other like peanut butter and chocolate.

Sights

★Tzushr Temple — TAOIST TEMPLE

(祖師廟, Zǔshī Miào; ☎tour 2671 1031) The centre of religious life in Sansia, the Tzushr Temple honours Qingshui Tsu-Sze, a Song-dynasty general worshipped by the people of Anxi, Fujian, for his power to protect their tea industry. First erected in 1769, the present structure hails from a late-1940s restoration that is still not finished.

In 1947, Tzushr Temple was in near total decay, as were many temples around Taiwan after WWII. Professor Li Mei-shu, scion of a wealthy and politically active family, was given the task of supervising the rebuilding. Li, a trained art professor, was the perfect man for the job. In addition to his formal training, which included a stint in Japan, Li had been a careful observer of temple crafts as a child. Li supervised reconstruction with an obsessive attention to detail and introduced numerous innovations, including bronze doors and wall relief and the use of gold foil over woodcarvings.

After Professor Li's death in 1983, however, the temple committee attempted to go the cheap route with the rest of the reconstruction. The master artisans were let go one by one, and a construction company was hired to oversee work. The ensuing public lambasting halted work, and these days everything still seems on hold.

Some standout features to look for include the 126 hand-carved stone pillars (the original design called for 156) and the astonishingly beautiful plafond (decorative ceiling), which recedes into a vortex. On every sculpted surface you'll find traditional motifs and auspicious symbols (such as bats, storks, frogs, crabs, cranes, peonies, pines, vases and turtles) and illustrated stories from history and mythology. Buy a copy of the *Shan-hsia Tsu-sze Temple Tour Guide* (NT$200) booklet at the temple for more details, or call for a private tour (available in Chinese only).

Minquan Old Street — STREET

Sansia's name (Three Gorges) reflects the fact that it sits at the confluence of three rivers. Once an important transport hub for charcoal, camphor and indigo dye, the town's prosperity is evident in this old block of red-brick merchant houses and residences dating from the end of the Qing dynasty through to the early years of the Japanese colonial era.

WORTH A TRIP

JUMING MUSEUM & JINBAOSHAN CEMETERY

Ju Ming (born 1938) is Taiwan's most famous living sculptor, having gained fame here in the 1980s, and internationally a decade later. His works are instantly recognisable, despite varying from giant stone abstractions and delicate wood pieces, to a series of nativist works that includes sculptures of historical figures as well as daily life scenes. Among the most popular of the artist's works are those in the 'Tai Chi' series, which feature gigantic blocky stone monoliths in various martial arts poses.

The majority of Ju Ming's works can be seen together at the **Juming Museum** (朱銘美術館, Zhūmíng Měishùguǎn; www.juming.org.tw; admission NT$250; ⏲10am-6pm Tue-Sun), which lies across a 15-hectare park in the hills above Jinshan. Most works are outdoors so make sure to bring an umbrella or a hat to protect against sun or rain.

Just up the street from the museum is the vast **Jinbaoshan Cemetery** (Chin Pao Shan, 金寶山, Jīn Bǎo Shān), which, odd as it may sound, is a sight not to be missed. This wonderland for the underworld will literally make you feel envious of the deceased for having one of the best living environments in Taiwan. There are well-tended gardens, beautiful carvings by master artists (such as Ju Ming), a towering golden columbarium (a building with niches for funeral urns to be stored), and row upon row of intricately carved and decorated graves looking over a gorgeous stretch of the northeast coastline and the East China Sea.

The most famous grave here is that of **Teresa Teng** (鄧麗君), a silky voiced pop singer who died tragically young in 1995 though not before achieving massive popularity (which endures) in the Chinese-speaking world. Tourism shuttle buses stop just across from her grave but you wouldn't miss it for the fresh flowers, pilgrims and giant workable keyboard in front. Go ahead and step on the keys. We've seen kids playing Für Elise on them.

Both the museum and cemetery are served by the Taiwan Tourism Shuttle Buses (www.taiwantrip.com.tw) from Tamsui or Keelung.

After a two-year restoration, the street now looks much as it did 100 years ago, and on weekends there's a lively market atmosphere as the little shops operating from behind dark-wood doors sell speciality snacks, tea and souvenirs. Street performers also work the area, making this a fun venue to take in after the spiritual and aesthetic treasures of Tzushr Temple.

As you walk the Old Street (民權老街) look for the diversity of styles in the shop facades: they incorporate late-Qing, Japanese and Western baroque elements. The mortar used for the bricks is a combination of sticky rice and crushed seashells.

To reach the Old Street turn right as you exit the temple and walk up the alley to Minquan (Minchuan) St.

Activities

★Wuliao Jian HIKING

(五寮尖, Wǔliáo Jiān) On the outskirts of Sansia, the Wuliao Jian trail doesn't cover much ground yet takes six hours to complete. After all, you need to tread slowly on a ridge that's less than a hand's-breath wide in places. Definitely don't go unless you have a good head for heights and are in the mood for a challenge.

As with other crazy ridge walks in the north, you'll find secure ropes and guide poles in place where they are needed. There are also rough maps in place and it's tough to get lost. But if you want a full description of all the twists and turns, consult Richard Saunders' *Taipei Escapes 2*.

The easiest way to get to Wuliao Jian is to take the MRT to Yongning station and then a taxi to the trailhead (NT$300 to NT$400). If you want to save money catch bus 916 from Exit 1 to Sansia's Taipei Bus Company and then catch a bus heading to Manyueyuan Forest Recreation Area.

At the temple at the end of the hike, you can usually ask for a taxi to come and pick you up.

Getting There & Away

From Yingge, you can take a taxi to Sansia (from Yingge Ceramics Museum to Tzushr Temple is NT$130) or bus 702 (NT$15) from the museum.

Manyueyuan Forest Recreation Area 滿月圓森林遊樂區

This **recreation area** (滿月圓森林遊樂區, Mǎnyuèyuán Sēnlín Yóulè Qū; www.forest.gov.tw; admission NT$100; ⏲8am-5pm) is truly a park for all seasons and all people. The first section has paved or cobbled paths, scenic pavilions and short walks to a number of gorgeous waterfalls. Once you get past this, however, you're on natural trails that climb for hours through sweet-smelling cedar forests.

The main trail starts up a short incline to the right of the toilets at the end of the paved route to Manyueyuan Waterfall. There are many side branches but the main route connects Manyueyuan with Dongyanshan FRA. However, there is no public transport to and from Dongyanshan, so if you walk there you must walk back. It's about a four-hour hike one way.

Two very worthy diversions on the main trail include up to **Beichatianshan** (北插天山, North Sky-Piercing Mountain; elevation 1727m), the highest peak in the north, and further afield to a stand of **giant ancient cedars** (神木, *shénmù*).

To get to Beichatianshan, take the main trail to its highest point and then turn left, following the English signs. It's a long day hike to the summit and back (expect it to take 10 to 12 hours), so many people make it an overnight trip. There's a wild campground near the base, beside a rushing stream.

The trail down to the old cedars follows the same path as to the base of Beichatianshan and then drops down a side trail, but this is not clearly marked in English. Get a copy of Richard Saunders' *Taipei Escapes 2* for directions, or follow another hiking group.

Autumn is a nice time to visit the park, as the leaves on the gum and soap-nut trees are changing colours. Fireflies come out in the spring and summer, and you can often spot monkeys and barking deer further into the park. Be aware that the park has its own microclimate and, while it may be sunny and dry in Taipei, it could be cool and wet here.

Public transport here is limited and complicated. First take the MRT to Yongning MRT station and outside Exit 1 catch bus 916 or a taxi to Sansia's **Taipei Bus Company** (台北客運三峽站 大勇路; ☎2671 1914; www.tpebus.com.tw) on Dayong Rd (this is the bus's final stop). From there catch bus 807 (NT$45). Buses leave weekdays at 7am, 9.30am and noon, and weekends at 6am, 8.30am and 11am and should go all the way to Manyueyuan parking lot (show the driver the characters so he is clear where you are going). If the bus doesn't go all the way to the park, it will drop you off at **Honeybee World** (蜜蜂世界) about 30 to 40 minutes' walk from the park entrance. If you can get a few people together, consider taking a taxi (NT$500) from Yongning MRT station directly to the park.

Hitching a ride back to town is usually easy. The last bus leaves the parking lot at 3.50pm on weekdays and 6.10pm on weekends (call the Taipei Bus Company to confirm).

HIGHWAY 2: THE NORTH & NORTHEAST COAST

☎02

The 166km coastal Provincial Hwy 2 winds along the top of the island from the mouth of the Danshui River to the alluvial plains of Ilan. It's a stunning route with a wide range of coastal landscapes: rolling grass hills, high rugged cliffs, sand beaches, pebble beaches, rocky terraces and windswept peninsulas.

Most of the area falls under the auspices of either the **North Coast & Guanyinshan Scenic Administration** (www.northguan-nsa.gov.tw; ⏲9am-5pm) at Baishawan Beach or the **Northeast & Yilan Coast Scenic Administration** (www.necoast-nsa.gov.tw; ⏲9am-6pm), which is headquartered in Fulong. You'll find travel information centres at both offices.

ℹ Getting There & Around

There are public buses to most places in the region. Between Tamsui and Keelung the brilliant Tourism Shuttle Bus (www.taiwantrip.com.tw; one-day pass NT$100) runs hourly on weekdays and every 30 minutes on weekends to the main sites, including the previously difficult to reach Juming Museum. The last buses leave/return around 5pm or 6pm.

Another shuttle bus line connects Juifen with Fulong Beach.

The highway is popular with cyclists, as are the side roads around Sanzhi, Fulong and Daxi.

Baishawan Beach 白沙灣

One of the better beaches in New Taipei City (this is not meant to be particularly high praise) is found at this little bay (Báishāwān), the name of which translates as 'white-sand bay' – though these days it is definitely more of a brownish colour. The entrance to the beach is down a side road 100m or so off Hwy 2 (there are brown signs in English around the 23km mark). Swimming is permitted from May to September, as is surfing.

For surfboard rentals and lessons, visit **CU Surf Paradise Taiwan** (台湾西元衝浪新樂園, Táiwān xīyuán chōnglàng xīn lèyuán; www.facebook.com/cu.surf.taiwan) on the main road where the bus drops you off.

Baishawan is formed by the stubby finger of rocky **Linshanbi Cape** (麟山鼻, Línshānbí) extending into the Taiwan Strait. This is a scenic part of the north coast and a several-kilometres-long **boardwalk** runs along the shoreline as part of a 10km bike path from Sanzhi to Shimen.

Tourism Shuttle Buses depart from Danshui MRT station and stop on Hwy 2 just before the beach's entrance. Or you can catch bus 862 (20 to 30 minutes, every 20 to 40 minutes) heading to Keelung. The first bus leaves at 5.50am.

Check the stop at Baishawan for the return schedule (there should be return buses until around 8.30pm).

Fuguei Cape 富貴角

The cape (Fùguìjiǎo) is the most northerly point in Taiwan, and the constant sea winds make the local vegetation grow dwarfed and twisted. There's a small park here with good views and a large **fisherman's wharf complex** where you can buy and eat fresh seafood. Tourism shuttle buses stop near the cape at the Shimen Wedding Plaza stop.

About a 10-minute walk southeast from Fuguei Cape is an area that is rather beautiful when the tide is low: the **Laomei Algal Reef** (老梅海岸, Lǎoméi Hǎiàn). Looking like a row of fallen monoliths carpeted with emerald green moss (in reality, it's just layer upon layer of algae), the reef is understandably a popular spot with photographers.

18 Lords Temple 十八王公

People sometimes refer to this temple (Shíbā Wánggōng) as the 'dog temple'. According to one version of the legend, 17 fishermen went missing one day and a dog pined for days for the return of his master until, unable to bear the suffering any longer, he leaped into the foaming sea and drowned himself. Local people were so impressed by this act of loyalty that they built a temple in honour of the dog. Later, the temple became associated with Taiwan's underworld and it's still common at night to see tattooed gangsters, prostitutes and other characters about.

When you arrive, local women will try to sell you small red packets used for worship. If you do buy one, you will be instructed to wave the package over burning incense, then wipe it on the dog statue's nose and head (and sometimes genitals) before placing it in the dog's mouth.

The temple is just off Provincial Hwy 2 in front of the first nuclear power plant. However, a few kilometres back in the hills is a larger, newer version of the temple with an astonishing **canine statue** in the parking lot that's well over 15m high.

Neither sight is served by the tourism shuttle buses, unfortunately, so you need your own vehicle.

Yeliu Geopark 野柳地質公園

Stretching far out into the East China Sea, this **limestone cape** (Yěliǔ Dìzhí Gōngyuán; admission NT$50; ⏲7.30am-6pm May-Sep, to 5pm Oct-Apr) has long attracted people to its delightfully odd rock formations. It's a geologist's dreamland but also a fascinating place for the day tripper. Aeons of wind and sea erosion can be observed first-hand in hundreds of pitted and moulded rocks with quaint (but accurate) names such as **Fairy's Shoe** (仙女鞋, Xiānnǚ Xié) and **Queen's Head** (女王頭, Nǚwáng Tóu), which truly looks just like a silhouette of the famous Nefertiti bust.

The **visitor information centre** (⏲8am-6pm) has an informative English brochure explaining the general conditions that created the cape and also the specific forces that formed different kinds of rock shapes, such as the mushroom rocks, marine potholes and honeycomb rocks. Tourism shuttle buses stop directly outside the park entrance.

Keelung (Jilong) 基隆

☎02 / POP 387,000

Keelung (Jīlóng) is a perennially wet, largely run-down port city, famous in Taiwan for its excellent night market and August/September ghost month festival. Thanks to its position, which has been of strategic importance over the centuries, the area also has a number of old forts.

Keelung's bus and train stations are adjacent to each other and located at the northern end of the city. There's a **visitor centre** (基隆遊客中心; ☎2428 7664; http://tour.klcg.gov.tw; ⌚9am-5pm; 📶) just outside if you need it and Richard Saunders' *Taipei Escapes 2* covers pretty much everything you could think of to do and see here.

Sights

Miaokou Night Market MARKET

(基隆廟口夜市, Jīlóng Miàokǒu Yèshì; ⌚hours vary) Probably the most famous night market in Taiwan, Miaokou became known for its great food during the Japanese era, when a group of merchants started selling snacks at the mouth of the **Dianji Temple** (奠濟宮). Nowadays, Miaokou is considered the best place in Taiwan for street snacks, especially seafood.

'Miaokou' means 'temple entrance' and also 'temple mouth', but the market covers several streets. To get here from the train station exit, cross the pedestrian walkway and head straight a few blocks (passing the harbour on the way). When the road narrows, turn right. The market entrance is

DON'T MISS

KEELUNG GHOST FESTIVAL

During the seventh lunar month, Keelung is host to Taiwan's most renowned **Ghost Festival** (中元節, Zhōngyuán Jié), a fascinating mix of Taoist and Buddhist beliefs and rituals. The festival lasts the entire month (usually August or September), and each year a different Keelung clan is chosen to sponsor the events. Highlights include folk-art performances, the opening of the Gates of Hell and the release of burning water lanterns.

Keelung's festival began in the mid-19th century as a way to bridge the rift between feuding groups of Hoklo immigrants. However, the belief in ghost month is widespread in Chinese culture. According to popular beliefs, during this month 'hungry spirits' (or 'good brethen' as they are also called) roam the earth and must be appeased and sated with elaborate banquets, festivities and a whole lot of ghost paper burning (asthmatics should seriously be very careful around this time).

The main events are as follows:

Day 1 The Gates of Hell are opened at noon at **Laodagong Temple** (老大公廟, Lǎo Dà Gōng Miào; 37 Lane 76, Le 1st Rd), west of Keelung Harbour.

Day 12 Lights are lit on the main altar of **Chupu Temple** (主普壇), the temple that overlooks Keelung Harbour from Zhongzheng Park.

Day 13 A large parade throughout downtown Keelung honours the 15 clans involved.

Day 14 An elaborate lantern-release ceremony (this is ghost month's main event) takes place. The ceremony begins with an evening street parade of floats which slowly make their way to Badouzi Harbour, southeast of downtown. Sometime around midnight (technically the 15th day so don't be misled by tourism information and show up later on that day) water lanterns shaped like houses and stuffed with ghost paper are released into the harbour and set alight.

Day 15 During the day, temples and private households hold Pudu rituals, in essence sacrificial offerings to deliver the wandering spirits from their suffering. You will see piles of food and money outside people's homes. The largest rites are held at Chupu Temple at 5pm. Late at night a Taoist priest also performs a ghost-expelling dance to remind ghosts they should return to their world after the end of the month.

Day 1, eighth lunar month At 5pm, the Gates of Hell are shut again at Laodagong Temple. According to folklore experts, the gates are closed on the first day of the eighth month to allow for potential tardy spirits.

For more information, see the Keelung City (www.klcg.gov.tw) website.

obvious just up the road. Stalls on the main street are all numbered and have signs in English, Japanese and Chinese explaining what's on the menu.

Ershawan Fort HISTORIC SITE
(二沙灣, Èrshāwān) Also known as Haimen Tianxian, this first-class historical relic was once used to defend Taiwan during the First Opium War (1839–42). Its imposing main gate and five cannons, still tucked into their battery emplacements, are a dramatic sight. To get here, take city bus 101 or 103 to Haimen Tianxian, walk up the stone footpath and take the second right.

If you have time afterwards, retrace your steps to the bus and continue another 10 minutes to the stop for **Heping Island** (和平島, Hépíng Dǎo), which is connected to the mainland by a short pedestrian bridge and features beautiful and bizarre limestone rock formations, as well as some old shrines. In April the green hillsides are splashed with the white of Formosan lilies.

Getting There & Around

Trains from Taipei (NT$41, 45 minutes) leave every 20 minutes or so.

Keelung's local buses (NT$15) start at the city bus hub across from the train station as you exit. **Tourism Shuttle Buses** (www.taiwantrip.com.tw) start from in front of the visitor centre.

Jiufen & Jinguashi

02 / POP 2000

Nestled against the mountains and hemmed in by the sea are the villages of Jiufen (九份, Jiǔfèn) and Jinguashi (金瓜石, Jīnguāshí), two of the quaintest stops along the northeast coast. Both villages were mining centres during the Japanese era and by the 1930s, Jiufen was so prosperous it was known as 'Little Shanghai'. Jinguashi later became notorious during WWII as the site of the prisoner-of-war camp Kinkaseki.

A gold rush began in the 1890s during the construction of the Keelung to Taipei railway. The rail work had attracted Cantonese miners who had taken part in the great Californian gold rush and among them were the Li family, who have long been credited with discovering the first gold deposits in Juifen. Following the discovery, the Taiyang Mining Corporation was formed and exploited the deposit until 1971.

After mining ceased, Jiufen and Jinguashi slipped into obscurity. With the release of the 1989 film *City of Sadness,* set in Jiufen in the aftermath of the 2-28 Incident, urban Taiwanese began to flock to the old villages in search of a way of life that had been all but swept away in the rush to modernisation. Rich in Japanese-style homes and narrow winding lanes, Jiufen and Jinguashi gave them exactly what they were looking for.

Any trip to the area should leave time just to wander the hills. If you can imagine a grassy emerald landscape, with a rugged topography dominated by jagged shale peaks and steep slopes dropping into the sea, then you've pictured something of this extraordinary bit of Taiwan.

Sights & Activities

Jiufen

Orienting yourself in Jiufen is fairly straightforward as there is only one main road and it winds up very steeply. The bus drops you off near the town's 7-Eleven, which is close to the sights.

Jishan Street STREET
(基山街, Jīshān Jiē, Jiufen Old Street) Narrow, covered Jishan St often leaves lasting impressions. It's really just one long covered lane, but spending a few hours here browsing the snack and craft shops is a lot of fun. Jiufen's famous stair-street, Shuqi St, which features an old theatre and teahouses used as sets in *City of Sadness,* intersects it a few hundred metres down.

One of the most popular activities on the street is snacking. Some distinctive snacks to look for include *yùyuán* (芋圓, taro balls), *yúwán* (魚丸, fish balls), *cǎozǐ gāo* (草仔糕, herbal cakes) and *hēitáng gāo* (黑糖糕, molasses cake).

Jishan St begins just to the right of the 7-Eleven on the main road.

Jilongshan MOUNTAIN
(雞籠山, Jīlóngshān) You just can't miss this emerald colossus for the way it dominates the skyline. At only 588m, Jilongshan may read like a rather puny giant, but it rises up so fast and steep, it's dizzying to stare at from below. You can climb the peak in about 40 minutes. The trailhead is up the main road from the 7-Eleven.

Fushan Temple TAOIST TEMPLE

(福山宮, Fúshāngōng) This Earth God (Tudigong) temple is an interesting blend of Japanese, Chinese and Western elements. The outside features two old toro shrines, while the interior sports a beautiful post-and-beam structure (made without nails), intricately carved stone pillars and panels, including one over the main altar with nude Western angels.

The Earth God has one of the lowest rankings in the Chinese pantheon, but, not surprisingly in these old mining towns, he is among the most exalted. In the 1930s, miners crowded the 200-year-old Fushan Temple daily, praying to the god to point them to a rich vein that would make them gentlemen overnight. After a decision to expand the temple caused panic ('What if it damages the efficacious feng shui?'), a larger structure was simply constructed over the original, giving Fushan the nickname 'the temple within a temple'. Alas, the damage appeared to have been done in any case (some claim that other gods were jealous to see Tudigong raised so high), and many blame the building of the larger temple for the decline of Jiufen not a decade later.

To reach the temple, walk up the main road to the top of the hill where the road splits. Left will take you to Jinguashi and right will take you to Fushan Temple in about 1km.

Jiufen Kite Museum MUSEUM

(九份風箏博物館, Jiǔfèn Fēngzhēng Bówùguǎn; www.cfkite.com.tw; 20 Kungwei Lane; admission NT$100; ⏲10am-5pm) This quirky private collection can seem underwhelming at first, but then it dawns on you: these things can really fly! Its collection ranges from the tiniest butterfly-shaped kites to a 3m-long phoenix with a fox in its mouth. Some kites even have musical instruments built into them so they drum or whistle when in the air.

The museum, which is located in a B&B down the main street about 300m to 400m from the 7-Eleven, is generally only opened to guests but if you show up and they aren't busy the owners will let you in. Alternatively, go to the visitor centre and ask them to take you there.

Jinguashi

Gold Ecological Park HISTORIC SITE

(黃金博物園區, Huángjīn Bówùyuánqū; www.gep.ntpc.gov.tw; ⏲9.30am-5pm Mon-Fri, to 6pm Sat & Sun) FREE This park, set high above the village in green, quiet hillsides, is a true slice of 1930s Taiwan, with restored Japanese-era residential and office buildings connected by narrow walkways bordered by aged brick walls. The remains of the gold-mining industry that once drove the local economy is also well preserved, including one of the original mine tunnels.

The **Crown Prince Chalet** (太子賓館, Tàizǐ Bīngguǎn) at the back of the park was built to house the Japanese royal family on their visit to Taiwan (which alas, never came). It's the best-preserved Japanese-style wooden residence in Taiwan, though unfortunately you can only wander the gardens and look inside.

The former working **Beishan Fifth Tunnel** (本山五坑, Běnshān Wǔkēng; admission NT$50) allows visitors to go inside and glimpse mining conditions of the old days, while the **Gold Building** (黃金博物館, Huángjīn Bówùguǎn) lets you touch what is reportedly the largest gold bar in the world. Sitting high on the steep slopes above the park, the ruins of the **Gold Temple** (黃金神社, Huángjīn Shénshè) look like something out of Greek mythology.

It may be interesting to note as you walk around that not all the gold in this area has been collected. Even today there remains a 250-tonne reserve estimated at more than NT$200 billion (US$6 billion) lying underground.

Golden Waterfall WATERFALL

(黃金瀑布, Huángjīn Pùbù) The water that forms this unusual fall has a yellow hue from the copper and iron deposits it picks up as it passes through Jinguashi's old mines. You'll find the waterfall down from the Gold Ecological Park as you head towards the sea (which is also a yellowish colour from the river water).

Remains of the 13 Levels HISTORIC SITE

Just across from the Golden Waterfall, on a sea-facing bluff, are the remains of a massive **copper-smelting refinery** (十三層, Shísāncéng) whose 13 levels descend towards the sea in rapid progression. The refinery inspires such a heavy, dystopian industrial awe that it has been used as a background for music videos.

If you want to get close, head up the side road just after the Golden Waterfall (on the right as you head down). The road winds up to the top level and then drops down to the village of Changren. There is a short flight of stairs across a parking lot to a lookout with a perfect vantage point over the remains. You can't take a bad photograph here.

Nanya Peculiar Rocks SCENIC AREA
(南雅海岸, Nányǎ Hǎi'àn) Just south of Jinguashi on Provincial Hwy 2 (KM81.5) is a quirky bit of eroded coastline. The most famous formation is a swirling tower that genuinely looks like a striped ice-cream cone.

The odd shapes and colours were formed by the sea and wind eroding sandstone rocks that just happened to have rich iron and copper deposits in them. As the metals were exposed to the air they oxidised leaving the outside of the stones striped with colourful bands.

Drinking & Nightlife

Apart from shopping, strolling and snacking, the main attraction in Jiufen is spending a few hours in a antique-laden traditional teahouse sipping fine *pào chá* (tea). The price is much the same everywhere: NT$400 to NT$900 for a 37.5g (one Chinese *liang*) packet of leaves and NT$100 per person for the water fee *(chá shuǐfèi)*.

★ **Jiufen Teahouse** TEAHOUSE
(九份茶坊, Jiǔfèn Cháfǎng; www.jioufen-teahouse.com.tw; 142 Jishan St, Jiufen; ⏲10am-10.30pm; 📶) This 100-year-old wood and brick building at the far end of Jishan St hosts what was reputedly the first teahouse in Jiufen. It's a solid choice for any traveller looking to step back in time among heavy wooden furniture and other furnishings from the past. The tea selection includes old pu'ers, roasted Oriental Beauty and a fruity Tieguanyin.

In the basement level of the teahouse there is a ceramic studio and exhibition area. The quality of work is much higher than in the souvenir shops on the main street.

Shu-ku Tea Store TEAHOUSE
(樹窟奇木樓, Shù Kū Qí Mù Lóu; Jiufen; ⏲10am-10.30pm) This darkly atmospheric two-storey teahouse from the Japanese era has the look and feel of a frontier gambling den. In the low-slung rooms you can still practically see the old miners squatting on the makeshift benches, shuffling cards and warming their hands on a metal teapot.

To get here follow Jishan Rd past the main tourist area where it starts to descend steeply. Just past a couple of homestays look for the English sign to the teahouse on the left.

Sleeping

A number of quaint B&Bs dot the hillsides, should you want to spend the night.

★ **Wu Fan Keng Gongyuan Bao** HOMESTAY $
(五番坑公園堡, Wǔ Fān Kēng Gōngyuán Bǎo; ☎0926-982 050; http://5park.isogi.net; 204 Jishan St, Jiufen; d/tw from NT$1000/2500; 📶) This friendly family-run guesthouse is down from the noise and hubbub of the tourist street. Some rooms have excellent sea views, but for something different try the lower rooms that are literally built into the side of the mountain. This unique feature of old Jiufen houses ensured they were stabilised on the very sloped terrain.

To get here just keep heading along Jishan Rd until it starts to descend steeply. The guesthouse is a little further down on the right.

Jiufen Shan Hai Guan Minsu HOMESTAY $$
(九份山海觀民宿, Jiǔfèn Shānhǎi Guān Mínsù; ☎0972-887 200; www.wretch.cc/blog/shanhaiguan/1058264; 217 Jishan St, Jiufen; d from NT$2000; 📶) This guesthouse is actually a number of individual, stylish midrange rooms set in various locations on the hillsides around Jiufen. Most have superb sea views. Check in is at a restaurant at 217 Jishan Rd.

Information

The **Jiufen Visitor Information Centre** (九份旅遊服務中心; ⏲8am-6pm) is worth a visit for the informative history sections (in English). It's just down the street on the opposite side from the Jiufen Kite Museum.

Getting There & Around

BUS

From Taipei, catch the frequent **Keelung Bus Company** (www.kl-bus.com.tw) bus 1062 at Zhongxiao Fuxing MRT (Exit 1) to Jiufen/Jinguashi (NT$100, one to two hours). Buses pass the Jiufen bus stop near the 7-Eleven first and then proceed to Jinguashi (the final stop). The two towns are 3km apart and are served by buses every 10 minutes or so (NT$15).

TRAIN

From Taipei (fast/slow train NT$76/49, 40/50 minutes) trains leave every 30 minutes. Exit at Ruifang, cross the road and catch a bus the last 15 minutes to Jiufen/Jinguashi. Expect to stand on the train.

Bitou Cape 鼻頭角

One of three beautiful emerald capes along the north coast, Bitou Cape (Bítóu Jiǎo) is of note for its sea-eroded cliffs, fantastic views along the coast, and the **Bitou Cape Trail** (鼻頭角步道, Bítóu Jiǎo Bùdào), which is like an easier version of the nearby and more majestic Caoling Historic Trail.

The trail starts near the cape's bus stop before a tunnel (head up the road on the left) and takes a couple of hours to walk. One excellent route follows the path along the bluffs towards the ligthhouse (passing what must be the nicest setting for an elementary school in Taiwan) and then heads down a set of steep stairs and returns along the seashore on a sea-eroded platform called the **Fisherman's Pathway**. It's a geological classroom down here as well as a fabulously scenic walk.

Maps of the route in English are located along the trails. To get here from Ruifang train station or Jiufen take a **Taiwan Tourism Shuttle Bus** (www.taiwantrip.com.tw; NT$50, 30 to 40 minutes) heading to Fulong. Buses run hourly from 9am to 4pm weekdays and 8am to 4pm weekends. You can also catch hourly buses in Keelung from the **Keelung Bus Company** (基隆客運; 02-2433 6111; www.kl-bus.com.tw) station.

Longdong 龍洞

Just through the tunnel past Bitou Cape is Longdong (Lóngdòng), a well-known diving and snorkelling spot. Within walking distance of the park is an area described as having the best **rock climbing** in Taiwan and some of the best coastal climbs anywhere. One standout feature of the area is the wealth of climbs at all levels. Pick up a copy of *Rock Climbing Taiwan* by Matt Robertson and check out his brilliant website (www.climbstone.com), which includes details on food and lodging in the area for climbers.

To get here from Ruifang train station or Jiufen take a **Taiwan Tourism Shuttle Bus** (www.taiwantrip.com.tw; NT$50, 30 to 40 minutes) heading to Fulong. Buses run hourly from 9am to 4pm weekdays and 8am to 4pm weekends. You can also catch hourly buses in Keelung from the **Keelung Bus Company** (基隆客運; 02-2433 6111; www.kl-bus.com.tw) station.

Fulong Beach 福隆海水浴場

The most popular **beach** (福隆海水浴場, Fúlóng Hǎishǔi Yùchǎng; admission NT$100; 8am-6pm May-Oct) in northern Taiwan, Fulong has a long sandy beach and clear waters that are suitable for sailing, windsurfing, surfing and other sports. The coastline is a popular cycling destination.

There are two parts to the beach, divided by the Shuangshi River. The left beach, a long and clean strecth of sand, sits behind the **Northeast Coast Scenic Administration** (www.necoast-nsa.gov.tw; 9am-5pm) building. This is the paid area and you'll have to use this section if you want to do any water sports that require rentals. If you head right and continue towards a large temple on the end of a peninsula (a 10-minute walk from the admin area), you'll get to the free beach. This is also a good place to swim or surf and is reasonably clean in summer.

Activities

In addition to all the water activities, Fulong has bike routes suitable for families with kids as well as for more-serious cyclists.

To the right of the train station a bike path leads to the **Caoling Old Tunnel** (舊草嶺隧道, Jiù Cǎolǐng Suìdào), a 2km train tunnel built in 1924. The tunnel essentially cuts through the cape, dropping you off on the southeast side where a brilliant coastal bike-only path (completely secure against cars) then takes you round the cape and back to Fulong or on to the fishing port of Aodi, all in all a 26km ride. You can rent cheap bikes suitable for this all around the train station.

For a more challenging ride head north out of Fulong on Hwy 2 and take the first left at the petrol station. Follow the road to the town of **Shuangxi** (雙溪) and just past a red bridge head right (not into the tunnel) and shortly look for a sign for the **Shuangtai Industry Road** (雙泰產業道路, Shuāngtài Chǎnyè Dàolù). This 30km route runs up through a quiet watershed area with superb views over densely wooded hills rolling down to the Pacific Ocean. The first section is very steep and seemingly endless but is followed by a long, gently rolling stretch with a final fast steep descent into Daxi.

Many cyclists also ride the Shuangtai Industry Rd as part of a long day trip from Taipei to the coast.

Festivals & Events

Hohaiyan Rock Festival MUSIC
(貢寮國際海洋音樂祭, Gònglião Guójì Hǎiyáng Yīnyuèjì; http://hohaiyan.com) Every July (dates vary) since 2000, Fulong has hosted the Hohaiyan Rock Festival, which has grown from a small indie event into the largest free outdoor concert in Taiwan, attracting hundreds of thousands over a three- to five-day period.

Sleeping & Eating

There are cheap restaurants and convenience stores all around the train station area. **Fulong Biandang** (福隆便當, Fúlóng Biàndāng; lunchbox NT$60; 9am-7pm) is a bit of an institution in the area, having served cheap but tasty lunchboxes for decades. The rustic shop is just to the left of the train station as you exit. Just go to the back of the shop and shout 'Biàndāng' if no one is out front.

Longmen Riverside Camping Resort CAMPGROUND $
(龍門露營區, Lóngmén Lùyín Qū; 02-2499 1791; entrance fee NT$70, 4-person site incl tent from NT$800, 2-/4-person cabins NT$2300/3500) This 37-hectare campground by the Shuangshi River has accommodation for up to 1600 people. To get here from Fulong train station, exit the station and turn left at the main road (Hwy 2). Just past the visitor centre a dedicated lane runs along the highway to the campground. It takes about 10 minutes to walk here from the station.

Fullon Hotel Fulong RESORT $$$
(福容大飯店, Fúlóng Dà Fàndiàn; 02-2499 2381; http://fulong.fullon-hotels.com.tw; d/tw incl breakfast NT$7200/9200;) This private garden resort sits just off the beach and offers high-end cabins with mountain or sea views. Though not large, access to bike paths through the forest and a long beachfront make it seem quite spacious. Rates drop up to 50% midweek and between September and May.

FUBAR BARBECUE $$
(0955-496 175; www.facebook.com/thefubar.fulong; pitas NT$200-300, grills from NT$250; noon-9pm Sat & Sun;) This South African-run beachside restaurant, specialising in barbecue, has a solid reputation among Taiwan's expat population. The grill menu is first-come-first-served, and varies each weekend, but there are also toasted pita sandwiches and salads. All meats are grass fed and organic. Catered events (which could include lamb or pig on a spit) are welcome.

FUBAR is found over by the free beach area, across from the enormous temple. Reservations for groups of four or more are recommended.

Information

DANGERS & ANNOYANCES

The beach is officially closed from October to May but people still come here to surf and swim. The beach is usually pretty dirty at this time unless a crew has been in recently to clean it up.

The currents at Fulong can be treacherous in places, especially where the river flows into the sea. The **Environmental Protection Agency** (EPA; www.epa.gov.tw/en) also recommends that people do not swim for several days after a typhoon, as many contaminants get washed into the sea from the land. During summer, the EPA makes regular announcements about the water quality here and at other beaches.

Getting There & Away

Trains from Taipei to Fulong (fast/slow train NT$128/99, one hour/one hour and 20 minutes) leave every 30 minutes or so. To get here from

DIVING OFF THE NORTHEAST COAST

Good diving spots can be found stretching from the limestone cape of Yeliu down to the high sea-cliff walls off Ilan. Visibility is generally good, averaging between 5m and 12m, while water temperature varies much more than down south: it can be a comfy 25°C to 28°C in summer, but in winter it can get down to 17°C. Bring a 5mm suit!

All entrances are shore based, and are a bit tough, with rocky shores, swells and currents to contend with. However, those same currents mean you'll find a rich variety of tropical and temperate sea life. Divers rave about the soft coral patches along coastal walls, and the large numbers of beautiful sea fans that can be seen in areas with particularly strong currents.

If you go out, note that the seas off Yeliu, Bitou Cape and Longdong Bay are very crowded with divers on summer weekends. However, during the week they can be delightfully empty (of people).

Jiufen take a **Taiwan Tourism Shuttle Bus** (www.taiwantrip.com.tw; NT$50; one hour) heading to Fulong. Buses run hourly from 9am to 4pm weekdays and 8am to 4pm weekends.

Caoling (Tsaoling) Historic Trail & Taoyuan Valley Trail 草嶺古道、桃園谷步道

If you can only do one hike in the north, make it this one: a trail that runs along rugged coastal bluffs forming the very northeasterly extent of the Snow Mountain Range. The first section takes you through thick woodlands and scrub, which are pleasant enough, but it's the many, many kilometres along high, grassy headlands overlooking the Pacific that make this hike such a treasure. To top things off, there are wild grazing buffalo to observe and a few boulder-sized historical tablets.

In 1807 the government in Taiwan built the Caoling Trail (Cǎolǐng Gǔdào) to provide transport between Tamsui and Ilan. The 8.5km section that remains today is one of the few historical roads left in Taiwan.

In recent times, a long addition was made to the trail called the Taoyuan Valley Trail (Táoyuángǔ Bùdào). Taoyuan Valley is not a valley but an emerald grassy bluff, kept trim by the water buffalo. It's stunningly beautiful up here and is a prime spot for picnicking. With the addition of the Taoyuan Valley Trail section, the entire Caoling Trail is about 16km long and takes five to eight hours to complete.

The trail is broad and simple to follow, with signposts and maps (in English), though it certainly is strenuous in places. There is not the slightest danger of getting lost, but do save the walk for the autumn or spring months. You'll roast at the top during summer, and during winter you'll understand exactly why there is a 10m-long boulder inscribed 'Boldly Quell the Wild Mists'.

There are many ways to tackle this trail, and several shortcuts, but the two most common starting and ending points are Fulong Beach and Daxi. The trailhead in Daxi is just north of town after the river. From Fulong, you can walk to the official trailhead, but it's easier to take a 10-minute taxi ride. You can pick up a map at the visitor centre in Fulong.

Wai'ao 外澳

This pleasant seaside village (Wài'ào, Waiao) has in recent years become a hub for surfing on the northeast coast as well as the new beach hangout for Taipei's foreign population. The strollable black-sand beach is wide and long, and there's a new modern boardwalk running a couple of kilometres in either direction. This connects with bike lanes, and nearby are hiking trails, hot springs, museums, dolphin- and whale-watching and a quirky tidal pool for snorkelling.

The two most recognisable structures in the area are a humungous yellow Mr Brown (a cafe chain shop) and what looks like a mosque but is actually the residence of a Taiwanese who has extensive business dealings in the Middle East. These two structures bookmark the town and beach and in between them you'll find a strip of sea-facing houses that have been converted in recent years into B&Bs, restaurants and cafes.

Sights

Lanyang Museum MUSEUM
(蘭陽博物館, Lányáng Bówùguǎn; 9am-5pm Thu-Tue) FREE Designed to imitate the cuesta rock formations in the area, this stunning glass and aluminum panelled structure is worth a visit just to admire the architecture. Exhibits focus on the ecology and history of the Lanyang Plain (or Yilan Plain), an alluvial fan formed by the Lanyang River.

The museum is just south of Wai'ao at Wushih Harbour (where there are dolphin-watching tours as well as boats to Turtle Island). You can walk here from Wai'ao train station in 20 minutes. Just cross the street as you exit the station and head right along the boardwalk.

Beiguan Tidal Park ROCK FORMATIONS
(北關海潮公園, Běiguān Hǎicháo Gōngyuán) FREE Just north of Wai'ao is this small seaside park with beautiful cuesta and 'tofu' block rock formations, and lookouts down the coast. You can snorkel here in summer.

Activities

Surfing & Swimming

Wai'ao is suitable for beginner to advanced surfers nearly all year round; the main beach has a sand bottom. From November to March, northeast winds bring consistent

1.2m to 1.5m swells. From April to October, southerly and eastern tropical depressions bring 1m to 1.5m swells, but July to September pre-typhoon weather can bring 2m to 2.5m perfect barrels.

Rising Sun Surf Inn offers English surfing lessons (and rentals) by an experienced coach and former lifeguard from California. Two-hour lessons including surfboard rental for the day and use of hostel showers cost NT$1500.

For swimming, stick to the beach areas across from the train station, and watch for currents. There is also a safe little protected area for children to swim around the mosque-like building. Some people call it the Mermaid's Hole.

Hiking

There is a large network of trails cutting through the hills of Wai'ao. The most accessible run through an afforestation area that was sponsored by King Car (the company that owns Mr Brown). Paths are wide and clear and offer fantastic views up and down the coast.

To get here take the side road across from the seaside Mr Brown Cafe (the giant yellow glass structure) and head up the steep road 2.5km to the end where there is a second enormous Mr Brown Cafe (this one looking like a castle). The trails begin just back from the parking lot.

Sleeping & Eating

There are half a dozen or so B&Bs, cafes and restaurants facing the beach. The foreign-owned **Rising Sun Surf Inn** (0938-330 35; www.risingsunsurfinn.com; dm NT$450-800, d NT$1000; wi-fi) offers mixed and female-only dorms. Amenities include free bikes, wi-fi, common areas, and a patio bar and restaurant open from 8am to 11pm serving Western breakfast and backpacker fare (burgers, sandwiches and Mexican) for lunch and dinner.

Wai'ao and nearby Toucheng and Jiaoxi are well known for fresh off the boat seafood.

EVERYBODY'S GONE SURFING!

Or so it seems. So popular has the sport become these past few years that in the summer months you could probably walk from Baishawan all the way to Wushih Harbour. We mean on the water, or, rather, on the endless floating boards just offshore.

Baishawan

Baishawan has a nice, safe, sandy beach break and can accommodate the needs of most surfers. **Jhong-jiao bay** (中角灣, Zhōngjiǎo Wān), further east and just north of Jinshan, is one of the hottest surfing destinations these days. Depending on the swell, the beach is suitable for beginner to advanced surfers but better surfers usually avoid the place. As at most popular venues, during peak season you will be sharing the waters with a lot of people who don't know what they are doing. We mean 'a lot' and there isn't much emphasis on skills or etiquette. To put it bluntly, as one veteran of the surf scene told us, the attitude on the water is basically, 'Me first'.

Daxi

At the town's southern edge (a short walk from the train station) is a surfing beach known as **Honeymoon Bay** (蜜月灣, Mìyuè Wān). Waves are generally chest to head high, though during the summer typhoon months they can be over 3m. Depending on the swells, conditions are suitable for beginner to advanced surfers. Daxi has a reputation for being a bit of a locals-only venue now so be respectful if you decide to surf here.

Wai-Ao

Just a little further south is Wai-Ao, which is quickly becoming the new surf and beach hot spot, but is still quiet during the week. Just south of Wai'ao, or just north of Toucheng, is **Wushih Harbour** (烏石港, Wūshí Gǎng), which can get unpleasantly crowded on summer weekends. If you take the beach road from Wai-Ao you will start to hit the shops that cater to the crowds here very quickly.

Surfboard rentals are available across all the above-mentioned places usually for NT$600 to NT$800 per day. Wetsuits are also available, though you can usually surf in the north in a swimsuit or shortie, with a wetsuit reserved for those cold snaps in January and February.

Getting There & Away

The train station is literally across the street from one of the beach entrances. There are hourly trains to/from Taipei (NT$113, one hour and 40 minutes). If you are looking to rent a scooter, head to Jiaoxi.

Jiaoxi (Jiaoshi) 礁溪

03 / POP 5000

Like most spa areas in Taiwan, Jiaoxi (Jiāoxī) is overdeveloped and crowded but landscaping impovements are proceeding to make it a more attractive place. The hotels roadside are cheapest, while those further back towards the mountains have the best water quality and facilities. Midweek the area is quiet and with the new Taiwan Tourism Shuttle Buses (www.taiwantrip.com.tw) you can make a good day trip here, visiting the three-layered **Wufengqi Waterfall** (五峰旗大瀑布, Wǔfēngqí Dà Pùbù) and the 6.5km **Paoma Historic Trail** (跑馬古道, Pǎomǎ Gǔ Dào) before you soak. Buses (NT$20) run on weekdays – hourly, on the hour – starting at the train station.

For a cheap, fun place to hot spring try **Art Spa Hotel** (中冠礁溪大飯店, Zhōngguàn Jiāoxī Dàfàndiàn; 6 Deyang Rd; per person unlimited time NT$250; 7.30am-11pm), which features the only hot-spring slide (that we know of) in Taiwan. To get here walk straight out of the train station, turn left on Zhongshan Rd and then right on Deyang Rd. If you fancy Japanese-style nude bathing (segregated) try the stylish **Tang Wei** (湯圍溝公園, Tāng Wéi Gōu Gōngyuán; 99-11 Deyang Rd; per person NT$80; 8am-11pm) further up Deyang Rd. This is the main spring area in town, with dozens of places big and small as well as myriad seafood restaurants, noodle shops and cafes.

There are frequent trains to Jiaoxi (fast/slow NT$199/128, 1½/two hours) from Taipei. If you want to explore the county, you can rent scooters outside the train station (NT$300 to NT$600) with an international driving permit.

National Centre of Traditional Arts 國立傳統藝術中心

This **arts centre** (國立傳統藝術中心, Guólì Chuántǒng Yìshù Zhōngxīn; www.ncfta.gov.tw; admission NT$150; 9am-6pm; @) occupies 24 hectares along the scenic Tongshan River and is a venue for the research and performance of folk music, opera, dance, toymaking and temple decorations. For visitors there is an exhibition hall loaded with artefacts and informative displays (in English), that change regularly but could be on everything from family shrines to the life of students under a Confucian education system.

Along the river sits a genuine traditional scholar's house that was rescued from the wrecker's ball and reassembled on the centre's grounds. The folk-art street shops sell good-quality glassware, paper cuttings and glove puppets in what is rather oddly a recreation of the various touristy 'old streets' one finds around Taiwan.

Trains to Luodong (羅東; fast train NT$238, 1½ hours, slow train NT$153, 2½ hours) leave Taipei about every half-hour. Once in Luodong, it's a short taxi ride to the arts centre or catch a Taiwan Tourism Shuttle Bus (www.taiwantrip.com.tw) from the station. Buses (NT$22) run every 30 minutes.

SU-HUA HIGHWAY: SUAO TO HUALIEN

Just past Luodong, Hwy 9 rejoins the coast and begins what is known as the Suao-Hualien Hwy (Su-Hua Hwy). The road stretches for 118km along the coastline and, at one of the most breathtaking sections, the Qingshui (Chingshui) cliffs, the highway is literally cut into towering walls of marble and granite that loom 1000m above the rocky seashore.

The beginnings of the route go back to 1874, when the Qing government ordered a road to be built along the east coast to end the region's isolation (and prove to the world they actually were sovereign over all Taiwan). The Japanese widened the road in 1920, battling with landslides and earthquakes the whole time. In fact, the road didn't officially reopen for public use until 1932.

Plans to turn the highway into a superfast freeway have been tossed about for decades but were finally scuttled in 2010 when the government announced that it would pay for an expansion of the existing highway, but not for a full freeway. At the time of writing the road was being widened, and straightened where possible using old tunnels, but

OFF THE BEATEN TRACK

TURTLE ISLAND (GUISHAN ISLAND)

This captivating volcanic islet (龜山島, Gūishān Dǎo), 10km off the coast of Ilan, is less than 3km long yet rises up to 398m. Once supporting a population of 750 people, the island was taken over by the military in 1977 then returned to civilian rule in 2000. These days Turtle Island is a protected marine environment and access is very limited.

In addition to fantastic views from the highest point, the island also has numerous quirky geological features. These include **underwater hot springs** that turn the offshore water into a bubbling cauldron, **volcanic fumaroles** that spout steam, and a **'turtle head'** that faces right or left depending on where you stand on shore.

Turtle Island is open from 1 March to 30 November, 9am to 5pm. If you wish to land on the island you must apply in advance for a special permit (it's a hassle but worth it). Download a copy of the application form from the **Northeast & Yilan Coast Scenic Administration** (☎02-2499 1115; www.necoast-nsa.gov.tw) website and fax it, along with your passport information, three to 20 days before you wish to sail. Once you get your permit, ask for a list of boat operators and make a reservation (none speak English so ask the scenic office for help).

If you just want to circle the island or whale- and dolphin-watch you don't need permits but you should still make a reservation. Call the Wushih Harbour reservation centre on ☎03-950 8199 (Chinese only so try going to a visitor centre in Taipei or elsewhere and asking for help).

Boats leave from Wushih Harbour. It costs NT$600 for a 1½-hour cruise to and around the island, and NT$1200 for a three-hour tour that includes a stop on the island. Combination tours involving stops on the island and **dolphin- and whale-watching** (April to September) are also available (NT$1600, 4½ hours).

To get to Wushih Harbour, take a train from Taipei to Toucheng (fast/slow train NT$184/119, 1½/two hours, every half-hour) and then a short taxi ride. Or take a train to Wai'ao and walk 15 minutes south along the beachwalk.

Call the **English Tourist Hotline** (☎0800-011 765) or Northeast & Yilan Coast Scenic Administration for more information. If you are staying at Rising Sun Surf Inn (p146) in nearby Wai'ao, staff can help arrange fast permits for the island.

nature was not cooperating and closures and delays due to washouts were and will probably remain a regular occurrence.

Nanao 南澳

☎03 / POP 500

The small coastal town of Nanao (Nánào) has a large crescent bay with a dark sandy beach that's visible from the highway as you make your descent from the hills. It's a great spot for strolling along and taking in the gorgeous coastal scenery. Heading towards the hills, the scenery and the ethnography change completely, from alluvial plains and the Hakka to deep-cut river valleys and the Atayal.

Though it covers a large area, it's easy to find your bearings in Nanao. Highway 9 runs through the centre, and you can clearly see the sea to the east and the mountains to the west.

History

Atayal aboriginals settled in the Nanao region about 250 years ago, and throughout the late Qing period were successful in repelling Taiwanese advancement. It was not until 1910, after a five-year campaign by the Japanese to 'pacify' aboriginal groups, that Taiwanese settlers were able to begin to develop the land for farming. These days the Atayal presence is still strong, and much of their traditional way of life, including hunting for deer and pigs, is visible as soon as you head off the highway.

Activities

Despite the town being snugly positioned between the sea and some very rugged mountains, Nanao's cycling is, for the most part, flat and leisurely. The alluvial plains on the east side of Hwy 9 offer hours of riding on empty roads through pretty farming fields. On the west side, a couple of roads head up the valleys formed by the North and South Nanao Rivers.

To reach the north river valley, head south out of town and at the Km133 mark turn right onto **Township Rd 55**, which was under heavy repair at the time of writing. A few kilometres past **Jin-yue Village** there is a set of free outdoor hot springs that should be open by the time you read this. After a dip in the waters, continue to the end of the road. It's gorgeous up here.

To reach the south river valley road, head down Hwy 9 south out of town to the Km136 mark and turn right on **Township Rd 57**. Ten kilometres up the valley, the road ends at the start of the **Nanao Historic Trail** (南澳古道, Nánào Gǔdào), an old Qing-dynasty cross-island road that's open for the first 3km. It's a beautiful walk up a deep river valley and the chances of hearing and spotting indigenous birds, monkeys, deer and even wild pigs are high. At the time of writing the trail was closed for repairs.

Also worth exploring is the **Jhaoyang Historic Trail** (朝陽步道, Zhāoyáng Bùdào) that runs over a lushly forested hillock and affords excellent coastal views from on high. To get to the trail turn left at the traffic lights just before the 7-Eleven on the main road (as you head south) and follow to the end (the harbour).

You can rent cheap bikes (per three hours NT$100) from a couple of shops just outside the train station.

Sleeping & Eating

There are small noodle shops and restaurants beside the highway, and a couple of lunchbox shops near the train station. There's also a 7-Eleven, a small grocery store and a night market near the town square.

At Km134.6 there is a large farmers' association outlet with dozens of stalls and shops inside selling all manner of local products, including honey, cooked sausages, ice cream and coffee.

Nan-Ao Recreation Farm CAMPGROUND
(南澳農場, Nánào Nóngchǎng; ☎988 1114; http://nanao-farm.e-land.gov.tw/html/link2.htm) FREE
This free, large, clean and green campground has shaded sites and hot showers (from 5pm to 10pm.) To reach it from Nanao, turn left at the Km134.5 mark just after crossing a bridge. Follow the road down about 1km to the obvious campground entrance.

If you keep driving past the entrance you'll reach a long **black-sand beach** in a few minutes with dramatic views down the rocky coastline.

Getting There & Away

There are trains every hour or two to Nanao from Taipei (fast/slow NT$305/196, 2½ to three hours).

NORTH CROSS-ISLAND HIGHWAY

If you're looking for wild scenery but want a change of pace from coastal waters and rugged shorelines, try a journey down National Hwy 7, also known as the Běihéng or North Cross-Island Highway (Běibù Héngguàn Gōnglù).

The highway starts in the old Taoyuan County town of **Daxi**, famous for its excellent *dòugān* (firm tofu) and the **Qing-dynasty facades** on Heping St. At first the road winds through the countryside, passing flower farms and settlements, including the mausoleum of former leader Chiang Kai-shek. After passing above Shimen Reservoir, the largest body of water in northern Taiwan, the road narrows and starts to rise and wind its way along steep gorges, across precipitously high bridges and, in general, through some pretty fantastic mountain scenery. You can drive across in four or five hours, but there are many great stops leading to waterfalls, caves, forest reserves, hot springs and stands of ancient trees.

At Chilan, the highway descends suddenly and an hour later enters the flood plains of the Lanyang River, which divides the Snow and Yushan Ranges and is home to the largest cabbage patch in Taiwan. The road then continues northeast to Ilan, with spur routes to Luodong and Wuling FRA.

It's best to have your own transport, as buses are few and far between. Cycling is popular, if challenging, and usually takes two days. In general, accommodation options are also few and far between; if you're spending the night, stay in the Baling area, about halfway across.

The best time to ride or drive the highway is autumn to spring on weekdays (avoid Chinese New Year). Be very aware of both other drivers and the natural hazards. This road is curvy and treacherous, and some part of the surface is always under repair due to typhoons and landslides.

Richard Saunders' *Taipei Escapes 2* covers many small sights on the highway that are worth checking out if you have time.

Getting There & Around

BICYCLE

The highway usually takes two days by bike from Taipei, with an overnight stop in Baling or Mingchi. Cycling is popular with many bloggers, so there's lots of information online.

BUS

The **Taiwan Tourism Shuttle Bus** (www.taiwantrip.com.tw) has these options:

Cihu Route To Daxi Old Street, Shimen Reservoir and Cihu. From Zhongli train station exit the front, turn left and look for the Taoyuan Bus Company station a short distance down Zhonghe Rd. Buses run hourly on weekdays and every 30 minutes on weekends from 9am to 5pm to Daxi Old Street, Shimen Reservoir and Cihu. All-day passes cost NT100.

Xiao Wulai Route To Daxi Old Street, Cihu and Xiao Wulai. From the back of Taoyuan train station, head up Yanping Rd 2 blocks to the Toayuan bus station on the right. Bus 502 runs on weekends only. Day passes cost NT$150. See the website for schedules.

CAR & SCOOTER

You can rent a car in Taipei or at the Taoyuan International Airport, or a scooter in Jiaoxi.

Cihu 慈湖

Cihu (Cíhú, Lake Kindness) is a quiet, scenic park where the remains of Chiang Kai-shek's body are entombed, awaiting a (hopeful) eventual return to China. It's also the site of one of Taiwan's oddest tourism attractions: the **Cihu Memorial Sculpture Park** (慈湖紀念雕像公園, Cíhú Jìniàn Diāoxiàng Gōngyuán; ⌚8am-5pm) **FREE**, where 152 unwanted Chiang Kai-shek statues have been sent over the past decade to escape being melted down or smashed.

This sculpture safehouse is a hoot (surely unintentionally), with promenades of Chiang busts and clumps of Chiangs standing facing each other as if in conversation. There are storytime Chiangs reading books to shorter Chiangs, salesmen Chiangs bowed at the waist and hat removed, avuncular Chiangs always smiling, and martial Chiangs, sword in hand, ready to defend the nation.

On a more serious note the park also gives insight into the cult of personality that was developed (and still exists for hardcore KMT supporters) around Chiang. You'll learn for example how his statues were placed at the front of every school, and often in pre-existing popular shrines so worshippers would be forced to pay homage whether they wanted to or not.

The sculpture park is free but if you want to see more of the area apply ahead of time on the **Taoyuan County** (http://backcihu.tycg.gov.tw/Cihu/index.aspx) website for the area called **Back Cihu** (後慈湖, Hòu Cíhú). This former command centre was used by Chiang in his plans to retake China. It's set around a pretty lake and takes a couple of hours to walk.

Shimen Reservoir 石門水庫

Biking out to the Shimen Reservoir (Shímén Shuǐkù) from Taipei is a popular day trip for stronger cyclists. You can take County Rd 110 from Bitan to Sansia and then Hwy 7乙, or ride the bike-only riverside bicycle paths that head along the west bank of the Tamsui (you'll pass Yingge on the way). The latter route is very scenic past Yingge.

Fuxing (Fuhsing, Fusing) 復興

☎03 / POP 1000

The aboriginal village of Fuxing (Fùxīng), 18km down Hwy 7 from Daxi, makes for an excellent pit stop, or an even better base from which to explore the whole area. If you want to stay the night, the **Youth Activity Centre** (青年活動中心, Qīngnián Huódòng Zhōngxīn; ☎382 2276; d/tw incl breakfast NT$2600/4300, 10% weekday discounts) has simple rooms in a pretty, landscaped park on a high ridge overlooking an arm of Shimen Reservoir. The land was formerly occupied by one of Chiang Kai-shek's summer villas (it burned down in 1992), which should clue you in to the fact that it's incredibly scenic here. YHA holders can stay for NT$800 per night.

On a small bluff to the right of the centre (head to the back of the car park and then down the wooden stairs) is **Shenlin Shui An** (森鄰水岸, Sēnlín Shuǐ Àn; ☎382 2108; www.facebook.com/loveforesthouse/info; set meals NT$320-420; ⌚10am-8pm), a rustic restaurant run by an aboriginal family. The view here is even more incredible than at the Youth Activity Centre and the food and coffee are far superior. The owner speaks some English and is a pub singer. If there are enough people around, or if he likes you, he will take out his guitar and play.

Shenlin Shui An has a well-built wooden **cabin** (NT$3800) that can sleep up to eight people. Call for directions down if you are driving.

In town you can get solid, aboriginal-style food, such as *tǔ jī* (土雞; free-range chicken), *zhútǒng fàn* (竹筒飯; rice steamed in bamboo tubes) and a variety of noodle dishes served with the mushrooms for which Fuxing is famous.

Xiao Wulai Waterfall 小烏來瀑布

This long cascading waterfall (Xiǎo Wūlái Pùbù) can be viewed up close or from a ridge almost half a kilometre away. On a foggy day, the sweeping scene of steep mountain peaks and the long waterfall bears a remarkable likeness to the famous Song-dynasty landscape painting *Travellers in Mountains and Streams*.

If you are driving, the turn-off to the falls is just past the Km20.5 mark. Two kilometres up County Rd 115 you'll run into a closed toll booth and just past that the ridge lookout. Further down is a parking area (NT$100) and entrance to a small trail system (and developing scenic area) that winds around the back of the falls and down to the base.

Lower Baling 巴陵

This small pit stop (Bālíng) on the highway is the usual overnight stop for cyclists. There are a couple of hotels roadside, including **Lower Baling Hot Spring Hotel** (下巴陵溫泉山莊, Xià Bālíng Wēnquán Shān Zhuāng; ☎03-391 2323; http://shabaling.mmmtravel.com.tw; d/tw NT$2500/4000; 📶), which has simply furnished rooms upstairs from the spacious 1st-floor restaurant.

Weekday prices are about 40% to 50% of weekend rates, and outside of summertime or holidays you should be able to negotiate lower rates at any time of the week. If the place isn't busy, see if they'll include breakfast and dinner in your room price.

Lalashan Forest Reserve 拉拉山國有林自然保護區

The imaginatively named Upper Baling (Shàng Bālíng) sits about 10km up the road from Lower Baling. Perched on a high, thin ridgeline, the village offers some splendid mountain views. More to the point for travellers, it's the site of the **Lalashan Forest Reserve** (拉拉山國有林自然保護區, Lālāshān Guóyǒ Lín Zìrán Bǎohùqū; ☎391 2761; ⏲8am-5pm) FREE, a 63.9 sq km expanse of mixed forest holding one of the largest stands of ancient red hinoki cypress trees left in Taiwan.

The most ancient of the ancients is over 2800 years old, but there are a hundred more that are not much younger. A 3.7km wooden boardwalk winds through the dense forest, and interpretative signs indicate the age, species, height and diameter of each giant.

To get to the reserve by car, exit Hwy 7 at Lower Baling onto County Rd 116 and continue up a very steep road. About 4km past Upper Baling you'll reach the official start of the park (and if you are taking a bus this is as far as it will take you). From here it's another 2.7km to a car park. The trail begins just up from here and there's a small **exhibition hall** (⏲9am-6pm) at the start where you can pick up maps and information.

It's possible to visit the reserve as a day trip from Taipei by public transport. First catch a train to Taoyuan station. Head straight out the front exit and walk one block up Zhongzheng St to Fuxing Rd. Turn right and look for the Zhongli Bus Station (really just a stop) about 50m down on the far side of the street. Bus 5301 (NT$208, 3½ hours) leaves at 6.30am and 12.30pm. The bus drops you off at Linbankou stop, which is at the start of the reserve but still 2.7km to the old tree area. Buses from Linbankou return at 9.30am and 3.30pm. Note that there are other buses that run only as far as Upper Baling.

If you are staying the night, **Magic World Country House** (富仙境鄉村渡假旅館, Fùxiānjìng Xiāngcūn Dùjià Lǚguǎn; ☎03-391 2115; http://country-house.lalashan.tw; d incl breakfast NT$2500, 30% weekday discount) just down from Upper Baling is a good choice. The house has fabulous views over the mountains from the rooms or outside on the long wooden deck.

LOCAL KNOWLEDGE

CHRIS NELSON: GRAVER

My hobby is 'graving', that is, I visit, research and document cemeteries around the world. It's not a hobby that endears me to superstitious locals here in Taiwan, but I think graving gives me insight into the history and culture of the places I visit.

Best Overall Gravesite

For an excellent introduction to the variety of Chinese graves, nothing beats the **Liuzhangli Cemeteries** in Taipei. There are Buddhist, Taoist, Christian and Muslim graveyards, as well as three White Terror cemeteries where people killed by the Kuomintang (KMT) are buried.

Foreign Graves

At the Tamsui Foreign Cemetery (p108) in Tamsui there are graves of dozens of foreign merchants, mariners and missionaries. Next to it is the Mackay Family Cemetery (p108), where George Leslie Mackay (p106) and his family are buried.

The grave of Nelly O'Driscoll is the remotest one I know of. It's a lonely grave at the **Hsiyu Lighthouse** in Penghu. Nelly was the daughter of a lighthouse keeper, but little else is known about her. Kind of sad, to be buried in such a faraway place.

Don't Miss

Cihu Memorial Sculpture Park (p150) is where Chiang Kai-shek (CKS) is entombed. It's interesting: even though CKS is widely reviled now, people still look on his tomb with awe and respect.

Most Kitschy Grave

Up the road from the Juming Museum (p136), there's the tomb of singer Teresa Teng, at **Jinbaoshan Cemetery**. Busloads of fans make pilgrimages here to pay homage to 'Taiwan's Sweetheart'. There are kitschy sculptures, piped-in music and even an oversized electronic keyboard you can play.

Best Time to Visit Graves

The best time to visit is during the Qing Ming Festival (also called Tomb Sweeping Day) when people return to their ancestors' graves for a once-a-year cleaning. The festival is usually held in early April.

For more cemetery information in Taiwan, and the locations of the places mentioned above, check out **Find a Grave** (www.tinyurl.com/taiwangraves).

Hikers should note that from the reserve it's possible to hike six hours all the way downhill to Fushan near Wulai on the Fu-Ba National Trail (see p127). Magic World staff can arrange for you to be picked up or dropped off at Lalashan (which is helpful, especially if you are hiking up from Fushan to Baling). Request this service in advance.

For eating options head to Upper Baling where there are plenty of restaurants serving up mountain cabbage and mushrooms, fried tofu, and mountain pig or chicken. Set meals for two people are between NT$400 and NT$600. Look for the signs 2人, 4人 (ie meals for two people or four people).

Mingchih Forest Recreation Area

明池森林遊憩區

This **forest recreation area** (明池森林遊憩區, Míngchí Sēnlín Yóuqì Qū; www.yeze.com.tw/mingchih/html/page002-1.htm) is a good base for exploration, and provides a retreat from the relentless heat of summer in the city. Lying at an altitude between 1000m and 1700m, even in July the average temperature is only 20°C.

There's not much in the reserve itself except pleasant little **Lake Mingchih** (明池, Míngchí Hú; admission NT$120; ⏲8am-5pm) across the highway. It's popular with ducks, and strolling around it when you first wake up is a great way to start the day. Nearby are wild hot springs and a stand of ancient trees (different from the ones at Lalashan).

Sights & Activities

★ Ma-Kou Ecological Park FOREST

(馬告生態公園, Măgào Shēntài Gōngyuán) This 16.5 hectare ecological park hosts a stand of ancient red and yellow cypress trees easily the match of those at other ancient forests in Taiwan including Lalashan. The oldest tree here is reportedly over 2500 years old.

The gated park is a few kilometres down Hwy 7 past Mingchih. Visitor numbers are limited each day, and you need to be on a tour. Tours leave three times a day from Mingchih (guests staying at the forest recreation area pay NT$600, nonguests NT$800). To make a reservation contact the front-desk staff at Mingchih.

Hot Springs

There are numerous hot springs within a short drive of Mingchih, some developed, as at Jioujheze on the way up to Taipingshan, and at Jiaoxi, but also some natural ones for those willing to do a little hiking.

Sileng Hot Spring HOT SPRING

(四稜溫泉, Sìléng Wēnquán) This beautifully set natural spring lies at the bottom of a steep ravine. Despite the rough trail down, it's one of the more accessible wild springs in Taiwan, and popular on weekends. The springs seep and gush down a rock slope, coloured with deposits from the waters, and gather in small pools on a shelf above the river.

To get here, head west from Mingchih exactly 7.1km (to around Km58.5). As you go around a sharp bend that juts out into the valley you'll see a small spot to park. Leave your car here then look for a hot-spring symbol on the cement barrier to your left. Cross the barrier and follow the trail down for 40 minutes or so until you reach the river. The springs are obvious on the other side, though you may get off track a few times. Give yourself plenty of time and be aware that you are going into a potentially dangerous situation.

Note you must cross the river at the end, so don't go after heavy rains, especially in spring and summer. River shoes are helpful.

Sleeping & Eating

Mingchih has rooms and cottages (from NT$3900, weekday discounts) set among tall cedar trees. Try to get a room away from the highway, though, as trucks come by at all times of day or night and can disturb your sleep. The log-style restaurant has a lovely sunroom area looking out onto the forest where you can enjoy an OK breakfast, lunch and dinner (average dishes cost NT$220 to NT$360).

Getting There & Away

Guests who are staying overnight at Mingchih can take a daily shuttle (NT$600, 9am, three hours) from Taipei MRT Sun Yat-Sen Memorial Hall station (Exit 4). Otherwise, you need your own transport.

Taipingshan National Forest Recreation Area 太平山國家森林遊樂區

During the 20th century, Alishan, Bashianshan and this 126 sq km **forest recreation area** (太平山國家森林遊樂區, Tàipíngshān Guójiā Sēnlín Yóulè Qū; http://tps.forest.gov.tw; admission NT$200, per vehicle NT$100; ⌚6am-9pm) were the three top logging sites in Taiwan. Taipingshan only became a protected area in 1983 and has since transformed itself into one of the best mountain retreats in Taiwan. Around a small wooden village set on the forested slopes are endless lookouts over the Snow Mountains, as well as Japanese shrines, hiking trails through old forests, and informative displays on the old logging industry.

The 30km ride up to Taipingshan from Hwy 7 takes more than an hour on the very steep and tortuous road. Be aware that this area is often very foggy and at times you may not be able to reach the village. The best time to visit the park is from April to November, especially in late autumn when the leaves are changing colour.

Sights & Activities

Logging in the 20th century mostly stripped Taiwan of its ancient camphor and cypress forests, but left intact huge tracts of hemlock, pine, beech and maple. Which means that as you hike the many trails around Taiping Village you're going to find yourself in some dense, beautiful old growth. A decent network of well-marked trails begins just up from the village but there are more trails starting off the road. Pick up a map at the visitor centre on the way up.

The tiny passenger **Bong Bong Train** (蹦蹦車, Bèngbèng Chē) was out of commission at the time of writing, but should it be running you can take it from the village on a 20-minute trip through the forest. At the end two trails split, one through lush forest, the other to the **Sandie Waterfalls** (三疊瀑布, Sāndié Pùbù).

Jioujheze Hot Springs HOT SPRING
(鳩之澤溫泉, Jiūzhīzé Wēnquán; public pools unlimited time NT$200; ⏲ 9am-7pm) The public facilities here feature simple rock-lined pools (and include two nude pools segregated by sex), while the private rooms feature wooden inset tubs (NT$500 to NT$800 per hour). The springs are mildly sulphurous and extremely hot. For fun, before you head off for a dip, join others who are boiling eggs in a special pool.

The springs are located down a side road less than halfway up to Taipingshan (already at an altitude of 520m but with another 22km to go).

★ **Lake Cuifeng** SCENIC AREA
(翠峰湖, Cuìfēng Hú) This very scenic small lake is set at 1900m above sea level and is reportedly the largest alpine lake in Taiwan. Two trails offer a chance to get away from it all, including the 3.9km **Cuifeng Lake Circle Trail** (翠峰湖環山步道, Cuìfēng Hú Huánshān Bùdào). Lake Cuifeng is 16km up the Taipingshan road from the villa area and is only accessible via your own transport.

Sleeping & Eating

There's only one place to sleep and eat here: in the lodge area called **Taipingshan Villa** (☎ 02-030 1176; http://tps.forest.gov.tw/en/food.html; tw from NT$2500, 20-30% weekday discount). Accommodation includes dinner and breakfast. A huge lunch is an extra NT$200. It's advisable to make room reservations in advance on weekends and summer. You can do so online up to a month in advance.

Getting There & Around

It's best to have your own vehicle for Taipingshan, but **Kuo Kuang Motor Transport** (☎ 02-2311 9893; www.kingbus.com.tw) has buses from Yilan (NT$226, 8.30am) on Saturday, Sunday and holidays. The bus stand is out the back exit of the Yilan train station in front of a Hi-Life convenience store. Buses arrive at Taipingshan at 12.20pm and leave the next day at 3.30pm. Note that buses don't run to Lake Cuifeng.

Wuling Forest Recreation Area (Wuling Farm) 武陵農場

☎ 04

About 1½ hours further south down Hwy 7 from the turn-off is Wuling Forest Recreation Area, better known as **Wuling Farm** (Wǔlíng Nóngchǎng; admission NT$160). Originally established in 1963 as a fruit-growing area by retired soldiers, the farm (elevation 1740m to 2200m) became part of Sheipa National Park in 1992, and these days only a few show orchards remain.

Many travellers come to Wuling to climb Snow Mountain, Taiwan's second-highest mountain, but Wuling also makes for a nice weekend getaway, or a cool break from the heat of summer. There is gorgeous alpine scenary all round which can be taken in at a leisurely pace. During the spring cherry blossom season the road from Yilan to Wuling is packed with cars, and there are daily limits to enter the recreation area.

Wuling Farm is well known for its efforts to preserve the indigenous and endangered Formosan landlocked salmon (櫻花鉤吻鮭, Yīnghuā Gōuwěn Gūi), also known as the masu salmon. Unlike other salmon, these never leave the cool freshwater rivers they were born in.

There's only one main road through Wuling, with an offshoot to the campground. From the Wuling National Hostel to Wuling Villa is about 7km. From the National Hostel to the trailhead for Snow Mountain is about 8.5km. The **visitor information centre** (旅遊客服務中心; www.wuling-farm.com.tw; ⏲ 9am-4.30pm Tue-Sun) near the bus stop (公車站) has maps and books but staff are generally not very knowledgeable and speak little if any English.

Activities

For people of average fitness, Wuling offers short walks down by the river or strolls along newly built paths beside the main road. It's also very pleasant to walk up to the highly scenic campground area and up to the trailhead for Snow Mountain (about 7.5km from the visitor centre). And do stop and lie down in the Yushan cane up here and bask in the high mountain glory. The cane may look prickly but it's actually very comfortable.

The 4.5km **Taoshan Waterfall Trail** (桃山瀑布, Táoshān Pùbù) starts from the end of the road near Wuling Villa hostel. The falls are 50m high (at an elevation of 2500m) and well worth the three-hour return hike. Try to schedule your return around dusk as you stand a good chance of seeing wildlife.

Bikes are available during daylight hours by the visitor centre for NT$150 to NT$200 for two hours.

Sleeping & Eating

For instant noodles and snack foods, there's a **convenience store** (便利商店; 7am-7pm) near the visitor centre.

Wuling Villa HOSTEL $
(武陵山莊, Wuling Mountain Hostel, Wǔlíng Shānzhuāng; 2590 1020; dm weekday/weekend NT$700/900) Despite the name, this is the hostel in the Wuling area. Normal rooms here have simple wooden interiors with a minimum of furniture and are grossly overpriced on weekends (doubles go from NT$4000). For dorm rooms ask for a *tongpu* (東埔; room with floor mat and thick quilt). Breakfast (congee and salty eggs) is included and lunch/dinner costs NT$150/350.

Campground CAMPGROUND $
(露營管理中心, Lùyíng Guǎnlǐ Zhōngxīn; 2590 1470; sites NT$400-1000, cabins NT$1800-2200) Set high on a gorgeous alpine meadow, this campground offers clean, modern facilities (including showers and a convenience store) with grass sites, platform sites and even platforms with pre-set army-style tents. Sites come both unpowered and powered; for the ultimate comfort try the little wooden cabins (without private bath).

Wuling National Hostel HOTEL, CABIN $$
(武陵國民賓館, Wǔlíng Guómín Bīnguǎn; 2590 1258; d/tw NT$3420/5190, 20% discount weekdays) A comfortable place to stay with forest views all around, the hostel (really a mid-range hotel) offers good-value rooms that include buffet-style breakfast and dinner.

Wuling Farm

Activities, Courses & Tours
1 Snow Mountain Trailhead & Ranger Station A2

Sleeping
2 Campground A2
3 Wuling National Hostel B6
4 Wuling Villa A1

Eating
5 Convenience Store B5

Information
Police Station .... (see 6)
6 Sheipa National Park Wuling Station B5
7 Visitor Information Centre B5

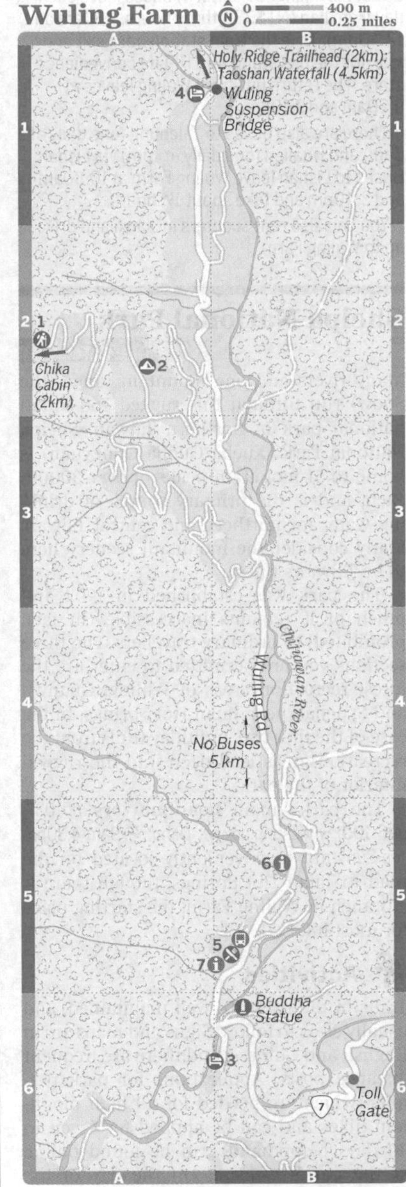

Meals (breakfast NT$150, set lunch NT$250 to NT$290, dinner NT$350) are also available for nonguests. There's wi-fi in the hotel lobby.

Getting There & Away

Two **Kuo Kuang Motor Transport** (☎ 02-2311 9893; www.kingbus.com.tw) buses leave each day from Ilan (NT$337, three hours, 7.30am and 12.40pm). Take the train station back exit and look for the bus stand by a Hi-Life convenience store. The return bus from Wuling leaves at 9.20am and 2.10pm.

There are also buses to Taichung (one daily at 8am) and Hualien (one daily at 1pm) via Lishan. Buses to Lishan leave Wuling Farm at 10.30am and 3.40pm and take about 1½ hours.

You can also rent scooters in Jiaoxi and drive up to Wuling Farm.

Sheipa National Park

雪霸國家公園

Many rivers and one mountain range (the Snow) run through this rugged 768-sq-km national park in northern Taiwan. Sheipa National Park (Xuěbà Guójiā Gōngyuán) is home to 51 mountain peaks of over 3000m each, and is the primary source of drinking water for northern and central Taiwan. Many consider the mountain scenery here to be Taiwan's finest.

The park was established in 1992 and much of it remains inaccessible (in fact, prohibited) to ordinary travellers. The three sections you are permitted to enter are the forest recreation areas of Wuling, Guanwu and Syuejian near Taian Hot Springs. In the case of the first two, multiday trails from the recreation areas lead deep into the rugged interior of the park.

The park's main **headquarters** (☎ 037-996 100; www.spnp.gov.tw; Dahu; ⏲ 9am-4.30pm Tue-Sun) are inconveniently located on the road to Taian Hot Springs, though there is a branch in Wuling Farm, the starting place for most hikes.

Activities

Trails in the park are well maintained, and usually clear to follow. Signs and maps are in English and Chinese, and there are frequent distance posts. Applications for park permits (which are needed for all high mountain hikes and can be applied for seven to 30 days beforehand) can be found online at the park's website. On the day of the hike, make sure you drop into the **Sheipa National Park Wuling Station** (雪霸國家公園武陵管理處) to apply for a mountain permit (different from park permits). At the trailhead for Snow Mountain the park's staff will check both permits and afterwards ask you to watch a movie on safety and acting responsibly in the park.

The best months for hiking in the park are October to December, and March and April. Winter hiking is becoming more popular, though you need to be prepared for snow and bitter cold. A good two-day option is simply to hike to the East Peak, staying in Qika Cabin overnight.

During April and May, seasonal heavy rains, including monsoons, are common, and if you don't hit any typhoons, July and August are good months to avoid the crowds.

Snow Mountain Main Peak HIKING

The first recorded climb of Snow Mountain (雪山主峰) was in 1915 – it was then called Mt Silvia, and is now also spelled Syueshan, Shueshan and Xueshan. Since then this sublime peak (Taiwan's second-highest) has attracted teams and solo hikers from all over the world.

The trail (from ranger station trailhead to summit) is 10.9km and takes 8½ to 11½ hours to complete (one-way). Because of the altitude gain, and the fact that most people are carrying heavy packs, this usually requires two days (with a third for the return).

➡ Trailhead to Chika Cabin: 2km, 1½ hours

➡ Chika Cabin to 369 Cabin: 5.1km, five to six hours

➡ 369 Cabin to Main Peak: 3.8km, three to four hours

The trail to the main peak is for the most part broad and clear, and requires mere fitness rather than any technical skill (unless you are going in winter). The first day's itinerary is always a bit tricky. If you have taken a bus and walked (or hitch-hiked) the 7.5km to the trailhead (2140m) then you aren't likely to get any further than Chika Cabin the first night. Nor should you, as it's best to acclimatise at this elevation before going further.

The second day's hike is a long series of tough switchbacks (one is even called the **Crying Slope**). But the views on a clear day are stunning, and the landscape is ever-changing: from forested cover to open meadowland and fields of Yushan cane. The

Sheipa National Park

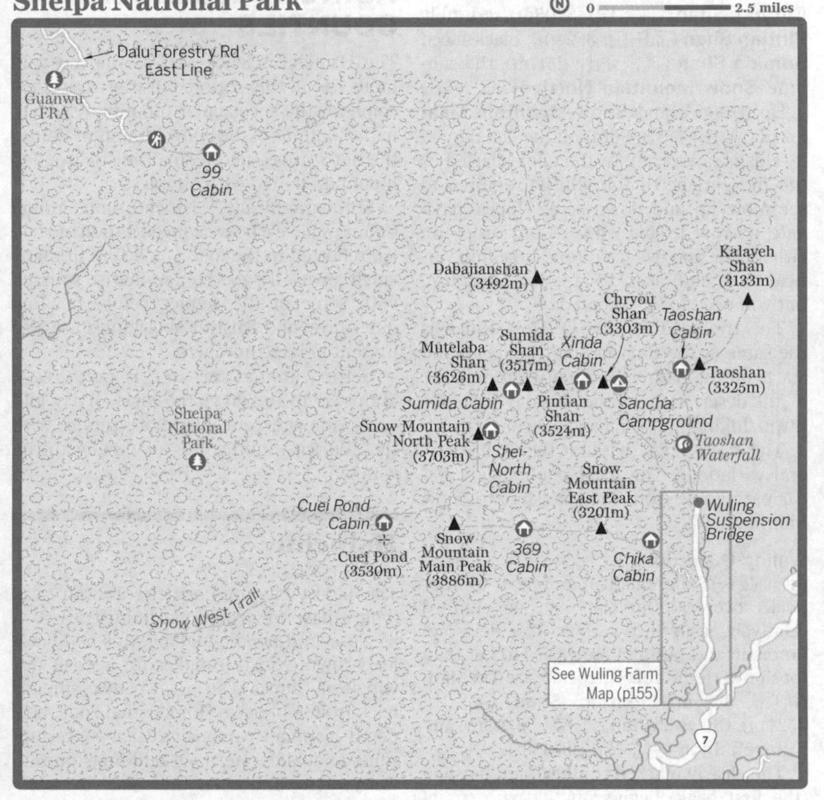

box-fold cliff faces of the Holy Ridge are unforgettable.

At 369 Cabin, a sturdy shelter nestled on a slope of Yushan cane, most hikers overnight, getting up at 2am so that they can reach the summit by daybreak. Unless you know the path to the top, it's really not advisable to do this.

So, assuming you get a reasonable start you'll soon be in the Black Forest, a moody stand of Taiwan fir. At the edge of the forest be on the lookout for troops of Formosan macaques. Note that the giant hollow before you is a **glacial cirque** formed by retreating ice-fields.

It's another 1km from here to the summit along more switchbacks. Unlike Yushan, the summit of Snow is rounded and requires no climbing to mount. But you'll want to linger here and take in the Holy Ridge and other surrounding peaks.

Hikers normally reach the summit of Snow and then return to the trailhead (and their vehicles) on the same day. You need to leave 369 Cabin no later than 6am to accomplish this before dark. For reference: from the Main Peak back to the trailhead takes about six hours (two hours back to 369 Cabin and a further four hours from there to the trailhead).

★O' Holy Ridge HIKING

(聖稜線O型縱走, Shènglíng Xiàn O Xíng Zòngzǒu)

The O stands for the circular nature of this hike (written as Shengleng Trail on the national park website), which begins and ends at Wuling Farm. It's also probably the shape your mouth will be in most of the time as you take in what may be the best high-mountain scenery in the country.

After a hard push on the first day to the ridgeline, you never drop below 3000m for the next four days as you reach the summit of a half-dozen peaks, including grassy **Chryou Shan** (池有山; 3303m), crumbly **Pintian Shan** (品田山; 3524m), black-faced **Sumida Shan** (素密達山; 3517m), the sublime **Snow Mountain North Peak** (雪山北峰; 3703m), and **Snow Mountain Main Peak** (雪山主峰; 3886m) on the last day.

This is not a trail for the faint-hearted or the inexperienced. You will be required to scramble up and down scree slopes, navigate narrow ledges with 1000m drops on either side, and use fixed ropes to climb vertical shale cliff faces. It's a grand adventure but you need to be prepared.

The trailhead for the O' Holy Ridge is the same as the Chryou Shan trailhead and starts off the path to Taoshan Waterfall. For a full description of the five-day hike see http://hikingintaiwan.blogspot.com.

The Holy Ridge (without the O) has several variations. The most popular is a linear path going from Dabajianshan to Snow Mountain.

Wuling-Quadruple HIKING

(武陵四秀) The quadruple refers to four peaks over 3000m that can be climbed relatively easily in two days. The views are fantastic and permits are easier to get than for Snow Mountain. The peaks are **Taoshan** (桃山; 3325m), **Pintian Shan** (品田山; 3524m), **Chryou Shan** (池有山; 3303m) and **Kalayeh Shan** (喀拉業山; 3133m).

The clearly marked trailhead for Taoshan (the first peak) begins off the path to Taoshan Waterfall in Wuling Farm.

Sleeping & Eating

Before and after hikes you can sleep and eat at Wuling Farm. On the trail there are cabins at the end of each day's hike with bunk bedding, ecotoilets, water, solar lighting and sometimes an outside deck. Cabins are unattended, so you must bring your own food supplies.

Getting There & Away

All hikes begin in the Wuling Farm section of Sheipa National Park. Kuo Kuang Motor Transport buses leave twice each day from Ilan (NT$337, three hours, 7.30am and 12.40pm) for Wuling Farm. Take the train station back exit and look for the bus stand by a Hi-Life convenience store. The return bus from Wuling Farm leaves at 9.20am and 2.10pm.

There are also buses to/from Taichung via Lishan. You can also rent scooters in Jiaoxi and drive up.

HSINCHU & MIAOLI COUNTIES

The Hsinchu Science Park is the most famous site in this region, but most travellers come for the spectacular mountain scenery in the foothills of the Snow Mountain Range, the hot springs, and a small mist-shrouded mountain dotted with temples.

Ethnographically, Hsinchu and Miaoli Counties have a heavy concentration of Hakka, reflected in the food you'll find in many small towns. It's good to familiarise yourself with some of the staples before heading out. Atayal and Saisiyat aboriginals are also present in large numbers.

Getting around the area is pretty easy. Trains go up and down the coast all day, and there is now decent inland bus service with the Tourism Shuttle Bus (www.taiwantrip.com.tw).

Hsinchu 新竹

☎03 / POP 416,000

The oldest city in northern Taiwan, and long a base for traditional industries such as glass- and noodle-making, this laid-back, leafy town (Xīnzhú) makes for a great day trip from Taipei. The town centre spreads back from a pretty restored canal zone, bordered by small personalised shops, restaurants and cafes. Heritage buildings pop up everywhere, and even the modern streets have pleasant arcades for strolling along. Out on the coast, Hsinchu boasts a scenic oceanside bike path, and a harbour with a lively restaurant and cafe scene.

Hsinchu sprang into the modern era in 1980 with the establishment of the Hsinchu Science Park, modelled on California's Silicon Valley. Today the park houses over 400 technology companies, and accounts for 10% of GDP (for all Taiwan). This probably has something to do with why the city was voted the happiest place in Taiwan in 2012.

Sights

At the time of writing Hsinchu was opening the NT$450 million **Taiwan Pavilion** (世博台灣館, Shìbó Táiwān Guǎn; day/evening NT$200/250; 10am-9pm), taken from the 2010 Shanghai World Expo and re-assembled in a location halfway between the train station and the High Speed Rail (HSR) station. Shaped liked a futuristic sky lantern, the pavilion is a showcase for Taiwan's cutting-

Hsinchu

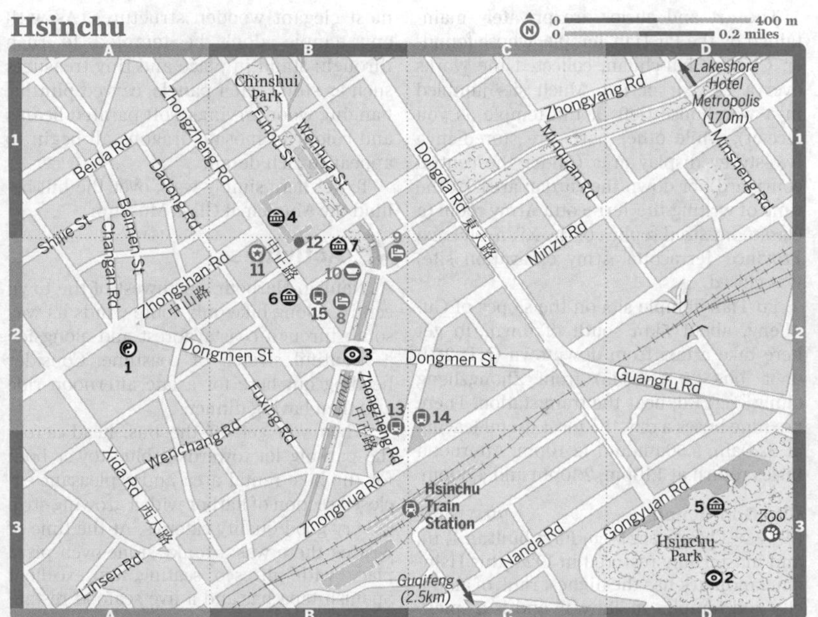

edge technology and is the centerpiece of an emerging high-tech industrial park. A taxi from the HSR or downtown will cost around NT$200.

Hsinchu was called Hsinchang by the early Chinese settlers, who built a *hsinchang* (bamboo fence) around the city to protect themselves from Taiya, Saisha and Pingpu aborigines. In 1826 a solid brick wall was constructed around the city. Only one portion of the wall remains today, the **Eastern Gate** (東門, Dōngmén), but it is in fine shape and a great central landmark.

A number of buildings from the Japanese era dot the urban landscape and are worth a nod as you wander about, including the train station, **City Hall**, the **Municipal Image Museum**, Taiwan's first air-conditioned movie theatre, and the **Reclamation Hall**. Beimen St, just north of the City God Temple, also has a number of old dwellings and traditional arcades.

★ **Guqifeng (Guqi Mountain)** ART COLLECTION
(古奇峰, Gǔqífēng; ⏲8am-6pm Sat) **FREE** This must-see art collection includes a life-size four-poster bed of pure jade, ivory dragon boats, hundreds of stunning wood and stone god statues and relief panels, and detailed carved-wood replicas (the size of two pool tables) of traditional villages and temples: the temple parade scene along the Japanese-era facades in the town of Hukou is simply marvellous.

Hsinchu

Sights

1	City God Temple	A2
2	Confucius Temple	D3
3	Eastern Gate	B2
4	Hsinchu City Hall	B1
5	Municipal Glass Museum	D3
6	Municipal Image Museum	B2
7	Reclamation Hall	B2

Sleeping

8	East City Hotel	B2
9	Sol Hotel	B2

Drinking & Nightlife

10	PAO	B2

Information

11	Foreign Affairs Police	B2
12	Hsinchu Foreigner Assistance Centre	B2

Transport

13	Bus to Guqifeng	B2
14	Bus to Nanliao Harbour	C2
15	Public Bus Hub	B2

The art and curios are privately maintained by the Pu Tian Temple, whose founder, Cheng Chai-chuan, collected the works over a 20-year period. Much sits jumbled in a warehouse (left of the temple as you face it), while other parts are stored in a two-storey display area (under the central courtyard), or down the garden area. At the time of writing the Terracotta Army room (a classroom-sized replica of the Xi'an, Shaanxi Province Terracotta Army excavation site) was closed.

Pu Tian Temple sits on the slopes of Guqifeng, about 5km south of town. To get here take a taxi from downtown (NT$250) or a bus 20 (NT$15) from Zhongzheng (Jungjeng) Rd, near the train station. There are nine buses a day, the most useful leaving at 8.20am, 9.50am and 12.40pm. Afternoon buses return at 1.10pm, 2.10pm and 4.30pm.

City God Temple TAOIST TEMPLE

(城隍廟, Chénghuáng Miào) First built in 1748, and masterfully restored in 1924, this Hsinchu landmark has the highest rank of all the city god temples in Taiwan, and is a splendid example of the fine work local artisans were capable of in the early 20th century.

Examples of this work include the elegant structure itself with sweeping swallowtail eaves, the shallow but vivid plafond ceiling, and the wealth of carved wooden brackets and beams: look for dragons, phoenixes and melons, as well as panels of birds and flowers (auspicious symbols when placed together). The *jiànniàn* (mosaic-like temple decoration) dragons on the roof are superb.

The temple is most lively during the seventh lunar month and on the 29th day of the 11th month, when the birthday of the temple god is celebrated.

Municipal Glass Museum MUSEUM

(玻璃工藝博物館, Bōlí Gōngyì Bówùguǎn; www.hcgm.gov.tw; 2 Dongda Rd, Sec 1; admission NT$20; 9am-5pm Tue-Sun) This little museum in a heritage building on the edge of a pleasant wooded park is dedicated to the local history of glassmaking, which goes back to 1880. The 1st floor exhibits recent works, while the 2nd highlights the history of glass (in Taiwan and around the world) and the various techniques used to produce glass art. A taxi here from downtown costs NT$100.

Confucius Temple CONFUCIAN TEMPLE

(孔廟, Kǒng Miào; 8.30am-4.30pm Wed-Sun) First built in 1810, this is one of Taiwan's most elegant wooden structures. As with any temple, don't be tempted to rush through: stand in place and tiny treasures such as stone relief panels, carved plinths, hanging woodcarvings, soft painted beams and colourful mosaic dragons all begin to appear in rich detail.

To get here simply walk over the hill behind the Municipal Glass Museum.

Activities

At Nanliao Harbour, northwest of the town centre, a long bike-only route winds its way south through coastal forest and alongside a beautiful stretch of coastline. Consider heading out here for a late afternoon ride and then having dinner.

When you get off the bus, head across the parking lot towards a blue tower both for the bike rental area and a pleasant enclosed section of harbor with a growing strip of very good quality eateries. At the time of writing there was a funky stone-oven pizza place with alfresco seating, an excellent Spanish tapa bar and a live seafood restaurant extending onto a boat.

To get to the harbour catch bus 15 (NT$15, 30 minutes, every 15 to 30 minutes) outside Sogo on Minzu Rd. The last return bus from the harbour is at 6.30pm. After that time, walk to Dongda Rd (the main road in) and then along that for five minutes to the bus stop across from a 7-Eleven. The last bus from here is at 9.20pm.

Sleeping

Hsinchu has lots of hotels that mostly serve the people working at the Science Park.

East City Hotel HOTEL $

(東城精品旅館, Dōngchéng Jīngpǐn Lǔguǎn; 522 2648; 1 Lane 5, Fuhou St, 府後街5巷1號; d/tw incl simple breakfast from NT$800/1200; @) Across from the canal and surrounded by restaurants and cafes, this is the obvious budget choice in Hsinchu. Doubles are a low NT$700 on weekdays.

Lakeshore Hotel Metropolis BUSINESS HOTEL $$

(煙波大飯店, Yānbō Dà Fàndiàn; 612 0000; www.lakeshore.com.tw; 177 Minsheng Rd; r from NT$3600, discounts of 30%; @) This branch of the Lakeshore chain is not near the lake, but it's an excellent-value midrange business hotel, with smart modern rooms and a great morning buffet spread.

Sol Hotel HOTEL $$$
(迎曦大飯店, Yíngxī Dàfàndiàn; ☎534 7266; www.solhotel.com.tw; 10 Wenhua St, 文化街10號; d/tw incl breakfast NT$5000/8000; @ 📶) A solid upmarket hotel, with good English-speaking service and in a great location just across from the canal. Book online for a 30% discount.

Eating & Drinking

In addition to Nanliao Harbour, the train station area is chock-a-block full of places to eat, both on the streets and in the shopping malls. The area around the City God Temple has a lively and well-known food market. If you enjoy sampling local fare try the meatballs (貢丸, *gòngwán*) and flat rice noodles (粄條, *bǎntiáo*). The latter are dried by wind, which means no one makes them like Hsinchu (the Windy City) makes them.

The canal area has a load of Japanese sushi, barbecue and lunchbox restaurants. **PAO** (卡莎蕾義式餐廳; 30 Lane 96, Zhongzheng Rd), on the 2nd floor above one of these, is a relaxing place for a coffee. Though closed at the time of writing, PAO should have reopened by the time you read this.

Information

Hsinchu City Website (www.hcccb.gov.tw) Excellent online guide to the city.

Hsinchu Foreigner Assistance Centre (☎521 6121; http://foreigner.hccg.gov.tw; 107 Zhongyang Rd; ⏲8am-5pm Mon-Fri; @ 📶) Travel, business, health and living information.

Getting There & Around

Roaming taxis are not numerous in Hsinchu. Get your hotel to call for a taxi before you head out, or keep the number of the driver you've found.

HIGH SPEED RAIL

Travel to/from Taipei costs NT$290 (35 minutes, every half-hour). Shuttle buses (30 minutes, frequent) connect the HSR and the public bus hub on Zhongzheng Rd. A taxi costs NT$300.

TRAIN

Hsinchu is on the main west-coast line so there are trains to all major cities. Frequent trains leave Taipei (fast/slow NT$177/144, one hour/1½ hours).

Around Hsinchu

The water is not the cleanest along the west coast but the conditions are great for windsurfing. For lessons and rentals contact **Spot X-Sport** (www.spot.com.tw), which also has simple lodging in the **Jhunan Seashore Forest Park** (假日之森, Jiàrì Zhī Sēn), 100m from the sea in a quaint little hamlet.

Dabajianshan 大霸尖山

The most famous climb in the Hsinchu area is to Dabajianshan (Dàbàjiān Shān; Big Chief Pointed Mountain; 3492m). The barrel-peaked Daba is one of the most iconic high mountain images in Taiwan and is a sacred spot to the Atayal.

The hike takes three days to complete, including two overnight stays on the mountain in **99 Cabin** (99山莊, Jiǔjiǔ Shānzhuāng) at 2800m. For an account of the hike with fabulous pictures check out **Hiking Taiwan** (http://hikingtaiwan.wordpress.com).

The route starts at **Guanwu Forest Recreation Area** (Guānwù Sēnlín Yóulè Qū; http://recreation.forest.gov.tw; ⏲7am-5pm), about 28km or an hour's drive from Qingquan. To begin, hikers walk a 19.5km (four to six hours) forestry road (closed to vehicles) to the old trailhead. This is followed by a 4km (three- to four-hour) hike to 99 Cabin. The next day, hikers leave 99 Cabin and hike 7.5km (four to five hours) to the base of Dabajianshan peak (you can't climb to the very summit anymore).

Most hikers return to 99 Cabin the same day, and then head back to Guanwu the following morning. But it is also possible to hike another three days from Dabajianshan to Snow Mountain along what is known as the Holy Ridge (p157).

Because Dabajianshan is within Sheipa National Park (p156), mountain and national-park permits are required to climb it.

Guesthouses in Qingquan can arrange transport to and from Guanwu FRA if you request this in advance.

Beipu 北埔

☎03 / POP 10,400

This small Hsinchu County town (Běipǔ) pulls in the visitors with its Hakka cultural heritage, and makes for an excellent morning or afternoon excursion (especially when combined with a drive through the picturesque surrounding countryside). There's an authentic feel to the town, and it's one of the best places to try Hakka pounded tea. Beipu is small and easy to navigate. The bus drops you off in the heart of things.

WORTH A TRIP

EMEI LAKE: HOME OF THE ORIENTAL BEAUTY

A short drive from Beipu, pretty **Emei Lake** (峨眉湖, Éméi Hú) serves as a reservoir for farmers growing Oriental Beauty tea. This highly oxidised oolong is renowned for several things: 1) Queen Elizabeth gave it its name; 2) it's completely lacking in astringency; and 3) it needs small crickets to bite the young shoots for the full flavour to come out.

When brewed the tea is red in colour, and has a naturally sweet and slightly spicy flavour. Like high-mountain oolong it's one of those teas that is immediately appealing, and countries such as China and India are now getting in on the action. From what we've heard, most of what is sold in the area is actually grown in China. For real Oriental Beauty it's best to shop in Pinglin.

While the tea is the lake area's claim to fame, visitors will most likely first notice an airport-terminal-sized (and -looking) monastery, and the 72m **Maitreya Buddha Statue**, built by the World Maitreya Great Tao Organization (www.maitreya.org.tw). You should be able to visit both by the time you read this.

Sights

The following is written as a short tour from the bus stop on Jhong Jheng Rd (中正路), across from an OK convenience store.

From the bus stop head towards the hill. In a minute or so you'll see old buildings on either side of the road. On the right is **Tian Shui Hall** (天水堂, Tiān Shuǐ Táng), the largest private traditional three-sided compound in Beipu. To the left is **Jinguangfu** (金廣福公館, Jīnguǎngfú Gōngguǎn), a heritage house from 1835. Unfortunately you can't go inside the buildings, but if you continue up the narrow alley between them you'll reach a very quaint teahouse, the Well.

Facing Tian Shui Hall, go right. Shortly you'll pass **Jian Asin Mansion** (姜阿新故居, Jiāngāxīn Gù Jū) on the left. This two-storey Western-style house was built by a rich tea merchant.

From the mansion it's just a hop to the **Zhitian (Citian) Temple** (慈天宮, Cítiān Gōng), a charming traditional temple (established in 1835) dedicated to Guanyin. Some notable features to look for include the carved **stone pillars**, both out front and especially within the main hall (which features tales in relief from *The Twenty-Four Filial Exemplars*, a classic work promoting Confucian values), the painted beams, the assorted carved wooden brackets, and the panels of excellent **cochin pottery** (brightly coloured, glazed pottery) to the right and left of the main hall. On the roof look for an assortment of crustaceans (representing official promotion) and shaggy yellow lions in *jiǎnniàn*.

To the left of the temple (as you face it) is a small passageway; walk to its curvy end. Notice a few loose stones? That's not an accident. In the wilder days of Taiwan's history the narrow passageways into Beipu were lined with the occasional loose stone so that intruders could be heard approaching.

As you exit the temple the street directly in front of you is **Beipu Street** (北埔街). There are a number of old buildings along the first few blocks and many pleasant snack shops, teahouses and cafes. There's also a tiny alley immediately to your left with a couple of old teahouses.

One block up Beipu Street, at the intersection with Nansing Rd (南興街), turn right and walk back to the OK convenience store. This is where you got off the bus, and where you can catch it again back to Jhudong.

Eating & Drinking

Beipu is almost 90% Hakka and in almost every restaurant you'll find Hakka staples explained with picture menus. Try mountain chicken (土雞, *tǔ jī*), fried tofu and *kejia xiaochao* (客家小炒; stir-fried strips of pork, squid, veggies and tofu).

Smaller shops sell a variety of dried goods (as a mobile people the Hakka relied on dried foods), in particular persimmons. Around town you will also find vendors selling tasty *lei cha* (擂茶, *léi chá;* pounded tea, see p166) flavoured ice cream.

People don't linger in Beipu, so expect most shops to close by early evening.

Well TEAHOUSE
(水井茶堂, Shuǐjǐng Chátáng; ⏲10am-6pm) One of the best places to try *lei cha* (擂茶, *léi chá;* pounded tea) is in this rustic Hakka house. You can sit inside at tables or on wooden floors, or even outside on a deck under the plum trees. A set of *lei cha* ingredients costs NT$300 plus NT$100 for each person.

Getting There & Away

From the Hsinchu High Speed Rail (Exit 4) catch a **Tourism Shuttle Bus** (www.taiwantrip.com.tw) heading to Lion's Head Mountain. Buses run from 8.22am hourly on weekdays and every 30 minutes on weekends. The last bus from Beipu leaves at 5.25pm on weekdays and 6.25pm on weekends.

Shitoushan 獅頭山

ELEV 492M

Shitoushan (Shītóushān) is a foothill on the border of Miaoli and Hsinchu Counties. Beautiful dense forests and rugged rock faces define the topography, but if you ask anyone it is the temples tucked into sandstone caves and hugging the slopes that have given the place its fame. Shitoushan is sacred ground for the island's Buddhists and draws big weekend crowds, with people coming to worship or simply enjoy the beauty and tranquillity of the mountain.

There are several ways to start your explorations. The easiest is from the **Quanhua Temple bus stop** (in a large car park). Head up the stone stairs and through the arch to **Futian Temple** (輔天宮, Fǔtiān Gōng), dedicated to the Ksitigarbha Bodhisattva, one of the most beloved divinities in Japan (where he is known as Jizō). To the left is an office where you check in if you are spending the night.

From this temple head up the stairs to the left (as you face Futian Temple) for an overview of the temple rooftop, a dazzling landscape of soaring swallowtail ridgelines and vivid decorative dragons, carps and phoenixes. At the top of the stairs is **Quanhua Tang** (勸化堂, Quànhuà Táng), built from 1900 to 1915. Dedicated to the Jade Emperor, it is the only Taoist temple on the mountain. Altogether there are 11 temples, five on the front side of the mountain, six on the back, as well as numerous smaller shrines, arches and pagodas. Give yourself at least three hours to explore the area, or an overnight stay for the full effect.

On the other side of the mountain, connected by a walking path/paved road, is the **Lion's Head Mountain Visitor Centre** (⌚9am-6pm). The centre is a pleasant place to grab a meal (set meals NT$180) or a map. There are several good short hikes starting from the centre.

Visitors (including non-Buddhists) are allowed to stay overnight at **Quanhua Tang** (Chuanhua Hall; ☎037-822 020/063; tw NT$1000). Excellent vegetarian meals are NT$80 each, but if that doesn't appeal to you there are stalls and shops lining the back car park and even a cafe on the way up the stairs to the hall. The old rules forbidding talk during meals or couples sleeping together are no longer enforced, but do be on your best behaviour.

Getting There & Away

If taking the bus it's highly recommended you go on a weekday. Shitoushan itself can be very crowded on weekends and buses jammed pack.

From the Hsinchu High Speed Rail (Exit 4) catch a Tourism Shuttle Bus (www.taiwantrip.com.tw) heading to Lion's Head Mountain. The trip is one hour and buses run from 8.22am, hourly on weekdays and every 30 minutes on weekends. The last bus from Lion's Head Mountain leaves at 5pm on weekdays and 6pm on weekends. Alight at the visitor centre and then either follow the hiking path/road to the temple areas or, better, catch the Lion's Head Mountain Nanzhuang Route (all-day pass NT$50) to the Quanhua Temple (the buses connect), the first stop on this line.

Nanzhuang 南庄

Off the travellers' radar until recent years, this former logging and coal-mining centre has changed little since Japanese times, and many streets and villages have retained their signature clapboard facades. The food is also delicious and varied, reflecting the diverse ethnic make-up of the residents: Hakka, Taiwanese as well as aboriginal Taiya and Saisiyat.

Nanzhuang is set in the foothills of the Snow Mountains, one of the greenest and most enchanting regions in northern Taiwan. There are only a couple of roads running through the region, so orienting yourself is not hard with a basic map. In essence, if you follow County Rd 124甲 as it makes a big loop off Provincial Hwy 3, you've covered most of Nanzhuang. If you take a side trip up Township Rd 21苗, you will have seen everything.

Sights & Activities

Nanzhuang Village VILLAGE

(南庄) A good place to start exploring in Nanzhuang Village is the **visitor information centre** (www.trimt-nsa.gov.tw/cht/main.aspx; ⌚8.30am-5.30pm). Across the street look for a stone washing area, still used by

OFF THE BEATEN TRACK

COMMUNITIES IN THE CLOUDS: SMANGUS & QINGQUAN

Some of the most remote places in Taiwan are small aboriginal hamlets tucked into the Snow Mountains. If you are looking to get truly off the beaten path and explore a way of life far removed from the coastal cities, consider the Atayal villages of Smangus and Qingquan.

Smangus

Deep in the forested mountains of Hsinchu County lies the Atayal settlement of **Smangus** (司馬庫斯, Sīmǎkùsī; www.smangus.org), the last village in Taiwan to be connected to the electric grid (in 1980). For centuries life went on pretty much as it always had, with hunting and farming for millet, taro, yams and bamboo forming the backbone of the local economy.

In the early 1990s a forest of **ancient red cypress trees** was discovered nearby and lowland Taiwanese began to flock here in numbers. There was intense competition between villagers for customers, until in 2004 a cooperative (modelled on the Israeli kibbutz) was formed to manage lodging and the area's resources. Fortunes could have been made selling out to developers but instead the village has admirably gone the local and sustainable route.

Directions to the village are posted on the website (in Chinese). It's a long drive – at least five hours from Taipei – but everyone knows the place once you get closer. **Homestay lodging** (☎03-584 7688; ⏲9am-6pm) is booked through one office and ranges from NT$1600 for a basic double to NT$5000 for a four-person cabin. Meals are taken in the communal dining hall.

The main attraction in the area, besides the chance to learn about Atayal life, is the old tree grove, which is reached by a clear 6km trail (about five hours return). The oldest tree is reported to be 2700 years old.

Qingquan (Cingyuan, Chingchuan)

County Rd 122 runs up a deep river valley in a rugged, chillingly beautiful part of the country that is often completely cut off from the rest because of landslides. The last major village along the road before Guanwu Forest Recreation Area is Qingquan (清泉, Qīngquán), like Smangus, another remote Atayal settlement that seems to be perputually drifting in and out of the mountain mist.

The village has a good **hot spring** (public pools NT$100; ⏲9am-6pm Mon-Fri, to 10pm Sat & Sun) overlooking the river, and not far away is the **Syakaro Historic Trail** (霞喀羅古道, Xiákèluó Gǔdào); you'll need a local to take you to the trailhead in a jeep. The 24km-long trail was used by Atayal for hunting and inter-village transport until the Japanese era when it became a patrol route. Also check out the local Catholic church. Father Barry Martinson has been living in the village for over 30 years and is a fount of local knowledge.

There are a number of restaurants in the area, including an outdoor eating area in the big parking lot as you enter town. If you want to stay in the village, try **Palm Tree House** (棕櫚居, Zōnglǘ Jū; ☎0911-255 766; htpp://palm.okgo.tw; d/tw incl breakfast NT$2500/4000, 20% weekday discounts) just behind the house of travel writer San Mao (三毛, Echo Chen). The attached restaurant serves good set meals (NT$250 to NT$420) of mountain chicken, fish or pork.

To get here from Hsinchu catch a frequent bus to Jhudong (竹東) from the Hsinchu Bus Company (新竹客運) station, just left of the Hsinchu train station as you exit. Get off at Xiagongguan (下公館; 50 minutes) where there are connections to Qingquan. There are eight buses a day: useful departures are 8.40am, 9.20am, 10.40am and 12.20pm. The last bus back to Xiagongguan from Qingquan is 4.55pm.

older residents for cleaning their clothes. Behind this starts a stone-stair alley called **Osmanthus Lane** (桂花巷, Guìhuā Xiàng), one of the more charming 'old streets' in Taiwan, with stalls and shops selling Hakka food and local snacks, many flavored with sweet *Osmanthus* (a type of flowering plant). This is also the place to go if you need a gourmet coffee while in town.

The visitor centre is the hub for buses coming from Shitoushan and Jhudong, as well as buses heading further into Nanzhuang.

Saisiyat Folklore Museum MUSEUM
(賽夏族民俗文物館, Sàixiàzú Mínsú Wénwù Guǎn; ⌚9am-5pm Tue-Sun) FREE This lakeside museum is dedicated to the Saisiyat (賽夏族) and their intriguing Festival of the Short People (賽夏族矮靈祭, Sàixiàzú Ǎlíngjì, the Pas-ta'ai Ritual). The Saisiyat ('the true people'), with just over 5000 members, are one of the smallest aboriginal groups in Taiwan and every three years they hold their festival in honour of the Ta'ai, a mythical pygmy race.

According to legend, the Ta'ai and Saisiyat once lived in peace, but after the Ta'ai began molesting Saisiyat women they were killed off. Famine resulted and the festival arose as a way of appeasing the vengeful spirits who were clearly at the root of the disaster. The festival is held beside the museum at Xiang Tian Hu (向天湖, Xiàngtiān Hú), a small lake nearly always shrouded in mist.

The festival is held on a full moon around the 15th day of the 10th lunar month every two years, with a particularly large event held every 10 years. The next regular festival will be held in 2014, with the big one to be held in 2016.

Buses to the lake and museum leave from the visitor centre.

Luchang Village VILLAGE
(鹿場; Lù Chǎng) If you continue along Township Rd 21苗 past the turn-off for Xiangtan Lake, you'll run up a deep rugged canyon and eventually to the high-altitude Luchang Village. It's stunningly beautiful up here and and a few kilometres further up the road is the trailhead to the 2220m-high **Jiali Mountain** (加里山, Jiālǐ Shān). Note that there is no bus to Luchang.

Sleeping & Eating

There are dozens of pleasant B&Bs scattered around Nanzhuang, most charging around NT$2000 to NT$3000 a night for a double. There's also a campground off Township Rd 21苗 in Donghe Village. The Tourism Shuttle Bus stops directly across from here (東河吊橋, Donghe Suspension Bridge stop). Nearby Shitoushan is also a good option.

For meals, head to Osmanthus Lane in Nanzhuang Village or to one of dozens of obvious restaurants off the main roads, which usually have set meals of four to five dishes for two people for NT$400 to NT$500. Locally raised trout is popular, as are Hakka staples such as mountain chicken (土雞, tǔ jī), fried tofu and *kejia xiaochao* (客家小炒; stir-fried strips of pork, squid, veggies and tofu). Most places have picture menus.

Pu Yuan Villa GUESTHOUSE $$
(南江璞園, Nánjiāng Pú Yuán; ☎0939-851 652; www.037825925.com.tw; d incl breakfast from NT$2000; ☏) Just outside town is this cosy two-storey guesthouse with large rooms and a garden setting. Excellent homemade breakfasts are included and the **East River Spa Garden** (東江溫泉, Dōngjiāng Wēnquán) hot springs (under reconstruction at the time of writing and slated to open in 2014) are just a 100m walk down the road.

To get here, take the Tourism Shuttle Bus from the visitor centre heading to Xiangtan Lake and get off at the Dongjiang He Tribe bus stop. You can also walk here from the visitor centre in about 20 minutes.

Getting There & Around

A superb area for biking or driving, Nanzhuang is now also easily visited by bus. It's best if you visit here from Shitoushan, but if you want to come directly catch a **Nanzhuang Route Tourism Shuttle Bus** (www.taiwantrip.com.tw) from Jhudong train station. Buses (NT$91, one hour) run hourly from 8.30am to 5pm. The last return bus is at 6.40pm.

To get to Xiangtan Lake and the campground, catch the Xiangtan Lake Route bus from the visitor centre. Buses (NT$44, 30 minutes) run about every hour from 9.30am to 5.30pm. The last bus leaves the lake at 6pm.

There's also a bus line that runs from the visitor centre down the scenic Penglai River to the giant Xianshan Temple.

Scooters (per day NT$500) can be rented on the main street in Nanzhuang with just an international driving permit.

Taian Hot Springs

泰安溫泉

☎037

There are hot springs all over Taiwan, and beautiful mountains for hiking too, but we still think Taian (Tàiān Wēnquán) is special. For one thing, it has hot-spring water so good that 100 years ago the Japanese built an officers' club here.

In a remote mountainous corner of southeastern Miaoli County, just on the boundary of rugged Sheipa National Park, Taian is not precisely defined on most maps, but is more or less the region that County Rd 62 runs through. Beginning just outside the town of Wenshui, County Rd 62 runs for 16km alongside the Wenshui River before ending in a car park just below the Japanese Police Officers' Club. Most visitors stay within the last 3km stretch, in an area known as Jinshui Village (Jǐnshuǐ Cūn; population 200).

As you drive up County Rd 62, pay attention to the make-up of the people in the villages around you. At the start, they will be almost exclusively Hakka (evident both in the look of the people and the food on offer), while further inland Atayal aboriginals predominate. (Taian is in fact the last remaining Atayal area with elderly women who have facial tattoos; the last Atayal man with tattoos died in 2013.)

This pattern is common in mountainous regions in Taiwan. As late immigrants to Taiwan, Hakka groups often found the best land on the plains long settled. By purchase or pressure, Hakka groups acquired their share, often forcing aboriginal groups even further into the hinterlands.

Activities

Hot Springs

Taian's alkaloid carbonic waters are clear, tasteless and almost odourless. They are reputedly good for treating skin problems and nervousness. Your skin will certainly glow after a soak, and with three spring sources there's plenty of water to go around. Most places offer good discounts on weekdays and in the low season, May to September.

★Cedarwood Villa HOT SPRING
(竹美山閣-溫泉會館, Zhúměi Shāngé Wēnquán Huìguǎn; ☎941 800; www.cedarwood-villa.com.tw; per hr NT$800-1000) Though slate walled and not made of cedarwood at all, this quiet and stylish hotel offers large marble soaking rooms with huge windows overlooking a superb stretch of Taian's mountain. It's the kind of place you take someone special to.

The hotel has rooms for overnight stays, and is found on its own on the side of a mountain up a rough side road.

Sunrise Hot Spring Hotel HOT SPRING
(日出溫泉渡假飯店, Rìchū Wēnquán Dùjià Fàndiàn; public pools unlimited time NT$450; ⏲8am-10pm) This wood-and-stone multipool outdoor complex is designed to let you take in the mountain views as you bathe. There are also private rooms for NT$1400 per hour.

Hiking

You should always check with locals about the conditions before heading out. This is a rough area. Try to finish higher trails before mid-afternoon, as fog can obscure the views and make it easy to get lost.

LEI CHA

If you pronounce it incorrectly, *lei cha* (擂茶, *léi chá*) sounds like 'tired tea', but this hearty brew was designed to do anything but make you sleepy. It was a farmer's drink, rich and thick and full of nutrients and calories. In the old days, Hakka farmers would drink it both during and after work in the tobacco fields in order to fortify their bodies. Or so the story goes.

Very likely, *lei cha* is a modern invention (like the Scottish tartan), or at best a family drink that has been cleverly promoted as an authentic part of Taiwan's Hakka heritage. In any case, it's everywhere now, and authentic or not, it's definitely part of the Taiwan experience.

Lei cha means 'pounded tea', and that's exactly what you must do before you can drink it. First you will be given a wooden pestle and a large porcelain bowl with a small amount of green tea leaves, sesame seeds, nuts and grains in the bottom. Using the pestle, grind the ingredients in the bowl to a fine mush. Your host will then add hot water and dole out the 'tea' in cups. At this moment, or perhaps earlier, you will be given a small bowl of puffed rice. Add the rice to the drink and consume it before the kernels get soggy.

If this sounds like your cup of your tea (and really, it is delicious), head to the teahouses around Beipu's Zhitian Temple, or further afield at Sanyi's Sheng Shing train station (p168), or Meinong.

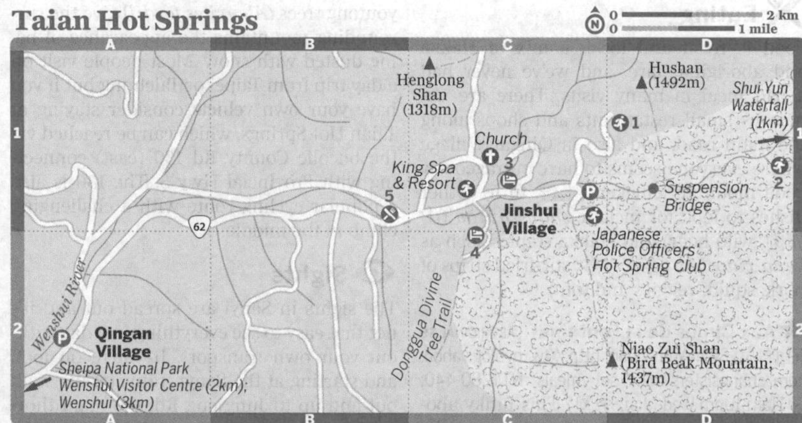

Taian Hot Springs

Activities, Courses & Tours

1 Cedarwood Villa ... D1
2 Shui Yun Waterfall ... D1
Sunrise Hot Spring Hotel ... (see 3)

Sleeping

3 Sunrise Hot Spring Hotel ... C1
4 Tenglong Hot Spring Resort ... C2

Eating

5 Aux Cimes de la Fontaine ... B1

Shui Yun Waterfall WATERFALL

(水雲瀑布, Shŭiyún Pùbù) The path to this thundering waterfall goes along a river, through a forest and up a canyon. The return trip takes three to four hours and there are several deep and safe swimming holes for cooling off along the way.

Start at the car park at the end of County Rd 62 and follow the trail by the river for 1km until you reach a suspension bridge. Cross it and climb the stairs on the other side. The trail now enters the forest and splits. Take the lower path (the upper leads to Hushan) and at the river follow the left bank up the canyon until it narrows at a rock face. The falls are just around the corner up a side channel.

Hushan HIKING

(虎山, Hŭshān) Getting to the top of craggy Hushan (1492m) is the most difficult of Taian's hikes. Start on the trail to Shui Yun Waterfall and when the path splits after the suspension bridge, take the upper route. Pay attention to the ribbons and markers as the route is not always clear. The return trip takes about five hours.

Sleeping

There are at least a dozen hotels in the area, the fancier ones charging NT$5000 to NT$8000 a night and the more basic charging NT$2000 to NT$3000 a night.

Tenglong Hot Spring Resort HOTEL $$

(騰龍溫泉山莊, Ténglóng Wēnquán Shānzhuāng; ☎941 002; www.teng-long.com.tw; campsite NT$500, 2-/4-person cabins NT$3000/4200, weekday discounts 25%) The cabins are basic but have hot-spring water pumped in, and the resort grounds are nicely cared for and surrounded by lush forest. Rooms include free use of the nude segregated hot-spring pools (otherwise per person NT$220). The campground is simple and includes hot showers but can be very noisy if a big student group is staying.

Tenglong (which looks like a little village as you drive past) is reached by a small side road and bridge across from the King Spa & Resort. In the summer the resort grounds swarm with swallowtail butterflies.

Sunrise Hot Spring Hotel HOTEL $$$

(日出溫泉渡假飯店; ☎941 988; www.hothotel.com.tw; d from NT$5500, 30% weekday discount) This stylish hot-spring hotel makes liberal use of wood and stone and Southeast Asian decor in its public areas. Rooms are a little more staid, but feature large stone tubs (big enough for two Westerners) with open mountain views. Breakfast is included in the room price, as is free use of the outdoor hot-spring complex.

Eating

Food is fresh and local, a mix of Hakka and aboriginal fare, and we've never had a bad meal in many visits. There are numerous small restaurants and shops along the main road, and also in Qingan Village where everyone seems to have outrageously good mountain chicken (土雞, tǔ jī). Other dishes to look for include *shān zhūròu* (山豬肉, wild boar) and Hakka staples such as *kejia xiaochao* (客家小炒; stir-fried strips of pork, squid, veggies and tofu).

★Aux Cimes de la Fontaine ABORIGINAL $$
(山吻泉, Shān Wěn Quán; http://tw.myblog.yahoo.com/changsisters-mkf; set meals NT$280-440; ⏲11am-10pm Wed-Mon;) This funky aboriginal restaurant and cafe overhangs the Wenshui River; its name in Chinese reads 'Mountain Kiss Spring'. The two aboriginal sisters who run the place whip up some fine meals (mostly hot pot and hot plates), and play good music to boot.

Information

The **Sheipa National Park Wenshui Visitor Centre** (www.spnp.gov.tw; ⏲9am-4.30pm Tue-Sun) sits at the start of County Rd 62. It doesn't have any information on travelling in Taian, but it does offer a good overview of the history of the Atayal and Hakka settlers in the area.

DANGERS & ANNOYANCES

Taian suffers frequent landslides, which can wash out roads and change the course and look of riverbeds. Avoid the area after heavy rains or earthquakes.

Getting There & Around

You need your own transport.

Sanyi 三義

☎037 / POP 5000

Over 100 years ago, a Japanese officer discovered that camphor grew in abundance in the hills around Sanyi (Sānyì), a small Miaoli County town. Since camphor makes for excellent wood products (it's aromatic, extremely heavy and can resist termites), the officer wisely established a wood business. Over time, Sanyi became *the* woodcarving region in Taiwan and today nearly half the population is engaged in the business in one way or another.

The best time to visit Sanyi is in April when the white flowers of the blooming youtong trees *(Aleurites fordii)* give the surrounding mountains the appearance of being dusted with snow. Most people visit on a day trip from Taipei or Taichung but if you have your own vehicle consider staying at Taian Hot Springs, which can be reached via the bucolic County Rd 130 (east) connecting with Provincial Hwy 3. The 130 is also a popular cycling route with a challenging climb in the middle.

Sights

The sights in Sanyi are spread out and it's not that easy to see everything in a day without your own transport. If you're on foot, and starting at the Sanyi train station, walk out and up to Jungjeng Rd, the main thoroughfare in town, and turn left (everything you want to see is left). The turn-offs for the old train station and the woodcarving museum (which are in opposite directions) are about 2km down the road. The Sheng Shing train station is another 5km away, however, and the museum is about 1km. The main commercial street with all the woodcarving shops is straight ahead. There are signs in English.

Woodcarving

Woodcarving is the lifeblood of the town, and on Jungjeng Rd alone there are over 200 shops selling an array of carved items. We're not talking dull signposts here, but 3m-tall cypress statues of savage-faced folk gods, delicate lattice windows and beautiful traditional furniture. You can come here with the intention of buying, but if you just like to browse and enjoy the work of skilled artisans you won't be disappointed.

Most stores are clustered on a few blocks of Jungjeng Rd just down from the wood museum, and around the wood museum itself. Stores close around 6pm, though a few stay open until 10pm or later on weekends.

Miaoli Wood Sculpture Museum MUSEUM
(苗栗木雕博物館, Miáolì Mùdiāo Bówùguǎn; ⏲9am-5pm) FREE Exhibits include informative displays on the origins of woodcarving in Sanyi, a knockout collection of Buddhas and Taoist gods, some gorgeous traditional household furniture and temple architectural features. Unfortunately, there is very little English.

Sheng Shing Train Station SCENIC AREA
(勝興火車站, Shèngxīng Huǒchēzhàn) Built during the Japanese era and without the use of

nails, this charming train station was once the highest stop (at 480m) along the Western Trunk Line. After it closed in 1997, a small tourist village soon popped up, filling the old brick houses with all manner of teahouses, cafes and Hakka restaurants.

Four kilometres past the station stand the picturesque ruins of the **Long Deng Viaduct** (龍騰斷橋, Lóngténg Duàn Qiáo), destroyed in a 7.3-magnitude earthquake in 1930. The terracotta brick arches are held together with a sticky-rice and clam-shell mortar.

If you have a vehicle (especially a bike) consider continuing up the road to pretty **Liyu Reservoir** (鯉魚潭水庫, Lǐyú Tán Shuǐkù).

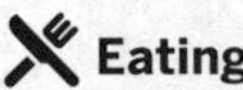

Eating

Near Sheng Shing train station or the museum there is no end of places to eat and drink traditional Hakka fare such as mountain chicken (土雞, *tǔ jī*), fried tofu and *kejia xiaochao* as well as *lei cha*. Most places have picture menus.

Getting There & Away

There are hourly afternoon trains from Taipei (NT$228, 2½ hours); 7.05am and 8.17am trains (NT$77, one hour) from Hsinchu; and hourly trains from Taichung (NT$50, 30 minutes).

Taroko National Park & the East Coast

Includes ➡

Best Views

- Taroko Gorge (p179)
- Sixty Stone Mountain (p196)
- Qingshui Cliffs (p182)
- Shitiping (p187)
- Luye Gaotai (p197)

Off the Beaten Track

- Walami Trail (p195)
- South Cross-Island Highway (p200)
- Liji Badlands (p198)
- County Road 197 (p198)
- Loshan Scenic Area (p196)

Why Go?

Much is made of the old Portuguese name for Taiwan, Ilha Formosa, which translates as 'the Beautiful Isle'. Well, it's this part of the country that they gave it to, and this part to which it still applies best.

The eastern landscape is dominated by towering sea cliffs and marble gorges, rice fields and wooded mountain ranges. There are no bad views here, and if you spot a worried look on a traveller's face, it means 'I hope they don't ever ruin the east'.

The east is Taiwan's premier outdoor playground, and cyclists have discovered an ideal environment combining knockout scenery, good roads and plenty of cosy little B&Bs. Others find the high concentration of indigenous people gives the region an appealing distinction – and a less manic vibe than the west. Just look at the top speed limit: 70km/h! You don't rush through the east; you savour it.

When to Go

Hualien

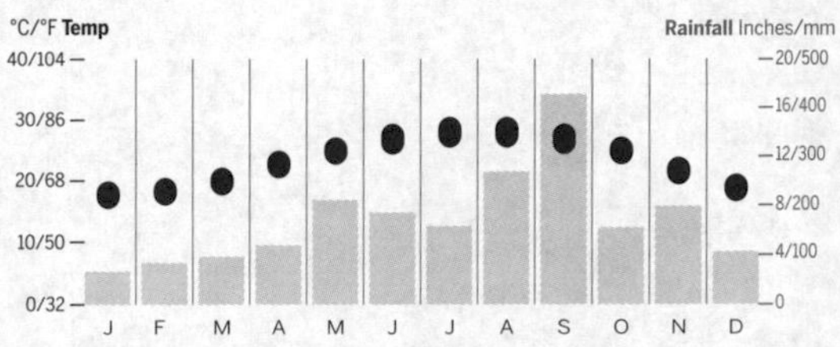

Jan Good time for beating the crowds at Taroko National Park.

Jul & Aug Aboriginal festivals all summer long.

Sep–Dec The best months for biking.

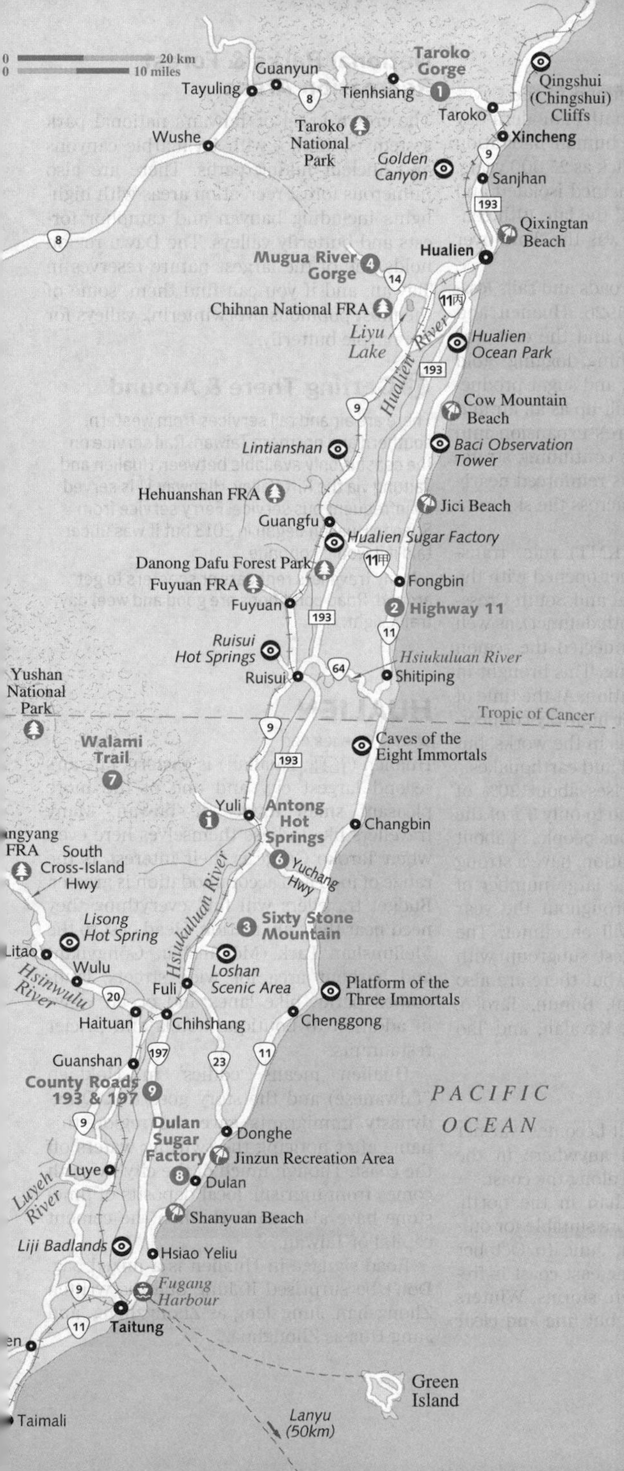

Taroko National Park & the East Coast Highlights

1. Hike ancient hunting trails and marvel at marble canyon walls in **Taroko Gorge** (p179).
2. Cycle down the winding coastline on **Highway 11** (p185).
3. Photograph the magical floral landscape on **Sixty Stone Mountain** (p196).
4. Swim in pools of crystal-blue water in the **Mugua River Gorge** (p190).
5. Join aboriginal festivals all summer long (p195).
6. Soak in wild and tamed hot springs like **Antong Hot Springs** all over the east (p194).
7. Retrace colonial history and nature-watch on the **Walami Trail** (p195).
8. Check out a thriving local art and music scene at **Dulan Sugar Factory** (p188).
9. Roam the back country on **County Road 197** (p198).

History

Archaeological remains found in the Caves of the Eight Immortals, south of modern-day Shitiping, date the first human habitation on the east coast as far back as 25,000 years. However, the region remained isolated and primarily aboriginal until the late 19th century. To Taiwanese, this was the 'land over the mountains'.

Under Japanese rule, roads and rails lessened the isolation (by 1926, Hualien and Taitung were connected) and the east was gradually opened to fishing, logging, gold mining, tobacco growing and sugar production. Taitung was also built up as an air and naval base for the empire's expansion into the Pacific. (The region's continuing strategic military importance is reinforced nearly daily with F-16s roaring across the sky from Chih-hang Air Base.)

Under Kuomintang (KMT) rule, transport to the east was further opened with the completion of the Central and South Cross-Island Highways (now both defunct), as well as railway lines that connected the region with Taipei and Kaohsiung. This brought in a fresh round of immigration. At the time of writing, a faster and safer highway connecting Suao and Hualien was in the works, but plagued by heavy rainfall and earthquakes.

The east coast comprises about 20% of Taiwan's land, but is home to only 3% of the population. The indigenous people, at about one-quarter of the population, have a strong influence, reflected in the large number of annual festivals held throughout the year and the food visitors will encounter. The Amis make up the largest subgroup with about 140,000 members, but there are also smaller groups of Atayal, Bunun, Taroko, Paiwan, Rukai, Puyuma, Kavalan, and Tao (on Lanyu).

Climate

As you go further south it becomes warmer and more tropical, and anywhere in the mountains is cooler than along the coast.

Summers are dryer than in the north, which makes the area more suitable for outdoor activities. However, June to October is typhoon season and the east coast is frequently battered by severe storms. Winters can be chilly and damp, but fine and clear days are common.

National Parks & Forest Recreation Areas

The crown jewel of Taiwan's national park system is Taroko, with its marble canyons and ancient hiking paths. There are also numerous forest recreation areas with highlights including banyan and camphor forests and butterfly valleys. The Dawu region holds one of the largest nature reserves in Taiwan, and if you can find them, some of the most populous overwintering valleys for the purple butterfly.

ℹ Getting There & Around

There are air and rail services from western, southern and northern Taiwan. Rail service on the coast is only available between Hualien and Taitung via the Rift Valley. Highway 11 is served by infrequent bus service. Ferry service from Suao to Hualien began in 2013 but it was uncertain if it would continue.

Many travellers rent cars or scooters to get around. Road conditions are good and weekday traffic light.

HUALIEN

☎03 / POP 108,000

Hualien (花蓮, Huālián) is eastern Taiwan's second largest city and one of the more pleasant small towns in Taiwan. Many travellers like to base themselves here even when Taroko Gorge is their interest as the range of food and accommodation is greater. Budget travellers will find everything they need near the train station. Head east to the Meilunshan Park (Měilúnshān Gōngyuán) and harbour area for wide streets, landscaped parks, bike lanes and ocean views in addition to boutique hotels and pricier restaurants.

Hualien means 'eddies' in Hokkien (Taiwanese) and the story goes that Qing-dynasty immigrants gave the region this name after noticing the swirling waters off the coast. Though much of the city's wealth comes from tourism, local deposits of limestone have also made Hualien the cement capital of Taiwan.

Road signage in Hualien is a mixed bag. Don't be surprised if Jung Shan is written Zhongshan, Jung Jeng as Zhongzheng, and Jung Hua as Zhonghua.

Sights & Activities

Seaside Parks

Hualien has three seaside parks, all joined by a walking and bicycle path that continues to Qixingtan Beach. The path starts at **Nan Bin Seaside Park** (南濱海濱公園, Nán Bīn Hǎibīn Gōngyuán), the southernmost park, which affords a bird's-eye view of the town and its dramatic mountain backdrop.

Qixingtan (七星潭, Qīxīng Tán, Chihsingtan), about 3km north of Hualien, looks down a coastline of high cliffs and green mountains. The water is too rough for swimming but it's a great spot for biking, strolling or picnicking. At the south end amid fishing villages are B&Bs and restaurants and the **Chihsing Tan Katsuo Museum** (七星柴魚博物館, Qīxīng Cháiyú Bówùguǎn; Qixingtan Beach, Hualien; ⌚9am-7pm) FREE, dedicated to dried bonito, an industry that was once of huge importance to Taiwan.

Cycling

The cycling path from Nan Bin Seaside Park to Qixingtan is mostly scenic but does pass through an industrial area for a couple of kilometres in the middle. At Qixingtan the path continues through a diverse coastal forest. Or connect with the quiet flat County Road 193 for an easy ride to Sanjhan and Taroko Gorge.

Giant Bicycles BICYCLE RENTAL

(捷安特, Jié Ān Tè; ☎823 4057; giant.d21100@msa.hinet.net; ⌚8am-6pm) To the left of the train station, Giant Bicycles has day (NT$300) and multiday rentals (per three days NT$1200). It's best to book in advance for the latter.

Water Sports

While the city has no swimming beaches, just down the coast is Jici Beach, a popular **swimming** and **surfing** venue in summer. **River tracing** the many astonishingly beautiful canyons around Hualien is also popular.

Tidal SURFING

(衝浪旅店, Tidal Chōnglàng Lǚdiàn; www.tidal.com.tw; 18-1 Jung Shan Rd; ⌚10am-10pm) Tidal rents surfboards and provides transport on weekends.

Hualien Outdoors WATER SPORTS

(www.hualienoutdoors.org) Hualien Outdoors runs custom river-tracing trips to Taroko Gorge and the Golden Canyon, as well as less challenging venues for those who just want a swim in crystal-clear waters surrounded by lush scenery. They also do trips to remote wild hot springs.

Other Sights

There are a number of interesting heritage sights around Hualien, including **Pine Garden** (松園別館, Sōngyuán Biéguǎn; ⌚9am-6pm) FREE, a former WWII command post for the Japanese Navy. Built in 1943, it was also where kamakazi pilots were wined and pleasured the night before their final missions. To get here, head up Jung Jeng Rd and look for the signs on the left at the intersection with Minquan 1st Rd.

Chingszu Temple BUDDHIST TEMPLE

(靜思堂, Jìngsītáng; 703 Jungyang Rd, Sec 3) Chingszu Temple's simple white and grey exterior is striking. Inside the 10-story modern building, a large exhibition hall showcases the Tzu Chi Buddhist organisation's activities around the world (see boxed text, p177). Exhibits are in English and Chinese. The temple is a couple of kilometres north of the train station in a Buddhist complex that includes a hospital and university.

Hualien Railway Cultural Museum HISTORIC BUILDING

(花蓮鐵道文化園區, Huālián Tiědào Wénhuà Yuánqū; 71 Jung Shan Rd; ⌚8.30am-5pm Tue-Sun) FREE This museum covers the grounds of the restored eastern railway depo, built in 1932. Further toward the harbour lies the old machine yard, which was part of a large restoration project at the time of writing.

Hualien Far Glory Ocean Park PARK

(花蓮海洋公園, Huālián hǎiyáng gōngyuán; www.farglory-oceanpark.com.tw; adult/child NT$890/590; ⌚9am-5pm, to 6.30pm 1 Jul–25 Aug) A large aquarium/amusement park south of Hualien off Highway 11. Attractions include dolphin shows and a water funpark. Young kids usually love this place.

Sleeping

Many travellers also stay at Taroko Village, Liyutan, Qixingtan, or even at one of the many B&Bs down Highway 11.

Amigos HOSTEL $

(阿美客國際青年旅館, Ā Měi Kè Gúojì Chīngnián Lǚguǎn; ☎836 2756; www.amigoshostel.tw; 68 Guo Lian 2nd Rd, 國聯2路68號; dm incl breakfast NT$450-550; @📶) Everything you want in a hostel: bright, clean, inexpensive and run by a friendly, well-travelled local who

Hualien

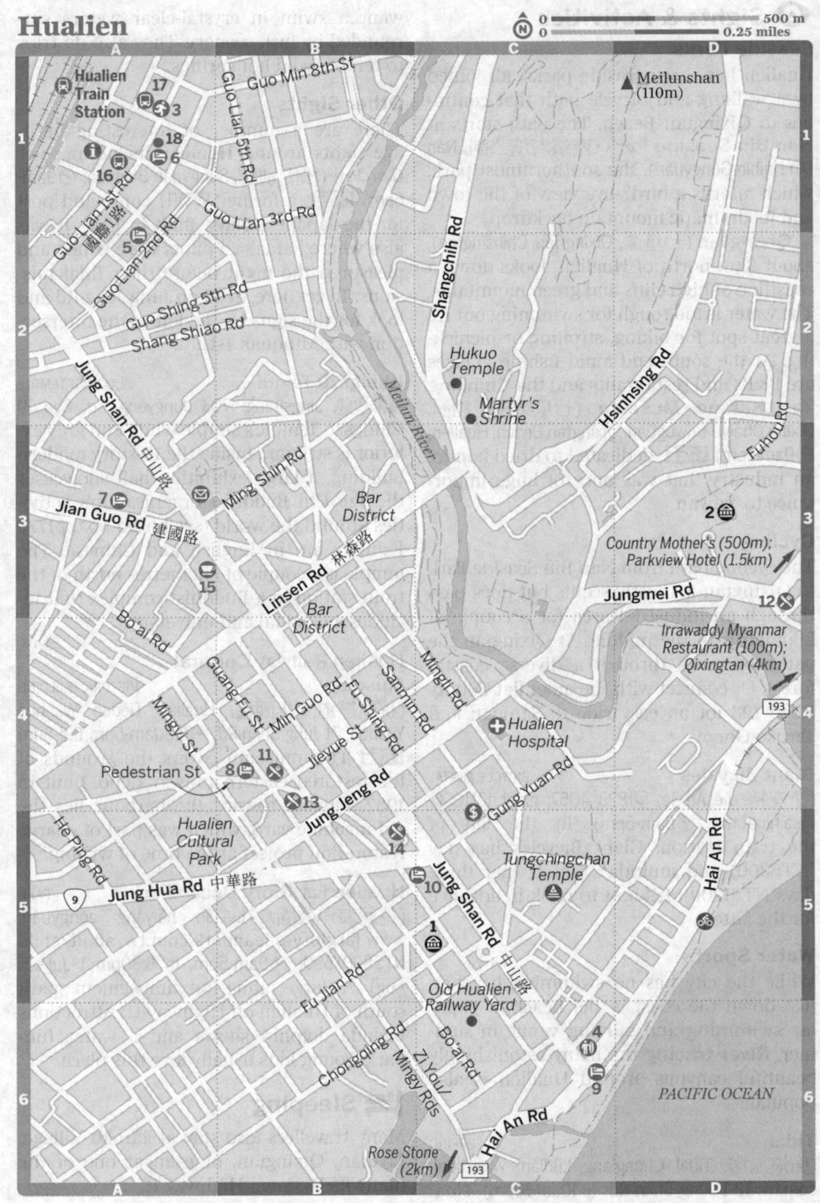

speaks your language (English anyway). It's also just a five-minute walk from the train station. There's a shared kitchen, free wi-fi, clean sheets and enough showers for everyone.

Amigos' owner can help with everything from scooter and bike rentals to whale-watching and river-tracing tours. Reservations are recommended from July through to September and for long weekends. Book online.

Hualien

Sights
1 Hualien Railway Cultural Museum ... C5
2 Pine Garden ... D3

Activities, Courses & Tours
3 Giant Bicycles ... A1
4 Tidal ... C6

Sleeping
5 Amigos ... A2
6 Ching Yeh (Green) Hotel ... A1
7 Formosa Backpackers Hostel ... A3
8 Kanjian Tiedao Guesthouse ... B4
9 View Ocean Hotel ... C6
10 Wai Tan 31 ... C5

Eating
11 Country Mother's Downtown ... B4
12 Dou Sang ... D3
13 Kimamaya ... B4
14 Night Market ... B5

Drinking & Nightlife
15 King Tang Cafe ... A3

Transport
16 Dingdong Bus Company ... A1
17 Hualien Bus Company ... A1
18 Pony Leasing & Rental Group ... A1

Formosa Backpackers Hostel HOSTEL $
(青年民宿; 835 2515; formosahostels@yahoo.com; 206 Jian Guo Rd, 建國路206號; dm NT$450, d with shared bathroom NT$1200;) Run by young, friendly, English-speaking Taiwanese, Formosa is great value for money. There's laundry service, a guest kitchen, a small cafe and bar, an English library, and free pick-up from the train station. Friday night activities were starting at the time of writing.

Ching Yeh (Green) Hotel HOTEL $
(青葉飯店, Qīng Yè Fàndiàn; 833 0186; www.green-hotel.com.tw; 83 Guo Lian 1st Rd, 國聯1路83號; d/tw incl breakfast from NT$1500/2400;) The Ching Yeh is one of the best budget options by the train station. Rooms are compact, but bright and very clean. Some have great views of the mountains. Staff speak some English.

Sea Sea House GUESTHOUSE $$
(惦惦看海, Diàndiàn Kàn Hǎi; 0988-585 376; http://038.hlbnb.net/index.htm; d/tw/tr incl breakfast NT$1500/2100/2500, weekday discounts 20%;) This sweet little guesthouse set in a Fujian-style *ping fang* (bungalow) is just a stone's throw from the sea and bike lanes at Qixingtan, the beach area north of Hualien city. Call (Chinese only) for train or airport pick-up, or catch the Tourism Shuttle Bus (www.taiwantrip.com.tw) towards Taroko and get off in Qixingtan. The guesthouse is just nearby.

Rose Stone HOMESTAY $$
(福園古厝客棧, Fúyuán Gǔcuò Kèzhàn; 854 2317; www.fulu.qov.tw; 48 Hai Bin Rd, 海濱路48號; d/tw incl breakfast NT$2280/2880, weekday discount 20%;) Set in a beautifully preserved traditional brick mansion, the Rose is such a maze of corridors, courtyards, chambers and gardens that you'll need to be shown to your room. Despite the old-time atmosphere, rooms offer modern comforts (but avoid the dull tower rooms). Home-cooked meals are served in an elaborately decorated tea room.

To get to the Rose, drive south down Jung Shan Rd (中山路) to the end and turn right onto County Road 193 (the last road at the coast). Continue until the Km19 mark. The turn-off for the Rose is just past this on the left. You can't really see the place until you are on top of it and the nearby area does not look promising. A taxi from the train station will cost about NT$200.

Kanjian Tiedao Guesthouse GUESTHOUSE $$
(看見鐵道民宿, KànjiànTiědào Mínsù; 832 9292; www.038329292.com.tw; 128-5 Ziyou St, 自由街128之5號; d/tw incl breakfast from NT$2580/3680, weekday discounts 20%;) Kanjian sits on the pedestrian-only lane (a former railway line) cutting across from Jung Hua to Min Guo. It's a quiet, atmospheric spot, with loads of excellent restaurants and cafes about. Rooms are modern and tastefully furnished, and there is a pleasant lounging area on the ground floor.

To get here turn west (right) off Jung Shan onto Jieyue St and head right when you reach the pedestrian street. The guesthouse is obvious on the right about 50m up.

Wai Tan 31 GUESTHOUSE $$
(外灘31, Wàitān 31; 831 1222; www.yt31.com.tw; 31 Jung Hua Rd; d NT$2400, weekday discounts 30%;) With low weekday rates (NT$1700 per night) and decor dreamed up by the

love child of Baudelaire and Hello Kitty, this quirky guesthouse just off Jung Hua Rd is a solid choice. The location puts you just across from the pedestrian-only lanes running up to Min Guo Rd and the pleasant shopping along Jung Hua.

View Ocean Hotel GUESTHOUSE **$$**
(海傳民宿, Hǎi Chuán Mínsù; www.view-ocean.com.tw; 4 Hai Bin Rd; d incl breakfast from NT$3600, weekday discounts 20%;) Unmistakable at the end of Jung Shan Rd, this towering guesthouse has large stylish rooms with superb ocean views. A buffet breakfast is included as well as bike rentals to use on the bike lanes that literally run behind the guesthouse. Staff speak good English.

Parkview Hotel HOTEL **$$$**
(美崙大飯店, Měilún Dàfàndiàn; 822 2111; www.parkview-hotel.com; 1-1 Lin Yuan, 林園1-1號; r from NT$5800;) In the hills above the harbour, this five-star hotel includes a golf course, tennis courts, pool and multiple food and beverage outlets. Book online (English available) for deep discounts.

Eating

Across from the train station on Guo Lian 1st Rd, you can pick up lunchbox meals (NT$80) from a number of places.

★**Country Mother's** WESTERN **$**
(34 Fu Qian Rd, 府前路34號; set breakfast NT$150-180, dishes NT$100-150; 6.30am-2pm;) Echoing its name nicely, Country Mother's serves some of the best Western breakfasts and sandwiches in Taiwan in a cosy venue up from the harbour. It also serves some of Taiwan's best Rome-style pizza and appetisers from a **downtown** (156 Bo'ai Rd, 博愛街156號; dishes NT$150-350; 11am-2pm & 5-9pm) location on the corner of Bo'ai and Jieyue Rds.

Ziqiang Night Market MARKET **$**
(自强夜市; cnr Heping & Ziqiang Rds) For local food head to this well-regarded market, southwest of the train station (a taxi costs around NT$130). Things to try include barbecued pork, spring rolls, stewed spare ribs (燉排骨, *dùn páigǔ*), coffin cake (棺材板, *guāncái bǎn;* different from the Tainan style) and fresh fruit drinks. On weekends some of the popular stalls can have very long waits.

Night Market MARKET **$**
(cnr Gongzheng & Jung Shan Rds) Just off Jung Shan Rd is a small night market with excellent cheap meat buns (包子, *bāozi*).

Kimamaya JAPANESE, BARBECUE **$**
(炭火燒肉工房, Tànhuǒ Shāoròu Gōngfáng; 144 Bo'ai Rd; dishes from NT$100; 5pm-midnight;) Popular with locals, this Japanese barbecue place has sunken tables for DIY comfort. Good Japanese beer is available and the atmosphere on weekends gets quite lively.

Dou Sang TAIWANESE **$$**
(多桑, Duō Sāng; 2 Jungmei Rd; dishes NT$100-250; 5-11pm) You have to pronounce the name of this restaurant in Taiwanese, if you want to get it right. It's the least you can do, since it does such a good job with the dishes. Set in an old Japanese-era wood house, and serving ultra-orthodox Taiwanese dishes, this is where locals take their visiting friends.

Dishes to try include barbecued pork (烤鹹豬肉), ginger intestine (薑絲大腸), minced pork (蒼蠅頭) and beef with scallion (蔥爆牛肉). There's no English menu.

Irrawaddy Myanmar Restaurant BURMESE **$$**
(伊江滇缅料理, Yījiāng Diānmiǎn Liàolǐ; www.irrawaddy.com.tw; 11-1 Minquan Rd, 民權路11-1號; dishes NT$120-220; 11am-2pm & 5-9pm, closed 3rd Monday of each month;) Run by a Burmese immigrant family, Irrawaddy serves up some fine curries. To get here cross the river on Jung Jeng Rd and head up the winding road. At Minquan 1st St, at a park, turn right and head down the hill to Minquan Rd. Irrawaddy is not far up on the left.

Drinking & Nightlife

Hualien has many trendy cafes and teahouses along its main streets. On Linsen Rd (林森路) east of Fu Hsing Rd, and up Fu Hsing itself, is a small bar district with places popping open and closed with regular frequency.

★**King Tang Cafe** CAFE
(金湯達人咖啡館, Jīn Tāng Dárén Kāfēi Guǎn; 431 Jung Shan Rd; 8am-10pm;) One of Hualien's best cafes, both for the quality of the coffee and the atmosphere, King Tang has an airy high-ceilinged indoor area, and a surprising back garden area that features an old air-raid bunker from WWII. Light, fresh meals are also available.

Shopping

Hualien's main export, marble, is all over the city. Numerous souvenir shops sell marble carvings but be aware that the mining of marble is having a devastating effect on the local environment.

Hualien's delicious cakes and cookies are available at bakeries and gift shops around town especially on Jung Hua Rd, which has pleasant arcades for strolling along. *Mochi,* a sticky rice treat, can be found elsewhere in Taiwan but many enjoy the Hualien variety most.

Information

Almost all hotels and hostels have free wi-fi, and it's common in restaurants and cafes. The Hualien County Information Centre also acts as an internet station for travellers, with free computer access and wi-fi.

THE MAVERICK: CHENG YEN

Her followers call her Shangren ('the exalted person') and consider her a living Bodhisattva. Business magazines think she is a powerful and effective CEO. If you listen in on one of her sermons, you might think Cheng Yen is a recycling plant owner. She isn't – but as the head of the worldwide Tzu Chi organisation, she does have her own TV station on which she spends more time talking about doing good in the world (which includes recycling) rather than expounding on scriptures. What kind of Buddhist nun is this, you may ask? A maverick, an iconoclast, a Made in Taiwan special.

Cheng Yen was born in 1937 to a wealthy business family in Taichung. Beautiful and deeply compassionate, she began her journey to Bodhisattva-hood after the death of her father compelled her to seek comfort with the Buddhist nuns living nearby. At 24 she made the extraordinary move of running away with another nun and spent the following years wandering the island, living in huts and caves, and studying scripture as a lay Buddhist.

Cheng Yen's devotion and spirit caught the attention of the Venerable Yinshun, a major advocate of reformist humanitarian Buddhism. Yinshun took Cheng Yen on as his last student and helped her to become ordained. For the next year the nun meditated, endured hardship and, according to her small number of disciples, performed miracles.

More significantly, Cheng Yen began to display her genius for organising people and she set about restoring dignity and rationality to monastic orders. Disciples were, among other restrictions, forbidden to take money for alms but had to work for their living. Such changes would pay off in the 1980s, when Taiwan's spiritually void but progressive middle class began looking for a faith that didn't smack of superstition and backwardness.

Two chance events in 1966 set the stage for the most important phase in Cheng Yen's life: the formation of Tzu Chi. In the first incident, Cheng Yen saw a poor aboriginal woman die of a miscarriage. In the second, not long after, Cheng Yen was challenged by three Catholic nuns over why Buddhists, with their concept of universal love, do no charity work.

Cheng Yen's response to the challenge came a few months later. Rather than accept a cushy position as a lecturer in Chiayi, she stayed in Hualien, and sensing the latent power of Taiwanese lay society to do good, started the Tzu Chi Buddhist Humanitarian Compassion Society.

The society (which is composed mostly of lay followers) grew slowly. In 1966 it was but a handful of housewives pledging 50 cents a day to charity. By 1979, however, it was large enough to attempt to build a hospital in then poor and mostly aboriginal Hualien. Against the odds, the Tzu Chi (Ciji) Buddhist Hospital opened in 1989 to islandwide acclaim.

In 1989 martial law had been lifted for only two years and Taiwanese, with their first taste of freedom, were forming civil associations with abandon. Membership in the established and well-respected Tzu Chi expanded rapidly.

By 2000 Tzu Chi was the largest formal organisation in Taiwan, with hundreds of thousands of lay volunteers working on projects as diverse as rebuilding houses after disasters to recycling. Tzu Chi has also been a leader in the development of hospice care in Taiwan, and its medical university places a unique stress on the moral cultivation of physicians.

Today, Tzu Chi is an international organisation with five million worldwide members and assets as high as US$9 billion. In Taiwan alone it runs four state-of-the-art hospitals, a recycling program, the medical university mentioned here, and a TV station.

For more, visit www.tzuchi.org or pick up a copy of Julia Huang's *Charisma and Compassion: Cheng Yen and the Buddhist Tzu Chi Movement*.

EAST COAST CYCLING

The east coast is Taiwan's top cycling destination. The scenery is outstanding, routes are varied, and you are never too far from a convenience store, restaurant or place to crash.

Most small towns have day-bike rentals. Good quality long-distance rentals are available in Hualien, Guanshan, and Taitung.

Most Common Routes

- Highway 9 or 11 between Hualien and Taitung

Don't Miss

- A ride through Taroko Gorge
- Highways connecting the 9 and 11
- County Roads 193 and 197

Serious Challenges

- Taroko Gorge to Hehuanshan: a 0m to 3275m climb in 86km

There are ATM machines all over town and in most 7-Elevens.

Bank of Taiwan (台灣銀行; 3 Gung Yuan Rd) Offers money changing and ATM service.

Hualien County (http://tour-hualien.hl.gov.tw) Good online introduction to the attractions in the area.

Hualien County Information Centre (⌚8am-10pm) On the right of the train station as you exit, this centre is good for brochures and very general information. Hostels are usually far better sources, especially for current events and recommendations.

Tzu-chi Buddhist Hospital (慈濟醫院, Cíjì Yīyuàn; ☎856 1825; 707 Jung Yang Rd, Sec 3) A hospital known for its excellent facilities. It's northwest from the train station, at the intersection of Jung Shan and Jung Yang Rds.

Getting There & Away

AIR

Hualien Airport (www.hulairport.gov.tw) Located north of town in Qixingtan, Hualien Airport has daily flights to Taipei, Taichung and Kaohsiung with **Mandarin Airlines** (www.mandarin-airlines.com) and **TransAsia Airways** (www.tna.com.tw).

BUS

Very few buses run the distance between Hualien and Taitung. In most cases you are better off taking the train, which is both faster and cheaper. There are hourly buses along Highway 11 to about Chenggong. Buses to Taroko Gorge leave outside the visitor information centre. For the schedule and price, see p185.

Dingdong Bus Company (鼎東客運; http://diingdong.myweb.hinet.net; 138-6 Guo Lian 1st Rd) There's no station, just a small bus stop to the left of the Hualien County Information Centre (as you face it). Buses to Taitung (NT$475, 3½ hours) depart daily at 1.10pm.

Hualien Bus Company (花蓮客運; www.hl.gov.tw/bus) The station to the left of the train station as you exit has buses to Taitung (NT$514, 3½ hours, 9.20am daily), which also stops at Dulan (NT$435), Lishan (NT$447, four to five hours, 8.40am) and Jici Beach (NT$121, one hour, hourly).

TRAIN

Frequent trains run north and south through the Rift Valley. When the line is electrified in 2014, travel times will be reduced. A fast/slow train to Taipei costs NT$345/266 and takes two/3½ hours.

Getting Around

TO/FROM THE AIRPORT

Hualien Bus Company runs buses to the airport (NT$38, 50 minutes, hourly).

CAR & SCOOTER

Vehicles are available for rent around the train station. Rental scooters cost NT$400 to NT$500 per day and cars NT$2000 per day and up (both exclude petrol). You need an International Driver's Permit and ID to rent a car. To rent a scooter, you need a Taiwanese driver's licence, except at **Pony Leasing & Rental Group** (小馬租車集團; www.ponyrent.com.tw; 國聯一路81號; ⌚7.30am-9pm), to the left of the Ching Yeh Hotel.

TAXI

Drivers congregate around the train and bus stations. To travel to and around Taroko costs up to NT$3000 per day.

TAROKO NATIONAL PARK

03

Just 15km north of Hualien sits Taroko National Park (太魯閣國家公園, Tàilǔgé Gúojiā Gōngyuán; www.taroko.gov.tw), Taiwan's top tourist destination. With its marble-walled canyons, lush vegetation and mountainous landscape, Taroko really puts the *formosa* (beautiful) in Ilha Formosa.

The park covers 1200 sq km and rises from sea level in the east to over 3700m further west. In fact, Taroko is 90% mountainous with 27 peaks over 3000m. Almost all the bio-geographical zones in Taiwan are represented here, providing a sanctuary for half the island's plant and animal species.

The blue-green Liwu River (called Yayung Paru – Great River – by the Taroko tribe) cuts through the centre, forging deep slitted valleys and ravines before emptying into the sea. In one stretch it forms Taroko Gorge, an 18km marble-walled canyon that many consider one of Asia's scenic wonders.

While most activities in the park take place within the gorge, increasingly people are exploring deeper. Hikers are now tackling high mountains such as Hehuanshan, Bilu Shan and Nanhudashan, while cyclists have discovered there's a remarkable ride in the 86km from the base to Wuling Pass at 3275m.

History

Although humans inhabited the park as long as 3000 years ago, the ancestors of today's Taroko tribe (recognised in 2004) began to settle along the Liwu River in the 17th century. The Taroko were known for their hunting and weaving skills, the use of facial tattoos, and ritual headhunting.

The Taroko lived in isolation until 1874 when the Qing began to build a road from Suao to Hualien to help open the area to Chinese settlers. In 1896 the Japanese marched in looking to exploit the forestry and mineral resources. After an 18-year bloody struggle, they finally forced the outnumbered and out-weaponed Taroko to submit, and most villages were relocated to the foothills or plains of Hualien.

The Japanese cut roads and widened existing trails (using Taroko labour) to form the 'Old Hehuan Mountain Rd' from the base of the gorge to Wushe in Nantou County. The road facilitated control over mountain aborigines and the extraction of the area's natural resources. It also spurred the first wave of tourism in the area, with hiking becoming a popular activity by the mid-1930s.

In the 1950s the KMT extended the road west as part of the first cross-island highway. Many of the road workers later settled in the area, often marrying Taroko women and becoming farmers. Plum Garden is one of the most well known of these settlements.

As with Yushan National Park, there were plans to turn the Taroko area into a national park in the 1930s. However, WWII scuttled that idea and it was not until the 1960s that the KMT government began to draft a national park act. Taroko National Park is Taiwan's fourth such park, officially established on 28 November 1986.

Dangers & Annoyances

Earthquakes, typhoons and landslides are having their effect on the strata of Taroko Gorge, and a small number of visitors have been killed in recent years from falling rocks. The park offers free helmets for visitors, although wearing them is optional.

Sights & Activities

The 18km marble-walled **Taroko Gorge** (太魯閣, Tàilǔgé) has been a popular walking and hiking destination since the 1930s. The park puts out an excellent guide called *Trails of Taroko Gorge and Su-Hua Areas*. Pick up a copy at the National Park Headquarters. Useful trail maps are included with clear

DON'T MISS

TAROKO'S TOP NATURAL SIGHTS

- **The Gorge** The marble-walled jewel in the national park's crown.
- **Jhuilu Trail** Witness spellbinding and vertigo-inducing views of the gorge.
- **Swallow Grotto** How can rock make such magical patterns?
- **Shakadang River** A green-blue river tossed with even more colourful boulders.
- **Baiyang Trail** A Chinese landscape painting brought to life.
- **Qingshui Cliffs** Classic towering sea cliffs
- **Golden Canyon** A deep marble-walled pool in which you can swim.
- **Eternal Spring Shrine** Poignant and picture perfect.

Taroko National Park

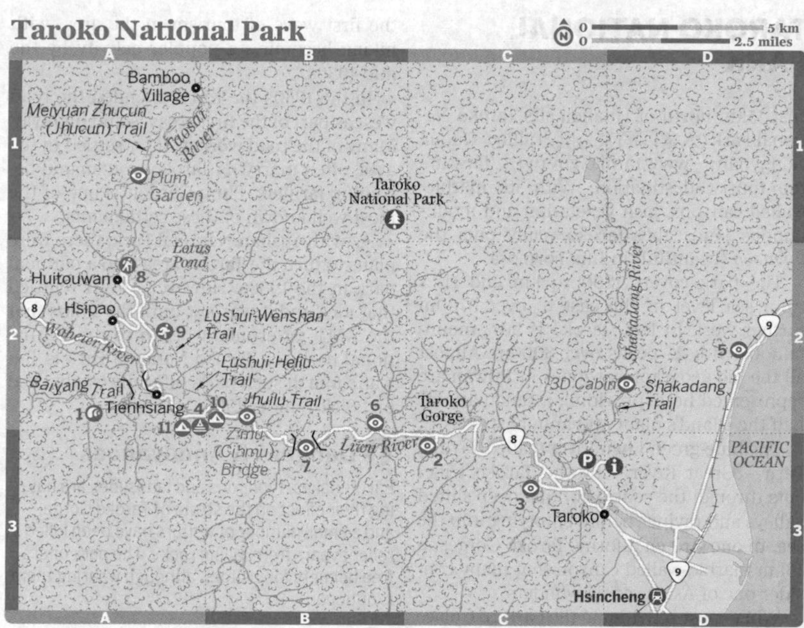

Taroko National Park

Sights

1 Baiyang Waterfall A2
2 Bulowan C3
3 Eternal Spring Shrine C3
4 Hsiangte Temple A2
5 Qingshui (Chingshui) Cliffs D2
6 Swallow Grotto B2
7 Tunnels of Nine Turns B3

Activities, Courses & Tours

8 Meiyuan Zhucun (Jhucun) Trail A2
9 Wenshan Hot Springs A2

Sleeping

10 Holiu B2
11 Lüshui A2

information on length, times, conditions and things to observe along the way.

Taroko Gorge began as coral deposits deep under the sea. Under pressure from geological forces, the coral was transformed into limestone and then marble, schists and gneiss. Five million years ago, as Taiwan was lifted from the sea by the collision of the Philippine and Eurasian plates, the gorge began to be formed. In essence, the upward thrust of hard rock, combined with the erosion of the soft layers from water and landslides, left towering canyon walls that are so narrow in places that you could play catch with someone on the other side.

The following are presented in the order you would encounter them starting out from the base of the gorge.

Shakadang Trail HIKING

(砂卡礑步道, Shākǎdāng Bùdào; one hour one way) Formerly the Mysterious Valley Trail, this flat 4.4km hike follows the crystal-clear Shakadang River as it winds through marble canyons and boulder-strewn flats. The curving riverbed creates massive pools of bluish green water (best seen in summer and fall).

Coming from the direction of the National Park Headquarters, the trailhead is to the right after emerging from the first tunnel. Follow the stairs down to the river to access the path. There's a parking lot just past the trailhead.

The Shakadang Trail officially ends at 3D (sometimes written as 5D) Cabin. However, if you have permits (you can apply for them the same day at the park's police stations), you can continue on the **Dali–Datung Trail** (大禮-大同步道, Dàlǐ–Dàtóng Bùdaò) to Dali and Datung, two isolated aboriginal villages. This trail should take about seven to eight hours, return.

Eternal Spring Shrine MEMORIAL

(長春祠, Cháng Chūn Cí) Not far from the park administration centre, overlooking the Liwu River from a cliff-side perch, sits this haunting shrine, dedicated to the 450 workers who lost their lives building the highway. A gushing spring that never dries pours out onto the rocks below, gracing the shrine with what looks like a hoary old beard.

Shuttle buses usually stop here on the way back from Tienhsiang.

Bulowan SCENIC AREA

(布洛灣步道, Bùluòwān Bùdào) Meaning 'echo', Bulowan is a former Taroko mountain village divided into a lower park-like terrace (with a small exhibition area) and an upper-level resort. Come here to watch Taroko Gorge transform from steep marble cliff walls into dense forest clinging to mist shrouded peaks.

You can walk up to Bulowan via a short flight of stairs (starting at Km178.8), or drive up a side road.

Swallow Grotto SCENIC AREA

(燕子口步道, Yànzǐ Kǒu Bùdào, Yanzikou) Along this half kilometre slice of the old highway (starting at Km178), the gorge twists and towers in one of its most colourful and narrow sections. It's a superb location for taking pictures. It's best to visit here before noon as tour buses literally fill the entire stretch later in the day.

If you are driving be aware that you can only proceed in a westerly direction. There's parking at the far end.

Tunnels of Nine Turns SCENIC AREA

(九曲洞, Jiǔ Qū Dòng) One of the most famous sights in the park, this 2km long pedestrian tunnel opens strategically to great masses of sublimely colourful stone walls. At the time of writing, however, access was closed due to heavy rockfall damage. There was no word on when it would reopen.

★ Jhuilu (Zhuilu) Old Trail HIKING

(錐麓古道, Zhuī Lù Gǔ Dào) One of the most spectacular of the accessible hiking paths in Taiwan, the 10.3km Jhuilu Old Trail (aka the Vertigo Trail) follows the last long remaining section of the Old Hehuan Mountain Rd. Justifiably famous in hiking circles, the trail gets its name from the section of the 1100m-high Jhuilu Cliff it traverses about 500m above the Liwu River.

At its narrowest and most exposed points, the trail is no more than 60cm to 70cm wide and is literally cut into the cliff face. The bird's-eye view of the gorge is spellbinding, and there are numerous now classic spots for taking photos showing you in the seemingly most precarious of positions.

The trail begins at Zimu (Cihmu) Bridge (Km172) and runs east along the north wall of the gorge before recrossing at Swallow Grotto (Km178). You need about seven hours to complete the full route. At the time of writing, only the last 3km of the route were open and hikers began at Swallow Grotto. There was no word on when the full route would reopen.

Applications for Zhuilu must be made at least a week in advance. See the park website for instructions.

Lüshui-Heliu Trail HIKING

(綠水-合流步道, Lûshuǐ-Héliú Bùdào) Part of the Old Hehuan Mountain Rd, this 2km trail runs above the highway along a cliff, with fantastic views of the Liwu River. Think of it as the Jhuilu Old Trail for the faint of heart. The trails starts behind a building to the right at Km170.7.

Lüshui-Wenshan Trail HIKING

(綠水文山步道, Lûshuǐ Wénshān Bùdào) After the Jhuilu Old Trail, this is Taroko's best day hike, a superb four- to five-hour tramp through subtropical forests with grand sweeping views down the peak-studded gorge. With few hikers about, you stand a good chance of seeing wildlife, including monkeys, barking deer, squirrels and various pheasants.

The trail affords the most dramatic scenery as you head downhill, but it's difficult to coordinate a start at the upper trailhead (it literally starts in the middle of a tunnel that begins at Km166). Easiest is to start at the same entrance to the Lüshui-Heliu Trail and head up. This also allows you to stop in at the Wenshan Hot Springs at the end of the hike (the hot springs are at the beginning of the tunnel at Km166). From here back to Tienhsiang it's a manageable 2.5km.

You need a mountain permit for this hike, which can be applied for on the spot at the Tienhsiang Police Station.

Hsiangte Temple BUDDHIST TEMPLE

(祥德寺, Xiángdé Sì) Just before Tienhsiang look for a suspension bridge leading to this temple on a ledge overlooking the gorge. The temple is named after the Buddhist monk who prayed for the safety of the workmen as they built the Central Cross-Island Hwy.

Baiyang Trail HIKING
(白楊步道, Báiyáng Bùdào) This 2.1km trail to **Baiyang Waterfall** (白楊瀑布, Báiyáng Pùbù) is one of the most popular short walks in the park so be sure to get on it early. Just before the falls, the trail splits to **Water Curtain Cave** (水濂洞, Shuǐ Lián Dòng). Don't miss this section of man-made tunnel where water rushes out from faults in the ceiling in beautiful showers.

The trailhead for the falls is 700m up the main road from Tienhsiang. Look for the entrance, a narrow 380m-long tunnel carved into the side of the mountain, just before the end of the car tunnel. Bring a torch as this and other tunnels are quite dark inside.

Wenshan Hot Springs HOT SPRING
(文山溫泉, Wénshān Wēnquán) Closed for years after a rockslide killed several bathers, the free, open-air hot springs have finally unofficially reopened. The location down at the riverside is wonderfully scenic, but do exercise caution coming here after heavy rainfall or earthquakes (and note you bathe at your own risk). The stairs down to the springs are at Km166, just before a tunnel.

Meiyuan Zhucun (Jhucun) Trail HIKING
(梅園竹村步道, Méiyuán Zhúcūn Bùdaò, Bamboo Village/Plum Garden Trail) About 6km up from Tienhsiang, at the Km164.5 mark on a switchback, this 12.4km trail runs up the rugged Dasha and Taosai River valleys along a path chiselled into cliff walls. At the Chiumei (Jiumei) suspension bridge (20 minutes hike up the main trail), a 2.1km side trail leads to **Lotus Pond** (蓮花池步道, Liánhuā Chí Bùdaò).

Though a popular hiking route (plan on eight hours for a return trip on the main trail, and three hours return if you only go to Lotus Pond), it's also the only outside access for two tiny farming villages that are deep in the mountains. Once the site of Taroko aboriginal settlements, the villages were resettled after the construction of the Central Cross-Island Hwy.

Qingshui (Chingshui) Cliffs SCENIC AREA
(清水斷崖, Qīngshuǐ Duànyá) Towering coastal cliffs are a regular feature of Taiwan's east. The most spectacular examples, known as the Qingshui Cliffs, extend 21km from Chondge, just north of where the Liwu River enters the sea, to the town of Heren. One classic location for cliff viewing is a little pullover park at Km176.4 on Highway 9.

The cliffs are composed of durable marble and schist walls, which rise 200m to 1000m above sea level. They form the easternmost section of the Central Mountains, and reportedly are the oldest bit of rock in Taiwan.

River Tracing

The Sanjhan North River (三棧北溪, Sān Zhàn Běi Xī) flows through southern Taroko National Park. A short 2km trail has been built along the river, following a canal built by the US government in 1952 (clean, clear water still flows down the canal). But the real reason to come is to river trace to the **Golden Canyon** (黃金峽谷, Huángjīn Xiágǔ), a beautiful gorge with numerous waterfalls and deep, blue-tinted swimming pools.

From spring to autumn, river-tracing outings are organised by various outfits. Most hostels in Hualien can arrange trips for you, though you might want to ask about conditions before you go: this place is getting increasingly overrun. The expat-run Hualien Outdoors (p173) also organises trips here and to other spots around the county.

Sanjhan sits just south of Taroko National Park. If you are heading to Hualien from

TOURING TAROKO

You can visit Taroko National Park any time of year, but during weekends and holidays the place is very crowded, especially on the road. The longer trails, however, are always quiet and tour buses cannot drive past Tienhsiang.

With increased Chinese tourism has come an increased number of tour buses (they peak February to April). However, these tend to get a late start so visit prime, easily accessible sights (such as Baiyang Trail and Yanzikou) as early as you can. Also note that after 6pm the park is nearly deserted allowing for sublimely peaceful dusk walks or rides down the gorge.

There's only one road through the park (Hwy 8), and only one real village (Tienhsiang). Food and accommodation are limited here, so many people base themselves outside the park, in Taroko Village, Liyu Lake or Hualien.

The park is slated to start charging an entrance fee of around NT$100 in 2014.

Taroko, turn right off Hwy 9 at the sign for Sanjhan (三棧, Sānzhàn, Sanchan). When you cross the bridge into the village, stay right along the river.

Cycling

Cycling Taroko Gorge grows in popularity each year, with the majority of riders making a day trip up to Tienhsiang (elevation 470m) and back. Bikes can be rented across from the Hsincheng (Xincheng) train station and also in Hualien and Qixingtan. Contact Mr Su at Taroko Lodge (p184) for bike rentals that include a drive up the gorge (with your bike) and drop-off at any point. While this may seem like cheating, it's ideal for the day tripper as it gives you time to see the sights, hike a few short trails (or one long one) and finish with a sublime coast down the gorge later in the day.

A great deal more challenging is the 75km ride from the base to Dayuling and then, for the brave, on to Lishan (another 29km) and, for the heroic, to Hehuanshan (another 11km): the latter takes you from sea level to 3275m at Wuling Pass, the highest section of road in East Asia.

It's a gruelling ride up switchback after switchback, with the air cooling and thinning at higher levels. The rewards, beyond the physical accomplishment, include world-class mountain vistas as your constant companion, and an ever-changing forest cover that eventually gives way to rolling fields of dwarf bamboo at the highest levels.

The ascent is not particularly steep to Tienhsiang but afterwards it becomes more relentless. Most riders spend the first night in the hostel at Guanyun (altitude 2374m), about 71km up from the base. A complete cross-island ride from Taroko to Taichung covers 200km of road and typically takes three days, with the second night's stop in Wushe.

Tours

All travel agencies in Hualien and Taipei can arrange full- or half-day tours of Taroko Gorge. Taking a tour is a convenient way to see the gorge but it doesn't leave enough time for exploring.

Taiwan Tour Bus BUS TOUR
(www.taiwantourbus.com.tw; half-/full-day tours NT$650/988) Leaves from the visitor information centre at Hualien train station. Staff at the centre can help with ticket purchases.

Festivals & Events

Taroko International Marathon MARATHON
The park has been the venue for this autumn event since 2000. Organisers like to stress that it's the only canyon marathon in the world. The event attracts runners from all over the world (there were 10,000 participants in 2009) and there are full and half marathons as well as a 5km run. Contact the Chinese Taipei Road Running Association (www.sportsnet.org.tw/en) for more information.

Sleeping

With your own transport, you have many options for sleeping.

Arrive early if you wish to stake out a spot at the campgrounds at **Holiu** (合流; cleaning fee NT$200) and **Lüshui** (綠水; camping free). Both campgrounds sit in superb locations on flats above the river, and bathrooms with showers are available. You can also erect a tent for free in the Baiyang Trail parking lot (about 700m up from Tienhsiang). Tents can only be put up after 3pm and must be taken down before 10am each day. Toilets and cold showers are available here.

Tienhsiang

Catholic Hostel HOSTEL $
(天祥天主堂, Tiānxiáng Tiānzhǔ Táng; ☎869 1122; dm NT$300, d without shower NT$700, d/tw with shower NT$1100/1400) The Catholic Hostel has been the principal budget hotel in Tienhsiang for 50 years. The place is getting a bit long in the tooth but it still offers dorms at no-nonsense prices.

Tienhsiang Youth Activity Centre HOTEL, HOSTEL $$
(天祥青年活動中心, Tiānxiáng Qīngnián Huódòng Zhōngxīn; ☎869 1111; www.cyct-syac.com.tw; dm NT$900, d/tw incl breakfast NT$2200/3000; [wi-fi]) Up the hill from the Catholic Hostel, the airy, expansive Youth Activity Centre offers far superior private and dorm rooms to the Catholic Hostel. Expect two-star comfort but a lot of space to hang out, including a cafe-bar with outdoor seating. Rooms are discounted by 15% midweek and there's a restaurant and laundry facilities on the premises.

Silks Place Hotel HOTEL $$$
(太魯閣晶英酒店, Tàilǔgé Jīngyīng Jiǔdiàn; ☎869 1155; http://taroko.silksplace.com.tw; r from NT$8000; [wi-fi] [pool]) Most likely the first building

you'll see upon entering Tienhsiang, the former Grand Formosa sports a new name and an updated style: think clean lines, liberal use of wood and stone, and red-tile floors. In addition to multiple eating and drinking venues, the hotel boasts a rooftop pool with big views of Taroko Gorge.

Shuttle buses can pick up guests from Hualien Airport or train station. See the hotel's website for seasonal and midweek discount packages.

Bulowan

★Leader Village Taroko CABIN **$$$**
(立德布洛灣山月村, Lìdé Bùluòwān Shānyuè Cūn; ☎861 0111; www.leaderhotel.com; cabins incl breakfast from NT$5100; 📶) In the upper level of Bulowan, on a high meadow surrounded by postcard-perfect scenery, the Leader Village Taroko offers 36 quality wood cabins with old-time porches to let you relax and take in the views. Endemic butterfly and bird species flit about year-round, and monkeys, civets and barking deer are often spotted at the edge of the forest.

Management encourages guests to be quiet here, so don't expect any loud entertainment (except a nightly hour of aboriginal music and dance). Book online for weekday/low-season discounts.

Taroko Village 太魯閣

In this little village just metres from the park entrance, and 5km from Hsincheng train station, you'll find a number of inexpensive restaurants and hotels lining the main road.

Liwu Inn HOSTEL **$**
(立霧客棧, Lìwù Kèzhàn; ☎861 0660, 861 0769; http://liwu.hoseo.tw/index.php; dm/d/tw incl breakfast NT$350/2000/2400; @📶) Just a stone's throw from the entrance to the park on the main road, this small guesthouse has basic rooms and a small simple dorm. The owner speaks some English and can help with bike and scooter rental.

★Taroko Lodge GUESTHOUSE **$$**
(嵐天小築民宿, Lántiān Xiǎo Zhú Mínsù; ☎0922-938 743; http://rihang.wordpress.com; d/tw incl breakfast NT$2000/3500; 📶) This well-run guesthouse at the base of Taroko Gorge sits on a large plot of land with mountain and ocean views. Rooms are spacious and Western breakfasts include a proper cup of coffee. Your host, Mr Su, offers train station pick-ups and a great bike rental service that includes an optional drive up the gorge (with your bike).

Taroko Hotel HOTEL **$$**
(太魯閣旅店, Tài Lǔ Gé Lǚdiàn; ☎861 1558; www.taroko-hotel.com.tw; d/tw incl breakfast from NT$1800/3000) Close to the entrance of the park on the main road is this spiffy family-run hotel with large rooms and free guest bike rentals (for short local trips). There's a 20% discount midweek.

Guanyun (Kuanyun)

Youth Activity Centre HOSTEL **$$**
(觀雲山莊, Guānyún Shānzhuāng; ☎04-2599 1173; http://kwan.cyh.org.tw/eng; dm/d/tw incl breakfast NT$500/1900/2800) At an altitude of 2374m, this activity centre in tiny Guanyun (觀雲), 57km up from Tienhsiang, offers inexpensive meals and accommodation literally in the clouds. The first night's stop for most cyclists on the way to Lishan or Hehuanshan, it's a bit too far away from the main sights to be of much use to most other travellers.

The centre is 400m off Hwy 7. Look for the sign in Chinese at around Km117.

Eating

Bland Chinese and aboriginal food is available at a few stalls and sit-down places at the back of the parking lot in Tienhsiang. There's also a convenience store here.

Tienhsiang Youth Activity Centre RESTAURANT **$$**
(Tienhsiang; lunch & dinner NT$180; ⏰7-8.30am, noon-1.30pm & 6-7.30pm) Meals are available to guests and nonguests. Buy tickets in advance. For breakfast (NT$120), buy a ticket before 9pm the night before.

Leader Village Taroko ABORIGINAL **$$**
(Bulowan; lunch & dinner set meals NT$380-580; ⏰noon-2pm & 6-8pm; 📖) At the Leader Village resort in Bulowan aboriginal chefs have brought their local cooking to a whole new level (as alluded to by the name of a popular set meal 'The Wild Boar Meets the Eiffel Tower'). Set meals are large, and might include barbecued wild pig or mountain chicken, soup, rice steamed in bamboo tubes, and exotic mountain vegetables.

Silks Place Hotel CHINESE, WESTERN **$$$**
(Tienhsiang; dinner buffet NT$800; ⏰noon-2.30pm & 5.30-9.30pm; 📖) Excellent breakfast

OFF THE BEATEN TRACK

HOT CROSS HIGHWAYS

There are two main highways (the 9 and 11) running north and south along the east, but there are innumerable smaller roads going in all directions. Taking time to explore at least a few of these quiet, intensely scenic routes should be considered mandatory. In addition to County Roads 193 and 197, consider the roads that cross directly over the Coastal Mountains, linking the two main highways.

Highway 11 甲

The first route connecting Highways 11 and 9, 11甲 runs along the Dingzilou River (丁子漏溪, Dīngzǐlòu Xī), over a narrow lushly forested ridge, and then past pretty fields before ending in Guangfu, 19km to the west. A good day trip from Hualien entails riding Highway 11 to the turn-off at Fongbin, the 11甲 to County Road 193, and then following that superb road back to Hualien.

Ruigang Hwy (Township Road 64)

More winding country road than highway, the 22km Ruigang Hwy (瑞港公路) follows the rugged contours of the Hsiukuluan River from a high-enough perch to let you take in all the surrounding natural beauty. If you're cycling, plan on taking about two hours to get to Ruisui – and bring water as there is only one small farming settlement along the way.

Highway 23

The last route connecting Highways 11 and 9, the 23 is windy, steep and sparsely populated – unless you count the numerous monkey troops that hang out on the sides of the road.

and dinner buffets are available as well as set meals for lunch.

Information

The **National Park Headquarters** (太魯閣遊客中心, Tàilǔgé Yóukè Zhōngxīn; www.taroko.gov.tw; ⌚8.45am-4.45pm, closed 2nd Monday of each month) has useful information on the status of trails and road conditions, and free maps and brochures of hiking trails. There's also a pleasant cafe and bookstore. This is the only visitor information centre in the park where you might find someone who can speak English.

There are no ATMs that take international cards in the park.

Getting There & Away

BUS

The yellow **Taroko Tourist Shuttle Bus** (www.taiwantrip.com.tw) is a decent way to get around the park. Buses run every hour or two from Hualien to Tienhsiang and stop at all major sights and trailheads, as well as the visitor information centre. You can pay for single portions or a day pass (NT$250). The first bus leaves Hualien train station at 7.50am and the last bus returns from Tienhsiang at 5pm. The schedule is written on every bus stop.

The Hualien Bus Company (p178) also has four buses a day (NT$172) from the train station to Tienhsiang. The earliest leaves at 6.30am and the last bus from Tienhsiang departs at 6.30pm.

TAXI

A day trip from Hualien to Taroko Gorge costs up to NT$3000, and a one-way trip from Hualien to Tienhsiang costs NT$1500.

TRAIN

Hsincheng Station (新城站, Xincheng), also known as Taroko Station, lies closest to the park entrance (about 5km away). It's used by travellers staying in Taroko Village or the gorge. All buses to Taroko Gorge stop here. A fast/slow train from Taipei to Hsincheng costs NT$403/311 and takes 2½/3½ hours.

HIGHWAY 11

Two main routes run north–south along the east coast – whichever road you choose to travel will make all the difference to your journey. Highway 9 cuts through the verdant East Rift Valley (Huādōng Zòng Gǔ), while Highway 11 winds down the narrow strip between the sea and the Coastal Mountains, a series of steep volcanic arcs. There are few large settlements but plenty of small aboriginal villages, fishing harbours, beaches and ocean terraces. There are several places to camp along the way, and more and more guesthouses seem to spring up every year.

Much of Highway 11 falls under the auspices of the East Coast National Scenic Area (www.eastcoast-nsa.gov.tw).

EAST COAST EATING

Hualien and Taitung Counties have a diverse mix of aboriginal, Hakka, Taiwanese and mainland Chinese descendents, all contributing to the culinary traditions of the area. Amis cooking is particularly influential and emphasises the natural flavours of fruits, flowers, taro and wild vegetables. Amis dishes made from betel-nut flowers, sorghum and rattan can be seen in various night markets and restaurants. For something very traditional head to Matai'an for hot pot brought to boil with heated rocks.

Fruit is abundant on the east coast and grown year-round. Something is always for sale roadside. The Luye region is known for its pineapples, Dulan its pomelos, and Beinan County its custard apples. The best of the latter are known as pineapple custard apples and really do have the consistency of custard.

Some of the best meals you can find along the east will often be at homestays or small guesthouses. Set meals usually include fresh mountain veggies, free range chicken, local rice and a soup of in-season ingredients.

Some specific regional delicacies to look for include the dumplings of Hualien, the steamed buns of Donghe (look for two shops in mid-town across from the 7-Eleven), and mountain boar in aboriginal areas. Fresh seafood is available all along the coast. Finally, if you need a quick bite, look for the giant agricultural association buildings off the main highways: they usually have simple but tasty lunchboxes made with locally grown produce as well as a host of dried and preserved snacks you can take away.

ℹ Getting Around

Personal transport (scooter, car, bicycle) is best for travelling Highway 11.

BUS

Dingdong Bus Company (鼎東客運; http://diingdong.myweb.hinet.net; 138-6 Guo Lian 1st Rd) Has buses from Hualien to Taitung (NT$475, 3½ hours, once daily at 1.10pm)

Hualien Bus Company (花蓮客運; www.hl.gov.tw/bus) A daily bus from Hualien to Taitung (NT$514, 3½ hours, 9.20am) and hourly buses from Hualien to Chenggong.

BICYCLE

The 180km from Hualien to Taitung (and perhaps on to Chihpen hot springs) comprises the most popular long-distance cycling route in Taiwan. An average cyclist will take three days, with overnight stops in Shitiping and Dulan. The road winds, but the only major climb, to the Baci Observation Tower, lies behind you after the first morning. From Hualien to Chihpen, the highway has a smooth, wide, double-lined shoulder marked for cyclists and scooters only.

Cow Mountain Beach 牛山

The beach (Niúshān) is a short but wide stretch of sandy coastline bookmarked by rocky cliffs about 27km south of Hualien. It's a lovely place to escape the crowds of the more developed beaches on the east coast, but there's no swimming here because of the rough surf and a quick drop off.

Besides the quiet beachside atmosphere, travellers come here to wander or even stay the night in the **Huting Recreation Area** (呼庭休閒區, Hūtíng Xiūxián Qū; ☎852 1875; admission NT$50; ⏲10am-7pm), an old grazing area (Cow Mountain is called Huting by the local aboriginals) developed by a friendly Ami family into a rustic resort. There's a cafe-restaurant serving Ami food, a simple campground (NT$150 per person) set up on the open grassy fields, and rustic driftwood cabins (d/tw with shared bath NT$1200/2200, 30% discount Sunday to Thursday).

The beach and recreation area are about 1.5km off the highway down a very steep road that is often washed out. Look for the sign with the cow head on it for the turn-off. Just a short distance further up Hwy 11 is **Baci Observation Tower**, a mandatory highway stop with a mesmerising cliff-side view over the blue waters of Jici Beach. For cyclists this is the summit of the longest climb on Highway 11.

Jici (Chichi) Beach 磯崎海濱遊憩區

This **beach** (磯崎海濱遊憩區, Jīqí Hǎibīn Yóuqì Qū; admission NT$120; ⏲9am-6pm) is one of only two you can swim at between Hualien and Taitung, so if you're looking for a dip, a paddle or a bit of surfing, don't pass by – at least between May and September. Surfers can rent boards (per day NT$500) at Tidal (p173) in Hualien. The company also provides transport to the beach for NT$200 on summer weekends, and surf lessons.

Jici Beach has showers, changing rooms and rental equipment, as well as a **campground** (☎03-871 1251; per site NT$500). All Hualien buses (NT$121) pass by the beach, so you should never have to wait more than an hour for a ride.

Shitiping (Shihtiping) 石梯坪

The Kuroshio Current runs closest to Taiwan at Shitiping (Shítīpíng, Shiti Fishing Village) and misty conditions along the coast make the vegetation greener and denser than elsewhere. The volcanic coastline has also eroded to form beautiful natural stone steps (Shitiping in fact means 'stone steps').

Shitiping is divided into a rough-hewn village, a fishing harbour below this, and a nicely landscaped park south of the harbour. Further south are a number of tiny Ami settlements where fishermen can be seen casting nets at the mouths of rivers, and wood craftsmen transforming driftwood into furniture and sculptures.

Shitiping is now a mandatory stop for Chinese tour buses and as such the entrance to the landscaped park can be unpleasantly crowded at times. If you simply pass the groups and head down toward the camping area, however, you'll find a quiet area of limestone rocks with lookouts down the coast that will leave you breathless.

At 80km from Hualien, Shitiping is usually the first night's resting area for cyclists. Note that as you head south, if you turn into Jingpu Village after crossing the bridge, it's a lovely ride along the ends of the Xiuguluan River and then along the sea. In two kilometres you reconnect with Highway 11.

Sleeping & Eating

In the park area of Shitiping, the national scenic administration runs a well-laid-out **campground** (☎03-878 1452; per site NT$300 Mon-Fri, NT$500 Sat & Sun) with raised platforms that face the sea. There are hot water showers (evenings only) and toilets available. Check in at the visitor centre at the end of the road.

Pakelang GUESTHOUSE $
(巴歌浪船屋民宿, Bāgēlàng Chuánwū Mínsù; ☎089-881 400; http://pakelang.e089.com.tw; d incl breakfast NT$1500, weekday discount 20%) At this beachside guesthouse you've got plenty of land to stretch out on, as well as a long beach (swimmable only in summer). The guesthouse is run by a local Ami family and seafood dinners are available for NT$800 per person.

Pakelang is a few kilometres past Shitiping, and just past the Tropic of Cancer monument at Km72.5. Look for a wooden sign marked 'Pakelang' and head down the narrow path.

A-zhen Seafood Restaurant GUESTHOUSE $
(阿鎮海鮮餐廳, Ā-zhèn Hǎixiān Cāntīng; ☎0937-980 0960; 106 Shihtiping; d/tw NT$1400/1800, weekday discounts 20%; Wi-Fi) Basic guesthouse accommodation is available above the restaurant, which, as the name suggests, serves some fresh (and cheap) seafood from 6am to 8pm. Xin Yang is to the right off Highway 11 as it runs through the village.

★ **Sea Fan Guesthouse** BOUTIQUE HOTEL $$
(石梯緣景觀咖啡 民宿, Shítī Yuán Jǐngguān Kāfēi Mínsù; ☎03-878 1828; www.seafan.idv.tw; d NT$2200-3200, midweek discounts 20%; Wi-Fi) This cosy boutique hotel at the start of the park has small well-furnished rooms with views that are hard to top. Get the sea-facing doubles and you can look north at 40km of undeveloped coastline that's all dark-green hills and blue ocean. Other rooms feature mountain views but it's so worth spending a little more to face the sea.

Meals are available and locally sourced by your humble, genial host, Mr Wang.

Caves of the Eight Immortals 八仙洞

This mandatory stop (Bā Xiān Dòng) for all tour buses going up and down the east coast is the site of the earliest human inhabitation of Taiwan. While a good place to spot wild monkeys, the insides of most caves have been turned into tacky Buddhist shrines. Archaeology is an afterthought.

Platform of the Three Immortals 三仙台

Also known as Sansiantai (Sānxiāntái), this is a series of arched bridges leading to a small coral island that was once a promontory joined to the Mainland. The island's three large stone formations have been likened to the three immortals of Chinese mythology – hence the name.

Sansiantai is a very pleasant spot to wander, although on holidays and weekends it's a bit of a madhouse with the tour-bus crowds.

Dulan (Doulan) 都蘭

POP 500

This funky little village (Dūlán) is by far the best spot along the coast to base yourself for an extended stay. There's good food, a range of accommodation, a secret local beach (ask the locals for directions) and a boatload of interesting characters. You'll meet Taiwanese big city kids who've dropped out of the rat race to open a guesthouse and live in paradise, expats who've done the same, dozens of artists who've set up woodcarving studios in an abandoned sugar factory, and musicians who make the town buzz on weekends with a live music show.

The Dulan area has been inhabited for thousands of years, as evidenced by the stone coffins and other archaeological ruins of the Beinan culture in the hills west of town. These days, it has one of the largest Ami settlements along the east coast, and the aboriginal presence in the arts scene is strong.

Dulan is small, in essence a couple of blocks on either side of Highway 11, and a few backstreets (which teem with bird and butterfly life) winding into the hills. And do take the time to ride or wander in those hills. As odd as it sounds, you'll feel like you've left Taiwan and set foot on some mysterious emerald tropical isle.

Sights & Activities

Dulan Sugar Factory ARTS CENTRE
(都蘭糖廠, Dūlán Tángchǎng; 61 Dulan Village; 24hr) FREE Once a busy processing plant and a source of local employment, the factory closed its doors in the 1990s. Local artisans and craftspeople soon began to reopen the abandoned warehouse space as makeshift studios: a genuine local art scene developed and continues to gain in reputation.

As you ride into Dulan from the north, it's easy to spot the factory on the right, near the edge of town. Weekdays the art scene is usually pretty quiet, but weekends you can usually watch carvers at work and also make purchases of some unique articles. The factory is also the setting for frequent east coast festivals and weekly live music concerts by aboriginal players on Saturday night.

Moonlight Inn ARTS CENTRE
(月光小棧, Yuèguāng Xiǎo Zhàn) FREE In the hills above Dulan sits a quaint old forestry building from Japanese times. Nicknamed 'Moonlight Inn', it hosts frequent local arts exhibitions. Handcrafted items are for sale inside a cafe area that's open till about 6pm.

To get to the inn, follow the English signs off Highway 11. Along the way there's a **stone coffin site** that's worth checking out.

Water Running Up NATURAL ODDITY
(水往上流, Shuǐ Wǎng Shàng Liú) FREE Just south of Dulan is the geological oddity known as Water Running Up. Can you figure out why it's doing this?

Sleeping & Eating

Hostels and guesthouses continue to open, and with the strong expat presence in the village, there's a growing range of food

SURFING THE EAST COAST

While the north of Taiwan has had a vibrant surf scene for close to a decade now, the east coast waves have until very recently been the exclusive domain of a tiny community of surfers around Donghe, Dulan and Taitung. That's fast changing. In 2011 Taitung's (and Taiwan's) first international surf event was held, and a year later, the country's biggest surf event, the Taiwan Open of Surfing – ASC Ultima Event, was held in Jinzun Harbour. The open was held once more in 2013, making it highly likely this will become a yearly event.

The Taitung surf environment has been given four stars out of six by the ASC. Prime is the area between Changbin and Donghe, in particular around Chenggong, Jinzun (金樽) and the Donghe River mouth (東河河口). A few surf shops have started to open in Donghe and Dulan, but it's still very much a DIY scene.

See the Taiwan Open of Surfing (www.taiwanopenofsurfing.com) website for more and contact WaGaLiGong (p189) in Dulan for board rentals.

(there's even a guy at the start of town selling excellent if pricey handmade bread). In the lane above Water Running Up, look for the daily fruit market.

★Taitung Sea Art Hostel – Motherland HOMESTAY $
(台東海之藝民宿, Táidōng Hǎizzhīyì Mínsù; ☎in Chinese 0935-061 578, in English 0988-243 108; http://taitung-sea-art-hostel.webs.com; d/tw NT$1000/2000; @) Up in the wooded hills above Dulan, one of the nicest couples you'll ever meet in Taiwan have set up a dreamy little rustic homestay in a traditional *ping-fang* (see p191), complete with funky rooms (designed by your host, Roman), a sweet outdoor shower block, DIY kitchen, and as much wildlife as you're likely to see anywhere outside a national park.

Motherland is a fair drive off the main road, so call first to make reservations (and a pick-up, if needed). There's a scooter for rent (per day NT$400) and your hosts are well connected to the local community if you need information on festivals or local activities. Also check out the website for art and alternative therapy classes.

For those after a private getaway, check out **Taitung Sea Art Guesthouse – Rainbow Forest** (台東海之藝民宿-成功彩虹森林; http://taitung-rainbow-forest-guesthouse.webs.com; cottage NT$2500) a little further north up the coast in Chenggong. This is a single-room cottage with bedding for four, another great outdoor kitchen and shower block, all sitting on a large slice of forested land that was lovingly restored with native plants by the previous aboriginal owner. The beautiful long **Rainbow Waterfall** is nearby.

Cottage rates drop to NT$1000 per day after the second night. You'll want your own vehicle if you stay here.

Backpacker Dog HOSTEL $
(背包狗, Bèibāo Gǒu; ☎0922-677 997; dm/s/d NT$450/600/1200; @ wi-fi) This friendly bright hostel is just off the main street, a few minutes' walk from the Sugar Factory. Facilities and amenities include bike rentals, kitchen and barbecue area, wi-fi, laundry and English-speaking staff. Bookings must be made through online booking services such as Hostelworld.com. Backpacker also runs another hostel in town with a jailhouse theme.

WaGaLiGong (Dulan 89) HOSTEL $
(哇軋力共, Wa Yà Lì Gòng; ☎0913-481 392; www.facebook.com/wagaligong; dm/d/tw NT$600/1200/1300, small weekday discounts; @ wi-fi) This new Taiwanese and expat-run surf hostel is on the main road and features a restaurant and bar as well as amenities like wi-fi and laundry. Surf boards can be rented for NT$500 per day.

Dulan Indian Cuisine INDIAN $$
(☎0910-762 434; curries NT$200; ⏲10am-dinner Wed-Sun; menu) An unexpected treat in the east, this Indian restaurant run by a Bangalore native, who just couldn't hack it as a local organic rice farmer, serves some delicious set curry meals. The chick pea is particularly good as is the handmade ice cream (NT$60), worth a special trip on its own.

To get here turn right after the bridge as you head south at the Km145 marker. Stay left up the valley about 500m and then pull into a walled area on the right.

☆ Entertainment

★Dulan Café MUSIC VENUE
(都蘭糖廠咖啡屋, Dūlán Tángchǎng Kāfēiwū; ☎089-530 330; http://dulancafe.pixnet.net/blog; Dulan Sugar Factory; ⏲10am-whenever; wi-fi) FREE It all began with the cafe, people say. Run by an Ami family who are heavily involved in the music and arts scene, the cafe sponsors the weekly live-music performances that have put Dulan on the map. If there is a heart to Dulan, this is certainly it.

The performances start every Saturday evening and go into the night. Most musicians are local Amis, but guest performers come from elsewhere. The cafe also frequently hosts art showings.

ℹ Getting There & Away

Dulan is a 30-minute drive north of Taitung. You can rent a touring bicycle, car or scooter (you must have a local licence to rent a scooter) in Taitung outside the train station. The East Coast Line of the **Tourism Shuttle Bus** (www.taiwantrip.com.tw) has six buses each day (NT$108, one hour) that run from the train station to Dulan. See the website for schedules.

There is also one bus a day from Hualien (NT$435, three hours) leaving at 9.20am.

Hsiao (Xiao) Yeliu 小野柳

Just a few kilometres north of Taitung is Hsiao Yeliu (Xiǎo Yěliǔ), a coastal park known for its bizarre rock and coral formations, formed over thousands of years by wind and water erosion. The landscape is truly unearthly here, with rocks curving and twisting into all manner of fantastic shapes.

There's a good **campground** (per site weekday/end NT$300/500) at the back of the park, with wooden tent platforms facing the sea. Fugang Harbour is also literally around the corner from here, meaning you can walk to seafood restaurants as well as to the boat for Green Island.

HIGHWAY 9 & THE EAST RIFT VALLEY

Highway 9 is the main transport artery through the East Rift Valley (www.erv-nsa.gov.tw), a long alluvial plain that just happens to sit right on the seam of the collision point between the Philippine and Eurasian plates. The valley has some of Taiwan's best farming country, to say nothing of rural scenery: bordered by the Central Mountains on one side and the Coastal Mountain Ranges on the other, there are stunning views in every direction.

ℹ Getting Around

There are good train services all down the Rift Valley, and most small towns have bike rentals.

BICYCLE

Highway 9 is flatter and straighter than Highway 11, but it has more traffic, especially trucks. At the time of writing, bike-only lanes had been built from Liyu Lake to around Fuli, but many cyclists still prefer to take highly scenic backcountry routes such as County Roads 193 and 197, popping back onto Highway 9 for meals and accommodation. If you are doing a loop of the east coast, it is easy to avoid scruffy Taitung city by taking the 197 past Luye.

Liyu Lake & Mugua River Gorge

Though the entire Rift Valley was most likely once a giant lake, it drained long ago, leaving 2km long Liyu Lake (鯉魚潭, Lǐyú Tán) as the largest natural body of fresh water on the east coast. Shaped somewhat like a carp (Liyu means 'carp' in Chinese), Liyu is tucked into the green foothills of the Central Mountain Range about 19km southwest of Hualien.

Families with small children who enjoy camping or picnicking will like it here. There are safe bike trails around the lake, **Chinan Forest Recreation Area** (池南國家森林遊樂區, Chínán Guójiā Sēnlín Yóulè qū; www.forest.gov.tw; admission NT$50; ⏲8am-5pm) has old trains and logging displays, and there are short hikes in nearby hills. In April fireflies are out in force. Just north of the lake are pleasant B&Bs, such as **Monet Garden** (莫內花園民宿, Mònèi Huāyuán Mínsù; ☎864 2243; www.monetgarden.com.tw; d/tw incl breakfast from NT$2300/3600), which also has an excellent cafe, and **Liyu Lake Campground** (鯉魚潭露營區, Lǐyú Tán Lùyíng qū; ☎03-865 5678; per site NT$800, A-frame cabins NT$1000).

Cyclists looking for a bit of adventure should come midweek, and out of summer months, and ride to the **Mugua River Gorge** (慕谷慕魚, Mùgǔ Mùyú), a chasm as dramatic in appearance as Taroko Gorge but far more raw. The gorge has a morning and afternoon limit of 300 visitors so get here by 5.30am (for the 6.30am opening) or 11am (for the noon opening). You need to register at the police station along the way to receive your permit. Bring your passport and note that headlights are essential for this ride.

Several popular swimming holes can be found in the gorge down a side road. After passing the police station, continue a few kilometres until you reach a large red bridge. Don't cross, but instead take the lower road to the left going upstream along the Chingshui River. Further up are some large marble-lined natural swimming holes filled with deep, bluish green, crystal-clear water. Recent restaurant and shop construction has ruined the atmosphere in places, but you can still find beautiful spots.

If you want to take a bus to Liyu Lake there are nine per day from Hualien (NT$82, 20 minutes). The Shoufong (壽豐, Shòufēng) bus (from Hualien) passes by the lake.

Lintianshan 林田山林業文化園區

At its heyday as a Japanese-era logging village, Lintianshan (Líntiánshān) housed a population of over 2000. The now near ghost town is definitely worth a visit if you are in the area. The surrounding mountains are lushly forested and there is a genuine historical atmosphere to the village, which is made entirely out of cypress. The main buildings and a couple exhibition halls that highlight logging, firefighting and woodcarving are opened from 8am to 5pm Tuesday to Sunday, but you can wander the village at any time.

If you are driving south, take the exit at Km243 on Highway 9 for Wanrong. The turn-off for Lintianshan (marked in English) is a few hundred metres down. From Hualien, there are four morning trains (NT$40 to NT$65, one hour). Get off at Wanrong Station (萬榮) and turn left down a short lane. Turn left again at the end and follow the road (Hwy 16) for about 2.5km.

Hualien Sugar Factory

Sugar became an important export in the late 19th century after the forced opening of ports following the second Opium War. Up until the 1930s it dominated the economy, and under Japanese colonial rule, sugar fields and processing factories were established all over the island. The **Hualien Sugar Factory** (光復糖廠, Guāngfù Tángchǎng; Guangfu) was built in 1921 and at its peak was processing 2600 tons of sugarcane a day.

The factory closed in 2002, and left a wealth of old wood dormitories, machines and storage buildings intact. After years of reconstruction the **houses** (日式木屋旅館式, Rìshì Mùwū Lǚguǎn Shì; ☎870 4125; www.hualiensugar.com.tw; d/tw NT$3240/4320, midweek discounts 30%) are now once again opened for overnight guests. Free bike rentals are included and there are a couple restaurants on the factory grounds.

Just south of the factory grounds is **Danong Dafu Forest Park** (大農大富平地森林園區, Dànóng Dàfù Píngdì Sēnlín Yuánqū), 11-hectares of reforested ground that was once planted with sugar fields. Nestled between the coastal and central range, the views here are breathtaking and the high grass teems with birdlife. The turn-off for the park is at Km256 on Highway 9, though you can also wend your way here from the sugar factory backroads.

Even if you don't plan to stay the night at the factory, stop for the **ice cream** (NT$45; 8am-8pm), and a wander around the factory grounds. Here's a bit of trivia for you: the large carp pools beside the ice-cream shop are craters from the US bombing of Taiwan during WWII.

The sugar factory is just south of the town of Guangfu (光復) on Highway 9. There are signs in English on the highway directing you there.

Matai'an 馬太鞍

☎03 / POP 500

On the west side of Highway 9, close to the Hualien Sugar Factory turn-off, is the wetland area known as Matai'an (Mǎtàiān). An ideal place for farming and fishing, Matai'an has supported generations of Ami. Recent efforts to protect wetlands have seen the area turned into a bit of an ecological classroom.

At **Shin-liu Farm** (欣綠農園, Xīnlǜ Nóngyuán; ☎870 1861; www.shin-liu.com; d/tw NT$2400/2800) – really more of a guesthouse – a network of wooden bridges and narrow walking paths criss-cross over a large picturesque section of wetland. In June look for lotus flowers in bloom, and in autumn and winter, glow-in-the-dark mushrooms sprout in the nearby hills. Fireflies

LITTLE HOUSE ON THE RIFT VALLEY

In addition to the knockout scenery, most visitors to Taiwan's east coast are charmed by the many frontier-style villages dotting the region. Among the most common dwellings (besides modern cement blockhouses often 'adorned' with the most amazing collection of old tires, cables, farm equipment, recyclables and, oddly enough, stacks of doors) are clapboard houses from the Japanese era, and a type of whitewashed bungalow, painted blue on the lower half, with a sloped tiled roof supported by two front columns.

This simple southern Chinese (Fujian) accommodation is called a *ping fang* (平房). A typical *ping fang* will have three rooms, which can be expanded (to support a bigger family) by adding front-facing extensions. The house is then known as a *sanheyuan* (三合院; three-side structure) which are commonly found on the west coast of Taiwan (such as around Meinong), though usually sporting a handsome red-brick exterior.

Historians claim that the white and blue colouring in the east is not traditional but done to imitate Greek-style housing. Some particularly good places to check out these frontier homes are Guanshan, Luye, County Roads 193 and 197, and the road to Liji.

are out most of the year and at any time it's worth a stop for a stroll. The farm is free to access and there are English interpretation signs about the place.

For an intimate homestay in the Matai'an area with a local family enquire at **Cifadahan Cafe** (紅瓦屋文化美食餐廳, Hóngwǎwū Wénhuà Měishí Cāntīng, Kwangfu Hong Wawu; ☎870 4601; www.facebook.com/cifadahan; 9-course set meal NT$350; ⏲11am-2pm & 5-8pm; 🗐), which is also called Hong Wawu Restaurant. Also, don't miss the food at this Matai'an institution. Run by a talented Ami artist whose aboriginal-themed carvings and furniture adorn the restaurant, dishes include a 19-vegetable salad and a hot pot (石頭火鍋) brought to the boil with fire-heated stones. The huge set meals offer a range of dishes to sample.

ℹ Getting There & Around

CAR & SCOOTER

Coming from the north, look for signs in Chinese at the Km251.5 mark on Highway 9. Turn right. Head straight until the road ends then turn left and follow the signs (now in English) to the farm or cafe.

TRAIN

From Hualien (fast/slow NT$98/76, 45 minutes/one hour, hourly). Exit at Guangfu Station and walk to Highway 9. Turn right and walk 1km south. Turn right at sign for Matai'an.

Fuyuan Forest Recreational Area 蝴蝶谷溫泉度假村, 富源國家森林遊樂區

In the late 19th and early 20th century Taiwan dominated the world market of camphor production. Extracted from the stately camphor tree, which grew in abundance at midlevel elevations, the substance was used in everything from embalming fluid to medicine to insect repellent.

A few kilometres off Highway 9, in an area of serene natural beauty, the 235-hectare **Fuyuan Forest Recreational Area** (Húdié gǔ wēnquán dùjiàcūn xiǎo zhú, Fùyuán Guójiā Sēnlín Yóulè Qū; www.bvr.com.tw; admission NT$100; ⏲6am-5pm), which is run by the Butterfly Valley Resort, protects the largest pure camphor forest left in Taiwan. Quiet trails run through the reserve to waterfalls and

PUBLIC LAND LEASING

In recent years, government expropriation of private land and cheap leasing of public land to developers has been a contentious issue in Taiwan.

Shanyuan Beach (杉原海水浴場, Shānyuán Hǎishuǐ Yùchǎng), the longest swimmable beach between Hualien and Taitung, is an example of public land leasing that has been hotly contested by locals. The beach was once public and serviced by a range of local businesses, from B&Bs to a campground and one of the best Italian restaurants in Taiwan. But in 2004, with the promise of bringing jobs to the region, the local government signed a build-operate-transfer (BOT) agreement with Taipei's Miramar Group, which required other businesses to vacate the beach.

No environmental impact assessment (EIA) was passed for this project, as Miramar's initial plans declared their hotel would be 0.9 hectares and, by law, EIAs are not required for projects under 0.9 hectares. However, after Miramar applied for exansion permits, and ended up with a resort six times the size of the original plans, the Environmental Protection Agency demanded the county government submit an EIA. The Taitung County quickly pushed one through in a meeting that consisted largely of its own county council members. The High Court and Supreme Court ruled several times that the EIA was flawed and construction must cease.

Taitung locals, headed by aboriginal groups, were at the forefront of the fight for the beach, holding protest concerts and and taking Miramar to court over building violations. In October 2013 the Supreme Administrative Court made a final ruling that the construction had been illegal from the start and must be terminated. Miramar accepted the results.

The court ruling may affect far more than Shanyuan Beach and its surrounding environment. Dozens of similarly large construction projects have been green-lit on the coast but, following the case of Shanyuan Beach, it's likely developers will rethink their approach.

special bird and butterfly corridors. About 100 species of birds can be found in Fuyuan, and you have a good chance of spotting the gorgeous Maroon Oriole. As for butterflies, this is one of the richest areas in the east: swallowtails are in abundance, including the exquisite Golden Birdwing.

A series of open-air stone and wood **hot-spring pools** (admission NT$250; ⏲10am-10pm) nestle under the camphor trees not far from the ticketing booth and are open late. The resort also has rooms starting at NT$8000 and guests and nonguests can eat at the **buffet restaurant** (breakfast/lunch/dinner NT$450/550/900; ⏲7am-10am, noon-2pm & 6-9pm), which has a wide variety of dishes including many rare seasonal local vegetables. There are also plenty of less expensive guesthouses on the road into the reserve.

It's a bit tricky getting here off Highway 9. If you are driving south, just past Km260 turn right onto a smaller road and follow this 1.1km to Guang Dong Rd (just past the police station and before a temple). Then turn right and follow this beautiful country road to the end.

From Ruisui there is a cycling path to the Fuyuan area and you can rent bikes or scooters outside Ruisui train station on weekends. Fuyuan also has a train station but it's a bit far to the forest park.

Ruisui (Rueisui) 瑞穗

☎03 / POP 5000

Ruisui (Ruìsuì) opens up into some very scenic countryside within a few minutes from the train station. In particular, a deep gorge cutting through the Coastal Mountains, formed by the longest river in the east. In the summer months Taiwanese flock here to raft and then later soak in Ruisui's carbonated hot springs.

At 70km from Hualien (depending on your route), and at the junction of three excellent cycling roads (Hwy 9, County Road 193 and the Ruigang Hwy), Ruisui is often used as an overnight stop for cyclists.

Activities

Ruisui Hot Springs HOT SPRING

(瑞穗溫泉, Ruìsuì Wēnquán) The carbonated Ruisui hot springs were first opened by the Japanese in 1919 reportedly as a rehab centre for injured soldiers. The water boasts a temperature of 48°C and is rich in iron, giving it a pale-brown colour and a slightly salty, rusty flavour (so we've heard). Many Taiwanese still believe that frequent bathing in the spring water increases a woman's chance of bearing a male child.

The hot-spring area (with a dozen or more hotels) is a few kilometres directly west of Ruisui town (on the other side of Hwy 9). As you drive down the highway there are English signs pointing to the area.

Rafting

Rafting trips (泛舟, Fànzhōu) can be arranged all year at the **Rueisui Rafting Service Centre** (瑞穗泛舟服務中心, Ruìsuì Fànzhōu Fúwù Zhōngxīn; ☎887 5400) at the start of the rafting route. The standard fee is NT$750, which includes transportation from and to Hualien, lunch, equipment and insurance. See the East Coast National Scenic (www.eastcoast-nsa.gov.tw) website for a list of companies.

The peak season is May to September. About 10 companies operate during this time, which means you can usually just show up in the morning and join a trip. Boats usually run between 7am and noon and take 3½ hours to complete the 24km-long route down the Xiuguluan (Hsiukuluan) River (Xiùgūluán Xī) from Ruisui to Dagangkou. For the most part, this is leisurely rafting, unless there has been a typhoon recently.

To get to the service centre on your own, head out from Ruisui train station and continue straight along Zhongshan Rd for about 4km to 5km. A taxi will cost around NT$100.

There's a good **campground** (per site weekday/weekend NT$300/500) with toilets and showers at the service centre.

Sleeping & Eating

Most hot-spring hotels have restaurants in them. Around the train station there are numerous small noodle stands and restaurants, as well as convenience stores for snacks, sandwiches and drinks.

Rueisui Hot Springs Hotel GUESTHOUSE $$

(瑞穗溫泉山莊, Ruìsuì Wēnquán ShānZhuāng; ☎887 2170; www.js-hotspring.com.tw; 23 Hongye Village; dm/d/tw NT$500/2400/3600) At over 90 years old, this place lays claim to being the first and longest-running hot spring and guesthouse in the area. Managed by a local family and offering tatami-style dorm rooms and bike storage, it's a popular place for cyclists to spend the night.

Double and twin rooms are pretty basic and can be a bit noisy so non-cyclists may prefer the more modern and stylish hotels nearby that go for NT$2000 to NT$3000 a night. The Rueisui Hot Springs Hotel is up a small road off the main road through the hot-spring area (there are signs in English).

Getting There & Away

There are hourly trains from Hualien to Ruisui (fast/slow train NT$110/143, one/1½ hours). You can rent scooters (per day NT$400) and good quality bikes outside the train station on weekends.

Yuli 玉里

03 / POP 3000

In the mid-19th century, Hakka immigrants from Guangzhou established Yuli (Yùlǐ) as one of the earliest non-aboriginal settlements on the east coast. Today, with the Central Mountains looking over its shoulder, and the Rift Valley under its nose, Yuli is well placed for day trips to hot springs, mountains covered with day lilies, the organic rice-growing valley at Loshan, and the eastern section of Yushan National Park.

Activities

Two popular day rides start from a marked path to the right of the train station (as you exit). The first leads to the Walami Trail (12km away); the second, to Antong Hot Springs via a section of abandoned rail line running through fields of rice and swaying betel-nut palms. The backcountry heading west toward the mountains is also filled with scenic farm roads. Head out toward the Walami Trail and follow your nose.

You can rent good bikes at the **Giant** (捷安特, Jié Ān Tè; 888 5669; 和平路47號; 8am-9.30pm) bicycle shop on Heping Rd (per day NT$200) for short or extended trips. To find the shop head straight from the train station and turn left at the second intersection. The shop is on the left a block up the street.

Sleeping & Eating

Yuli's eponymous noodles (玉裡麵; Yùlǐ miàn) won't strike you as much different from Ruisui or Taipei noodles, but they are cheap (per bowl NT$45), filling and ubiquitous.

Two budget hotels sit across the road from the train station. We like **Walami Inn** (瓦拉米客棧, Wǎlāmǐ Kèzhàn; 888 6681; 214 Datong Rd, 大同路214號; d NT$800-1600, tw NT$1800-2500;) best because of the name, the friendly front desk staff, wi-fi, and the slightly more-updated rooms.

★ **Wisdom Garden** HOMESTAY $$
(智嵐雅居民宿, Zhìlán YǎJū Mínsù; 0921-986 461; www.wisdom-garden.com; 玉里鎮大禹里5鄰酸甘98-1號; r from NT$2200; @) This country-quaint guesthouse just outside town is *the* place to stay in the Yuli area. The house sits in an orchard high above the Rift Valley, looking across to Chikha Mountain. Rooms all have their own character, and are flooded with light. The owner, a Buddhist and former hotel manager, has made a true retreat here.

If you're driving, the turn-off for Wisdom Garden is at the Km289.4 mark on Hwy 9. Just follow the signs from here. If you make prior arrangements the owners will pick you up from Yuli train station.

Shalom TEAHOUSE $
(五餅二魚複合式茶舖, Wǔbǐng Èryú Fùhéshì Chápù; 174 Zhongshan Rd, 中山路二段174號; set meals NT$160; 11am-10pm;) Set in a 100-year-old former police station, this teahouse offers simple meals and drinks with very friendly service. To reach the shop, head straight out from the train station and turn left on Zhongshan Rd.

Getting There & Away

Frequent trains run from Hualien to Yuli (fast/slow train NT$190/146, one hour and 20 minutes/two hours).

Antong Hot Springs 安通溫泉

About 8km south of the town of Yuli off Hwy 26, Antong (Antung) Hot Springs (Āntōng Wēnquán) have been soothing tired bodies since Japanese times. The clear alkaline waters (slightly odorous) have a temperature of 66°C and are drinkable. In fact, hotels here use it to make coffee (the only place we know of in Taiwan that does so).

Modern hotels with a range of rooms and pools have popped up in the upper and lower village: the latter are most enjoyably reached by bicycle from Yuli along the old train tracks. An excellent option for spending the night is in the upper village at **New Life Hot Springs Resort** (紐澳華溫泉山莊, Niǔàohuá Wēnquán Shānzhuāng; 03-888 7333; www.twspring.com.tw; dm with IYH card NT$800, r incl breakfast from NT$2600, midweek discounts

ABORIGINAL FESTIVALS ON THE EAST COAST

Dates for festivals are only roughly the same each year, so it's important to find out the exact schedule before you go. Call the 24-hour **tourist hotline** (☎0800-011 765) or contact the **East Coast National Scenic Administration** (www.eastcoast-nsa.gov.tw).

Ami Harvest Festival The largest aboriginal festival in Taiwan takes place from July through September in various towns around Hualien and Taitung Counties. In June tribal chiefs choose the exact dates.

Bunun Ear Shooting Festival (Malahodaigian) The festival is held in towns throughout the East Rift Valley around the end of April. It's meant to honour the legendary hunting heroes of the tribe and to teach young boys how to use bows and arrows.

Rukai Harvest Festival One highlight of this harvest festival is watching tribal youth play on giant swings. The festival takes place every July or August in Beinan Township, Taitung County.

Tiehua Music Village (鐵花村音樂聚落; http://tw.streetvoice.com/users/tiehua; 26 Lane 153, Xinsheng Rd) In Taitung city, this is the site of weekly music events from mostly aboriginal performers and a few local indie bands. Major performances are Saturday nights, while up-and-coming groups and individuals perform during the week. Show times are Wednesday to Saturday 8pm to 10pm, and 4pm to 6pm Sunday.

If you are interested in exploring aboriginal Taiwan in more depth, Cheryl Robbins' books (a three-part guide to travel in aboriginal areas all over Taiwan), website (www.tribe-asia.com) and tour company are a great place to start. There are few, people more expert on the subject than this long-term expat who is also a certified tour guide.

20%). The resort is more like a wood lodge, with wide decks and open halls for relaxing. Rooms are airy, wood panelled and open to views across the Coastal Mountains. The more expensive suites have their own private hot-spring area: not just a tub but a whole separate room. To get to the hotel look for the English sign as you ride into the hot-spring area.

Walami Trail 瓦拉米古道

A must-do hike, the Walami Trail (Wălāmĭ Gŭdào) begins high above the Nanan River, about 12km southeast of Yuli in the Nanan section of Yushan National Park. Along the path there are high waterfalls, suspension bridges, lookouts, sections cut straight into the cliff walls, and the constant sound (and occasional sight) of monkeys crashing through the trees. It's a subtropical jungle out there – and one of the best preserved in Taiwan. The views down the valley and across the mountains are chillingly beautiful.

The trail hails from the Japanese era and was built to facilitate the opening of the east as well as maintain a careful eye on aboriginal tribes. In fact, the Walami Trail forms part of the much-longer Japanese-era Batongguan Traversing Route, which cuts right across Yushan National Park.

You can hike the first couple of kilometres without permits. With permits you can hike the 14km (six to seven hours) up to the attractive Walami Cabin and spend the night. The A-frame cabin has water and room for 24 hikers.

Apply at least a week ahead of time for a permit (see www.ysnp.gov.tw). On the day of your hike check in at the **Nanan Visitor Centre** (南安遊客中心; ☎03-888 7560; www.ysnp.gov.tw; ⏲9am-4.30pm, closed 2nd Tue of each month) and then pick up a mountain permit at the police station. If you plan to return the same day you can pick up a one-day pass (on the same day) at the visitor centre provided you apply earlier than 9am.

If you don't have your own transportation, a taxi from Yuli to the visitor centre will cost about NT$400 – more if you want the driver to wait while you arrange permits and then drive you the last 6km to the trailhead.

Consider renting a bike in Yuli. You'll first pass old Hakka villages dating back to the 1850s, then along open fields, and finally up the deep wooded Nanan River gorge (passing **Nanan Waterfall**, 南安瀑布, Nánān Pùbù), which just gets more lush and wild with every kilometre.

OFF THE BEATEN TRACK

SIXTY STONE MOUNTAIN

One of the east coast's most mesmerising landscapes sits high above the Rift Valley. As you ride the ever winding road up, it seems as if this is 'simply' yet another journey through beautiful lush subtropical forest. But wait for the top, where cleared forest gives way to a 400-acre table of undulating farmland dotted with homesteads and pavilions. Imagine the English midlands 1000m up with a backdrop of dark emerald mountains fast descending to a valley floor where they seem to anchor themselves to earth with giant hooked fingers.

And there is more: once a typical mid-altitude rice-growing area, Sixty Stone Mountain (六十石山, Liùshí Dàn Shān; 952m) became a centre for growing day (tiger) lilies (金針, *jīnzhēn)* a few decades ago. The orange-coloured lilies are popular with Taiwanese consumers who eat them fresh or dried in tea drinks and a host of other products. During the harvest time from August to early September the plateau is carpeted with orange blossoms and this already dreamy landscape turns pure wonderland.

There are a number of guesthouses at the top of the mountain should you wish to stay the night. Try **Wangyou Yuan Guesthouse** (忘憂園民宿小築, Wàngyōu yuán mínsù xiăo zhú; ☎03-882 1368; http://60stonedaylily.hlbnb.tw; d/tw NT$2000/3000, 20% discounts midweek) if you want to make a reservation during the busy day lily season.

You need your own transport to get here. The turn-off on Hwy 9 is just past Yuli at Km308.5. Look for the sign reading 'Lioushihdan Mountain'.

Loshan (Luoshan) Scenic Area 羅山風景區

Just south of Sixty Stone Mountain, in an area called the rice barn of Taiwan, lies this stunning valley (Lóshān) that Hakka farmers have transformed into the centre of the organic rice industry in Hualien. Loshan is rural Taiwan at its best: bucolic splendour running in every direction, with green rice fields lying between not just one but two dramatic mountain ranges. Ride up the main road through the valley toward the steep and densely forested Coastal Mountains and minute by minute, curve by curve, the landscape changes. A few stops to make include the quaintly photogenic villages, the 120m-long **Luoshan Waterfall** (羅山瀑布, Lóshān Pùbù) and a number of small bubbling mud volcanoes.

The **visitor centre** (☎03-882 1725; ⏲8.30am-5.30pm) runs a free campground. Call ahead (Chinese only) to reserve a tent platform. You can also rent bikes for free here.

The centre can help with homestays and with joining a group to make the area's speciality cuisine: 'volcanic tofu'. A good nearby option for sleeping is at the spacious **Luntian Recreation Area** (綠海天際渡假村, Lû Hăitiān Jì Dùjià Cūn; ☎03-884 6099; http://greencurb.hlbnb.tw; d/tw incl breakfast NT$3040/3840, 25% discounts midweek; 📶). The duplex cabins feature a high level of comfort, and an open airy design that allows natural light to flood in. To get to the area turn right off Hwy 9 just past Km309 and follow the signs for about a kilometre.

If you are looking for a quick bite, the giant agricultural association building just north of the Loshan entrance has good lunchbox meals for NT$80 to NT$100.

Guanshan (Kuanshan) 關山

POP 2000

For most of Taiwan's history, the Guanshan region was Ami territory until the Japanese opened the area to logging and farming in the late 19th century. Today, Guanshan is renowned for its rice, and most residents work in the farming sector. For the traveller it makes a pleasant base for exploring the region. The town retains much of its Japanese-era atmosphere, with tree-lined streets, clapboard houses, and the only remaining wood train station on the entire Rift Valley line (it's to the right of the new station as you exit).

Guanshan is best known these days for a short (12km) but scenic bike path through rice paddies and fields of colza and sugarcane, but it's not really worth a special trip here. However, there is excellent riding all around, including down to Luye, and along County Road 197. Dozens of bike rental shops are set up around the train station including **Giant** (捷安特關山站; ☎089-814 391; http://tw.myblog.yahoo.com/giant-guanshan; ⏲9am-6pm Fri-Sun) that has bikes for day (NT$200) and multiday rides (per three days NT$1200 including saddle bags; book in advance). The shop is just to the right of the train station as you exit.

Sleeping & Eating

Corner House GUESTHOUSE $$
(☎0922-982 873; www.cornerhome.url.tw; d/tw incl breakfast NT$2200/3200; 📶) Corner House has near boutique-level rooms that include free bike rental and a locally made and delivered traditional breakfast. To get here turn right on Zhongshan Rd as you drive the main road through town (Hwy 9). The guesthouse is on the corner with Sanmin Rd. There's a 20% midweek discount on room rates.

Guanshan Meatball Restaurant TAIWANESE $
(關山肉圓老店, Guānshān Ròuyuán Lǎo Diàn; 60 Zhonghua Rd; dishes NT$30-100; ⏲6am-3pm) This well-known, family-run shop across from the Matsu Temple (look for the temple's big red arch off the main road through town) serves a variety of local dishes, including their namesake meatballs. There's a picture menu.

Getting There & Around

There are frequent trains to Guanshan from Hualien (fast/slow train NT$276/213, two/three hours).

Luye 鹿野

The township that ugliness forgot, Luye (Lùyě) was first settled by Amis and Puyuma aboriginals who hunted the abundant herds of deer. After the Japanese settled the area in the 1920s, they reportedly claimed this was the best place to live in Taiwan. Today, the township is a prosperous tea-growing region, a popular retirement destination and, rather incongruously, a centre for paragliding and the **Taiwan International Balloon Fiesta** (熱氣球嘉年華, Rèqìqiú Jiāniánhuá; http://balloontaiwan.taitung.gov.tw). This hot-air balloon event, held each summer from June to mid-August, is getting wildly popular, and in 2013, free-riding (which means sailing on the balloons untethered) was added to the roster.

Township Rd 33 is the main route through Luye (turn off Hwy 9 at Km344.5). Keep in mind the sprawl around the Luye train station off Hwy 9 is not at all representative of the region.

Sights & Activities

★Luye Gaotai SCENIC AREA
(鹿野高台, Lùyě Gāotái) Luye's pastoral charms don't grow on you, they embrace you fast, like a person you want to marry after a first date. And do! There's no better place to fall for the township than the area known as the Gaotai, a fecund plateau rising sharply above the alluvial plains.

In addition to the orderly fields of tea and pineapples, and panoramic views, the lower villages of Longtian (龍田村) and Yongan (永安村) have maintained much of their historical character as Japanese immigrant villages, and are worth a visit. The easiest way to find these villages is to take Township Rd 34 off Hwy 9 just past the train station.

The Gaotai used to be a popular venue for tandem paragliding, but the future of that sport is uncertain. Contact the **Luye Visitor Centre** (☎551 637) for more information.

To get to the Gaotai, take Township Rd 33 at Km344.5 and follow the signs up.

Hongye Hot Springs HOT SPRING
(山月溫泉館, Shān Yuè Wēnquán Guǎn; per person NT$150; ⏲2-11pm Mon-Fri, 10am-11pm Sat & Sun) These pleasant outdoor hot springs are just a quick hop from Luye; you could walk from the Zixi Garden Lodge in about 20 minutes. At Km356 on Hwy 9, turn right and follow the signs for Hong Ye Hot Springs (the old name for this place).

Sleeping & Eating

The plateau has a half dozen or so well-run B&Bs and an equal number of cafes and restaurants. Agricultural products are on sale at various shops. Fulu Tea, a type of oolong, is the region's most popular product, and in many ways is the source of its modern prosperity.

Frog & Pheasant B&B GUESTHOUSE $$
(青蛙與雉雞民宿, Qīngwā Yǔ Zhìjī Mínsù; ☎0973-829 665; www.travel123.com.tw/bnb/fp.htm; r from NT$3000; 📶) Run by an Australian expat and his Taiwanese wife, this cheerful guesthouse sits down on the rice growing tableland above the Beinan River. Rooms are large and set off an airy bright living room. Call for

OFF THE BEATEN TRACK

COUNTY ROAD 197 & THE LIJI BADLANDS 利吉惡地

This made-for-touring (bike, car or scooter) route skirts the Beinan River Valley as its shores change from dense subtropical forest cover buzzing with bird and butterfly life to a fantastical muddy, barren moon-world of sheer slopes, deep ravines and pointy ridges: and that's just on one side! On the opposite bank, the more durable cliffs have been eroded into kilometres of craggy ridges and steep-sided outcrops. The area goes by the name Little Huangshan (小黃山), after the famous Chinese landscape, while the moon-world is called the Liji Badlands.

County Road 197 begins around Guanshan, but there is a long gravel section so it's best to start just past Luye by turning left at Km350.5 toward Luanshan. On the opposite side of the bridge (across the Beinan River), turn right and follow the 197. Later, at the sign for Liji, turn right onto 東45.

In addition to the badlands and the crags, the village of Liji itself is a picturesque place, and there are a number of guesthouses should you want to stay the night.

東45 eventually leads into Taitung but if you want to avoid the sprawling town, you can loop up to coastal Highway 11 at Km8.5 on 東45 by literally doing a U-turn up onto the bridge. This puts you on Hwy 11乙. After crossing a pretty stretch of fields, you'll connect to Hwy 11 just north of Taitung city.

reservations and directions as the place is a bit tricky to find. There are 15% discounts midweek.

Zixi Garden Lodge LODGE **$$**
(紫熹花園山莊, Zǐxī Huāyuán Shānzhuāng; ☎089-550 617; www.tzyy-shi.com.tw; d/tw incl breakfast NT$3460/4950, midweek discounts 30%; 📶) This enormous lodge sports wood-panelled rooms, Chinese- and Japanese-style wings, and a mezzanine reading floor. If coming from the north, turn right on County Rd 33 just past Km356. Zixi Garden Lodge is on the left about a kilometre up from Hwy 9. Look for the wooden arch fronting the grounds.

Getting There & Around

The **Taiwan Tourism Shuttle Bus** (www.taiwantrip.com.tw) runs every hour or two from Taitung train station to Luye train station and Gaotai, but it's best to have your own transport.

Taitung 台東

☎089 / POP 110,192

TRANSPORT HUB

There's little reason to visit this sprawling, traffic congested town, except for the fascinating Lunar New Year festival Bombing Master Handan (p200) or the live music at Tiehua Music Village (p195). If you need a base in the region consider Dulan or Guanshan.

The train station is inconveniently placed on the outskirts of town and you cannot rent a scooter here without a local licence.

Sleeping & Eating

There are a few small restaurants around the train station. Otherwise head to the old train station in the downtown area.

Longxing Holiday Cabins HOTEL **$**
(龍星花園渡假木屋, Lóngxīng Huāyuán Dùjià Mùwū; ☎228 005; www.long-xing.com.tw; 625 Xinxing Rd, 新興路625號; d/tw from NT$1100/1700; 📶) The cabins, actually connected rooms around a central garden, are in a perfect location if you're arriving late or heading out early from the train station. It's just two blocks straight ahead on the right from the station exit.

Getting There & Away

AIR

There are flights from Taitung's **Fong Nian Airport** (www.tta.gov.tw) to Kaohsiung, Taichung, Lanyu and Green Islands with **Daily Air Corporation** (www.dailyair.com.tw). **Uni Air** (www.uniair.com.tw) has flights to Taipei.

BUS

The East Coast Line of the Tourism Shuttle Bus (www.taiwantrip.com.tw) has six daily buses from the train station to Fugang Harbour (for boats to Green Island and Lanyu), Xiao Yeliu, Shanyuan Beach, Dulan, Jinzun, Donghe and Sanxiantai. There is also a line to Luye. See the website for schedules.

There are a few daily buses to Kaohsiung and two daily to Hualien, but they are slower and more expensive than the train. There are no buses to Kenting.

TRAIN

Hualien (fast/slow train NT$345/266, 2½/3½ hours, hourly)

Kaohsiung (fast/slow train NT$362/279, 2½/3½ hours, hourly).

Getting Around

TO/FROM THE AIRPORT

Taxis are plentiful, or take the Tourism Shuttle Bus (www.taiwantrip.com.tw), which run six times daily (NT$23, 15 minutes) at 6.52am, 8.22am, 9.52am, 11.52am, 1.22pm and 2.52pm.

CAR & SCOOTER

You can rent cars and scooters from both the train station and airport; however, you must have a local Taiwanese licence to rent a scooter. For a car, bring an International Driver's Permit.

South of Taitung

South of Taitung there are a few interesting little stops where you can enjoy bathing in hot springs, beachcombing and a fascinating banyan forest.

Cyclists can continue riding south (Hwy 11 is a nicer ride out of Taitung than the 9) to connect with the 199 to Kenting, but be aware that the cycling shoulder lane ends past Chihpen. Many find sharing the twisting and rising road with speeding trucks more of a challenge than they care for. Consider taking the train down to Dawu or getting a very early morning start. Either way most riders can make it to Kenting in a day.

Chihpen (Zhiben) 知本

Chihpen (Zhībě) lies about 15km southwest of Taitung in a canyon at the foot of the Dawu Mountains. It's a popular hot-spring area, with rows of five-star hotels, garish KTVs and traffic clogging the road into the canyon on weekends. At the far end of the canyon is a lush jungle park with a beautiful banyan forest.

Sights & Activities

★Chihpen (Zhiben) Forest Recreation Area FOREST PARK
(知本森林遊樂區, Zhīběn Sēnlín Yóulè Qū; www.forest.gov.tw; admission NT$80; ⏲7am-5pm) This enchanting forest park features a path of giants; giant white-bark fig trees, that is. These 'weeping figs' have hanging ariel roots that form a complex spiderweb-like design. In the forest it's also common to see Formosan macaques and even catch a glimpse of the tiny Reeves' muntjac deer (barking deer), which makes a barking sound like a dog.

The recreation area is at the end of the road through the hot-spring area.

Hot Springs

The quality of the sodium bicarbonate spring water (colourless, tasteless and 90°C) was first recognised by the Japanese, who built a resort here in the early 20th century. They dubbed the area 'Chihpen', meaning 'source of wisdom'. Most hotels have hot-spring facilities that are open to nonguests.

Toyugi Hot Spring Resort & Spa HOT SPRING
(東遊季溫泉渡假村, Dōngyóujì Wēnquán Dùjiàcūn; www.toyugi.com.tw; admission NT$300; ⏲8am-10pm) This resort sits on a large shelf above the river valley, giving it a private feel in the madhouse that is Chihpen. Facilities include a multipool complex, restaurant, and rooms and cabins (from NT$3500 per night). To get to the hotel look for the sign a few kilometres down the main road reading 'Journey to the East'.

Eating

The main road through Chihpen (Longchuan Rd) has plenty of small restaurants and noodle stands selling decent local food at standard prices.

Getting There & Away

From Zhiben Train Station (just south of Taitung) catch bus 8129 (NT$63). Morning buses run at 6.40am, 7.55am, 9.10am, 10.30am and 11.45am. The last return bus is at 10pm.

Taimali 太麻里

This small Bunun village (Tàimálǐ) running up the emerald coast hillsides has become known locally for efforts to revitalise traditional aboriginal culture (including the skills needed to genuinely live off the land). Outside of the Harvest Festival in August, travellers are unlikely to see any of this but do stop in for the beach, the long, beautiful palm-studded beach that stretches on and on. There's no swimming (it's far too rough) but the crashing surf, the wide soft-sand beach, the green mountains rising to the west and the long coastline sweeping out to the north make this an absolutely fabulous

WORTH A TRIP

BOMBING MASTER HANDAN

Taitung's most popular Lantern Festival activity only began in 1954, and is intimately tied to the gangsterism that has long plagued small town life in Taiwan. Called **Bombing Master Handan** (炸寒單, Zhà Hándān), the festival is, depending on which legend you believe, a celebration of a former Shang dynasty general (and god of wealth and war) who hates the cold, or a more recent thuggish leader who asked for his followers to blast him to death in payment for his crimes. Either way, 'warming' him with firecracker and bottle rockets as he passes by is considered a good way to win this god's favour.

The twist in the Taitung festival is that volunteers accompany the Handan statue on his platform as he is carried across town. Wearing nothing but red shorts and a few protective items (googles, gloves, scarf, amulet), they willingly subject themselves to the same treatment Handan is getting. Few last more than a few minutes of the barrage which is one reason why this strange festival is linked to organised crime: today, as in the past, many of the volunteers are current or ex-gangsters looking to show their courage, or atone for their sins.

Though banned for years because of its connection with mobsterism, the festival has been growing in popularity in recent years, and is now up there with the Matsu Pilgrimage, the Yenshui Fireworks Festival, and the Pingxi's sky lantern release as one of Taiwan's top folk events. Unfortunately it takes place at the same time as the latter three, which means a hard choice must be made come Lantern Festival time.

For a behind the scenes look at the festival, check out Ho Chao-ti's *The Gangster's God: A Film of the Taiwanese Underworld*.

place for a couple hours of strolling. There's also plenty of driftwood, should you want to build a fire, and no one would object if you set up a tent and camped out.

The BBC chose this beach as one of the 60 best places in the world to watch the sunrise of the new millennium on 31 December 1999.

SOUTH CROSS-ISLAND HIGHWAY

In August 2009 Typhoon Morakot wiped out large sections of this old mountain highway (南部橫貫公路), one of Taiwan's grandest. At the time of writing there was still no access on the west side from Meishan to Yakou, though rumors persisted that eventually some kind of road would reopen (though it's highly unlikely). We've included coverage up to Siangyang Forest Recreation Area, but ask about road conditions before you head out as many sections are still under repair. You need your own vehicle for this route.

Wulu 霧鹿

POP 100

The first real stop on the way up the highway, about 20km from Haituan, the tiny Bunun village of Wulu (Wùlù) sits on a ledge over the wild S-shaped **Wulu Canyon** (霧鹿峽谷, Wùlù XiáGǔ). As you ride through the area, watch for steamy fumaroles and hot-spring water spitting out from cracks in the canyon walls, and long cliff faces stained with colourful mineral deposits.

At the start of the village, take the side road to the left to the **Wulu Fort Memorial Park** (霧鹿炮臺紀念公園, Wùlù Pàotái Jìniàn Gōngyuán) to see the **Wulu Battery**, a pair of rusting canons that were built by the Russians in 1903, lost to the Japanese during the Russo-Japanese War, and then brought to Wulu in 1927 to suppress aboriginal revolts against the opening of the region for mineral extraction. They are the real thing, not reproductions, and sit atop a high crag perch still facing the village of Motian, which they shelled more than 80 years ago.

Wulu's hot-spring water is odourless and silky to the touch. One of the best places to try it is the **Chief Spa Hotel** (天龍飯店, Tiānlóng Fàndiàn; ☎089-935 075; www.chiefspa.com.tw; r incl breakfast from NT$3600, 30% discount weekdays), which looks out onto the canyon. Guests and nonguests can also cross the chasm on the highest suspension bridge in the east. Just up the road from the hotel on the left is a **sichuan restaurant** with OK food and an English menu.

Wulu is well known to birdwatchers, and organised tours frequently stop there. Endemic species to watch include the Taiwan partridge, mikado pheasant and rusty laughing thrush.

Lisong Hot Spring
栗松溫泉

Arguably the most beautiful natural hot spring in Taiwan, Lisong (Lìsōng Wēnquán) is a must-visit for any lover of the sublime in nature who's also up for a challenging hike. For here, at the base of a deep river valley, aeons of mineral deposits have painted a small limestone grotto shades of deep green, white, red and black. Steam rises from the rocks, and hot-spring water bubbles and spits and streams from fissures and cracks in the canyon walls. Stand in the right place and you're in a hot-spring shower. It's as good as it sounds.

To get to the springs, exit the highway around Km168 (about 8km to 9km up from Litao) onto a narrow marked farm road in the village of **Motian** (摩天, Mótiān). Follow the road for a kilometre or so to the trailhead and then head down. The way is exceptionally steep; be careful not to impale yourself on the 'trail improvements'. When you reach the river, the springs are to the left, and require a couple of crossings. It's best to save this for the dry winter months.

Siangyang Forest Recreation Area & Jiaming Lake National Trail
向陽森林遊樂區、嘉明湖

Another 12km along from Lisong Hot Spring, this forest recreation area (Xiàngyáng Sēnlíng Yóulè Qū; elevation 2300m) was at the end of the drivable road at the time of writing. Not a bad end, all things considered, as Siangyang offers prime birdwatching in the old cypress and pine forests, and a three-day national trail to **Jiaming Lake** (嘉明湖, Jiāmíng Hú). The elliptical alpine lake (elevation 3310m), gem-like on a sunny day, attracts a great deal of wildlife and your chances of spotting endemic yellow-throated martens and sambar deer are good. In fact, recent surveys put the number of deer in the area at a whopping 70 to 80 per square kilometre.

You only need a mountain permit for the hike which can be picked up at the police station near the **visitor centre** (☎0912-103 367; ⏲8.30am-4.30pm) on the day of the hike. However, you must prebook your cabin beds in advance (difficult without reading Chinese) with the **Forestry Bureau** (http://recreation.forest.gov.tw/askformonhouse/AskForPaperMain.aspx).

The 10.9km trail to the lake from Siangyang is clear and well marked, though fog at higher altitudes can make navigating difficult. The route begins in a pine and hemlock forest, but once you ascend the ridgeline it's all rolling hills of dwarf bamboo dotted with rhododendron bushes and wind-twisted alpine juniper.

Depending on the time you arrive at Siangyang and arrange permits, you can hike two to three hours up a very steep trail to the spacious wood **Siangyang Cabin** (向陽工寮, Xiàngyáng Gōngliáo), which has water and basic toilet facilities, or five to seven hours to the well-worn **Jiaming Lake Cabin** (嘉明湖避難山屋, Jiāmíng Hú Bìnàn Shānwū; 3350m). Note the water supply here is unreliable.

From Jiaming Lake Cabin, the trail runs along the lower edge of a ridge skirting a chain of rugged peaks. The lake itself is down from **Mt Sancha** (三叉山, Sānchā Shān; 3496m) in a wide hollow carpeted in soft dwarf bamboo. Camping is permitted but be sure to make your latrine on the other side of the watershed. Lake water can be drunk after purifying it.

From Jiaming Lake Cabin to the lake and back takes six to eight hours. It's another four to five hours back to the visitor centre.

Yushan National Park & Western Taiwan

Includes ➡

Best Hikes

➡ The Yushan Peaks (p205)

➡ Yuanzui–Shaolai–Xiaoshue National Trail (p211)

➡ Taichi Gorge (p235)

➡ Aowanda National Forest Recreation Area (p236)

➡ Hehuanshan Forest Recreation Area (p238)

Best Temples

➡ Chenghuang Temple (p214)

➡ Fengtian Temple (p216)

➡ Chaotian Temple (p216)

➡ Nanyao Temple (p222)

➡ Longshan Temple (p224)

➡ Glass Matsu Temple (p226)

➡ Chung Tai Chan Temple (p232)

Why Go?

If you're looking for variety in your Taiwan travel experience, look west. The Matsu Pilgrimage, one of the country's biggest and holiest celebrations, is definitely a highlight. This nine-day parade across half of Taiwan is an extravaganza of feasting, prostrating, praying and great acts of generosity.

Keen on hiking or trekking? Head to Yushan National Park to climb the highest peak in Northeast Asia; if you continue down the back route trails you'll be in total wilderness for days at a time. Alternatively, hike Dasyueshan or Hehuanshan, two awe-inspiring, high-altitude forests of pristine alpine scenery. For a glimpse of indigenous traditions, spend the night at one of the firefly-lit aboriginal villages in the Alishan Range.

For a bit of nostalgia, look no further than the quaint Japanese-era railway legacy in Alishan or the frozen-in-time streets in villages such as Lukang, both of which provide beautiful examples of the Taiwan of yore.

When to Go

Taichung

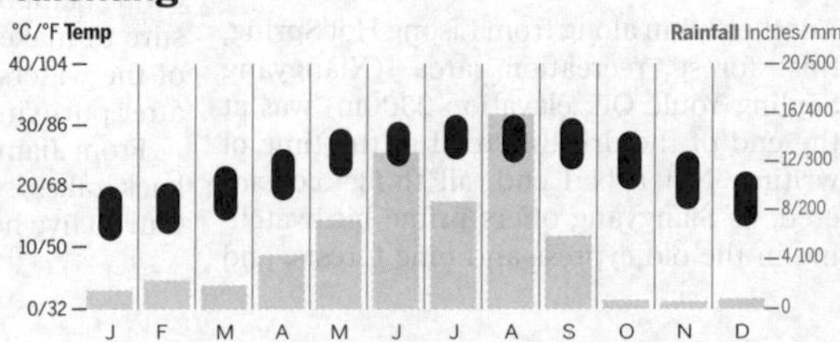

Apr Colourful nine-day Matsu Pilgrimage honours the patron of seafarers and fisherfolk.

Mar–Jun Firefly-watching in Alishan.

Sep–Dec Best time for hiking in Yushan National Park.

National Parks & Forest Recreation Areas

Western Taiwan has its share of parks, including pristine Yushan National Park, home of the 3952m-high Yushan (Jade Mountain), the highest peak in Taiwan. Rather tame by comparison, the Alishan Forest Recreation Area is its polar opposite, with an old alpine train and cherry-blossom trees as the main draws. Dasyueshan Forest Recreation Area and Aowanda National Forest Recreation Area offer the best birdwatching venues in the country, while rugged Hehuanshan Forest Recreation Area offers scenic hikes above the treeline. Huisun, Sitou and Shanlinhsi Forest Recreation Areas are cool mountain retreats with short hikes and plenty of good scenery.

The Linnei area has a bird reserve for the globally threatened fairy pitta, and is also a mass gathering point on the purple crow

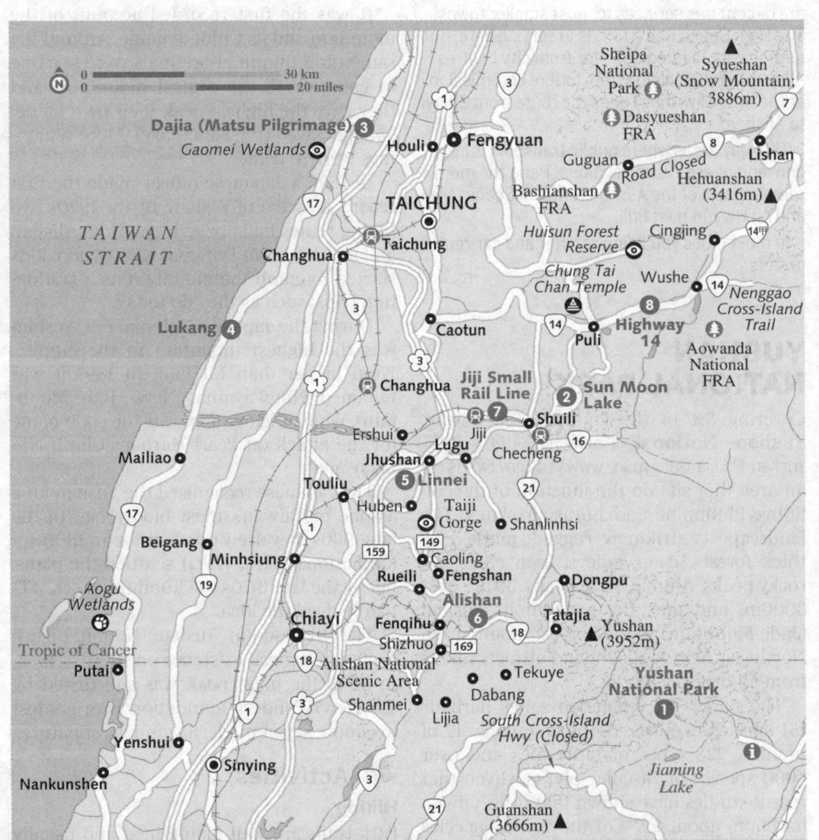

Yushan National Park & Western Taiwan

Highlights

1 Climb Yushan, Northeast Asia's highest mountain, in **Yushan National Park** (p204).

2 Cycle, boat and stroll along **Sun Moon Lake** (p228).

3 Seek the spiritual at the **Matsu Pilgrimage**, which starts in **Dajia** (p212).

4 Get lost in the old streets of **Lukang** (p224).

5 Bird- and butterfly-watch around **Linnei** (p227).

6 Explore ancient forests at **Alishan** (p217).

7 Take in the quaint countryside around **Jiji Small Rail Line** (p233).

8 Revel in the picture-perfect mountain scenery of **Highway 14** (p236).

butterfly's yearly migration (p227). Changhua's Baguashan is one of the best places to watch migratory raptors in the spring. Visit the Formosan macaque nature reserve in Ershui to see monkeys in the wild.

Getting There & Around

Taichung has one airport for both international and domestic services.

Regular trains run frequently down the coast, connecting all major and minor cities, and there are decent bus services to most smaller towns. The High Speed Rail (HSR) is in service here, but stations are located quite far from city centres. A narrow-gauge alpine train (out of commission at the time of writing) does the route from Chiayi to Alishan.

The only areas where public transport is inconvenient are Yushan National Park, the more remote parts of the Alishan National Scenic Area and on Hwy 14 past Puli.

In most cities you'll find scooter and car-rental outlets.

YUSHAN NATIONAL PARK

Covering 3% of the landmass of Taiwan, **Yushan National Park** (玉山國家公園, Yùshān Guójiā Gōngyuán; www.ysnp.gov.tw) is in an area that sits on the junction of the colliding Philippine and Eurasian plates. The landscape is strikingly rugged, marked by thick forests, deep valleys, high cliffs and rocky peaks. Among these peaks, 30 are over 3000m, and one, the eponymous Yushan (Jade Mountain), is the highest mountain in Northeast Asia at 3952m and attracts hikers from all over the world.

The park's six vegetative zones harbour 151 species of birds, 34 of mammals, 17 of reptiles, 228 types of butterflies and over 4000 species of vascular plants. Given that recent studies have shown that little Taiwan harbours about 2.5% of the world's species of plants and animals, this national park is rightly considered a natural treasure trove.

Yushan National Park covers areas of Chiayi, Nantou, Kaohsiung and Hualien Counties. A 20km drive west will take you to the Alishan Forest Recreation Area. From Yuli in the east, you can reach the Nanan section of the park, with its fantastic Walami Trail. The South Cross-Island Hwy, which skirts the southern borders of the park, is no longer passable.

You can visit the park year-round for hiking or sightseeing. In general, the area is wet in summer and dry in winter.

History

In 1697 Chinese travel writer Yu Yung-ho wrote, 'Yushan stands amidst 10 thousand mountains. It is white like silver, and appears at a distance covered in snow. It can be seen, but not reached. The mountain is like jade.'

It was the first recorded account of the mountain and its Chinese name. Around the same time Bunun aboriginals were starting to emigrate to the central mountains and they gave the highest peak their own name: Tongku Saveq (the Sanctuary). More renamings were to come.

In 1896 a Japanese officer made the first recorded ascent of Yushan. By the 1920s two hiking routes had opened: one from Alishan and another from Dongpu. High-school kids started to climb the mountain as a graduation trip, much as they do today.

During the Japanese colonial era, Yushan was the highest mountain in the empire, 176m higher than Mt Fuji. In 1897 it was renamed Niitakayama (New High Mountain), which incidentally was the code name for the attack on Pearl Harbor: 'Climb Niitakayama'.

The Japanese recognised the Yushan area as one of Taiwan's most biodiverse. In the late 1930s they drew up plans for an 1800-sq-km national park. WWII scuttled the plans, but by the late 1970s the Kuomintang (KMT) had revived the idea.

The 1050-sq-km Yushan National Park came into official existence on 10 April 1985. In 2009 the main peak was shortlisted by the New7Wonders foundation in a contest to choose seven modern wonders of nature.

Activities

Hiking

Park trails are well maintained and usually clear to follow. Signs are in English and Chinese. Before beginning a hike to the main peaks make sure you drop into the Tataka Squad and Paiyan Visitor Centre to get your permits in order.

The best time to hike in the park is during autumn and early spring (October to December and March to April). May has seasonal monsoon rains, and typhoons are a problem from June to September. In winter the main peaks are usually closed for almost

Yushan National Park

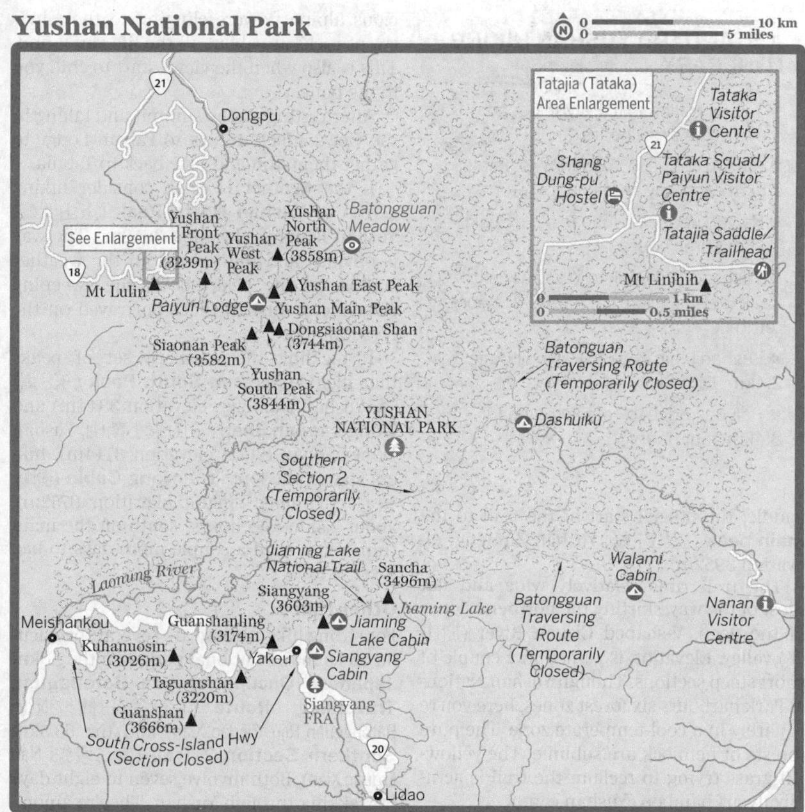

two months to give the environment a rest, though the day hikes around Tatajia are open year-round.

Day Hikes

Most day hikes are concentrated at Tatajia (塔塔加, Tǎtǎjiā) around the Km108 mark on Hwy 18. As these can get over 2800m, bring adequate warm, all-weather clothing, food and water before you head out. Pick up a copy of the excellent *Tatajia: Guide to the Tataka Recreation Area* at any visitor centre for an overview of the system.

A pleasant 1.7km walk through grassland and pine forest runs from the Tataka Visitor Centre (塔塔加遊客中心) to the Tataka Squad (塔塔加小隊, Tǎtǎjiā Xiǎoduì) and adjacent Paiyun Visitor Centre.

From the Tataka Squad you can follow the road an easy 3.5km to the **NCU Lulin Observatory** (鹿林天文台, NCU Lùlín Tiānwéntái). Another paved route runs south 2km to **Tatajia Anbu** (塔塔加鞍部, Tǎtǎjiā Ānbù, Tatajia Saddle), the start of the trail to Yushan. From Tatajia it's 1km of steep trail up to **Mt Linjhih** (麟芷山, Línzhǐ Shān; elevation 2854m) or you can take an easier 1.8km route that skirts the peak from the south.

Mt Lulin (鹿林山, Lùlín Shān; elevation 2881m) can be tackled from the road to the observatory or on a trail connecting with Mt Linjhih. The area is largely open grassland, with superb views. Give yourself all day if you plan to hike the whole circuit.

Overnight Hikes

Yushan Peaks

HIKING

The trail to the main peak is straightforward and can be done by anyone in decent shape. From the Tataka Squad and Paiyun Visitor Centre (a short walk up a sideroad from Hwy 18) where permits are processed, a shuttle bus transports hikers to Tatajia

A STANDARD YUSHAN HIKING ITINERARY

- Tatajia trailhead to Paiyun Lodge: 8.4km, four to six hours
- Paiyun Lodge to Yushan West Peak: 2.5km each way, three hours return
- Paiyun Lodge to Yushan Main Peak: 2.4km, three hours
- Yushan Main Peak to Yushan North Peak (detour): 3km each way, 2½ hours return
- Yushan Main Peak to Paiyun Lodge: 2.4km, 1½ hours
- Paiyun Lodge to Tatajia trailhead: 8.4km, four hours

Saddle, the official start of the trail to the **main peak** (玉山主峰, Yùshān Zhǔfēng; elevation 3952m).

The trail runs relatively wide and flat most of the way, skirting the northern slopes of the deep, V-shaped Cishan River (旗山溪) valley. Elevation is gained in a couple of short steep sections. Though Yushan National Park harbours six forest zones, here you're squarely in a cool-temperate zone. The pure forests of hemlock are sublime. The yellowish grass trying to reclaim the trail is actually dwarf bamboo (Yushan cane).

At **Paiyun Lodge** (排雲山莊, Páiyún Shānzhuāng; elevation 3402m) hikers rest for the night in preparation for the ascent on the main peak. Be on the lookout for yellow-throated martin at the cabin, and even serow (goat-antelope) on the slopes.

If you arrive early at Paiyun Lodge and still have energy to spare, you can tackle **Yushan West Peak** (玉山東峰, Yùshān Dōngfēng; elevation 3518m). The trail starts to the left of the cabin.

The next day most hikers get a 3am start in order to reach the summit by daylight. It's switchback after switchback until a loose gravel slope. At the top of the slope hikers enter a steel cage, exit onto a tiny rocky pass, and then make a final scramble up the roughest and most exposed section of the trail to the ingot-shaped peak.

On the way up, watch for the hemlock and spruce forest giving way to fields of rhododendron and stands of juniper, at first tall and straight and then twisted and dwarfed. At the highest elevations, lichens and tenacious alpine flowers clinging to the windswept rocks are about all the life you'll find. This is also when the views start to chill you to the bone.

After resting on the summit and taking in the views, hikers return to Paiyun Lodge to gather their stuff and hike back to Tatajia.

If the weather is clear, consider hiking across to **Yushan North Peak** (玉山北峰, Yùshān Běifēng; elevation 3858m). The way is obvious and the view from the weather station on the peak shows the sweeping ridgeline of Yushan that's portrayed on the NT$1000 note.

If tackling the southern set of peaks that include **Yushan South Peak** (玉山南峰, Yùshān Nánfēng; elevation 3844m) and **Dongsiaonan Shan** (玉山東小南山, Yùshān Dōngxiǎonán Shān; elevation 3744m), hikers stay at the lofty **Yuanfong Cabin** (圓峰營地, Yuánfēng Yíngdì; elevation 3752m), about 2.5km (1½ hours) south off the main trail. You'll need a couple more days to bag these extras.

Other Hikes

For strong hikers, there are several spectacular treks in the national park, like the 90km **Japanese Occupation Era Batongguan Traversing Route** (八通關日據越道線, Bātōngguān Rìjù Yuèdào Xiàn) and the 63.5km **Southern Section 2 Trail** (南二段線, Nán Èrduàn Xiàn). Both involve seven to eight days of trekking through Yushan. They're among the best hikes in Taiwan but the trails are yet to be restored after typhoon and earthquake damage in 2013. Keep an eye out for updates on the national park website (http://mountain.ysnp.gov.tw).

Bird- & Butterfly-Watching

About 150 bird species can be sighted in the park. Rusty laughing thrush and Yushan Yuhina are commonly seen on the trails. At Tatajia Saddle the endemic mikado pheasant can be spotted as often as not.

Butterflies can be found all over the park, but Tatajia is the funnel point of a remarkable and little-understood butterfly corridor. In late spring, winds from Puli sweep the immense valley below Tatajia, carrying every little winged creature upwards. Hundreds of butterflies can pass the saddle per minute, and even in late June we have watched awestruck as dozens were blown up overhead every minute, spun around in the turbulence and then carried away.

About 100 species can be spotted, including a good number of migratory purple crows, who have either got caught in the wrong winds (they should be following the currents north) or have taken a detour to look for food. Mid-May mornings are the best time to see this phenomenon, though it continues until late June.

Tours

The park organises hikes to Yushan Main Peak twice monthly from October to December. Call for reservations.

Sleeping & Eating

On the trail, cabin quality varies. Paiyun Lodge below the summit of Yushan has bunk bedding, flush toilets, running water, solar lighting and a cafeteria.

Other cabins around the park are usually sturdy A-frames, with open floors for crashing out on (some have a nice thick, black underpadding), a loft for extra bedding, solar lights, a water source and ecotoilets. Some cabins also have clear space around them for camping and a deck for cooking and lounging.

You can book meals at Paiyun Lodge (breakfast NT$150, lunch NT$300, dinner NT$300). This gives you access to a multi-course buffet prepared by Bunun porters. In the morning you get rice porridge and hot water.

Other cabins are unmanned, so you must bring your own supplies.

Shang Dung-pu Hostel HOSTEL $
(東埔山莊, Dōngpǔ Shānzhuāng; ☎049-270 2213; dm NT$300) The only place to stay in the park if you're not on a trail is this hostel at Tatajia. The rustic old wooden building has simple bunk dorm beds, showers and toilets. Simple meals can be arranged if you give advance notice, but you can buy instant noodles and snacks at the front desk. Book ahead if you want to stay here.

Information

There are no banks in the park. Wi-fi is available on the summit of Yushan (no kidding!). All of the following visitor centres provide maps in English, brochures and information on current trail conditions.

Nanan Visitor Centre (南安遊客中心; ☎03-888 7560; 83-3, Choching; 9am-4.30pm)

Tataka (Tatajia) Visitor Centre (塔塔加遊客中心; 9am-4.30pm)

Yushan National Park Headquarters (玉山國家公園管理處; www.ysnp.gov.tw; 515 Jungshan Rd, Sec 1, Shuili, Nantou County, 水里鄉中山路一段515號; 8.30am-5pm)

IF YOU CAN'T CLIMB YUSHAN, TRY…

With over a thousand people applying for the 90 permits to climb Yushan each day, you need some options if you want to climb a 3000m-plus mountain in Taiwan. Here are a few worthy alternatives that are easier to secure permits for.

- **Snow Mountain** (p156) Taiwan's second-highest peak. Amazing geology and vistas.
- **Wuling-Quadruple** (p158) Climb four peaks in two days, with superb views over the Holy Ridge.
- **Beidawushan** (p272) Most southerly 3000m-plus peak. Long, sweeping ridgeline walk to the summit. Only a police permit needed.
- **Hehuanshan Peaks** (p238) Series of short hikes starting above the treeline. No permits needed.
- **Dabajianshan** (p161) The holy peak of the Atayal, with a magical landscape.
- **Jiaming Lake** (p201) Sublime high-alpine scenery at a young meteor lake. Only a police permit needed.
- **Nenggaoshan North Peak & Chilai South Peak** (p236) In the heart of the central mountains. Big views. Only a police permit needed.
- **Holy Ridge** (p157) Five-day adventure on a thin ridgeline that never dips below 3300m.
- **Nenggao–Andongjun Trail** (p237) Six days through alpine lake country. Unlikely to see another person after the first day. Only a police permit needed.

Getting There & Away

Public transport is nonexistent in the park. If you don't have your own vehicle or driver, you might be able to hire a taxi in Alishan, or catch the sunrise-tour buses.

Dongpu (Tungpu) 東埔

POP 500 / ELEV 1200M

Just over the northern tip of Yushan National Park sits the hot-spring village of Dongpu (Dōngpǔ). The carbon-acid hot spring delivers high-quality, clear, odour-free water with an average temperature of 50°C.

Dongpu's status as a gateway to Yushan National Park is threatened by severe washouts on the trail up to the Batongguan meadows (a junction of trails that includes a back route to Yushan Main Peak). Even before Typhoon Morakot hit in 2009, this section was in such rough shape that Bunun porters were reluctant to take it.

There are plenty of hot-spring hotels in Dongpu. For an inexpensive option, try the **Youth Activity Centre** (青年活動中心, Qīngnián Huódòng Zhōngxīn; ☎049-270 1515; r from NT$700) at the high end of town.

Yuanlin Bus Company (員林客運; ☎049-277 0041) runs buses between Dongpu and Shuili (NT$152, 80 minutes) approximately hourly between 6am and 5.40pm.

GREATER TAICHUNG

Taichung 台中市

☎04 / POP 2,690,000

Under Japanese, and later KMT, economic planning, Kaohsiung became the centre of heavy industry, Taipei the centre of colonial administration, and Taichung? The centre of light industry. If your image of Made in Taiwan still conjures up visions of cheap toys, shoes and electrical goods, then you've got old Taichung in mind.

Today the name Taichung tends, among locals anyway, to conjure up visions of great weather. Taipei and Taichung may have very similar average temperatures but Taichung is much drier, receiving around 1700mm of rain a year compared with Taipei's 2170mm.

Taichung is a transport hub of western Taiwan and you are likely to stop over or even spend a night or two here especially if you plan to head inland. In 2010, the city and county of Taichung were merged to form a greater municipality. The city centre has several attractions for travellers, and it's a good base to make side trips to the outer area, which has a lot more to offer.

Sights & Activities

National Taiwan Museum of Fine Arts MUSEUM

(台灣美術館, Táiwān Měishù Guǎn; ☎2372 3552; 2 Wuquan W Rd; ⏲9am-5pm Tue-Fri, to 6pm Sat & Sun) FREE The open, modern design is visually sophisticated; high-quality exhibits of both Taiwanese and foreign artists are featured. Exhibits change often. For children there is a good, hands-on play area and storybook centre on the lower floors. To get to the museum take bus 71 or 75 (westbound) from the train station.

Taichung Folk Park CULTURAL SITE

(台中民俗公園, Táizhōng Mínsú Gōngyuán; 73 Lu Shun Rd, Sec 2; admission NT$50; ⏲9am-5pm, closed Mon) The park is divided into several sections but most of the interesting material is to the far right as you enter the park. Don't miss the collections of folk artefacts, which includes everything from ceramic pillows to farming implements. Board bus 58 at the train station.

Paochueh Temple BUDDHIST TEMPLE

(寶覺寺, Bǎojué Sì; 140 Jianxing St; ⏲8am-5pm) This Buddhist temple features one of the largest and fattest Milefo (laughing) Buddhas in Taiwan. Board bus 31 at the train station.

Rainbow Village VILLAGE

(彩虹眷村, Cǎihóng Juàncūn; Lane 56, Chun'an Rd) Found to the west of the city, this aptly named ageing village has been revitalised into a whimsical 'outdoor gallery', bedecked with vibrant colours and drawings on every inch of the walls by Mr Wong, the nonagenarian 'resident painter' who's also a KMT veteran of the Chinese Civil War (1945–49).

To get there, take bus 27 (50 minutes) from the train station. Alight at Gancheng 6th Village (干城六村, Gānchéng Liùcūn), cross the road, walk through the archway (春安路, Chun'an Rd), pass a primary school and then turn left into an alley and walk to the end.

Gaomei Wetlands SCENIC AREA

(高美濕地, Gāoměi Shīdì; ⏲24hr) FREE The prime spot for a bird-and-sunset-watching combo in the greater Taichung

Taichung

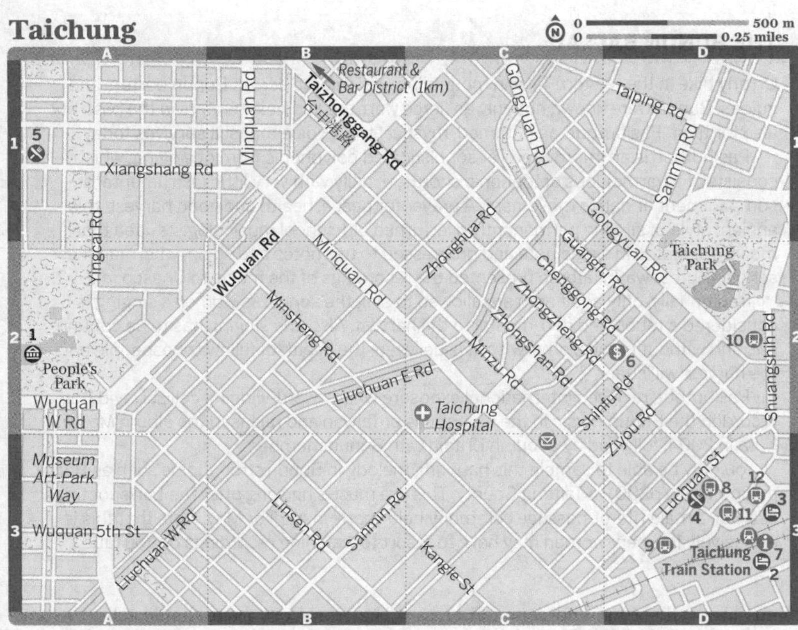

Taichung

Sights
1 National Taiwan Museum of Fine Arts A2

Sleeping
2 Hotel Mi Casa D3
3 Plaza Hotel D3

Eating
4 Miyahara D3
5 Weng Ji Restaurant A1

Information
6 Bank of Taiwan D2
7 Visitor Information Centre D3

Transport
8 Bus to Rainbow Village D3
9 Fengyuan Bus Company D3
10 Nantou Bus Company D2
11 Taichung Bus Company Station D3
12 UBus D3

area. Take a local train to Qingshui (清水), then board bus 178 (NT$20, 30 minutes). There are only five buses a day, so consider taking a taxi (NT$250).

Dakeng SCENIC AREA
(大坑, Dàkēng) To the east of the city is a hilly area known as Dakeng. If you're going to spend any time in the city, Dakeng is worth exploring, as there are pleasant hiking trails and even a few hot springs.

Festivals & Events

Taichung Jazz Festival MUSIC
(www.taichungjazzfestival.com.tw) One of the most famous annual events in Taichung is the Taichung Jazz Festival, a nine-day extravaganza held mainly at the Civic Square and along Jingguo Boulevard Parkway in October.

Sleeping

The area around the Taichung train station has been cleaned up a bit in recent years and makes for a decent base, having all your life-support systems nearby.

WoW Backpacker HOSTEL $
(☎2465 2058; 3rd fl, 166-81, Xitun Road, Sec 3, 西屯路三段166-81號3樓; dm from NT$450, tw NT$1400; @ 📶) This hostel is quite out of the way (it's northwest of the city) but travellers rave about it and find the staff very helpful. Dorms (sleeping between three and six) and

THE BUNUN BALLAD

On any hike in the western Taiwan mountains, you'll come across Bunun porters and guides. Bunun were known not only as fierce warriors and headhunters in the past, but also for their 'Pasibutbut', an untamed, mystical tribal voice that still survives today.

'Pasibutbut' is an improvised yet sophisticated polyphonic form of singing, which consists of a harmonious octophonic chorus, usually with very little instrumental accompaniment or dance movement. A prayer for peace, health and good harvest, this ancient style of singing permanently overturned old-school musicologists' idea that music originated in single note and progressed to two notes and so on, when Japanese scholar Kurosawa Takatomo presented the recordings of the music to Unesco in 1952.

Traditionally, only adult men are allowed to sing the songs, as women's singing is considered a taboo and detrimental to the harvest. Also, the singing has to be continuous and without breaks; otherwise, it is believed, the health of fellow tribespeople and the harvest will suffer.

'Pasibutbut' received international exposure when award-winning cellist David Darling recorded the Bunun music in the mountains of Taiwan and released the album *Madanin Kata* in 2004, followed by a tour in Britain with Bunun members.

You may be able to sample this haunting melody in Bunun strongholds such as Dongpu and Wulu (p200) in Taitung County. This is a must-sing song after the Ear-shooting Festival, a male rite-of-passage ceremony held yearly in April or May. Note that this is exclusively for men; women may have to resort to watching recordings on YouTube.

rooms are well set up, and common areas are spacious.

Hotel Mi Casa HOTEL **$$**
(米卡沙旅店, Mǐkǎshā Lǚdiàn; ☎2229 5353; www.mi-casa.com.tw; 8 Alley 5, Lane 149, Fuxing Rd, Sec 4, 復興路4段149巷5弄8號; s/d/tw NT$1350/1650/1900; @) This stylish business hotel stands out for its Japanese minimalist design, good prices and extras such as complimentary breakfasts. It's located behind the train station.

Plaza Hotel HOTEL **$$**
(達欣商務精品飯店, Dáxīn Shāngwù Jīngpǐn Fàndiàn; ☎2229 3191; www.plazahotel.com.tw; 180 Jianguo Rd, 建國路180號; s/d/tw incl breakfast NT$1400/1880/2080; @) Just a stone's throw from Taichung train station, this smart-looking business hotel is a great bargain for business people and tourists alike. Not all doubles have windows, though. The singles are a superb deal.

Eating

A few popular areas for restaurant dining are the streets south of the National Taiwan Museum of Fine Art (for lunch and dinner only) and the restaurant and bar district marked on our Taichung map.

Weng Ji Restaurant TAIWANESE **$**
(翁記剝骨鵝肉, Wēngjì Bōgǔ éròu; 99-1, Xiangshang Rd, Sec 1; dishes NT$20-180; 5pm-1am) The crowd out front should tell you something about this much-loved eatery specialising in goose meat. Try the smoked (燻鵝, *Xūn'é*) or drunken variety (醉鵝, *Zuì'é*), or the Taiwanese-style foie gras (鵝肝, *É Gān*).

Miyahara ICE CREAM **$**
(宮原眼科, Gōngyuán Yǎnkē; 20 Zhongshan Rd; ice cream from NT$120; 10am-10pm) Both the ice cream and the heritage building that houses the shop are awe-inspiring. Try the freshly made ice cream with Hakka *lei cha* (擂茶, *léi chá*) or other seasonal fruit flavours. The splendidly decorated restaurant upstairs serves both Taiwanese and Western fare, with a minimum charge of NT$385 per person.

Fengjia Night Market MARKET **$**
(逢甲夜市, Féngjiǎ Yèshì; 20 Zhongshan Rd) A sprawling night market well known for its innovative and cheap street food. A taxi from Taichung train station is about NT$220.

Finga's Base Camp EUROPEAN, DELI **$$**
(風格餐廳, Fēnggé Cāntīng; 61 Zhongming S Rd; dishes NT$150-400; 10am-10pm) A deli, restaurant and bakery all in one.

Drinking & Nightlife

Chun Shui Tang Teahouse TEAHOUSE
(春水堂, Chūn Shuǐ Táng; Chingming St; 8.30am-11.30pm) Taiwan bubble tea is famous worldwide – this is supposedly the company that

began it all. On the pedestrian-only street, this modern teahouse has outdoor seating and is pleasant on cool evenings.

Smooth Bar & Grill BAR
(☎2329 3468; 5-7 Lane 50, Jingcheng Rd; drinks from NT$180; ⏰3pm-1am) This long, long-running bar and grill is well stocked and has a big-screen TV for watching sports. There's also an international menu offering curries, steaks, pastas, goulash and more.

ℹ Information

There are plenty of banks and 7-Elevens with ATMs around Taichung train station, and further up along Zhongzheng and Taizhonggang Rds.

Bank of Taiwan (台灣銀行; 144 Zhongzheng Rd) Offers money-changing facilities and an ATM.

Taichung County Government (www.taichung.gov.tw) The county's official website.

Visitor information centre (☎2221 2126; ⏰9am-6pm) Located in Taichung train station. Staff speak English and have an abundance of useful information.

Welcome to Taichung (http://english.tccg.gov.tw) The city government's website.

ℹ Getting There & Away

Taichung has an **airport** (www.tca.gov.tw), but it's unlikely you'll ever use it.

BUS

Near Taichung train station, **Nantou Bus Company** (南投客運; www.ntbus.com.tw; ☎04-2225 6418; 35-8 Shuangshi Rd) has frequent buses to Puli (NT$135, one hour) and Sun Moon Lake (NT$272, 1½ hours), though you can also catch the bus at the HSR station.

UBus (統聯客運; www.ubus.com.tw) has frequent buses to Taipei (NT$260, 2½ hours) and Kaohsiung (NT$310, 4½ hours).

HIGH SPEED RAIL

A commuter train connects the HSR station with central Taichung and Taichung train station (NT$18, 10 minutes, every 20 minutes). Shuttle buses also travel to central Taichung from the HSR station (average price NT$30, 20 to 40 minutes, every 15 minutes).

An HSR train travels to/from Taipei (NT$700, 60 minutes, three trains hourly). There are also buses from the HSR station to Sun Moon Lake, Puli and Lukang.

TRAIN

There is train service from Taipei (fast/slow train NT$375/289, two/three hours) and Kaohsiung (fast/slow train NT$469/361, 2½/three hours).

ℹ Getting Around

The public transport system is slowly improving, but do check with the visitor information centre for the latest on the services and schedules available. An EasyCard (p104)entitles you to 8km of free bus rides anywhere within the greater Taichung area.

At the time of writing, construction had begun on two Mass Rapid Transit (MRT) lines.

Dasyueshan Forest Recreation Area 大雪山國家森林遊樂區

At the western edge of the Snow Mountain Range, the **Big Snow Mountain Forest Recreation Area** (Dàxuě shān Guójiā Sēnlín Yóulè Qū; admission NT$200; ⏰8am-5pm) rises from 1000m to just under the gold standard of 3000m. The area was closed at the time of writing, due to the landslides caused by Typhoon Soulik in 2013. When it is open, expect some fantastic hiking opportunities and great wildlife viewing, in particular birdwatching. The climate is humid and cool with an average temperature of 12°C, making it a popular summer retreat.

Sights & Activities

Forestry Road 200 SCENIC AREA
The 49km-long 200 from Dongshi to the end of the line is an incredible route that offers the fastest change of landscapes, going from a subtropical forest of fruit orchards, through a magical mixed zone where cypress and cedar trees stand beside giant tree palms and ferns, to a pure high-mountain coniferous forest in just 1½ hours.

Hiking

Yuanzui–Shaolai–Xiaoshue National Trail HIKING
(鳶嘴稍來小雪山國家步道, Yuānzuǐ Shāolái Xiǎoxuěshān Guójiā Bùdào) Though the total length of this popular trail is only 15.5km, it takes two days to complete. You are required to register at the Dadong police station (at the Km15 mark of the trail) before you hit the road.

Most hikers just do a small portion starting at the Km27 mark. It's about one to 1½ hours uphill on a great path to **Yuanzui Shan** (鳶嘴山; elevation 2130m), where an observation tower gives you views of Yushan.

From here another two to three hours along steep rocky ledges takes you to **Shaolai Shan** (稍來山; elevation 2307m). Another

THE MATSU PILGRIMAGE

The unquestioned patron deity of Taiwan, Matsu, although often referred to as the Goddess of the Sea, is officially Tianhou (Empress of Heaven). Her divine jurisdiction extends from protecting fisherfolk and helping women in childbirth to restoring social order.

Matsu was once Lin Mo-niang (林默娘; born AD 960) from Meizhou, Fujian. As a young girl Mo-niang was noted for her quickness to master magical arts and soon began to be regarded as a female shaman. Her particular forte was helping fishermen survive at sea: one of her most famous exploits was rescuing her own father.

Mo-niang died young, aged 28, but almost immediately people in Meizhou began to worship her. As word of her divine efficaciousness spread, so did her cult. Her highest title, Empress of Heaven, was conferred after she reportedly assisted in overthrowing Dutch rule in Taiwan – by stemming the tides, as legend has it.

Matsu worship came to Taiwan with the earliest settlers and her oldest temples date back to the 16th century. Today there are more than 500 Matsu temples around the island. Statues of the goddess usually depict her with black skin, a beaded veil and a red cape. Standing next to her are her loyal attendants, Eyes That See a Thousand Miles and Ears That Hear upon the Wind, two demons that she subjugated and rescued from hell.

The Pilgrimage

The pilgrimage is the largest and most celebrated religious and folk activity in the country. Hundreds of thousands of pilgrims and spectators from all over the island and abroad escort a palanquin, graced by a statue of Matsu, from Dajia to Hsinkang in southern Taiwan, and then back again, covering a distance of over 350km. The goddess is carried through 50 towns; over a million people see her pass their homes.

Many devotees will follow Matsu for the full nine days. They'll jostle each other to touch the sedan chair, while the most devout will jump to the front and actually kneel down on the road to allow the goddess to be carried over them. According to legend, touching the palanquin will confer good luck for a whole year.

The dates for the pilgrimage are announced every year in March. *Bwah bwey* (casting moon blocks) are used to determine the starting dates, though the goddess is only given weekends as a choice. The first, fourth (when the palanquin reaches Fengtian Gong) and last days are the most spectacular, but now many subordinate temples are starting to let their own statues and palanquins arrive early to avoid overcrowding and the frequent gang fights that erupt on the last day.

If you decide to join the pilgrimage, note that temples and volunteers along the way will provide water, basic meals and accommodation. The schedule is usually as follows:

- Day 1: Pilgrims leave **Chenlan Temple** (鎮瀾宮) in Dajia around midnight and end their walk at **Nanyao Temple** (南瑤宮), Changhua city.
- Day 2: **Fuhsing Temple** (福興宮) in Siluo Township, Yunlin County.
- Day 3: **Fengtian Temple** (奉天宮) in Hsingang Township, Chiayi County.
- Day 4: Main blessing ceremony and a second night at Fengtian Temple.
- Day 5: **Fuhsing Temple** (福興宮) in Siluo Township, Yunlin County.
- Day 6: **Chengan Temple** (奠安宮) in Beidou Township, Changhua County.
- Day 7: **Tienhou Temple** (天后宮) in Changhua city.
- Day 8: **Chaohsing Temple** (朝興宮) in Qingshuei Township, Taichung County.
- Day 9: Pilgrims return to Chenlan Temple in Daija.

For information on the dates and events of each year's pilgrimage, check the website www.dajiamazu.org.tw.

To reach Dajia take a train from Taipei. Chenlan Temple is a few blocks straight ahead as you exit from the front of the train station.

hour takes you back to the main road at the Km35 mark. It's possible to continue walking to **Anmashan** (鞍馬山; Ānmǎshān) and down to the village at the Km43 mark, but that would take another day.

No matter which route you take, be prepared. In 2010 a group of foreign hikers wandered off the (clear) trail and spent a bitterly cold night in the mountains before being rescued in the morning.

Syueshan Sacred Tree Trail HIKING
(雪山神木步道, Xuěshān Shénmù Bùdào) An easy and popular hike is this 2km trail that runs from the parking lot at the Km49.5 mark to Tianchih, a pond filled with water year-round at 2600m, and onwards to the 1400-year-old Formosan red cypress. The walk takes around two hours return.

Wildlife-Watching

Despite being a former logging area, much of the forest cover here was not cut, which is one reason it is still so stocked with wildlife. Commonly seen are martins, weasels, white-faced flying squirrels, barking deer and Formosan macaques.

Even the casual visitor will be rewarded with a little time spent birdwatching on Forestry Road 200, long regarded as Taiwan's top birding location. At least 12 of the 17 endemic species to Taiwan can be spotted here. Some prime spots include the Km23 mark on Forestry Road 200 for the majestic Swinhoe's pheasant, and the Km47 mark for the mikado pheasant.

It's easy to see flying squirrels at night in the trees from the parking lots outside the cabins (after the Km43 mark), while barking deer and serow can be seen on the grassy slopes behind the cabins. Bring a good torch.

Festivals & Events

Dasyueshan International Bird Race EVENT
The Dasyueshan International Bird Race is held annually around April. Contact the Chinese Wild Bird Federation (www.bird.org.tw) for details.

Sleeping & Eating

There are very pleasant wood **cabins** (☎04-2587 7901; d Mon-Fri NT$2200, Sat & Sun NT$3400) at the village at the Km43 mark. You can book online (http://tsfs.forest.gov.tw; in Chinese) but do call afterwards to confirm. Set meals (NT$150) are also available, but it's best to bring your own food.

Information

The **visitor information centre** (遊客中心; ⌚9am-5pm) in the village at the Km43 mark has simple maps of the recreation area.

Getting There & Away

You will need your own transport.

ALISHAN NATIONAL SCENIC AREA

☎05

If you want to see Taiwan's natural environment raw in tooth and nail, visit a national park. If you want to see how humans have tried to make a go of settling on landslide-prone mountains and battered escarpments (as spectacular as they are to merely gaze upon), come to the Alishan National Scenic Area.

From a starting altitude of 300m in the west at Chukou, the 327-sq-km scenic area quickly rises to heights of more than 2600m. The great diversity of climate, soils and landscapes allows for the growing of everything from wasabi and plums to high-mountain oolong tea, the latter some of the best in the world. From the Tsou aboriginals, the original settlers, come foods you've never heard of, such as bird's-nest fern, tree tomatoes, *ai yu* jelly and millet wine.

Tourists have been finding their way to this region since the early days of the Japanese period. They come for the local specialities, the natural and human-designed landscapes (who doesn't like terraced tea fields?) and, more recently, the legacy of the colonial period, which includes a very rare narrow-gauge forest train.

Tourism took a massive hit in 2009 after Typhoon Morakot wiped out roads, villages and large sections of the railway tracks. Today, the area is getting back on its feet. Hwy 18 is passable, but the railway was still out of commission at the time of writing.

Chiayi

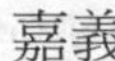

☎05 / POP 271,291

While Chiayi (Jiāyì) is not part of the Alishan National Scenic Area, almost every traveller will have to pass through here on the way there. The narrow-gauge train to Alishan leaves from Chiayi train station, as do buses and taxis. There are a few sights worth checking out in and around Chiayi, so plan to spend a day or so before moving on.

Central Chiayi is small enough to walk across in 30 minutes, though air pollution often makes it unpleasant to do so.

History

Chiayi is the capital of Chiayi County and was once the home of plains aborigines, but during the Dutch occupation of Taiwan, Fujian farmers began to settle in numbers. The name Chiayi was given by the Emperor Chien-lung, intended as a reward for Chiayi citizens taking the 'right' side in an 18th-century island-wide rebellion. The city prospered under Qing and later Japanese rule (when it was the capital of the sugar industry and one of the most modern cities in Taiwan), but these days, sadly, there is too little of this prosperity remaining.

Sights

★Chenghuang Temple TAOIST TEMPLE
(城隍廟, Chénghuáng Miào) This is the spiritual centre of Chiayi and is dedicated to the City God. First constructed in 1715, many of the best parts of the temple hail from a 1941 reconstruction. Look for the gorgeous spiderweb plafond (decorative) ceiling and two rows of lively cochin (koji; brightly coloured, glazed ceramic) figures on the walls of the main hall (found behind a glass pane).

The traditional double-eave roof sports elegant swallowtail ridges and colourful figures in *jiǎnniàn* (mosaic-like temple decoration). You can check it out from the upper floors of the back annex.

Alishan Forest Railway Chiayi Garage MUSEUM
(阿里山森林鐵路嘉義車庫, Ālǐshān Sēnlín Tiělù Jiāyì Chēkù; 2-1 Linsen W Rd; 8.30am-5pm) FREE The tree-lined garage is actually a park with an extragavanza of old steam locomotives. Train buffs and kids alike will certainly love it. Look for the SL13 (built in 1910), the oldest in the collection.

Koji Ceramic Museum MUSEUM
(交趾陶館, Jiāozhǐtáo Guǎn; 275 Jungshiao Rd; 9am-noon & 1.30-5pm Wed-Sun) FREE A museum dedicated to cochin a low-fired, brightly coloured glaze style of ceramic traditionally used for temple decoration. It's in the basement of the **Chiayi Cultural Centre** (嘉義市文化中心, Jiāyìshì WénHuà Zhōngxīn).

Prison Museum MUSEUM
(獄政博物館, Yùzhèng Bówùguǎn; 362 1873; 140 Wei Hsin Rd; 9.30am, 10.30am, 1.30pm & 2.30pm Tue-Sun) FREE Offering a taste of life behind bars, free admission to this museum includes a guided tour, which is repeated four times per day. The museum is on the site of the old Chiayi Prison, built in the 1920s and the only wooden prison structure in Taiwan that has survived from the Japanese era. Check out the fan-shaped cell complex and the Japanese shrine atop the central control room.

All tours are conducted in Mandarin, but the architecture speaks for itself. English-speaking guides may be available if you call ahead. Arrive 10 minutes before the tour starts and register with your ID. Each tour lasts about an hour.

Chiayi Park PARK
(嘉義公園, Jiāyì Gōngyuán) This huge park is a repository of natural and urban history of the city, with numerous features on offer: old trees, landscaped hills, a moat, Qing-dynasty steles, a Confucian temple, Japanese shrine, steam engines, a war memorial and fountains. The park is 3km east of the train station. To get there, go east on Mincyuan Rd, then turn right to Qiming Rd (啟明路).

Sleeping

Assemble! Backpackers HOSTEL $
(嘉聚旅人之家, Jiājù Lǚrén Zhījiā; 0978-101 770; assemble.backpackers@gmail.com; 279 Xirong St, 西榮街279號; dm/d NT$550/1250;) This IKEA showroom–like hostel has squeaky-clean dorms and rooms, a well-equipped kitchenette and welcoming hosts who are a fount of knowledge on the city.

Maison de Chine HOTEL $$
(兆品酒店, Zhàopǐn Jiǔdiàn; 229 2233; 257 Wenhua Rd, 文化路257號; d/tw NT$3600/4000;) One of the top hotels in town, offering a 30% discount on weekdays. Facilities include a business centre, small fitness room, VIP lounge, restaurant and cafe. English service is available.

Country Hotel HOTEL $$
(國園大飯店, Guóyuán Dàfàndiàn; 223 6336; fax 223 6345; 678 Guangzai St, 光彩街678號; d/tw NT$1660/2800;) This is very much a business hotel, with purely functional decor and few frills. It offers a car park next door and free snacks in the evening.

Chiayi

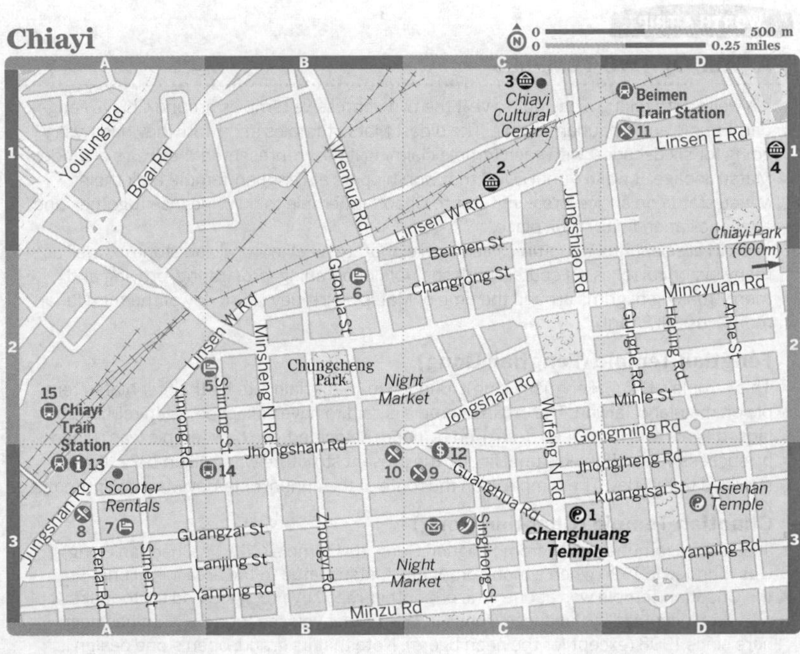

Chiayi

Top Sights
1 Chenghuang Temple C3

Sights
2 Alishan Forest Railway Chiayi Garage C1
3 Koji Ceramic Museum C1
4 Prison Museum D1

Sleeping
5 Assemble! Backpackers B2
6 Maison de Chine B2
7 Country Hotel A3

Eating
8 Gongbing Vegetarian Restaurant A3
9 Night Market C3
10 Pen Shui Turkey Rice B3
11 Yushan Inn Cafe D1

Information
12 First Commercial Bank C3
13 Visitor Information Centre A3

Transport
14 Chiayi Bus Company B3
15 Kuo Kuang Hao Bus Company A2

Eating

There are many inexpensive generic restaurants and cafes on Jhongshan and Renai Rds and around Chungcheng Park.

If you head east on Minzu Rd for 1km to 2km past the boundaries of our Chiayi map (the road turns into Daya Rd), you'll hit the new business area of town. Many nice cafes and restaurants have opened up here recently.

Pen Shui Turkey Rice TAIWANESE $
(噴水火雞飯, Pēnshuǐ Huǒjīfàn; 325 Jhongshan Rd; bowl NT$40; ⊙8.30am-9.30pm) Everyone in Taiwan knows that Chiayi is famous for its turkey rice dish (火雞肉飯, *huǒ jī ròu fàn*). This is the place that started it all 60-odd years ago.

Yushan Inn Cafe CAFE $
(玉山旅社咖啡, Yùshān Lǚshè Kāfēi; 410 Gonghe Rd; dishes from NT$150; ⊙10am-7pm) Housed in a charming Japanese-era wooden building in front of the historical Beimen train station, Yushan Inn Cafe serves decent sandwiches, pastries and coffee. The tatami common space on the upper floor provides very basic lodgings should you want to stay here.

WORTH A TRIP

A TALE OF TWO TEMPLES

It's well worth taking a day out to visit the two impressive temples around Chiayi: Fengtian Temple and Chaotian Temple. The oldest Matsu temples in Taiwan, they had rivalry going for six decades, with each temple claiming it best represented the area's orthodox Matsu lineage. It wasn't until 2009 that worshippers at Fengtian Temple took their Matsu statue on an 'ice-breaking' visit to Chaotian Temple to burn incense together, and a reconciliation finally took place.

Both are beautiful structures filled with elaborate relief in wood and stone, as well as many historical relics. Of course, both see riots of parading, prostrating, praying and merry-making pilgrims around the time of Matsu's birthday (23rd day of the third lunar month, usually April).

Fengtian Temple (Fengtian Gong)

This temple (奉天宮, Fèngtiān Gōng), founded in 1622, claims to be the first Matsu temple on mainland Taiwan. The original temple is said to have collapsed, been rebuilt, collapsed again and then been destroyed by flood. Relocated, the new temple was ruined by successive earthquakes until finally, the present structure was built in 1922. It has survived to this day. The temple is on the route of the annual nine-day Matsu Pilgrimage.

Chaotian Temple (Chaotian Gong)

Just a few kilometres away from Fengtian Gong, this temple (朝天宮, Cháotiān Gōng) was founded in 1694 when a monk brought a Matsu statue to the area. Like Fengtian, the Chaotian Temple was at one time or another razed by fire, flood and earthquake. It was even occupied by Japanese troops in 1895. What you see today is what has been here since 1908 (except for the neon tigers). Note that its grand, open stone design is quite unlike any other temple in Taiwan.

Getting There & Away

Buses to Beigang leave frequently from the **Chiayi County Bus Company station** (嘉義縣公車站; fare NT$62), located by the Chiayi train station. The trip takes 45 minutes and Chaotian is just a couple of minutes' walk from the station. To get to Fengtian Temple, catch a taxi from Beigang.

Gongbing Vegetarian Restaurant VEGETARIAN $
(宮賓素食館, Gōngbīn Sùshí Guǎn; 457 Renai Rd; average meal NT$150; ⏲6.15am-7.30pm; ☑) Long-running, buffet-style vegetarian restaurant.

Night Market MARKET $
(Wenhua Rd) Good for cheap food. Located between Mincyuan and Chuei Yang Rds.

Information

Internet cafes are located around the train station; ask at the visitor information centre for the latest details. Most hotels offer free ADSL.

There are numerous banks and ATMs on Renai Rd near Chiayi train station.

Chiayi City Government (www.chiayi.gov.tw) Good for general information about the city, including sights and activities for tourists.

First Commercial Bank (第一商業銀行; 307 Jhongshan Rd) ATMs and currency exchange.

St Martin De Porres Hospital (天主教聖馬爾定醫院; ☎275 6000; 565 Daya Rd, Sec 2)

Visitor information centre (遊客服務中心; ☎225 6649; ⏲8.30-5pm) The centre is located inside Chiayi train station; it provides English brochures and travel information about Chiayi and Alishan. Staff speak English.

Getting There & Away

Chiayi is the gateway to the Alishan National Scenic Area.

BUS

Chiayi Bus Company (嘉義客運; ☎275 0895; 503 Jhongshan Rd) has buses to Guanziling (NT$81, one hour, every 30 minutes).

Taiwan Tour (台灣好行; ☎379 9056) runs buses from early morning to late afternoon to Alishan (NT$221, 2½ hours, hourly).

There is also frequent service to Beigang (NT$64, 45 minutes) and Budai Port (NT$121, 1½ hours, hourly), and less-frequent service to Rueili and Fenqihu (see the visitor information centre for the schedule).

Kuo Kuang Hao Bus Company (國光客運公司; www.kingbus.com.tw) offers buses to Taipei (NT$350, three hours, every 30 minutes) and other cities on the west coast. Buses leave from the company's new bus station at back of the train station. Other intercity bus companies also leave from here.

BOAT

All Star (www.aaaaa.com.tw) runs in the summer months between Putai Port (near Chiayi) and Makung on Penghu (NT$1000, 1½ hours).

HIGH SPEED RAIL

A free shuttle bus connects the HSR station with Chiayi train station (40 minutes, every 20 minutes). The shuttle bus stop is at the back of the train station, near the intercity bus companies.

Trains travel frequently to Taipei (NT$1080, 90 minutes, four trains hourly).

TRAIN

At the time of writing the famous narrow-gauge train to Alishan was out of commission until mid-2014 at the earliest (though parts were repaired further up the line).

Trains travel to/from Taipei (fast/slow train NT$600/386, three/4½ hours) and Kaohsiung (fast/slow train NT$246/158, one/two hours).

Getting Around

Scooter rentals (機車出租; per day NT$300 to NT$400) are available from shops across from Chiayi train station. An International Driving Permit (IDP) and ID are required.

Alishan Forest Recreation Area 阿里山

05

The high-mountain resort of **Alishan** (Ālǐshān; admission NT$200) has been one of Taiwan's top tourist draws since the 1920s. Today, it's most popular with decidedly senior Chinese tour groups who arrive by the busload virtually every day of the year. True, there may be similar – and less-visited beauty – elsewhere in Taiwan, but do not let the crowds at Alishan spoil your visit, as they usually only stay for a couple of hours in the morning. Apart from the standard attractions such as the charming old narrow-gauge railway, the glorious sunrises, sunsets and the 'sea of clouds' phenomenon, there are some walking and hiking options, and you can have the high mountain beauty to yourself if the time is right.

In spring the cherry trees in Alishan are in bloom, while summer is busy with city folk looking for a cool retreat. Anytime between March and early June is a good time to see fireflies.

Summer temperatures average from 13°C to 24°C, while those in winter are 5°C to 16°C. You should bring a sweater and a raincoat no matter what time of year you visit.

It's simple to get your bearings in Alishan. Most people stay in Zhongzheng Village, though most just refer to it as Alishan Village. This village comprises a car park, post office, bus station, visitor centre, and most of the hotels and restaurants.

History

In former times the recreation area was probably home to Tsou hunting grounds rather than the site of permanent settlements. Modern development began with the Japanese, who became aware of the abundant stands of cypress (hinoki) growing in the misty mountains. In 1906 the first railway into the mountain was established and by 1913 the tracks had reached Alishan at Chaoping station.

Logging was the mainstay of activity in Alishan, but the area attracted hikers and sightseers early on. In 1926 the Japanese opened a 43km trail from Chaoping to the summit of Yushan, later shortening it by extending the railway to Tatajia.

Logging continued into the 1970s, when the first steps towards creating a forest park were taken. In the 1980s Hwy 18 opened, and the fast connection between Alishan and Chiayi caused an explosion in tourism. In 2001 the Alishan National Scenic Area (which covers far more than just this recreation area) opened with the mandate to regulate and limit development. These days the administration's hands are filled repairing typhoon damage and getting things back to how they were.

Sights & Activities

Alishan Forest Train — OLD TRAIN

The train used to run on narrow-gauge track (762mm), ascending to 2216m from a starting altitude of 30m in just 3½ hours. The total length of track is 86km, spanning three climatic zones. At the time of writing, however, the line was operating only from Chiayi to its outskirts, and from Alishan village to the Chushan sunrise area. There's no guarantee when the whole line will be restored.

As you ride up it may feel like the train is going backwards. It is! The track

WORTH A TRIP

A HIKING & HOT-SPRING COMBO

The old Central Cross-Island Hwy 8 has yet to be fully restored after typhoon and landslide damage in 2004, but you can travel east as far as the hot-spring town of **Guguan** (谷關, Gǔguān) and the **Bashianshan Forest Recreation Area** (八仙山國家森林遊樂區, Bāxiānshān Guójiā Sēnlín Yóulè Qū; www.forest.gov.tw; admission NT$150; ⌚8am-5pm).

Guguan was devastated by the 921 earthquake in 1999 and subsequently by typhoon, but is getting back on its feet. **E-Daw Hot Spring** (伊豆溫泉, Yīdòu Wēnquán; www.e-daw.com.tw; NT$350; ⌚8am-midnight) is a gorgeous Japanese-style hot spring with indoor and outdoor pools, and the mist-shrouded mountains of Baishianshan as the backdrop. Bring your own towel. To get there, take the alley beside the 7-Eleven and walk uphill for about five minutes.

Baishianshan Forest Recreation Area is located 7km west of Guguan. The area was closed at the time of writing, but you can expect beautiful day-hike options there when it reopens.

Fengyuan Bus Company (豐原客運; ☎2222 3454) has buses to Guguan (NT$197; 1½ hours) departing from Taichung HSR station five times a day on weekdays and roughly hourly on weekends between 7am and 6pm. For Bashianshan, alight at Duming Bridge (篤銘橋, Dǔmíng Qiáo), just 2km before the bus reaches Guguan; from there it's a 5km walk to the Baishianshan visitor centre.

arrangement employs a unique system of switchbacks that allow it to traverse slopes ordinarily too steep for trains.

Sunrise

Sunrise viewing is *de rigueur* here. There are two main viewing venues: the summit of **Chushan** (祝山, Zhùshān; elevation 2489m) and **Tatajia** (塔塔加, Tǎtǎjiā), a mountain pass 2610m above sea level in nearby Yushan National Park.

To reach Chushan you can either take the train from Alishan station (expect a long queue at the ticket booth), or hike up along the **Chushan Sunrise Viewing Trail** (祝山觀日出步道, Zhùshān Guānrìchū Bùdào). The train takes about 25 minutes, while hiking can take up to 1½ hours if you start in the village.

If you wish to see the sunrise at Tatajia, pay for a seat on one of the sunrise-tour minibuses (NT$300, three hours). Any hotel can arrange it for you. Buses come directly to your hotel.

The minibus has several advantages over the train, one being that it stops at numerous scenic locations, such as the monkey-viewing area and the site of a few ancient trees, on the way back from the sunrise viewing.

Hiking

There are many trails in the park, ranging from strolls around flower gardens to hikes up mountaintops requiring several hours or more to complete. On the **Giant Tree Trail** (巨木群棧道, Jùmùqún Zhàndào) you'll find majestic old cypresses up to 2000 years old. This trail is best done towards dark, when the crowds have left.

For a bit of peace and quiet and a few hours' workout on a natural path, the **Duei-Kao-Yueh Trail** (對高岳步道, Dùigāoyuè Bùdào) is just the ticket. The Chushan Sunrise Viewing Trail, and the viewing platform on it, are busy at dawn but empty of people by late morning.

For more information, including times and distances for trails, pick up the brochure at the visitor centre.

Festivals & Events

Cherry Blossom Festival FESTIVAL

The Cherry Blossom Festival runs in March or April for two weeks, while the trees are in bloom. This is an extremely busy time for the park.

Sleeping

Most hotels are in the village below the car park. The high season is during Chinese New Year and the Cherry Blossom Festival. Saturday nights have increased rates, too.

Catholic Hostel HOSTEL $

(天主堂, Tiānzhǔtáng; ☎267 9602; dm/d/tw NT$500/1200/2400) Nothing fancy, but this is it for rock-bottom budget accommodation in Alishan. The hostel, down a side road to the left of the park entrance gate, is not always open (especially on weekdays) so call before you go.

Shermuh HOTEL $$
(神木賓館, Shénmù Bīnguǎn; ☎ 267 9666; http://alisan.hotel.com.tw; d/tw NT$3200/4500) Rooms are comfy and clean enough but unsurprising. The hotel is located off a lower road, which you can reach by taking a set of stairs beside the visitor centre.

Alishan House HOTEL $$$
(阿里山賓館, Ālǐshān Bīnguǎn; ☎ 267 9811; www.alishanhouse.com.tw; r from NT$8000) The old-world charm from this Japanese-era hotel is a bit faded, but it's still Alishan's top hotel. The food in the restaurant is so-so, but the outdoor cafe has a lovely setting among the cherry trees. Make sure to get the hotel to pick you up as it's a bit of walk from the village car park or train station.

Eating

Most of the restaurants in Alishan are clustered around the car park and serve similar decent fare at similar prices: hot pots, stir-fries, and local vegetable and meat dishes for around NT$150 to NT$250. Most are open for breakfast, lunch and dinner. English menus are available.

In the car-park area is a 7-Eleven selling sandwiches, noodles and drinks.

Shopping

Alishan high mountain tea (阿里山高山茶, Ālǐshān Gāoshān Chá), dried plums, cherries, fruit liqueurs, *moji* (sticky rice) in almost every conceivable flavour and aboriginal crafts are sold in the shops just back from the car park.

Information

There's free internet at the Chunghua Telecom (中華電信) office in Alishan Village. Both the village post office (郵局) and the 7-Eleven have ATMs but we advise that you bring cash with you.

Alishan National Scenic Area (www.ali-nsa.net) The English version has not been updated to reflect the typhoon damage.

Public Health Clinic (衛生所, Wèishēngsuǒ; ☎ 267 9806) The clinic has irregular hours, but is always open in the mornings and usually the afternoons, too. It's just down the road from the Catholic Hostel, near the entrance gate to the park.

Visitor centre (旅客服務中心; ☎ 267 9917; ⏲ 8.30am-5.30pm) Located below the entrance to Alishan House, and a five-minute uphill walk from the car park. An excellent English map is available here.

Getting There & Away

BUS

Buses to Chiayi train station (NT$221, 2½ hours, hourly) run from 9.10am to 5.10pm and leave from in front of the 7-Eleven. There are two buses to Chiayi HSR station (NT$255, three hours) leaving at 2.40pm and 4.40pm.

TRAIN

There are four train stations in Alishan.

Alishan Station In Zhongzheng Village (main train station).

Chaoping Station A few minutes by train up the track.

Chushan Station Twenty-five minutes by train up the track. It's where passengers watch the sunrise.

Shenmu Station Five minutes by train up the track. It's a spur line to the trailhead of Giant Tree Trail.

Fenqihu 奮起湖

A former repair and maintenance station for the Alishan railway, Fenqihu (Fènqǐhú) sits about halfway up the line at an altitude of 1405m. Once a popular stop for both tour bus and rail passengers, the future of this old Hakka village is uncertain.

Sights & Activities

The **train station** platform is an obvious place to begin your exploration of Fenqihu, especially the garage, which accommodates two old engines. Across the tracks and up a small set of stairs to the left is a fenced-in strand of the curious **square bamboo** (四方竹, *sìfāng zhú*).

You can hike the 7km **Fenqihu–Rueili Historic Trail** (奮瑞古道, Fèn-Ruì Gǔdào) from Fenqihu all the way to Rueili in about three to four hours. Much of the trail runs through bamboo forests that look like something out of a *wushu* (martial arts) film. In Rueili the trail ends (or begins) on the main road into town, close to hotels, restaurants and the visitor centre. The trail is mapped and signed in English.

Sleeping

Catholic Hostel HOSTEL $
(天主堂, Tiānzhǔtáng; ☎ 256 1134; http://aj-centersvd.myweb.hinet.net; dm/d with shared bathroom NT$300/500) Run by a sweet Swiss

sister, the hostel (on the grounds of the Arnold Janssen Activity Centre) is a cosy, quiet place to stay. The hostel is a few minutes' walk downhill from the train station.

Eating

Restaurant hours in Fenqihu are not fixed but expect places to close early (or not open at all) on weekdays. Some local specialities to look for include fresh Alishan wasabi and 'tree tomatoes' (樹番茄, *shù fānqié; Cyphomandra betacea*), which tastes like a combination of tomato and passionfruit.

Fancylake Hotel TAIWANESE $
(奮起湖大飯店, Fènqǐhú Dàfàndiàn; lunchbox NT$100) Just behind the train station at the start of the 'old street', Fancylake is famous for its lunchboxes (鐵路便當, *tiělù biàndāng*) of rice, veggies and meat, served in special wooden souvenir containers.

Getting There & Away

At the time of writing the railway line between Chiayi and Fenqihu had not yet been restored after being struck by Typhoon Morakot in 2009. There are two buses going to Fenqihu (NT$181, two hours) from Chiayi train station at 7am and 3.10pm daily.

Rueili (Juili) 瑞里

POP 970 / ELEV 1000M

Rueili (Ruìlǐ) was one of the first places established as a permanent settlement by 18th-century Fujian pioneers in the Alishan region. Today the small, quiet, tea-growing community is gradually rebuilding from the devastation of Typhoon Morakot in 2009, and has started attracting visitors back.

In addition to panoramic mountain scenes, bamboo forests, waterfalls and historic walking trails, pesticide-free Rueili offers one of the best venues in Taiwan for watching fireflies.

Sights & Activities

Rueili has several beautiful waterfalls, including **Cloud Pool Waterfall** (雲潭瀑布, Yúntán Pùbù), just past the Km22 mark on County Rd 122.

The **Ruitai Old Trail** (瑞太古道, Ruìtài Gǔdào) was once used for transporting goods between Rueili and Taihe. It's now part of the overall hiking system that connects Fenqihu to Rueili.

Fireflies (螢火蟲, *yínghuǒchóng*) show off their bioluminescent skills from March to June. The mountainsides literally sparkle throughout the night.

Sleeping & Eating

The Ruitai Tourist Centre can help with homestays and hotel bookings.

Most hotels and homestays have their own restaurant (set meals NT$100 to NT$250) and there are scattered places to eat around town as well.

Roulan Lodge HOTEL $$
(若蘭山莊, Ruòlán Shānzhuāng; ☎250 1210; fax 250 1555; 10 Rueili Village; d/tw NT$1800/2400, cabins from NT$3200) One of the most popular places to stay in Rueili, especially during the firefly season. The owners of the lodge have been recognised nationwide for their efforts at preserving the natural heritage of Rueili. There is a weekday discount of 30%.

Information

Rueitai Tourist Centre (瑞太遊客中心; ☎250 1070; 1-1 Rueili Village; ⏲8.30am-5pm) offers brochures, internet and a very knowledgeable, friendly staff of locals.

Getting There & Around

If you aren't hiking from Fenqihu, there are buses to/from Chiayi. See the Chiayi visitor centre for the latest schedule.

You will need your own transport to get around Rueili.

County Road 169

The 13km southern stretch of County Rd 169 that starts from Shizhuo (石桌, Shízhuō) leads you to the strongholds of the Tsou people. While damages caused by Typhoon Morakot in 2009 can still be seen, the landscape of the valley is visually stunning. There's an explosion of colours in spring when the cherry trees are in full bloom; likewise in autumn, when the turning leaves remain on the maple trees. The night sky is filled with fireflies from March to June.

The villages of **Dabang** (達邦, Dábāng) and **Tefuye** (特富野, Tèfùyě) are of particular importance among the Tsou communities, as only they have the honour of housing a Kuba – a men's meeting hall where decisions concerning tribal affairs are made, and warring skills, along with history of the tribe, are passed down to younger generations. The Kuba can be easily identified: it's a large, thatch-roofed wooden platform on stilts. Note that female visitors are not allowed to enter the Kuba.

Dabang is the biggest Tsou village and is a great place for birdwatching. The white-eyed nun babbler (regarded as a sacred bird among the Tsou), as well as Swinhoe's pheasant, can be spotted on the 1km **Bird Divination Pavilion Trail** (鳥占亭步道, Niǎozhàntíng Bùdào). The trailhead is near the Km34.2 mark.

At the Km33.5 mark, the road to the left takes you to Tefuye, which has an easy walking trail, a suspension bridge and tea plantations.

Head back to County Road 169 and drive to the end of the road to find the lovely village of **Lijia** (里佳, Lǐjiā) sitting on the riverbank. The village boasts several bucolic short walks near its centre, with the most challenging one in **Jushiban** (巨石板, Jùshíbǎn), 5km southwest of the village. Beautiful Jushiban is a 700m-long flat rock surface that you can walk on through to the trailhead of **Limei Refuge Trail** (里美避難步道, Lǐměi Bìnàn Bùdào), a 1.6km steep trail descending to **Danayigu Ecological Park** (達那伊谷自然生態保育公園, Dánàyīgǔ Zìrán Shēngtài Bǎoyù Gōngyuán) in Shanmei. The hike takes three to four hours return.

Sleeping & Eating

Your only option is a homestay in the villages; it's wise to book in advance, as availability is scant. Most homestays provide breakfast and can serve indigenous cuisine or barbecue for dinner (NT$250) if advance notice is given.

★ Jiana Homestay HOMESTAY **$$**
(嘉娜民宿, Jiānà Mínsù; ☎251 1383, 0933-505 101; jiana0616@gmail.com; 61, Lane 3, Lijia Village, 佳里3鄰61號; r incl breakfast from NT$1920) Jiana is run by two energetic widows and is superbly located in the centre of Lijia Village. Rooms are neat and pleasant, while the terrace on the 2nd floor is a perfect stargazing deck. Ms Lin, one of the hosts, speaks communicable English. Jiana is across from the Km49.5 mark.

Keupana Guesthouse HOMESTAY **$$**
(給巴娜民宿, Gěibanà Mínsù; ☎251 1688; 108 Lane 5, Dabang Village 達邦村5鄰108號; r incl breakfast from NT$1600) This five-room guesthouse is just a stone's throw from the centre of Dabang Village. Rooms are simple but clean, and the garden is huge. To get there, turn left at the first intersection after the Km33.5 mark on County Rd 169.

Information

Dabang Tourist Centre (達邦遊客中心; ☎251 1982; 6 Lane 1, Dabang Village; ⏲8.30am-5pm) offers brochures and maps of the Tsou region.

Getting There & Around

Buses run from Chiayi to Dabang (NT$208, two hours) twice on weekdays and three times on weekends. While the centre of each village is small enough to walk around, you'll need your own transport to get around the area.

THE TSOU & THE MAYASVI

The Tsou, an aboriginal group living mainly in Alishan, used to be fierce warriors who regarded the hunting of enemies' heads as a sign of bravery and heroism. But this practice was discontinued during the Japanese period, and many other Tsou traditions and customs were phased out when the group converted to Christianity in the 1940s. However, the Mayasvi, a warring ceremony, has survived up to this day, remaining a very important Tsou tradition that is used to thank the gods and ancestral spirits for their protection. A number of rituals are performed, including a procession led by the tribe's chief, a pig sacrifice and chanting to welcome the deities. The finale is an ambulatory ritual to send off the gods.

Mayasvi is considered a very solemn ritual. Visitors are allowed to take photos but they're reminded to not interfere with the smooth running of the proceedings in any way. Also, a respectful distance has to be kept from the Kuba and nearby trees that the locals consider sacred. After the ritual is performed, there's singing and dancing at night, which visitors are welcome to join in.

The ceremony used to be held several times a year; now it's usually held on 15 February, alternating between the Kuba (tribal meeting hall) in Dabang and Tefuye Villages.

Yuyupas Park 優遊吧斯鄒族文化部落

Literally meaning 'affluent' or 'wealthy' in the Tsou language, **Yuyupas** (Yōuyóubasī Zōuzú Wénhuà Bùluò; NT$300) is an eco-tourism initiative meant to help rebuild the livelihood of the Tsou villagers in the destructive aftermath of Typhoon Morakot in 2009. At an elevation of 1300m, the theme park is designed mainly for tour groups, but it's also a family-friendly destination.

Inside the thatched-roof houses are exhibition halls with displays on the culture and history of the Tsou, as well as shops, restaurants and tea-tasting rooms. Outside are verdant tea plantations, paved walkways and an outdoor theatre that holds evening performances on weekends.

To get there, turn right at the Km61 mark on Hwy 18.

CHANGHUA & YUNLIN COUNTIES

Changhua 彰化市

04 / POP 236,463

Changhua City (Zhānghuà), the capital and political heart of Changhua County, has usually been thought of as a gateway to the old town of Lukang, but there are some treats in the town itself, including stately old temples, a giant hilltop Buddha and a rare fan-shaped train garage that nestles a half-dozen old steam engines.

Birders should note that Changhua is on the migratory route of the grey-faced buzzard and that the hilltop with the Great Buddha statue affords a 360-degree panoramic view.

Changhua is not a compact city, but you needn't wander too far from the train station during your stay. Even the Great Buddha statue is only a couple of kilometres to the east.

Sights & Activities

Confucius Temple CONFUCIAN TEMPLE

(孔廟, Kǒng Miào; 30 Kungmen Rd; 8am-5pm, closed national holidays) This 1726 beauty both ranks as one of the oldest Confucian temples in Taiwan and as a first-class historical relic. Inside the ancestral hall, there's an inscribed plaque donated by the Qing dynasty emperor Chien Long. Every year on Confucius' birthday (28 September) there is a colourful ceremony at dawn.

Baguashan SCENIC AREA

(八卦山, Bāguàshān) Changhua is best known for the 22m-high **Great Buddha statue** (八卦山大佛像, Bāguàshān Dàfóxiàng) that sits atop Baguashan looking down over the city.

The Great Buddha was added in 1962, while the Baguashan slopes were for centuries a military observation zone. The area affords views not only over the whole of the city, but far out to sea. It's a pleasant place to stroll, especially in the spring, when the snow-white flowers of the youtong trees are in bloom.

Baguashan is a prime **birdwatching** area. During late March and early April migratory grey-faced buzzards and Chinese sparrow hawks appear in great numbers. Contact the **Changhua County Wild Bird Society** (728 3006) for information.

Fan-Shaped Train Garage NOTABLE BUILDING

(扇形車庫, Shànxíng Chēkù; 724 4537; 1 Changmei Rd; 8am-5pm) FREE The fan-shaped train garage is the last of its kind in Taiwan. In essence, a single line of track connects with a short section of rotatable track from which 12 radial tracks branch out. A train engine rides up onto the short track, rotates in the direction of its garage, and then proceeds inside for maintenance and repairs.

The garage accommodates the oldest steam-powered train engine in Taiwan (CK101, built in 1907). Visitors need to show ID to enter the garage area, but you are allowed to walk right up to the engines and across the radial tracks.

Nanyao Temple TAOIST TEMPLE

(南瑤宮, Nányáo Gōng; 43 Nanyao Rd; 6am-8pm) Located 2km south of Changhua train station, this remarkable temple is one of the stops on the Matsu Pilgrimage. The distinctive character of the complex lies in the hall in the middle: check out the Doric columns, Baroque-style decor and Japanese shrines that adorn the space. The sanctum, a 1920s addition, honours Guanyin, the bodhisattva of mercy.

To get to the temple, head south on Jhongjheng Rd from the train station, then turn left to Ren'ai Rd. When you reach the intersection with Nanyao Rd, turn right.

Changhua

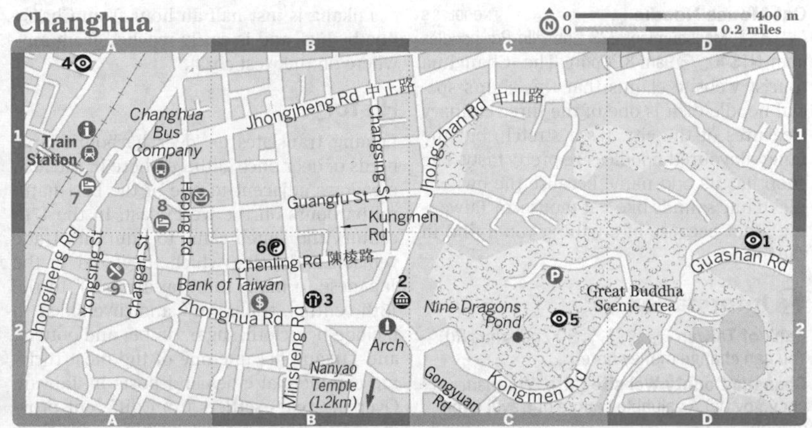

Changhua Arts Museum & Hongmao Well MUSEUM
(彰化藝術館, Zhuānghuà Yìshù Guǎn; 542 Jhongshan Rd, Sec 2; ⏲1.30-9pm Wed-Fri, 9am-9pm Sat & Sun, closed Mon) FREE The museum sits in a lovely heritage building, and on the grounds of the museum is the 300-year-old **Hongmao Well** (紅毛井, Hóngmáo Jǐng), the last of the original Dutch-built wells (hence the name Hongmao, meaning 'red hair') in central Taiwan.

Yuanching Temple TAOIST TEMPLE
This splendid southern-style temple (元清觀, Yuánqīng Guàn; founded in 1763), just a stone's throw away from the Confucian temple, boasts elegant, swallowtail rooftop eaves and a wealth of fine interior woodcarvings. The resident deity is Jade Emperor.

Cycling

The rolling hills between Baguashan and Ershui offers some fine road cycling. There are a number of marked routes, but you can just follow roads such as the **County Rd 139**, a sweet rural route down to Jiji.

OK-quality **bikes** (per day NT$150) can be rented across from the train station.

Sleeping

Rich Royal Hotel HOTEL $
(富皇大飯店, Fùhuáng Dàfàndiàn; ☎723 7117; www.fuhong.com.tw; 97 Changan St, 長安街97號; d from NT$800-1200, tw NT$1800) This place feels like a love hotel when you walk down the long garage to the check-in counter but it is, in fact, popular with families. Rooms are ageing a bit, but it's probably the best value for money in town.

Changhua

Sights
1 Baguashan D2
2 Changhua Arts Museum & Hongmao Well B2
3 Confucius Temple B2
4 Fan-Shaped Train Garage A1
5 Great Buddha Statue C2
6 Yuanching Temple B2

Sleeping
7 Hotel Taiwan A1
8 Rich Royal Hotel A1

Eating
9 Cat Mouse Noodle A2

Hotel Taiwan HOTEL $$
(台灣大飯店, Táiwān Dàfàndiàn; ☎722 4681; www.hoteltaiwan.com.tw; 48 Jhongjheng Rd, Sec 2, 中正路二段 48 號; d/tw NT$1750/2100; @📶) The recently refurbished Hotel Taiwan is the best midrange accommodation in Changhua. The rooms are decently sized and modern. The hotel's location – right next to the train station – is an additional convenience.

Eating & Drinking

Changhua is famous for its *ròu yuán* (肉圓, meatballs) and you'll find many places to try them out on Chenling Rd.

For cheap eats and cafes, there are plenty of places around the train station to try. There are also cafes on Guangfu St. If you're in the mood for a beer, head up Chengling Rd, past Heping Rd.

Cat Mouse Noodle NOODLES $
(貓鼠麵, Māoshǔmiàn; 223 Chenglin Rd; noodles from NT$40; ⏲9am-8.30pm) The Changhua tourist website claims that this shop's special noodle dish is one of the three culinary treasures of the city. It's a stretch, but the tangy-flavoured noodles are pretty tasty. The shop has its odd name because the owner's nickname sounds like 'cat mouse' in Taiwanese – not because of anything you'll find in the food.

ℹ Information

Bank of Taiwan (台灣銀行; 90 Zhonghua Rd) You can change money here.

Changua County Website (http://tourism.chcg.gov.tw) A valuable source of travel information.

Changua City Website (www.changhua.gov.tw) Very helpful information for visitors.

Visitor centre (☎728 5750; ⏲9am-5pm) Located in the train station. English maps of Changhua county are available.

ℹ Getting There & Away

Buses to Lukang (NT$56, 30 minutes, every 15 to 30 minutes) depart from the **Changhua Bus Company** (彰化客運; ☎722 4603; 563 Jhongjheng Rd) station, located near the train station.

Trains travel from Taipei (fast/slow train NT$415/320, 2½/three hours) and Kaohsiung (fast/slow train NT$429/331, two/three hours) to Changhua.

Lukang (Lugang) 鹿港

☎04 / POP 86,065

Ninety percent of Lukang (Lùgǎng) is as nondescript as most small towns in Taiwan...but then there is that other 10%. Comprising some of the most gorgeous temples in the country, and featuring curiously curved streets, heritage buildings, and dusty old shops where equally old masters create colourful handicrafts, it is this small part of Lukang that justifiably brings in the crowds.

People call Lukang a 'living museum' and this is true as much for the food as it is for the buildings and streets. Traditional dishes are cheap and readily available near all major sights. Look for the enticingly named phoenix-eye cake, dragon whiskers and shrimp monkeys, among many other dishes.

You can cover most sights on foot in one long day and there are many more worthy ones than we can list.

Lukang is just half an hour from Changhua by bus, and is easily reached from anywhere on the west coast.

History

Lukang translates as 'deer harbour': large herds of deer once gathered here in the lush meadows adjacent to one of the best natural harbours on the west coast. In the 17th century the Dutch came to hunt and trade venison and pelts (which they sold to the Japanese to make samurai armour). In the 18th century, trade grew and diversified to include rice, cloth, sugar, timber and pottery, and Lukang became one of the most thriving commercial cities and ports in Taiwan. Over the years settlers from different provinces and ethnic groups in China made their home here and left a legacy of temples and buildings in varying regional styles.

In the 19th century silt deposits began to block the harbour, and the city began to decline. To make matters worse, conservative elements in Lukang refused in the early 20th century to allow trains and modern highways to be built near their city. Lukang became a backwater, only to be reborn decades later when modern Taiwanese began to search for a living connection with the past.

👁 Sights

★**Longshan Temple** BUDDHIST TEMPLE
(龍山寺, Lóngshān Sì) Built in the late 18th century, Longshan Temple remains a showcase of southern Taiwanese temple design. The temple is expansive, covering over 10,000 sq metres within its gated walls, so give yourself a few hours to take in the grandeur and admire the minutiae.

Some highlights include the front **mountain gate**, with its elegant *dǒugǒng* (special bracketing system for Chinese architecture) and sweeping eaves. Before the front of the Hall of Five Gates you'll find the most famous **carved dragons** in Taiwan: note that the head of one runs up the column while its twin runs down.

Also check out the hall's window lattice for two fish that curl around each other in the shape of the **yin and yang symbol.** Inside the hall you'll find one of the most stunning **plafonds** in Taiwan, as well as brackets and beams carved into a veritable smorgasbord of traditional symbols: there are clouds, dragons, bats, lions, melons, elephants, phoenixes, fish and more.

Lukang (Lugang)

Top Sights
- 1 Longshan Temple C4

Sights
- 2 Breast Touching Lane (Mo-Lu Lane) B4
- 3 Din Family Old House C3
- 4 Folk Arts Museum C3
- 5 Matsu Temple B1
- 6 Nine Turns Lane (Chinseng Lane) C3
- 7 Old Market Street B1

Sleeping
- 8 Matsu Temple Believer's Hotel B1
- 9 Tai 17 Backpacker C3

Eating
- 10 Yu Chen Chai C3

Shopping
- 11 Mr Chen's Fan Shop B1
- 12 Wan Neng Tinware C4
- 13 Wu Tun-Hou Lantern Shop B1

The resident deity at Longshan Temple is the Bodhisattva Guanyin. You'll find her shrine at the back worship hall.

Matsu Temple TAOIST TEMPLE

(天后宮, Tiānhòu Gōng) This holy structure was renovated in 1936, a high period in Taiwan's temple arts. The woodcarvings are particularly fine in the front hall, and the high plafond is simply gorgeous.

The Matsu statue in this temple is now called 'the Black-Faced Matsu', as centuries of incense smoke have discoloured her original complexion.

The area around the Matsu Temple is pedestrian-only and great crowds gather here on weekends, though the atmosphere feels festive and not touristy. Vendors and the surrounding stores sell a variety of traditional snacks, sweets and drinks.

Folk Arts Museum MUSEUM
(民俗文物館, Mínsú Wénwùguǎn; 152 Jhongshan Rd; admission NT$130; ⏲9am-5pm, no entry after 4.30pm, closed Mon) The Folk Arts Museum has always been one of our favourite heritage sites in Lukang. Built in the Japanese era and originally the residence of a wealthy local family, the museum houses a large collection of daily-life artefacts from a bygone age.

Din Family Old House HISTORIC BUILDING
(丁家進士古厝, Dīngjiā Jīnshī Gǔcuò; 132 Zhongshan Rd; ⏲9am-5pm) FREE This beautifully restored Fujian-style house is the last remaining imperial scholar's home in Lukang.

Glass Matsu Temple TAOIST TEMPLE
(玻璃媽祖廟, Bōlí Māzǔ Miào; 30 Lugongnansi Rd) A remarkable structure standing inside the coastal park 8km west of the old town, this new Lukang attraction is built with 70,000 pieces of glass, while the mountain behind the Matsu statue is made with 1400 pieces of the same stuff layered one on top of the other. Come visit at night when the LED lights are on.

Old Market Street STREET
(古市街, Gǔshì Jiē) The merchant streets of old Lukang are well represented by the shops lining both sides of the curved, red-tiled lanes of what is now called Old Market St. You can shop for traditional items, try some local delicacies or just enjoy a stroll through history.

Nine Turns Lane (Chinseng Lane) STREET
(九曲巷, Jiǔqū Xiàng) Don't bother counting the turns as you wend your way past some of the oldest and most charming residences in Lukang on Nine Turns Lane. The number nine refers to the ninth month – cold winds blow down from Mongolia at this time of year and the turns function as a natural windbreak.

Breast Touching Lane (Mo-Lu Lane) STREET
(摸乳巷) The narrowest alley in Lukang gets its comical label from the fact that a man could not pass a woman down the narrow inner passageway without her breasts brushing against him. The true gentleman would always wait for a lady to pass through first.

Tours

Taiwan Tour Bus BUS
(☎0800 011 765; www.taiwantourbus.com.tw) Has day tours of Lukang (NT$1500) leaving from the train station, HSR stations and major hotels in Taichung.

Festivals & Events

Folk Arts Festival FESTIVAL
Every year Lukang hosts a four-day folk arts festival that begins three days before the Dragon Boat Festival (p24). This is a crowded but rewarding time to visit Lukang.

Matsu's Birthday RELIGIOUS
The birthday of Matsu, held on the 23rd day of the third lunar month (usually in April), is cause for intense celebration at both Matsu temples.

Sleeping

Tai 17 Backpacker HOSTEL $
(☎777 9212; http://tai17backpacker.blogspot.com; 3-1 Jingfu Lane, 景福巷3-1號; dm from NT$500; 📶) This is a brand new hostel, so everything is spick and span. Other perks include free use of the kitchenette and laundry. It's hidden in an alley, so download the map and directions from the website before you go.

Matsu Temple Believer's Hotel HOTEL $
(鹿港天后宮香客大樓, Lùgǎng Tiānhòugōng Xiāngkè Dàlóu; ☎775 2508; 475 Zhongshan Rd, 中山路475號; d/tw NT$1200/1300) You don't have to be a believer to stay here, though it might help you to ignore how bland the rooms are. Be aware that the entire hotel may be booked out months in advance of Matsu's birthday and other important festivals.

Eating

There's hardly a street in Lukang that doesn't offer wall-to-wall eating, and the pedestrian-only zone around Matsu Temple is a lively market of food stalls and eateries. Some famous local dishes include steamed buns, shrimp monkeys (溪蝦, *xī xiā*), oyster omelettes (蚵仔煎, *é ā jiān*), and sweet treats such as cow-tongue crackers (牛舌餅, *níushé bǐng*) and dragon whiskers (龍鬚糖, *lóngxū táng*).

Yu Chen Chai SWEETS $
(玉珍齋食品有限公司, Yùzhēnzhāi Shípǐn Yǒuxiàn Gōngsī; 168 Minzu Rd; ⏰8am-11pm) This fifth-generation shop sells pastries based on original Qing-dynasty recipes. Try the phoenix-eye cake (鳳眼糕; *fèngyǎn gāo*) or the green-bean cake (綠豆糕; *lǜdòu gāo*).

Shopping

Lukang offers great shopping if you're in the market for original crafts. Down near the end of Zhongshan Rd is a row of old furniture makers, still plying their trade in such items as sedan chairs for carrying touring gods. Just browsing is welcome.

Wan Neng Tinware HANDICRAFTS
(萬能錫舖, Wànnéng Xīpù; ☎777 7847; 81 Longshan St) The master here is in fact a fourth-generation tinsmith. His elaborate dragon boats and expressive masks cost thousands but are worth the price for their beauty and craftsmanship.

Mr Chen's Fan Shop HANDICRAFTS
(陳朝宗手工扇, Chéncháozōng Shǒugōngshàn; ☎777 5629; 400 Zhongshan Rd) The shop is just

OF BUTTERFLIES & BIRDS

For serious birders and butterfly buffs, Linnei Township (林內) in Yunlin County has two remarkable things not to be missed: a butterfly migration corridor and a reserve for the globally endangered fairy pitta.

Purple Butterfly Migration

Every spring hundreds of thousands of purple crow butterflies migrate from the warm, sheltered valleys of the south to the north to breed. In Linnei Township, the western migrants converge before crossing the Choshui River (濁水溪). It isn't easy to see the migration unfold as much depends on the weather conditions. However, the peak action hours should be from 7am to 9am daily between 20 March and 10 April.

The best place to see the butterflies on the move is **Linbei Village Chukou** (林北村觸口, Línběicūn Chùkǒu), where Provincial Hwy 3 and National Fwy 3 almost touch. To confirm you've got the right spot, just look up at the freeway overpass. If you don't see 600m of netting, designed to help the butterflies pass over the highway safely, you are in the wrong spot.

In addition to Linbei Village Chukou, the ridgetop tea-growing village of **Pingding** (坪頂, Píngdǐng) is a good place to spot the butterflies.

Fairy Pitta

A 17.4-sq-km area between the villages of Pingding and **Huben** (湖本, Húběn) has been designated as a major wildlife habitat by Taiwan's Forestry Bureau, and an Important Bird Area (IBA) by BirdLife International. The habitat is the world's largest breeding ground for the globally threatened fairy pitta (八色鳥; *bā sè niǎo*). This enchanting migratory bird, aptly called the eight-coloured bird in Chinese, arrives in Taiwan in April for the breeding season, which lasts till May. By August the adults and their young have started migrating south, some travelling as far as Borneo.

There are various trails and interpretation signs in the areas, mostly with English translations.

Sleeping & Eating

Pitta Cafe (湖本生態合作社, Húběn Shēngtài Hézuòshè; ☎05-589 0375; hubenpitta@gmail.com; 56 Sanquan Rd, Huben, 湖本村三權路56號; dm Mon-Fri NT$450, Sat & Sun NT$500) This cafe offers very basic dorm lodging on tatami mats. Reserve in advance. Meals and drinks are also available. The cafe is 2.5km up Township Rd 67 (the road that connects with Pingding) off Provincial Hwy 3 in Huben.

Getting There & Around

During the butterfly migration period a free shuttle bus (8am to 4.30pm) runs from Linnei train station to Chukou on weekends. If driving, take National Fwy 3 south and exit at the Linnei Interchange. Head east on Provincial Hwy 3 and look for signs for Huben Eco Village, Pingding or Linbei Village Chukou.

on the right before you enter the pedestrian-only area near Matsu Temple. Fans range from a few hundred dollars to many thousands for the larger creations. Mr Chen has been making fans since he was 16.

Wu Tun-Hou Lantern Shop HANDICRAFTS
(☎777 6680; 312 Zhongshan Rd) Mr Wu has been making lanterns for 70 years and has collectors from all over the world come to make purchases. These days you're more likely to see his sons (highly skilled themselves) and grandsons at work outside.

Information

Lukang website (www.lukang.gov.tw) An informative introduction to the town's history and sights.

Visitor centre (遊客中心; ☎784 1263; Fusing Rd; ⌚9am-5.30 Mon-Fri, to 6pm Sat & Sun) This new visitor centre is easy to spot, located in a large field/car park across from the Changhua Bus Company station. Pick up a brochure in English for more sights than we can cover.

Getting There & Away

There are direct buses from Taipei's main bus station to Lukang (NT$350, three hours) with **U-bus** (統聯汽車客運; www.ubus.com.tw). Buses to Changhua (NT$53, 30 minutes, frequent) leave from the **Changhua Bus Company Station** (彰化客運站; ☎722 4603; Fusing Rd). The last bus returns at 9pm.

Taiwan Tour Bus (www.taiwantrip.com.tw) runs buses from Changhua to Glass Matsu Temple (NT$76) via the old town of Lukang five/10 times a day on weekdays/weekends, with the last bus back at 7.24pm.

SUN MOON LAKE NATIONAL SCENIC AREA

Sun Moon Lake 日月潭

☎049

Sun Moon Lake (Rìyuè Tán) is on the itinerary of every Chinese group tour to Taiwan, so expect hordes of tourists year-round. But do not be deterred by the crowds – at an altitude of 762m, this largest body of fresh water in Taiwan is one of the island's most lovely natural vistas. While boating is popular, hiking and biking allow you to get off the beaten path while staying on the tourist trail.

Sun Moon Lake is part of the 90-sq-km Sun Moon Lake National Scenic Area under the control of the central government. Accommodation is more than plentiful, with the majority of hotels centred in Shueishe Village (水社村) and Itashao (伊達邵). Itashao is not the quiet backwater it once was, though the strong presence of the Thao aborigines (the area's original inhabitants) is a very obvious contrast to the predominantly Taiwanese atmosphere at Shueishe.

Sights

Shueishe Village VILLAGE
(水社村, Shǔishè Cūn) People often refer to Shueishe Village as Sun Moon Lake Village. The area by the **Shueishe Pier** (水社碼頭, Shǔishè Mǎtóu) is a great place to hang out. Lakeside walking paths extend from the village in either direction. Going east you can walk all the way to Wenwu Temple.

Meihe Garden (梅荷園, Méihé Yuán), on a ledge above the village, is a heavenly spot to hang out on a sunny day (and the night view is pretty charming, too).

Sun Moon Lake Ropeway CABLE CAR
(日月潭纜車, Rìyuètán Lǎnchē; return NT$300; ⌚10.30am-4pm weekday, to 4.30pm weekend, closed 1st Wed every month) The seven-minute, 1.9km ride offers an unparalleled bird's-eye view of the lake as you rise into the nearby hills. The gondola terminates at the **Formosan Aboriginal Cultural Village** (九族文化村, Jiǔzú Wénhuà Cūn), an amusement park–cum–culture venue.

Wenwu Temple TAOIST TEMPLE
(文武廟, Wénwǔ Miào) This temple has superb natural lookouts and faux northern-style temple architecture.

Syuanzang Temple BUDDHIST TEMPLE
(玄奘寺, Xuánzàng Sì) Syuanzang Temple stores a fragment of the skull of Tripitaka (AD 600–664), the monk immortalised in the novel *Journey to the West*.

Tsen Pagoda MONUMENT
(慈恩塔, Cíēn Tǎ) This temple was built by Chiang Kai-shek in honour of his mother.

Activities

Boating

Boat tours (NT$100 each way) are a popular way to take in the scenery and sights; they leave every 30 minutes between 9am and 6pm. You can get on or off at any of the three

Sun Moon Lake

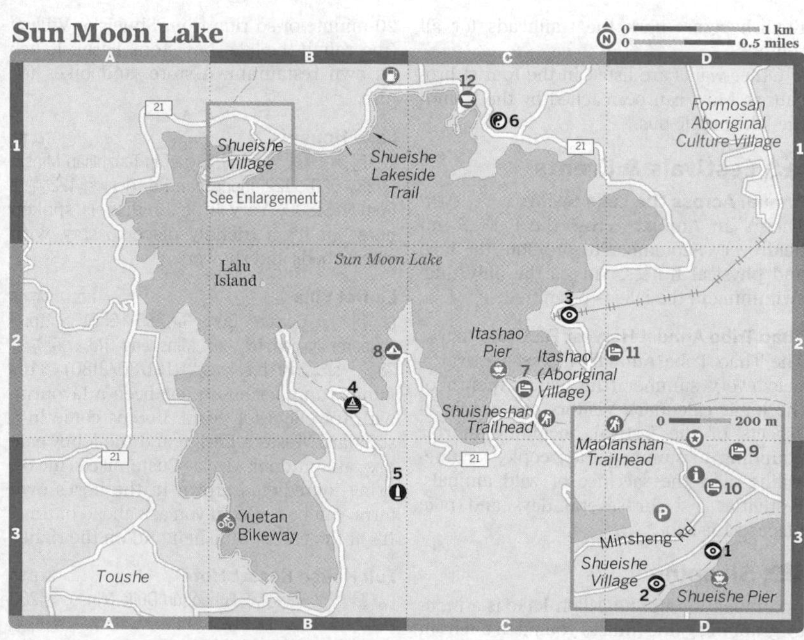

Sun Moon Lake

Sights

1 Meihe Garden ... D3
2 Shuieshe Village ... D3
3 Sun Moon Lake Ropeway ... C2
4 Syuanzang Temple ... B2
5 Tsen Pagoda ... B3
6 Wenwu Temple ... C1

Sleeping

7 Full House Resort Hotel ... C2
8 Holy Love Campground ... B2
9 Lake House ... D3
10 Laurel Villa ... D3
11 Youth Activity Centre ... D2

Eating

Full House Resort ... (see 7)

Drinking & Nightlife

12 Eau Cloud Cafe ... C1

piers, wander round and catch the next boat out. You can also take bikes on the boats.

Most hotels will sell you a ticket without commission. Otherwise, pick one up at any pier.

Cycling

While circling the 29km round-the-lake road is the most popular option, many cyclists are now riding down to towns along the Jiji Small Rail Line via County Rd 131. The 18km from the lake to Checheng (the end of the Jiji line) passes quiet villages, thickly forested hills and a final stretch following the downstream flow of the Shuili River, dammed in several places to store water released from Sun Moon Lake for the generation of hydroelectric power.

You can now ride on the new path that joins Shueishe Village with the 8km **Yuetan Bikeway** (月潭自行車道, Yuètán Zìxíngchē Dào) and a circular route through **Toushe** (頭社, Tóushè), a scenic peat soil basin south of the lake.

The Giant bicycle shop has a variety of bikes for rent. It's located beneath the visitor information centre.

Hiking

Sun Moon Lake offers some very pleasant hiking, and on the longer trails you are sure to leave the tour groups behind. The trails to **Maolanshan** (Māolán Shān; two hours return) and **Shueisheshan** (Shǔishè Shān; seven to eight hours return) are the longest.

English signs mark the trailheads for all routes.

Other walks are listed in the tourist brochures. Most can be reached by the round-the-lake public bus.

Festivals & Events

Annual Across the Lake Swim EVENT

There's an Annual Across the Lake Swim held every September to promote the lake and physical fitness. This is the only time swimming in the lake is permitted.

Thao Tribe Annual Harvest Festival FESTIVAL

The Thao Tribe Annual Harvest Festival is held every summer (the eighth month of the lunar calendar). Visitors can watch all aspects of the festival, including mortar pounding to summon the people, fortune-telling, and the sacrifice of wild animals. Festivities last for several days and take place in Itashao.

Sleeping

Accomodation in Sun Moon Lake is a money-grabbing game (unless you pitch a tent in one of the campgrounds).

Homestays on the main road are a better option than the hotels. As you wander down from the visitor information centre towards the village (around the 7-Eleven), there are a dozen small homestays, with a picture board at the entrance so you can see what you're getting.

Holy Love Campground CAMPGROUND $

(聖愛營地, Shèng'ài Yíngdì; ☎0925-150 202, 285-0202; www.holylove.org.tw; 261-10 Jhongjheng Rd, 中正路261號之10號; dm NT$500, campground per person NT$300) Run by a Catholic church group, this secluded campground beside the lake offers good views and better water quality. There are on-site showers, a kitchen, and kayak rental. Advance booking is a must.

To reach the campground, take a round-the-lake bus to Tutingzai Hiking Trail (土亭仔步道, Tǔtíngzǐ bùdào). Walk uphill until you see a green letterbox between the Km9.5 and Km9.6 marks. Take the path behind the letterbox; it's a 10-minute walk to the campground. For five people or more, a boat shuttle from Itashao pier can be arranged.

Youth Activity Centre HOSTEL $$

(日月潭青年活動中心, Rìyuètán Qīngnián Huódòng Zhōngxīn; ☎285 0071; www.cyh.org.tw; 101 Jhongjheng Rd, 中正路101號; dm with IYH card NT$750, d/tw 1760/3000) This centre is a 20-minute-or-so ride from Shueishe Village (the round-the-lake bus stops here). It has its own restaurant, a store, and bikes for hire.

Lake House HOTEL $$

(日月潭-潭之戀民宿, Rìyuètán-Tánzhīliàn Mínsù; ☎285 5207; 122 Jhongshan Rd, 中山路122號; r from NT$1800) Very little English is spoken here but it's a friendly place to stay, with proper beds and showers.

Laurel Villa HOMESTAY $$

(桂月村, Guìyuè Cūn; ☎285 5551; http://en.laurelvilla.com.tw; 28 Minsheng Rd, 名勝街28號; s/d incl breakfast NT$1780/2180) This family-run guesthouse has been a favourite with travellers for years. Rooms come in a standard Western design and the lobby cafe has an outdoor deck. Customised meals, using ingredients grown in the host's own farm, can be served if you ask ahead of time. It's at the end of Minsheng Rd on the right.

Full House Resort Hotel B&B $$

(富豪群渡假民宿, Fùháoqún Dùjià Mínsù; ☎285 0307; www.fhsml.idv.tw; 8 Shueishe St, 水秀街8號; d/tw from NT$2200/3200) This B&B is set in a two-storey wooden house behind a small garden in Itashao. The owner is a painter; his works adorn the lobby and rooms. All rooms are large, with all-wood interiors, solid wood furniture and antique decorations, and each enjoys a private balcony.

Eating

The general breakdown for eating is Shueishe for Chinese food and Itashao for aboriginal. If you are on a budget there's a 7-Eleven in Shueishe for noodles and sandwiches, and cheap stir-fries and filling set meals are available from the nearby restaurants (dishes from NT$90, set meals NT$250). Most of the expensive hotel restaurants don't serve anything better than the shops on the main street.

Restaurants in Itashao are largely set up for groups, but solo travellers can head to the snack street across from the pier for all manner of aboriginal-style foods, including mountain pig and chicken, sticky rice and wild vegetables.

Full House Resort TAIWANESE $$

(set meals from NT$220; ⏲24hr) Tasty and filling set meals with a veggie option. The outside garden gets a bit too much noise from the streets, but it hasn't completely lost its charm.

Drinking & Nightlife

Along the waterfront, both in Shueishe and Itashao, many hotels run cafes where you can take in the lake views from your table. The Starbucks beside the Del Lago Hotel in Shueishe actually has one of the nicest views, so don't knock it off your list.

Eau Cloud Cafe CAFE
(雲水坊, Yún Shuǐ Fang; 23 Jhongjheng Rd Rd) On the 3rd floor of Fleur de Chine Hotel is this cafe that boasts fantastic lake views and serves the locally grown Assam black tea. During Japanese times the tea enjoyed a worldwide reputation that it's slowly regaining.

Information

There are no banks here, but the 7-Eleven on the main road up from the village has an ATM.

Sun Moon Lake National Scenic Area (www.sunmoonlake.gov.tw) Excellent online resource, with bus information for both getting there and around.

Visitor information centre (遊客服務中心; ☎285 5668; 163 Jhongshan Rd, Shueishe Village; ⏲9am-5pm) This centre is in a large modern building off the main road just before the turn-off for the village. English-speaking staff are usually on hand to help with all your needs.

Getting There & Away

Purchase bus tickets at the kiosk outside the visitor information centre. On the kiosk side of the road, **Nantou Bus Company** (南投客運; www.ntbus.com.tw) has hourly buses to Puli (NT$62, 30 minutes), Taichung HSR (NT$190, 1½ hours) and Taichung city (NT$190, two hours).

Across the street from the kiosk, **Green Transit Bus** (Fengrong Bus Company, 豐榮客運; ☎285 5219) has buses to Sitou (NT$194, 90 minutes, every one or two hours) via Jiji (NT$86, 50 minutes) and Shuili Snake Kiln (NT$58, 20 minutes).

Getting Around

The round-the-lake bus (all-day pass NT$80, every 30 minutes from 6.40am to 5.30pm) leaves from in front of the visitor information centre and turns back at Xuanguang Temple. An English schedule is available at the visitor information centre.

Good-quality scooters (NT$500 per day) can be hired from shops on the main street of Shuishe. An international driver's licence is needed.

Puli 埔里

Thirty minutes north of Sun Moon Lake, Puli (Pǔlǐ) is known in modern times as the epicentre of the 921 earthquake in 1999 and the home of Shaohsing wine. The area was once a centre for butterfly exports. It still flitters with winged life year-round and is the source of the mysterious butterfly dispersal over Tatajia every May and June.

Accommodation in Puli is as expensive as in Sun Moon Lake, but dreary.

Sights & Activities

Paper Dome CHAPEL
(紙教堂, Zhǐ Jiàotáng; 52-51 Taomi Lane, Taomi Village; NT$100; ⏲9am-8pm Sun-Fri, to 9pm Sat) The chapel was originally built as a post-disaster recovery project by survivors of the 6.8-magnitude earthquake that struck Kobe, Japan, in 1995. It later found its permanent home in Puli, the epicentre of the 921 earthquake in 1999. With its supporting pillars, dome and benches made of rolled cardboard and paper materials, and the outer protection a structure of weatherproof translucent plastic, the chapel is especially photogentic after dark when the lights are on.

You'll also find landscaped gardens, eco-farms, outdoor galleries and cafes around the chapel. Paper Dome is 6km south of Puli off Hwy 21. A taxi from Puli is about NT$250.

Puli Wine Museum & Factory MUSEUM
(埔里酒廠, Pǔlǐ Jiǔchǎng; 219 Zhongshan Rd; ⏲8am-4pm Mon-Fri, 8.30-5pm Sat & Sun) FREE The history of the Puli winery is tied with the monopoly system established by the Japanese (and continued by the KMT) on core industries such as alcohol, tobacco and logging. In 1917 the factory began producing sake, and some five decades later switched to Shaohsing wine, traditional Chinese firewater made from glutinous rice and wheat. The amber-coloured liquid has a kick and a bite, and while rarely appreciated by the Western palate, the jugs and jars it comes in are attractive and make for nice gifts.

On the 1st floor of the factory a sample area now lets you try the beverages and a number of Shaohsing-flavoured items, such as popsicles, cakes and sausages. Upstairs the entire history (in English) of the factory and other monopoly industries – and even Chinese spirits in general – is laid out in mesmerising detail.

A taxi from the bus station to the factory will cost less than NT$100.

Hot Springs

Carp Lake (鯉魚潭, Lǐyú Tán) is a pretty, willow-lined pond with a lush mountain backdrop on the outskirts of Puli. Here, you'll find hot springs (*wēnquán*) at **Solas Resort** (天泉溫泉會館, Tiānquán Wēnquán Huìguǎn; www.solasresort.com; unlimited time NT$250; 5-10pm Mon-Fri, 2-10pm Sat & Sun), which is a nice, modern set-up spilling over from a covered area to the edge of the lake. Bring your own towels.

Sleeping & Eating

Hotels in Puli are overpriced. For a cheap and cheerful place to stay, head to the Japanese-run **Guest House Puli** (埔里背包客之家, Pǔlǐ Bèibāokè Zhījiā; 0931-347 432; www.guesthousepuli.com; 6 Lane 303, Dongrong Rd, 東榮路303巷6號; dm/r NT$560/1300). The guesthouse is 800m north of the bus station. From the bus station, turn right on to Zhongshan Rd; from there take another right immediately and walk four blocks to Beihuan Rd. Cross the road and turn right into the first alley. The guesthouse is to your left.

Sumama Rice Ball (蘇媽媽湯圓, Sūmāmā Tāngyuán; 118 Zhongshan Rd, Sec 3; dishes from NT$45; 11am-9pm Thu-Tue) is highly recommended by locals. The salty rice balls stuffed with juicy pork (鮮肉湯圓, *xiānròu tāngyuán*) are al dente; the sweet ones (甜湯圓, *tián tāngyuán*) are equally delicious.

Getting There & Away

Hourly buses are available with **Nantou Bus Company** (南投客運; www.ntbus.com.tw) between Puli and Sun Moon Lake (NT$52, 30 minutes).

The Sun Moon Lake route operated by **Taiwan Tour Bus** (台灣好行; www.taiwantrip.com.tw) stops at Taomi Keng, from where it's a five-minute walk to the Paper Dome.

You'll need a taxi to get around Puli.

Chung Tai Chan Temple 中台禪寺

This 43-storey **temple** (Zhōng Tái Chán Sì; www.chungtai.org) is more than just one of the quirkiest buildings in Taiwan (think tiled mosque meets rocket ship) – it's a global centre of Buddhist academic research, culture and the arts. Opened in 2001, it represents an international branch of Buddhism founded by the Venerable Master Wei Chueh, the master who is said to have revived the Chan (Zen) tradition in Taiwan.

The temple was designed by Taipei 101 architect CY Lee, who embraced, rather than shunned, modern technology in its design, which is why it has won numerous awards for its lighting and design. From the entrance doors with their giant wooden guardians to the 18 delightful Lohan reliefs, only highly skilled artists (both Taiwanese and foreign) were employed, and top-quality materials used, for the temple's construction. A highlight is the seven-storey indoor pagoda, built without any metal nails or screws.

Several resident nuns speak good English, and it is their responsibility to give guided tours to any and all visitors. Reservations must be made three days in advance.

There are also weekly meditation classes held in English, and weeklong retreats during Chinese New Year and summer. Other retreats, lasting three days, are held on an irregular basis. During retreats, guests stay at the temple.

You can get to the temple in a taxi from Puli (NT$300). If you are driving, head north on Jungjeng Rd out of Puli and then follow the signs. The temple is about 6km away.

Don't miss the superb **Chung Tai Museum** (中台山博物館, Zhōngtáishān Bówùguǎn; www.ctmuseum.org; NT$100; 9.30am-5.30pm), adjacent to the main temple building – a fabulous showcase of Buddhist artefacts that date from as early as AD 386. If you're wondering why one Buddha has a medicine ball in his hand while another is holding a lotus, you can find the answers on the touchscreen panels in the exhibits. These tools will also help you understand the history of Buddhism and its statues, motifs and iconography, as well as the 22 physical markings of the Buddha.

Huisun Forest Reserve 惠蓀林場

Located 25km from Puli, this forest research station-cum-recreation park offers a range of trails for light hiking (from two to six hours). The **reserve** (Hùisūn Línchǎng; http://huisun.nchu.edu.tw/home.php; admission NT$150; 7am-10pm) is also a prime site for spotting endemic bird and butterfly species.

There are pleasant rooms and cabins for rent (from NT$2400; check the website for details). Meals (breakfast NT$90, lunch or dinner from NT$220) are served in the centre at the end of the reserve (about 5km from the entrance gate on the lone road).

Nantou Bus Company (南投客運; ☎049-299 6147; www.ntbus.com.tw) runs services to Huisun (NT$137, 40 minutes) leaving from Puli's Zhongzheng Rd at 8.50am and 2.15pm.

JIJI SMALL RAIL LINE

☎049

Branching off the west-coast trunk line in flat, rural Changhua, the train on this 29km narrow-gauge railway (集集小火車線, Jíjí Xiǎohuǒchē Xiàn) chugs past some lovely stretches of rural Taiwan before coming to a halt in Checheng, a vehicle yard and former logging village in the foothills of Nantou County.

While the ride takes just 45 minutes, the list of things to see and do at the seven stops is long: you can cycle, hike and monkey-watch, as well as visit temples, museums, kilns, dams and historical buildings. The most visited stations are Ershui, Jiji, Shuili and Checheng. You can sometimes get a map at the train stations, but they're only in Chinese.

Most of the towns have 7-Elevens with ATMs.

History

Completed in 1922 under Japanese rule, the Jiji line supported the construction of the Daguan Power Station downstream from Sun Moon Lake. This was the first hydro-electric plant in Taiwan; the power it generated was used as far away as Taipei. Tourism began in earnest in the early 2000s; along with farming, it now forms the core of the local economy.

Getting There & Around

BUS

Nantou Bus Company has six buses going from Sun Moon Lake to Shuili (NT$58, 25 minutes) and Jiji stations (NT$86, 35 minutes).

TRAIN

A Jiji line all-day train pass costs NT$80, with 13 daily trains in either direction running from 6am to 10pm. The schedule is available at any station along the small rail line.

Ershui, the first station of the Jiji Small Rail Line, is connected to the main west coast line, but not every train stops here. Trains run frequently from Changhua (fast/slow NT$73/56, roughly every 40 minutes), taking 30 minutes.

When you arrive at Ershui station, alight and transfer to the Jiji Small Rail Line.

Ershui 二水站

POP 300

Ershui is the first station on the Jiji line and it's where you'll transfer if coming by train from Changhua. It's worth a few hours' stop to cycle the dedicated bike paths through the farm fields. There's a visitor centre at the station.

Sights & Activities

Ershui Formosan Macaque Nature Preserve WILDLIFE RESERVE
(二水台灣獼猴自然保護區, Èrshuǐ Táiwān Míhóu Zìrán Bǎohùqū; ☎04-879 7640; ⏲9am-5pm, closed Mon) FREE The 94-hectare park covers the slopes of Songbo Ridge and contains well-preserved mid-elevation forests favoured by the Formosan macaque, the island's sole monkey species. They are easiest to spot in the morning.

The reserve and exhibition halls are 6km east of Ershui off County Rd 152 (look for the English sign 'Ershui Formosan Macaque Education Hall'), which is a pleasant rural route to take should you wish to ride the 20km to Jiji.

Cycling

The cycling-only **bike path** *(jiǎotàchē zhuānyòng dào)* begins to the right of the train station, and intersects with quiet country roads. The countryside is picturesque, with lush fields and temples, traditional brick villas and pagodas popping up in unexpected places. Just to the north stands Songbo Ridge, which is a holy spot for Taiwan's Taoists.

You can rent bikes outside the train station (per day NT$100 to NT$200).

Jiji (Chi Chi) 集集

POP 12,035

Lying at the feet of Great Jiji Mountain, Jiji (Jíjí), the fifth stop down the Jiji Small Rail Line, has a real country charm, with banana fields, betel-nut trees, grapevines and cosmos flowers lining the roads. The old cypress train station is a reproduction of the original Japanese-era station, which was levelled in the 921 earthquake.

The visitor centre is just 100m north of the train station.

Sights & Activities

Endemic Species Research Institute MUSEUM
(特有生物研究保育中心, Tèyǒu Shēngwù Yánjiù Bǎoyù Zhōngxīn; www.tesri.gov.tw; 1 Minsheng East Rd; admission NT$50; ⏲8.30am-4.30pm) This research centre-cum-natural history museum for plant and animal species endemic to Taiwan boasts highly informative displays and features full English text. It's about 1km east of the train station on the bike path.

Wuchang Temple TAOIST TEMPLE
(武昌宮, Wǔchāng Gōng) Wuchang Temple made its name after the 921 earthquake collapsed its lower floors, leaving the roof to stand in ruins. To reach this photogenic temple in its state of disrepair, turn right as you leave the train station and walk for about 10 minutes to Ba Zhang St (八張街). Turn left and walk for another 10 minutes.

Cycling

Jiji's **bike path** is for the most part scenic and easy to follow, with distance markers and clear turning signs. Note that when you get down near the weir the bike path takes you back to town, but it's fun to explore this area as well. Riding up County Rd 152 takes you through the **Green Tunnel** (綠色隧道, Lûsè Suìdào), a section of road with a high canopy formed by interlocking camphor-tree branches, while County Rd 27 rises to take you past the trailhead to **Great Jiji Mountain** (集集大山, Jíjí Dà Shān; elevation 1390m) before a fast descent into Shuili.

You can rent bicycles (per day NT$150) at numerous locations around the train station.

> **ROAD BIKING AROUND THE LINE**
>
> Ershui and Jiji have short cycling paths but the rural roads all over this area are great for longer rides:
>
> - Ershui to Jiji on County Rd 152 (20km)
> - Jiji to Shuili on Township Rd 27 (7km)
> - Jiji to Changhua on County Rd 139 (50km)
> - Shuili to Sun Moon Lake on County Rd 132 (22km)

Sleeping & Eating

Jiji is a pleasant alternative to base yourself in if you find accomodation in Sun Moon Lake too expensive and the Sitou area too remote. You'll find places to eat both around the train station and at various stops along the bike routes. There's a night market on Tuesday and Saturday.

Jiji Hotel HOTEL $
(集集大飯店, Jíjí Dà Fàndiàn; ☎276 0778; http://chichi.nantou.com.tw; 113 Minsheng Rd, 民生路113號; d/tw incl breakfast NT$1100/1900; wi-fi) This budget hotel provides clean and decently sized rooms and a good location, as well as perks such as a free self-service laundry and wi-fi. The only disappointment is the breakfast – you'll be heading to a local breakfast joint as soon as you see what's on offer.

To get to the hotel, turn left from the train station on to Minsheng Rd (民生路), and then another left at the first intersection.

Mountain Fish Water Boutique Hotel HOTEL $$
(山魚水渡假飯店, Shān Yú Shuǐ Dùjià Fàndiàn; ☎276 1000; www.mfwhotel.com.tw; 205 Chenggong Rd, 成功路205號; d/tw incl breakfast NT$2280/4080; @ pool) Off a quiet leafy road, this hotel boasts big mountain views and cosy rooms that offer comfort and style beyond their costs. Use of the swimming pool (fed with mountain spring water), steam room and spa are included (summer only). To reach the hotel, go north from the train station to Cheng Gong Rd (成功路) and turn right.

Shuili 水里

POP 1000

The penultimate stop on the Jiji Small Rail Line, bland Shuili (Shuǐlǐ) serves mostly as a base for travelling somewhere else.

The **Yushan National Park Headquarters** (玉山國家公園管理處, Yùshān Guójiā Gōngyuán Guǎnlǐchù; ☎277 3121; www.ysnp.gov.tw; 515 Jungshan Rd, Sec 1, 水里鄉中山路一段515號'; ⏲8.30am-5pm) has English brochures and films about the park, as well as the latest road and trail information. Usually you'll find someone who speaks English.

Getting Away

Buses to Sun Moon Lake (NT$58, 30 minutes, hourly) are available with **Green Transit Bus Company** (Fengrong Bus Company, 豐榮客運; ☎277 4609; www.gbus.com.tw). **Yuanlin Bus**

Company (員林客運; ☎277 0041; www.ylbus.com.tw) has buses to Dongpu (NT$152, one hour 20 minutes, eight buses daily). Note that buses to these places run during daylight hours only (6am to 5pm or so). To reach the Yuanlin Bus Company, exit the train station and turn left on Minquan Rd. The bus station is just opposite the 7-Eleven. The Fengrong Bus Company is further down the road on the same side.

Checheng 車埕

At the end of the Jiji Small Rail Line, Checheng's (Chēchéng) fortunes were closely tied to the railway's functions as a supply stop for local hydroelectric development and logging.

Sights & Activities

A few decades ago more than 2000 residents lived in Checheng, most working for the Chen Chang Corporation, which had won the rights to log the region in 1959. A moratorium on logging in 1985 left Checheng nearly a ghost town. The remains of the logging industry and the old wood and brick houses now form the backbone of this charming little stop. The upper village exists more or less as it was, while the lower village has been gentrified, with a nice mix of wooden walkways, grassy parks, open decks, new cedar wood buildings, cafes and restaurants.

Checheng Wood Museum (Logging Exhibition Hall) MUSEUM
(車埕木業展示館, Chēchéng Mùyè Zhǎnshìguǎn; admission NT$40; ⏲9am-5pm) This stylish museum, under an enormous wood A-frame, highlights the area's logging history.

Mingtan Reservoir SCENIC AREA
(明潭水庫, Míngtán Shuǐkù) This reservoir feeds a power station billed as the largest pumped-storage generating plant in Asia. The system uses surplus electricity at night from the 2nd and 3rd nuclear power plant to pump water back up to the original source of the reservoir's water (Sun Moon Lake). During the day, the water is released to generate extra power.

Sitou (Hsitou) & Shanlinhsi 溪頭、杉林溪

The old forest reserves of **Sitou** (Xītóu; elevation 1150m; admission NT$200), 26km south of Jiji, is noted for beautiful stands of bamboo, China fir and cedar, but can be shockingly overrun on weekends. The whole area is often shrouded in mist but the trails are paved and well marked.

Just south of Sitou is another forest-resort area called **Shanlinhsi** (Shānlínxī, Sun Link Sea). The area is less developed than Sitou and offers longer hikes.

For sleeping check out the **Youth Activity Centre** (青年活動中心, Qīngnián Huódòng Zhōngxīn; ☎049-261 2160; http://chitou.cyh.org.tw; dm with IYH Card NT$600, d NT$1900) in Sitou. The area outside the entrance of Sitou has recently been developed into a Japanese-themed village and offers plenty of eating options.

Nantou Bus Company (南投客運; www.ntbus.com.tw) has buses between Sun Moon Lake and Sitou via Jiji (NT$194, roughly every two hours, 90 minutes), running six times a day between 7am and 5.30pm.

Buses (NT$175, roughly every 30 minutes) to Sitou operated by **Taiwan Tour Bus** (台灣好行; www.taiwantrip.com.tw) leave from Taichung train station and HSR station between 7am and 3pm.

From Sitou, there are five buses daily going to Shanlinhshi (NT$59).

Taichi Gorge 太極峽谷

It's not hard to see why a 1986 rockslide that killed 28 visitors closed **Taichi Gorge** (Tàijí Xiágǔ; admission NT$50; ⏲7.30am-5pm) to the public for over two decades. The precipitously high, narrow and rocky terrain just doesn't allow for easy trail development. Kudos to the forestry bureau for the wall-hugging wooden steps and the thrilling 136m **Ladder to Heaven** (天梯, Tiāntī) – it's one of Taiwan's longest suspension bridges, and certainly the only one with built-in steps (to help you descend faster). You'll need a few hours here if you want to explore some of the narrower chasms, as well as the waterfall pools at the bottom of the gorge.

Taichi Gorge is 15km south of the town of Jhushan (竹山, Zhúshān) – itself about 20km southwest of Jiji – on Township Rd 49. It's best to have your own vehicle to get there but public transport is also possible. **Yuanlin Bus Company** (員林客運; ☎264 2005) has three buses (each direction) running between Jhushan and the entrance of Taichi Gorge (NT$71, 50 minutes) daily at 8.20am, 12.50pm and 4.20pm. Buses back from the gorge to Jhushan depart at 9.10am, 1.40pm and 5.10pm. Jhushan itself is connected by buses to and from Jiji, Sitou, Douliu and Taichung.

Should you want to stay in Jhushan, **Min Sheng Hotel** (民生旅店, Mínshēng Lǔdiàn; http://min-sheng.98inn.com.tw; 125 Jhushan Rd; d from NT$850) has very decent rooms. From Yuanlin bus station, walk north for one block and turn right on to Jhushan Rd. The hotel is opposite a 7-Eleven.

HIGHWAY 14

Although it begins just south of Taichung in the bland town of Caotun, Hwy 14 makes up for a poor start in no time. After Puli, the elevation rises and one turn after another brings stunning mountain views. Along the way you can break for sightseeing and some of the best hiking in Taiwan.

Hwy 14 ends at Tayuling, just north of the forest recreation area of Hehuanshan (which sits at over 3300m), and from here you can go east to Taroko Gorge or north to Wuling Farm and Ilan. Public transport is not good along the highway. Only Puli has anything like regular bus service from Taichung. By driving and not stopping much, you can cover the route in four to five hours, but we recommend giving yourself at least two days to explore here.

Aowanda National Forest Recreation Area 奧萬大國家森林遊樂區

As you drive along the scenic Hwy 14 east of Puli, you reach the mountain community of **Wushe** (霧社; elevation 1150m) in less than an hour.

Half an hour south, down a long and winding road, is the national **forest recreation area** (Àowàndà; http://trail.forest.gov.tw/index.aspx; admission NT$200) of Aowanda. It's well worth an overnight stay in the quaint **wooden cabins** (NT$1800) surrounded by plum and maple trees. Aowanda has a **visitor centre** (049-297 4511; 8.30am-5pm) offering maps and brochures in English.

The park ranges in altitude from 1100m to 2600m, making it a cool retreat from the heat in summer. On the developed trails you can walk from one end of the reserve to the other in about two hours. All signs are bilingual and trails are simple to follow.

Aowanda is famous for its **maple trees** (*fēngshù*). November to late January, when the leaves change colours, is a busy time for the park. **Birdwatching** is also popular here: in all, 120 species of bird live in the park, and 10 of the 30 bird species endemic to Taiwan can be found here, including Swinhoe's pheasant and the Taiwan partridge. The park has set up a birdwatching platform (*shǎngniǎotái*) and benches.

From Taichung, the **Nantou Bus Company** (04-2225 6418; 35-8 Shuangshi Rd) usually runs buses on the weekends from autumn to spring. Call for the schedule.

Nenggao (Neng-Gao/ Nengkao) Cross-Island Trail 能高越嶺國家步道

This 200-year-old high-mountain trail (Nénggāo Yuèlǐng Guójiā Bùdào) was first used by the Taiya to help them ply their trade between Puli and Hualien. During the Japanese occupation it was expanded and used, ironically, to police aboriginal tribes. During the later half of the 20th century, the path was expanded further by Taipower, which used it when laying high-voltage power lines.

For strong hikers, it is possible to hike from Nenggao to Hehuanshan. Usually three to five days are required.

Activities

Taiwan Adventures (www.taiwan-adventures.com) can arrange hikes and permits.

Nenggaoshan North Peak & Chilai South Peak HIKING

Also called the Nenggao West section, this trail starts at **Tunyuan** (屯原; elevation 2041m) at the end of Hwy 14 and ends the first day at **Tienchi** (天池; elevation 2860m), with the average hiker taking about five or six hours to walk in. You'll find beds and water in the brand new **Tienchi Cabin** (天池山莊, Tiānchí shānzhuāng; 236 5226; http://tconline.forest.gov.tw; weekend/weekday NT$480/450). You can also camp here.

On the next day, **Nenggaoshan North Peak** (能高北峰; elevation 3184m) and **Chilai South Peak** (奇萊主山南峰; elevation 3358m) can be climbed in one long day (including a return to Tienchi cabin).

The return to Tunyuan takes three hours.

WORTH A TRIP

HUASHAN COFFEE AREA

Locals claim coffee has been grown in the foothills of Gukeng Township (古坑鄉, Gŭkēng Xiāng) since the Dutch occupation of Taiwan. If true, it was only after – you guessed it – the 921 earthquake in 1999 destroyed everything that locals turned to coffee as their saviour. The timing was fortuitous, to say the least: coinciding with Taiwan's recent coffee craze, Gukeng has since become one of its most prosperous rural townships.

The Huashan Coffee Area (華山咖啡園區, Huáshān Kāfēi Yuánqū) is built on the steep hillsides east of National Fwy 3. It's all narrow roads lined with orchards, betel palms and coffee fields, with the occasional house offering a deck or a garden for sipping a pot of Gukeng coffee (古坑咖啡, *gŭkēng kāfēi*). A number of B&Bs in the area rent out rooms should you want to spend the night.

To get to Gukeng, take County Rd 149 towards Caoling and then follow the signs.

Nenggao–Andongjun HIKING
An epic six-day hike across the spine of Taiwan, the Nenggao–Andongjun (能高-安東軍, Nénggāo–Āndōngjūn) hike is for the very fit and experienced only. The first day's hike follows the same route as the others to Tienchi but after that veers south to cross a rugged, high-mountain landscape of deep-set lakes, rolling meadows of dwarf bamboo, deep-cut valleys and endless dark ranges. There is great beauty here and deeper solitude. The last day's hike down the Aowanda River ends in the Aowanda National Forest Recreation Area.

Be prepared to carry your own supplies, including a tent, for the whole trip. A guide who knows the route is an absolute necessity; contact Taiwan Adventures (p236).

Information

The Nenggao Cross-Island Trail is part of the National Trail System. Only a mountain permit is needed to hike; you can get one at the **police station** (☎049-280 2520) in Wushe.

Getting There & Away

You need your own vehicle. Note that past Wushe, Hwy 14 splits into Hwy 14甲, which heads north, and Hwy 14, which heads east to the trailhead at Tunyuan. Alternatively, one of the eateries opposite the 7-Eleven in Wushe can arrange a 4WD to drop you off and pick you up (NT$1000 one way); look for the sign with this phone number on it: ☎0963-211 840.

Cingjing 清境

Between Wushe and Hehuanshan, **Cingjing** (Qīngjìng; www.cingjing.gov.tw) was once a cattle ranch of the Seediq; it wasn't until the 1960s that this place was turned into farmland, providing livelihood to KMT veterans from the Chinese Civil War. Today, Cingjing covers more than 700 hectares of rolling meadow, and is a hill station especially popular with Taiwanese, Singaporean and Chinese visitors.

Most visitors come here for the **Evergreen Grasslands** (青青草原, Qīngqīng Căoyuán; admission NT$200; ⏲8am-7pm), an agricultural attraction which offers sheep and dog shows and a farm experience (lamb feeding) for city slickers. It's located near the Km10 mark.

Small Swiss Garden (小瑞士花園, Xiăo Ruìshì Huāyuán; admission NT$120; ⏲8am-7pm) is a well-maintained garden, with an evening water-themed show in the summer months. It's located right opposite Cingjing Veterans Farm Guest House, the landmark hotel of the area.

There are six **walking trails** in Cingjing that meander through tea plantations and fruit orchards and offer splendid views of the mountains of Hehuan and Nenggao. Each walk takes between 40 and 60 minutes to complete.

If Cingjing is on your itinerary, try to visit during the week to avoid the huge weekend crowds.

Sleeping & Eating

Homestays have sprouted up in Cingjing but avoid the roadside ones: they're noisy at night when trucks trundle back and forth along the highway.

Cingjing has the highest concentration of restaurants and cafes along Hwy 14甲. Baiyi cuisine from Yunnan, China, is a speciality here, thanks to the KMT veterans and their aboriginal wives from Yunnan who settled and brought their home cuisine here. Most homestays also serve meals.

Shangrila Hanging Garden & Resort B&B $

(香格里拉空中花園, Xiānggélǐlā Kōngzhōng Huāyuán; ☎280 2166; www.shangrila-resort.com.tw; 8, Rongguang Lane, Datong Village, 大同村榮光巷8號; per person with IYH card incl breakfast NT$1000, r from NT$2350) This faux-Swiss holiday cottage is an HI-affiliated B&B with bright rooms that ooze rustic charm. To get there, take the side road next to Cingjing Veterans Farm Guest House (near the Km7.5 mark) and walk about 150m.

Cingjing Veterans Farm Guest House HOTEL $$

(清境國民賓館, Qīngjìng Guómín Bīnguǎn; ☎280 2748; http://hotel.chingjing.com.tw; 170 Renhe Rd, Datong Village, 大同村仁和路170號; d incl breakfast from NT$2400) This is the only hotel in Cingjing, offering standard midrange hotel rooms with no wow factor – but they are very comfortable. The rates include admission to Evergreen Grasslands and the Small Swiss Garden. It's located near the Km7.5 mark.

ℹ Getting There & Away

Nantou Bus Company (南投客運; ☎049-299 6147) runs nine buses daily to Cingjing (NT$127; one hour 30 minutes) from Puli.

Hehuanshan (Hohuanshan) Forest Recreation Area 合歡山森林遊樂區

The last interesting stop on Hwy 14甲 before the descent into Taroko Gorge is **Hehuanshan** (Héhuān Shān Sēnlín Yóulè Qū; www.forest.gov.tw). At over 3000m, the recreation area sits mostly above the treeline, and the bright, grassy green hills of the Mt Hehuan Range roll on and on, often disappearing into a spectacular sea of clouds. Driving up from the western plains of Taiwan, the change in a few hours from urban sprawl to emerald hills is miraculous.

Hwy 14甲 passes right through the park, and at Wuling Pass (not to be confused with the forest recreation area called Wuling) it reaches the highest elevation of any road in Taiwan (and East Asia) at 3275m. It snows up here in winter, and when it does the road becomes a skating rink, parking lot and playground for the Taiwanese. It's best to avoid the area at this time as it gets crowded.

Summer is delightfully cool and highly scenic as different alpine flowers bloom from May through to September. Autumn and spring are excellent times for hiking.

THE WUSHE INCIDENT

In 1930, Wushe witnessed the last large-scale (and the bloodiest) revolt against the Japanese, who in turn massacred the Seediq aborigines who began it.

In October of that year, Mona Rudao, one of the leaders of the Seediq tribe, held a wedding banquet for his son, Daho Mona. A Japanese policeman was on patrol, and was offered some local liquor by Daho, but he refused as Daho's hands were tainted by blood from slaughtering animals for the banquet. This led to a brawl and the policeman was injured. Though Mona Rudao tried to make amends, he was rebuffed.

Fearing the police would take revenge, and with already-simmering local resentment now starting to boil over, the Seediq decided to launch an indiscriminate attack in Wushe on 27 October, killing 134 Japanese people (including women and children).

This shocked the Japanese authorities, who immediately sent 2000 troops to Wushe, forcing the Seediq to retreat into the mountains. The battle continued for more than a month, seeing 354 Seediq members either killed in battle or caught and executed. Determined to end the battle quickly, the Japanese forces started dropping tear-gas bombs by plane. Mona Rudao and his tribespeople, who fought with bare hands or primitive weapons, knew their days were numbered; he and 290 members of the tribe committed suicide to avoid dishonour.

The incident was depicted in the epic film of *Warriors of the Rainbow: Seediq Bale*, directed by Taiwanese director Wei Te-sheng in 2011; today, traces of the dreadful carnage can hardly be found in Wushe. At its **Mona Rudao Memorial** (莫那魯道紀念碑, Mònà Lǔdào Jìniànbēi) you'll find Mona Rudao's tomb, as well as the collective tomb of 30-odd Seediq victims of the bloodshed. The memorial, marked by a white arch, is located up the main road of Hwy 14, on the left before you reach Wushe.

In the autumn the 'sea of clouds' formations are at their best.

Despite its chilly temperatures (12°C average), Hehuanshan has a remarkable amount of plant and animal life to admire. Check out the website for details.

Activities

There are a number of short hikes starting close to the former Hehuan Cabin, which is planned to be repurposed as an information centre and clinic. You are advised to still get a proper map of the area, and be aware that fog or rain can come in suddenly in the mountains, so always be prepared with warm clothing and rain protection. Be aware also that if you have driven straight up from lower altitudes, your body may need some time to get used to exercising at 3000m-plus elevation.

No permits are needed to tackle the following hikes.

The trail to **Hehuanshan East Peak** (合歡山東峰, Héhuān Shān Dōngfēng; elevation 3421m) starts next to the Ski Villa. It's a two- to three-hour return hike to the top.

The marked trailhead to **Hehuanshan North Peak** (合歡山北峰, Héhuān Shān Běifēng; elevation 3422m) starts at 200m north of Taroko National Park Hehuanshan Station at Km37. It's a three- to four-hour return hike.

The trailhead for **Shimenshan** (石門山, Shímén Shān; elevation 3237m) is just north of the former Hehuan Cabin on the east (left) side of the road. It's a short walk to the top. People often come here to watch the sunrise.

The paved path up to **Hehuanshan Main Peak** (合歡山主峰, Héhuān Shān Zhǔfēng; elevation 3417m) starts at the 30.5km mark (just before Wuling) and is about a two-hour return hike.

The trail up to **Hehuan Jian Shan** (合歡尖山, Héhuānjiān Shān; elevation 3217m) starts just behind the former Hehuan Cabin. It takes about 15 minutes to reach the top.

For overnight hikes, check the Hehuanshan website.

Sleeping & Eating

Camping is possible in the parking lot at the information centre.

The restaurant in Song Syue Lodge is the only place to eat on the mountain.

Ski Villa HOTEL **$$**

(滑雪山莊, Huáxuě Shānzhuāng; ☎04-2522 9797; dm incl breakfast & dinner NT$1000, d incl breakfast from NT$2440) You can stay overnight in the Ski Villa, found down the lower lane from a toilet block opposite the former Hehuan Cabin. The upper lane leads to the overpriced Song Syue Lodge (松雪樓).

Getting There & Away

The **Fengyuan Bus Company** (☎2222 3454) runs one bus daily to Hehuanshan from Taichung (NT$464, four hours, 8.50am). If you want to continue north from Hehuanshan, catch the next day's Fengyuan bus as it passes Hehuanshan heading to Lishan. The bus arrives in Lishan at around 2.30pm, where you can connect to a bus at 4pm to Wuling Forest Recreation Area, and the next day continue by bus down to Ilan or Taroko Gorge.

Southern Taiwan

Includes ➡

Best Temples

- Confucius Temple (p242)
- Matsu Temple (p243)
- Nankunshen Temple (p261)
- Foguangshan (p263)
- Temple clusters in Lotus Pond (p256)

Best Bike Rides

- Kenting National Park (p273)
- County Road 185 (p275)
- Dongshan Coffee Road (p253)
- Houbi (p252)
- Anping in Tainan (p247)
- Kaohsiung (p259)

Why Go?

Southern Taiwan is a land of timeless rituals and strong folk culture. The yearly calendar is chock-full of some of Taiwan's most unforgettable festivals: when they're not burning boats to honour their indomitable ancestors, southerners let off fierce fireworks to seek supernatural protection for the future.

Tainan, the island's former capital, is the city most worth visiting outside Taipei. Expect a feast of original street snacks, flamboyant temples and enduring relics available at every turn. Outside the cities, the wonderful biking routes and beaches offer enough activities to impress action travellers, and the wild landscape simply stirs the blood. From the jagged mountains and beautiful coastal cliffs of Pingtung County to the geological oddity of mud volcanoes outside Kaohsiung, this is Formosa at its most formidable. No wonder millions of purple and yellow butterflies return yearly to overwinter in the verdant mountain valleys around Maolin and Meinong. They've chosen well.

When to Go

Tainan

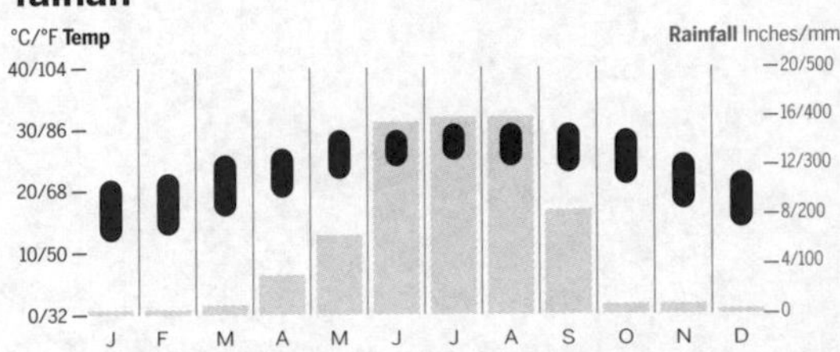

Feb Yenshui fireworks festival.

Apr The Spring Scream music festival takes over Kenting.

Sep–Oct Raptor migration over Kenting National Park.

National Parks & Forest Recreation Areas

There are three national parks in the south: Kenting, a beach playground with some well-protected areas into which few people venture; Taijiang, Taiwan's newest national park and a storehouse for ecological and cultural heritage along the southwest coast; and Yushan, unfortunately now inaccessible from the south because of typhoon damage. Maolin Forest Recreation Area is a stronghold for aboriginal culture and also holds an important overwintering valley for the purple butterfly, while Shuangliou Forest Recreation Area has a gorgeous waterfall.

Southern Taiwan Highlights

1. Marvel at Taiwan's temple heritage in and around the old capital of **Tainan** (p242).
2. Swim, surf and cycle year-round in **Kenting National Park** (p273).
3. Discover the bizarre yet interesting Martian landscape of **Wushanding Mud Volcanoes** (p266).
4. Bird- and butterfly-watch at protected areas including **Taijiang National Park** (p252) and **Meinong** (p263).
5. Enjoy a bike ride along charming back-country routes such as **County Road 185** (p275).
6. Climb **Beidawushan**, the most southerly of the 3000m-plus peaks in Taiwan, and admire the view from the clouds (p272).
7. Get rained on by fireworks at **Yenshui** (p258).
8. Snorkel or soak up some sun at Taiwan's only coral island, **Little Liuchiu Island** (p269).
9. Watch a ceremonial boat burn to the ground in **Donggang** (p267).

Getting There & Around

There's excellent train, High Speed Rail (HSR) and bus transport between cities. You'll find decent public transport within major cities, but alternatives are definitely needed outside them. Scooter and car rental is available in major cities and in Kenting.

TAINAN CITY

06 / POP 770,000

You'll almost certainly receive looks of jealousy from any Taiwanese person if you mention you're going to Tainan (台南市), and it's not hard to see why. Traditional culture continues to thrive in Tainan, the oldest city in the country. Inside temples that are hundreds of years old, people *bwah bwey* (cast moon blocks) to determine the best course of action, just as their ancestors did when the temples first opened. Outside, Tainanese are fastidious about food, and a number of dishes are exclusive to the region but renowned all over the country.

Tainan is best visited in winter: it's warm (in the high 20s) and dry, but there are few tourists. Traditional festival days are, of course, a great time to come, as are the local birthdays of temple gods.

Most of the sights in Tainan are concentrated around the city centre west of the train station and in the Anping District. Both areas are compact enough to get around on foot, though you may want a taxi or bus to take you from one area to the other.

History

Fujianese first settled in the Tainan area in the late 1600s, but it was the Dutch East India Company (VOC) that encouraged immigration. After being booted off Penghu by the Qing dynasty, the Dutch established Tainan as an operational base for their trade with Japan and China. However, unable to persuade Taiwanese aborigines to grow rice and sugar for export, and unable to persuade Dutch rulers to allow immigration, the VOC looked to China for cheap labour.

When the Ming loyalist Koxinga defeated the Dutch, he established a central government in Tainan and started building up the city (a project later continued by his sons). Koxinga's son constructed Taiwan's first Confucian temple, helping to establish Tainan as a cultural and educational centre.

In 1683, when the Qing dynasty gained control of Taiwan, Tainan was chosen as the capital. The city remained the political, cultural and economic centre under the Qing, but lost this status in 1919 when the Japanese moved their colonial capital to Taipei. To the discerning eye, Tainan's pedigree is apparent from the stately quality of the city's temples and historic sites.

Modern Tainan has industries producing metals, textiles and machinery, and a few old masters working on traditional crafts, as well as a new science park that promises to bring the city into the avant-garde of Taiwan's high-tech revolution. Tainan City and County merged into one municipal area in 2009.

Sights

Central Tainan

★Confucius Temple CONFUCIAN TEMPLE
(孔廟, Kǒng Miào; http://confucius.cca.gov.tw; 2 Nanmen Rd; admission NT$25; 8.30am-5pm) Confucian temples usually exude the calm, grace and dignified beauty of traditional Chinese culture and this, the first such temple in Taiwan, doesn't disappoint.

Entry to the temple grounds is free, but you must pay to enter the palace area. Look out for the stone tablet on the right as you enter the Edification Hall. It explains the school rules (the site was once a centre for Confucian studies), such as prohibition of gambling, drinking and cheating.

The temple is part of a larger cultural zone that includes the **Old Tainan Martial Arts Academy** (台南武德殿, Táinán Wǔdé Diàn), a renovated Japanese dojo built in 1926 that was once used to train the colonial police force (not open to the public).

Across the street from the temple entrance is a **stone arch** (泮宮石坊, Pàngōng Shífang) that was crafted by masons in Quanzhou, Fujian, in 1777. It's now the gateway to a pedestrianised street filled with cafes and small eateries.

★Chihkan Towers HISTORIC SITE
(赤崁樓, Fort Proventia, Chìkǎn Lóu; 212 Minzu Rd; admission NT$50; 8.30am-9pm) This old fort is a splendid place to roam around, or to enjoy an outdoor concert on weekends.

Chihkan has gone through many masters – Ming, Qing and Japanese, and the Kuomintang (KMT; China's Nationalist Party) – since the foundations were first laid by the Dutch in 1653. At that time the seashore reached the fort's outer walls. Our favourite features are the nine stone turtles with tablets on their backs. These stelae hail from the Qing dynasty. If you check the backs you can see where the carver made a mistake on one and, rather than starting over with a fresh slab, simply turned the stone over and redid everything on the other side.

★Matsu Temple TAOIST TEMPLE
(大天后宮, Dà Tiānhòu Gōng; 18 Lane 227, Yongfu Rd, Sec 2) This lively temple once served as the palace of Ning Jin, the last king of the Ming dynasty. If you wish to confirm visually that a king's status is lower than an emperor's, count the steps to the shrine. There are only seven; an emperor would get nine.

Right before the king's death, the palace was converted to a Matsu temple according to his last wish. Some features to note at this particular temple include the 300-year-old Matsu statue and, in the back, the shrine to Matsu's parents in an area that used to be the king's bedroom. Look up and you'll see the roof beam from which the king's concubines hanged themselves so many years ago (see Wufei Temple, p244).

Official God of War Temple TAOIST TEMPLE
(祀典武廟, Sì Diǎn Wǔ Miào, Sacrificial Rites Temple; 229 Yongfu Rd, Sec 2) This is the oldest and most impressive temple in Taiwan dedicated to Guandi (Guangong), a Han-dynasty general deified as the God of War and the patron of warriors and those who live by a code of honour.

The temple's overall structure was established in 1690, although much splendid artwork and many historically valuable objects have been added over the years. The long, deep-rose-coloured walls of this temple have always been one of its highlights. Other interesting features include the beggar seats around the doorframe that the poor used to beg alms from every visitor, and the high threshold at the entrance (originally designed to keep women out!).

Dongyue Temple TAOIST TEMPLE
(東嶽殿, Dōngyuè Diàn; 110 Mincyuan Rd) People come here to communicate with the dead through spirit mediums. It's a fascinating place to catch a glimpse of Taiwanese folk culture.

The first chamber of the temple holds the God of Mount Tai, the Taoist king of the underworld; the second, Ksitigarbha Bodhisattva, who vowed to not attain Buddhahood as long as there is still one suffering soul in hell; the last, a number of demon gods who rule the underworld.

The grim murals on the walls of the second chamber are as graphic as the depictions of hell by Hieronymus Bosch, including depictions of disembowelments, eye gougings, stabbings and boilings.

City God Temple TAOIST TEMPLE
(城隍廟, Chénghuáng Miào; 133 Cingnian Rd) The City God (Chenghuang), officially the protector of towns, also tallies this life's good and bad deeds after we die. Hence it is not unusual that his image appears in the last chamber of Dongyue Temple, which is dedicated to the underworld, nor that these two temples sit near each other.

When you enter the temple, look up for the two large abacuses used to calculate whether you have done more good than bad in life; check out the gold scripted plaque: it translates roughly as 'You've come at last', meaning death escapes no one.

In the worship hall look for pink slips of paper on the altar. They're from students asking for help to pass an exam. Yep, school is hell everywhere.

Koxinga's Shrine HISTORIC SITE
(延平郡王祠, Yánpíng Jùnwáng Cí; 152 Kaishan Rd; ⏲8am-6pm) FREE In 1661 Ming loyalist Koxinga (Cheng Cheng-kung) led his army to Taiwan with plans to restock supplies and then retake the mainland, which by that point had been all but conquered by the Manchus. He found the Dutch already here, but after nine months' battle they surrendered and departed Taiwan. Koxinga did much to improve conditions on the island. But, like the KMT of modern times, he did not live to see the mainland retaken. He died after only a year in Taiwan, and his grandson surrendered to the Manchus in 1683.

The original southern-style temple was rebuilt in a northern style by the KMT government in the '60s. Many of the artefacts are historical, however, including the boxes in the shrine that hold the original imperial edict from 1874, which permitted the shrine's construction.

Lady Linshui's Temple TAOIST TEMPLE
(臨水夫人媽廟, Línshǔi Fūrén Mā Miào, Chen Ching Gu Temple; 1 Jianye St) For generations, women have come to this temple to ask Lady Linshui to protect their children. This is demanding work and the goddess employs 36

Central Tainan

assistants (three for each month), whose statuettes can be seen in little glass vaults around the inside walls of the temple.

In addition to offerings of incense, you'll often see flowers, face powder and make-up left at the temple. If you are extremely lucky you might see the unique southern-temple spectacle associated with Lady Linshui called the **Twelve Grannies Parade**.

Wufei Temple — TAOIST TEMPLE

(五妃廟, Wǔfēi Miào; 201 Wufei St; 8am-6pm) When Koxinga's grandson surrendered to the Manchus in 1683, all hope of restoring the Ming dynasty ended. King Ning Jin, the last contender for the Ming throne, knew his time was up. Before he committed suicide, his concubines, claiming their honour was as important as the king's, hanged themselves on a roof beam in the bedroom of his palace. The palace is now the shrine to Matsu's parents at the Matsu Temple and the beam is still in place.

The dainty Wufei Temple was constructed in the concubines' honour and now sits in a 2000-sq-metre garden park off Wufei Rd. Note that the real tombs of the concubines are behind Koxinga's Shrine and are covered with cement.

Great South Gate — HISTORIC SITE

(大南門城, Dà Nánmén Chéng; Lane 34, Nanmen Rd; 8.30am-5pm) FREE This old city gate is the only one in Tainan that still has its defensive wall intact. The inner grounds feature several cannons and a section of the old wall that is marvellously overgrown with thick roots. At the far end of the park a collection of handsome **stelae** commemorates centuries of battles, bridge constructions and official promotions.

National Museum of Taiwanese Literature — MUSEUM

(國家台灣文學館, Guójiā Táiwān Wénxué Guǎn; www.nmtl.gov.tw; 1 Jungjeng Rd; 9am-9pm)

Central Tainan

Top Sights
1 Chihkan Towers ... B1
2 Confucius Temple ... B2
3 Matsu Temple ... A1

Sights
4 Altar of Heaven ... B2
5 City God Temple ... C2
6 Dongyue Temple ... C2
7 Great South Gate ... B3
8 Koxinga's Shrine ... C3
9 Lady Linshui's Temple ... C3
10 National Museum of Taiwanese Literature ... B2
11 Official God of War Temple ... B1
12 Old Tainan Martial Arts Academy ... B2
13 Stone Arch ... B2
14 Wufei Temple ... B4

Sleeping
15 JJ-W Culture Design Hotel ... A2
16 Fuqi Tainan Hostel ... B2
17 Ing Wang Hotel ... B1
18 Shangri-La's Far Eastern Plaza Hotel ... D1
19 Takatama Hotel ... D1
20 Your Fun Apartment ... A1

Eating
21 A Cun Beef Soup ... A2
22 A Xia Restaurant ... B2
23 Chi Kin Dandanman ... B1
24 Guli Restaurant ... B1
25 Jade Room Restaurant ... C1

Drinking & Nightlife
26 A Chuan Melon Drink ... B1
27 Daybreak 18 Teahouse ... C2
28 Gandan Café ... C2
29 Lily Fruit Shop ... B3
30 TCRC Bar ... B1

Shopping
Tainan Kuang Tsai Embroidery Shop ... (see 26)

Information
National Museum of Taiwanese Literature ... (see 10)
31 Visitor Information Centre ... D1

Transport
32 City Bus North Station ... D1
33 City Bus South Station ... D1
34 Ho-Hsin Bus Company ... D1
35 Hsingnan Bus Company ... D1
36 Scooter Rentals ... D1

FREE Honestly, this museum highlighting the development of Taiwanese literature from the time of the pre-Han aborigines up to the modern era is very uninteresting, but it's worth coming here just to wander the halls and relax in the foyer, as it's a gorgeous example of Japanese colonial architecture (built in 1916): it was once the Tainan District Hall.

Altar of Heaven TAOIST TEMPLE
(天壇, Tiāntán; 16 Lane 84, Jhongyi Rd, Sec 2) Tainan families have been coming here for generations on the 1st and 15th of every month, to pray to the supreme Taoist entity, the Jade Emperor, for good luck. The temple has no statue of the god as the original temple was only meant to be temporary – 300 years ago! There's a famous *Yī* (One) inscription over the altar signifying that there is only one true way for heaven and earth: humanity and righteousness.

Anping 安平區

The western district of Anping (Ānpíng) has one of the most interesting concentrations of relics and temples in southern Taiwan. The centre of Anping is the intersection of Anping Rd and Gubao St. Buses from central Tainan (bus 2 or 88) stop just west of here across from the square in front of the Anping Matsu Temple. This is a good place to start your explorations.

History

When the Dutch established their colony on Taiwan, they built their first fort and commercial centre here in Anping. Anping was a very different harbour back then, being part of a giant inland sea called Taijiang (now the name of the eighth national park). But silting has always been a major problem for western seaports and in 1822 most of Taijiang was filled in.

In 1858 the Tianjin Treaty opened Anping to Western powers and their business interests, something that's readily apparent in the number of old merchant houses about town. By the early 20th century, however, continued silting had made Anping lose almost all function as a workable harbour.

Former Tait & Co Merchant House and Anping Tree House HISTORIC BUILDING
(德記洋行暨安平樹屋, Déjì Yángháng Jì Ānpíng Shùwū; Gubao St; admission NT$50; ⏲8.30am-6pm) The merchant house was built in 1867 and holds a permanent exhibit of household artefacts from the 17th century. Through a series of decorated rooms, the exhibit highlights the lifestyle of Dutch, Chinese and aboriginal families.

But nobody comes for that. Instead, it's the **Anping Tree House** (Ānpíng Shùwū) that draws in the curious with its massive banyan strangling the gutted roofless walls of the back quarters.

Both houses are up Gubao St and behind the primary-school grounds.

Anping Matsu Temple TAOIST TEMPLE
(安平天后宮, Ānpíng Tiānhòu Gōng; 33 Guosheng Rd) This temple is one of many claiming status as the oldest in Taiwan. Its interior is more elaborately decorated than most in central Tainan, and features a splendidly ornate and deep plafond (decorative ceiling) above the main shrine. Near the altar, little packets of 'safe rice' are available to help keep you and your family safe.

Anping Fort HISTORIC SITE
(安平古堡, Ānpíng Gǔbǎo, Fort Zeelandia; admission NT$50; ⏲8.30am-5.30pm) Behind the Matsu Temple, the fort was a stronghold of Dutch power until its capture by Koxinga in 1661 after a nine-month battle. Most of it has been reconstructed but it's still an impressive site. A small **museum** on the grounds highlights the history of the Dutch occupation of Taiwan.

Anping Old Streets STREETS
To the right of the Anping Fort entrance you'll find some of the oldest streets in Taiwan. As you wander about, look for **stone lion masks** (劍獅, *jiànshī*) with swords across the mouth. They were once used to protect a house against evil but today there are only a few dozen left.

Siaojhong Street (效忠街, Xiàozhōngjiē) is an interesting street that leads to a number of back alleys with restored brick buildings.

Yenping Street (延平街, Yánpíngjiē) is the site of the first market in Taiwan. Now it has been turned into a dull tourist lane, although it's worth a visit to sample traditional Tainan foods.

Eternal Golden Castle HISTORIC SITE
(億載金城, Yìzài Jīn Chéng; admission NT$50; ⏲8.30am-5.30pm) This photogenic fort was built in 1876 to shore up Taiwan's defences against the Japanese threat. Not much remains of the original fortress; oddly, though, the intact arched front gate was built with bricks pilfered from Anping Fort. City buses 2 and 14 stop at the Eternal Golden Castle, as does tour bus 88.

WORTH A TRIP

THE FORGOTTEN SOULS

When you leave Anping Matsu temple (p246), turn right (westward) on Anping Rd, walk about 100m, and you'll see a group of splendidly restored **Fujian-style tombs** (明清古墓群, Míngqīng Gǔ Mùqún) dating from the Ming and Qing dynasties on a knoll to your left. This was once the site of the Dutch-built Fort Utrecht, which was completely ruined in 1662 when Koxinga's troops dropped hundreds of bombs on it in a single day.

Not much of the fort remains today, but look out for 12 column-shaped Japanese tombs, collectively known as the **Tombs of the Anping Military Porters** (安平十二軍伕墓, Ānpíng Shí'èr Jūnfū Mù), among the sea of Chinese-style graves. This is the final resting place of 12 Anpingers who were conscripted as military porters by the Japanese and died in battle in China during the Second Sino-Japanese War (1937–1945). More than 400 conscripts, mostly in their 20s, were recruited from Anping. Most of them thought that it was just an unskilled labourer's job with a higher pay; it's only when they boarded the boat to Shanghai that they realised they were going to the front line. The youngest victim among the 12 buried in Anping was only 17, while the oldest was in his 40s. Five of them are honoured at the controversial Yasukuni Shrine in Tokyo, which marks Japan's WWII dead, including convicted war criminals.

The tombs are quite close to the roadside; a large information panel stands in front of them.

Activities

Anping has lots of flat, open areas and pavements, so walking or cycling are both good ways to get around. A **riverside bike path** runs west coastwards, where you can continue north through Taijiang National Park or south along the Taiwan Strait and into the harbour area.

Bikes can be rented from the Tainan City program at Anping Fort, Eternal Golden Castle and Anping Tree House.

Tours

Taiwan Eco Tours NATURE TOUR
(www.taiwanecotours.com) Richard, a Tainan-based guide, offers custom-made tours outside the city, with a focus on hiking, flora and fauna.

Festivals & Events

Traditional Chinese holidays such as the **Dragon Boat Festival**, which falls on the fifth day of the fifth lunar calendar month; **Lunar New Year**, usually in January or February; and **Lantern Festival**, on the 15th day of the eighth lunar calendar month, are celebrated in a big way in Tainan. The birthdays of the various temple deities – **Matsu** (the 23rd day of the third lunar month), **Confucius** (28 September) – usually feature colourful and lively events at the respective temples.

Sleeping

Budget and midrange options can be booked solid on weekends and public holidays. Reserve well in advance.

★**City Hut 1828** HOSTEL $
(Dorm 1828; ☎276 2740; www.dorm1828.com; 28, Lane 18, Dasyue Rd, 大學路18巷28號; dm/tw NT$600/1400; @📶) Also called Dorm 1828, this hostel is a magnificent choice comparable to midrange digs. In addition to a variety of cosy dorms (both mixed and female-only) and rooms, it has nice furnishings, strong rainforest showers, a fully equipped kitchen and a relaxed communal area with blue-and-white checked floor tiles. The owner, Jasmine, has unlimited tips on outdoor activities.

To get to the hostel, go to the rear exit of Tainan train station, follow Dasyue Rd and turn right when you see a Hang Ten boutique shop. The hostel is at the end of the lane. The walk is about 15 minutes.

Ing Wang Hotel HOTEL $
(英王商旅, Yīngwáng Shānglǚ; ☎2263 3151; www.ingwang.com; 26 Lane 233, Jhongyi Rd, Sec 2, 忠義路2段233巷26號; r incl breakfast from NT$1280; @) A popular budget hotel just a stone's throw from Chihkan Towers (down the back alleys). The newly renovated rooms are small but bright, and a small breakfast is thrown into the deal. From the corner of Chenggong and Jhongyi Rds, head south. Look for the turn for Lane 233 about 50m up on the right.

Fuqi Tainan Hostel HOSTEL $
(台南福憩客棧, Táinán Fúqì Kèzhàn; ☎703 4543; http://fuqitainanhostelen.blogspot.com; 76 Jhongjheng Rd, 中正路76號; dm/d NT$500/1400) Fuqi has two charming doubles and bright dorms for six to 12 people. The staff are very helpful and hospitable, and the central location means most attractions are within walking distance.

Your Fun Apartment B&B $$
(有方公寓, Yǒufāng Gōngyù; ☎223 1208; www.trip235.com; 9 Lane 269, Hai'an 2nd Rd, 海安路二段269巷9號; r from NT$2100; 📶) With a mix of vintage and designer furniture in the huge communal area, and rooms that combine old-world charm with a modern, minimalist style, this B&B, housed in an early republican-era building, has stolen the heart of many a visitor to Tainan. The best way to get there is to enter from Lane 259; its blue entrance is to your right.

JJ-W Culture Design Hotel BOUTIQUE HOTEL $$
(佳佳西市場旅店, Jiājiā Xīshìchǎng Lǚdiàn; ☎220 9866; http://jj-w.hotel.com.tw/eng/; 11 Zhengxing St, 正興街11號; d from NT$3200; 📶) The sophisticated style of the designer rooms in this hotel attracts returning visitors from Hong Kong and Japan. The hotel is awash with art-inspired designer cool, and each of the 30 rooms is funky and unique. The only downside is you can't pick the room you want as you'll be allocated what's available upon arrival.

Takatama Hotel HOTEL $$
(高玉商務飯店, Gāoyù Shāngwù Fàndiàn; ☎220 1006; www.takatamacoco.com.tw/hotel.php; 3rd fl, 2 Chenggong Rd, 成功路2號3樓; d/tw incl breakfast from NT$1200/1790; 📶) Don't be put off by the awful building exterior because inside, on the 3rd floor, this budget hotel provides well-sized and clean rooms, good breakfast

and an excellent location right opposite the train station.

★Shangri-La's Far Eastern Plaza Hotel HOTEL $$$
(香格里拉台南遠東國際大飯店, Xiānggélǐlā Táinán Yuǎndōng Guójì Dàfàndiàn; ☎702 8888; www.shangri-la.com/tainan/fareasternplaza-shangrila; 89 Dasyue Rd, 大學路89號; d/tw/ste incl buffet breakfast NT$3350/5800/7000;) Superbly located right behind the train station, this grand dame of Tainan boasts 333 rooms with plush beds and impeccable service that has come to be expected from any Shangri-La hotel. Most rooms offer a view of the city, and the rooftop pool makes for a great escape after a long day out in the humid city.

Eating

Tainanese brag about their food and, indeed, this place is famous throughout Taiwan for its great variety of street snacks. The strong foodie culture here means you'd be hard pressed to find any city street not chock-a-block with eateries.

For traditional food you can't beat the areas around Chihkan Towers and Anping Fort. Look for *dan zai mian* (擔仔麵, *dànzǎi miàn;* a soupy bowl of noodles with braised pork topping), coffin cake (棺材板, *guāncái bǎn*) and milkfish belly soup (虱目魚肚湯, *Shīmù Yúdùtāng*).

Some of the best areas for casual eating in Tainan are down narrow back alleys. Bao'an Rd, a narrow old street a few blocks west of Confucius Temple, is lined up with shops and stalls selling traditional dishes, as is Yenping St in the Anping area, which dates back to a Dutch-era market.

In central Tainan the leafy old street directly east of the Confucius Temple (through the gate) is another pleasant pedestrian-only area with cafes and small restaurants.

The mouth of Shennong St (off Hai'an Rd just north of Mincyuan St), an old character-filled alley, hosts a number of outdoor eateries serving beer and fried dishes.

Central Tainan

Chi Kin Dandanman TRADITIONAL SNACKS $
(赤崁擔仔麵, Chì Kǎn Dànzǎimiàn; 180 Minzu Rd, Sec 2; dànzǎi miàn bowl NT$60; 11am-9pm;) Set in a Japanese-era merchant's house, this is a fun place to try traditional *dànzǎi miàn*, a simple, refreshing dish that mixes noodles with a tangy meat sauce. *Dànzǎi*, literally 'two baskets and a stick', refers to the baskets used to carry the noodles around for sale. This shop uses no MSG.

A Cun Beef Soup TAIWANESE $
(阿村第二代牛肉湯, Ācūn Dì'èrdài Niúròutāng; 7 Lane 41, Bao'an Rd; soup NT$100; 4am-midday & 6pm-midnight) Beef soup (*niúròutāng*), a Tainan speciality is served as early as 4am for breakfast, right after the cattle are slaughtered in the middle of the night. One of the best places to savour the soup and the meat at its freshest is A Cun, a streetside stall that has been feeding carnivores for more than four decades.

Guli Restaurant VEGAN $$
(穀粒蔬食自然風味料理, Gǔlì Shūshí Zìrán Fēngwèi Liàolǐ; 242 Mincyuan 2nd Rd; set meals from NT$150, hot pot from NT$280; lunch & dinner;) A paradise for the health and environmentally conscious, this restaurant only uses naturally farmed and locally sourced produce. Their food, a fusion of Japanese and Taiwanese fare, is beautifully presented and tasty. The English menu should be available by press time.

A Xia Restaurant SEAFOOD $$$
(阿霞飯店, Āxiá Fàndiàn; ☎221 9873; 7 Lane 84, Jhongyi Rd, Sec 2; dishes NT$500-700, 2-person set meals NT$1500; 11am-2.30pm & 4.30-9pm Tue-Sun;) A popular venue for weddings and other celebrations, now sporting a modern look. Not really suitable for single diners.

Jade Room Restaurant CHINESE, WESTERN $$$
(翡翠廳, Fěicuì Tīng; 1 Chenggong Rd; buffet lunch/dinner NT$780;) This long-running restaurant inside the Hotel Tainan has one of the best buffets in town.

Anping

The area close to Fort Anping is also well known for its local foods. Some snacks to look out for include shrimp rolls (蝦捲, *xiājuǎn*) and fish-ball soup (魚丸湯, *yúwántāng*).

An-Ping Gui Ji Local Cuisine Cultural Restaurant TAIWANESE $
(安平貴記美食文化館, Ānpíng Guìjì Měishí Wénhuàguǎn; 93 Yenping Jie; set meals NT$149; 11am-8pm) This restaurant offers a host of traditional Tainan snacks at low prices. The shop features a big photo display of traditional foods and a multilanguage brochure to help visitors. The restaurant also

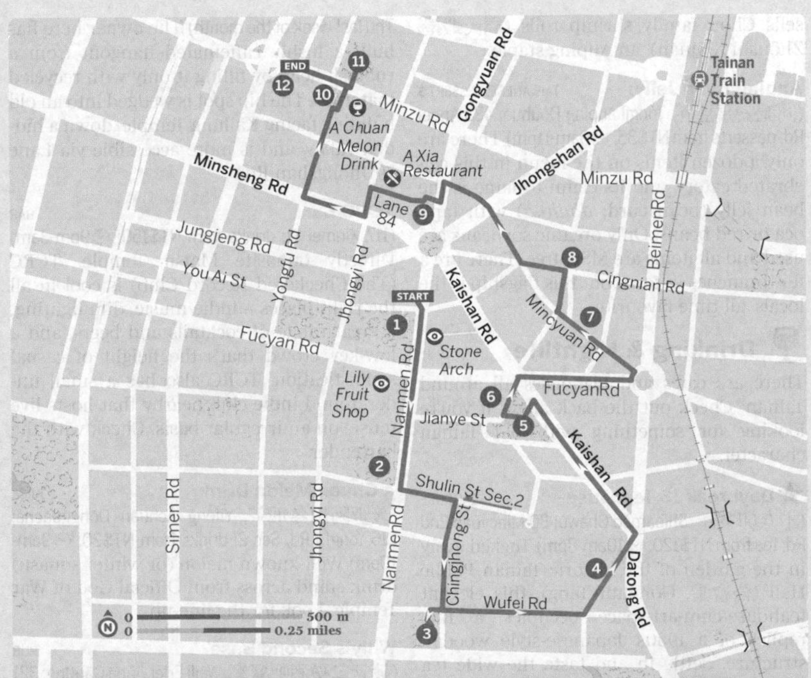

Walking Tour Tainan Temples

START CONFUCIUS TEMPLE
FINISH MATSU TEMPLE
LENGTH 6KM; FOUR HOURS

After admiring the classical layout of **1 Confucius Temple** (p242), head south. After passing martial **2 Great South Gate** (p244) turn left on Shulin St and then take the first right. When you reach Wufei Rd, check out **3 Wufei Temple** (p244), shrine to the concubines of the last contender for the Ming Empire.

Head east down Wufei Rd and turn left just past building No 76. You'll soon see the grounds of the 300-year-old **4 Fahua Temple**.

Continue up the alley until you reach a large intersection. Head north up Kaishan Rd until you see the stately **5 Koxinga's Shrine** (p243) on the left. When you leave the compound, take the back right gate to visit **6 Lady Linshui's Temple** (p243). You'll mostly see women here, asking for their children to be protected.

Now get back on Kaishan Rd and turn right at the intersection. Head east down Fucyan Rd and turn left at the big intersection onto Mincyuan Rd. At **7 Dongyue Temple** (p243) check out the terrifying paintings of hell.

Continue up Mincyuan to Chenghuang Rd and turn right. At the end of this short street you'll see **8 City God Temple** (p243).

Now head west down Cingnian and turn right up Mincyuan. Cross Gongyuan and turn left. You'll see a bank and then a small alley. Turn right into the alley to get to **9 Altar of Heaven** (p245). Say a prayer for protection from any bad luck.

When you leave the alley, it's a quick left and then a right onto Minsheng Rd. A block later, turn right up Yongfu Rd. Two blocks ahead you'll see the beautiful deep-rose-coloured walls of the **10 Official God of War Temple** (p243).

Now continue to the end of Yongfu Rd to **11 Chihkan Towers** (p242). On the opposite side of the street, a tiny alley leads to **12 Matsu Temple** (p243). Don't forget to check out the door gods and roof beams.

sells Chou family shrimp rolls (周氏蝦捲, Zhōushì Xiājuǎn), an Anping staple.

Anping Bean Jelly TAIWANESE, DESSERT $
(同記安平豆花, Tóngjì ānpíng Dòuhuā; 433 Anbei Rd; desserts from NT$35; ⊙9am-11pm) There are only a dozen items on the menu in this celebrated eatery, and its claim to fame is the bean jelly (bean curd; *dòuhuā*) with tapioca or red beans. Only organic soybeans are used and all items are MSG-free. There are a few branches in town but this flagship is the locals' all-time favourite.

Drinking & Nightlife

There are cafes and teahouses all around Tainan. Check out the back alleys if you're looking for something with old Tainan character.

★ **Daybreak 18 Teahouse** TEAHOUSE
(十八卯茶屋, Shíbāmǎo Cháwū; 30 Mincyuan 2nd Rd; tea from NT$120; ⊙10am-8pm) Tucked away in the garden of the historic Tainan Public Hall (公會堂, Gōnghuì Táng), this elegant teahouse-cum-art-space occupies a fine replica of a 1930s Japanese-style wooden structure. Settle in and taste the wide tea selection – black, white, green, oolong, fruit and herbal brews – or buy beautiful pots and boxes of healing leaves.

Lily Fruit Shop JUICE
(莉莉水果店; 199 Fucyan Rd, Sec 1; fruit drinks NT$50; ⊙11am-11pm, closed 2 Mon per month) Across from the Confucius Temple is this well-known shop that serves up delicious *bào bīng* (刨冰, shaved ice and fruit) and fruit drinks.

Former Julius Mannich Merchant House PUB
(德商東興洋行, Déshāng Dōngxīng Yángháng; beer from NT$100; ⊙10am-10pm Sun-Thu, to midnight Fri & Sat) The First Opium War between the British Empire and China led to the opening of ports in Taiwan to European trade. This fine old wood-and-brick structure is mildly interesting to tour as a site but is also highly enjoyable as a place to hang out. The garden restaurant serves good German beer and sausage plates.

The merchant house is just a few minutes' walk from the Tree House, and just behind a row of houses across from Anping Fort.

Gandan Café CAFE
(甘單咖啡, Gāndān Kāfēi; 13 Lane 4, Mincyuan Rd; coffee from NT$150; ⊙1pm-9.30pm, closed Mon-Thu last week of the month) The owner here has built a lushly caffeinated hangout from a rubbish heap by filling it only with recycled materials. The hip spot is wedged into an old building facing Kailung Temple, down a hidden valley, and is more accessible via Lane 79 Jhongshan Rd.

TCRC Bar BAR
(117, Xinmei St; drinks from NT$150; ⊙9pm-3am) Directly opposite Matsu Temple, TCRC (The Checkered Record Club) is cool in all the right places – indie music, dim lighting, a great range of cocktails and beers, and a low-key crowd that's the height of casual sophistication. TCRC also has a small underground indie club nearby that hosts live music on an irregular basis. Check with the bartender.

A Chuan Melon Drink JUICE
(義豐阿川冬瓜茶, Yìfēng Āchuān Dōngguāchá; 216 Yongfu Rd, Sec 2; drinks from NT$20; ⊙9am-10pm) Well-known melon (or winter squash) drink stand across from Official God of War Temple. Look for the line-up.

Willy's Second Base PUB
(葳苙二壘酒吧餐廳, Wēilì Èrlěi Jiǔbā Cāntīng; 321 Jiankang Rd, Sec 2; drinks from NT$100; ⊙6pm-2am) Loud and fun, with good British pub fare on offer (meals NT$200 to NT$300).

Shopping

Tainan Kuang Tsai Embroidery Shop HANDICRAFTS
(府城光彩繡莊, Fǔchéng Guāngcǎi Shòu Zhuāng; ☎227 1253; 186-3 Yongfu Rd, Sec 2; ⊙8am-10pm) Mr Lin, one of the last remaining embroidery masters in Tainan, has been working at his craft for more than 50 years and now he and his daughter have taken the craft to a new, modern level. All his pieces have the light touch and expressiveness of a craftsman truly at the peak of his skills.

The most famous samples of his work are the long Eight Immortals panels, which used to be popular at weddings and other special occasions. Such panels cost tens of thousands of Taiwanese dollars but this doesn't stop buyers from all over the world coming to the shop. Smaller pieces can be purchased for a few thousand, and even those just wanting to browse are more than welcome (as the sign outside the shop says).

Information

After Taipei, Tainan is probably the most English-friendly city in Taiwan. Nearly every sight worth seeing has English interpretation signs around it.

There are ATMs in most 7-Elevens (which are everywhere) in Tainan. You can use the ATMs or change money at the Bank of Taiwan. ADSL is widely available in hotels. Free wi-fi is available at many sites including Chihkan Towers, Anping Fort, Anping Tree House, Eternal Golden Castle and Koxinga's Shrine.

National Cheng Kung University Hospital (成大醫院; www.hosp.ncku.edu.tw; 138 Sheng Li Rd) Reputable local hospital across from the north side of the National Cheng Kung University campus.

National Museum of Taiwanese Literature (www.nmtl.gov.tw; 1 Jhongjheng Rd; ⏲8am-5pm Tue-Sun) Internet access is free in the museum library.

Tainan City Government (http://tour.tainan.gov.tw) Website with a wealth of information on everything to see, do and consume in the city.

Visitor information centre (遊客服務中心; ☎229 0082; ⏲9am-6pm) The most convenient one for travellers is right in the train station. Staff speak English and can provide maps of the city and greater Tainan.

Getting There & Away

BUS

Ho-Hsin Bus Company (和欣客運; www.ebus.com.tw; 23 Beimen Rd) This company takes you to Taipei (small/large seat NT$400/600, five to six hours, every 30 minutes), as do other bus companies nearby.

HIGH SPEED RAIL

The HSR station is a 30- to 40-minute drive or bus ride south of the city centre. Trains to Taipei (NT$1350, two hours) leave every half-hour.

TRAIN

Tainan is a major stop on the Western Line with fast/slow trains to Taipei (NT$738/569, four/5½ hours) and Kaohsiung (NT$106/82, 30 minutes/one hour).

Getting Around

TO/FROM THE AIRPORT & HIGH SPEED RAIL

Bus 5 connects the airport with City Bus North Station (NT$18, 20 minutes). HSR shuttle buses connect HSR station with City Bus North Station (free, 40 minutes, every 20 minutes).

BUS

City Bus

The **City Bus** (http://ebus.tncg.gov.tw) covers most of the city. Basic fares are NT$18, and buses run every 30 to 60 minutes. The hub across from the train station is divided into **City Bus North Station** and **City Bus South Station**. Most city buses stop at both stations, as do the tourist buses.

Tourist Bus

Tour bus 88 runs daily (NT$18, every 30 minutes from 9am to 6pm) to all major historic sites. Tour bus 99 runs to Sihcao Dazhong Temple, in Taijiang National Park, or Taiwan Salt Museum, only on weekends (NT$18; every 30 minutes from 9am to 5.15pm). The visitor information centre has a map of all routes and stops.

BICYCLE

The city has a government bicycle-rental program (per four hours NT$50, from 9am to 5pm). Rental sites include Chihkan Towers, Koxinga's Shrine, Eternal Golden Castle, Anping Fort and Anping Tree House. You can return bikes to any station.

SCOOTER

Rentals (機車出租) cost NT$300 to NT$400 per day and are available at **shops** behind the train station. You only need an International Driving Permit and ID.

SOUTHWEST COAST

National Museum of Taiwan History 國立臺灣歷史博物館

Eight kilometres north of the city centre of Tainan, this three-storey **museum** (國立臺灣歷史博物館, Guólì Táiwān Lìshǐ Bówùguǎn; www.nmth.gov.tw; 250, Sec 1, Changhe Rd; admission NT$100; ⏲9am-4pm Tue-Sun) opened in 2011 and is a good introduction to the ethno-cultural history of Taiwan.

The visually appealing exhibits and multimedia installations give an overview of Taiwan's history covering the early settlement of the aboriginal groups, the Dutch occupation, the Japanese era, the KMT takeover, and today's democracy. Note that the 2-28 Incident (p330) is significantly downplayed, as are other episodes of political suppression by the KMT.

The museum also has a well-designed park which includes lakes, an ecological education centre, walking paths and bird-watching areas. The combined treat is certainly worth the time it takes to get there.

Bus 18 (NT$18) leaves from the hub opposite Tainan train station for the museum every 30 minutes on weekends. On weekdays, there are six buses going in each direction between 7am and 7.55pm.

Taijiang National Park 台江國家公園

The eighth and newest national park in Taiwan, **Taijiang** (Táijiāng Guójiā Gōngyuán; www.tjnp.gov.tw) covers a patchwork of coastal lands north of Anping Harbour (see the website for a map of the areas included). The almost 50 sq km of land and 340 sq km of sea include tidal flats, lagoons, mangrove swamps and wetlands that are critical habitats for rare fish, crustaceans, mammal and bird species, including the endangered black-faced spoonbill.

Taijiang covers an area dear to the hearts of Taiwanese, as it was here that their ancestors first landed after the dangerous crossing of the Black Ditch (the Taiwan Strait). Once a giant inland sea, Taijiang silted up during the 18th century, facilitating the development of local salt and fish-farming industries. These days only the fish farms remain active.

Cycling is possible in Taijiang, as the land is flat, the climate is sunny year-round and parts of the new bike trail have been completed.

Sights & Activities

You can take a boat ride through the mangrove swamps and further out to the estuary of the Yenshui River from a pier close to the **Sihcao Dazhong Temple** (四草大眾廟, Sìcǎo Dàzhòng Miào). A 30-minute ride through the **Mangrove Green Tunnel** (紅樹林綠色隧道, Hóng Shùlín Lùsè Sùidào) is NT$150 while the 70-minute ride that goes out to larger channels and into the mouth of the Yenshui River is NT$200. Boats leave when full, so on most weekdays you will be waiting a long time.

Bus 10 (NT$36, every hour) from Tainan runs out to the temple daily while the tourist bus 99 (NT$18, every 30 minutes) runs from 9am to 5.15pm on weekends. You can take bikes on the buses.

Taiwan Eco Tours (p247) offers kayaking through the mangroves.

Black-Faced Spoonbill Reserve 野生動物保護區

This **reserve** (Yěshēng Dòngwù Bǎohùqū; ☎06-786 1000; Cigu Township) is a small section of wetlands on the west coast of Tainan that's dedicated to protecting the extremely rare black-faced spoonbill. The bird spends summers (May to September) in Korea and northern China and migrates to Tainan for the winter. Once down to just a few hundred individuals, numbers are now over a thousand, though this is still a tiny population and the species' future is by no means assured.

If you visit the reserve you won't be able to see the birds up close, but there are high-powered binoculars you can use for free. To get to the reserve head north up Hwy 17 from Tainan and look for the English signs around the Km162 mark after crossing the Zengwen River, or contact Taiwan Eco Tours (p247) for private tours.

Houbi 後壁

Houbi (Hòubì), 50km north of Tainan, has been regarded as the 'granary of Taiwan' because of the excellent quality of grains it produces. To visitors, the miles of farmland mean there are easy cycling opportunities and it makes a good day-trip option from Tainan or Chiayi.

Opened in 2012, **Togo Rural Village Art Museum** (土溝農村美術館, Tǔgōu nóngcūn měishùguǎn; 86-12 Tugou Village) comprises galleries and workshops housed in traditional courtyard homes in Tugou Village. There are a lot of alleys but getting lost is part of the fun and every turn can be a surprise when you see paddy fields aesthetically adorned with roadside artworks. The village is 3km northeast of Houbi train station.

Jingliao (菁寮, Jīng liáo) is another charming village on County Rd 82, 2km northwest of the train station. The unmissable **Saint Cross Church** (菁寮天主堂, Jīngliáo Tiānzhǔtáng), a Roman Catholic church designed by German architect Gottfried Boehm in the 1950s, is the highlight.

To get there, take a local train from either Tainan or Chiayi to Houbi. There are bike rentals (NT$150 per three hours) right outside Houbi train station.

Taiwan Salt Museum 台灣鹽博物館

This **museum** (Taìwān Yén Bówùguǎn; Cigu Township; admission NT$130; ⌚9am-5pm, closed 3rd Wed of month) makes for a nice diversion on a long day exploring Taijiang National Park. The 1st floor has English interpretation signs, and there are several movies to watch. The 2nd-floor display of salt crystals from around the world is fascinating in its variety. Next to the museum are several **salt mountains** (admission NT$50; ⌚9am-6pm) that kids can climb.

The museum and salt mountains are off Hwy 17 north of Tainan. Look for the turn-off's English signs that are near the Km156 mark.

Aogu Wetlands & Forest Park 鰲鼓濕地森林園區

The sprawling 15-sq-km wetland park known as Aogu (Áogǔ Shīdì Sēnlín Yuánqū) includes mud beaches, marshes, lagoons, fish farms, beefwood forests and tracts of thick shrub. Dozens of bird species can be spotted here with nothing more than one's naked eyes. These include drongos, egrets, cranes, ducks, cormorants, hawks and eagles. In total, 245 species have been recorded in the wetlands, with the majority being migratory.

Aogu is easily reached off Hwy 17 if you have your own vehicle, but be aware that the reserve is a maze of dirt roads.

Guanziling (Kuanziling) 關子嶺

☎06 / POP 2000

Only three places in the world can lay claim to having mud hot springs, and Guanziling in the hilly northern Tainan is one of them.

The Guanziling area is essentially one long dip off County Rd 172 on leafy Township Rd 96. The village, on the eastern end of the dip, is divided into lower (the older part of town) and upper sections that are joined by a series of stone steps for walking. There's an ATM in the 7-Eleven in the lower village.

It's possible to visit Guanziling as a day trip from Tainan or Chiayi. Should you want to stay here, there are a few hotels remaining from the Japanese era in the lower village. The posher resorts are in the upper village.

Sights

On the ride up to Guanziling the road passes two popular Buddhist temples, the expansive **Dasian Temple** (大仙寺, Dàxiān Sì) and the Ming-dynasty era **Biyun Temple** (碧雲寺, Bìyún Sì) dedicated to Guanyin, the Goddess of Mercy. The latter commands excellent views over the plains.

Red Leaf Park PARK

(紅葉公園, Hóngyè Gōngyuán) This Japanese-built park boasts clear, unspoiled views of Dadongshan and the sight of maple leaves changing colours in autumn. To reach the park, head up from the 7-Eleven in the lower village and look for a wooden arch to the left about 200m along. The stairs lead directly to the park.

Water & Fire Mix NATURAL SITE

(水火同源, Shǔihuǒ Tóng Yuán) Five kilometres southwest of the hot-spring area is this natural oddity, a small grotto where fire and water really do mix – natural gas from underground bubbles up through a pool of water and ignites spontaneously on the surface. The result is a surreal dance of flames atop pure water.

WORTH A TRIP

DONGSHAN COFFEE ROAD

Guanziling's mountain roads see little traffic during the week and offer some fine road cycling. A particularly scenic route is County Rd 175.

Some signs refer to County Road 175 as the Dongshan Coffee Road. From the roadside you won't see much sign of coffee growing, but you will get expansive views over the alluvial plains of rural Tainan and the choppy foothills of the Central Mountains.

A good place to sample the exceptional quality of Dongshan coffee is **Ta Chu Hua Chien** (大鋤花間, Dàchú Huājiān; ⌚10am-8pm Mon-Sun), a beautiful alfresco cafe located off the Km11.5 mark.

It's 25km of rolling pitch from the start of the 175 to Nansi. If you want to continue riding through more undeveloped natural landscape, head up the east side of Tsengwen Reservoir.

Activities

Hot-springing is de rigueur in Guanziling. The mud hot-spring water isn't really muddy but is rather a light grey colour, owing to the heavy concentration of minerals it picks up on the way to the surface. The Japanese built the first hot-spring resort in Guanziling and considered the muddy waters (found elsewhere only in Japan and Sicily) particularly therapeutic. If you are staying overnight, look for bargains in the lower village hotels.

King's Garden Villa HOT SPRING
(景大渡假莊園, Jǐngdà Dùjià Zhuāngyuán; ☎682 2500; www.myspa.com.tw; admission NT$450; ⏰9am-10pm) King's Garden Villa has a set of stone and wood pools, as well as a swimming pool and mud-bath room for you to while away the time. Look for the English signs as you drive up the main road in the upper village.

Eating & Drinking

There are plenty of eateries around Guanziling. Across from the bus stop sits a row of barbecue stalls that serve group-sized portions. Most of the hotels have restaurants, and decent *tàocān* (set meals) can be had for around NT$250.

Central Kaohsiung

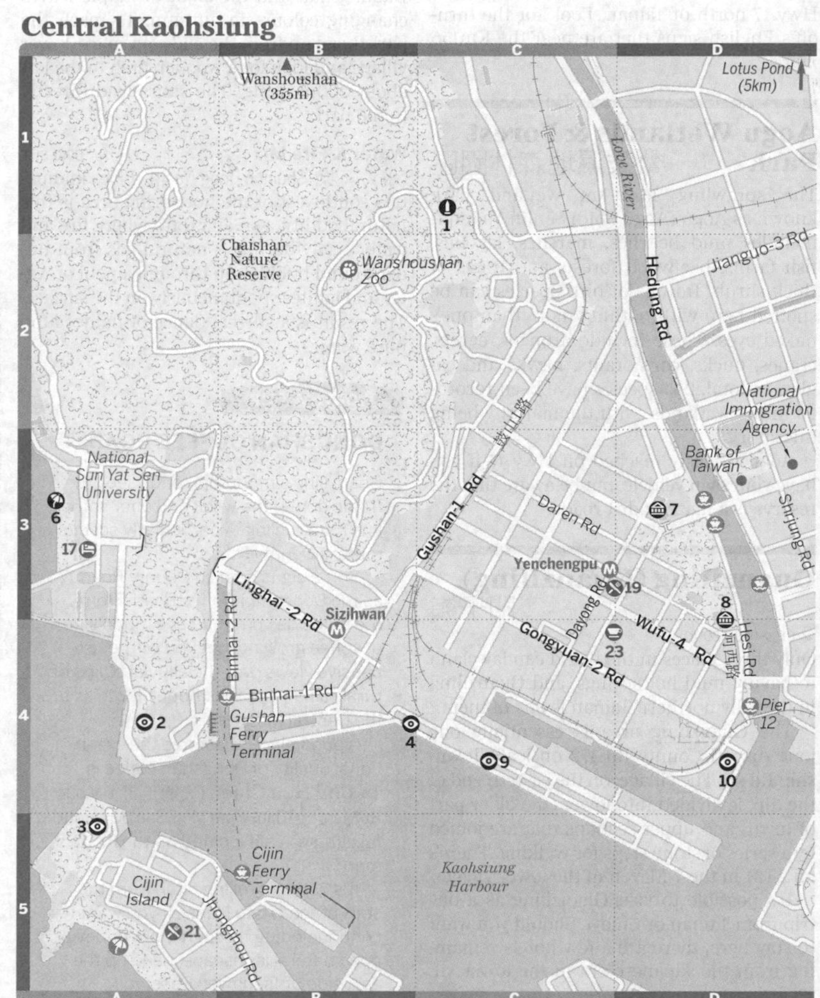

Getting There & Around

You can catch a train from Tainan or Chiayi to Xinying, and then a bus to Guanziling. The bus station is opposite the railway station in Xinying. But since the sights are so spread out, it's best to take your own transport. Consider hiring a scooter in Chiayi (NT$300 to NT$400 per day).

Kaohsiung City 高雄市

07 / POP 2,778,920

The southern city of Kaohsiung (Gāoxióng) is Taiwan's largest port, its second-largest city and the centre of the country's heavy and petrochemical industries.

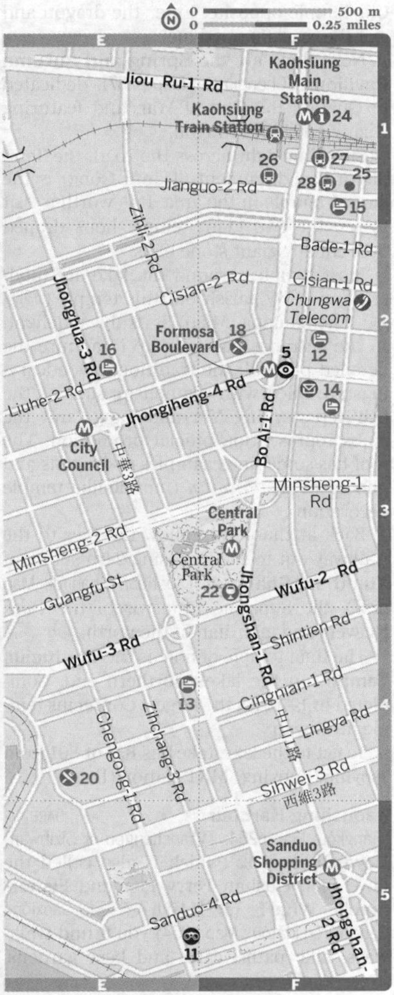

Today's Kaohsiung has largely been transformed from grim industrial warrens into a modern urban landscape of shiny cafes, wide streets, river- and harbour-side parks, public transport, bicycle lanes, and cultural venues that have embraced the manufacturing past. There are also two swimming beaches within the city area, and 1000 hectares of almost-pristine forest right on its doorstep.

Most of what you want to see in Kaohsiung is clustered in a few areas that are within walking distance or a short bus ride (or cycle) from a Kaohsiung Mass Rapid Transit (KMRT) station: the harbour and lower

Central Kaohsiung

Sights

1 2-28 Memorial C1
2 British Consulate Residence at Takou (Dagou) A4
3 Cijin Island Lighthouse A5
4 Fisherman's Wharf B4
5 Formosa Boulevard KMRT Station F2
6 Hsitzuwan Beach A3
7 Kaohisung Museum of History D3
8 Kaohsiung Film Archives D4
9 Kaohsiung Harbour C4
10 Love River D4
11 Tuntex Sky Tower E5

Sleeping

12 Angels Backpack F2
13 Cozy Planet Hostel E4
14 Hotel Dua F2
15 Hwa Hung Hotel F1
16 Legend Hotel E2
17 Sunset Beach Resort & Spa A3

Eating

18 Liuhe Night Market F2
19 Mars C3
20 Vegetary Restaurant E4
21 Ya Jiao Seafood Restaurant A5

Drinking & Nightlife

22 Brickyard Beer Garden F3
23 Dog Pig Art Cafe C4

Information

24 Train Station Visitor Centre F1

Transport

25 Car Plus F1
26 City Bus Hub F1
27 Kaohsiung Ke Yuan F1
28 Kuo Kuang Bus Company F1
Kuo Kuang Bus Company Station .... (see 28)

Love River area (in the Yancheng, Gushan and Sizihwan Districts); the Lotus Pond area in Tsoying District in the north; and Cijin Island.

In 2010 Kaohsiung city and county were merged into one giant metropolitan area.

History

The Chinese settled on Cijin Island in the late Ming dynasty, and throughout the Qing period Kaohsiung was an administrative centre for the Taiwan territory. As usual, the Japanese were responsible for its modern character. 'Rice in the north and sugar in the south' was the colonialist policy, and under it Kaohsiung became a major port for the export of raw materials. During this time the grid pattern of streets was laid out, the harbour was expanded and rail lines were built.

The Japanese called the harbour area Hamasen, a name still used by older residents and the tourism bureau. The area lay in ruins after Allied bombing at the end of WWII but was slowly rebuilt under the KMT. Once again, with central planning, Kaohsiung became the heavy industry centre.

Under mayor Frank Hsieh (1998–2005) the city started to clean up and to shift its industrial base towards tourism, high technology, automation and other capital-intensive industries. These days a massive land-reclamation project called South Star is creating space for a pop-music centre, and for the expansion of Kaohsiung's yacht-building industry, already the largest in Asia.

Sights

Kaohsiung has two decent beaches right within the city borders, open for swimming from May to October. At both you'll find showers and changing rooms.

Ciaotou Sugar Factory NOTABLE BUILDING
(橋頭糖廠, Qiáotóu Tángchǎng) Ciaotou consists of a defunct factory (which you can walk into, and explore the old mechanisms and vats) and an old village that retains most of its early-20th-century flavour. There are also some handsome old offices in what is called the Japanese Dutch Colonial style.

The sugar factory and village grounds begin as soon as you exit Ciaotou Sugar Factory KMRT station. There are good English interpretation signs around.

Lotus Pond SCENIC AREA
(蓮池潭, Liánchí Tán) The pond in the north of the city has been a popular destination since the Qing dynasty and is well known for the 20 or so temples dotting the shoreline and nearby alleys. At night coloured lights give the lake a very festive appearance.

Starting from the southern end and heading clockwise around the lake, you'll first encounter sections of the **Old Wall of Fengshan** (Fèngshān Jiùcháng), built in 1826. The intact north gate wall runs along Shengli Rd.

Extending out onto the pond itself are the **Dragon and Tiger Pagodas** (Lónghǔ Tǎ; Map p257), built in the '60s as an extension of the Ciji Temple opposite. Enter the dragon and exit the tiger for good luck.

Next along are the **Spring and Autumn Pavilions** (Chūnqiū Gé; Map p257), dedicated to Guandi, the God of War, and featuring Guanyin riding a dragon.

Standing right across the road, the Temple of Enlightenment (Tiānfǔ Gōng) is the largest temple in the area. It is worth a visit to see the two giant temple lions draped over equally giant stone balls.

Most temples around the lake are modern and fairly garish but this temple (城隍廟; Chénghuáng Miào) is truly a delight. In the entrance hall look up to admire the detailed plafond; the traditional woodcarvings are filled with symbolism, such as the fish representing Yin and Yang, and the crabs representing official promotion. The roof has some fine examples of dragons and phoenixes in *jiǎnniàn* (mosaic-like temple decoration).

Back at the pond, follow the pier to the walkway out to the imposing 24m statue of **Xuantian Shang-di** (Xúantiān Shàngdì; Map p257), the Supreme Emperor of the Dark Heaven, and guardian of the north.

The final temple of note is the **Confucius Temple** on the lake's northern end. Completed in 1976, it's the largest Confucius temple in Taiwan.

To get to the lake, take bus R51 or 301 from Tsoying (Zuoying) MRT station (Exit 2).

Kaohsiung Harbour HARBOUR
(Gǎngkǒu; Map p254; M Yanchengpu or Sizihwan) Down by Pier 12 (which is also called the Love Pier, Gushan Ferry Pier and **Fisherman's Wharf** (高雄港漁人碼頭, Gāoxióng Gǎng Yúrén Mǎtóu ; Map p254) you'll find walkways, bike paths, cafes and beer gardens.

Lotus Pond

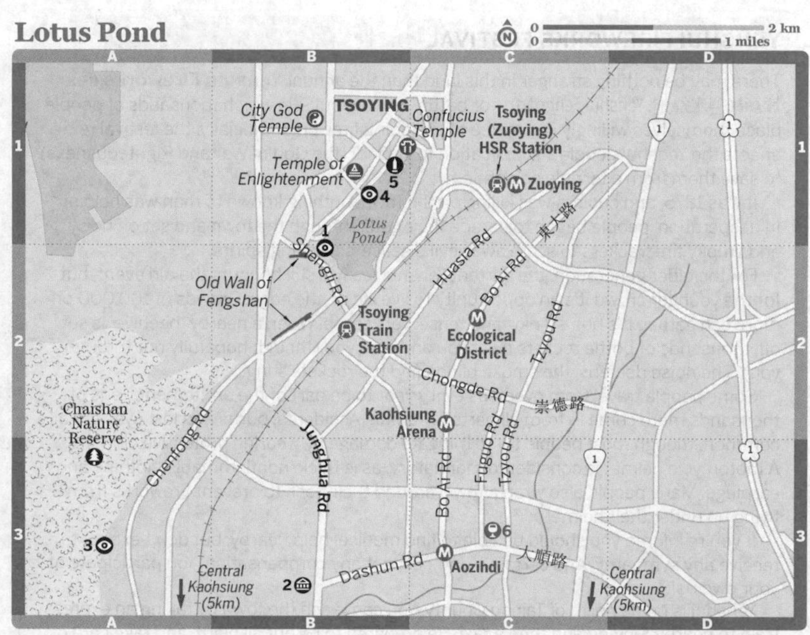

Check at the train station visitor centre about harbour cruises.

Pier-2 Art District NEIGHBOURHOOD
(駁二藝術特區, Bóèr Yìshù Tèqū; Ⓜ Yanchengpu) This is an old warehouse area that was renovated into art studios. Exhibitions and concerts are frequently held indoors and out. Check at the visitor centre for the events schedule.

British Consulate Residence at Takou (Dagou) HISTORIC SITE
(打狗英國領事館, Dǎgǒu Yīnguó Lǐngshì Guǎn; Map p254; 20 Linhai Rd; admission NT$30; ⏲9am-midnight) Built in 1865, this handsome red-brick consulate residence sits 70m above the mouth of Kaohsiung Harbour, a perfect location for watching giant container ships sail through the tiny mouth of the harbour. There's also an interesting clash of cultures to observe here as Chinese tourists react in bewilderment to the open presence of Falun Gong posters decrying the Beijing government.

While in the area, check out a tiny **temple** to the left of the larger temple beside the consulate. It's the only shrine in Taiwan to deify 17th-century Dutch naval commanders, much in the way old Chinese generals have been deified over the centuries.

Lotus Pond

Sights

1 Dragon & Tiger Pagodas....B2
2 Kaohsiung Museum of Fine Arts....B3
3 Longcyuan Temple....A3
4 Spring & Autumn Pavilions....B1
5 Xuantian Shang-di....B1

Drinking & Nightlife

6 Lighthouse Bar & Grill....C3

The consulate is a five-minute walk from Sizihwan Beach.

Cijin Island SCENIC AREA
(旗津, Qíjīn) This thin island acts as a buffer to the harbour and extends down the city coastline. It's a popular day trip from the mainland, with its frenetic seafood street (Hǎichǎn Jiē), beach, **lighthouse** (Qíjīn Dēngtǎ; Map p254; admission free; ⏲9am-4.30pm) and biking routes being the main attractions.

You can rent bikes on Cijin or take your bike over on the ferry (NT$15, 10 minutes), which runs from 5am to 2am between the Gushan Ferry Terminal (map p254) (鼓山碼

YENSHUI FIREWORKS FESTIVAL

There may be nothing stranger in this land than the annual **Yenshui Fireworks Festival** (鹽水蜂炮, Yénshǔi Fēngpào) – or battle, or blow-out – in which thousands of people place themselves willingly in a melee of exploding fireworks. Officially, the festival re-enacts the Yenshui people's supplication to Guandi (the God of War and Righteousness) to save them from a terrible epidemic.

It was 1875, and cholera was killing off the town; nothing known to man was helping. In desperation, people began to parade their gods through the town and set off noisy and smoky firecrackers to scare away evil disease-spreading spirits.

For the older generation, the current Yenshui festival still honours the old event, but for the younger crowd it's an opportunity to live life on the edge. Crowds of 100,000 or more can gather. It's hot, smoky, and tense, very tense. When a nearby 'beehive' is set off, thousands of bottle rockets fly at you and over you (though hopefully not through you). The noise deafens, the smoke blinds and the rockets sting.

Some people travel from overseas every year to be part of the excitement. Tens of thousands more come in from all parts of Taiwan. Accidents, burns and lost eyes are all common, though most people try to mitigate damage by wearing protective clothing. A motorcycle helmet is considered mandatory, as is thick, nonflammable clothing and earplugs. Many people also wrap a towel around their neck to prevent fireworks from flying up under their helmet.

If you're injured you should be able to find medical help nearby, but don't expect to receive any sympathy. And certainly don't expect any compensation. You participate at your own risk.

Yenshui is in the north of Tainan County. You can reach the town by taking an express train to nearby Sinying and then a taxi. Be prepared to be out all night, and take care of your valuables. The festival takes place every year during the Lantern Festival, two weeks after Chinese New Year.

頭, Gǔshān Mǎtóu) and the Cijin Ferry Terminal (map p254).

The beach on Cijin Island is just a five-minute walk from the Cijin Ferry Terminal. When going in the water, be aware that there are serious rip tides along the more-open parts of the beach.

Matsu Temple TAOIST TEMPLE
(天后宮, Tiānhòu Gōng; 93 Miaojian Rd) The oldest temple in the Kaohsiung area is Cijin's Matsu Temple, the origins of which go back to the late 17th century when the area was the first commercial centre in Kaohsiung. Many of the excellent stone relief and pillar carvings go back to the 18th century.

Love River SCENIC AREA
(愛河, Ài Hé; Map p254; Ⓜ MRT Yanchengpu) Love River was once an open sewer and it has seen a remarkable transformation in recent years. The waters flow clean and the riverside promenades with their benches, shady trees and outdoor cafes are popular hangouts for both locals and visitors.

You can cruise along the river day and night (20-minute boat rides are NT$80, and run from 4pm to 11pm).

Hsitzuwan Beach BEACH
(Sizi Bay, Xīzǐwān; Map p254; admission NT$70; ⏲8am-6pm; Ⓜ MRT Sizihwan) Hsitzuwan Beach is smaller than Cijin, but it's a calmer swimming beach and an excellent place for hanging out and watching the sunset.

Kaohsiung Film Archives MUSEUM
(高雄市電影館, Gāoxióngshì Diànyǐngguǎn; Map p254; 10 Hesi Rd; ⏲1.30-9.30pm Tue-Sun) FREE Just back from the Love River is the wonderful Municipal Film Archives, where you can enjoy on-site private and public viewings of the archives' films.

Kaohsiung Museum of Fine Arts MUSEUM
(高雄美術館, Gāoxióng Měishùguǎn; Map p257; http://english.kmfa.gov.tw; 80 Meishuguan Rd) FREE Has a stylish interior with exhibits highlighting Taiwanese artists and local themes. Exhibits change frequently. Take Bus 35 from KMRT Aozihdi station.

Kaohsiung Museum of History MUSEUM
(高雄市立歷史博物館, Gāoxióng Shìlì Lìshǐ Bówùguǎn; Map p254; http://khm.gov.tw; 272 Jhongjheng-4th Rd; ⏲9am-5pm Tue-Sun) FREE This lovely museum is housed in what

was the city government building during Japanese times. Tucked into neat rooms down the blond-wood and marble hallways are photographic displays, a permanent **2-28 Memorial** (Map p254), and exhibits that change quarterly.

National Science & Technology Museum MUSEUM

(科學工藝博物館, Kēxué Gōngyì Bówùguǎn; www.nstm.gov.tw; 720 Jiou Ru Rd; admission NT$100) Features an hourly IMAX show and high-quality, hands-on science exhibits designed for children. The exhibit on the industrial history of Taiwan, one of the few in English, is so informative that it alone is worth the price of admission. Take bus 60 to the museum from the main train station.

Formosa Boulevard KMRT Station NOTABLE BUILDING

(Map p254) Stop to see the resplendent **Dome of Light** (光之穹頂, Guāng Zhī Qióng Dǐng), by Italian glass artist Narcissus Quagliata. Formosa Blvd is south of the main train station.

Tuntex Sky Tower LOOKOUT

(Map p254; Gāoxióng 85 Dàlóu, 高雄85大樓) This was the tallest building in Taiwan before Taipei 101, with a look inspired by the character 高 (gāo), meaning 'tall'. Take the elevator (NT$100) to 75th floor for sunset views.

Activities

Hiking

The 1000-hectare **Chaishan Nature Reserve** (Cháishān Zìrán Gōngyuán), which was started by the Japanese, is famous for its macaque population, which has been getting increasingly aggressive with visitors and locals alike. Don't carry food into the area and watch out that the monkeys don't steal your camera!

To reach the start of the trails into the reserve take Red Bus 32 from Aozihdi KMRT station (outside Exit 1) to **Longcyuan Temple** (龍泉寺; Map p257), where the trails begin (access via Lane 25, Gushan 3rd Rd). The reserve is northwest of the city centre.

Cycling

Kaohsiung has 100km (and growing) of bike paths around the city. The cheap and effective **C-bike** (www.c-bike.com.tw; per hour NT$30) program has 119 stations around the city – you can rent a bike with a credit card at one location and drop it off at any other location when you have finished. There are obvious-looking stands for the green bikes outside every KMRT and also at major tourist sights.

You can pick up a map of the bike routes at the visitor centre. The most interesting route runs along the Love River and through the old warehouse district at the harbour.

Festivals & Events

International Container Arts Festival FESTIVAL

(國際貨櫃藝術節, Guójì huògùi yìshù jié) As befitting a port city, a quirky International Container Arts Festival is held biannually (in odd-numbered years). Containers are used as art material.

International Lion Dance Festival & Competition FESTIVAL

(高雄戲獅甲藝術節, Gāoxióng Xìshījiǎ Yìshùjié) The colourful International Lion Dance Festival & Competition held every December in Kaohsiung Arena is a raucous folk extravaganza. The two-day event drew 30,000 visitors from Taiwan, China, Malaysia and Singapore in 2012. Tickets sell out fast. Check www.k-arena.com.tw for details.

Sleeping

Cozy Planet Hostel HOSTEL $

(Map p254; ☎0921-576 577; www.cozy-planet.com; 8th fl, No 2, 331 Jhonghua-4th Rd, 中華四路331號8樓之2; dm/d from NT$550/1540; @ 📶) Tucked away in two storeys of a residential building, this hostel really makes you feel at home. Dorms (from two-to six-bed) are spick and span, and the private rooms are simple yet pleasant. Perks include free laundry service, bike rental and a fully equipped kitchen.

Angels Backpack HOSTEL $

(Map p254; ☎0970-050 139; angelsbackpack@gmail.com; 159-2, Liohe 1st Rd, 高雄市六合一路159-2號; dm NT$378-600; @ 📶) This extremely popular hostel rocks with its fab location and well-equipped en-suite dorms. If you arrive in Kaohsiung keen for company, this could be the place for you since it attracts young backpackers and action-loving crowds. The staff are uberhelpful and hospitable.

Hwa Hung Hotel HOTEL $

(華宏大飯店, Huáhóng Dàfàndiàn; Map p254; ☎237 5523; www.hhhotel.com.tw; 243 Jianguo-2nd Rd, 建國2路243號; d/tw NT$950/1600; @) The fresh, funky interior of this hotel looks like it was taken out of a comic book. Rooms are large, casually furnished and, overall, great value for money. The only downside is the neighbourhood. The train station is nearby if you need it, but otherwise this is a depressing part of town.

Legend Hotel HOTEL $$
(秝芯旅店, Lìxīn Lǚdiàn; Map p254; ☎287 7766; www.legendhotel.com.tw; 55 Xinsheng 1st St, 新盛一街55號; s/d incl breakfast NT$1180/1780; @☜) Just a short walk from either the City Council metro station or Liuhe Night Market, this good-value choice is the best gateway to the market action, but is also far enough away not to be disturbed by it. The 49 rooms are all reasonably sized and bright. The decor won't wow you, but you'll get a good night's sleep.

Sunset Beach Resort & Spa HOTEL $$
(西子灣沙灘會館, Xīziwān Shātān Huìguǎn; Map p254; ☎525 0005; www.seasbay.com.tw; 51 Lianhai Rd, 蓮海路51號; s/d/tw NT$2112/3300/4200; @) The rooms provide good bedding and other midrange comforts but it's the location that really sells this place. It is literally on the beach, and the hotel has its own private entrance. There are seasonal and midweek discounts.

Hotel Dua HOTEL $$
(Map p254; ☎272 2993; www.hoteldua.com; 165, Linsen 1st Rd, 林森一路165號; d from NT$3080; @☜) This hotel has 158 ultramodern and sleek rooms with enormous beds, inside a completely renovated building. The dark-hued furniture blends well with the wooden-planked walls and muted contemporary decor. There's also a beautiful rooftop lounge where you can enjoy breakfast or sip cocktails.

Eating

There's food everywhere in Kaohsiung, at all times of day or night. Fuguo Rd east of Bo'ai (near Aozihdi MRT station) is filled with midrange restaurants and has a good range of Thai, Italian, barbecue and seafood. Kaohsiung arena, north of the city centre, is another good area.

Locals recommend the food at **Ruifong Night Market** (瑞豐夜市, Ruìfēng Yèshì; ⊙closed Mon & Wed; Ⓜ MRT Kaohsiung Arena), though there is little space to even move here. **Liuhe Night Market** (Liùhé Yèshì; Map p254; Ⓜ MRT Formosa Boulevard) is famous islandwide for its 100-plus food stalls, and you'll see a convoy of tourist buses bringing tour groups there in the evening.

Other places to try traditional foods include the Lotus Pond area, especially on Shengli Rd, and around the Gushan Ferry Terminal.

Escape 41 WESTERN $$
(海洋天堂歐風餐館, Hǎiyáng Tiāntáng Ōufēng Cānguǎn; ☎525 0058; 41-2 Caishan, Gushan District, 鼓山區柴山路41之2號; dishes NT$120-450; ⊙noon-11pm) With a quiet location down the slopes of a mountain and sitting just a few metres above the blue sea, Escape is worth the effort to trek out to. Good attention is paid to the food: the pizzas are the biggest draw but there are also good veggie options and a broad cocktail and wine selection. Taxis from Sizihwan station will cost about NT$200.

Vegetary Restaurant VEGETARIAN $$
(李記素食工坊, Lǐjì Sùshí Gōngfǎng; Map p254; 191 Cingnian 2nd Rd; set meals from NT$290; ⊙6.30-9.30am, 11am-9pm; ✎) A comfortable veggie place with set meals and à la carte dishes. The speciality here is hot pot.

Mars WESTERN $$
(睦工場, Mù Gōngchǎng; Map p254; 80 Dayong Rd; sandwiches from NT$180, set meals from NT$220; ⊙10am-10pm Tue-Sun;) This stylish cafe whips up fresh sandwiches, pastries, pasta and soups. It also serves good brunches.

Ya Jiao Seafood Restaurant SEAFOOD $$
(鴨角活海產店, Yājiǎo Huóhǎichǎn Diàn; Map p254; 22 Miaoqian Rd, Cijin Island; ⊙10.30am-11pm) For fresh seafood the locals recommend Ya Jiao on Cijin Island. It's the kind of place you go to eat freshly cooked seafood or sashimi, drink cheap beer, and be loud like the locals. Just tell the staff how much you want to spend and they will arrange dishes for you. Try the stir-fried clams with basil (塔香海瓜子, *tǎ xiāng hǎi guāzǐ*) and blanched shrimps (白灼蝦, *báizhuóxiā*).

Drinking & Nightlife

Cafes, tea shops, fruit stalls and the like are everywhere. Along the Love River, outdoor cafes offer shade in the daytime and stay open into the late evening. Some serve beer at night. Fisherman's Wharf has a row of outdoor bars; Wufu-4th Rd, a traditional pub street, is looking very tired these days.

Dog Pig Art Cafe CAFE
(豆皮文藝咖啡館, Dòupí Wényì Kāfēiguǎn; Map p254; ☎521 2422; 2nd fl, 131 Wufu-4th Rd; coffee NT$90-150; ⊙5-11pm Tue-Fri, 2-11pm Sat & Sun)

WORTH A TRIP

TEMPLE TOURING ON THE SOUTHWEST COAST

The southwest coast contains some of the most ancient temples in Taiwan. In most cases these centre on the stars of southern folk faith: Matsu and the Wang Yeh (the Royal Lords, general protectors).

At Luermen, look for the massive **Luermen Matsu Temple** (鹿耳門天后宮, Lùěrmén Tiānhòugōng), which is near where Koxinga is said to have landed during his campaign against the Dutch. Close by is the **Orthodox Luermen Matsu Temple** (聖母廟, Shèngmǔ Miào), which reached its outlandish size after a battle for spiritual (and funding) supremacy with the Luermen Matsu Temple in the 1980s. Both temples are near the Sihcao Dazhong Temple and can be reached by bike.

Two temples off Provincial Hwy 19 are well worth the effort to find if you have any interest in traditional temple arts. The **Zhenxing Temple** (振興宮, Zhènxīng Gōng) in Jiali (佳里), just past the Km119 mark, contains some fantastic tableaux of figures in *jiǎnniàn* (mosaic-like temple decoration). However, these figures are not on the roof, as is usual, but on the sides of the entrance portico.

At the front of the temple, check out the unique cochin (brightly coloured, glazed ceramic) figures of an old man and woman crouching as if to support crossbeams. They were created by Master Yeh Wang (see Koji Ceramic Museum, p214) and are called *The Fool Crouching to Raise the House*.

About 5km north of Jiali, in the town of Xuejia (學甲), the **Ciji Temple** (慈濟宮, Cíjì Gōng; 170 Jisheng Rd, 濟生路170號) protects more of the remaining works of Master Yeh Wang. The beautiful works are collected in a four-storey **museum** (admission free; ⏲8.30am-noon & 2-5pm) beside the temple. Ciji itself is a lovely southern-style temple, with a graceful swallowtail roof and stone work and woodcarvings from the 19th century.

From Xuejia, head coastwards for Provincial Hwy 17 and you'll reach **Nankunshen Temple** (南鯤鯓代天府, Nánkūnshēn Dàitiān Fǔ) within 15 minutes. Established in 1662, this temple is the centre of Wang Yeh worship (don't confuse these gods with Master Yeh Wang). The size of Nankunshen is the direct result of rivalry with a local upstart over who had paramount status in the world of Wang Yeh. Nankunshen won.

On most Sundays the temple explodes with exuberant displays of ritual devotion: there are fireworks, parades and chanting. If possible, try to visit during the Welcoming Festival for Wang Yeh (20 April, lunar calendar).

Madou Temple (麻豆代天府, Mádòu Dàitiānfǔ) in Madou (麻豆), 15km southeast of Xuejia, is the nearest rival of Nankunshen. What you see today comes from 1956 onwards (the original temple dates back to the Ming dynasty) and all Tainanese can claim a common childhood memory of receiving an unorthodox moral education inside the garish, gigantic dragon behind the main temple. To re-create what they went through, pay NT$40 to go to hell from the dragon's tail, or to ascend to heaven from its mouth. The experience beats Singapore's Tiger Balm Villa as the demons here don't stay still; it's so kitsch it's fun.

This is a long-running cafe and art space in Kaohsiung. Documentary movies and alternative theatre can be watched on the 3rd floor on weekends. The cafe serves good curries and has a decent foreign-beer selection.

Brickyard Beer Garden BAR
(Map p254; cnr Jhongshan-1 & Wufu-3rd Rd; ⏲5-11pm Mon-Sun) Inside Central Park, this beer garden enjoys a popular reputation among locals and expats alike. It also serves sandwiches, burgers and Chinatown-style Chinese food.

Lighthouse Bar & Grill BAR
(燈塔美式酒館, Dēngtǎ Měishì Jiǔguǎn; Map p257; 239 Fuguo-1st Rd; ⏲6pm-late) A popular hangout in the Tsoying District, with good service, live sports broadcasts and a wide selection of bar favourites such as pizza and sandwiches.

☆ Entertainment

Art-house movies and documentaries are shown nightly except Monday at the Municipal Film Archives (p258).

Dog Pig Art Cafe has alternative theatre and documentary showings at weekends.

Pier-2 Art District (p257) is often the site of concerts and outdoor performances. Pick up a seasonal events calendar at the visitor centre.

Shopping

Shiquan Road Flea Market MARKET
(十全路跳蚤市場, Shíquánlù Tiàozao Shìchǎng; cnr Shiquan Rd & Jhonghua 2nd Rd; ⏲8am-5.30pm Sat & Sun) This long-standing market is lined with small shops and stalls selling furniture, books, silver, vinyl, porcelain, vintage toys, paintings and trinkets. Open Saturday and Sunday only.

Information

There are banks and ATMs everywhere, including most 7-Elevens. You can change money at the **Bank of Taiwan** (台灣銀行; Map p254; 264 Jhongjheng-4th Rd).

ADSL is widely available in hotels. There's free wi-fi at the Kaohsiung Cultural Centre, as well as outside the MRT station at Central Park.

Chung-Ho Memorial Hospital, Kaohsiung Medical University (高雄醫學大學附設中和紀念醫院; www.kmuh.org.tw; 100 Zihyou 1st Rd) Just east of Houyi KMRT Station.

Kaohsiung City (http://khh.travel) Excellent city tourism website.

Train station visitor centre (火車站遊客服務中心; Map p254; ⏲9am-7pm) In the main train station. Staff speak English and are a good source of information.

Getting There & Away

AIR

The airport, south of the city, connects seamlessly to downtown by KMRT. Domestic and international terminals are joined and you can quickly walk from one to the other.

There's a visitor information centre in each terminal. Staff speak passable English and can help with hotels, tours, MRT travel, car rentals etc.

Nine kilometres south of the city is **Siaogang Domestic Airport Terminal** (www.kia.gov.tw; 2 Jhongshan 4th Rd), which has flights to Kinmen and Penghu. **Uni Air** (www.uniair.com.tw) and **Daily Air Corporation** (www.dailyair.com.tw) fly from here.

Siaogang International Airport Terminal has flights to most Southeast Asian countries, Japan, Korea and China. **EVA** (www.evaair.com) and China Airlines (p378) fly from here.

BOAT

Taiwan Hangye Company (www.tnc-kao.com.tw/Shipdate_1.aspx) has year-round boats from Kaohsiung to Makung, Penghu (NT$860, 4½ hours). The schedule changes every three months and is unreliable in winter. It's best to go directly to the ticketing office to check the schedule with them and buy tickets on the spot.

BUS

Kaohsiung Ke Yuan (高雄客運; Map p254; ☎746 2141; 245 Nanhua St) has buses to Donggang (NT$125, 50 to 70 minutes, every 15 to 30 minutes), Foguangshan (NT$80, 40 minutes, eight per day), Kenting (every 30 minutes, 24 hours a day) by Kenting Express (NT$413, 2½ hours) or regular bus (NT$383, 3½ hours), and to Meinong (NT$134, 1½ hours, every one or two hours).

Kuo Kuang Bus Company (國光客運東站; Map p254; ☎236 0962; www.kingbus.com.tw; 306 Jianguo-2 Rd) is located at Kuo Kuang Bus Company Station. It has buses to Taipei (NT$530, five hours, every half-hour, 24 hours a day) and Taitung (NT$300, four hours).

HIGH SPEED RAIL

The HSR travels from Tsoying station to Taipei every half-hour (NT$1490, two hours).

TRAIN

Kaohsiung is the terminus for most west-coast trains. Trains run frequently from early morning until midnight to Taipei (fast/slow NT$845/650, five/six hours) and Taichung (fast/slow NT$375/289, 2½/three hours).

Getting Around

TO/FROM THE AIRPORT & HIGH SPEED RAIL

Taking the KMRT Red Line to the airport and HSR costs NT$35. Taxis to the airport or HSR cost NT$320 from the city centre.

BUS

The city has a decent bus system that ties in with the KMRT. The bus hub is directly in front of the train station, and buses have English signage at the front and electronic English displays inside indicating the next stop.

Routes are clearly mapped in English at every KMRT station, and a one-zone fare is NT$12.

CAR

Both of the following have English-speaking staff and do pick-ups:

Car Plus (Map p254; ☎0800-222 568; www.car-plus.com.tw; 264 Jianguo-2 Rd)

Central Auto (☎802 0800; www.rentalcar.com.tw; 400 Gaotie Rd)

KAOHSIUNG MASS RAPID TRANSIT

Locals complain that Kaohsiung's MRT **system** (www.krtco.com.tw; ⏲5.55am-11.40pm) doesn't go where they live, but it does go where travellers want to visit. Abundant English signs and maps make the system easy to use.

Individual fares start at NT$20 and can be purchased at every station. A day pass costs NT$130 (plus NT$70 deposit) – buy directly from any staffed station booth. A bus/MRT/ferry combo pass is NT$200 (no deposit).

AROUND KAOHSIUNG

Foguangshan 佛光山

07

A massive temple complex, **Foguangshan** (Light of Buddha Mountain, Fóguāngshān; www.fgs.org.tw) is about a 50-minute drive from Kaohsiung. The complex consists of a monastery, a meditation centre and a new museum. It's considered the centre of Buddhism in southern Taiwan.

Sights

Buddha Memorial Center MUSEUM

(佛陀紀念館, Fótuó Jiniànguǎn; 656 3033, ext 4002; www.fgsbmc.org.tw; 9am-8pm Mon-Fri, to 9pm Sat & Sun) FREE The latest addition to Foguangshan is this eye-catching museum complex that houses 12 symmetrically arranged pagodas and a giant Buddha sitting atop the main hall. Inside the main hall you'll find a 4D theatre, a museum exhibiting Buddhist artefacts, and several new Buddhist shrines.

Great Buddha Land BUDDHIST

(大佛城, Dàfóchéng) Here in Great Buddha Land you'll see a 36m Amitabha Buddha towering over a garden of 480 smaller Buddha statues.

Pure Land Cave BUDDHIST

(淨土洞窟, Jìngtǔ Dòngkū) FREE The rather Disneyland-like Pure Land Cave has animated figures and a light show.

Courses

Weekend Temple Retreats MEDITATION, COOKING

(英語寺院生活體驗營, Yīngyǔ Sìyuàn Shēnghuó Tǐyàn Yíng; 656 1921, ext 1374; www.fgs.org.tw/events/wkend_retreat/index.html; weekend retreat NT$500) Weekend retreats are held every second weekend of the month and include meditation, chanting, calligraphy, cooking and philosophy classes.

Tours

Half-day tours in English can be arranged with the nuns at the **reception** (656 1921, ext 6203-05) of the main temple (大雄寶殿, Dàxióngbǎodiàn). Temple tours stress the ceremonial aspects of Buddhism and you will be requested to bow and kowtow. In return, you will be instructed in Buddhist thought, history and iconography.

Sleeping & Eating

Pilgrim's Lodge LODGE $$

(Cháoshān Huìguǎn; dm/d NT$300/2000) The lodge invites devotees and tourists to spend the night. The accommodation is surprisingly good. The Front Hall of the Buddha Memorial Center has a Starbucks, several vegetarian restaurants, and an all-you-can-eat veggie canteen (NT$100) on the 2nd floor.

Getting There & Around

There are 11 buses a day between the temple and Kaohsiung (NT$80, 50 minutes); 15 buses run between Tsoying HSR station and Buddha Memorial Center (NT$65, 40 minutes). The temple and the memorial centre are within walking distance of each other, but you can also hop on the shuttle buses (NT$20, every 20 minutes) that link the two places.

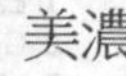

Meinong 美濃

07 / POP 42,374

In 1736 the intrepid Lin brothers led the first Hakka immigrants to settle the plains of Meinong (Měinóng). While the Hakka make up about 14% of the population of Taiwan, in Meinong the percentage is around 95%. Hardworking people who value higher education, the Hakka of Meinong can count a disproportionate number of PhDs (and in the past, imperial scholars) among their population.

Thoroughly rural in character, and once the centre of a well-protected tobacco industry, Meinong was hit hard by Taiwan's entry into the World Trade Organization (WTO) in 2002. With the monopoly system abolished, the town began to refashion itself into a country retreat. Hakka culture, historic sites and butterfly-watching became the cornerstones of the new economy.

Winter is a great time to visit, as the weather is perfect – warm and dry – and tourists are few. Summer is the season of the yellow butterflies; in the valleys to the northeast they swarm in the hundreds of thousands.

Meinong

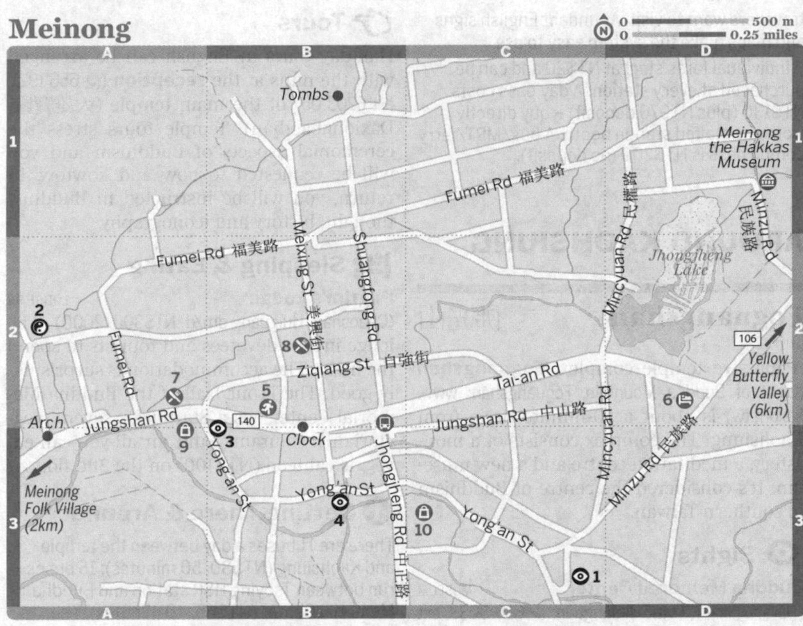

Sights & Activities

One of the most pleasant things to do in Meinong is to get on a bike and ride through the countryside. Postcard scenes of old brick houses fronted by lush fields are everywhere. Some of the best cycling is off the main road towards the mountains and out to the Yellow Butterfly Valley. **A Lin Bicycle Shop** (阿麟的店, Ā Lín De Diàn; 166 Jungshan Rd, Sec 1) has a good selection of bikes.

Yellow Butterfly Valley BUTTERFLY VALLEY
(黃蝶翠谷, Huángdié Cuìgǔ) Late spring and summer are the best time to visit the valley. Over 100 species can be found here, and the chances of having a dozen species flittering about you at any moment are high. In late July you may see half a million individuals within a couple of hectares of open riverbed and the surrounding forest.

The flighty, midsized yellow emigrant butterfly (*Catopsilia pomona*) is the most commonly seen species. It breeds in spring and explodes in numbers in summer. Around July it is common to see swarms of yellows crossing Hwy 10 as they disperse to richer pastures.

The valley is 7km northeast of downtown Meinong. Head north from Minzu Rd and follow the English signs to the valley.

Yong'an Street STREET
(永安路, Yǒngān Lù) This was the first street in Meinong, and some of the oldest family residences can still be found in the narrow back alleys.

Just behind the **East Gate** (東門, Dōngmén) at the end of the street is a famous **Bogong shrine** (伯公神壇, Bógōng Shéntán), dedicated to the Earth God and especially popular among the Hakka. In old Hakka style no statue is used – just a stone tablet and incense. There are over 400 Bogong shrines around Meinong but this is the most valued. Bow three times to this or any other shrine to bring peace to your life.

Meinong residents have long placed a high premium on book learning. Oblation furnaces such as the 235-year-old **Minong jhuang Oblation Furnace** (瀰濃庄敬字亭, Mínnóngzhuāng Jìngzìtíng) at the start of Yong'an St were designed to dispose of paper that contained written text, thus signifying such paper's exalted status.

Guangshan Temple TAOIST TEMPLE
(廣善堂, Guǎngshàn Táng) 'If you don't stop fighting we're going to build a temple.' It doesn't sound like much of a threat, but in 1915 Gu A-Jhen and 12 other local worthies were true to their word and, miraculously, after they constructed this temple in 1918, peace was restored to Meinong. It's a showpiece of a southern temple complete with beautiful swallowtail roof.

Meinong Folk Village TOURIST VILLAGE
(美濃民俗村, Měinóng Mínsú Cūn; 80 Lane 421, Jungshan Rd, Sec 2; ⏲8am-5.30pm) FREE This artificial re-creation of an old-fashioned neighbourhood is definitely touristy but you can still watch traditional crafts being made, sample Hakka *lei cha* (擂茶, *léi chá;* pounded tea) and other tasty snacks, and purchase well-made paper umbrellas, fans and bamboo baskets.

Sleeping

Guangshan Temple HOSTEL $
(廣善堂, Guǎngshàn Táng; ☎681 2124; s/d NT$800/1000) The temple has a small and basic pilgrim's house in which you can stay, if you reserve in advance.

Lin Home HOMESTAY $$
(林家民宿陶坊, Línjiā Mínsù Táofang; ☎0921-245 800; www.minsu.com.tw/076820658; 53-7 Minzu Rd, 民族路53-7號; r incl breakfast from NT$1800) This B&B-cum-pottery workshop has four modernly furnished rooms in its traditional courtyard complex. Bikes are free for guests. There is no English signage but the entrance is lined with pottery. Advance booking a must.

Eating

Meinong Traditional Hakka Restaurant HAKKA $
(美濃古老客家菜, Měinóng Gǔlǎo KèJiācaì; 362-5 Jungshan Rd, Sec 1; dishes NT$120-280; ⏲9am-2pm & 5-9pm) This good eatery dishes out simple bowls of *bantiao* (炒粄條, chǎobǎntiáo; flat rice noodles) as well as other famous Hakka treats, such as the mouthwatering but artery-clogging *méigān kòuròu* (梅干扣肉; succulent fatty pork on dried leaf mustard).

Meixing St HAKKA $
(美興街, Měixìng Jiē; Meixing St; noodles from NT$40) This street in downtown Meinong is lined up with *bantiao* noodle joints and each has a different recipe. Needless to say, every Meinonger has their own pick of perfect noodles here.

Shopping

Artisans have been making umbrellas in Meinong for almost a century. The umbrellas are made of paper and bamboo, and are hand-painted and then lacquered to make them durable and waterproof. They make great decorations and gifts.

Guan De Xin Paper Umbrella Shop HANDICRAFTS
(廣德興紙傘, Guǎngdéxīng Zhǐsǎn; 361 Jungshan Rd, Sec 1) If you're looking to buy, this is one of the best places. An umbrella here costs between NT$400 and NT$1500.

Jing Shing Blue Shirts Shop CLOTHING
(錦興行藍衫店, Jǐnxīngháng Lánshāndiàn; 177 Yong'an St; ⏲7.30am-9pm) This little family-run shop opened in the 1930s making traditional Hakka-style indigo clothing and accessories. A loose-fitting shirt costs NT$3000.

Getting There & Around

Buses between Meinong and Kaohsiung (NT$134, 1½ hours) run every one or two hours.

Meinong is small but the surrounding countryside is expansive and you'll need a vehicle or bicycle to get around. B&B owners may be able to help you hire a scooter.

Maolin Recreation Area 茂林遊憩區

☎07

The drawcard of the mountainous **recreation area** (Màolín Yǒuqì Qū; www.maolin-nsa.gov.tw) is the Purple Butterfly Valley, one of

WORTH A TRIP

WUSHANDING MUD VOLCANOES

In the boondocks between Kaohsiung and Meinong you'll come across some of the most unusual sights in Taiwan – mud volcanoes. While they aren't the same as those amazing spectacles in Azerbaijan, which has the lion's share of the world's mud volcanoes, and are not destructive like the variety found in Indonesia, they are still serious geological curiosities worthy of a day's exploration.

One of the most volatile hydrothermal areas in Taiwan is the **Wushanding Mud Volcanoes** (烏山頂泥火山, Wūshāndǐng Níhuǒshān) in Yanchao (燕巢, Yàncháo), 27km north of Kaohsiung. This, the smallest nature reserve (just under 5 hectares) in Taiwan, has two volcanoes and, although their height and shape change constantly with the weather, they are normally no taller than 1.5m so you can get really close to the craters to see the boiling pot of gray goo. Visitors have to show some form of ID to the makeshift office at the entrance of the volcano area.

Unique geothermal reactions can be seen in a pair of gurgling pools in **New Yangnyu Mud Pond** (新養女湖, Xīn yǎngnǚhú) near Wushanding. Buy a tea egg from the store in front of the pools and the chap will light the methane gas that bubbles up from the depths.

To get to Wushanding, first take Hwy 1 to the Gangshan Interchange, then head east out of Yanchao on route 38. The volcanoes are to the north of Kaohsiung National Normal University. There are bilingual signs to Wushanding, though we can't guarantee that you won't get lost. From Wushanding the road to New Yangnyu Mud Pond is signposted.

If you are on the way to Meinong from Tainan, **Tianliao Moon World** (田寮月世界, Tiánliáo Yuèshìjiè; 36 Yueqiu Rd, Chongde Village, 崇德里月球路36號; ⌚10am-5pm), a geopark off Hwy 28 in Tianliao, is also worth a visit. The strange Martian landscape here will make you wish you'd paid attention in geography class. Moon World is also accessible by public transport. Red bus 70 leaves from Gangshan South MRT Station in Kaohsiung six times a day between 8am and 6pm. The last bus back is at 7.40pm.

It's also worth heading out from Tainan to **Mt Tsao Moon World** (草山月世界, Cǎoshān Yuè Shìjiè), a grimly picturesque landscape of barren eroded cliffs and pointy crags. There are places in Taiwan that feel as remote, but few that feel as bewitchingly desolate. To reach the Moon World, follow Hwy 20 and turn left around the Km27 mark towards Nanhua on Hwy 20甲 . Proceed about 1km and then turn right at the sign for Moon World. Five kilometres further, turn left at the next set of signs. From here it's 9km to Hill 308, which has panoramic views over the badlands.

15 overwintering sites that stretch across southern Taiwan from Maolin to Dawu in Taitung. Other than that, you'll discover pristine mountain landscapes, vertiginously high suspension bridges, waterfalls, natural swimming pools and strong Rukai aboriginal culture in this remote yet beautiful valley.

The only road that runs through the area, County Rd 132, connects two Rukai settlements: Maolin village at the start and Dona at the end.

Sights & Activities

Purple Butterfly Valley BUTTERFLY VALLEY
(紫蝶幽谷; ⌚9am-5pm) The valley is not one geographical location, but a number of sites around the recreation area. Some will be signed as you drive along the main road, but enquire at the visitor information centre for good butterfly-watching locations. The centre is located where County Rd 132 meets Hwy 27, before the entrance of the recreation area.

The best time to watch the butterflies is between 9am and 11am. On cooler or rainy days the butterflies remain motionless, hanging from the trees like garlands. It's possible to arrange a tour with De En Gorge Guesthouse.

Waterfalls WATERFALLS
You can drive up to the first of the five levels of **Qingren Valley Waterfall** (情人瀑布, Qíngrén Pùbù). Now only the first three levels of it are accessible by a trail. The next waterfall in the park is **Maolin Gorge Waterfall** (茂林谷瀑布, Màolíngǔ Pùbù). As you drive down into Maolin Gorge Valley

there is a sign for the waterfall. The road was closed at the time of writing but is likely to be reopened by the time you read this.

Road to Dona (Duona) SCENIC AREA
County Rd 132 from Maolin Village to Dona features a number of roadside attractions, including the **Dona High Suspension Bridge** (多納吊橋, Duō nà diàoqiáo), the **Snake Head mountain** (蛇頭山, Shétóu Shān) and the **Dragon Head mountain** (龍頭山, Lóngtóu Shān), which are odd-shaped mounds in the river valley.

Dona (多納, Duō nà) is a stronghold for Rukai aboriginal culture and stonework. However, the village was damaged by natural disasters and now there's a mix of traditional shale buildings and makeshift houses.

Sleeping

There are guesthouses in Dona charging around NT$1500 a night for a double. Just walk around and you will see them.

De En Gorge Guesthouse HOMESTAY $$
(Dé Ēn Gǔ Mínsù; ☎0989-579 751; http://tw.myblog.yahoo.com/maolin-deengorge; dm/2-person cabin NT$500/2500) Run by a friendly local family that offers good ecotours in English, De En Gorge Guesthouse is the default accommodation in Maolin. Camping is permitted on the grass bluff (per person NT$200; bring your own equipment), while the cabins, made of grey stone, offer some modern comfort.

To get to the guesthouse head up County Rd 132 until you see the signs for Maolin Valley (茂林谷; Màolíngǔ, also Maolin Gorge). Turn right down a side road and cross the bridge. When the road ends at a fork, head left and up about 1km. The first building you see is the guesthouse.

Eating

Options for eating are very limited in Maolin. Little stalls are set up on the main road in Maolin Village but be aware that these places close early (by 6pm or 7pm).

Information

The new **visitor information centre** (茂林遊客中心; ⏲9am-5pm) stands where County Rd 132 meets Hwy 27, right before you enter Maolin Village. It has exhibitions on the region's topography and stocks a good brochure that introduces the butterflies and flora in the valley.

Getting There & Away

Maolin can be reached from Meinong via the new Shinwei Bridge (新威大橋, Xīnwēi Dàqiáo), which links Hwys 28 and 27 – a much quicker route than going via Liugui. You need your own vehicle. Consider renting a car or scooter in Kaohsiung or Tainan.

PINGTUNG COUNTY

Oddly, Taiwan's poorest county has some of the country's best beaches, most fertile farmland, richest fish stocks and balmiest weather. Also, Pingtung County (屏東) boasts one of the most exuberant festivals in Taiwan, the Burning of the Wang Yeh Boats, and there are outdoor pursuits aplenty – swimming, snorkeling and birding at Kenting National Park, and cycling along the quiet county roads that roll slowly past calming fields and foothills.

Donggang 東港

POP 49,097

During the Qing dynasty, Donggang (Tungkang) was one of three main commercial ports in Taiwan, the landing site for the ancestors of millions of modern Taiwanese (in particular the Hakka), and a rather prosperous little town. Today the town of about 50,000 people remains an important centre for fishing, especially the prized blue-fin tuna and mullet, but its heyday is long gone.

Festivals & Events

★Burning of the Wang Yeh Boats TAOIST FESTIVAL
(www.dbnsa.gov.tw) This is one of Taiwan's top folk festivals. It involves inviting gods to earth, feasting them, and then asking them to carry trouble-causing demons and plague away with them on a boat. In the spectacular conclusion to the festival, the boat is torched to the ground on the beach.

In Donggang, what makes the festival so highly enjoyable is that everyone around you, the faithful and the spectators, are so taken in by it. Sublime, dignified, bizarre, entertaining and stirring: the boat burning is all that, and for most people, usually all at once.

The festival is sponsored every three years by the resplendent **Donglong Temple** (東隆宮, Dōnglóng Gōng), established in 1706 and long one of the centres of folk faith in southern Taiwan. The exact dates vary, but the festival always starts on a Saturday and ends on a Friday night (into Saturday morning). The next boat burning will take place in autumn 2015.

History

The origins of boat-burning festivals go back over 1000 years to the Song dynasty and are connected with the Wang Yeh, deities once worshipped for their ability to prevent disease.

The festivals were brought to Taiwan by Fujian immigrants in the 18th and 19th centuries, and have continued into modern times. Many southern temples still hold their own small boat burnings, but a greater number have simply merged their traditions with Donglong Temple.

The meaning of boat burnings has changed considerably today, and they are now held as prayers for peace and stability. But the dark and solemn plague-expulsion rituals remain central to the festival.

Known officially as the **Sacrifice of Peace and Tranquillity for Welcoming the Lords** (東港迎王平安祭典, Dōnggǎng Yíngwáng Píngān Jìdiǎn), the festival runs for eight consecutive days. Most visitors (and you can expect tens of thousands of them) attend the first and last.

The Ceremony

Day One (Saturday): Inviting the Gods

Around noon a procession leaves Donglong Temple for the beach, where it meets five Wang Yeh who are returning to earth for this year's festival. At the beach, **spirit mediums** (*jītóng*) write the names of the quintet in the sand when they sense their arrival. When the leader of the five Wang Yeh arrives, his surname is written on a large yellow banner. Usually the procession doesn't get back to the temple till late afternoon.

At around 7pm local Donggang leaders carry the Wang Yeh (on sedan chairs) over live coals before they enter Donglong Temple.

Things to watch for on this day include people with **paper yokes** around their necks. Square yokes indicate that a wish has been made. A fish or round yoke means a wish has been fulfilled.

Down at the beach there will be hundreds of other temple representatives with their gods and sedan chairs. Many will take the chairs into the ocean for a rough, watery blessing. Painted troupes representing the **Soong Jiang Battle Array** will also be around, though they usually perform earlier.

Days Two to Seven

The Wang Yeh are carried around town on an inspection and are then feasted. The boat is also blessed.

Volunteers **parade the boat** through town to allow it to collect every bit of misfortune and evil that it can. The boat returns to Donglong Temple around 7pm and is loaded with all manner of goods, as if truly going on a voyage.

Between 10pm and 11pm, **Taoist priests** burn pieces of paper spell and chant in the courtyard. This ritual relieves hundreds of gods and their thousands of foot soldiers from the duties they have performed this past week. After 11pm, watch (and have your camera ready) a priest with a wok, *ba gua* (Chinese religious motif) symbols, broom, rice sifter and sword as he leads a large group of priests to dance and perform rituals to direct the demons onto the boat.

Around midnight the leaders of the temple offer the Wang Yeh one last special **feast** of 108 dishes, which include famous traditional palace foods, local snacks, fruit and wine. This is one of the most solemn and beautiful rites of the festival, but it's hard to get near enough as there is an ocean of people, so you may want to wander around town a bit as many of temples are also holding interesting celebrations and rituals.

Around 2am the boat is dragged on wheels out of the temple grounds through a famous **gold foil arch** (it's a sight you'll never forget) and down to the beach. Expect a lot of exploding fireworks.

At the beach hundreds of tonnes of ghost paper is packed around the ship to help it burn, and the anchors, mast, sails (made of real cloth), windsock and lanterns are hoisted into place.

Finally the five Wang Yeh are invited onto the boat and firecrackers are used to start a fire, which slowly engulfs the entire ship. The **burning** takes place between 5am and 7am and it's proper to flee as soon as the boat is lit, to avoid having your soul taken away. But these days only older locals follow this custom.

Eating

Bluefin tuna (黑鮪魚, *hēi wěiyú*) is Donggang's second claim to national fame. One place to try it (or perhaps not, as environmental groups are calling for an outright ban on bluefin tuna fishing) and other delicacies such as mullet roe (烏魚子, *Wūyúzǐ*) and sea grapes (海葡萄, *hǎi pútáo*) is **By the Sea** (海這裡餐廳, Hǎi Zhèlǐ Cāntīng; www.bythesea.com.tw; 53 Xinsheng 1st St, 新生一路53號; dishes from NT$200; ⏲10.30am-9pm Tue-Sun), which is actually more 'by the port'.

Getting There & Away

Buses from Kaohsiung (NT$115, 50 to 70 minutes, every 15 to 30 minutes) and Pingtung (NT$85, 40 minutes, every hour) drop you off near the McDonald's in central Donggang. Facing McDonald's, turn left and left again at the first intersection. The temple is about 500m down the road on the left.

After the festival consider taking a bus or taxi down to Kenting. You'll need some rest.

Little Liuchiu Island

小琉球

☎08 / POP 13,000

This pretty coral island (Hsiao Liuchiu Island, Xiǎo Liúqiú) offers sea vistas, convoluted caves, sandy beaches, odd rock formations and temples to keep you happy for a long, long day. Best of all, it's simple to get to and to get around.

Going green has never looked better on the island: in 2013, the destructive practice of gill-net fishing was banned to protect the corals and the 200 endangered green sea turtles inhabiting the coasts. During the turtles' spawning season (May to July), residents and visitors alike are not allowed access to certain parts of the coast after dusk.

You can visit Liuchiu all year round, but winters are lovely: warm and dry, with temperatures averaging in the mid-20°C range.

History

The original inhabitants of Little Liuchiu, Siraya aborigines, called it Samaji. During the Dutch occupation, the island was under VOC control and when the crew of the shipwrecked *Golden Lion* were killed by the Siraya, the Dutch forcibly removed the entire population. This act included a notorious slaughter of several hundred Siraya. The massacre is now remembered (and bowdlerised) in the legend on the plaque in front of the Black Dwarf Cave.

In the 18th century, Taiwanese fisherfolk started to settle in small numbers. Until recently, about 80% of the island's residents made their living from fishing.

Sights & Activities

You can ride around the island on a scooter in about 30 minutes but give yourself at least half a day. This island was made for exploring.

Some attractions to look out for are **Vase Rock** (花瓶岩, Huāpíng Yán), a giant eroded coral with a thin base and large head, **Black Dwarf Cave** (烏鬼洞, Wūgǔi Dòng; ⏲8am-5pm) and **Beauty Cave** (美人洞, Měirén Dòng; ⏲8am-5pm). Note that some sites require an entrance ticket; one ticket for NT$120 is good for all of them.

Other must-sees include the narrow, twisting, root-strangled coral passageways at **Shanzhu Ditch** (山豬溝, Mountain Pig Ditch, Shānzhū Gōu) and **Lingshan Temple** (靈山寺, Língshān Sì), just up from the pier. The temple offers fine, clear views across the Taiwan Strait.

The ginormous **Sanlong Temple** (三隆宮, Sānlónggōng) sponsors a boat-burning festival every three years. The festival takes place in the autumn a couple of weeks after Donggang's Donglong Temple holds its festival.

The best place for a swim is at **Zhong Ao Beach** (中澳沙灘, Zhōng Ào Shātān). The beach at **Vase Rock** is nice for wading or snorkelling, while the tiny but picturesque stretch of shell-sand beach at **Geban Bay** (蛤板灣, Gébǎnwān) makes for a sweet picnic spot.

To find out more about the marine life of Little Liuchiu, evening guided tours to **Shanfu Ecological Corridor** (杉福生態廊道, Shānfú Shēngtài Lángdào), the only inter-tidal zone on the island open to the public, can be arranged at most of the homestays. To maintain the ecological integrity of the area, only 300 visitors are allowed there per day.

Be sure to wear something on your feet if you go into the water as the coral rocks can really cut you up. Also, don't go more than 20m from shore unless you are wearing fins; there is a nasty undertow around the island.

Sleeping & Eating

Accommodation costs around NT$1600 to NT$2600 a night on the island. Homestays are centred in two areas: across the port as soon you get off the boat; and down County Rd 201, which is reached by following the main road uphill out of the port. At the four-way intersection (which is one block from the port) you'll see a narrow lane with

Little Liuchiu Island

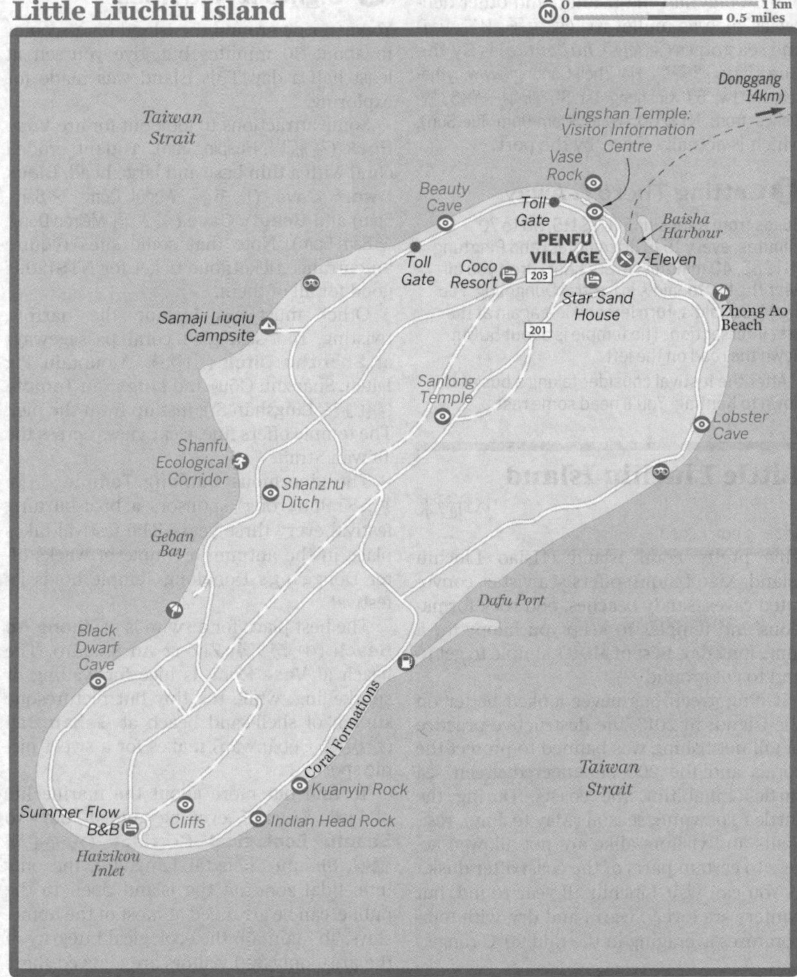

the 201 road sign in front (to your right is a 7-Eleven, and to your left, a temple).

The village at Baisha Harbour has many small eateries. You can eat expensive fresh seafood or simple stir-fries for less than NT$100. You can also buy sandwiches and drinks from the village's 7-Eleven.

Samaji Liuqiu Campsite CAMPGROUND **$**
(沙瑪基島露營渡假區, Shāmǎjīdǎo Lùyíng Dùjiàqū; ☎861 4880; www.samaji.com.tw; per site NT$400, cabins from NT$1600) The cheapest accommodation on Little Liuchiu, Samaji offers terrific views from its expansive cliffside perch on the west side of the island. Tents are provided but if you bring your own it's NT$100 cheaper. It offers an onsite restaurant and bike rental (NT$100 per hour).

Summer Flow B&B B&B **$$**
(夏琉民宿, Xiàliú mínsù; ☎861 4756; www.facebook.com/summerflowbnb; 16 Zhongxiao Rd, 忠孝路16號; per person from NT$2650; 📶) At the southern end of the island, this new homestay is diagonally opposite **Haizikou Inlet**, where you can swim. Rooms are simple but bright and airy. The host, Hsiao Long, is a certified eco-guide and offers sea-life tours.

His partner, Stella, can interpret in English for him. Room rates include round-trip ferry tickets and scooter rental.

Coco Resort CABIN $$

(椰林渡假村, Yélín Dùjiàcūn; ☎861 4368; www.coco-resort.com.tw; 38-20 Minzu Rd, 民族路38-20號; 2-/4-person cabins NT$2600/3800) An old standby down County Rd 203 (Minzu Rd) that still looks as well tended as ever. It's just a minute's scooter ride from the island's one and only 7-Eleven.

Information

There's an ATM in the 7-Eleven in Penfu Village. The **visitor information centre** (遊客服務中心; ☎861 4615; www.tbnsa.gov.tw; ⏲9am-5pm) is just above Lingshan Temple on the cliff. Very little English is spoken but the view up here is good.

Little Liuchiu Island is part of the Dapeng Bay National Scenic Area. If you are so inclined, check out the website (www.tbnsa.gov.tw) for more information.

Getting There & Away

BOAT

Boats to Baisha Harbour leave Donggang hourly in the morning from 7am, and every 1½ hours in the afternoon (round trip NT$410, 30 minutes). The last return boat to Donggang leaves at 5.30pm.

BUS

Buses stop in central Donggang diagonally opposite McDonald's. From here catch a quick taxi (NT$100) to the harbour ferry terminals. Use the first terminal on the right before the fish market.

To Donggang, buses leave from Pingtung every 20 minutes (NT$85, 40 minutes), and from Kaohsiung (NT$115, 50 to 70 minutes) every 15 to 30 minutes.

Getting Around

The island is only 9km around so you could easily walk it in a day. Electric bikes (NT$300 per day) and scooter hire (NT$250/300 per half-/full day) are available at the harbour – you don't need ID or a licence.

Sandimen 三地門

☎08 / POP 7505

This small aboriginal community (Sāndìmén), 30km east of Pingtung, is a stronghold of the Rukai and Paiwan. The region was lashed by Typhoon Morakot in 2009 and, today, traces of rockslides remain obvious. But the local communities are slowly getting back on their feet and it's now possible to go further into the mountains to very remote aboriginal villages, such as Wutai and Dewen.

If you come from Kaohsiung or Pingtung, you are likely to arrive first at the lowlands of Shuimen (水門, Shuǐmén), on the southern bank of Ailiao River. You'll find most of the facilities you need there, including hotels and the bus station. Sandimen is on the northern bank and there are two bridges linking the two townships.

Sights

Indigenous People's Cultural Park PARK

(台灣山地文化園區, Táiwān Shāndì Wénhuà Yuánqū; www.tacp.gov.tw; Majia Village; admission NT$150; ⏲8.30am-5pm Tue-Sun) The park, set in forested mountains, displays true-to-life examples of traditional aboriginal houses and communal structures. A museum near the entrance has exhibitions of daily, ceremonial and martial items, though there is less emphasis these days on showing artefacts and more on videos.

Highway 24 SCENIC AREA

The last section of Highway 24 is a gorgeous winding highway that leads you deep into the mountains. Not for the fainthearted, some parts of the road run along very steep cliffs. Do check the road conditons before you set off, as the area is often inaccessible when there are heavy rains. You have to register at the police station (at 26.8km mark) before you enter the Wutai area.

This section of the road, between Sandimen and **Wutai** (霧台, Wùtái), is 18km long and the altitude changes from 100m to above 1000m. Expect head-spinning views of the river, valleys, waterfalls, cliffs and aboriginal villages. Wutai (after the Km39 mark) is one of the most attractive settlements of the Rukai, with a striking **Presbyterian church** and traditional **slate-walled houses** straddling the road.

From Wutai, you can continue the last 8km to the abandoned village of **Ali**, or head back and make a detour to **Dewen** (德文, Déwén), a beautiful coffee-growing village sitting 800m to 1200m above sea level. To get to Dewen, switch to County Rd 31 (northbound) before you reach the police station (if you're going downhill). From this turn-off, it's just a 6km drive to the village.

Sleeping & Eating

Homestays can be found in Sandimen and Wutai at around NT$1200 for a double room. Noisy karaoke restaurants straddle Hwy 24; their speciality is barbecued pork (烤山豬肉, *kǎo shānzhūròu*). In Shuimen, eateries are concentrated on the section of Chenggong Rd near Shuimen Bridge.

Rinari Village HOMESTAY $
(禮納里永久屋, Lǐnàlǐ Yǒngjiǔwū; ☎799 7198, 0925-043 288; ngedre_druluan@yahoo.com.tw; Majia County, 瑪家鄉; per person incl breakfast NT$600) Rinari is a resettlement of three Paiwan and Rukai villages destroyed by Typhoon Morakot. To help villagers find new livelihoods, 40 families received hospitality training and converted their new homes into homestays. The contact person for this initiative is Li Jinlong. He doesn't speak English but he can get someone to translate English emails for him. Advance bookings are a must.

All two-storey houses are brand new and look alike. Usually the hosts live on the ground floor while guests stay on the 2nd floor. Dinner is an extra NT$350. Rooms are basic but clean.

The village is in Majia County. From Shuimen, follow the signs to the Aboriginal Culture Park. Before the entrance to the park, switch to County Rd 35. The village is right after the Km2.5 mark.

Pingshan Hotel HOTEL $
(屏山旅館, Píngshān Lǚguǎn; ☎799 1803; http://087991803.tranews.com; 339 Jungshan Rd, Shuimen Village, 水門村中山路339號; d from NT$1200) There are few frills but rooms are comfortable, clean and quiet. It's on the northern part of the main drag, Jungshan Rd, in Shuimen, but just south of the channel.

Qiuyue Restaurant CAFE $$
(秋月的店, Qiūyuè de diàn; 150 Jhongjheng Rd, Sec 2; dishes from NT$150; ⏰10am-midnight; 📵) A beautiful cafe perched on the cliff with a huge terrace overlooking the valley. The bathrooms have a terrific view. The cafe is after the Km24 mark on Hwy 24 (if you go uphill).

Drinking & Nightlife

Gu Liu Fang CAFE
(古琉坊, Gǔ Liú Fang; 31 Chenggong Rd, Shuimen Village; coffee from NT$180; ⏰10am-5pm Mon-Sun) At the front, it's a shop selling indigenous clothing and handicrafts; the back is a cute cafe that serves excellent coffee from Dewen. It's a three-minute walk from Pingshan Hotel. Turn left from the hotel, cross the bridge and take another left.

Getting There & Around

Driving or riding north on County Rd 185 takes you to Maolin Recreation Area. It's best to have your own vehicle to get here and around.

Beidawushan 北大武山

A side route off County Rd 185 south of Sandimen takes you to the trailhead to Beidawushan (Běidàwǔshān), the most southerly mountain in Taiwan, which rises to over 3000m. A holy peak, home to spirits of the Rukai and the Paiwan, it now requires a tough two-day hike to reach it, instead of the easy overnight excursion it once was, after the huge landslide caused by Typhoon Morakot pushed the trailhead much lower and further back. From the summit you can observe both the Pacific Ocean and the Taiwan Strait, and look down upon a reserve that might be the last refuge of the clouded leopard.

The trail to the summit is about 12km in length. Signposts are in both English and Chinese.

Activities

The new trailhead is 2km south of the old one, and begins at an elevation of 1160m. In an hour or two of steep climbing (400m up) you'll reach the old trailhead. From here the trail is wide and clear, and it's a 4km hike to **Kuaigu Cabin** (aka Cedar Valley Lodge), which has running water, flush toilets and a campground. Note that you need to reserve online with a Taiwanese ID should you want to stay in the cabin (but not the campground). Allow yourself six hours to go from the new trailhead to the campground, as you're looking at a 1000m climb. Formosan macaques and flying squirrels can be spotted en route.

The next day you need to be on the trail by 6am. Expect a lot of switchbacks, with some tricky rope sections before the ridge. Some highlights include a **1000-year-old red cedar** (with a 25m circumference), a Japanese-era shrine, and forests of rare hemlock spruce. Keep your eyes open for **raptors**: grey-throat eagles, crown eagles and black kites are all fairly common.

The last couple of hours to the summit run along a wooded ridgeline. It is not particularly challenging to navigate this section. The summit is the end of the line and you simply retrace your steps to reach the trailhead.

Getting There & Away

You need your own vehicle to get to the new trailhead and we aren't going to promise that you won't get lost at least a few times getting here. As you ride along County Rd 185 heading south, turn left just past the Km40 mark, heading towards the hills and Jiaping Village (佳平村, Jiāpíng Cūn), also known as Taiwu Village.

One kilometre up the hill, stop at the police station to apply for mountain permits. From then on, consult a good map.

Jin-Shui Ying Old Trail 浸水營古道

This Qing-dynasty road (Jìnshuǐ Yín Gǔ Dào) once started at Fangliao and crossed the entire southern part of the island. Today it still covers about half of the island and takes a full six hours of downhill walking to reach the end of the trail near Dawu on the east coast. Along the way you pass the remains of a Qing-dynasty army camp, a nature preserve and a rich butterfly valley near the suspension bridge at the end of the trail.

The trail begins in the mountains east of Fangliao and runs along a jungle that receives the second-highest rainfall in Taiwan. You have a good chance of spotting local wildlife en route, including the Formosan macaque, the Reeves' muntjac, wild boar, wild pangolin and over 80 species of birds.

The last section of trail after the suspension bridge is washed out and it's a bit tricky to navigate the new paths over the ridge and onto the back roads to Dawu. Only during the winter months you can walk the last 5km stretch along the dry bed of the Dawu River, almost 1km across at this point.

To hike the trail you need a police permit and your own transport.

Kenting National Park 墾丁國家公園

08

Kenting National Park (Kěndīng Guójiā Gōngyuán) attracted massive attention first as one of the settings for Taiwanese director Wei Te-sheng's hit movie *Cape No. 7* in 2008, and later for Ang Lee's *Life of Pi* in 2012. But long before this period of cinema-fuelled tourism spike, the park, which occupies the Hengchun Peninsula (the entire southern tip of Taiwan), was already drawing in flocks of visitors who came to swim, surf, snorkel and dive, visit museums, hike and enjoy a little nightlife – all year round. The average January temperature is 21°C and it's usually warm enough for you to swim. In July it can get to a scorching 38°C.

Low mountains and hilly terraces prevail over much of the land in the park, along with rugged high cliffs and sandy deserts. The swimming beaches with yellow sands and turquoise waters are wonderfully suited to recreation, and sightseeing on a scooter or bicycle is highly enjoyable.

The park is a sanctuary for wildlife, including the reintroduced sika deer. In autumn, migratory raptors can be spotted overhead in the tens of thousands, and these are just a few of the 310 bird species recorded in the park.

GREAT MIGRATIONS

With 39 species representing seven families, Kenting National Park has the highest diversity of land crabs in the world. The crustaceans that leave their solitary burrows in the inland areas for the coast, normally between August and October, are driven by a clear purpose: to breed and spawn.

You can easily spot them between Sail Rock and Eluanbi on Hwy 26 during the spawning season and, needless to say, crushed crabs are a common sight. The park now closes parts of the road in the evenings when the spawning season is at its peak (usually during the Mid-Autumn Festival, ie the full moon in September or October) and volunteers are recruited to help escort the crabs cross the highway. During other times, drive slowly to help protect this declining population.

Twitchers will be happy to know that during the land-crab migration, they can see hawks take off en masse at dawn.

The national park covers 180 sq km. At the time of writing only the area of Eluanbi required entrance fees, but there were plans to charge entry to more sites from 2014.

Sights

Kenting Forest Recreation Area SCENIC AREA
(墾丁森林遊樂區, Kěndīng Sēnlín Yóulèqū; admission NT$150; ⏲8am-5pm) Once an undersea coral reef, the forest area is now a quirky landscape of limestone caves, narrow canyons and cliff walls strangled with the roots of banyan trees. It's one of the most visited places in the park, so try to arrive early.

Sheding Nature Park WILDLIFE RESERVE
(社頂自然公園, Shèdǐng Zìrán Gōngyuán; ⏲8am-5pm) FREE This well-protected expanse of scrubby hills and open grasslands is a favourite with picnickers and ecotourists. The reintroduced sika deer is often spotted in the brush, as are endemic bird species, dozens of butterfly species (in particular, colourful swallowtails) and even wild boar.

National Museum of Marine Biology MUSEUM
(國立海洋生物博物館, Guólì Hǎiyáng Shēngwù Bówùguǎn; www.nmmba.gov.tw; 2 Houwan Rd, Checheng; admission NT$450; ⏲9am-6pm) The

Kenting National Park & Around

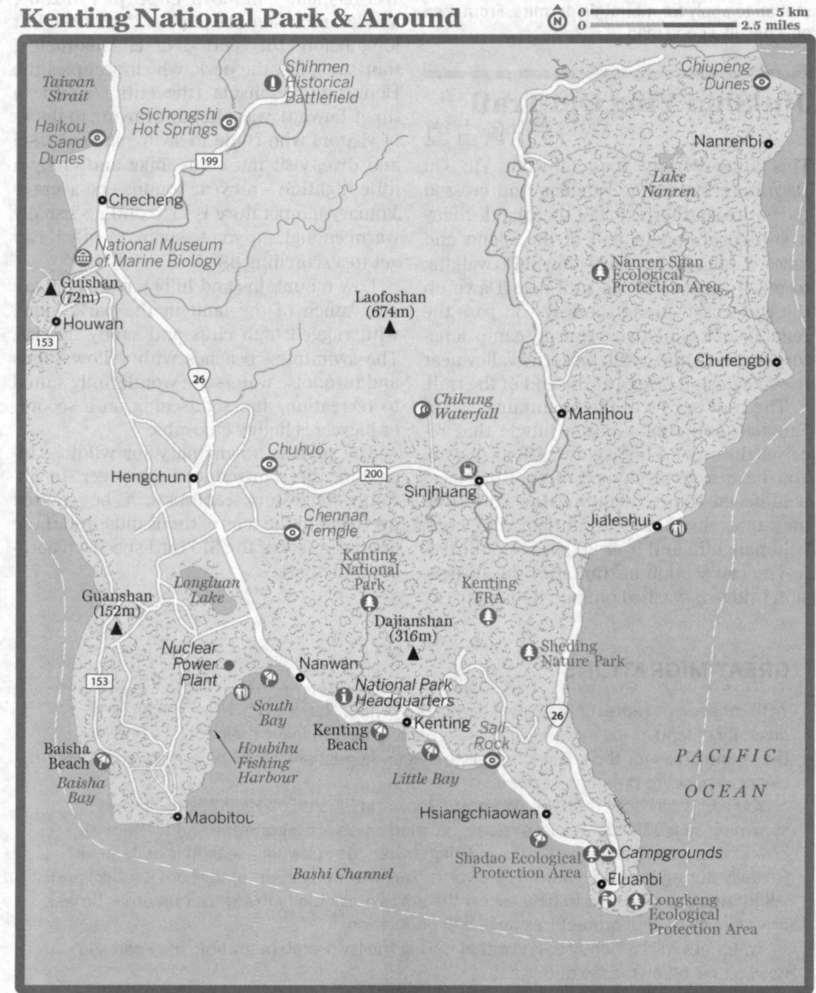

museum is rated highly by visitors for the live displays of incredibly diverse marine life that are professionally and imaginatively designed.

Jialeshui SCENIC AREA

(佳樂水, Jiālèshuǐ; admission NT$100; ⏲8am-5pm) A 2.5km-long stretch of coral coastline with rocks eroded into quirky shapes.

Reserve Areas

The park maintains strict access controls over ecologically sensitive regions, such as the area around **Lake Nanren** (Nánrén Hú) and the beautiful coastal area at **Longkeng** (Lóngkēng). You can apply on the park's website for permits to enter these areas.

Activities

Swimming

Taiwan's waters have treacherous currents and undertows not far offshore. Some sound advice from a long-term expat is to go no deeper than where your feet can still touch the sand.

Kenting Beach is the longest swimming beach in the area.

The beach across from the Caesar Hotel is smaller but set in picture-perfect **Little Bay** (小灣, Xiǎowān). It has a beach bar and showers (free for Caesar Hotel guests, a nominal fee for others). This beach is very family oriented.

The vibe at **Nanwan** (南灣, Nánwān, South Bay) is young and brash. The beach has been cleaned up a lot but expect tractors on the beach, and jet-ski heroes making runs at the sand with complete disregard for whoever might be in their way.

The sweet little crescent beach at **Baisha Bay** (白砂灣, Báishā Wān) is a little further afield but is now in the limelight after Ang Lee shot parts of *Life of Pi* here. Still, it's the least crowded beach around.

Jumping off the chin (and other protuberances) of **Sail Rock** (船帆石, Chuánfán Shí), aka Nixon Rock, and swimming round the landmark is also a popular swimming option.

Surfing, Snorkelling & Diving

The waters around **Jialeshui** and the nuclear power plant at **Nanwan** have the best surfing waves. Jialeshui is by far the more laid-back and less crowded of the two. You can hire surfboards (NT$800 per day) almost everywhere.

> **SANDIMEN TO KENTING NATIONAL PARK**
>
> The top attraction in the south is Kenting National Park, and getting there is half the fun if you take the right route. The most delightful way to reach Kenting, and the only way to go by bike, is to start in Sandimen and ride to Fangliao on County Road 185. This absolutely idyllic road runs flat for 46km. From Fangliao, it's another 50km to the edge of Kenting. There's bad traffic on this stretch, but you can minimise it by taking the coastal roads into Kenting once you pass Checheng.

For snorkelling, check out the coral formations near **Sail Rock**. You can hire gear across the road.

For snorkelling and scuba tours, as well as lessons, contact **John Boo** (☎0913-388 065; scuba_diving1@yahoo.com).

Birdwatching

With 310 species of birds, Kenting is a twitchers' paradise, and the National Park HQ has several good birdwatching brochures. **Eluanbi** (鵝鑾鼻, Éluánbí), **Sheding Nature Park** and Manjhou are prime spots. **Longluan Lake** (龍鑾潭, Lóngluántán) has an educational **visitor centre** and observation area.

The Hengchun Peninsula is one of the most important sites for raptor migration in East Asia and is one of the top 20 raptor-migration sites worldwide. In a single autumn day, over 50,000 raptors have been recorded flying overhead. Among the more famous to sail the Kenting skies are the Chinese goshawks and grey-faced buzzards. Goshawks start arriving early to mid-September on their journey south to Indochina. The best time and place to see them is morning in Sheding Nature Park.

Around 10 October, grey-faced buzzards pass through the park, also on their way to Indochina. The best times and places to see these 'National Day Birds' are Sheding in the mornings, and Manjhou between 3pm and 6pm.

Cycling

Hengchun Peninsula is one of Taiwan's best cycling destinations, and it's important to choose the right route to avoid the pollution in the industrial area. Hwy 26 from

COUNTY ROAD 199

This idyllic country road rewards at every turn with a rich history and a varying landscape of hills, ponds, farms, aboriginal villages and open fields. It's a preferred route for those continuing at a leisurely pace on to the east coast (Hwy 9 is faster but thick with speeding buses and trucks), or vice versa.

The first historical sight of note is the **Tomb of Ryukyuan Sailors** (琉球藩民墓, Liúqiú Fānmín Mù) just off County Rd 199 near the Km36 mark (look for the Japanese-style stone lantern on the roadside). It's a collective tomb of 54 sailors from Ryuku (today's Okinawa), murdered by Paiwan aborigines in 1871. The incident subsequently ignited the battle between the Japanese and the Paiwan in Shihmen in 1874. Note that the first three characters on the stele, literally saying 'Greater Japan', have been blotted out.

Heading east, **Sichongsi (Szchongshi) Hot Springs** (四重溪溫泉, Sìchóngxī Wēnquán) is a real treat, and a soak in an outdoor pool in the cooler evenings is especially recommended.

Seisen Hot Spring (清泉日式溫泉館, Qīngquán Rìshì Wēnquánguǎn; 5 Wenhua Rd; unlimited time NT$220; ⏲6am-11pm) was a honeymoon destination for the then Japanese crown prince Hirohito and his wife in 1915. The Japanese *onsen*, now restored, has lovely indoor and outdoor pools. It's accessible via the alley next to the 7-Eleven.

East of Sichongsi, on a high meadow, the **Shihmen Historical Battlefield** (石門古戰場, Shímén Gǔzhànchǎng) is worth a visit more for the views than for any historical remains. After this, for the next few dozen kilometres just kick back and enjoy as the road winds and curves through an ever-thickening forest cover. Human settlements are few, but flocks of endemic birds such as the Taiwan partridge are often seen by the roadside.

Just before the coast, you have the choice of taking 199甲 to the photogenic grasslands around Syuhai (Xùhǎi), or continuing up the 199 to Hwy 9 and turning left to reach **Shuangliou Forest Recreation Area** (雙流森林遊樂區, Shuāngliù Sēnlín Yóulèqū; www.forest.gov.tw). The park offers an easy day hike with two trails to some gorgeous waterfalls and wooded hills.

Checheng to Kenting is congested and best avoided.

The 100km-long **Kenting coastal loop** is a popular and scenic cycling route. From Checheng, take County Rd 153 along the coast down to Nanwan; from there, swtich to Hwy 26 and head east to Jialeshui. The roads are usually not busy and run through a beautiful landscape of beaches and coastal bluffs. From Jialeshui, the 200 takes you back to Hengchun via beautiful Manjhou.

At Checheng, another good alternative is to head east on County Rd 199, one of the sweetest rural roads in the south.

Festivals & Events

Spring Scream MUSIC

(www.springscream.com) Indie-music fans should definitely try to time their Taiwan visit for April when Spring Scream takes over Kenting. The country's longest-running music festival, this multistaged event brings together names big and small in Taiwan's indie-music scene, along with some imported bands. It's currently held in Eluanbi.

Sleeping

Summer (approximately May to September), Chinese New Year and other public holidays are considered the high season. Discounts of 40% or more for midrange and top-end hotels are standard on weekdays and during the low season.

KENTING VILLAGE

Kenting Village has the lion's share of hotels along the main strip (usually charging less than NT$1000 on low-season weekdays) but this street is a noisy, charmless place to stay.

Kenting Youth Hostel HOSTEL $

(淳青背包客棧, Chúnqīng Bèibāo Kèzhàn; ☎886 1409; www.ktyh.com.tw; 243-1 Kenting Rd, 墾丁路243-1號; dm NT$499; 📶) This backpacker hostel is nothing to write home about but the beds and the bathrooms are reasonably clean. All rooms are windowless but there are ACs. It's the cheapest yet decent option in the park, so it fills up quickly, especially on weekends. The hostel is next to KFC.

Tz Shin Resort Hotel HOTEL $$
(澤信旅店, Zéxìn Lǚdiàn; ☎276 006; http://tzshin.myweb.hinet.net; 260 Dawan St, 大灣路260號; d from NT$2400) Dawan St has a row of stylish three-storey B&Bs all facing onto the car park and the beach. To reach this street, turn right just past McDonald's as you enter Kenting Village. At Tz Shin, rooms are spiffy and feature large beds and big windows. Low-season midweek prices for a single traveller can go down to NT$850.

Chateau Beach Resort RESORT $$$
(夏都沙灘酒店, Xiàdū Shātān Jiǔdiàn; ☎886 2345; www.ktchateau.com.tw; 451 Kenting Rd, 墾丁路451號; r from NT$7780; @ 🏊) There's a light, breezy, whimsical and secluded feel to the pastel-coloured Chateau, the only resort in Kenting to sit right on the beach. Room interiors could have come from anywhere, but the dazzling views of the sea and mountains are pure Kenting.

SAIL ROCK

Hainan Island Resort B&B B&B $$
(海南島精品旅店, Hǎinándǎo Jīngpǐn Lǚdiàn; ☎885 1689; 668 Sail St, 船帆路668號; d from NT$2400; 📶) This three-storey B&B boasts rooms with middle-class levels of comfort and design, and large balconies from which to enjoy coastal views. It's to your left just 50m past the 7-Eleven as you enter the Sail Rock area.

JIALESHUI

Winson House GUESTHOUSE $$
(☎880 1053; www.tbay.com.tw; 244 Chashan Rd, 茶山路244號; dm/d NT$700/2500) Run by the well-known local surfer Winson, this guesthouse finally had a facelift and provides reasonably comfortable rooms and beds. Surfing lessons are available, as are surf tours and equipment hire. The surfing beach, considered the best in the Kenting area, is just down the hill from the house, 100m before the toll booth into Jialeshui.

Hotel de Plus BOUTIQUE HOTEL $$
(☎880 2277; www.hoteldeplus.com; 36 Xinghai Rd, 興海路36號; d from NT$3000; 📶) You won't miss this photogenic hotel on your way to Jialeshui. Behind the whitewashed facade there are 12 rooms, each individually decorated in a bright, minimalist style, and they come equipped with high-quality designer furniture and ocean views to boot. The 1st-floor cafe serves good grub and cocktails.

SHADAO

You can pitch a tent at one of the privately run **campgrounds** (per person NT$150) facing the beach of Shadao. All provide bathroom facilities.

HENGCHUN

Surf Shack HOSTEL $
(☎0958-856 645; www.taiwansurfshack.com; 224 Hengnan Rd, Hengchun, 恆春鎮, 恆南路224號; s/d without bathroom NT$400/800; 📶) Run by a Canadian and his local wife, this hostel-cum-restaurant pulls in a young, fun crowd from all over the world. The owners are a fount of knowledge of Kenting's aquatic secrets. Rooms are basic but clean. It's a 10-minute walk south from the Hengchun bus station and it's to your left. Breakfast is NT$200.

Eating & Drinking

Kenting Village is a tourist town and there is no shortage of food, including Thai, Italian and even South African. Prices are reasonable and most places are open late. Many restaurants, such as Warung Didi's and Amy's, also serve as bars (beer from NT$150), with music played loudly in the evenings. The **Caesar Hotel** (Kǎisà Dà Fàndiàn; beer from NT$140; ⏰11am-10pm) runs an outdoor bar-cafe on Little Bay Beach.

Hengchun and the strip in Nanwan are also loaded with restaurants, while Sail Rock has big seafood joints.

Warung Didi THAI, MALAYSIAN $$
(迪迪小吃, Dídí Xiǎochī; ☎886 1835; 26 Wenhua Lane, Kenting Rd, Kenting Village; dishes NT$200; ⏰5.30pm-1am) This long-running restaurant draws crowds every night with the promise of excellent Thai and Malay curries, good music, beer and a lively beach atmosphere. Reservations recommended on weekends.

Amy's Cucina ITALIAN $$
(Nánxīng Dàfàndiàn; 131-1 Kenting Rd, Kenting Village; dishes NT$240; ⏰10am-late) This was the first place in Kenting to serve pizza and it still has some of the best Italian food in the park. Its casual design makes it suitable for hanging out and enjoying a nice meal.

Bossa Nova Beach Cafe CAFE $$
(巴沙諾瓦, Bāshānuòwǎ; 100 Nanwan Rd, Nanwan; dishes NT$180; ⏰11am-late; 📶) This cafe sits on the main drag in Nanwan, across from the beach. Sandwiches are filling. Should you want to stay in the Nanwan area, the cafe also runs a B&B.

OLD ALANGYI TRAIL: EXPENSIVE EXERCISE

The 12km stretch of coastline between Syuhai (旭海, Xùhǎi) in Pingtung County and Nantian (南田, Nántián) in Taitung County is the last coastline in Taiwan that hasn't yet been paved by highways. **Alangyi Old Trail** (阿塱壹古道, Ā lǎngyī Gǔdào), which follows this coastline and boasts magical ocean-meets-mountains views, is a spectacular five-hour hike. The trail was first used by the aborigines, then by both the Qing soldiers and civilians during the 1870s to commute between the east coast and Hengchun Peninsula. It remained relatively undisturbed until the 2000s, which was when the government proposed a plan to add a highway to bridge the southern and eastern coasts of Taiwan.

The highway, if built as planned, would significantly save travel time and could serve as an alternative route if Hwy 9 (which links the eastern and western coasts) is closed due to frequent rockslides. However, the plan sparked a public outcry, as the road would run alongside the trail, stealing away not only its natural beauty and serenity, but also putting 49 protected species, including the endangered sea turtles, under serious threat.

After several rounds of tug-of-war between development and conservation, in 2012 Pingtung County Government finally declared that section of the coastline to be a nature reserve, and the construction of the highway was halted – a victory for the wildlife and ecosystem of the coast.

The trade-off? Trail quotas (a maximum of 300 people a day) are imposed and an exorbitant guiding fee of NT$3000 (for a group of no more than 20 people) is mandatory even if you are hiking alone and the trail is just a single track. And it's unlikely that the guide will speak English.

Permits have to be applied for online one month in advance from **Pingtung County Government** (www.pthg.gov.tw/Syuhai/index.aspx). A heads-up: even if you are planning to start at Nantian in Taitung County, you still have to apply for the permit, otherwise you'll be subject to a hefty fine of NT$30,000.

Zuo'an Homestay & Campground (左岸民宿露營區, Zuǒ'àn Mínsù Lùyíngqū; ☎0931-942 126; www.5658.com.tw/0931942126/default.aspx; 1-3 Syuhai Village, 旭海村1-3號; per tent NT$450, d from NT$1400) in Syuhai can help arrange permits and transport to the trailhead and back if you stay there. It's located where 199甲 meets Hwy 26, right opposite the police station.

Syuhai is on the eastern end of 199甲. Pingtung Bus has two buses (NT$116) leaving from Hengchun to Syuhai at 6am and 4pm.

ℹ Information

There's free wi-fi at the National Park Headquarters, and you'll find ATMs in the 7-Elevens in Kenting Village.

National Park Headquarters (國家公園管理處; ☎886 1321; 596 Kenting Rd; ⊙8am-5pm) You'll find English-speaking staff and several useful English brochures and maps. The centre is a few kilometres north of Kenting so you'll probably need to check into your hotel and rent a scooter before visiting.

ℹ Getting There & Away

BUS

From Kaohsiung, the Kenting Express (2½/3½ hours NT$413/$383) leaves every 15 minutes. Buses from the HSR station are less frequent (NT$413, three hours, every hour). Both buses are nonstop from Kaohsiung to Kenting Village, but they take different routes. Kenting Express goes via Hwy 88, which has less traffic.

TAXI

Taxis take groups of passengers from the main train station in Kaohsiung to Kenting Village for NT$350 per person (1½ hours). Single travellers can wait until the taxi fills, which usually doesn't take long. However, it's difficult for a single traveller to take a shared taxi from the HSR (per person NT$400) unless your hotel has arranged this.

ℹ Getting Around

Kenting Shuttle Bus (墾丁街車, Kěndīng Jiēchē) has four routes; it runs roughly every 30 minutes and stops at almost all major sights in the park. A day pass costs NT$150. Hotels can arrange car, 4WD or scooter rental. Scooter-rental shops (per day NT$400 to NT$500) are to the right as you enter Kenting Village from the north. Some shops now refuse to rent to travellers unless they have a Taiwanese driver's licence.

Taiwan's Islands

Includes ➡

Best Wildlife Spots

- ➡ Hungtou Eco-Education Trail (p310), Lanyu
- ➡ Across Mountain Trail (p314), Green Island
- ➡ Lake Tai (p288), Kinmen

Best Village Homestays

- ➡ Qin Inn (p288)
- ➡ Banli Dazhai Homestay (p297)
- ➡ Erkan B&B (p307)

Why Go?

Taiwan's outlying islands have yet to give in to mass tourism. There's plenty to discover off the grid, from unspoiled golden-sand beaches to secluded mountain trails and coves where you'll see more wildlife than other travellers.

Kinmen and Matsu, lying in the Taiwan Strait, have preserved some of the country's oldest villages and a rich legacy of Cold War struggles that saw the islands turned into battlefields. Today, it's also a twitcher's dreamland. Lanyu, Taiwan's furthest outpost, combines a volcanic landscape with the deep charms of an indigenous people living off the sea.

In Green Island and Penghu, divers and beach lovers will find much to like about the perfect sand beaches, pristine waters and coral reefs. Each location has a top draw you won't find anywhere else: Green Island boasts one of the world's rarest seawater hot springs, while Penghu is Asia's top windsurfing destination.

When to Go

Makung (Penghu Island)

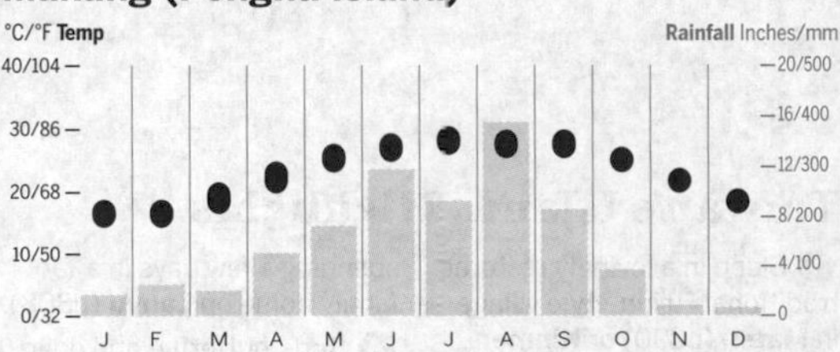

Mar–May Flying Fish Festival on Lanyu, the most important yearly event for the Tao people.

Apr Welcoming the City God parade on Kinmen, a vibrant pilgrimage.

Sep–Mar World-class windsurfing around Penghu.

Taiwan's Islands Highlights

1. Sleep in a lovingly restored traditional Fujian-style village in **Matsu** (p290) or **Kinmen** (p281).

2. Indulge yourself in **Chaojih Hot Springs** (p314), a rare seawater spring just off the beach on Green Island.

3. Absorb the traditional seafaring way of life by spending a few days in a Tao family home on **Lanyu** (p308).

4. Bird-, butterfly- and deer-watch in the parks and on the ponds and beaches of Taiwan's islands.

5. Windsurf in **Penghu** (p298), a windswept archipelago of almost 100 islands.

6. Dive the dreamy waters of **Green Island** (p313), home to more than 200 species of coral.

7. Delve into the remains of the Cold War between the Chinese communists and Nationalists, on **Kinmen** (p281).

National Parks & Forest Recreation Areas

Though you'll find higher mountains and larger stretches of green in Taiwan proper, the outer islands have things well covered when it comes to parkland. Reforested Kinmen itself is a national park, and there's talk of eventually turning Green Island into one, too. Mountainous Lanyu is almost entirely covered by forests, and its indigenous Tao inhabitants are quite militant about fighting any improper development. Most of the Penghu Archipelago consists of volcanic islands covered with low-lying cacti and other succulents. Trees in Penghu's Lintou and Chitou Parks tend to all grow at a pronounced angle thanks to the persistent wind.

KINMEN

☎082 / POP 116,570

Kinmen (金門, Jīnmén), lying only 2km off the coast of mainland China, is an odd remnant from the bitter civil war between communist and Nationalist forces. Along with Matsu, Kinmen is a small chunk of Fujian province occupied by Republic of China (ROC) forces and administered from Taiwan. This once heavily guarded island now greatly appeals to military history buffs, but in fact, has something to offer to every visitor.

Well-restored villages dating from the Ming and Qing dynasties can still be found in Kinmen today; they retain an old world charm not found anywhere in the rest of Taiwan. Also, the pollution-free islands boast open fields, sandy beaches, thick forests, landscaped parks and artificial lakes that attract hundreds of species of migratory birds. Cyclists and twitchers will find paradise here.

Kinmen is a fairly well-developed place. Roads double as runways (just in case!) so they are wide and well-maintained. Parks are everywhere, and in general the atmosphere is relaxed. But don't forget the fact that Kinmen remains a military outpost – restricted areas still exist.

History

Settlers began arriving on Kinmen as early as the Tang dynasty (AD 618–907). Originally called Wuzhou, it was changed to Kinmen (literally 'Golden Gate') after fortified gates were put up to defend the island from pirate attacks. During the Ming (AD 1368–1644) and Qing (AD 1644–1912) dynasties, increasing numbers of Chinese migrants settled on Kinmen's shores. The Ming loyalist Koxinga, also known as Cheng Cheng-kung, used Kinmen as a base to liberate Kinmen and Penghu from the Dutch. In the process, he chopped down all of Kinmen's trees for his navy, something the residents still grumble about. Koxinga's massive deforestation made Kinmen vulnerable to the devastating soil-eroding winds that commonly sweep across the strait.

Kinmen remained fairly peaceful until 1949, when Chiang Kai-shek transformed the island into a rear-guard defensive position against the communist forces that had driven his own Nationalist army off the Mainland. Though his original plan was to have his soldiers recuperate on the island before launching a full-fledged attack on Mao Zedong's armies, this never happened. Instead, the island became the final flashpoint of the Chinese Civil War and was subjected to incessant bombing from the Mainland throughout the 1950s and '60s.

Since martial law was lifted from Kinmen in 1993, this once off-limits military zone has turned into a national park and a tourist destination. Demining efforts on the island were finally completed in 2013.

ℹ Getting There & Away

AIR

In spring **Kinmen Airport** (www.kma.gov.tw) is often fogged in, leading to cancelled flights; in summer you'll need to book ahead. Flights operate to/from Taipei (one-way NT$2220), Kaohsiung (one-way NT$2120) and other west-coast cities with **Mandarin Airlines** (www.mandarin-airlines.com), **TransAsia Airways** (www.tna.com.tw) and **Uni Air** (www.uniair.com.tw).

BOAT

At the time of writing, foreign travellers could use the hourly ferry service to Xiamen (NT$750, 80 minutes) provided they had a visa for China in their passport. Tickets available at Kinmen Airport.

ℹ Getting Around

TO/FROM THE AIRPORT

Kinmen Airport is 8km east of Kincheng city. The hourly Bus 3 service links Kincheng, Shanwai and the airport. From the airport to Kincheng taxi drivers charge a flat fare of NT$250.

Kinmen

0 — 5 km
0 — 2.5 miles

CHINA
Mashan Observatory
Kuanao
KINSHA DISTRICT
Weitou Bay
Hsiyuan
Mt Lion Howitzer Station
Shanhou Folk Culture Village
Hsishanchien Village
Shamei
Tunghen Village
Bishan
Pupien
Chingtien Reservoir
Yangchai
Toumen
Huandao North Rd
Mt Taiwu (262m)
Mt Taiwu Cemetery
Neiyang
Huandao East Rd
KINHU DISTRICT
Qionglin Village
Lan Lake
Ming Lake
Shanwai
Chungyang Hwy
Lake Tai
August 23 Artillery War Museum
Hsipien
Hsinshih
Huchien
Military Brothel Exhibition Hall
Hsiahsing Village
Chenggong Village
Liaolo Bay
Tung Tsun
Liaolo
Hsinhu Fishing Harbour
TAIWAN STRAIT
Kinmen Airport
KINMEN
Beishan Broadcasting Station
Shuangli Lake
Nanshan
Guningtou War Museum
Shuangli Wetlands Area Centre
Beishan
Lake Ci
Angqi
Huhsia
KINNING DISTRICT
Huandao North Rd
Houpanshan
Tingpao
Boyu Rd
Peimen
Panglin
Hsimen
Kincheng
Tungmen
Kinmen Harbour
Koxinga Shrine
Juguang Tower
Juguang Lake
Huandao South Rd
Sihu Beach
Shuitou Harbour
KINCHENG DISTRICT
Shuitou Village
Jhushan Village
Tungsha
Ou Cuo Beach
Wuntai Pagoda
Takukang
Kukang Lake
Jhaishan Tunnels
Little Kinmen (Liehyu Island)
Huchingtou War Museum
LIEHYU DISTRICT
Huangtso
Hsiamen Harbour
Hsihuang
Pata Memorial
Tunglin
Lingshui Lake
Shanglin
Siwei Tunnel
Qing Yuan Lake
Chinchih

BICYCLE

Free-to-hire bicycles are available at many locations around the island. Obtain a map from the visitor information centre at the airport or Kincheng bus station.

BUS

Buses run around the island every one or two hours between 6am and 5pm. Schedules and destinations are posted in the bus stations in Kincheng, Shanwai and Shamei.

CAR & SCOOTER

Kinmen has very little traffic and the easiest way to see the island is by car or scooter. Vehicles can be rented at the airport (cars/scooters from NT$1300/400 per day). Cars can also be rented in Kincheng (ask at your hotel).

TAXI

Drivers prefer to ask for a flat fare rather than use the meter. Taxi tours cost NT$3000 a day; it's unlikely your driver will speak English.

TOURIST BUS

Four tourist bus routes – each taking about three hours to complete – serve the island's major sights. Buy tickets at the tourist information centres by the Kincheng or Shanwai bus stations.

Kincheng (Jincheng) 金城

Kincheng (Jīnchéng) may be the busiest town on the island, yet it's still a very laid-back place that's filled with winding alleys, brick-paved market streets, temples and old architecture.

Sights

Kincheng is a great place to explore on foot.

★Kuei Pavilion HISTORIC SITE

(奎閣, Kuí Gé; 44 Zhupu East Rd; 8.30am-5pm) Built in 1836 for the worship of the god of literature, the elegant two-storey pavilion is surrounded by a number of stately Western-style buildings and a whole neighbourhood of old dwellings connected by narrow lanes. The pavilion is down a side alley to the left just past the Memorial Arch to Qiu Liang-Kung's Mother. It's a bit of a maze but there are signs and the pavilion is no more than 100m from the arch.

Mofan Street HISTORIC SITE

(Mófàn Jiē) Built in 1924, the buildings on this charming little street have brick exteriors and arched door fronts modelled after both the Japanese and Western architecture that was in fashion back in the day.

Memorial Arch to Qiu Liang-Kung's Mother HISTORIC SITE

(Qiū Liánggōng Mǔ Jiéxiào Fǎng) Qiu Liang-Kung was a Kinmen native who rose to become governor of China's Zhejiang province. He erected this Kincheng landmark in 1812 to honour his mother who chose to live 28 years as a widow instead of remarrying after his father's death.

Kinmen Qing Dynasty Military Headquarters HISTORIC SITE

(清金門鎮總兵署, Qīng Jīnménzhèn Zǒngbīngshǔ; 53 Wujiang St; 10am-8pm) This is the oldest surviving Qing government building in Taiwan. It's lit at night with lanterns.

Wu River Academy HISTORIC SITE

(Wú Jiāng Shū Yuàn; 35 Zhupu North Rd; 9am-5pm) FREE This walled complex was built in 1780 to house one of Kinmen's ancient schools. Inside, the **Chutzu Shrine** (朱子祠, Zhūzǐ Cí) honours neo-Confucian scholar Chu Hsi, who sought a revival of Confucian values during the Sung dynasty (AD 960–1279).

Festivals & Events

Welcoming the City God TRADITIONAL FESTIVAL

On the 12th day of the fourth lunar month the **City God Temple** (城隍廟, Chénghuáng Miào) in Kincheng hosts this mass festival. A parade runs down the western side of the island and you'll find traditional opera and dancing, fireworks and costumed troupes en route. One unique part of the festival involves children dressed as characters from history and mythology. Depending on the village the kids will be riding on tricycles or rickshaws.

Sleeping

A number of homestays have opened up in restored dwellings in the traditional villages around Kinmen. These are infinitely preferable to the uninspiring hotels in Kincheng, though you'll still be likely to return to town for meals.

Ru Yi Jia HOMESTAY $

(如一家, Rúyìjiā; 322 167; ru.jia@msa.honet.net; 35-1 Zhupu North Rd, 珠浦北路35-1號; d/tw NT$1280/1980;) A friendly homestay right in the heart of Kincheng. Rooms feature modern decor and furnishings. It's almost directly across from the old Wu River Academy.

Kincheng

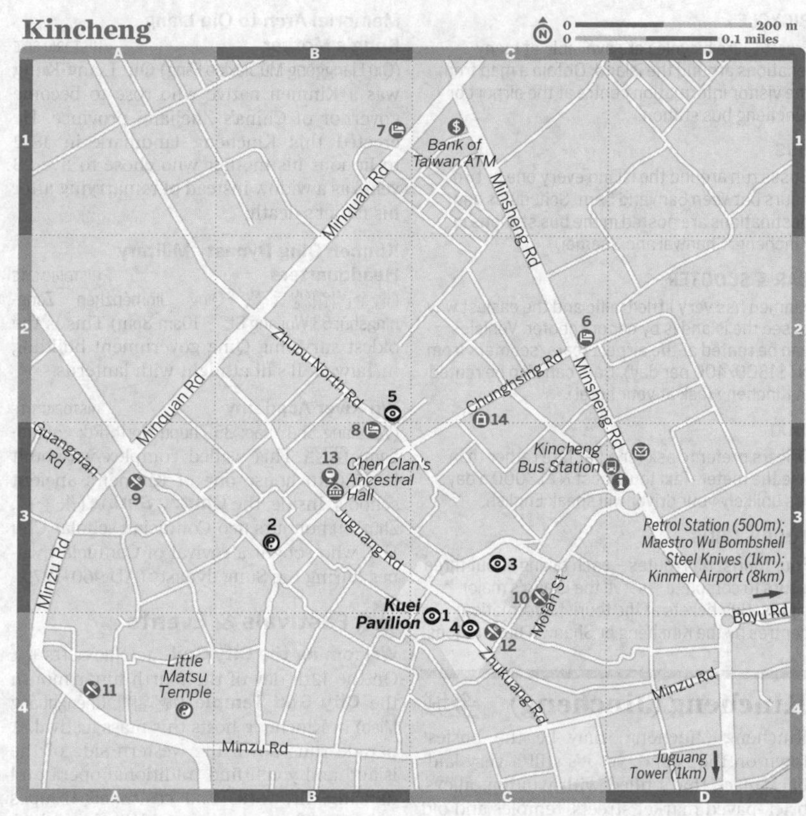

Kincheng

Top Sights
1 Kuei Pavilion C4

Sights
2 City God Temple B3
3 Kinmen Qing Dynasty Military Headquarters C3
4 Memorial Arch to Qiu Liang-Kung's Mother C4
5 Wu River Academy B2

Sleeping
6 In 99 Hotel C2
7 Quemoy Hotel B1
8 Ru Yi Jia B3

Eating
9 Damiaokou A3
10 Jessica's Restaurant C3
11 Niu Jiazhuang A4
12 Shou Ji Kuangtung Zhou C4

Drinking & Nightlife
13 White Lion Café Pub B3

Shopping
14 Kinmen Minsu Wenwu Chih Jia C2

In 99 Hotel HOTEL $$
(精品旅館, In jiǔshíjiǔ Jīngpǐn Lǚguǎn; ☎324 851; www.in99hotel.com; 16 Minsheng Rd, 金城 民生路16號; d/tw incl breakfast NT$1800/2200; ❄📶) An interior facelift has turned this centrally located business hotel into a decent mid-range choice. Rooms are small but clean, and modernly furnished. It's just down the road from the Kincheng bus station.

Quemoy Hotel HOTEL $$
(金瑞旅店, Jīnruì Lǚdiàn; ☎323 777; www.quemoyhotel.com.tw; 166 Minquan Rd, 金城 民權路 166號; d/tw NT$2000/2300;) Quemoy enjoys a good reputation among travellers and tour groups, meaning it's often fully booked. Rooms are unpretentiously well equipped.

Eating

The area around Mofan St is chock-a-block with small stands and eateries selling a variety of Kincheng snacks and sweets. Some of Kinmen's specialities include *gòng táng* (貢糖, hard candy), *miàn xiàn* (麵線, sticky rice noodles) and *chǎo shāchóng* (炒沙蟲, fried sandworms). Go to the market in the early morning or evening to get the best of what's on offer.

For small restaurants check out Juguang Rd and Minzu Rd. Minzu Rd is also loaded with fruit shops.

Niu Jiazhuang NOODLES $
(牛家莊, Niújiāzhuāng; 5 Lane 318, Minzu Rd; beef noodles NT$80; ⊙5-10pm) Different parts from a cow feature across the menu in this popular restaurant. The perennial favourite *níu'ròu miàn* (beef noodles) is cooked in the traditional Kinmen way. It's just off Minzu Rd down an alley across from the county stadium.

Shou Ji Kuangtung Zhou CHINESE $
(壽記廣東粥, Shòujì Guǎngdōng Zhōu; 50-1 Zhukuang Rd, Sec 1; congee NT$60; ⊙6.30am-noon) While Chinese rice porridge hardly makes an instant hit with Western travellers, this well-loved restaurant has been ladling up bowl after bowl of fabulous Cantonese-style congee for the past 80-plus years. Locals favour the *zhū dù* (pig stomach) congee but there are other varieties available.

Jessica's Restaurant TAIWANESE $$
(戀戀紅樓, Liànliàn Hóng Lóu; 24 Mofan St; set meals NT$180-250; ⊙10am-10pm) This place is extremely funky, with walls covered in political art representing both sides of the cross-Strait conflict. Set meals are great value and rather tasty. The menu features hot pot, rice dishes and a fair amount of pseudo Western fare.

Damiaokou SEAFOOD $$
(新大廟口, Xīn Dàmiàokǒu; cnr Minquan & Guangqian Rds; dishes NT$80-200; ⊙5pm-midnight) This restaurant serves up some mighty fine seafood. Weather permitting, management sets up tables so guests can sit outside and feast next to the **Waiwu Temple** (外武廟, Wàiwǔ Miào).

Drinking & Nightlife

White Lion Café Pub BAR
(Báishīzi Jiǔbā; 7 Lane 110, Juguang Rd; ⊙6pm-midnight Mon-Thu, 4pm-midnight Fri-Sun) Run by a Canadian-Taiwanese couple, this small pub is the spot to start the night with good craft beers. It's located next to the Chen Clan's Ancestral Hall.

Shopping

A potent liquor made from sorghum and sharp knives constructed from spent shell casings lobbed over from the Mainland are the island's most famous products.

At 58 proof, Kaoliang liquor (Gāoliáng jiǔ) is sold all over the island; try a few shots at a local bar before purchasing any serious quantities to take home. As for the knives, these unusual souvenir items are made from melted-down artillery shells and are some of the best cutting knives. The knives are available all over Kinmen and come in various shapes and sizes.

Kinmen Minsu Wenwu Chih Jia SOUVENIRS
(金門民俗文物之家, Jīnmén Mínsú Wénwù Zhī Jiā; Lane 1, 124 Chunghsing Rd; ⊙8am-7pm) A wonderful curio shop in central Kincheng, where you can find all sorts of ceramic knick-knacks, dishes and one-of-a-kind items to take home.

Information

Bank of Taiwan ATM (台灣銀行; Minsheng Rd) On the west side of Minsheng Rd, just before Minquan Rd.

Kinmen County Tourism (www.kinmen.gov.tw) Excellent online resource for background on sights and general cultural information.

Visitor Information Centre (遊客服務中心; ⊙9am-9.30pm) Located beside the bus station; has brochures and information on free bike rentals and bus tours.

Around Kincheng

Kinmen is easy to get around by bike or scooter. This 20km-long island is a national park dotted with ancient towns, battlefield monuments, lakes and forests. We recommend you spend at least two days on the island if you want to see what it has to offer.

Sights

Kinmen has the best collection of old dwellings in one small area in all Taiwan. In seven of the villages, much of the original feng-shui-beholden layout and clan structure can still be found; elsewhere, newer constructions stand unobtrusively among old yet well-maintained houses.

Kinmen's traditional dwellings feature the long, elegant swallowtail roof that you usually find only on temples elsewhere. The reason for this is that Kinmen was once a very wealthy place and swallowtail roofs symbolise high social position.

Many of Kinmen's old houses also feature fabulous-looking high gable fronts, which are usually painted with traditional symbols. Moreover, there are many more dwelling features like stone courtyards and woodcarvings to take in. To enjoy these beautiful clusters of architecture, spend a night in one of the renovated old dwellings, or simply go village-hopping by bike.

With its beautiful lakes, forests and bird sanctuaries, Kinmen truly is, as locals say, 'a garden built upon a fortress'. So much so that the island attracts visitors with no interest in military history.

Juguang Tower HISTORIC SITE

(莒光樓, Jǔguāng Lóu; ⊙8am-10pm) Just southeast of Kincheng, this three-storey tower, built in 1952 as a memorial to the fallen soldiers of Kinmen, should be your first stop for an overview of the rich history and culture of Kinmen. The 1st floor covers food, architecture and wind lions; the 2nd floor is dedicated to the Welcoming the City God festival; and the 3rd explains the origin of the tower itself.

★Shuitou Village ANCIENT VILLAGE

(水頭村, Shuǐtóu Cūn) The 700-year-old community of Shuitou Village boasts one of the best collections of old houses, both Chinese- and Western-style, in all of Taiwan.

There are over 100 western buildings around Kinmen, all built by Kinmen emigrants who made a bundle across Southeast Asia during the late 19th and early 20th centuries. The **Deyue Mansion** (得月樓, Déyuè Lóu), probably the most famous, was built in 1931 by the Huang clan (the earliest settlers in Shuitou) and features an unmistakable four-storey gun tower that was for years Kinmen's tallest structure.

The Huang clan also built the rows of traditional Fujian houses near Deyue Mansion. Follow the signs from Deyue Mansion to **Youtang Villa** (酉堂, Yǒu Táng), a 200-year-old former school that is a fine example of traditional design.

Jhushan Village ANCIENT VILLAGE

(珠山村, Zhūshān Cūn) During the late 19th century emigrants from Jhushan Village made huge profits from trading and shipping in the Philippines and sent much of it back to build the gorgeous houses you see today. In the centre of the village is a large brick-lined pond; at the back a hillock. In the world of feng shui it doesn't get much better than this potent wealth-retaining arrangement.

Beishan & Nanshan ANCIENT VILLAGE

The two villages of Beishan (北山, Běishān) and Nanshan (南山, Nánshān) around Shuangli Lake – and Lake Ci is just a little further away – retain much of their old character, adding a charming backdrop to the lakes.

The most visited of the old dwellings is the **Beishan Old Western-style House** (北山古洋樓, Běishān Gǔ Yánglóu). It's still riddled with bullet holes from the Guningtou battle in 1949 (p287). To find the house, head straight when you see the sign for the turn-off to the 'Nature Centre' (the Shuangli Wetlands Area Centre). The house is about 100m further up the road.

Shanhou Folk Culture Village ANCIENT VILLAGE

(山后民俗文化村, Shānhòu Mínsú Wénhuà Cūn) Shanhou consists of 18 Fujian-style buildings, all interconnected by narrow alleys. The village was built over a 25-year period in the late Qing dynasty; money made in Japan funded the construction. Go in the morning if you want to take pictures – the back of the village faces west and the late-afternoon sun makes it difficult to shoot.

Qionglin Village (Cyonglin or Chiunglin) ANCIENT VILLAGE

(瓊林村, Qiónglín Cūn) Qionglin Village in Kinhu is famous for having more shrines than any other village on Kinmen. Head off the main road for the best atmosphere and buildings.

Chenggong Village (Cheng Kung) ANCIENT VILLAGE

(成功村, Chénggōng Cūn) The major attraction in Chenggong Village is the splendid Western-style **Chen Ching Lan's Mansion**

DON'T MISS

WATCHING THE MAESTRO AT WORK

Living under bombardment has taught the people of Kinmen to make the best of things. One place where you can see this done with unique aplomb is at the **Maestro Wu Bombshell Steel Knives** (金合利鋼刀, Jīnhélì Gāngdāo; 236 Bóyù Rd, Sec 1; ⏲8.30am-6.30pm). It's here where old propaganda-laden shells lobbed by the communist Chinese in the 1950s and '60s are transformed into one-of-a-kind knives. The spent casings are shaped into beautiful steel blades for both kitchen and ornamental use. Prices start at around NT$950, and if you want to watch yours being made, don't come between noon and 2pm – that's when Maestro Wu rests.

The current Maestro Wu is the third generation owner of his family business, which was founded in 1937. He studied smithing and weapon crafting under the tutelage of his father (another Maestro Wu, as the title is passed down). Wu says unlike regular shells, which are designed to shatter into killing fragments, propaganda shells are ideal for making knives because they are made of high-grade steel, designed to split neatly open and demoralise the opponent.

(陳景蘭洋樓, Chénjǐnglán Yánglóu). It was built in 1921 by the eponymous businessman with the fortunes he made in Southeast Asia. The awe-inspiring architecture was later turned into a hospital and then a recreation centre for military officers during wartimes. It's now a museum with dull displays of the building's history.

Guningtou War Museum MUSEUM
(古寧頭戰史館, Gǔníngtóu Zhànshǐ Guǎn; ⏲8.30am-5pm) FREE Guningtou was the site of a ferocious battle between the communists and the Kuomintang (KMT) in 1949. The museum, on the actual battlefield site, provides a glimpse into a conflict that saw 5000 soldiers from both sides lose their lives over a 56-hour period. Beishan and Nanshan, two villages nearby, still bear the scars of the battle on some old buildings. It's to the right before the turn-off for the Shuangli Wetlands Area Centre (marked 'Nature Centre' on the road sign).

Beishan Broadcasting Station MILITARY SITE
(北山廣播站, Běishān Guǎngbò Zhàn) About 1km north of the Guningtou War Museum, the now defunct Beishan Broadcasting Station stands on a cliff right by the sea. The concrete wall boasts 48 speakers, each with a reported range of 25km, that used to crank out propaganda like 'Our steamed buns are bigger than your pillows!' to the communists. These days, the speakers prefer the more mellow numbers of the late Teresa Teng, Taiwan's best-loved songbird.

Jhaishan Tunnels HISTORIC SITE
(翟山坑道, Zhaíshān Kēngdào; ⏲8.30am-5pm) FREE Blasted out of solid granite by soldiers in the early 1960s, these tunnels stretch 357m to the ocean and were designed to protect boats from bombs during wars. You can walk through the spooky interior or follow a bridge over the entrance that leads to the piers.

August 23 Artillery War Museum MUSEUM
(八二三戰史館, Bā Èr Sān Zhànshǐ Guǎn; ⏲8.30am-5pm) FREE This museum documents the horrific battle that occurred on 23 August 1958, when the communists launched an artillery attack against Kinmen that lasted for 44 days and pummelled the island with almost 500,000 shells. Outside are fighter planes, tanks and cannons used during the siege.

Mt Lion Howitzer Station MILITARY SITE
(獅山砲陣地, Shīshān Pàozhèndì; ⏲8.30am-5pm) This recently opened military station carries multimedia displays of weapons used during the August 23 Artillery War in its 508m-long tunnel. The exhibition eventually leads you to the casemate where a howitzer is installed and a mock military drill is performed by volunteer residents and students six times a day. It's just 500m east of Shanhou Folk Culture Village.

Military Brothel Exhibition Hall MUSEUM
(特約茶室展示館, Tèyuē cháshì zhǎnshìguǎn; 126 Xiaojing, Jinhu; ⏲8.30am-5pm) Euphemistically called a 'special teahouse', this whitewashed complex used to be one of the brothels that were established on the island to entertain officers and soldiers stationed there between 1951 and 1990. Today, it's a museum documenting the teahouse's busiest years for guests of a different kind.

Lake Ci SCENIC AREA

(慈湖, Cí Hú) Saltwater Lake Ci did not even exist until the 1970s. Once an open harbour, the lake was formed after the Nationalists constructed a causeway along the western seashore following the battle of Guningtou. Today, the causeway is the perfect spot to take in the beautiful lake and its great variety of birds.

Lake Tai SCENIC AREA

(太湖, Tài Hú) Just south of Shanwai is Lake Tai, a 5m-deep body of water that was dug entirely by hand in the 1960s. The views from the south side take in Mt Taiwu, which from this angle looks far more imposing than its 262m height would suggest.

Mt Taiwu SCENIC MOUNTAIN

(Tàiwǔ Shān) The highest mountain on Kinmen, Mt Taiwu rises a colossal 262m above sea level. A road takes you about halfway up to a shrine and a **soldiers' cemetery** *(gōng mù)* built in 1952 to honour the ROC soldiers who died in battle.

From here a walking path takes you to the top (the walk takes about one hour). Be on the lookout for a famous stone inscription of one of Chiang Kai-shek's favourite one-liners, 'Wú Wàng Zài Jǔ' or 'Don't forget the days in Ju', which is an exhortation to recover the Chinese mainland based on a legend from the Warring States period in ancient China.

WIND LIONS

When you're travelling around Kinmen, you'll notice an abundance of stone lions. These are Kinmen's Wind Lions (風獅爺, Fēngshīyé), traditional totems said to have the power to control the winds and keep the land fertile. According to locals, these totems began appearing after Kinmen was deforested to build Koxinga's navy around the early Qing era (early 17th century). The locals, forced to turn to supernatural aid as the denuded soil of their island ceased bearing crops, began placing the lions around the island. The Wind Lions can still be found in almost every village around the island. Many stand upright and are draped in flowing capes.

For a complete list with locations, check out http://tour.kinmen.gov.tw.

Koxinga Shrine SHRINE

(延平郡王祠, Yánpíng Jùnwáng Cí) To the southwest of Kincheng sits the Koxinga Shrine, built in memory of the Ming general who fought against the Dutch occupation. As you leave the temple, turn right for 150m to find a lane running left down to the sea. This leads to a walkway over to an islet that you can reach during low tide.

Wuntai Pagoda HISTORIC SITE

(文臺寶塔, Wéntái Bǎotǎ) Considered one of the oldest constructions in Taiwan, the five-level hexagonal Wuntai Pagoda was built in 1387 for the Ming emperor Hungwu as a place to honour the stars and celestial deities.

Ou Cuo Beach & Sihu Beach BEACH

The connected beaches of Ou Cuo (歐厝沙灘, Ōu cuò shātān) and Sìhu (泗湖沙灘, Sìhú shātān) are two lesser-visited beaches on the southern side of the island. They are two of the few beautiful sandy beaches in Kinmen that didn't have anti-landing poles installed. There are no shower facilities though.

Sleeping

There are homestays aplenty around Kinmen, most offering rooms in dwellings over a century old. For a complete list (in Chinese only), see http://guesthouse.kmnp.gov.tw.

★**Qin Inn** HOMESTAY **$$**

(水頭一家親, Shuǐtóu Yījiāqīn; ☎0910-395 565; http://qininn.tumblr.com; 63-64 Shuitou Village, 水頭63-64號; s/d incl breakfast NT$1200/2400; ❄📶) Housed in a renovated traditional compound, this good-value B&B has seven pristine wood-beamed rooms. The host, Jiang Lin, is a conservationist and a fount of knowledge on architecture in Kinmen.

★**Piano Piano B&B** B&B **$$**

(慢漫民宿, Mànmàn Mínsù; ☎372 866; www.pianopiano.com.tw; 75 Jhushan Village, 珠山75號; s/d NT$1400/1800; ❄📶) In the splendid village of Jhushan is this charming B&B which offers both traditional- and contemporary-style rooms. There's a kitchenette for guest use.

Lexis Inn HOMESTAY **$$**

(來喜樓, Láixǐlóu; ☎325 493; http://lexisinn.blogspot.com; 82 Jhushan Village, 珠山82號民宿; s/d NT$1400/1600; ❄📶) This house in Jhushan was built in a Western style by emigrants who made their fortune in the Philippines in the 19th century. Rooms are simple but everything else is full of character, history and beauty.

BIRDWATCHING ON KINMEN

Lying along the migratory routes of hundreds of bird species and boasting a variety of habitats, Kinmen is rightly seen as a paradise for birdwatchers. Over 300 species of birds have been recorded, with about 40 resident species and the rest migratory. Lake Ci is one of the top twitching spots, especially in winter when thousands of great cormorants come to nest.

To the east, Lake Tai is a feeding ground for cormorants and ospreys, species best seen in the early morning. Later in the day look for the resident woodpecker-like hoopoe feeding in the grass of nearby Banyan Park.

On Little Kinmen, Lingshui Lake is a popular twitching venue. It's also a good place to spot fiddler crabs in the mudflats.

For more information on the birds of Kinmen, visit the **Shuangli Wetlands Area Centre** (雙鯉溼地自然中心, Shuānglǐ Shīdì Zìrán Zhōngxīn; ⌚8.30am-5pm), a research facility devoted to wetlands preservation. Also pick up a copy of *Birdwatching at Kinmen*, available at most visitor information centres.

Shuitiaogetou HOMESTAY **$$**
(水調歌頭, Shuǐdiào Gētóu; ☎322 389, 0932-517 669; www.familyinn.idv.tw/a01.asp; 40 Shuitou Village, 水頭40號; s/d incl breakfast NT$1800/2400) The rooms in this traditional Fujian-style house feature wood and red-brick interiors and lots of lovely old touches. The owner runs two other equally beautiful homestays in the same village.

Visit Kinmen Guesthouse HOMESTAY **$$**
(忘了飛民宿, Wànglefēi Mínsù; ☎352 058; www.visit-kinmen.com; 84 Shanhou Village, 山后84號; d incl breakfast NT$1600) Should you want to stay on the eastern side of the island, this Fujian-style house located right behind Shanhou Folk Culture Village (p286) has four rooms offering modern comforts and private facilities. The hosts speak English and are knowledgeable birdwatchers.

Eating & Drinking

Some of the smaller towns have a noodle shop or restaurant and there are a few 7-Elevens on strategic corners. It's probably best to carry lunch if you're going out all day.

Cheng Gong Dumplings TAIWANESE **$**
(成功鍋貼館, Chénggōng Guōtiēguǎn; 99-5 Chenggong Village; dumpling per piece NT$7, dishes from NT$160; ⌚11am-2pm & 5-8pm Wed-Mon) This nondescript eatery in Chenggong Village is famous for its *guōtiē* (鍋貼, pan-fried dumplings) and oyster omelettes. From Chen Ching Lan's Mansion (p286), head back to the main road (Huangdao Rd), turn right, and it's two blocks on the left off the main road.

Jin Shui Restaurant TAIWANESE **$$**
(金水食堂, Jīnshuǐ Shítáng; 48 Shuitou Village; dishes from NT$200; ⌚11am-2pm & 5-9pm) Right beside Deyue Mansion in Shuitou Village (p286), this much-loved restaurant is famous for its taro and *Yùtou pâigǔ* (pork ribs stew), a local speciality.

Quemoy Garden Cafe CAFE
(金門苍園, Jīnmér Huāyuán; 126 Xiaojing; coffee from NT$100, pastries from NT$70; ⌚midday-6pm Wed-Mon; 📶) From the patio of a former 'military brothel', this lovely cafe serves arguably the best coffee in Kinmen. They also do refreshing teas and pick-me-up juices.

Little Kinmen (Liehyu Island) 小金門

If Kinmen is an outpost, then Little Kinmen (Xiǎo Jīnmén), the common name for Liehyu Island (Lièyǔ Xiāng), is an outpost of an outpost. This 15-sq-km patch of land west of the main island is so close to the People's Republic of China (PRC) that mobile phones automatically switch to Fujian-based networks when you arrive. Pretty and windswept, Little Kinmen is an island park that just happens to sit atop the 1958 war's last front lines.

Sights & Activities

Cycling is the best way to see Little Kinmen and the price can't be beat – the Kinmen tourism department loans visitors bikes for free! Just head left towards the Siwei Tunnel when you get off the boat from Kinmen and head up the stairs to the main Liehyu visitor information centre (not the one at the harbour).

Little Kinmen's perimeter is ringed by an 18.5km bike path passing through lovely forests and coastal scenery. There are a couple of small stores that sell local specialities such as deep-fried oyster cakes, but you'd be wise to carry a lunch with you.

Siwei Tunnel HISTORIC SITE
(四維坑道, Sìwéi Kēngdào; ⏲8.30am-5pm) FREE This is the top tourist attraction on the island. The 790m underground Siwei Tunnel, which was blasted through a granite reef, is twice as large as the Jhaishan Tunnels on Kinmen. The Liehyu visitor information centre is right next to the tunnel entrance.

Lingshui Lake SCENIC AREA
(陵水湖, Língshǔi Hú) The pretty, artificial, saltwater Lingshui Lake is home to a number of species of waterbirds native to Fujian province.

Huchingtou War Museum MUSEUM
(湖井頭戰史館, Hújǐngtóu Zhànshǐ Guǎn; ⏲9am-5pm Tue-Sun) FREE The Huchingtou War Museum contains war memorabilia and an observation room with binoculars from which you can see Xiamen on a clear day.

Warriors' Fort & Iron Men's Fort MILITARY SITE
(勇士堡和鐵漢堡, Yǒngshìbǎo Hé Tiěhànbǎo; ⏲8am-5pm) The two intact forts in Huangtso were built in the 1970s and each has a web of underground tunnels, including a 200m-long one that connect the two structures.

Getting There

There are frequent ferries from Shuitou Harbour on the main island (NT$60, 20 minutes) to Little Kinmen (7am to 9pm). From Little Kinmen to Shuitou Harbour, ferries operate between 6.30am and 8.30pm.

MATSU

☎0836 / POP 11,300

Look no further than this green archipelago of 18 islands right off the coast of mainland China's Fujian province if you're seeking the off-the-beaten-path Taiwan. Like Kinmen, Matsu (馬祖, Matzu) retains much of its feel as a perpetual military outpost. The Matsu vibe is a bit more martial, however, and half the people you run into here are in uniform. Be prepared to scurry down narrow tunnels and, emerging to the clear light of day, enjoy a superb ocean lookout with a real 80mm anti-aircraft cannon at your side.

The people of Matsu speak a dialect derived from Fuzhou in mainland China, which is mostly unintelligible to speakers of Taiwanese. Most folk identify with their kin across the narrow strait that separates

THE AUGUST 23RD ARTILLERY WAR

In August 1955, Sino–US talks about the status of Taiwan had left China feeling bitter and angry. The US insisted that Beijing renounce the use of force against Taiwan. China retorted that Taiwan was Chinese territory and it had the right to liberate it from Chiang Kai-shek. Dead centre in the dispute, Taiwan declared a state of emergency and prepared for the full force of a Chinese attack.

That came on the morning of 23 August 1958, as Beijing launched a ferocious bombardment on Kinmen. In just two hours the island was hit with over 42,000 shells. Alarmed, the US realised that if Kinmen fell, Taiwan would likely be next, so it swiftly sent the Kuomintang (KMT) a shipment of jet fighters and anti-aircraft missiles, plus six supporting aircraft carriers, in order to strengthen the island's defence.

China created a tight blockade around Kinmen's beaches and airstrip in an effort to prevent any military supplies from reaching the Nationalist military. In response, the US sent several warships into the Taiwan Strait to escort a convoy of Taiwan military supply ships. The convoy got within 5km of the blockade and was surprised that the communists refused to fire.

Instead, Beijing offered Taiwan a very odd ceasefire – it would fire on Kinmen only on odd-numbered days. On even-numbered days the island would be left alone. The Chinese held to the ceasefire and continued to bomb Kinmen throughout September and October on odd-numbered days. By November tensions had eased and the bombing stopped. Tragically, almost 500,000 shells had struck Kinmen, killing over 3000 civilians. More than 1000 soldiers were also killed or wounded.

them. For over a generation they could only watch their brethren in Fuzhou through binoculars; today, the latter forms a substantial part of the visitor population.

Matsu islands are grouped into townships; the main townships, which are connected by ferries, are Nangan, Beigan, Dongyin and Jyuguang.

History

The development of Matsu began in the 1400s with the arrival of Fujianese mainlanders escaping political turmoil in their homeland. The migrant waves of the 1600s from mainland China to Taiwan saw an increase in Matsu's population as boatloads of Fujianese fishermen arrived on the island. They brought with them the language, food, architecture and religious beliefs of their ancestors, much of which is still around today.

Throughout the 1700s and 1800s piracy plagued the islands, causing residents at various times to temporarily abandon their homes to seek shelter elsewhere. Matsu was largely politically insignificant until the Nationalists fled to Taiwan in 1949 and established Matsu, along with Kinmen, as a front-line defence against the communists. The quiet islands were transformed into battlefields and the Mainland bombed Matsu intermittently until the deployment of the US 7th Fleet in 1958 prevented any further escalation.

Martial law was lifted from Matsu in 1992, a number of years after it was lifted over in 'mainland' Taiwan. In 2001, when the 'Three Small Links' policy was instituted, Matsu (along with Kinmen) became an early stepping stone in cross-Strait travel, permitting direct trade and travel between ROC- and PRC-controlled territories. Cross-Strait direct flights were started in 2008, and the government is now set on transforming this military zone into a major tourist destination.

In 2012 the residents of Matsu approved gambling on their island in a referendum, and a draft bill governing casino operations was railroaded in 2013. However, few people believe that a casino is ever going to be built as the bad weather often shuts down transport, making access to Matsu unreliable. The government has also said that the casinos will not open until 2019 at the earliest. Many speculate that this was just a trial run for what would be much more controversial referendums to introduce casinos to Kinmen and, eventually, Penghu.

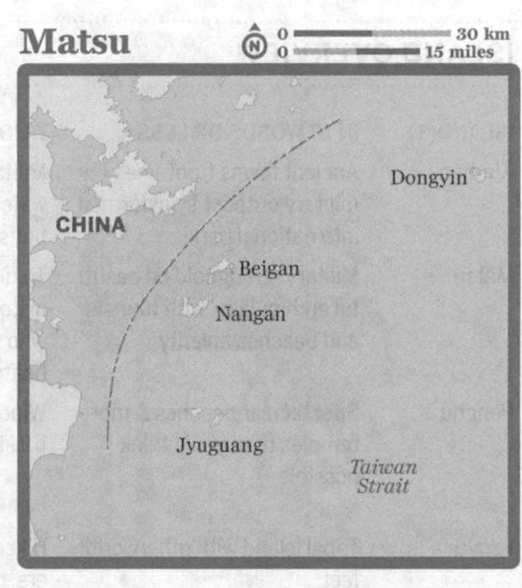

Dangers & Annoyances

Travellers in Matsu, especially Nangan, should be mindful of the fact that live-firing exercises are conducted regularly. Warning signs should be obeyed and straying too far off marked roads is a bad idea.

Nangan 南竿

The largest island in Matsu, Nangan (Nángān, Nankan) is a veritable hive of activity compared with the rest of the archipelago. Nangan's biggest settlement is **Jieshou Village** (介壽村; also spelled Chiehshou), which is where you'll find places to rent scooters and the island's only bank. The walk to Jieshou from the airport takes about 20 minutes. Ferries to outlying islands leave from **Fu'ao Harbour** (福澳港, Fúaò Gǎng), just a few kilometres northwest of Jieshou. The central bus station is in Jieshou Village, at the end of the main road just before the start of the seaside park.

Sights

The main roads of Matsu roll with the hilly terrain. Riding on a scooter means endless pretty scenes unfolding before your eyes, in particular the deep-blue sea dotted with green islets, and it's well worth the petrol. The northwestern corner of Nangan is a particularly lovely area.

Matsu is replete with forts, tunnels and sights connected with the islands' important

ISLAND OVERVIEW

ISLAND(S)	IN 10 WORDS OR LESS	WHO SHOULD GO	BEST TIME TO VISIT
Kinmen	Ancient towns front-line military outpost transformed into national park	Military enthusiasts, cyclists, bird-watchers, traditional-architecture buffs	Summer, autumn
Matsu	Military stronghold on beautiful archipelago, with tunnels and beaches aplenty	Traditional-architecture buffs, war historians, butterfly lovers, people who want to get seriously off the beaten path	Summer, autumn
Penghu	Spectacular beaches & more temples than you'd think possible	Windsurfers, beachcombers, spiritual travellers	Spring, summer, autumn, (winter if you like high winds)
Lanyu	Tribal island with otherworldly feel	Hikers, butterfly lovers, birdwatchers, those interested in authentic aboriginal culture	Spring, summer, autumn
Green Island	Yesterday's prison, today's playground	Political-history enthusiasts, snorkellers, divers, hot-spring lovers	Year-round (but it's crowded in summer)

position in the struggles between communist and Chinese Nationalist forces. Authorities claim the islands have the highest concentration of tunnels and warrens in the world. Some of these sites are now open for tourism; expect more in the coming years.

Temples in Matsu are largely uninspiring modern restorations, interesting more for their histories than anything else. Some, however, do sport striking-looking high gable ends that jut up like waves on the ocean, or licking flames. In fact, the roofs are called fire walls, and you'll not find them anywhere else in Taiwan.

Not surprisingly, numerous Matsu temples can be found on Matsu's islands. Many feature statues of the goddess as a sweet-faced young woman, which is something found only in this part of Taiwan as her likenesses elsewhere in the country are invariably dark-faced.

Most sights and activities on the islands are free.

Iron Fort MILITARY SITE

(鐵堡, Tiě Bǎo) One of the most impressive military sites is the abandoned Iron Fort, a rocky strip of coral jutting out over the sea and hollowed out to house Matsu's amphibious forces. Visitors are allowed to enter and have a look at the spartan living quarters of the soldiers who once lived there.

Be sure to look out over the ocean through sniper slots. Gruesome stories are told by Matsu residents of how Mainland frogmen would sneak inside the fort at night, slit the throats of the Taiwanese guards on duty and carry back an ear to show their comrades.

Beihai Tunnel MILITARY SITE

(北海坑道, Běihǎi Kēngdào; ⏲8am-5pm Mon-Fri) Carved out of a sheer rock face by soldiers using only simple hand tools, construction of this 700m tunnel began in 1968 and took three years to complete, with many losing their lives in the process. It was used as a hiding place for military boats and is supposedly large enough to hide 120 small vessels in case of attack. Kayaks are available for rent (NT$350) to paddle through the slightly mazy layout inside the tunnel.

Dahan Stronghold MILITARY SITE

(大漢據點, Dàhàn Jùdiǎn) Just across a rocky beach from the Beihai Tunnel is Dahan Stronghold, a fortification built directly into a granite peninsula. A warren of narrow and low tunnels leads visitors to emplacements where real 80mm anti-aircraft cannons and machine guns peak out from caves overlooking the sea.

Fushan Illuminated Wall MILITARY SITE

(枕戈待旦, Zhěngē Dàidàn) Overlooking Fu'ao Harbour is the Fushan Illuminated Wall, a concrete billboard that faces mainland China and warns communist forces to 'sleep on spears'. Translation: Chiang Kai-shek is coming to get you (one day).

Matsu Temple TAOIST TEMPLE
(馬祖天后宮, Mǎzǔ Tiānhoù Gōng) This particular Matsu Temple is considered one of the most sacred spots in Taiwan. Legend has it that during an attempt to save her father from a shipwreck, Matsu herself drowned and was washed ashore here. Show up on Matsu's birthday (the 23rd day of the third lunar month) for a lavish festival in her honour.

Matsu Cultural Village RELIGIOUS
(媽祖宗教園區, Māzǔ Zōngjiào Yuánqū) The brand new Matsu Cultural Village, a cultural and religious complex with a colossal 29m statue of the goddess atop the hill to the northeast of the temple, should be opened by the time you read this book.

Huakuang Tati Temple TAOIST TEMPLE
(華光大帝廟, Huáguāng Dàdì Miào) In the Ming dynasty, a villager dreamt that the god of fire told him an incense burner was buried in Fu'ao. The man later discovered it and Huakuang Tati Temple was built in the god's honour.

White Horse God Temple TAOIST TEMPLE
(白馬文武大王廟, Báimǎ Wénwǔ Dàwáng Miào) The small White Horse God Temple is devoted to a deified general who once defended Fujian. During storms a mysterious light appears to guide ships.

Jinsha Village ANCIENT VILLAGE
This collection of beautiful old stone houses lies just back from the sea in a sheltered cove. The bunker by the entrance to the beach is filled with paintings that bear the classic KMT propaganda slogan: 'Fight against the communists, resist the Russians, kill Zhu De, and remove Mao Zedong'.

Matsu Folklore Culture Museum MUSEUM
(馬祖民俗文物館, Mǎzǔ Mínsú Wénwùguǎn; 135 Qingshui Village; ⌚9am-5pm Tue-Sun) FREE With many old photos, artefacts, life-size dioramas and interactive films, this four-storey museum is a good introduction to the culture and lifestyle on Matsu. The displays are visually appealing and there are now more English explanations than before.

Activities

Matsu Distillery DISTILLERY
(馬祖酒廠, Mǎzǔ Jiǔchǎng; 208 Fuxing Village; ⌚8.30-11.30am & 1.40-5pm Mon-Fri, 1.40-4.40pm holidays, last tour 40min before closing) FREE The factory produces two of Matsu's best-loved products: *Gāoliáng jǐu* (高粱酒, Kaoliang liquor), made from sorghum, and *làojiǔ* (老酒, medicinal rice wine). There's honestly not much to see, but tagging along a Chinese-language tour allows you to partake of the samples that are given out liberally at the end of each session.

Bird- & Butterfly-Watching

Matsu's offshore islets attract thousands of breeding terns in the spring and summer months. In 2000, the area around Snake Island, a tiny bit of land off the northwestern shore of Xijju, was declared a **tern reserve** and serious twitchers can hire boats to take them around this and other locations. See www.birdingintaiwan.org for more.

Matsu is one of the best places in summer to see a variety of Taiwan's large and exquisite **swallowtail butterflies**. You don't need to search for them because there are colonies literally everywhere. Most of what you'll see are common species such as **Great Mormons** but the sheer numbers floating about roadside will astound anyone with the slightest naturalist impulses.

Some places to see them swarm in the hundreds are the coastal road past Jinsha Village, the road up from the **Chiang Ching-Kuo Memorial**, and the road to **Yuntai Mountain** (Yúntái Shān; 248m), Nangan's highest peak. Butterflies are for the most part quite used to people and you can get up pretty close for photos.

Sleeping

Homestays are springing up in the villages of Fuxing, Jinsha and Qingshui, which have restored their traditional houses to make the towns a better match to the lovely surroundings. There are also a few inns and hotels in Nangang should you prefer staying in conventional accommodation.

Matsu 1st Hostel HOSTEL $
(馬祖1青年民宿, Mǎzǔ Qīngnián Mínsù; ☎23353; www.matsuhostel.com; 71 Jinsha Village, 津沙村71號; per person NT$900; ❄📶) Housed in a beautiful Fujian-style stone house, this hostel offers capsule-style female-only rooms as well as four-bed and eight-bed mixed dorms. All are basic but spotless. The rate includes pick-ups, breakfast and scooter rental. To top it off there's a small swimming beach 50m down the road.

Nangan

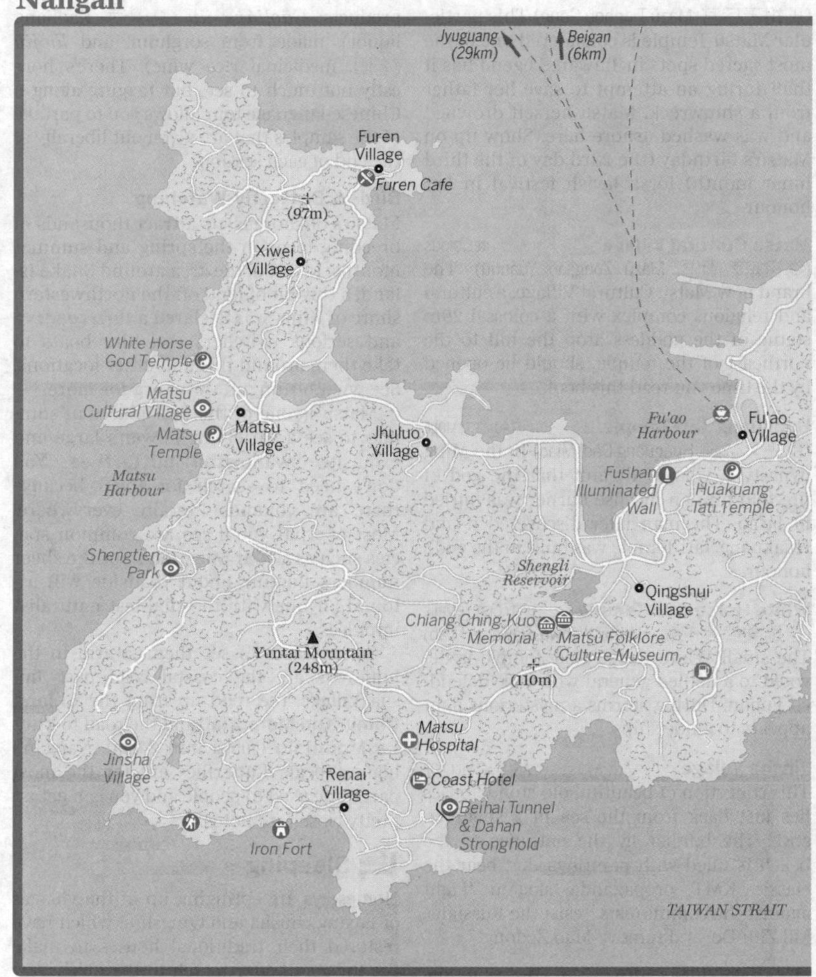

Niulan Homestay HOMESTAY $
(牛嵐民宿, Niú lán Mínsù; ☎215-898; http://tour.matsu.idv.tw/hotel_niulan.php; 124 Fuxing Village, 復興村124號; s/d NT$800/1000; ❄📶) Niulan has seven rooms, three of which are wood-plank rooms in an artsy traditional village house while four newer ones are in a concrete building next door. The alfresco terrace boasts good views of the village and the coast. It's just a five-minute walk (downhill) from Matsu Distillery.

Listen Sea Homestay HOMESTAY $$
(聽海民宿, Tīnghǎi Mínsù; ☎23003; http://tour.matsu.idv.tw/hotel_listensea.php; 32 Jinsha Village, 津沙村32號; d from NT$1200; ❄📶) The dull, grey stone exterior of this former village home may not look inviting, but the wooden interior structure is well preserved and the four double rooms are airy and comfortable. The sunny terrace out the front demands lazy afternoons spent enjoying coffee.

Coast Hotel BOUTIQUE HOTEL $$$
(日光海岸海景旅館, Rìguāng Hǎiàn Hǎijǐng Lǚguǎn; ☎26666; www.coasthotel.com.tw; Renai Village, 仁愛村; s/d/ste incl breakfast NT$3200/3500/4200; ❄📶) This small bou-

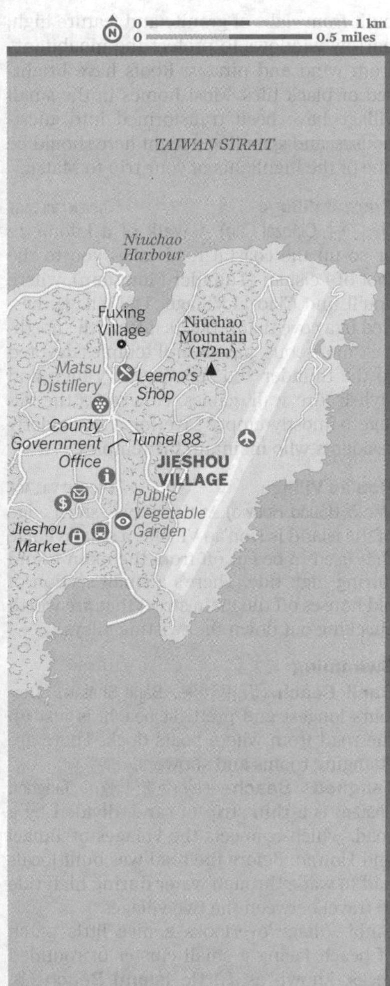

tique hotel boasts a Japanese minimalist design, sweeping ocean views, and an excellent restaurant and coffee shop serving both Western and Asian dishes.

Eating

There are a number of Taiwan-style restaurants along the main streets in the villages of Jieshou, Matsu and Fu'ao. The morning market in Jieshou (Jièshòu Shìzi Shìchǎng) is a good place for a traditional breakfast including fish noodles, oyster pancakes and a variety of cakes.

Furen Cafe CAFE $
(夫人咖啡館, Fūrén Kāfēiguǎn; www.furen.com.tw; 40-1 Furen Village; dishes NT$150; ⏲10am-10pm) This cafe cum hostel serves excellent coffee and simple dishes on the stone patio overlooking the sea.

Leemo's Shop SEAFOOD $$
(依嬤的店, Yīmā de Diàn; http://hogoema.pixnet.net/blog; 72-1 Fuxing Village; set meals NT$350; ⏲11am-2.30pm & 5-8.30pm; ) Unless you come with a group your only option is the one *tǎocān* (set meal): all nine dishes of it, which includes in-season seafood, soup, vegetables and fruit.

To get to the restaurant, first head down the side road to the right of the Matsu Distillery (towards Fuxing Village, aka Niujiao Village). Take the first right (following the English signs to Leemo's) and then another right in 50m. Look for the stone house with big glass windows.

Information

Taiwan's tourism department has information booths at the airport, the ferry terminal and any number of attractions. There's now finally a small supply of English materials, including the super-informative brochure *Let's Backpack in Matsu*.

Internet access is less uncommon on the island now. The airport and most homestays provide wi-fi.

Bank of Taiwan (台灣銀行, Táiwān Yínháng; Jieshou Village) The only place in Matsu to change money; it also has a 24-hour ATM on the Cirrus network. You'd be smart to take what you expect to spend on Matsu.

Getting There & Away

AIR

Uni Air (www.uniair.com.tw), and only Uni Air, flies to Matsu. There are six flights daily from Taipei (NT$1962, 55 minutes) to **Nangan Airport** (Nángān Jīchǎng).

BOAT

Shinhwa Boat Company (☎ in Keelung 02-2424 6868, in Nangan 22395; www.shinhwa.com.tw) runs an overnight boat from Keelung (9.50pm, eight hours, NT$1000). Boat schedules alternate, going directly to Nangan one night and to Nangan via Dongyin the next. The service is very unreliable, however; expect cancellations without notice. Even the tourist information centres recommend you call *every day* to confirm sailings.

Getting Around

TO/FROM THE AIRPORT

It's a 20-minute walk to Jieshou or Fuxing Villages from the Nangan Airport; most hotels offer airport pick-up.

BUS

There are two bus lines on the island: mountain and shore. Services run hourly around the island (NT$15 per trip, from 6.10am to 5.45pm); schedules are posted at bus stops except, oddly, at the central bus station.

SCOOTER

Rental costs NT$500 per day, including petrol. The information counter at the airport can help with bookings, but you might have a hard time finding your hotel the first time, so it's probably best to get your hotel to help with scooter rental after you've checked in.

TAXI

Drivers are supposed to use the meter (NT$100 for the first 1.25km, NT$5 for every additional kilometre).

Beigan 北竿

A quick ferry takes you from Nangan to Beigan, a less boisterous island which boasts spectacular coastal scenery, fine beaches and wonderfully preserved Fujian villages you can stay in overnight.

Ferries to Beigan dock in Baisha Harbour. The island's largest settlement is **Tangci Village** (塘岐村, Tángqí Cūn, Tangchi). Beigan is relatively small, but with all the steep hills, rent a scooter if you want to see the whole place in a day.

Sights & Activities

★Peace Memorial Park MILITARY SITE

With its high, rocky peninsula, the eastern edge of Beigan was once an important part of the ROC's military defence of Matsu. The entire zone, now a memorial park, is one of the island's most intriguing military sites, consisting of many 'strongholds' where you'll find tunnels, foxholes, forts, outdoor displays of real tanks and anti-aircraft cannons pointing out to sea.

Cinbi Village ANCIENT VILLAGE

(芹壁村, Qínbì Cūn) Chief among the preserved villages of Beigan is Cinbi Village, comprising interconnected stone homes built into the side of Pishan (Bi Mountain), overlooking **Turtle Island**. The houses are built from slabs of granite and feature high, narrow windows to protect the inhabitants from wind and pirates. Roofs have bright-red or black tiles. Most homes in the small village have been transformed into guesthouses, and spending a night here should be one of the highlights of your trip to Matsu.

Ciaozai Village ANCIENT VILLAGE

(橋仔村, Qiáozǎi Cūn) A walk of a kilometre or so up the coastal road takes you to the foot of Leishan (Thunder Mountain), where you'll find Ciaozai Village. The village, nestled in a cove that protects it from the north-east monsoons, has several temples devoted to the thunder god sporting very high and stylish 'fire wall' gables. Nowadays the village is mostly empty save for a few elderly residents who maintain the temples.

Hou'ao Village ANCIENT VILLAGE

(后澳, Hòuào, Houwo) At the very eastern edge of the island is Hou'ao Village, a small village that used to be cut off from the main island during high tide. There's a small section of old houses off the main street that are worth checking out down the twisting alleys.

Swimming

Banli Beach (坂里沙灘, Bǎnlǐ Shātān), Beigan's longest and prettiest beach, is just up the road from where boats dock. There are changing rooms and showers.

Tanghou Beach (塘后道沙灘, Tánghòu Shātān) is a thin strip of sand, divided by a road, which connects the villages of Tangci and Hou'ao. Before the road was built locals had to wade through water during high tide to travel between the two villages.

Cinbi Village overlooks a nice little patch of beach facing a small cluster of rounded rocks, known as **Turtle Island Beach** (龜島沙灘, Guīdǎo Shātān). It's a lovely place to swim most of the year.

Sleeping & Eating

Old villages, including Cinbi and Banli, have seen once neglected Fujian-style stone houses turned into B&Bs with pleasant, breezy rooms and ocean views.

If staying in a stone building doesn't do it for you, there are a number of hotels in Tangci Village, though you'd be better off staying on Nangan and just coming over for the day. There are eateries in Tangci Village but opening hours and days are subject to random change so just look for whatever's open that day.

Beigan

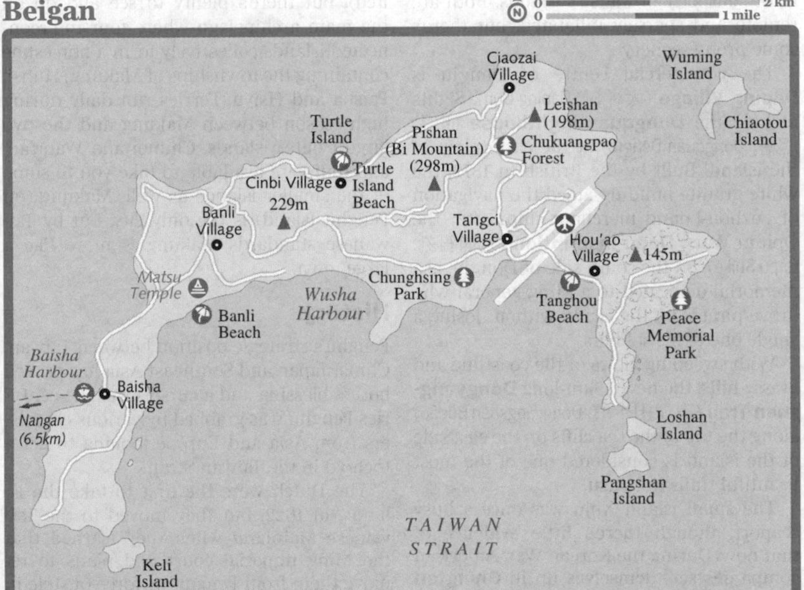

★Banli Dazhai Homestay HOMESTAY **$**
(坂里大宅, Bǎnlǐ Dàzhái; ☎55663; http://tour.matsu.idv.tw/hotel_banli.php; 48 Banli Village, 坂里村48號; s/d incl breakfast NT$800/1200; ❄📶) Opened in 2013, this new homestay in Beigan is a Qing-dynasty stone mansion with 14 attractive rooms. It's just a two-minute walk to the beautiful Banli Beach.

Chinbe No. 25 Guesthouse Homestay HOMESTAY **$$**
(芹壁村25號民宿, Qínbìcūn Èrshíwǔhào Mínsù; ☎55628; www.chinbe.com.tw; 25 Cinbi Village, 芹壁村25號; d NT$1800-3200; ❄📶) This homestay occupies three quaint stone buildings in the hilly Cinbi Village. Rooms are pleasantly appointed, if nothing fancy.

ℹ Getting There & Away

AIR

Uni Air (www.uniair.com.tw) has three flights daily from Taipei (NT$1862, 55 minutes) to **Beigan Airport** (Běigān Jīchǎng), which is at the end of Tangci Village's main street.

BOAT

Hourly services run to/from Nangan (NT$160, 10 minutes) from 7am to 5pm.

ℹ Getting Around

Hourly buses run around the island (NT$15) or drivers charge a flat rate: anywhere on Beigan is NT$100.

Scooter rentals at the airport or boat harbour cost NT$400/600 per four/24 hours, including petrol.

Matsu's Outer Islands

Northeast of Beigan, **Dongyin** (東引, Dōngyǐn) is the largest of the three outer islands and generally regarded to be the most beautiful section of the archipelago. Dongyin's landscape consists of steep cliffs, grassy hills and wave-eroded coastline. The main town of the same name is where you'll find hotels and restaurants.

Dongyin's most famous landmark is the **Dongyung Lighthouse** (東湧燈塔, Dōngyǒng Dēngtǎ). The lighthouse was built by the British in 1904 and remains an important part of Taiwan's coastal defence system. Birdwatchers shouldn't miss the steep **Andong Tunnel** (安東坑道, Āndōng kēngdào) from the 1970s; black-tailed gulls breed here during summer.

The islands of **Jyuguang Township** (莒光鄉, Jǔguāng xiāng), **Dongju** (東莒, Dōngjǔ, Tongchu) and **Xijju** (西莒, Xījǔ, Hsichu), are the most southerly of Matsu's islands. Both are remote and sparsely inhabited, but there's some pretty scenery.

The commercial centre of Dongju is **Daping Village** (大坪村, Dàpíng Cūn). Sights include the **Dongquan Lighthouse** (東犬燈塔, Dōngquǎn Dēngtǎ) at the eastern tip of the island. Built by the British in 1872, the white granite building aided the navigation of Fuzhou-bound merchant ships after the Opium Wars. **Dapu Inscription** (大埔石刻, Dàpǔ Shíkē), on the south side of Dongju, is a memorial dedicated to a Ming general who drove pirates off the island without losing a single one of his soldiers.

With sweeping views of the coastline and grassy hills, the new 1.5km-long **Dongyangshan Trail** (東洋山步道, Dōngyángshān Bùdào) along the top of the sea cliffs on the east side of the island is considered one of the most beautiful trails in Matsu.

The small island Xijju was once a busy seaport, though there's little evidence of that now. During the Korean War, American companies set themselves up in **Chingfan Village** (青帆村, Qīngfán Cūn) and nicknamed it 'Little Hong Kong'.

Getting There & Away

From Nangan there's one boat daily to Dongyin (NT$350, two hours) and three boats daily to Jyuguang's two islands (NT$200, 50 minutes).

PENGHU

06 / POP 98,843

Penghu (澎湖, Pénghú), also known as the Pescadores, is famous for its great beaches, glorious temples and the traditional Chinese-style homes surrounded by coral walls. In the summer months Penghu is hot and beautiful, while in winter and spring the archipelago is possibly the windiest place in the northern hemisphere. Many consider Penghu a windsurfing mecca and the Canary Islands of the Orient.

A flat, dry place covered mostly with low bush and grasslands, Penghu is significantly different from Taiwan proper geologically speaking, being formed from the solidified lava of volcanic eruptions some 17 million years ago. The stunning rock formations and towering basalt columns seen everywhere date from that time.

Penghu County includes almost 100 islands (only a quarter of which are inhabited), but there's plenty to see and do on the main archipelago where four interconnected islands collectively form a horseshoe containing the townships of Makung, Huhsi, Paisha and Hsiyu. Ferries run daily during high season between Makung and the two largest outer islands, Chimei and Wang'an, and tours are available to take you to some of the smaller islands as well. Makung (on Penghu Island) is the only city, but by Taiwanese standards Makung is more like a large town.

History

Penghu's strategic position between Taiwan, China, Japan and Southeast Asia has proved both a blessing and a curse. Over the centuries Penghu was grabbed by various colonisers from Asia and Europe looking to get a toehold in the Taiwan Strait.

The Dutch were the first to take the islands, in 1622, but they moved to the Taiwanese Mainland when they learned that the Ming imperial court had plans to remove them from Penghu by force (a stele in the Matsu Temple in Makung inscribes this threat). In 1662 the Ming loyalist Koxinga was sent to oust the Dutch from Taiwan for good. Penghu was a convenient place to station his troops as he drew up his battle plans. Some troops stayed in Penghu after the Dutch were gone and set up their own regime, which was short-lived, however, because the Qing court threw them out in 1683. The French were the next to arrive, in 1884, followed by the Japanese, in 1895, who settled down and stayed for the next 50 years, only to be replaced by the Nationalists in 1945.

Penghu is rich with historical relics, evidence of its long colonial history. To capitalise on this history and boost a drooping economy, the islands were transformed into a beach mecca for local and foreign visitors. The Penghu Archipelago has been designated a national scenic area and the main islands have at least been given a makeover that nicely blends tradition with modern comforts.

Getting There & Away

AIR

There are over 50 daily flights between **Makung Airport** (www.mkport.gov.tw) and Taipei (NT$2050, 40 minutes), Kaohsiung (NT$1718, 40 minutes) and other west-coast cities with **Mandarin Airlines** (www.mandarin-airlines.

Penghu

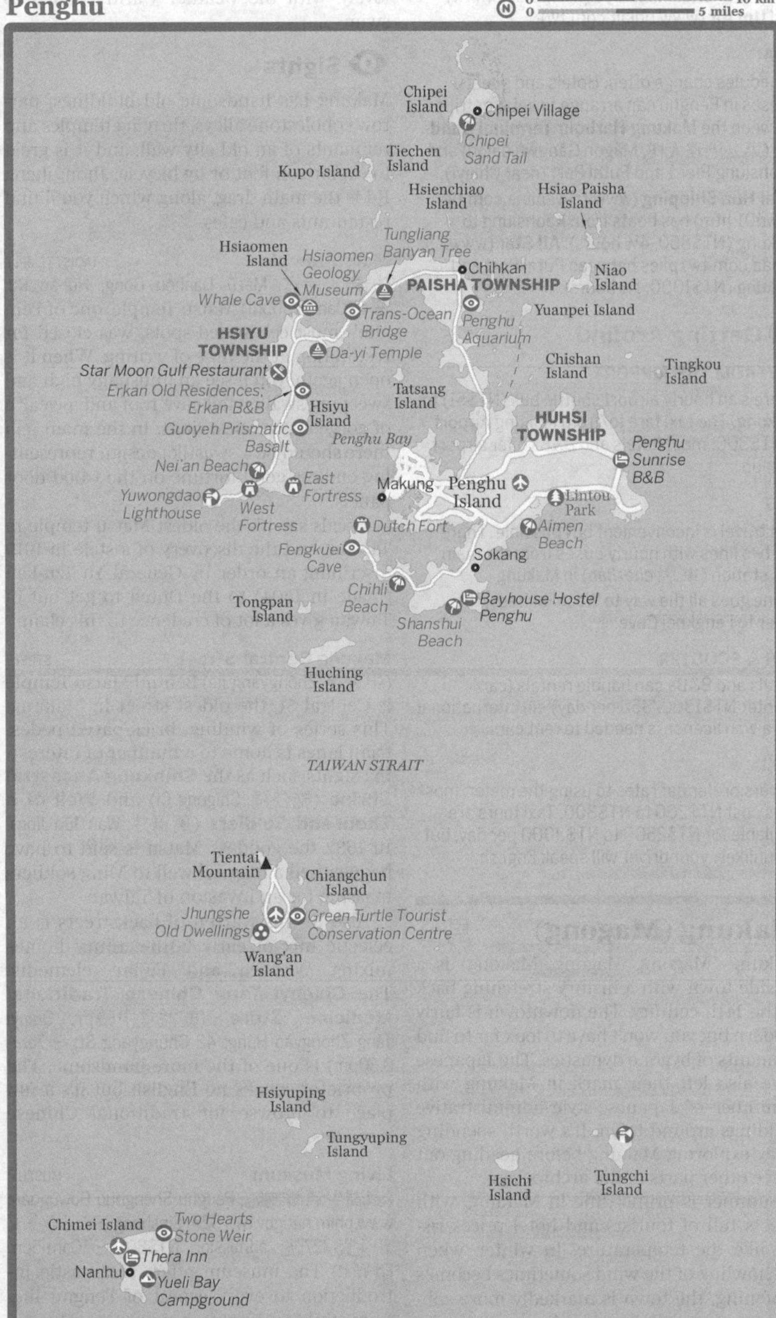
0 10 km
0 5 miles
Chipei Island
Chipei Village
Chipei Sand Tail
Tiechen Island
Kupo Island
Hsienchiao Island
Hsiao Paisha Island
Tungliang Banyan Tree
Hsiaomen Island
Hsiaomen Geology Museum
Chihkan
Niao Island
PAISHA TOWNSHIP
Whale Cave
Trans-Ocean Bridge
Penghu Aquarium
Yuanpei Island
HSIYU TOWNSHIP
Da-yi Temple
Star Moon Gulf Restaurant
Chishan Island
Tingkou Island
Erkan Old Residences; Erkan B&B
Tatsang Island
Hsiyu Island
HUHSI TOWNSHIP
Guoyeh Prismatic Basalt
Penghu Bay
Penghu Sunrise B&B
Nei'an Beach
East Fortress
Makung
Penghu Island
Lintou Park
Yuwongdao Lighthouse
West Fortress
Dutch Fort
Aimen Beach
Fengkuei Cave
Sokang
Chihli Beach
Tongpan Island
Bayhouse Hostel Penghu
Shanshui Beach
Huching Island
TAIWAN STRAIT
Tientai Mountain
Chiangchun Island
Jhungshe Old Dwellings
Green Turtle Tourist Conservation Centre
Wang'an Island
Hsiyuping Island
Tungyuping Island
Hsichi Island
Tungchi Island
Chimei Island
Two Hearts Stone Weir
Thera Inn
Nanhu
Yueli Bay Campground

com), **TransAsia Airways** (www.tna.com.tw) and **Uni Air** (www.uniair.com.tw).

BOAT

Schedules change often. Hotels and guesthouses in Penghu can arrange tickets for trips between the **Makung Harbour Terminal Building** (馬公港務大樓, Mǎgōn Gǎngwù dàlóu) and Kaohsiung Pier 1 and Putai Port (near Chiayi).

Tai Hua Shipping (www.taiwanline.com.tw/taiwu01.htm) has boats from Kaohsiung to Makung (NT$860, 4½ hours); **All Star** (www.aaaaa.com.tw) plies between Putai Port and Makung (NT$1000, 1½ hours).

Getting Around

TO/FROM THE AIRPORT

There's an hourly airport shuttle bus (NT$51) to Makung. The taxi fare to/from Makung Airport is NT$300; most hotels and B&Bs offer airport pick-up.

BUS

Bus travel is inconvenient but possible. There are two lines with hourly buses from the main bus station (車站, *chēzhàn*) in Makung.

One goes all the way to West Fortress, the other to Fengkuei Cave.

CAR & SCOOTER

Hotels and B&Bs can handle rentals (car/scooter NT$1300/350 per day); an international or Taiwan licence is needed to rent cars.

TAXI

Drivers prefer flat rates to using the meter; most trips cost NT$200 to NT$300. Taxi tours are available for NT$2500 to NT$3000 per day, but it's unlikely your driver will speak English.

Makung (Magong) 馬公

Makung (Mǎgōng, Magong, Makong) is a seaside town with a history stretching back to the 14th century. The downtown is fairly modern but you won't have to look far to find remnants of bygone dynasties. The Japanese have also left their mark in Makung with a number of Japanese-style administrative buildings around town. It's worth spending a day exploring Makung before heading out to see other parts of the archipelago.

Summer is prime time in Makung, with streets full of tourists and hotel prices rising like the temperature. In winter, when the howling of the wind sometimes becomes deafening, the town is markedly more subdued. Autumn and spring, however, can be lovely, with the weather warm enough to swim.

Sights

Makung has handsome old buildings, narrow cobblestone alleys, thriving temples and remnants of an old city wall, and it is great to explore on foot or by bicycle. Jhongjheng Rd is the main drag, along which you'll find restaurants and cafes.

Matsu Temple TAOIST TEMPLE

(馬祖天后宮, Mǎzǔ Tiānhòu Gōng; Hui-an Rd; ⏲4.30am-8.30pm) Matsu Temple, one of Penghu's most celebrated spots, was closed for restoration at the time of writing. When it is open again, you'll see an unusually high and sweeping swallowtail eave roof and a wealth of gorgeous woodcarvings. In the main hall there should be a swastika design representing endless good fortune on the wood door panels.

Locals say it's the oldest Matsu temple in Taiwan, and the discovery of a stele in 1919 inscribing an order by General Yu Tzu-kau (made in 1604) to the Dutch to get out of Taiwan gives a lot of credence to this claim.

Makung Central Street STREET

(中央街, Zhōngyāng Jiē) Behind Matsu Temple is Central St, the oldest street in Makung. This series of winding, brick-paved pedestrian lanes is home to a number of interesting sights such as the **Shihkung Ancestral Shrine** (施公祠, Shīgōng Cí) and **Well of a Thousand Soldiers** (萬軍井, Wàn Jūn Jǐng). In 1682 the goddess Matsu is said to have bequeathed a magical well to Ming soldiers massing for an invasion of Taiwan.

Also in this warren of backstreets is an eclectic mix of early 20th-century homes mixing Western and Fujian elements. The **Chienyi Tang Chinese Traditional Medicine Store** (乾益堂中藥行, Qiányì Táng Zhōngyào Háng; 42 Chungyang St; ⏲7am-9.30pm) is one of the more handsome. The proprietor speaks no English but it's a fun place to browse for traditional Chinese remedies.

Living Museum MUSEUM

(澎湖生活博物館, Pénghú Shēnghuó Bówùguǎn; www.phlm.nat.gov.tw; 327 Sinsheng Rd, 馬公市新生路327號; admission NT$80; ⏲10am-5pm Fri-Wed) The museum offers a fantastic introduction to every aspect of Penghu life: from child-rearing techniques to religious customs.

Makung (Magong)

Makung (Magong)

Sights
1 Kuanyin Pavilion A2
2 Makung Central Street B3
3 Makung Old Wall A4
4 Matsu Temple B3
5 Peichen Temple B3
6 Penghu Reclamation Hall C2
Shihkung Ancestral Shrine .... (see 7)
7 Well of a Thousand Soldiers B3

Activities, Courses & Tours
8 Liquid Sport B3

Sleeping
9 Bowa Hotel B4
Makung Traditional Homestay .... (see 7)
10 MF Hotel Penghu C4

Eating
11 Jang Jin Restaurant B4
12 Pengniang's Kitchen C2
13 Sha Ai Chuang C2

Drinking & Nightlife
14 Freud Pub C2

Shopping
15 Chienyi Tang Chinese Traditional Medicine Store B3
16 Peichen Market D1

Displays are filled with real artefacts (there's even a full-size traditional junk on the 2nd floor) and explanations in English are finally available.

Confucius Temple HISTORIC BUILDING
(孔廟, Kǒng Miào; 104-7 Xinsheng Rd; ⌚10am-5pm Wed-Mon) Next to the Living Museum is this very grand structure, which was formerly the Wenshi College, an important centre of

learning during the Qing dynasty. The name of the college was changed to the Confucius Temple during the Japanese occupation to take advantage of the Japanese respect for Confucius, in the hope that the college wouldn't be torn down.

Makung Old Wall HISTORIC SITE
A quick walk west along Jhonghsan Rd takes you to Shuncheng Gate and a section of the Makung Old Wall. City walls were constructed around Makung as a defensive measure. After the occupying French left the city in 1885, the walls were mostly knocked down by the Japanese. Today, parts of the remaining wall are overrun by cacti and aloe plants the size of ponies. The old neighbourhood around the wall is worth exploring.

Kuanyin Pavilion BUDDHIST TEMPLE
(觀音亭, Guānyīn Tíng; ⌚5am-8pm) Hugging Makung's western shoreline is the city's fabulous waterfront park and the enclosed bay here is great for swimming. The 300-year-old Kuanyin Pavilion in the park is dedicated to the goddess of mercy; this is the most important place for Buddhist worship in Penghu and the most important artefact in the temple is the old bell, which dates back to 1696.

Penghu Reclamation Hall MUSEUM
(澎湖開拓館, Pénghú Kāituò Guǎn; 30 Chihping Rd; admission NT$30; ⌚10am-5pm Wed-Sun, closed national holidays) Stylish Japanese-era building with displays of Penghu culture and history.

Peichen Temple TAOIST TEMPLE
(北辰宮, Běichén Gōng) Just off Jhongjheng Rd is the large, ornate Peichen Temple.

Festivals & Events

Lantern Festival LUNAR FESTIVAL
(元宵節, Yuánxiāojié) Though the Lantern Festival is a sight to behold anywhere in Taiwan, Penghu's festival is truly a unique celebration. It takes place on the 15th day of the first lunar month (about 15 days after the first day of Chinese New Year).

Penghu's celebrations include a bacchanalian parade with dancers and fireworks through the streets and past the many temples of Makung. One twist particular to Penghu is the parading of gigantic golden turtle effigies through the streets. In the days before the festival, most bakeries in town devote half their oven space to the production of turtle cakes, which are given away and eaten during the course of the festival. **Peichi Temple** (北極殿, Běijí Diàn) in Sokang near Shanshui Beach is a hub of activity at this time of year.

Sleeping

During summer, hotel prices in Makung rise dramatically, and rooms are hard to come by on weekends and holidays. But with hundreds of B&Bs around the archipelago, there's likely to be something available at any time.

Autumn through spring is low season, and though it's windier than in summer, the weather is usually still hot in autumn and spring; sizeable discounts are available at even the most expensive hotels.

Penghu Moncsor International Youth Hostel HOSTEL $
(澎湖滿客舍國際青年旅舍, Pēnghú Mǎnkèshě Guójì Qīngnián Lǚshě; ☎921 9681; http://penghu-moncsor.wix.com/hostel; 10 Lane 27, Minyu St, 民裕街27巷10號; dm/d NT$550/1300; ❄@📶) Located on the eastern outskirts of Makung, this HI-affiliated hostel has one well-maintained double and 19 comfy bunks distributed in three-bed and four-bed dorms. The host, Jeffrey, is super-hospitable and speaks good English. Other perks include free laundry service and bike rentals. It's a five-minute scooter ride from downtown Makung. Detailed directions are available on the hostel website.

MF Hotel Penghu HOTEL $$
(和田大飯店, Hétián Dàfàndiàn; ☎926 3936; www.mhoteltw.com; 2 Minchuan Rd, 民權路2號; d/tw NT$3000/2200; ❄📶) The bland exterior of this hotel gives no hint of the modern and well-appointed rooms within, and most rooms come with a harbour view. The staff are helpful and attentive, and the restaurant serves a decent Western breakfast and afternoon tea. The hotel is just a stone's throw from most places of interest in Makung.

Makung Traditional Homestay HOMESTAY $$
(馬公老街民宿, Mǎgōng Lǎojiē Mínsù; ☎926 6161; www.069266161.com; 8 Alley 1, Jhongyang St, 中央街1巷8號; d NT$2000; ❄📶) This homestay offers simple modern comforts and friendly hosts. And the location, of course. If you don't mind a bit of noise, get a room with a balcony over the old street. To get to the homestay head down the alley beside Matsu Temple. The entrance to the B&B is just past the Shihkung Ancestral Shrine.

Bowa Hotel HOTEL $$
(寶華大飯店, Bǎohuá Dàfàndiàn; ☎927 4881; www.bowahotel.com.tw; 2 Jhongjheng Rd, 中正路2號; s/d/tw incl breakfast NT$2600/2800/3800;) This hotel is a very handy, competitively priced option by Makung Harbour. Some of the spotless rooms include ocean views. Discounts of 15% are available midweek and in the low season.

Eating

Makung is a seafood-lover's paradise, though locally caught seafood is expensive (much of what you'll find at restaurants is flown in from other parts of Taiwan). Raw *lóng xiā* (龍蝦, lobster) and fried *wǔ xiāng cìhétún* (五香刺河豚; 'five-flavour' balloonfish) are favourites. In addition, look for the following local specialities: *jīnguā mǐfěn* (金瓜米粉; pumpkin rice noodles), *xián bǐng* (咸餅; salty biscuits), *shāo ròu fàn* (燒肉飯; grilled meat with rice) and *hēi táng gāo* (黑糖糕; brown-sugar sponge cakes). Penghu is famous for the latter.

There are restaurants all over town and you'll find street food cooking in front of just about any temple. Jhongjheng and Guangfu Rds are particularly rich in places to eat or just nibble.

Sha Ai Chuang TAIWANESE $
(傻愛莊, Shǎ Ài Zhuāng; 14 Sinsheng Rd; ⊙10am-midnight) Loosely translated as 'foolish lovepub', this handsome colonial building was once the home of Penghu's first county chief. It's now a restaurant serving standard Taiwanese fare in a chic tea lounge and tatami dining rooms.

Good Friend Vegetarian House VEGETARIAN $
(好朋友, Hǎo Péngyǒu; 320 Sanduo Rd; dishes from NT$120; ⊙10am-2pm & 5-9pm Fri-Wed, 10am-2pm Thu;) This vegetarian restaurant on the northern edge of Makung makes some of the best Taiwanese *niúròu tāngmiàn* (beef noodle soup) we've ever eaten. Quite the paradox, eh? To get to the restaurant head up Guangfu Rd and then turn left on Sanduo Rd.

Pengniang's Kitchen SEAFOOD $$
(澎娘海鮮廚房, Pēngniang Hǎixiān Chúfáng; 36 Jianguo Rd; dishes NT$120-240; ⊙lunch & dinner) While most seafood restaurants cater to large groups, this new, small eatery has a thoughtful menu for solo or independent travellers who want to sample fish and other sea creatures freshly caught from the Penghu waters. There is a picture menu and the owner speaks a little English.

Jang Jin Restaurant SEAFOOD $$
(長進餐廳, Chángjìn Cāntīng; 9 Minzu Rd; dishes NT$200-350; ⊙lunch & dinner) A loud and popular seafood place with a wide range of fresh dishes. Not really suitable for one person as dishes are designed for sharing.

Drinking & Nightlife

For cafes and fruit or tea shops, head to the little alleys around the Matsu Temple and off Jhongjheng Rd.

Freud Pub BAR
(弗洛伊得, Fúluòyīdé; 2-l Sinsheng Rd; ⊙6pm-2.30am) The house special in this slightly cramped but laid-back sports bar is the potent 'Absolutely Drunk' cocktail, made with six kinds of alcohol.

Shopping

Makung is full of shops selling all kinds of Penghu speciality items such as pink and black coral, shells and veined stones. We recommend against buying coral items as it only hastens the destruction of coral reefs and the decline of the marine creatures living within them.

Edible items are especially popular with Taiwanese tourists, and stores selling squid jerky, smoked fish and dried seafood can be found all over Makung. You can also buy just about anything edible, from freshly caught fish and oysters to local vegetables and cooked snacks, at the bustling **Peichen Market** (北辰市場, Běichén Shìchǎng) in central Makung.

Information

Penghu's not the most wired of places, but more and more hotels and guesthouses offer wi-fi connections.

Bank of Taiwan (台灣銀行; 24 Renai Rd) Foreign-currency exchange and ATMs.

South Seas Tourist Service Centre (Nánhǎi Yóukè Fúwù Zhōngxīn; ☎info 926 4738; Makung Harbour Third Fishing Dock; ⊙8am-5pm) This centre provides information about Chimei, Wang'an and Tongpan Islands, as well as boat tickets. They also provide a free left-luggage service.

Tourist Information Centre (澎湖遊客服務中心, Pénghú Yóukè Fúwù Zhōngxīn; http://tour.penghu.gov.tw; 171 Kuanghua Lane; ⊙8am-5pm) Inconveniently located, so pick up travel brochures at the airport or ferry terminal travel kiosks. Your best source for boat and plane schedules, and other information, will be your hotel or guesthouse.

Around Penghu Archipelago

Though it's actually four islands, this horseshoe-shaped archipelago is referred to by most locals as the main island, or simply Penghu. The U-shaped route 203 shoots north from Makung on the west side of the main island, passing through the Paisha Township before heading on to Hsiyu Island via the Trans-Ocean Bridge. Hsiyu is a long, narrow island, and route 203 continues to the West Fortress and Yuwongdao Lighthouse on its southern tip. The total distance of the one-way trip is just under 37km, so you can spend a full day exploring the sights along that road on a scooter and still make it back to Makung before dark.

Sticking to the main roads is not advisable unless you are in a hurry to get from sight to sight. Much of the magic of Penghu is found in its endless seaside hamlets with their stocky grey houses and narrow winding roads bordered by low coral walls.

Sights

Some call Penghu the Hawaii of Asia, but how many temples does Hawaii have? We lost count of how many we saw in Penghu, but we think the person-to-temple ratio is 10 to one. Travelling around Penghu you'll undoubtedly stumble across some. On the wide, flat plains the huge, colourful complexes are a bit hard to miss. Inside, listen for the often cacophonous chattering of birds (mostly buntings and swallows) – something rarely heard in temples on Taiwan proper.

★Erkan Old Residences TRADITIONAL VILLAGE

Set on emerald slopes above the blue sea, **Erkan Village** (二崁古厝, Èrkǎn Gǔ Cuò) oozes charm from every coral wall, stone walkway and brick facade. The 50 or so houses are built in a melange of southern Fujian, Western and Japanese styles, and they mostly hail from the early 20th century. Residents on the main street keep their front gates open and invite visitors to check out their unique homes and possibly sample a few local treats.

Guoyeh Prismatic Basalt SCENIC AREA

(大菓葉柱狀玄武岩, Dàguǒyè Zhùzhuàn Xuánwǔyán) Just down the road towards the coast is the Guoyeh Prismatic Basalt, a beautiful example of the basalt cliffs formed from the cooling lava that created Penghu.

Whale Cave SCENIC AREA

(鯨魚洞, Jīngyú Dòng) The western coast of Hsiyu is visually dramatic, full of steep

TURTLES OF PENGHU

Fifteen days after the start of the lunar year, on the evening of the Lantern Festival, Penghu residents crowd into temples around the islands and offer sacrificial turtle-themed offerings to the deities. They pray for prosperity and give thanks for the good things that happened to them the previous year. The sea turtles that migrate through the coastal waters off Penghu have a special meaning to the islanders, who believe that they represent longevity and fortune. Rice cakes and dough are formed into the shape of turtles and offered to temple deities. Sacrificial turtles are also made from gold coins, noodles, sponge cakes and sometimes offered live. Turtles can be offered to any of the gods or goddesses, though Matsu seems to be the local favourite. During the festivities, parades are held with men carrying giant palanquins down the streets bearing local gods and goddesses, accompanied by singing, dancing and plenty of fireworks.

Some of the beliefs about turtles come from ancient Chinese myths about the reptiles being special conduits between heaven and earth and capable of divining the future through marks on their shells. The turtle, along with the dragon, chimera and phoenix, were considered the four sacred beasts in the ancient times and they were thought to possess magical powers.

Unfortunately, there are more rice-cake turtles in Penghu now than the real things. Once dispersed throughout Taiwan's coastal regions, sea-turtle nesting sites are now found only on Penghu, Lanyu and the Taitung coastline.

For more on the plight of the green sea turtle and efforts to revive its numbers visit the Green Turtle Tourist Conservation Centre (p307) on Wang'an Island.

cliffs, basalt formations, shallow coves and headlands. Whale Cave is a hole in a rock that kinda-sorta looks like a whale. Visiting it gives you a fine excuse to ride over the Trans-Ocean Bridge, of which Penghu folks are quite proud.

Hsiaomen Geology Museum MUSEUM
(小門地質博物館, Xiǎomén Dìzhì Bówùguǎn; 11-12 Xiaomen Village; ⌚8am-5pm) FREE Not far away from Whale Cave is the Hsiaomen Geology Museum, a good introduction to the stuff that makes up the archipelago.

Dutch Fort SCENIC AREA
(風櫃尾紅毛城遺址, Fēngguìwěi Hóngmáochéng Yízhǐ) The ruins of the Dutch Fort, abandoned when the Dutch were driven out of Penghu by the Ming army in 1624, are at the end of the peninsula. There's nothing left of the fort to see, but the grassy terraces offer some fine walks and even finer views. To get to the fort, follow the signs to **Snakehead Hill** (蛇頭山, Shétóu Shān).

Sokang Pagodas TAOIST
(鎖港子午寶塔, Soǔgǎng Zǐwǔ Bǎotǎ) On the way to Shanshui Beach on County Road 25 are the Sokang Pagodas, two venerated stone towers. Blessed by a Taoist priest, they are reputed to contain supernatural powers that ward off evil and protect residents from natural disasters.

The towers are about two blocks from each other. From the north-facing tower just keep heading down the main road and look for the south-facing tower to the left down a side road.

Penghu Aquarium AQUARIUM
(澎湖水族館, Pénghú Shǔizú Guǎn; 58 Chitou Village; admission NT$200; ⌚8am-5pm) The two-storey marine exhibition centre provides information on all the aquatic creatures swimming around Penghu. Kids and adults alike will have a great time communing with the sea turtles. The highlight of the aquarium is the 14m glass tunnel allowing visitors and fish to meet eye to eye.

East & West Fortresses FORT
(東台古堡和西台古堡, Dōngtái Gǔbǎo Hé Xitái Gǔ Bǎo; admission each NT$30; ⌚8am-5.30pm) Both fortresses were built in 1887 following the end of the Sino-French War. Five thousand soldiers were once stationed in West Fortress, the largest of five fortresses in Penghu. East Fortress, though smaller, has a better shape and nicer views.

Yuwongdao Lighthouse LIGHTHOUSE
(漁翁島燈塔, Yúwēngdǎo Dēngtǎ) FREE In the 19th century, British lighthouse keepers stayed here on 10-year shifts. Look for the stone cross marking the grave of Nellie O'Driscol, the daughter of one of the keepers.

Tungliang Banyan Tree TAOIST TEMPLE
(通梁古榕, Tōngliáng Gǔróng) The astonishing 300-year-old Tungliang Banyan Tree wraps and creeps and twists round a cement frame that stabilises the tree like the lattice arch of a bower. The spread of branches and aerial roots cover 600 sq metres, enough to give shade to you and the endless tour bus loads of visitors.

It's said that during the Qing dynasty a ship sunk off the coast of Penghu and a small seedling floated to shore and was planted by locals. A temple complex was built later, and the tree and hall of worship are now inseparable.

A little snack shop by the temple sells cactus-fruit sorbet, something you won't find anywhere else in Taiwan. Well worth trying.

Da-yi Temple TAOIST TEMPLE
(大義宮, Dàyì Gōng) On Hsiyu Island, the 200-year-old Da-yi Temple is dedicated to Guandi, the god of war and the patron of warriors. Some say that when the French tried to attack Penghu, mysterious forces kept them away from the temple.

The temple is a massive structure with 4m bronze guardians of Guandi, **Guānpíng** (關平) and **Zhōucāng** (周倉), flanking the stairs. The interior features several large and detailed ceilings, some good dragons in *jiǎnniàn* (mosaic-like temple decoration) and, brace yourself, an **underground coral cavern** with a collection of giant (living) sea turtles. The legality of this is a grey area, but we'd be remiss not letting you know about it.

The temple is off route 203, down a side road towards the sea. There is an English sign for it after you cross the Trans-Ocean Bridge.

Activities

Beaches

The archipelago has several hundred kilometres of shoreline with more than 100 beaches. The following are among the best found on Penghu and, indeed, anywhere in Taiwan.

Shanshui Beach BEACH
(山水沙灘, Shānshǔi Shātān) Southeast of Makung the excellent Shanshui Beach has white sand and breaking waves. On weekends the beach is fairly crowded, but during the week you may have the beach to yourself. The beach is popular with Penghu's surf set when the waves are up.

Chihli Beach BEACH
(蒔裡沙灘, Zhílǐ Shātān) Up the coast from Shanshui to the northwest, Chihli Beach is a great little spot with a real community feel. The shell-sand beach stretches for over 1km and is popular with beach-sports enthusiasts and sunbathers.

This stretch of coast is also known for its bizarre rock formations, created thousands of years ago by cooling basalt magma. Sea erosion has created many unusual gullies and crevices. **Fengkuei Cave** (風櫃洞, Fēng Guìdòng), on Penghu's southwest shore, is a sea-eroded gully that reportedly makes a peculiar sound when the strong wind rushes through it.

Aimen Beach BEACH
(隘門沙灘, Àimén Shātān) Aimen Beach is a favourite among locals for all kinds of water sports and beach activities. The nearby expanse of pines in **Lintou Park** (林投公園, Líntóu Gōngyuán) borders a white-sand beach that's superb as a picnic spot but not so suitable for swimming as the coral is very sharp.

Nei'an Beach BEACH
(內垵沙灘, Nèiǎn Shātān) Tranquil and less touristy, white-sand Nei'an Beach is a great place to watch the sunset.

Windsurfing

With wave and wind conditions similar to Gran Canaria's Pozo Izquierdo, or the Columbia River Gorge in USA, Penghu is fast becoming Asia's premier spot for windsurfing – in winter! From September to April the same Arctic-Mongolian cold fronts that send temperatures falling in Taipei also blast strong winds down the Taiwan Strait. Wind speeds around Penghu can reach 50 knots.

In 2010 the Asian RSX championships were held in October for the first time. Organisers are hoping that the archipelago can become a serious training ground for Asia's Olympic windsurfing athletes.

Windsurfing lessons and equipment rental are available at Penghu Sunrise B&B (p306) in Guoyeh Village and **Liquid Sport** (www.liquidsportpenghu.com; 36 Huimin 1 Rd, 惠民一路36號; ⏲10am-9pm) in Makung. The first lesson is NT$1500, including equipment. September and October are the best windsurfing months because of the good weather and wind conditions that have yet to get too extreme.

Diving & Snorkelling

Though it was possible to get in some great snorkelling and diving even off the main beaches just a few years ago, a freak cold snap killed most of the shallow-water coral in 2008. The coral is growing back, but it will be years before the reefs return to their former glory.

There are still great sites on the smaller islands and in less accessible locations on the main archipelago. Liquid Sport does diving lessons and easy day trips in summer and now has clear-bottomed sea kayaks for rent – a marvellous way to see the underwater world.

Another reputable local dive instructor and guide is **Mr Liu** (☎0928-370 035; padi470704@yahoo.com.tw), who is based in Makung; by appointment only.

Sleeping & Eating

There are hundreds of B&Bs around the archipelago and you can find a place to stay almost anywhere. While nearby food options will probably be limited, Makung is no more than a 30-minute ride from any of the following.

Bayhouse Hostel Penghu HOSTEL $
(澎湖北吉光背包客民宿, Pēnghú Běijíguāng Bèibāokè Mínsù; ☎995 3005; www.bayhouse.tw; 17-26 Shanshui Village, 山水里山17-26號; dm from NT$600; ❄@📶) Just back from Shanshui Beach, this is a bright and cheerful hostel with clean mixed and female-only dorms and a well-equipped kitchen. The helpful staff speak good English. Bayhouse offers free airport and ferry pick-ups and shuttles to and from Makung twice a day.

★**Penghu Sunrise B&B** B&B $$
(澎湖民宿-菓葉觀日樓, Pénghú Mínsù-Guǒyè Guānrìlóu; ☎992 0818; www.sunrisebb.idv.tw; 129-3 Guoyeh Village, 菓葉村129-3號; s/d incl breakfast NT$1400/1800; ❄📶) Run by windsurfing fanatics Jan and his daughter Karen, the Sunrise in Guoyeh Village is a bona fide B&B with ocean views, fresh morning coffee and English-speaking hosts. Rooms are bright and comfortably furnished, and there's a

communal lounge area with a panoramic view of the ocean. Scooter, bicycle, windsurfing and sea-kayaking equipment are available for rent.

Erkan B&B HOMESTAY **$$**
(二崁民宿, Èrkǎn Mínsù; ☎998 4406; www.erkan-homestay.com; d NT$2400;) This block of old residences in the charming Erkan Village gives you a glimpse of rural life in Penghu without compromising modern comforts. The rooms, part of a larger family complex, are at the end of the village. Head towards the temple, turn left, then make a quick right, before bending your way around a knoll.

Star Moon Gulf Restaurant SEAFOOD **$$**
(星月灣餐廳, Xīngyuèwān Cāntīng; 132 Dachih Village; per person NT$200; 11.30am-2pm & 5.30-9pm) There is no formal menu here as the owner churns out dishes from the day's freshest catch and what is available in his own organic farm. For a NT$200 *tàocān* (set meal) you get six tapas-size seafood dishes and one soup.

The restaurant is just a 10-minute drive from Erkan Village on Hsiyu Island.

Outer Islands

The two largest of Penghu's outer islands are Wang'an and Chimei. Both are south of the main island and have boat and air service to Makung. The third largest is Chipei, north of Paisha, which has some great beaches. Tongpan is a small island ringed with some fantastic basalt column cliffs. Several of the smaller islands encircling the archipelago are reserves for migratory waterfowl.

Wang'an 望安鄉

About 30 minutes by boat from Makung harbour, Wang'an (Wàng'ān) is home to the **Green Turtle Tourist Conservation Centre** (綠蠵龜觀光保育中心, Lùxīguī Guānguāng Bǎoyù Zhōngxīn; 8.30am-5pm) FREE. Inside are bilingual exhibits about the state of sea turtles in Taiwan and around the world. There's also information on wildlife preservation efforts in the Strait Islands and Taiwan proper.

The protected areas for the turtles are on the southwest side of the island. However, green turtles are extremely rare and even during the breeding and hatching season (May to October) you are very unlikely to see one. But the beaches here are golden and can be swum during the day (after 8pm all activity is prohibited).

The **Jhungshe Old Dwellings** (中社古厝, Zhōngshè Gǔ Cuò) are a group of abandoned but well-preserved houses in **Jhungshe Village** (Zhōngshè Cūn). Nearby is the highest point on the island, **Tientai Mountain** (天台山, Tiāntái Shān), which is actually a grassy hill. Tientai Mountain is the oldest bit of basalt on Penghu but is most famous for the footprint of Lu Tungbin, one of China's Eight Immortals, impressed on a rock here.

Chimei 七美鄉

Chimei (Qīměi) means 'Seven Beauties' and refers to a legend involving seven women who, in the Ming dynasty, threw themselves into a well rather than lose their chastity to Japanese pirates. The island's coastline is one of the finest on Penghu and it's well worth your time to explore the cliffs and coves.

The **Two Hearts Stone Weir** (雙心石滬, Shuāng Xīn Shí Hù), a ring of stones literally shaped like two hearts, is a Penghu icon and probably the most photographed sight on the islands. The original purpose of the weir was to catch fish during low tide.

There are several excellent **snorkelling** spots in the shallow coves around Chimei, and one-day tours (NT$1100 to NT$1300, including transport and food) can be arranged beforehand by your hotel or homestay.

Nanhu Harbour has several seafood restaurants and a couple of homestays. Should you want to spend the night on Chimei, **Thera Inn** (希拉小宿, Xīlā Xiǎosù; ☎0972-727 103; www.thera.com.tw; 11 Nanhuqitou, Nangang Village, 南港村南滬崎頭11-1號; r from NT$1900) is recommended. It's just a five-minute scooter ride from the harbour on County Road 42. The new **campground** (鮪鯉灣露營區, Wěilǐwān Lùyíngqū) in Yueli Bay (鮪鯉灣, Wěilǐ Wān) is free and has shower facilities.

Chipei 吉貝

With its lovely sand-shell beaches, Chipei (Jíbèi) buzzes with tourists in summer but shuts down almost completely in winter. **Chipei Sand Tail** (吉貝沙尾, Jíbèi Shāwěi) is the most popular beach on the island and the only one that isn't trashed with garbage. This long strip of golden sand juts out into the water, its size changing with the coming and going of the tides. During summer, windsurfing, boating and even parasailing and karaoke singing are popular activities here. Equipment is available for rent at the beach resort or in the small shops around the beach. During winter you'll have the whole place to yourself.

Chipei Village has an assortment of homestays and small hotels but most people just come over for the day.

Tongpan 桶盤嶼

The shoreline of this small island is barricaded by walls of natural basalt columns, giving it an imposing appearance. Boats to Chimei will slow down to let you observe the columns, and some will even stop for an hour, just enough time to walk around the island and observe the walls up close.

Getting There & Away

AIR

Daily Air (www.dailyair.com.tw) has daily flights between Kaohsiung and Chimei (NT$1754, 35 minutes), and Chimei and Makung (NT$1028, 15 minutes).

BOAT

North Sea Tourist Service Centre (北海遊客服務中心, Běihǎi Yóukè Fúwù Zhōngxīn; ☎993 3082; Chihkan, Paisha Island; ⏰6.30am-9.30pm) Operates boats to Chipei (round-trip NT$300, 15 minutes, every 30 minutes) and some smaller islands north of Paisha.

South Seas Tourist Service Centre (南海遊客服務中心, Nánhǎi Yóukè Fúwù Zhōngxīn; ☎926 4738; No 3 Fishing Harbour, Makung Harbour; ⏰6.30am-9.30pm) Has boats to Chimei, Wang'an and Tongpan, as well as options for day trips in the high season. A full-day tour (NT$850) hits three or four islands with one- or two-hour stops depending on how many islands you are visiting. Book at your hotel: hotels often arrange 20% discounts or more.

Getting Around

Rental scooters are available on Chimei, Wang'an and Chipei for NT$400 to NT$500 a day or for NT$150 if you are just stopping as part of a one-day island tour. Tongpan is small enough to walk around in the hour that most tours give you.

LANYU

☎089 / POP 4700

The Tao people call their island home 'Pongso No Tao' (Island of the People), while the Taiwanese started calling it Lanyu (蘭嶼, Lányǔ, Orchid Island) post-WWII, after the flowers that have since been picked to near extinction. A volcanic island covered with a carpet of tropical rainforest, Lanyu lies about 65km southeast of the city of Taitung, making it the southernmost outpost of Taiwan.

Lanyu's status as a far-flung outpost isn't merely geographical, but cultural as well, as the island is by far the least Chinese part of Taiwan. The Tao people are of Australasian descent, speak their own distinct language, and have a culture well removed from that of the people 'on the Mainland' (as they sometimes refer to the Taiwanese).

The tropical island is sacred land to its inhabitants, but it had been mistreated for decades by a larger colonising neighbour. The opening of the island to tourism in the 1960s, coupled with controversial government policies, has seen the Tao struggle to retain their culture in the face of increasing outside influences. The Tao are well aware that most Taiwanese visitors view them as an oddity, so any visitors to Lanyu should take note of these sensitivities.

Summer is high season on Lanyu, and plane tickets are hard to get and accommodations scarce and more expensive. After mid-September, however, and in the spring, Taiwanese visitors are few and far between (especially during the week), despite the fact that the weather leans towards the idyllic end of the scale.

Lanyu is made up of two steep, jungle-covered mountains which are surrounded by a thin strip of coastal land with six villages on it. The 37km road circling both mountains can be driven in about 1½ hours; a shorter, twisting road winds between both mountains from just south of the village of Hungtou on the west coast to the village of Yeyin on the east. This road also branches off to reach the weather observation centre atop Hongtoushan (Red Head Mountain).

History

The Tao had been the only tribal group on their island up until the mid-20th century which was when outsiders began to seriously disturb their way of life.

During the Japanese period, the Japanese were fascinated by the Tao's customs and did little to interfere with their way of life. However, things changed drastically after the Kuomintang (KMT) came to power and attempted to introduce Chinese language and culture to the Tao.

Boatloads of mainland Chinese were shipped to the island in the hope that interracial marriages would Sinicise the Tao population. The Tao resisted this encroachment and years of fighting with the mainlanders ensued. In the late 1960s Soong Mei Ling (wife of Chiang Kai-shek) declared that the traditional underground homes of the Tao were not fit for humans and ordered they be torn down and new cement structures built in their place. The houses were poorly made and couldn't hold up to the typhoons that lashed the island every year. At about the same time the island was opened up to tourism and Taiwanese tourists began to arrive in droves. Christian missionaries soon followed, converting a large percentage of the population who are, to this day, primarily Christian.

The relationship between the Taiwanese government and the Tao took a turn for the worse when the government unilaterally decided that the island would be a good place to dump nuclear waste. Long Men (Dragon Gate), at the southern tip of the island, was selected as a temporary storage facility for mid- and low-level nuclear waste. The site, which government representatives told locals was 'a fish cannery', became a depository for up to 100,000 barrels of nuclear waste in 1982. When islanders discovered the truth from news reports, they raised a furious outcry, protesting both on Lanyu and in front of the various government buildings in Taipei.

Despite government promises that the dump would be removed, the barrels remain and there is evidence that approximately 20% of the original barrels are beginning to leak and the concrete trenches they are buried in are cracking. Soil samples from the south end of the island show higher than normal levels of radioactivity and the possibility of health problems resulting from long-term contamination is of great concern to Tao people.

The Tao are doing their best to preserve their culture in the face of various social issues not uncommon in aboriginal communities. Alcoholism is a problem on the island,

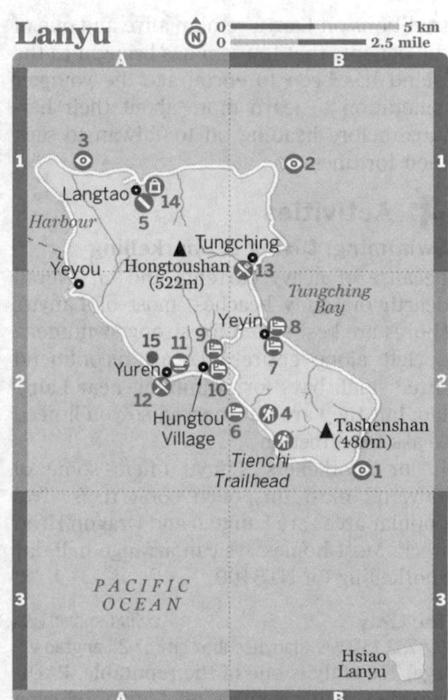

Lanyu

Sights

1	Dragon Head Rock	B2
2	Two Lions Rock	B1
3	Virgin Rock	A1

Activities, Courses & Tours

4	Hungtou Eco-Education Trail	B2
5	Tec Only	A1

Sleeping

6	Blue Ocean House	B2
7	Enhui Mingsu Zijia	B2
8	Fa'ai Homestay	B2
9	Lumai Home	A2
10	Meni's Place	A2

Eating

11	Epicurean Cafe	A2
12	Piaoliumu	A2
13	Three Sisters	B1

Shopping

14	Canaanland Workshop	A1
	Three Sisters	(see 13)

Transport

15	Lan En Foundation	A2

as is the overall brain drain caused by so many young people leaving to find greater economic prosperity in Taiwan. Even so, Tao traditions on Lanyu remain alive and one of the benefits that tourism has brought to the island has been to encourage the younger generation to learn more about their heritage before heading off to Taiwan to seek their fortunes.

Activities

Swimming, Diving & Snorkelling

Because of heavy currents and an overall dearth of sandy beaches, most of Lanyu's shores are best suited for strong swimmers, or left alone entirely. Locals recommend three small bays for swimming near Langtao, but they are not marked so you'll need to ask for directions.

For snorkellers, Lanyu offers some of Taiwan's most unspoiled coral reefs. Two popular areas are Langtao and Dragon Head Rock. Most homestays can arrange half-day snorkelling for NT$400.

Tec Only DIVING, SNORKELING
(☎732 151; www.lanyuscuba.com; 17-2 Langtao Village) Tec Only is one of the reputable, PADI-certified diving centres on Lanyu, offering introductory 'leisure courses'.

Wildlife-Watching

Despite its relatively small size, Lanyu is home to a few endemic butterfly and bird species. The diminutive **Lanyu scops owl** is relatively common in the more remote forests and most homestays can arrange for a night visit where the odds of spotting a few are high.

The new 1km-long **Hungtou Eco-Education Trail** (紅頭森林生態步道, Hóngtóu Sēnlín Shēngtài Bùdào) is an excellent place to spot special birds of Lanyu such as **Japanese Paradise Flycatcher** and **Whistling Pigeon**. The trailhead is at the Chung'ai bridge, 1km south of Hungtou Village, and it will lead you down into the gully that continues up to the river bed.

The gorgeous **Magellan's iridescent birdwing butterfly** has one of the widest wingspans in the world: up to 20cm across for males. Just riding around the main roads in April and May or October and November you may spot one or two, but for a tour of prime areas contact Mr Si, a well-known local carver, at his **Si Kang Chai Art Studio** (希岡菜木雕工作室, Xī Gāng Cài Mùdīao Gōngzùoshì; ☎0989-729 966; 38 Tungching Village).

Rock Formations

Visiting Lanyu is an otherworldly experience indeed and one of the features that gives Lanyu a vaguely Lovecraftian vibe is the twisted, jagged volcanic rocks jutting dramatically out of the ground and out to the sea. Taiwanese tourists like to pose before formations with imaginative monikers such as **Dragon Head Rock** and **Two Lions Rock**. On the north coast of the island one rock has been dubbed **Virgin Rock**, likely because the elliptical rock is hollow. Come see for yourself. In any event, the rocks' monikers have been assigned by the Taiwanese and not the Tao themselves (who generally find the names silly).

Hiking

The interior of the island has some magnificent hiking and one of the best hikes on Lanyu leads up to **Tienchi** (Tiānchí, Heaven Lake), an often-dry pond formed inside a volcanic crater on top of **Tashenshan** (Tashen Mountain). The hike to the lake and back is moderately difficult, with one section requiring hikers to navigate their way through a large, rocky ravine. As you climb higher into the jungly elevations the views open up and there are good opportunities for both bird- and butterfly-watching. Allow three to four hours to do the round-trip hike.

Tours

Most homestays can arrange snorkelling and wildlife tours. If you have an interest in a special part of Tao culture, contact Canaanland Workshop (p312), about 500m from the main strip in Langtao. Look for the really big canoe on the left.

Teresa (☎0988-263 187; tbunnyteresa@yahoo.com.tw), who's employed as a nurse at the island's health clinic and is one of the few fully fluent English speakers on Lanyu, also serves as a guide for those interested in Tao culture. Rates for her guide service go from NT$4000 per day for groups of no more than eight people. She also knows the various Flying Fish Festival dates.

Festivals & Events

Flying Fish Festival ABORIGINAL FESTIVAL
(飛魚季, Fēiyú Jì) The Flying Fish Festival is a traditional coming-of-age ceremony for young men whose societal standing was based on how many fish they could catch. The springtime festival is a very localised

affair and each village celebrates it on a different day chosen by the elders.

During the festival the men of the village wear traditional Tao loincloths, bark helmets and breastplates, and smear the blood of a freshly killed chicken on the rocks by the sea, all the while chanting 'return flying fish' in unison before heading out to sea in their canoes. According to custom, women are not allowed to view the festival, but most villages will make exceptions for visitors.

The festival usually takes place between March and May. If you have at least eight companions, you can arrange for fishermen to take you out fishing during the flying fish season.

Sleeping

Most villages offer homestays varying from rooms with a basic bed to fancy digs. Though the families running these places have limited to zero English, they're generally pleased to have Western guests. Accommodation tends to be overpriced in Hungtou, the most developed village on the island. All homestays listed here offer free pick-ups, and can arrange snorkelling, nighttime owl and sea-life tours.

Enhui Mingsu Zijia HOMESTAY $
(恩惠民宿之家, Ēnhuì Mínsù Zhījiā; ☎732 979; Yeyin Village, 野銀部落; d & dm per person NT$400) Li Ge and Li Sao, a husband-and-wife team, provide four spotless doubles and a large dorm on the upper floor in their home, which is located on a hill in Yeyin on the east side of the island. Li Ge, an excellent guide, also offers visits to his parents' underground house in the mornings.

Lumai Home HOMESTAY $
(魯邁民宿, Lǔmài Mínsù; ☎732 508; www.facebook.com/lumaihomelanyu; 142 Hungtou Village, 紅頭村142號; per person NT$500; ❄📶) With two cosy dorms, Lumai Home is an excellent budget choice in Hungtou. If you come from the airport, the homestay is on the slope before you reach the police station in the village. Their two canine members will greet you at the entrance with a surfboard beside it.

Fa'ai Homestay HOMESTAY $
(法艾民宿, Fǎài Mínsù; ☎0978-641 587; www.facebook.com/lanyufaai; 91 Yeyin Village, 野銀村91號; dm/d NT$500/1500; ❄@) Rooms are simple but clean in this new two-storey homestay with a pleasant sky blue and lilac look. The friendly owner, Hsiao Chiang, has an encyclopaedic knowledge of the island and can show you his family's underground houses just 200m south of the homestay.

Meni's Place HOMESTAY $$
(墨泥家, Mònì Jiā; ☎0978-719 003; www.facebook.com/menis.place; 87 Hungtou Village, 紅頭村87號; d from NT$1800; ❄@📶) This fancy guesthouse is especially popular among Taiwanese and other Asian travellers. There are five beautifully renovated rooms, three of them boasting ocean views. Kitchen use is possible with advance notice. Rooms can be booked solid even on weekdays so reserve well in advance.

Blue Ocean House CABIN $$
(藍海屋, Lánhǎi Wū; ☎0988-331 116; www.boh.com.tw/room/list.php; 1-8 Hungtou Village, 紅頭村1-8號; d NT$3600; ❄📶) The Blue Ocean dive shop and restaurant has added some new wooden cabins just across the road. Rooms are spacious and the open porches are made for chilling out in the ocean breeze. Good snorkelling and diving packages are available if you have four people or more (from NT$2350 per person).

TAO, DAWU OR YAMI?

The Tao – a word which means 'people' in the tribe's native tongue – were called the Yami, or northern islanders, during the Japanese occupation, thanks to the Japanese anthropologist Torii Ryuzo (1870–1953). Today, the aboriginal group is still officially known as the Yami, but in fact, since the 1990s, newer generations of the Tao, feeling an intense longing to rediscover their roots and reclaim their identity, have started to reject that term in favour of Tao or Dawu (Tao in Chinese pinyin). Though Yami isn't derogatory, most Tao people on Lanyu now rarely identify themselves as such and it won't go wrong to respect what they want to be called.

Eating & Drinking

The Tao diet consists primarily of fish and locally grown vegetables, with a bit of pork and goat on special occasions. In addition to enjoying homestay meals you can eat and drink at a growing number of restaurants and cafes on both sides of the island.

LOCAL KNOWLEDGE

QUAN YUMAN: RESPECTING LOCAL TRADITIONS

The majority of Tao on Lanyu were raised traditionally and it's important for visitors to travel carefully. Local craftswoman Quan Yuman (全玉滿) is part of Canaanland Workshop, an association in Langtao working to educate both visitors and locals on the culture, history and ecology of Lanyu. Here are her suggestions for minimising cross-cultural misunderstandings:

- In general, Tao do not like being watched when performing their common daily activities, and bristle at being looked upon as exotic or different.
- Following the above point, don't take photos without asking for permission. This applies not just to people, but to their houses and their possessions, including livestock.
- Don't touch or sit or pose by traditional canoes without asking for permission. The canoes are private property and not placed on the beach for tourists.
- During the flying-fish season, don't stand or walk under or take pictures of racks of drying fish. This is considered extremely impolite.
- If you see someone hauling in a large catch of fish don't comment on how many fish there are. As with many traditional cultures, the Tao feel this not only jinxes the fisherman (meaning his next catch will be small) but also puts an obligation on him to give you some of his catch.
- The traditional platforms you see everywhere are for resting during the day and cooling off. Tao dislike having their picture taken when they are sitting or sleeping in these. Visitors are free to use the platforms but ask first and be aware that the owner always has right of way.
- Tao men fish at night and so often sleep or hang about in the daytime. Suggestions that they have an easy or lazy life because they never seem very busy are not appreciated.
- Tao graves are often not marked, so don't go wandering off the trails in the forest as you might inadvertently step on one. In general, keep to the roads and paths. This applies to bird- and butterfly-watchers, too. If you want to explore, get a guide.
- If you are curious about Tao culture it's best to ask your homestay or the association to find someone who is willing to answer your questions. Local people don't always appreciate a lot of direct questions from strangers and may just make up their answers.

Three Sisters TAIWANESE $
(三姐妹, Sān jiěmèi; 23 Tungching Village; drinks from NT$80, dishes from NT$150; 11am-8pm) Adjacent to the Three Sisters gift shop, it's the most decent eatery on the eastern side of the island.

Piaoliumu CAFE $$
(漂流木, Piāoliúmù; 24-2 Yuren Village; drinks from NT$180, meals NT$200-390; 11am-2am) This cheerfully decorated roadside cafe and bar serves up arguably the best freshly brewed coffee and homemade pastries on the island. The thoughtful menu (written in Chinese but the owner speaks English) features locally sourced and seasonal dishes.

Epicurean Cafe CAFE
(無餓不坐, Wúè Búzuò; 77 Yuren Village; drinks from NT$70, meals NT$180-300; 11am-8.30pm;) The food here won't turn your head, but the hillside perch of this cafe-restaurant-bar is a great spot for sipping a coffee or beer while you enjoy views of Lanyu's coral coastline. If there are customers the cafe will stay open late, in effect turning into a late-evening bar.

Shopping

One of the most important Tao cultural traditions is the building of elaborately carved wooden canoes, made from 27 individual pieces of wood, ingeniously held together without nails. Buying a canoe is unfeasible unless you intend to row it home (not advisable).

Canaanland Workshop HANDICRAFTS
(迦南園工藝坊, Jiānányuán Gōngyìfāng; 0912-103 639; 224 Langtao Village; 8am-6pm) Canaanland Workshop sells good wooden canoe replicas, as well as other crafts at their Langtao shop.

Three Sisters HANDICRAFTS
(三姐妹, Sān Jiě Mèi; 23 Tungching Village) Three Sisters sells woven bracelets, woodcarvings and paintings.

Information

The cancellation of flights is common, so prepare extra cash for unplanned days. There are no international ATMs on Lanyu.

Wi-fi is available at a growing number of cafes, restaurants and homestays. Yeyin and Hungtou Villages have one internet cafe (網咖, *wǎngbā*) each.

Getting There & Away

AIR

Daily Air Corporation (☎362 489; www.dailyair.com.tw) has seven flights a day (NT$1345, 20 minutes) between Taitung and Lanyu. The 19-seat planes fill up quickly year-round, so book both ways as far ahead as possible. In the winter months scheduling is unreliable because of the weather.

BOAT

From April to October there are boats (NT$1000, two hours) running between Fugang Harbour (Taitung) or Houbitou (Kenting) and Lanyu (just north of Yeyou Village). Schedules are dependent both on weather and the number of passengers. Booking further than a day in advance can be unreliable; verify on the day of travel with the travel agency in Taitung or at the harbour.

In the summer months there are boats going from Lanyu to Green Island (NT$800, 40 minutes) twice a week, but not vice versa. Again, cancellation of services is not uncommon.

Getting Around

TO/FROM THE AIRPORT

Hotels and homestays provide transport to and from the airport if notified in advance.

BICYCLE

Bicycle rentals (NT$250 per day) are available at **Lan En Foundation** (蘭恩基金會, Lán ēn Jījīn Huì; 147 Yuren Village; ⏲8am-4.30pm Thu-Tue), a 10-minute walk from the airport. Look out for the towering, brightly coloured canoe prows at the entrance.

CAR & SCOOTER

There's a rental shop next to the Lanyu Hotel in Hungtou but any hotel or homestay can arrange rental (car/scooter NT$1800/400 per day). In winter renting a car is safer and more comfortable than a scooter because of slippery road conditions.

GREEN ISLAND

☎089 / POP 3482

Boasting lush mountains, good beaches and one of only three seawater hot springs in the world, Green Island (綠島, Lǜdǎo) is a popular resort destination for Taiwanese looking for rest and recreation. But in the not too distant past, the phrase 'off to Green Island' didn't conjure up visions of leisure pursuits in the Taiwanese psyche. For once upon a time the very name of this tiny volcanic island, 30km east of Taitung, was synonymous with repression. It was where, under martial law, political opponents of the regime were sent to languish at the island's notorious prison camp.

Today, this once potent place of repression has been transformed into a museum and human-rights memorial. To a new generation of Taiwanese the island is thought of not primarily for its infamous past, but as a place to see pristine coral reefs and gorgeous tropical fish, hang out on the beach and soak in the hot spring under the night sky.

Green Island is ringed by a 19km road that you can get around on a scooter in 30 minutes. With one main road hugging the shore and another leading up to Huoshao Mountain, getting lost is pretty difficult. The island was devastated by Typhoon Tembin in 2012 and was slowly recovering at the time of research.

Sights

★ **Green Island Human Rights Cultural Park** MEMORIAL PARK
(綠島人權文化園區, Lǜdǎo Rénquán Wénhuà Yuánqū; ⏲8am-5pm) FREE Standing forlorn on a windswept coast, its back to a sheer cliff, this complex is a sobering reminder of Taiwan's White Terror and Martial Law periods (1949–87). The park site is a former prison, sardonically referred to as **Oasis Villa** (綠洲山莊, Shānzhuāng), where those at odds with the KMT were sent.

Visitors are welcome to walk around the prison area and inspect the cells where former prisoners such as Taiwanese writer Bo Yang (author of *The Ugly Chinaman*) once spent years. Parts of the compound now house a museum and an exhibition hall dedicated to the survivors and those who died.

It's a sombre place, of course, so visit here first and devote the rest of the trip to more cheerful pursuits.

Little Great Wall VOLCANIC CRATER
(小長城, Xiǎo chángchéng) Green Island has some intriguing volcanic-rock formations. The 300m-long promontory called Little Great Wall is the northern wall of the crater of the volcano that formed Green Island. It leads to a pavilion where you can see **Haishenping** (海參坪, Hǎishēn Píng), the crater bay.

Across the bay is **Sleeping Beauty Rock** (睡美人, Shuì Měirén), one of the formations that actually does resemble its name (once you figure out the neck, the rest of the figure will fall into place).

Kuanyin Cave TAOIST SHRINE
(觀音洞, Guānyīn Dòng) The underground Kuanyin Cave is dedicated to Guanyin (the Goddess of Mercy) and features a stalagmite wrapped with a red cape. Legend has it that during the Qing dynasty a fisherman became lost at sea and a fiery red light came down from the sky and led him to safety in the cave.

The fisherman believed the light to be the Goddess Guanyin and the stalagmite in the cape to resemble the form of the goddess. The cavern remains a sacred spot on the island and people come here from all over Taiwan to pay their respects.

Yutzu Lake SCENIC AREA
(柚子湖, Yòuzǐ Hú) Not a lake but a sheltered cove, Yutzu Lake is the site of the first village on the island. Some old stone houses still remain and nearby is a sea-eroded cave worth a look.

Green Island Lighthouse LIGHTHOUSE
(綠島燈塔, Lùdǎo Dēngtǎ) The 33m-high Green Island Lighthouse was built in 1937 under the Japanese after the American ship *President Hoover* struck a reef and sank.

Pahsien & Lunghsia Caves CAVE
A cool collection of sea caves, **Pahsien Cave** (八仙洞, Bāxiān Dòng) and **Lunghsia Cave** (龍蝦洞, Lóngxiā Dòng) are just off the main road.

Activities

Diving & Snorkelling

Thanks to nutrients deposited in the water by the hot spring on the southern tip, Green Island boasts 205 types of coral and 602 types of fish around the coast, and the government has gone to considerable lengths to protect the reefs.

Most hotels and guesthouses can arrange snorkelling and diving trips. Equipment can be rented at shops in Nanliao Village. Rates depend on how many people you have in your group and the type of equipment you need to rent.

Dabaisha Beach (大白沙, Dà Báishā) has fine white coral sand and is known for its stunning coral reefs, making it a good spot for snorkelling, as is the small stretch of beach east of the Green Island Lighthouse.

Blue Safari Diving Centre DIVING, SNORKELING
(藍莎潛水中心, Lánshā Qiánshuǐ Zhōngxīn; ☎671 888; www.blue-safari.com.tw; 72 Gongguan Village) A reputable dive shop, run by diving enthusiasts Vincent and Eva.

Taiwan Dive DIVING
(www.taiwandive.com) For experienced divers, Kaohsiung-based Taiwan Dive can organise trips to see the hammerhead shark migration off Green Island as well as adventure dive trips.

Hot Springs

★**Chaojih Hot Springs** HOT SPRING
(朝日溫泉, Zhāorì Wēnquán; admission NT$200; ⏲5am-2am) Chaojih Hot Springs is one of the planet's three known seawater hot springs. It is clear and odourless, and the water temperature varies from 53°C to 83°C. Under an evening sky in autumn or winter, a soak in the hot pools followed by a quick dip in the sea is blissful.

There are two sets of pools to choose from: the older circular stone hot-spring pits down by the beach and the modern tile pools in the better-lit part of the complex. The latter set features pools of varying temperatures, from just above freezing to just below scalding, artfully shaped artificial privacy grottos and a good number of massage showers (overhead pipes jetting down spring water at jackhammer frequencies).

If you want to visit the beachside pools at night, take a torch with you.

Hiking

The two main trails on Green Island, imaginatively called the **Across Mountain Ancient Trail** (過山古道, Guòshān Gǔdào) and the **Across Mountain Trail** (過山步道, Guòshān Bùdào), both begin within a few hundred metres of each other on the mountain road to Huoshao (281m), the highest peak on the island.

You can't climb Huoshao because of the military base at the summit, but these two trails heading down to the seashore more than make up for that.

Green Island

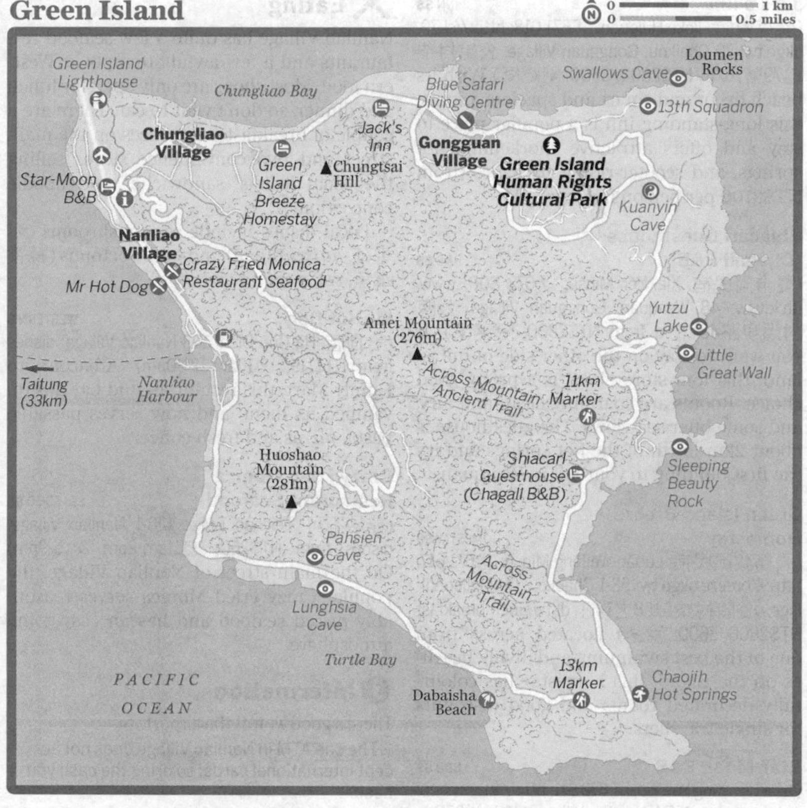

Both trails are about 1.8km long and run through thick, natural tropical forest. Paths are wide and clear, and have informative signs that explain the common English names of plants. Best of all, the chances of spotting sika deer or the tiny barking deer are high.

Tours

Green Island Adventures TOUR
(www.greenislandadventures.com) Green Island Adventures arranges year-round transport to the island, accommodation, and tailor-built tour packages including snorkelling, diving, hiking and hot springing. It also arranges the use of a glass-bottomed boat for tours around the island's fabulous coral reefs.

Sleeping

The greatest concentration of accommodation is on the main street in Nanliao Village close to the harbour, but these tend to be older hotels. Newer and more modern B&Bs have recently opened up around the island. Almost all hotels and guesthouses on the island offer free pick-ups from the airport and the ferry terminal, as do packages that include round-trip ferry tickets and scooter rental.

Green Island is a popular summer destination for Taiwanese tourists, which means that most hotels will be booked solid on weekends. During the low season (or even weekdays in summer) most hotels offer discounted prices.

Blue Safari Diving Centre HOSTEL $
(藍莎潛水中心, Lánshā Qiánshuǐ Zhōngxīn; ☎671 888; www.blue-safari.com.tw; 72 Gongguan Village, 公館村72號; dm incl breakfast NT$600;) Blue Safari is a dive shop that doubles as a well-maintained 12-bed mixed dorm hostel. It's the best budget option on the island so it's always heavily booked. The owner Eva can arrange free pick-ups and scooter rental if you reserve in advance.

Jack's Inn INN $$
(傑克會館, Jiékè Huìguǎn; ☎671 018; http://ck79.okgo.tw; 79 Chaikou, Gongguan Village, 公館村柴口79號; d/tw NT$2800/3600;) With its beach decor and smart and spacious rooms, this long-standing inn is a popular place to stay and offers attractive snorkelling, hot springs, and scooter-riding packages (from NT$2700 per person in summer).

Shiacarl Guesthouse (Chagall B&B) B&B $$
(夏卡爾民宿, Xiàkǎ'ěr Mínsù; ☎672 800; www.ith.idv.tw; 48 Wenquan, Gongguan Village, 公館村溫泉路48號; d from NT$2800;) If you want to stay on the other side of the island, this four-storey B&B is a pretty good choice. Rooms are sparkling clean and airy, and some offer sea views. The guesthouse is about 2km north of the hot springs and it's the first building to your left in Wenquan.

Green Island Breeze Homestay HOMESTAY $$
(綠島微風民宿, Lùdǎo Wēifēng Mínsù; ☎671 617; http://breeze.okgo.tw; 58-1 Chaokou, Chungliao Village, 公館村柴口58之1號; d/tw incl breakfast NT$2600/3600;) Located across from one of the best swimming and diving beaches on the island, this homestay has colourfully decorated rooms and good discounts for single travellers.

Star-Moon B&B B&B $$
(星月屋, Xīng Yuè Wū; ☎672 911; http://star-moon.hotel.com.tw; 255-1 Nanliao Village, 南寮村255之1號; d/tw incl breakfast NT$2000/2800;) This friendly B&B has 20-plus simple and homey rooms. It's located diagonally opposite the visitor information centre and is just a stone's throw from the airport.

Eating

Nanliao Village has quite a few seafood restaurants and a few awful attempts at Western food. Most shops are only open for lunch and dinner, so don't wait to eat. There are a couple of breakfast-only places on the main street and two convenience stores selling the usual drinks, sandwiches and noodle concoctions.

Local dishes include sea mushrooms (海香菇, *hǎi xiānggū*) and garlic octopus (蒜香章魚, *suàn xiāng zhāngyú*).

Mr Hot Dog WESTERN $
(哈狗店, Hā Gǒu Diàn; 103 Nanliao Village; dishes from NT$119; ⏰10am-12.30am) Adjacent to Family Mart, this restaurant and bar has revamped its menu and now serves passable pasta, pizzas and fresh coffee.

Crazy Fried Monica Restaurant Seafood SEAFOOD $$
(非炒不可, Fēichǎo Bùkě; 126-1 Nanliao Village; dishes from NT$250; ⏰11am-2pm & 5-9pm) On the main street of Nanliao Village, the popular Crazy Fried Monica serves reasonably priced seafood and has an easy-going atmosphere.

Information

There's good wi-fi at the airport.

The one ATM in Nanliao Village does not accept international cards, so bring the cash you need.

Visitor Information Centre (遊客中心, Yóukè Zhōngxīn; ☎672 027; 298 Nanliao Village; ⏰8am-5pm) A minute's walk from the airport, the centre has maps and information about the island's history, culture and ecology.

WORTH A TRIP

SWALLOWS CAVE & THE 13TH SQUADRON

If you go to the northeastern tip of the island from Green Island Human Rights Cultural Park (p313), there are a few sites en route that will provide memorable confrontations with the most gruesome chapters in the island's history. Not far from the main prison gate is a half-buried **pillbox** right by the sea which doubled as a water cell where the most disobedient prisoners were kept during high tides and left to the mercy of the elements.

The notorious **Swallows Cave** (燕子洞, Yànzi Dòng), 500m northeast of the park, is a natural sea cave where inmates rehearsed plays and which also served as an execution ground and a mortuary. Before you reach the cave, pay attention to the overgrown graveyard set by the cliff to your right. There were 12 groups of inmates in Oasis Villa (p313) and those who died in prison with no one to collect their bodies were collectively buried here, hence they were poignantly known as the **13th Squadron** (十三中隊, Shísān zhōngduì). About 40 gravestones remain but the actual number of burials is still unknown.

Getting There & Away

AIR

Daily Air Corporation (☎362 489; www.dailyair.com.tw) has three daily flights between Taitung and Green Island (NT$1028, 15 minutes) on small 19-seat propeller planes. During winter flights are often cancelled due to bad weather. In summer you must book several weeks ahead. The airport on Green Island is at the edge of Nanliao Village, about 500m from the main drag.

BOAT

From April to September boats run hourly between Taitung's Fukang Harbour and Green Island (NT$460, 50 minutes). The first boat leaves Fukang at 7.30am, Green Island at 8.30am. The schedule outside summer changes daily and is unreliable because of weather conditions. At all times it's a very uncomfortable ride that makes most people seasick.

Getting Around

BICYCLE

There's free rental at the visitor information centre outside the airport if you've flown to Green Island; you'll need to show a passport or Alien Resident Certificate (ARC) and boarding pass.

CHECKING IN & OUT

Green Island hotels have a strict 2pm check-in, so book ahead if you are catching an early ferry or flight. You'll wait in the lobby for a long time if you just show up. Also, take advantage of pick-ups, especially from the airport, which has no scooter rental nearby.

Be aware that most hotels also have a 10am checkout. You can usually store your bags if you have a later flight, but be sure to take them out of your room on time or you will be charged extra.

BUS

Buses circle the island eight times a day, stopping at various tourist points, and can be flagged down anywhere. Schedules are posted at each stop.

SCOOTER

Scooter rentals (NT$300 to NT$400 per day) are available at the harbour or from your hotel; none are available at the airport.

Understand Taiwan

Taiwan Today

In so many ways, Taiwan is stalled. The economy has suffered anaemic growth for years (starting wages are back to mid-'90s levels) and politically the country is acting at cross purposes: voting to strengthen ties with China but resisting any attempt to dilute local identity or autonomy. And yet, despite the contradictions, Taiwan continues to develop as Asia's most open, tolerant and liberal society. If there's a national mood these days, it might be sunny pessimism.

Best in Film

Cape No 7 (Wei Te-sheng; 2008) This romantic comedy revived both interest in and funding for Taiwanese cinema.

Seediq Bale (Wei Te-sheng; 2011) This two-part epic wowed audiences across the country with the tale of the Wushe Rebellion.

City of Sadness (Hou Hsiao-hsien; 1989) This film of the events around the 2-28 Incident finally broke the taboo against discussing the tragedy.

Eat Drink Man Woman (Ang Lee; 1994) A must-see for those interested in Taiwanese culture.

Best in Print

Formosa Betrayed (George Kerr; 1965) A compelling account from an American diplomat of post-WWII Taiwan including the 2-28 Incident.

Taipei People (Pai Hsien-yung; 1971) A short story collection from one of Taiwan's best writers about mainland immigrants in Taipei in the 1950s.

A Chinese Pioneer Family: The Lins of Wu-feng, Taiwan, 1729–1895 (Johanna Menzel Meskill; 1979) A readable historical account of one of Taiwan's most powerful families, from the first impoverished immigrant to contemporary business and cultural leaders.

The Mewling Tiger

Taiwan's economy once more than held its own against rival Asian Tigers South Korea, Hong Kong and Singapore. But in the last decade it has consistently posted the lowest growth, the least direct foreign investment and, more importantly, the lowest salaries. Average salaries in South Korea, for example, are now 2.8 times higher than in Taiwan.

Where did it all go wrong? The story is still being written but a few clear themes are emerging.

First of all there has been gross over-investment in China. Since the late '90s, Taiwanese firms, with their advantages in language and culture, have invested some US$120 to US$200 billion in China, but only a fraction of that at home.

There's also been a lack of R&D and business upgrading. Too many Taiwanese companies moved to China for the cheap manufacturing rather than as part of a sophisticated industrial restructuring. Now with wages rising in China, and firms there capable of handling production (and design), many Taiwanese companies are finding themselves outdated and unneeded.

Some one to two million Taiwanese have also relocated to China in search of better wages and opportunities and this brain drain is only worsening. China is also directly poaching skilled Taiwanese from industries it wants to develop. When Fujian province officials wanted to modernise and expand their tea growing industry, for example, they simply flew to Taiwan and offered land and loans to hundreds of farmers.

Identity Questions

In recent polls on national identity, 95% said they considered themselves either Taiwanese exclusively or Taiwanese and Chinese (with the latter usually referring to ethnicity and not nationality). Only a tiny percentage considered themselves Chinese only. This is a massive change from 20 years ago, when less than 17% considered themselves Taiwanese. More and more locals identify with Taiwan as both their nation and homeland and resent China's persistent moves to block their participation in international events and organisations (unless under the name Chinese Taipei).

Interestingly, the election in 2008 of Ma Ying-jeou, a KMT leader committed to closer ties with China, has not dampened this momentum in the least. Nor has it dampened real desire for independence. Though most say they support the status quo (de facto independence but no formal declaration), when asked how they would choose if they were not worried about China's response over 75% say they would vote for formal independence.

But China's response does matter, and its repeated threats of invasion should Taiwanese vote 'the wrong way' has its influence. In the 2012 election it became clear that Taiwan's major companies and business leaders had also decamped to the unification side, with some openly warning their employees not to vote 'the wrong way'. If Taiwan is to maintain its distinction and autonomy a consensus must be reached soon on how to keep China at bay politically while at the same time developing trade and cultural exchanges.

The Other Big Issues

In addition to national identity and the economy, you can be certain to hear lots of other issues discussed on the news and on the streets.

For example, Taiwan badly needs educational, judicial, police, health care, taxation and pension reforms (current public-sector worker pensions would make pre-crisis Greeks envious). Every move, however, has been countered or watered down by special interest groups.

Rising inequality is another concern. Warren Buffet may note that his secretary pays a higher percentage of taxes than he does, but according to reports by *Commonwealth Magazine,* wealthy Taiwanese often pay less in real dollars than most workers by parking their wealth in property and stock purchases (which are effectively tax free). This is starving the government of needed revenue to fund everything from infrastructure to education.

Connected with the above, housing in northern Taiwan, especially Taipei, is becoming unaffordable, with costs at 15 to 20 times average yearly income.

Nuclear energy is another hot topic these days, especially after the Fukushima disaster in Japan. Many young Taiwanese are also highly concerned with media monopolisation, especially with large companies with pro-China agendas appearing more than willing to stifle free expression.

One of the most contentious issues of the day is land confiscation. The Taiwanese government

POPULATION: **23,299,716**

GDP: **(PPP) $918 BILLION**

UNEMPLOYMENT: **4.19%**

HIGHEST POINT: **YUSHAN (3952M)**

GEOGRAPHY: **35,883 KM2**

LITERACY RATES: **96.1%**

if Taiwan were 100 people

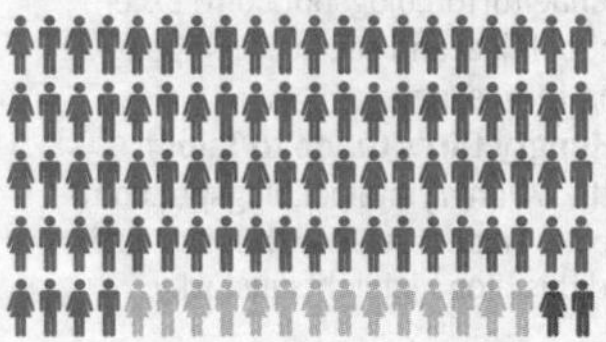

84 would be Taiwanese & Hakka
14 would be Mainland Chinese
2 would be Indigenous

belief systems

(% of population)

Folk religion(s) | Buddhist | Taoist

3 Protestant | 2 I-Kuan Taoist | 25 Other or not religious

population per sq km

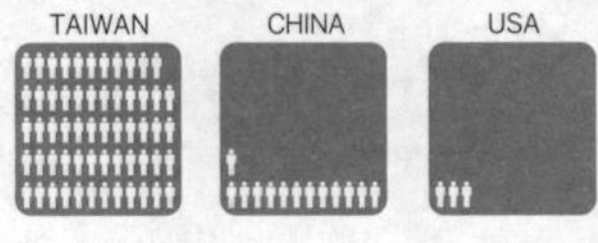

≈ 11 people

Myths

➡ Despite the Made in Taiwan reputation, Taiwan is not one giant factory but still largely rural and mountainous.

➡ Taiwan was once called Free China not because it was free, but because it was a counterpoint to communist China.

➡ It is true that both instant noodles and bubble tea were invented by Taiwanese.

Best Blogs

The View From Taiwan (http://michaelturton.blogspot.com) Excellent political and social coverage by a long-term expat.

A Hungry Girl's Guide to Taipei (http://hungryintaipei.blogspot.com) Food is an obsession with Taiwanese and this blog highlights just why.

Best Religious Festivals

Matsu Pilgrimage Taiwanese are devoted to their gods as this nine-day event in spring makes clear.

Keelung Ghost Festival Like many cultural celebrations in Taiwan, this one has been heavily localised and is a riot of colour and activity.

expropriates enormous amounts of land from farmers each year to provide space for development projects. Many people are fighting back and things often turn violent.

Government & Politics

A multiparty democracy, Taiwan's government is dominated by the KMT (Chinese Nationalist Party) which now controls both the executive and legislative branches. The main opposition party is the independence-supporting DPP (Democratic Progressive Party).

With the continual rise of China, both economically and militarily, the DPP are struggling to formulate a realistic China policy acceptable to both their core supporters and China. The KMT leadership, on the other hand, accepts China's One China Principle, and is open to unification as the desired outcome for Taiwan. But as is usual, current president Ma Ying-jeou ran on a platform of maintaining the status quo and for now voters in Taiwan are trusting that their democracy is mature enough and that their true interests won't be sold out no matter who is in power.

As his second term runs its course, however, Ma has been steadily losing support and trust. His economic policies have not brought growth to Taiwan, but have strengthened Taiwan's dependence on China. In 2013 his approval rating averaged around 15%.

The Future of Taiwan

Taiwan is down on the ropes but hardly out cold. It may be a small, resource poor, politically marginalised island, but it's also an IT powerhouse with a highly educated and entrepreneurial population. It may be coveted by the People's Republic of China (PRC) for nationalistic and strategic purposes but the US and Japan (and most of ASEAN) also hope to keep it as a democratic ally and bulwark against Chinese expansion.

Politically Taiwan may be divided about the future, but few have any desire to be ruled by Beijing. In the coming presidential elections in 2016, neither the KMT or DPP has a standout candidate and both are likely to face a continuing economic slump about which neither has any fresh solutions.

What's the future of Taiwan? An uncertainty wrapped in a layer of unpredictability.

History

Taiwanese believe they have a distinct society, and that is largely because of their history. Primarily aboriginal until the 17th century, Taiwan later saw centuries of immigration (coupled with colonisation by multiple empires), which resulted in localised arts, cuisine, religious worship patterns and social structures. The country's long road from authoritarianism (which sought to destroy that localisation) to democracy is another key part of the distinction people feel, and understanding this is essential for grasping the issues of the day.

Early History

Archaeological sites on the east coast, in particular the Baxianshan Caves, show humans existing in Taiwan as early as 50,000 years ago, as part of what is known as the Changbin Culture.

The ancestors of today's aboriginals likely came to Taiwan by sea from southeast China around 6000 years ago, landing in such places as Bali on the north coast and various spots down the west coast. They brought agriculture and advanced forms of culture (such as pottery) and quickly spread all over the island. Around 2000 BCE they even began to move off the island and there is good linguistic and archaeological evidence that this diaspora was the source of all of today's Austronesian peoples.

History Online

A vast collection of detailed and balanced articles on Taiwan's history can be found online at the Encyclopedia of Taiwan (http://taiwanpedia.culture.tw).

The Dutch Colonial Era

Though Chinese fisherman began to settle in Penghu around 1000 years ago, until the 16th century Taiwan was isolated and almost exclusively aboriginal. Official Chinese records were even unclear if it was one island or many until the late Ming dynasty. What happened to change the status quo? Trade. This was the era of increasing maritime commercial activity throughout East Asia and Taiwan quickly became a critical link in the routes between China (mostly Fujian), Japan, Manila and Macau.

Of particular importance were the routes established by the Dutch East India Company (abbreviated VOC). In 1602 the VOC was given a trade monopoly in the East. Unfortunately for it, the company was very

TIMELINE

50,000–10,000 BC

Human skeletons found in eastern Taiwan and in the Taipei Basin point to prehistoric human habitation of the island during the late Paleolithic era.

c 10,000 BC

Ancestors of Taiwan's present-day aboriginals first come to the island by sea and begin settling around the island.

AD 1544

Passing Portuguese sailors become the first Europeans to lay eyes on Taiwan; they are so enchanted they name the island Ilha Formosa (Beautiful Island).

late in the game and to become a serious player it had to first break the Spanish and Portuguese monopolies.

In the style of the age, the VOC fleets launched indiscriminate attacks on Portuguese and Spanish ships. By 1622, realising they needed a secure base in the region, the VOC sailed to Penghu (aka the Pescadores), an island group they had explored earlier, and built a small fortress.

In 1603, Ming troops landed in an attempt to root out piracy and illegal trade. From this came the first personal Chinese record of Taiwan: Dong Fan Zhi's *An Account of the Eastern Barbarians*.

From Penghu, the Dutch launched raids off the Fujian coast and disrupted Chinese trade with Manila (under Spanish control). The exasperated Chinese offered the Dutch permission to trade from Taiwan proper. The VOC caught the veiled threat, and left Penghu for Tayouan (what is now the Anping area of Tainan) where they established Fort Zeelandia.

The Dutch initially considered using Taiwan as an entrepot but quickly realised they would not be safe from aboriginal and Chinese attacks, and also trade rivals Spain and Japan, unless they could control the island. With this in mind they set out to pacify Plains aboriginals, import Chinese labour and destroy rival Spain. They also began the first modernisation program of Taiwan, establishing schools, missions (to convert aboriginals) and kilns, as well as issuing licences to Chinese fisherman and taxes on the deer meat trade. Their work was noted, and not always favourably.

In the early 17th century, Spain controlled the trade route between Fujian and Manila. The new Dutch presence on Taiwan, an island separated from Fujian by a narrow strait, was perceived as a major threat. In 1626 the Spanish landed and occupied the northern area of Taiwan around what is now Keelung and Tamsui. Over a 10-year period they established four forts, including Fort Santo Domingo in Tamsui, which remains intact to this day.

Though the Spanish engaged in military actions as far down the coast as Yilan and Hualien, their presence was always small. When the Manila governor, unimpressed with trade, further reduced troops, aboriginal groups attacked outposts. The Spanish withdrew to Keelung where they were then hit by the Dutch. By 1642 they had withdrawn from Taiwan entirely, giving the Dutch control from north to south.

In the 1640s instability in China (the Ming dynasty lost its capital to the Qing in 1644) was causing a wave of immigration from Fujian province into Taiwan. The new settlers chafed at European colonial rule and staged a revolt in 1652. Though the Dutch were successful in quelling that uprising, 10 years later they would be defeated and driven off Taiwan by a Chinese admiral and Ming Loyalist called Cheng Cheng-kung.

Cheng Cheng-kung, known in the west as Koxinga, was a colourful character, the son of a pirate turned admiral and his Japanese concubine. When Qing forces began to conquer China in the 1640s, the father capitulated but Koxinga fought on for the Ming's Yongli Emperor.

1622–62

The Dutch establish colonies on both Taiwan Island and Penghu to facilitate trade with China and Japan. They also encourage the first large migration of Han Chinese to Taiwan.

1662

After a two-year campaign, Dutch forces are driven off Taiwan by Ming loyalist Admiral Koxinga; they surrender to him in Tainan.

1662–83

Following Koxinga's death in 1662, son Zheng Jing sets up the first Han Chinese government on Taiwan, as a base to try to regain China from the Qing dynasty.

1683

Following Zheng Jing's death in 1682, son Zheng Keshuang rules briefly before being defeated at the Battle of Penghu, resulting in a surrender to Qing forces.

After a massive defeat in 1659, Koxinga sought refuge with his troops on Kinmen. There, a deputy suggested he invade Taiwan and overthrow the Dutch. Koxinga declined at first, but when both Dutch and Qing policies began to cut into his ability to trade and re-provision his troops, the stage was set.

Koxinga built a new fleet on Kinmen and in April 1661 sailed first to the Penghu Islands, before moving onto Taiwan proper. The outnumbered and outmaneuvered Dutch surrendered Fort Provenitia to him in five days. By February 1662 they had surrendered Fort Zeelandia. The 38 year colonisation of Taiwan by the Dutch was over.

Around 25,000 to 30,000 Chinese came to Taiwan with Koxinga (adding to a population that was around 100,000 aboriginals and a smaller number of Chinese). With them the admiral set out to create a military base for the re-taking of the mainland. As with the Dutch he continued to expand the agricultural system (soldiers had a dual role as farmers), but also introduced Ming-style administration and cultural elements: he built Taiwan's first Confucius Temple and introduced civil service exams. However, his dreams of overthrowing the Manchu were never realised. Koxinga died a year after landing on Taiwan at the age of 37.

After the admiral's death, his son Zheng Jing ruled Taiwan as sovereign of the Tungning Kingdom (1661–83). The young ruler encouraged trade, industry and immigration, not just of farmers and soldiers, but also scholars and administrators who did not want to serve the Qing. His death in 1681 led to bloody fights over succession, and in 1683, the Qing, under Admiral Shi Lang, moved in and captured Taiwan.

Afterwards, in one of the pivotal moments of Taiwan's history, Shi Lang convinced the skeptical Kangxi Emperor of the island's strategic importance. The emperor agreed to annexation, and Taiwan became Taiwanfu, a prefecture of Fujian province with a capital in present day Tainan.

Taiwan in the Qing Dynasty

Taiwan developed rapidly under the Qing. The population grew and Han Chinese became the dominant ethnic group as they spread over the western plains and across the Taipei Basin. Sugarcane production had dominated the economy under the Dutch, but now rice growing was added. With increased migration to the centre and north of the island, as well as the development of irrigation systems, almost all the arable land became utilised over time.

Immigration from China also increased but the imbalance of men to women led to increasing social problems, including the formation of secret societies. Grievances often led to violence and the Fujian Imperial

In the 16th century, Taiwan was a haven for pirates, who were driven to its isolated ports by Ming dynasty antismuggling campaigns. Ironically, these campaigns saw Taiwan become a base for secret trade between Japan and Chinese merchants.

1683–1885
Taiwan is governed by the Qing dynasty as a prefecture of Fujian province. Early years are marked by frequent rebellion, riots and civil strife.

1729
The Qing Emperor forbids immigration to Taiwan on pain of death. The order is later rescinded but immigration is officially limited for decades.

1787
The Lin Shuang-wen Rebellion, the largest popular revolt against Qing rule, takes over a year to suppress. The revolt shows the general dissatisfaction in Taiwan with Qing rule.

1861–64
The Treaty of Tianjin forces open Taiwan ports of Anping, Tamsui, Keelung and Kaohsiung to Western trade. Taiwan's camphor and tea exports enter the world markets.

Inspector Bian Baodi once noted famously that Taiwan had 'a revolt every three years and a rebellion every five years'.

During this period almost all immigrants came from the same three areas in China: Zhangzhou and Quanzhou in Fujian, and various locations in Guangdong province. The first two regions are the source of almost all ethnic Taiwanese (Hoklo); the latter the Hakka.

Though Taiwan was becoming Chinese during this era, it was also evolving unique associations and traditions to deal with the unusual immigrant circumstance. For example, lacking family ties, immigrants created social structures based on shared names, village origins and worship of similar folk gods. Even small differences could be a source of conflict: the Zhangzhou-Quanzhou distinction, for example, would be the cause of many small but deadly battles in Taiwan's history.

The latter half of the 19th century was a period of great turmoil for the Qing. Among other crises, they had to contend with the Taiping Rebellion, and forced trade with Western powers. Much of this directly and indirectly influenced Taiwan in profound ways.

THE RAW & THE COOKED

Controlling a large frontier such as Taiwan was no easy task. As with most colonial governments throughout history, both the Dutch and later Qing administrations had to find a way to maintain law and order without draining the coffers. Both also had to contend with aboriginal inhabitants who wouldn't conveniently accept their dominion.

When the Dutch arrived in southern Taiwan in 1622 they found it relatively easy to purchase land for their forts, and also form alliances with the neighbouring tribes. Military force was used when necessary, but Christian missions were vital for keeping the peace once areas had been pacified (by 1643 over 5000 aboriginals had been baptised). Elsewhere, the Dutch employed a divide and conquer strategy which resulted in an unstable political landscape of constantly shifting alliances.

Under the Qing *lifan* (aboriginal management policy) aboriginals were classified as raw (*shengfan*) or cooked (*shufan*). The cooked were those already pacified by the Dutch and so subject to taxation, education and military service. The raw were those living free of imperial obligations. To separate the two, the Qing literally drew a line down Taiwan: on one side was the civilised world, on the other the savage. This policy lasted until 1875, at which point the Qing, anxious to show the world they controlled all of Taiwan, reversed direction and attempted to open the interior and east coast by force.

Throughout the Qing era, cooked aboriginals were required to participate in the defence of Taiwan. Under a military habitation system (*tuntian*) young healthy aboriginals were conscripted to serve in self-supporting garrisons. In their dual role as farmer and soldier these aboriginals provided an invaluable service shielding Taiwan from both internal and external conflict.

1871

Japanese sailors stranded on the southern tip of Taiwan are killed in a conflict with local Paiwan tribespeople. The Japanese government demands compensation from the Qing court.

1874

A Japanese assault on Taiwan is repelled by a combination of locals and Qing troops. Japan withdraws its troops after suffering casualties caused by both battle and disease.

1885

Taiwan is made a separate province of the Qing Empire in response to growing interest in the island's strategic importance and resources by Japan and Western powers.

1885–91

Under the first provincial governor, Liu Mingchuan, a railway is built from Keelung to Taipei, the first in all of China. Liu also establishes a telegraph and postal system.

After the second Opium War ended (1860), for example, Taiwan was opened to trade with the West. Into the now free ports of Tamsui, Keelung, Anping and Kaohsiung flowed Western merchants, missionaries, soldiers, diplomats and scholars. Foreign trade increased rapidly, merchant houses such Jardine, Matheson & Co flourished, and Taiwan's economy became linked to global trade. The island became the largest camphor supplying region in the world, and its excellent teas were traded widely.

In early 18th-century Europe, much of what was known of Taiwan was picked from *An Historical and Geographical Description of Formosa* by George Psalmanazar. The Frenchmen, who claimed to be a native of the island, was later revealed to be a complete fraud.

Nearly all the major Western powers also had some kind of skirmish or 'incident' on Taiwan soil in the 19th century. The most significant was the Mudan Incident (1874) in which Japan sent 3600 troops on a punitive mission to the south over the butchery of 54 Japanese sailors by Paiwan aboriginals in Mudan, Pingtung County, three years earlier.

The incident revealed to the world both the weakness of the Qing government and their limited control over Taiwan (the Japanese had tried to bring their grievances to the Qing court only to be told that Paiwan aboriginals were outside Chinese control). A decade later French troops invaded and occupied Keelung during the Sino-French War. At last recognising the strategic importance of Taiwan, the Qing began to shore up its defences and spur development. Taiwan was made a province in 1885, with Liu Mingchuan the first governor.

Liu, a former general who had fought the French in Vietnam, believed in Taiwan self-reliance. Among his many initiatives were building cross-island roads (the present Highway 9 from Taipei to Ilan mostly follows his route), pacifying mountain aboriginals, and improving the economy. He implemented land reform, built the first railway from Taipei to Keelung, established a postal system, laid a submarine cable to Fujian, and created bureaus to handle railways, mining, telegraphs and other modern specialties.

Not all of Liu's reforms were successful, but it didn't much matter. Taiwan would not be Chinese territory for very much longer.

The Japanese Colonial Era: 1895–1945

In 1894 war broke out between Japan and China over the Japanese invasion of Korea. China's poorly equipped navy was no match for Japan's modern fleet, and in April of 1895 China signed the Treaty of Shimonoseki which ceded the Ryukyu Islands (Okinawa), Taiwan and the Penghu Archipelago to Japan.

On Taiwan locals responded to the treaty with alarm. Social and political leaders encouraged Governor Tang Jingsong to issue a statement of self-rule, which led to the declaration of the Taiwan Democratic Republic on 23 May. Any hopes that foreign powers would intervene were quickly lost, however, and by 3 June, Japanese forces had taken Keelung. Tang

1895 (April)

After being defeated by Japan in the first Sino-Japanese War, a Qing delegation signs the Treaty of Shimonoseki, ceding Taiwan and the Penghu Islands to Japan in perpetuity.

1895 (May)

Unhappy with being incorporated into Japan, local Taiwanese (assisted by disenchanted Manchu officials) establish the Taiwan Republic, the first independent republic in Asia.

1895 (October)

After a five-month campaign during which Japanese forces capture towns in a southward march, Republican forces surrender the capital of Tainan, ending the short-lived Taiwan Republic.

1921

Taiwanese elites form the Taiwan Cultural Society to press the Japanese Diet for local representation. Historians consider this the beginning of Taiwan-centred identity.

fled and with chaos engulfing the city, elites in Taipei asked Koo Hsien-jung (a businessman whose family is still influential in Taiwanese politics and business) to open the gates to the Japanese.

In international sporting events, and many international organisations, Taiwan goes by the name 'Chinese Taipei.' It's a compromise title since the People's Republic of China (PRC), a UN Security Council Member, refuses to allow either Taiwan or the Republic of China (ROC) to be used.

Resistance continued in the south in the name of the Republic but when the Japanese army entered Tainan on 21 October, the Republic fell for good. On 18 November the Japanese declared Taiwan 'pacified', though violent, localised resistance would continue for years, especially among aboriginal groups who were treated as savages to be conquered and pacified during the entire colonial era.

In general, though, Japan set out early to turn Taiwan into a model colony, attempting in part to show Western powers that they could match, or outdo, them in every way. They began with thorough studies of Taiwan's land, climate, people, history and natural resources. In 1899 they formed the Bank of Taiwan to facilitate investment; by 1914 Taiwan was not just financially self-sufficient but contributing taxes.

Over the coming decades, hundreds of kilometres of roads were constructed, and rail lines linked Keelung to Kaohsiung, and Hualien to Taitung. Schools and teaching colleges were established, a relatively fair legal system was implemented based on Western concepts of the rule of law, and cities and towns were redesigned on modern principles of urban planning (which included provisions for sanitation). Advanced agricultural practices saw food production increase over 10-fold and living standards and life expectancy rose rapidly. Taiwan's population surged from 2.6 million in 1896, to 6.6 million by 1943. And this was just the start.

Within Taiwanese society and culture, huge changes were also taking place. From a rural, superstitious and clan-based people, Taiwanese became increasingly urban and modern. A professional class developed, and while there was still great inequality, it was less entrenched than before. By the 1940s more than 200,000 students had studied higher education in Japan and 60,000 had received college degrees.

As early as the 1920s, the economy began changing from primarily agricultural to a mix which included light manufacturing and industries such as petrochemicals and machinery. With rising wages and living standards, Western-style leisure activities were indulged in. People attended movies, concerts, sporting events, and engaged in tourism. Civic associations also began to form among housewives, teachers and youth groups.

The early colonial experience also nurtured a growing sense of a unique Taiwanese (as opposed to Chinese) identity. This identity is sometimes said to have been sparked by the formation of the Formosan Republic in 1895, but it certainly began to take shape during the 1920s as Taiwanese chafed under colonial rule (which still treated them as second-

1927
Formation of Taiwan People's Party, the first political party in Taiwan, with the goal of pushing for local rights and representation. The party is suppressed three years later.

1930–31
In the 'Wushe Rebellion', Japanese authorities and members of the Seediq tribe in Nantou County clash in a series of battles. This is the last large-scale revolt against colonial rule.

1945
After Japan's defeat in WWII, Taiwan is placed under administrative control of Chiang Kai-shek's Republic of China. Taiwan's social order is thrown into chaos.

1947
A clash between a black market cigarette vendor and Monopoly Bureau agents leads to an islandwide revolt against KMT rule. This becomes known as the 2-28 Massacre.

class citizens in their own land) and local leaders pushed for civil rights and self-representation.

One of the most important figures in colonial rule, Gotō Shinpei, Chief of Civil Affairs from 1898 to 1906, has been called the father of Taiwan modernisation. Gotō was quick to suppress dissent, but he also believed that Taiwan should not be exploited for the benefit of Japan. As such, he helped lay the foundation for transportation systems, public buildings and urban planning, health care and a modern economy.

The Japanese colonial era is usually divided into three periods, which reflect the government's distinct developmental policies. After the first several decades of laying the groundwork for economic development, the colonial government began to assimilate the Taiwanese socially. Education policies began to mimic those in Japan, as did local governance and laws.

In 1937, after the outbreak of the second Sino-Japanese War began, the Japanese government initiated the Kominka Movement, in which Taiwanese were encouraged to become truly Japanese by changing their names, abandoning Chinese folk worship for Shintoism, speaking Japanese, and pledging allegiance to the Emperor. The policy was successful to a degree and many older Taiwanese still living, such as President Lee Teng-hui (born 1923), have said they believed at the time that they were Japanese. Lee himself went by the name Iwasato Masao.

During the war, Taiwan's economy saw industrial production surpass agriculture. The southern and eastern ports became bases for the Imperial navy, as well as training grounds for Kamikaze pilots. Around 140,000 Taiwanese would serve in the war, with some 30,000 dying. This, along with the population's widespread adoption of Japanese cultural traits, did not sit well with the Chinese when they gained control of Taiwan following WWII.

Taiwan Under KMT Rule

Taiwan's history after WWII is intimately tied to the Republic of China (ROC), founded in 1911 (in China) after the Qing dynasty was ended by the revolution of Sun Yat-sen (a doctor and Chinese revolutionary considered the father of the modern Chinese nation). Though Taiwan was little discussed in the early decades of the republic, after the start of the Sino-Japanese War it became part of a rallying call demanding the restoration of territory the Chinese considered stolen by Japan.

That demand was met on 25 October, 1945, in a ceremony at Taipei's Zhongshan Hall. There, Chinese General Chen Yi, on behalf of Generalissimo Chiang Kai-shek, leader of the Chinese Nationalist Party (Kuomintang or KMT) accepted the Japanese instrument of surrender on behalf of the Allied Powers. Though mandated only to administer

Koxinga, the Ming admiral who expelled the Dutch from Taiwan, is revered by many locals as a deity. He is worshipped at numerous temples across Taiwan, and a major university in Tainan is named for him.

1949 The Nationalist army is driven from mainland China by the communists. Chiang Kai-shek moves the ROC government to Taiwan with the intention of using the island as a base to retake the mainland.

1951 Japan signs the Treaty of San Francisco, formally relinquishing all claims to Taiwan and its surrounding islands. However, the treaty does not cede Taiwan to another country.

1954 The First Taiwan Strait Crisis begins when the People's Liberation Army (PLA) shells ROC-occupied Kinmen and Matsu. The conflict leads to the Sino-American Mutual Defense Treaty.

1958 The Second Taiwan Strait Crisis erupts when the PLA again attempts to seize Kinmen and Matsu from the ROC. Despite intense shelling the ROC maintains control of the islands.

Taiwan, Chen Yi quickly declared the island was once again Chinese territory. Pro-independence Taiwanese sometimes point to this moment as the beginning of what they consider the KMT's illegal occupation of Taiwan.

However, at first, Taiwanese were mostly pleased with being returned to Chinese rule, and local elites hoped that they would finally have the chance at the autonomy they had struggled for under the Japanese.

THE 2-28 INCIDENT

In the postwar years, the KMT (Kuomintang) government under Chen Yi continued and even expanded the monopoly system begun under the Japanese. However, a combination of graft and mismanagement led to the creation of a large black market of goods, of which tobacco was no small part. On 27 February, 1947, agents from the Tobacco Monopoly Bureau in Taipei seized contraband cigarettes and money from a middle-aged widow and pistol-whipped her into unconsciousness. Angry crowds formed and attacked the officers, one of whom responded by shooting into the crowd, killing an innocent bystander.

The next morning businesses closed in protest, and crowds gathered outside the Taipei branch of the Monopoly Bureau, attacking employees and setting the offices on fire. This was followed by an afternoon protest outside the governor-general's office. Here, security forces again fired into the crowds, killing a number of protestors. Violent protests now erupted all over Taiwan and for several days the island was in chaos.

Order was restored by the Taiwanese themselves, and on 2 March local leaders established a Settlement Committee with a list of 32 Demands, which included an end to government corruption and free elections. Chen Yi stalled. He promised to meet and discuss the demands, but in secret he waited for the Nationalist troop reinforcements he had requested from Chiang Kai-shek.

The troops arrived on 8 March, and according to witnesses, began a three-day massacre of civilians. This was followed in the coming weeks by the round-up and summary execution of protest leaders, intellectuals, high-school students and anyone else held suspect by the government. An estimated 18,000 to 28,000 people were killed during this period. Taiwan lost nearly its entire native elite.

Until the lifting of martial law in 1987, there was little open discussion of the event. In 1992 President Lee Teng-hui made a public apology to victims on behalf of the government. Three years later he declared 28 February (2-28) a public holiday, and created a memorial foundation to deal with compensation. Taipei Park was also renamed 2-28 Peace Memorial Park, and a 2-28 Memorial Museum was opened in the former radio station that had been taken over following the initial February protests. The museum exhibits were redone in 2010 in response to complaints that under KMT Mayor Ma Ying-jeou (now president) the museum had whitewashed the KMT's, and especially Chiang Kai-shek's, involvement in the massacre.

1971

UN General Assembly Resolution 2758 transfers the UN seat from the Republic of China to the People's Republic of China. The UN no longer recognises the ROC as a sovereign nation.

1975

Chiang Kai-shek dies aged 87; the government declares a month of mourning and Chiang's body is entombed in his former residence in Taoyuan County.

➡ Liberty Square (p59), Taipei

Unfortunately, under Governor Chen Yi, goodwill would be short-lived. Chen Yi refused to share power (he, as many KMT leaders, considered the 'Japanicised Taiwanese' as deracinated and degraded beings), and began allowing his ragtag army and civil service to loot, confiscate property and businesses, and monopolise trade. Basic public services, such as garbage collection, that people had grown used to under the Japanese were also abandoned. The economy went into a tailspin, hyperinflation hit, and in 1947, riots against the government broke out, leading to the deaths of tens of thousands of civilians.

Meanwhile, in China, Chiang Kai-shek's Nationalist regime was engaged in a civil war with the Communist Party for control of China: and they were losing badly. On 1 October, 1949, Mao Zedong proclaimed the creation of the People's Republic of China (PRC). Two months later on 10 December, Chiang fled to Taiwan, followed by two million refugees comprising soldiers, businessmen, landowners, monks, artists, gangsters, peasants and intellectuals.

Despite bringing all of China's gold reserve with them, Chiang's regime was broken. Many predicted it would fall soon to the communists, but the Korean War convinced the US that Taiwan was too strategically valuable to hand over to the Chinese Communist Party (CCP). In 1950 US President Truman ordered the US Navy to protect the Taiwan Strait. US monetary aid followed, and for the next two decades it was vital in keeping the Chiang government afloat and funding in part or in whole nearly every public works project.

Chiang kept alive the hope of retaking the mainland until his death and his rule was quick to crush any political dissent, real or imagined. However, concurrent with the brutality and paranoia, there were also sound economic reforms that would soon make Taiwan one of the wealthiest countries in Asia. Among the most famous of these were US-guided land reforms, which saw rents reduced, leases extended and government land sold off cheaply. Tenant farmers went from 49% of the total in 1949, to 10% in 1960. Agricultural productivity rose, which helped fuel more demand for industrial goods. At the same time, the reforms shifted the huge land capital of Taiwan's gentry class into investment in small- and medium-sized industrial enterprises. By 1960 industry had once again replaced agriculture as the largest share of GDP.

The political changes in this era were no less startling. In 1971 the UN Security Council admitted the PRC. Chiang Kai-shek responded by withdrawing the ROC. The following year, US President Nixon travelled to China to normalise relations. In 1979, under President Carter, the US switched official recognition from the ROC to the PRC. US policy towards Taiwan would now be dictated by the Taiwan Relations Act, which allows the US to provide defensive arms to Taiwan, and considers any move to

1976

Taiwanese Stan Shih starts a small company called Multitech in Hsinchu with his wife and an investment of US$25,000. Later renamed Acer, the company goes on to become a global computer producer.

1978

Chiang Ching-kuo becomes ROC president. While continuing many of his father's autocratic policies, the younger Chiang brings more Taiwanese into government.

1979

The Taiwan Relations Act is passed by US Congress following the breaking of official relations between the US and Taiwan. The Act establishes quasi-diplomatic relations between the two countries.

1979

Known as the Kaohsiung Incident, a major gathering for Human Rights Day in Kaohsiung sees demonstrators clash with military police, and well-known opposition leaders are arrested.

settle the status of Taiwan with military force to be a threat to US security. The act also officially ended US recognition of the ROC government.

When Chiang Kai-shek died in 1975, Yen Chia-kan became president for a three-year term and was then replaced by Chiang Ching-kuo (CCK), Chiang Kai-shek's only biological son. CCK had held various positions in the KMT government, including head of the secret police, and later premier. In the latter role, and as president, he initiated a series of major infrastructure projects which helped accelerate Taiwan's economic growth and per capita income.

CCK also began to bring native-born Taiwanese into the highest levels of government. The most important of these was Lee Teng-hui, who had served as agriculture minister and Taipei mayor. Lee was appointed vice-president.

The final years of CCK's presidency saw unexpected concessions to a rising democratic spirit within Taiwan. In 1986, with martial law still in effect, the president chose not to suppress Taiwan's first opposition party, the Democratic Progressive Party (DPP), after they announced their formation. In 1987 he also declared the end of martial law. The following year he passed away and Lee Teng-hui became the ROC president. For Taiwan, a new era had truly begun.

MARTIAL MADNESS

In 1948, in the closing years of the civil war with the Chinese Communist Party (CCP), Chiang Kai-shek declared Martial Law on most of China. A year later Taiwan was also subjected to the 'temporary provisions effective during the period of communist rebellion', which would prove anything but temporary. In fact, Taiwan's Martial Law period was one of the longest in world history, and was a time when there was no right to assembly, protest or free speech, and the Garrison Command had sweeping powers to arrest and detain anyone.

According to recent government studies, over 140,000 people were arrested during this period (many tortured and shipped off to detention on Green Island) with some 3000 to 4000 executed. This period is known locally as the White Terror.

As a locus of Taiwanese identity, folk culture was also held suspect, and elaborate festivals banned. (At the same time, statues of Chiang Kai-shek were placed in popular shrines so that people would be forced to worship his image.) The Hokkien, or Taiwanese, language was likewise proscribed in schools and media broadcasts and many older Taiwanese can still remember being beaten for speaking their native language in the classroom.

After Chiang's death in 1975, enforcements relaxed, but martial law would stay in effect until 1987.

1984

Henry Liu, a popular writer and frequent critic of the KMT, is assassinated in his home in California. The assassins, organised crime members, claim in trial the ROC government ordered the hit.

1986

The opposition DPP (Democratic Progressive Party) is formed in September; in December, Taiwan holds its first two-party elections.

1987

After 38 years, martial law is lifted in Taiwan, setting the stage for the island's eventual shift from authoritarian rule to democracy. Taiwanese citizens are once again allowed to travel to China.

1988

Chiang Ching-kuo dies of heart failure at age 78. He is succeeded by Lee Teng-hui, the first native-born president of Taiwan.

The Post-Martial-Law Period: 1988–2000

In the late 1980s Taiwan had its first native born president, but it was still a far cry from a democracy. In the first place, Lee had not been elected by the people, but appointed by Chiang Ching-kuo and voted in by the National Assembly, a body that had last been elected in China in 1947 and was still officially in session over 40 years later – and with largely the same people.

Lee initiated constitutional changes to allow for direct elections of the president and Legislative Yuan (Taiwan's parliament) as well as for the eventual dissolving of the National Assembly. He also ended the provisions that had allowed for martial law and the suspension of civil liberties. In 1991 he officially ended the state of war between the ROC and China.

Lee furthered CCK's policy of bringing more native Taiwanese into government and concurrently began a process of 'localisation' or 'Taiwanisation'. In effect this meant de-stressing a pan-China (and mostly northern China) focused view of history and culture. Taiwan was now its own centre, with a history and culture worth studying and promoting. In practice this meant emphasising Taiwan's southern Chinese roots, its strong folk religious traditions, its Dutch and Japanese influences, and its multiethnic makeup: Hakka, Hokkien, aboriginals and mainlanders.

The elections in 1996 were a watershed moment in Taiwan's advancement toward democracy. For the first time, Taiwanese would directly elect their leader. Lee ran against democracy advocate Peng Ming-min (and a host of others).

China, outraged that free elections were going to be held in Taiwan, and suspicious that Lee held independence sentiments (which he did as it turned out), held a series of missile tests from July 1995 to March 1996. The US responded with a build up of ships in the region, the largest military display in Asia since the Vietnam War. The people in Taiwan, more angry than scared, responded by giving Lee a clear majority vote (54%).

Lee's second term was marked with deteriorating social order, especially in the first year, which saw three high-profile murder cases involving organised crime figures terrify the public. Many openly longed for the the return of martial law and Lee himself was blamed. More interestingly, critics blamed Lee for using *heidao* (gangsters) himself in order to keep the KMT in power.

However, the infiltration of politics by organised crime figures, both predates the Lee presidency, and continues to this day. Even in 1996 intelligence reports showed that 40% of town representatives, 27% of city councilors, and 3% of national representatives had organised crime backgrounds. Criminologist Ko-lin Chin says Taiwan is pretty much

For a descriptive history of Taiwan's transition from colonial holding to vibrant Asian democracy, check out J Bruce Jacob's *Democratizing Taiwan.*

1990

A student demonstration quickly sees 300,000 people gather in Liberty Square. This eventually helps lead to direct presidential and National Assembly elections six years later.

1991

Lee Teng-hui announces the end of the 'Period of National Mobilization for the Suppression of the Communist Rebellion.' This formally ends the state of war between the ROC and PRC.

1992–93

In the Koo-Wang Talks, representatives from the ROC and PRC meet to discuss cross-Strait relations. From this arises the '92 Consensus in which each side claims the right to interpret One China in their own way.

1996

Lee Teng-hui is re-elected in Taiwan's first fully democratic presidential election, winning 54% of the vote in a three-way race.

unique for having such a high level of gangsters in elected office (not even Italian mafia, he says, dare to run openly but try to influence from behind closed doors).

On a more positive note, Lee's second term also saw the continuation of democratic and civil reforms. With respect to cross-Strait relations, the president argued that with the legitimacy of Taiwan's government now solely in the hands of Taiwan voters, the notion that the ROC 'represented' all of China could no longer hold. In 1999 Lee declared that China and Taiwan now held 'special state to state relations'. Neither the Chinese nor the Americans were amused by what they saw as a push towards a formal declaration of independence.

In 2000, Lee, unable to run for a third term, appointed the wooden Lien Chan as his successor. The popular and charismatic James Soong, former Provincial Governor, believing he should have been chosen to represent the KMT, ran as an independent. By splitting the KMT vote, the DPP's long-shot candidate Chen Shui-bian won with a little over 39%

THE KAOHSIUNG INCIDENT

For Taiwan, the late 1970s and early '80s was an era of storms: not just internationally, with de-recognition from the UN and the US, but increasing within its own society. Political dissent, which included calls for democracy and civil rights, was growing. One of the most noteworthy uprisings of the late martial-law period occurred in December 1979. Called the Kaohsiung Incident, it is still widely regarded as a turning point in Taiwan's shift from authoritarian rule to democracy.

The incident began with the editors of *Meilidao,* a publication often critical of the government, organising a rally to celebrate International Human Rights Day. On the day of the rally, after scuffles broke out between police and protestors the situation turned into a full-scale riot. The authorities rounded up 50 prominent dissidents and put them on trial. Among these included Taiwan's future vice-president Annette Lu, and democracy advocate Lin Yi-hsiung. (In February of the following year, Lin's mother and twin daughters were murdered in their Taipei home. It is widely believed the KMT had ordered the killing.)

The trial of the activists, though it ended with long prison terms, did not quite have the effect the government wanted. In the first place, it gave the voice for independence a wide audience (many foreign reporters were in attendance). It also created the reputation of the next generation of activists. These included two of the lawyers who represented the accused: future Taiwanese president Chen Shui-bian, and future vice-president Frank Hsieh.

The majority of people in Taiwan also sympathised with the accused and were horrified at the brutal crackdown by their government. The incident brought increased support for democratic reform which eventually led to the lifting of martial law and the formation of opposition parties.

1999

Taiwan is hit by a massive earthquake measuring 7.3 on the Richter scale. Centred in Nantou County, the quake causes massive damage, and thousands of deaths throughout the island.

1999

Lee Teng-hui declares to a German reporter that after his government amended the constitution in 1991, Taiwan and China now have a special state-to-state relationship.

2000

Former Taipei Mayor Chen Shui-bian is elected ROC president, winning 39.3% of the popular vote in a three-way race, ending over 50 years of Kuomintang (KMT) rule in Taiwan.

2000

In an early sign of thawing relations between Taiwan and China, the 'Three Small Links' commence, opening limited trade between China and the Taiwanese-held islands of Kinmen and Matsu.

of the vote. Over 50 years of continuous KMT rule came very unexpectedly to an end.

Taiwan in the 21st Century

Chen would serve Taiwan as president for eight years, during which time many long-term trends in politics and society became settled and mainstream. By the end of Chen's second term, for example, both the military and the civil service had generally become neutral bodies, loyal to the country and not just the KMT. Judicial reforms gave people Miranda Rights (such as the right to an attorney) but attempts at education reform, land use legislation, police reform and streamlining government either failed or stalled.

Lee Teng-hui's localisation and de-sinicisation policies were kicked up a notch and the names of many public companies and institutions were changed from 'China' to 'Taiwan'. Chiang Kai-shek International Airport was renamed Taoyuan International Airport, though attempts to rename CKS Memorial Hall resulted in a backlash. Still, increasingly, Taiwanese of all stripes began more and more to identify with Taiwan; even the children of mainlanders began to call themselves Taiwanese and not Chinese.

To many, though, it sometimes seemed this era was nothing but pure chaos. It began well. Recognising that he had won less than 50% of the vote and lacked a clear mandate (to say nothing of lacking control of the legislative, civil service or military), Chen filled his cabinet with many KMT appointees. He spoke of representing all Taiwanese, including mainlanders and his message to China was simple: don't attack us and we won't declare formal independence. The president's initial approval rating reached 80%.

Things began to slide when Chen cancelled construction of the fourth nuclear power plant in October 2000, incensing the KMT whose patronage networks across Taiwan are intimately linked to big construction projects. The following year Taiwan was hit with two economic whammies: the fallout in the agricultural sector from admission to the WTO (Taiwan was forced to open its markets to imported rice) and a recession that resulted from the dot.com bust. As is usual in Taiwan, the president was blamed, and many people openly wondered if the DPP could be trusted to run the economy.

In terms of economic policy, Chen moved away from Lee's slow and careful investment approach to China and there was an exodus of business, talent and investment across the Strait. Though GDP growth remained reasonably good in Taiwan, stagnating wages and opportunities again left many critical of the president. Among the economic success of

Jonathan Manthorpe's *Forbidden Nation* is a very readable overview of Taiwan's history, with plenty of informed opinions and balanced analyses of the political status of Taiwan.

2004

Chen Shui-bian is re-elected by the slimmest of margins; the day before the election both president and vice-president are mildly wounded by the same bullet in a botched assassination attempt.

2005

China enacts an 'anti-secession law', formalising its commitment to use military force if Taiwan declares independence. Protests against the law draw huge crowds around Taiwan.

2006

Chiang Kai-shek International Airport is renamed Taoyuan International Airport as part of a general movement to erase homages to the former dictator.

2007

Taiwan's High Speed Rail (HSR) begins operation to much fanfare and publicity. With speeds of up to 350km/h, the HSR cuts rail travel from Taipei to Kaohsiung to 90 minutes.

ECFA: TRADE AGREEMENT OR TROJAN HORSE?

In June 2010, after two years of negotiations that began nearly as soon as Ma Ying-jeou was sworn in as president, Taiwan signed a preferential trade agreement with China called the ECFA (Economic Cooperation Framework Agreement). The pact, similar to those signed between China and Hong Kong and Macau, aims to reduce tariffs and ease trade. Opponents claim it is nothing but a disguise for unification by subsuming Taiwan's economy into China's.

Large-scale protests were held from the time of the first visit by Chinese negotiator Chen Yunlin until 2010. But to no avail. A total of 18 agreements have been signed so far after eight rounds of negotiations.

The Ma government argued (and argues) that ECFA would give Taiwan a needed boost in GDP and job growth. More importantly, it would reverse the country's marginalisation as other regional powers connected themselves with free-trade agreements.

The results to date have hardly been spectacular. GDP growth is anaemic, foreign investment near zero, and trade with China appears to be growing less than with other regional economies. In a bad sign, fresh fruit exports (which are growing) are being purchased not by wholesalers, but Chinese officials eager to win the hearts of local farmers.

ECFA's secondary effects look more promising. In July 2013 Taiwan signed an economic cooperation agreement with New Zealand, its first with a developed country. The government was also in talks with India, Singapore and Indonesia.

the Chen years, the creation of a tourism industry ranks high. Inbound tourist numbers doubled from 2002 to 2008 and continue to rise today.

Relations with China, which had deteriorated under Lee Teng-hui, went from bad to worse. The nadir was reached in 2005 when China promulgated an Anti-Secession Law that codified China's long-standing threat to attack Taiwan should the island's leaders declare independence. The move was met by mass protest rallies throughout Taiwan.

Chen won re-election in 2004 by a tiny margin. The day before the election both the president and vice-president were mildly wounded in a botched assassination attempt. The KMT immediately cried foul and led weeks of mass, violent protests. To this day, many are convinced (though without evidence) that Chen was behind his own shooting.

Chen's second term was a classic lame duck, as the KMT dominated legislative assembly blocked his every move. In 2006 Chen's approval rating hit 20% as a series of corruption scandals implicated both his wife and son-in-law.

After stepping down in 2008, Chen Shui-bian immediately lost presidential immunity; within six months, he was arrested on charges of money laundering, bribery and embezzlement of government funds.

2008

Former Taipei mayor and long-time KMT favourite Ma Ying-jeou is elected president, regaining control of the executive branch after eight years of Democratic Progressive Party (DPP) rule.

2008

As part of the Ma government's opening to China, regularly scheduled direct flights between the two countries begin. Ma also declares that Taiwan, as the Republic of China, is part of China.

2009

Typhoon Morakot causes severe damage to the island, particularly in the southern counties. The storm kills hundreds and causes billions of dollars in damage.

2009

Former president Chen Shui-bian is sentenced to life imprisonment (later reduced to 20 years) on corruption charges; supporters of the former president claim the charges are politically motivated.

Chen was sentenced to life imprisonment in September 2009, reduced to 20 years in June 2010 as later trials found him not guilty of embezzling government funds. Taiwan observers claim Chen's conviction did enormous long-term harm to his party and to the cause of Taiwan independence.

In early 2008 the KMT won a decisive victory in the legislative elections. Two months later former Justice Minister and Taipei Mayor, Ma Ying-jeou, won the presidency with 58% of the vote. Ma Ying-jeou's clear victory that year (and again in 2012) signalled possibly yet another new era for Taiwan. The Hong Kong born Ma began a radical departure from Lee and Chen policies, especially concerning cross-Strait relations. Once again, under Ma the ROC has been declared the legitimate government of all China, and relations between Taiwan and the mainland are merely those of special regions to regions within that country. This does not, however, mean accepting PRC rule over Taiwan.

Despite years of rapprochement with China under the Ma Ying-jeou government, the PRC currently has over 1600 cruise and ballistic missiles pointed at Taiwan.

Since coming to power, Ma has focused on streamlining government (successfully), ending corruption (very unsuccessfully), re-sinicising society and bringing economic and cultural relations between China and Taiwan closer and closer. The latter highlights include signing an economic agreement (ECFA) covering trade, finance, services and security; opening Taiwan to direct cross-Strait flights and ferries; encouraging Chinese students and professionals to study and work here; and facilitating the rise of mass Chinese tourism.

2010

President Ma signs the Economic Cooperation Framework Agreement (ECFA), a trade agreement between the PRC and ROC governments, lowering economic barriers between the two sides.

2012

Ma Ying-jeou wins a second term as president, promising to continue policies of opening Taiwan's economy to China. Within months his popularity has sunk to 15%.

2012

Taiwan's economy is stalled. Foreign Direct Investment is the second lowest in the world. With wages stagnated for over a decade, many young people are looking to emigrate.

2013

Taiwan and Japan squabble over the Senkaku Islands, and with the Philippines over the death of a Taiwanese fisherman in disputed waters.

The People of Taiwan

First-time visitors to Taiwan often expect to find a completely homogenised society, with little difference in thinking, customs and attitudes from one generation to the next, from city to countryside, or even from person to person. But while the diversity of Taiwan is not as obvious as, say, in a large North American city, the country is accurately described as a multiethnic melting pot. Customs and traditions go back and forth between groups, evolve over time, and these days, family background and life experience is far more indicative of a person's attitudes and beliefs than simple ethnicity.

If you want to get a good sense of the national character, especially the capacity for mocking humour and creativity, check out a few Next Media Animations (http://tw.nextmedia.com).

Ethnicity

About 98% of Taiwan's inhabitants are ethnically Han Chinese, with the other 2% being aboriginal. Hoklo and Hakka are often referred to as *benshengren* (本省人, *běnshěngrén;* home-province person), while mainlanders, or those who came with Chiang Kai-shek (and their descendants), are *waishengren* (外省人, *wàishěngrén;* outside-province people). These titles are gradually falling out of use, however, especially with the younger generation.

Hoklo (Taiwanese)

Accounting for about 70% of the population, these are the descendents of Chinese immigrants between the 17th and 19th centuries from Fujian province. While nearly all speak Mandarin, many also speak Hoklo, or Taiwanese, as their native language. Hoklo are found all over Taiwan.

Hakka

About 15% of the population are Hakka, descendants of immigrants from Guangdong province. Taoyuan, Hsinchu and Miaoli Counties are Hakka strongholds, but you'll also find significant populations in Pingtung and Taitung.

Mainlanders

Around 13% of the people are those and their descendents who immigrated following WWII and the defeat of the Nationalist Army by the communists in 1949. They tend to be concentrated in urban areas such as in Taipei, Taichung and Kaohsiung and are among the most educated, connected and wealthy of citizens, but also among the most poor. Intermarriage and a Taiwan-centered consciousness among the young has made the label somewhat passe, though one still hears the phrase 'high-class waishengren' used as a mark of distinction in certain circles.

Indigenous People

The population of Taiwan's 14 officially recognised aboriginal tribes is around half a million (2% of the total population). Villages are concentrated along the east coast and the mountainous interior, though many young aboriginals work in the major cities. Although aboriginal people are by far the least prosperous, and most discriminated against, group in Taiwan, in recent years many villages have seen a rebirth of indigenous practices and pride and have begun building a sustainable and non-exploitative tourism industry around traditional culture.

Nearly all aboriginals speak Mandarin in addition to their own tribal languages. DNA tests have shown that 88% of ethnic Taiwanese have some aboriginal blood in them, likely owing to the lack of Chinese female settlers in the early days.

Aboriginal tribes in Taiwan include the following:

Amis (population 184,000) Mostly live on the east coast in Hualien and Taitung Counties.

Paiwan (population 88,000) Live in Kaohsiung and Pingtung County.

Atayal (population 80,000) Across the central and north mountainous regions with Wulai (near Taipei) their most northerly extent.

Bunun (population 51,000) Live in the central and southern mountains as well as Taitung County.

Truku (Taroko; population 26,000) Live in Taroko Gorge and other parts of Hualien.

Tao (Yami; population 3900) Live only on Lanyu Island.

Recent Immigrants

Several hundred thousand Southeast Asians and Chinese have immigrated to Taiwan in the past decade, many as mail-order brides for rural Taiwanese men. There are also a small number of Westerners who have become Republic of China (ROC) citizens and thousands who have become permanent residents.

One of the best books for a quick understanding of the Taiwanese character in all its quirks and qualities is Steve Crook's *Dos and Don'ts of Taiwan*.

Taiwanese Women Today

Taiwanese society leads Asia in sexual equality. The ROC constitution forbids discrimination on the base of gender, educational opportunities are equal for boys and girls, and in working life women are found in the upper echelons of many companies, religious organisations and government departments. From 2000 to 2008 the vice president's position was held by Annette Lu, and in 2012 the opposition candidate (gaining 46% of the vote) was London School of Economics–educated Tsai Ing-wen. The percentage of female legislators is also high: 33.6%, compared with 7.9% in Japan, and 17.8% in the US.

Among young women, marriage and child bearing are being delayed longer and longer (the average age now is 29 to 30, higher than most Western countries), with the result that Taiwan has one of the lowest birth rates in the world. What exactly is behind the low rates is multifold.

ETIQUETTE: DOS & DON'TS

- If a Taiwanese gives you a gift, put it aside to open later to avoid appearing greedy. Expect the same for a gift you have given.
- Don't leave your chopsticks upright in a bowl of rice. It reminds Taiwanese of funeral incense.
- Present and accepts things (such as business cards) with both hands as a sign of respect.
- Don't be afraid to talk politics. But if someone says they are tired of it, they're probably sincere and not being cautious.
- Don't give four of anything as a gift or white flowers. They are both associated with death.
- Don't worry about being cheated by a taxi or small business owner. Taiwanese are generally honest this way and will even offer you the same discount they would a local.

In part it's simply that Taiwanese women have more choices, but economic stagnation also plays a large role: young Taiwanese simply cannot afford their own families.

Boys are still favoured over girls in some families, and it is not uncommon to hear of a mother who is pregnant once again because her first three children were girls. But this is getting less and less common and comes down to individual family pressure rather than societal.

After giving birth, Taiwanese women partake of the month-long *zuo yuezi*, an ancient custom of postpartum recuperation with specific dietary and movement restrictions. These days *zuo yuezi* nursing centres provide 24-hour assistance in a hotel-like setting.

Lifestyle

Despite the low birth and marriage rate, family still remains central to Taiwanese life. Both young and old are generally deeply committed to each other. Parents dote on and indulge children in a way that seems developmentally harmful to many Westerners, while adult children continue to defer to their parents for major decisions. Male offspring take their role as guardian of the family name with utter seriousness.

Most people in Taiwan live in crowded urban conditions. However, with low taxes, cheap utilities, fresh local foods, to say nothing of excellent low-cost universal medical care, people enjoy a good balance between the cost of living and living quality. (On the other hand, stagnating wages are a major problem for young people; see p320.) Life expectancy is 83 years for women and 77 years for men.

One of the most unfortunate parts of Taiwanese life is education: an emphasis on rote learning means kids are burdened with long hours of homework and evenings spent at cram schools. Elementary school is fairly low pressure, but junior and senior high schools are true soul crushers and suicide is common among teens.

Like their peers in the West, young Taiwanese have taken to pop culture, casual dating, sexual experimentation, (limited) drug and alcohol use, and expressing themselves with fashion choices. They have been labeled the Strawberry Generation in that they look perfect but can't bear pressure. While often true, many in this generation are also proving to be devoted to social causes and willing to put themselves on the line in protests as shown in 2013 when 250,000 mostly under-30s protested in front of the Presidential Palace over the death-by-torture of a young army recruit. Strawberries are also more than willing to drop out of the rat race to pursue a dream.

In general, relationships are the key to Taiwanese society and this is expressed in the term *guānxi*. To get something done, it's often been easier to go through a back door, rather than through official channels. This has serious implications for the rule-of-law, however, as well-connected people are often able to get away with anything, even violent crime.

The Taiwanese Character

Many adults in Taiwan have no social life, or skills, due to a lifetime concentrated on intense study and long working hours. It's estimated there are 620,000 single women in their 30s, and 871,000 men.

Taiwanese have often been characterised as some of the friendliest people in the world. Reports from Western travellers and officials in Taiwan in the 1930s read like modern accounts which suggests friendliness is a deep long-standing quality. Some claim this likely has to do with Taiwan's immigrant background in which trust among strangers was paramount.

The important concept of 'face' can seem scary to those prone to social gaffes, but in reality the idea is largely about not causing someone else to lose status or dignity in front of their peers. Locals may often appear humble and polite but they have a fierce pride. Taiwanese men seem to have an instinctive way of defusing tension, but once things go too far, then extreme violence is often the end result.

Taiwanese stress harmony in relationships, and if the choice is to be made between maintaining harmony and telling the truth, many people opt for the former. It's best to see this as an expression of different values. The concept of a white lie is very broad for Taiwanese.

Associated with this is flattery. Travellers are often told how beautiful they are or that their Chinese is terrific. The best response is a smile and a humble reply in the negative, to avoid sounding arrogant. On the other hand people are often shockingly direct once they know you and will tell you directly you have gained weight, gotten ugly, are wearing unflattering clothing, and so on. And between friends and even loved ones a bossy, pushy, insulting tone is often taken. However, one of the best parts of the Taiwanese character is the general capacity for very open, sincere and lifelong friendships.

Taiwan has a literacy rate of 96.1%. No mean feat considering the country uses traditional Chinese characters to read and write with, and the average adult must learn to write and recognise thousands.

Sports

Despite their propensity for work and study, Taiwanese are a sports-loving people. Basketball and baseball are the most popular organised spectator sports: both have their own leagues in Taiwan and games are popular with local audiences, especially baseball. In fact, Taiwanese baseball players regularly make it to the big leagues in Japan (which introduced the sport to Taiwan in 1906) and America, with players like Chien-Ming Wang now household names around the world.

Taiwanese are also quick to embrace athletes such as pro-basketball star Jeremy Lin, born in the US to Taiwanese parents, as one of their own. And with the ascension of Yani Tseng and Lu Yen-hsun, golf and tennis are seeing a resurgence of interest.

When the five-day (more or less) workweek was established in 2001, Taiwanese began to take up biking, hiking, surfing and travel in record numbers. Today, a sporting and leisure society mentality is well entrenched, something that often confounds visitors from mainland China.

As with most activities, Taiwanese localise some aspects of their sports. Hikers always get up pre-dawn, for example, to watch the sunrise (a chi enhancing activity), while cyclists can't bear to be seen outside without the latest flashy gear and clothing.

TRADITIONAL FESTIVALS

In addition to scores of local cultural holidays and events, Taiwanese celebrate the big traditional Chinese festivals such as Lunar New Year. These are mostly family affairs but it's good to know a little about them as they are integral parts of local culture, and you might find yourself invited along at some point. For aboriginal festivals, see p195.

Chinese Lunar New Year (春節, Chūnjié) Celebrated for two weeks (people get four to nine days public holidays) in January or February, this is the most cherished holiday of the year. Activities include a thorough clean of the house; decorating doorways with couplets expressing good fortune; and a family reunion dinner on New Year's Eve. On the second day of New Years, married daughters return to their parents' home. The last days of the public holidays are for visiting friends and travelling. The 15th, or final day, is the Lantern Festival (p131), which in Taiwan is celebrated with a number of exceptional activities.

Tomb Sweeping Day (清明節, Qīngmíng Jié) Ancestor worship is among the most important features of Taiwanese culture, and on this day (Gregorian calendar, 5th April) families return to tend to their ancestral graves (though many now are interned in a columbarium).

Mid Autumn Festival (中秋節, Zhōngqiū Jié) Originally a harvest celebration, this public holiday falls on the 15th day of the eighth lunar month. Families gather to barbecue, eat mooncakes, gaze at the full moon, and recount the story of the fairy Chang'e and a jade rabbit who lives on the moon and mixes a mean elixir of immortality.

Religion in Taiwan

A funny thing happened to Taiwan on the way to its future. Instead of losing its religion as economic growth, mobility and education brought it into the developed world, the very opposite happened. There are more Buddhists today, for example, than ever before, and in fact, you'd be hard-pressed to find a larger (per capita) monastic population in all of Asia.

A god's ability to grant requests is critical to popularity. In the past he or she might be asked for protection against plague. Today, it could be advice on which job to take; help passing an important test; or even, as we saw once on a prayer card at Donglong Temple, that the young believer grow to over 160cm tall.

But the old Taoist gods, and the old acts of worship, have hung on, too. When a modern Mr Wang is troubled he is as likely to burn incense and joss paper, toss moon blocks (*bwah bwey*) and pray at the altar of a favourite deity as his ancestors were. Of course, before asking Baosheng Dadi to help cure his glaucoma, Wang will take the medicine his doctor prescribed knowing full well which one is more efficacious. But if he is cured, it's still the temple that will get the fat donation.

Perhaps the biggest change has been the way the media, feeding the public demand for religious content, has made nationwide stars of regional temple cults and festivals. Religious associations understand this very well, and several Buddhist and Taoist groups now control their own image by running independent TV stations. Probably only in the US, with its tradition of fiery evangelists spreading the word of God on TV, can you find such a potent fusion of technology with tradition.

All of which is to say that the more things change in Taiwan, the more they stay the same. No matter what form it's received in or propagated, religion in Taiwan continues to foster a sense of shared culture and identity, and to provide the individual with satisfying rites of passage and intimations of the divine.

A Brief History

The early immigrants to Taiwan faced conditions not unlike the settlers in the New World did: a harsh environment, hostile natives, a lack of wives and a host of devastating diseases. Faith in the local cults of their home village in China was vital in forming new and strong community bonds in Taiwan.

During the late Qing dynasty into Japanese times, a period of increasing wealth and mobility, many temples began to expand their influence beyond the village level. Famous pilgrim sites arose, and Matsu started her rise to pan-Taiwan deity status.

The Kuomintang (KMT) at first tolerated local religion but then attempted to both suppress and coopt it, fearing that it was at best superstitious nonsense and at worst a rallying point for Taiwanese independence. They were largely unsuccessful and even before the lifting of martial law had abandoned trying to direct local culture.

Three Faiths (Plus One)

The Taiwanese approach to spirituality is eclectic and not particularly dogmatic; many Taiwanese will combine elements from various religions to suit their needs rather than rigidly adhering to one particular spiritual path. Religion in Taiwan is largely about an individual relationship to a deity, dead spirit or even spiritual leader. Many of the gods, customs and festivals have little to do with any of the three official religions and are sometimes described as part of an amorphous folk faith. But don't expect anyone to ever tell you they are a believer in this faith: instead, they will say they are Taoist or Buddhist.

Temples have many statues of the same god because different statues can play different roles. In Tainan's Matsu Temple, the Great Matsu statue oversees the local neighbourhood; a second watches over the internal affairs of the temple; another is a helper of the Great Matsu. Each is said to have a different personality and be receptive to different requests.

Confucianism

Confucian values and beliefs *(Rújiā Sīxiǎng)* form the foundation of Chinese culture. The central theme of Confucian doctrine is the conduct of human relationships for the attainment of harmony and overall good for society. Society, Confucius taught, comprises five relationships: ruler and subject, husband and wife, father and son, elder and younger, and friends. Deference to authority and devotion to family are paramount.

The close bonds between family and friends are one of the most admirable attributes of Chinese culture, a lasting legacy of Confucian teachings. But Confucianism's continuing influence on modern Taiwan society is often overstated. The effects of modernisation, which include greater mobility, mass education (for both males and females) and democratic elections (which allow ordinary citizens to make demands of their rulers) are all centrifugal forces acting to push society away from a simple adherence to Confucian values.

Taoism

Taoism *(Dàojiào)* is easily the most confusing facet of Chinese culture, consisting of a vast assembly of philosophical texts, popular folk legends, various organised sects, a panoply of gods and goddesses numbering in the thousands, alchemists, healers, hermits, martial artists, spirit-mediums, alcoholic immortals, quantum physicists, New Age gurus… and the list goes on. Controversial, paradoxical and – like the Tao itself – impossible to pin down, it is a natural complement to rigid Confucian order and responsibility.

Taoism began with Lao-Tzu's *Tao Te Ching*. Its central theme is that of the Tao – the unknowable, indescribable cosmic force of the universe. Organised Taoism came into being in the 2nd century at which time there was an emphasis on mystical practices to cultivate immortality. Taoism reached a high point during the Tang dynasty when there was a fierce (but productive) battle with Buddhism and when many branches became increasingly tied to popular religion.

RÉNJIĀN FÓJIÀO: THIS-WORLDLY BUDDHISM

You won't get far understanding the Buddhist influence on modern Taiwanese society if you simply try to grasp doctrine and schools. In the past 40 years a special form of socially active Buddhism (*Rénjiān Fójiào*; this-worldly Buddhism) has emerged to redefine what that religion means to its practitioners. Rénjiān Fójiào draws inspiration from the thoughts of the early-20th-century reformist monk Taixu in China, but has been completely localised by masters such as Chengyan of Tzu Chi.

A central tenet of Rénjiān Fójiào is that one finds salvation not by escaping in a monastery but by bringing Buddhist compassion into ordinary life and adapting the dharma to the conditions of modern life. Taiwanese Buddhist groups stress humanitarian work, and teach that traditional beliefs, such as filial piety, should be expanded to encompass respect and consideration for society at large. With a combined de-emphasis on ritual and a central role for lay followers to take in the organisations, Taiwanese Buddhist groups have made themselves the religion of choice for middle-class urbanites and professionals. The older folk gods, on the other hand, remain more typically attractive to the working class.

In modern Taiwan, Taoist priests still play a vital role in the worship of deities, the opening of temples, the exorcising of bad luck (and sometimes illness) and the presiding over of funeral services.

For a more thorough look at Taoism, including the myriad deities, see the Daoist Encyclopedia (http://en.daoinfo.org/wiki).

Buddhism

Buddhism (*Fójiào*) came to Taiwan in the 17th century with the Ming loyalist Koxinga, but there were few orthodox associations until Japanese times. Many Japanese were devout Buddhists and supported the growth of the religion during their occupation.

In 1949, thousands of monks, fearing religious persecution in China, fled to Taiwan with the Nationalists. Under martial law, all Buddhist groups were officially organised under the Buddhist Association of the Republic of China (BAROC). By the 1960s, however, independent associations were emerging, and it is these maverick groups that have had the most influence in modern times.

WHO'S WHO ON THE DOOR?

In Taiwan the most commonly encountered deities aren't statues of Matsu or Buddha inside temples, but the colourful door gods that are practically everywhere. These supernatural bouncers are spotted not only at temple entrances, but also on city gates, house doors or even indoors as bedroom guardians. The function of door gods is to frighten away evil spirits; they are right on the frontline when it comes to securing the well-being of a temple or a family at home.

Among the panoply of predominantly male door gods, the most common are warriors from Chinese folklore while legendary members of the traditional mandarin class are also featured. If their origins appear too prosaic, they know that the holy door-keeping profession is also graced by the presence of celebrated eunuchs and youthful virgins.

Door gods of the same kind generally stand sentinel in pairs and some of the most famous partnerships are introduced below. Sometimes one can tell the kind of deity that's worshipped inside a temple or the religious faith of a house owner just by looking at the door gods they've chosen.

Taoist temples and homes are usually guarded by the likenesses of two Tang dynasty generals, Qin Shubao and Yuchi Gong. Typically, one of them is fair-faced while the other has a dark appearance, yet both share a penchant for long beards and wield weapons. They are also very popular door gods for city gates and ancestral halls.

Buddhist deities Skanda (Wei Tuo) and Sangharama (Jia Lan) are the most commonly seen door gods at Buddhist temples, and they are sometimes found at Taoist temples, too. Skanda is portrayed as a young, beardless military general while the localisation of Sangharama has seen him metamorphose into Guandi.

Occasionally, Buddhist temples are protected by Generals Heng and Ha, a fierce door god double act known for their unorthodox ways to vitiate an assailant. With a sullen pout and snort, bile-faced General Hang fires blazing rays from his nose. Similarly, when General Ha opens his menacing jaws, a blast of amber gas is thundered to show who's boss. These mean tricks are used to rob an enemy of their soul.

If a temple is dedicated to a high-ranking deity (for example, Baosheng Dadi or the City God), or one who was previously an emperor or an empress, the door gods would be palace maids or even eunuchs. Images of the latter are not noted for any facial hair, of course, but they would sport a dust brush and long fingernails (hinting at a life of little toil). At Tainan's Wufei Temple, which honours five Ming dynasty concubines, the door gods are played by palace maids and their emasculated counterparts.

Constantly battered by the elements, door gods have to be periodically restored and, in some cases, completely replaced when the weight of battle scars forces them into retirement. Most door gods that are on duty in Taiwan today were painted after the 1960s, but older ones do exist, and they may well have been watching you all along.

Buddhism in Taiwan is largely Chan (Zen) or Pure Land, though few groups are strictly orthodox. The main Buddhist associations are Foguangshan (the Light of Buddha), Dharma Drum, Tzu Chi and Chung Tai Chan.

The Bodhisattva Guanyin, the embodiment of mercy, is the most popular Buddhist deity in Taiwan.

Want to learn more about religious life in Taiwan? Pick up a copy of Mark Caltonhill's *Private Prayers and Public Parades: Exploring the Religious Life of Taipei.*

Folk Religion

Beliefs about ancestor worship permeate almost every aspect of Chinese philosophy. Most homes in Taiwan have their own altar, where family members pay their respects to deceased relatives by burning incense and providing offerings.

Closely tied to ancestor worship is popular or folk religion, which consists of an immense celestial bureaucracy of gods and spirits, from the lowly but important kitchen god (*zào jūn*) to the celestial emperor himself (*tiāndì* or *shàngdì*). Like the imperial bureaucrats on earth, each god has a particular role to fulfil and can be either promoted or demoted depending on his or her job performance. Offerings to the gods consist not only of food and incense, but also opera performances, birthday parties (to which other local gods are invited) and even processions around town.

Other Faiths

Presbyterians are few in number but are politically influential. Aboriginals tend to be overwhelmingly Catholic or of other Christian faiths; church steeples are a common fixture in villages as are ageing nuns and priests from Europe.

In addition Taiwan has a small number of Tibetan Buddhists, Muslims, and a number of followers of cults such as Falun Gong, Yiguan Dao and those that occasionally arise around a single person.

The Main Folk & Taoist Deities

Those outlined here are just a few of the dozens, even hundreds, of folk and Taoist gods you will come across in temples. Among the most important deities in the south, the Wang Yeh (the Royal Lords), who number in the hundreds, were either once real historical figures (such as Koxinga) or plague demons. Today, they are regarded as general protectors.

Matsu (Empress of Heaven) is the closest thing to a pan-deity in Taiwan. She is worshipped as a general protector.

GuanGong, or Guandi, is the so-called God of War, but better thought of as a patron of warriors and those who live by a righteous code. More generally he is worshipped as a god of wealth and literature. He is easy to recognise by his red face, beard and halberd.

At the Dizang Temple in Xinzhuang, Taipei County, thousands of people come yearly to file indictments with Bodhisattva Dizang against people who they believe have wronged them in some way. A bit of an indictment against the legal system, too, we would say.

Baosheng Dadi (the Great Emperor Who Preserves Life) is the god of medicine. He played an important role for early immigrants faced with a host of diseases and plagues.

The top god in the Taoist pantheon, the Jade Emperor, fulfils the role of emperor of heaven. In Taiwan he is usually represented by a plaque rather than a statue.

The City God (protector of cities), also officially the Lord of Walls and Moats, is also the moral accountant of the world, recording people's good and bad deeds for their final reckoning. People pray to him for protection and wealth.

Tudi Gong, the Earth God (and minor god of wealth), has the lowest ranking in the Taoist pantheon. As governor of local areas, he was very important in pre-industrial Taiwan and his shrines can be found everywhere. Look for statues of an old bearded man with a bit of a Santa-like visage.

Pilgrimage

As an integral part of the religious life in Taiwan, it's not surprising that pilgrimage fulfils many roles besides worship: it gives people an excuse to travel; it helps reinforce the relations between daughter and mother temples; and it's a major source of funding.

Jìnxiāng, the Chinese term for pilgrimage, means to visit a temple and burn incense to the god. But not any temple will do. Famous pilgrim sites have a reputation for divine efficacy (靈, *ling*), which is the magical power to answer a worshipper's prayers. Pilgrims visiting such sites expect to have a direct experience of the god's powers, and to return home with both good-luck trinkets and good results (such as prayers granted). In return they usually make a donation to the temple.

The most famous pilgrimage in Taiwan is in honour of Matsu. But there are many others, such as those to Beigang's Chaotian Gong, Maokong's Zhinan Temple, Tainan's Nankunshen Temple and Donggang's Donglong Gong.

Top Festivals

- Matsu Pilgrimage
- Burning of the Wang Yeh Boats, Donggang
- Ghost Festival, Keelung
- Yenshui Fireworks Festival
- Welcoming the City God, Kincheng
- City God's Birthday, Taipei
- Bao'an Folk Arts Festival, Taipei
- Qingshan Temple Night Patrol, Taipei

Religious Festivals

In all phases of Taiwan's history, the wealthier society got, the bigger the religious festivals. Well, there's never been a wealthier Taiwan, which means bigger, flashier, more extravagant festivals than ever. Good places to catch random celebrations are Lukang and Tainan.

A common sight at religious festivals are the spirit mediums (*jītóng* in Mandarin, *tangki* in Taiwanese). Not sure who these are? Look for wild bare-chested guys lacerating themselves with swords and sticking blades through their cheeks to prove the god is within them.

Acts of Worship & Prayer

Worship is known as *baibai* and doesn't have to take place in a temple, as most families have a household shrine devoted to their ancestors. In addition to the following, typical acts of worship include offerings of food, candles and thanks, as well as fasting or refraining from eating meat.

It's been said that the most important part of a temple is not its statues but its incense censer. In every temple in Taiwan you will see worshippers holding burning incense in their hands as they do the rounds, bowing first before the main deity and then the host of sub-deities. Afterwards the incense is placed in the censer.

Burning joss paper is another common act of worship and there are four different types, with each used for a variety of purposes, such as supplicating the gods, worshipping ancestors and literally providing spirits with money to use in the afterlife.

Going to a temple to ask gods or ancestors for answers to questions is common. The most typical form of divination is *bwah bwey,* which involves tossing two wooden half-moon divining blocks after a yes-or-no type question has been asked. If the two *bwey* both land curved-side up, the request has been denied. If one is up and one down, the request has been granted. If they both land curved-side down, it means the god is laughing at your request or suggesting you try again. There is no limit to how many times you can perform *bwah bwey* but if you get the same answer three times in a row, you should accept it.

The Temples of Taiwan

In Taiwan anyone can have a temple built, and it seems almost everyone does. Government statistics from 2009 show there are 14,993 registered temples, or approximately one for every 1500 residents (just a little higher than the average for convenience stores). This figure does not include unregistered temples, family shrines and the ubiquitous Earth God shrines. What's more astonishing is that the majority of these temples are relatively new. In 1930 there were 3336 registered temples; by 1981 there were 5331.

Taiwanese clearly love their temples. And why not? In addition to being houses of worship, temples fill the role of art museum, community centre, business hall, marketplace, recreation centre, orphanage, pilgrim site, and even recruitment centre for criminal gangs and fronts for money laundering.

Homonyms are an important part of Chinese visual art. Bats, for example, are commonly used motifs because bat (蝠, *fú*) sounds like 福 (fú) which means good fortune. Other common homophonic symbols include a vase (*píng*, meaning peace), a pike and chime (*jíqìng*, or auspicious), and a flag and ball (*qíqiú*, or to pray for). For examples see Xiahai City God Temple in Taipei.

History

Historians generally divide temple development in Taiwan into three periods. In the early immigrant stage (16th to 17th centuries), settlers, mostly from Fujian province, established branch temples based upon the gods worshipped in their home villages. These temples were sometimes little more than a thatched shrine covering a wood statue brought from China.

In the 18th and 19th centuries, as Taiwan grew wealthier, the small shrines were replaced with wood and stone temples. Wages for craftsmen were high and top artisans from China were eager to work here. Most materials were imported. This era also saw the establishment of Hakka temples.

The modern period began with the colonisation of Taiwan by the Japanese in 1895. Though Chinese masters were still used, several highly talented local schools developed and much of the fine work you'll see today comes from them.

Architectural Features

The basic characteristic of any temple hall or building is a raised platform that forms the base for a wood post-and-beam frame. This frame is held together by interlocking pieces (no nails or glue are used) and supports a curved gabled roof with overhanging eaves. Think of any pagoda you have seen as a ready example.

The layout of most temple complexes follow a similar and comprehensible pattern of alternating halls (Front, Main, Rear) and courtyards, usually arranged on a north–south axis. Corridors or wings often flank the east and west sides, and sometimes the whole complex is surrounded by a wall, or fronted by a large gate called a *pailou*. Exploring the variations of this theme is one of the pleasures of visiting multiple Taiwanese temples.

Temple Roofs

Stand outside a traditional Taiwanese temple and look up at the roof. It will be single or multitiered (with two or even three levels). The roof's ridgeline, slung low like a saddle, will curve upwards at the end, tapering and splitting prettily like the tail of a swallow. Not surprisingly this is known as a swallowtail roof, and is a distinctive feature of southern temples.

The ridgeline is always decorated with dragons in *jiǎnniàn* (mosaic-like temple decoration). Sometimes a pearl sits in the centre (which the dragons are reaching for); sometimes three figures (福祿寿, Fu Lu Shou) who represent the gods of good fortune, prosperity and longevity; and sometimes a seven-tier pagoda.

Slopes are covered with tiles (long and rounded like a bamboo tube) and much is fabulously decorated with vibrant cochin pottery and figures in *jiǎnniàn*. Fish and some dragon figures on the ends symbolise protection against fire (always a threat with wood structures).

Bracketing

Wooden brackets help to secure posts and beams but they are also decorative features. They vary from dragons and phoenix to flowers and birds, or tableaux of historical scenes unfolding as if on a scroll. Examples are Bao'an Temple in Taipei, Yinshan Temple in Tamsui, and Longshan Temple in Lukang.

TEMPLE STYLES

South vs North

Traditional Taiwanese temples are constructed in a southern style (sometimes called Minnan). What does this mean? Well, during the Ming and Qing dynasties, architecture in China moved away from the aesthetic principles of the Song dynasty (a high period of art) towards a stiff, formal and grandiose expressiveness best exemplified by Beijing's Forbidden City.

In more remote regions (such as Fujian), however, Song principles of beauty, playfulness, ornamentation and experimentation persisted. As all early Taiwanese emigrated from the south, they naturally constructed their temples in the style they knew. So don't rush through your next temple visit. It's heir to a thousand-year-old high tradition now found only here and a few scattered Chinese communities in Southeast Asia.

Buddhist vs Taoist vs Confucius

One of the easiest ways to distinguish between temples is to look at the actual name. A Buddhist temple will almost always end with the character 寺 *(sì)*, while a Taoist temple will end with the character 宮 *(gōng)* or 廟 *(miào)*. A Confucian temple is always called a Kǒng Miào (孔廟).

The general architectural features (such as a raised structure with a post-and-beam frame) will be the same for all three types, though modern temples can incorporate foreign influences such as the mosque-meets-rocket-ship design of the Chung Tai Chan Monastery in Puli. Older Buddhist temples such as the various Longshan Temples are harder to distinguish from Taoist, but modern Buddhist temples are usually built in a northern Chinese 'palace style' and have fewer images and less elaborate decorations.

Confucian temples are always large walled complexes and generally sedate, except on 28 September, the Sage's birthday. Taoist temples on the other hand will generally be loud, both in noise level and decoration. They tend to be very enjoyable to explore because of this.

RICHARD I'ANSON/GETTY IMAGES ©

Detail of a mural at Bao'an Temple (p65), Taipei

Dǒugǒng

Stand under the eaves of a temple roof and look up. Notice the complex system of two- or four-arm brackets? These brackets (very apparent when you see them) are called *dǒugǒng* and are unique to Chinese architecture. In fact, they are considered the very heart of the system.

Dǒugǒng gives builders a high degree of freedom during construction and is one reason why Chinese architecture can be found across a wide region so varying in climate.

Spiderweb Plafond Ceilings

This type of inverted ceiling (like in a cathedral) is constructed with exposed *dǒugǒng* arms that extend up and around in a spiderweb pattern (sometimes swirling like a vortex). Plafond ceilings are probably the most striking of all temple architectural features.

Examples are Confucius Temple and Qingshan Temple in Taipei, Anping Matsu Temple in Tainan, Tzushr Temple in Sansia, and City God Temple in Hsinchu.

A temple can seem raucous and worldly compared to a church, but before holy festivals it will undergo rites to transform it into a sacred space. Check out the *Five Day Completion Rituals To Thank Gods* at Bao'an Temple in Taipei every spring.

Temple Decorative Arts

Jiǎnniàn

One of the most delightful of the folk arts, *jiǎnniàn* (剪粘; cut-and-paste) is a method of decorating figurines with coloured shards. Imagine a three-dimensional mosaic.

True *jiǎnniàn* uses sheared ceramic bowls for raw material. The irregular pieces are then embedded by hand into a clay figurine. These days many artists use pre-made glass pieces but still embed them by hand. Some temples save money by simply buying prefab whole figurines.

Jiǎnniàn is usually found on the rooftops of temples (which can often be reached by stairs). Figures include humans, dragons, phoenix, carp, flowers and the eight immortals.

Examples are Bao'an Temple and Qingshan Temple in Taipei, Kaohsiung's City God Temple, and Zhenxing Temple in Jiali.

Cochin Pottery

A type of colourful low-fired, lead-glazed ceramic, cochin (also spelled *koji*) is one of Taiwan's unique decorative arts. The style is related to Chinese tri-colour pottery and came to Taiwan in the 18th century. Common themes include human figures, landscapes, flowers and plants, as well as tableaux depicting stories from mythology and history.

TOURING THROUGH TAIPEI'S BAO'AN TEMPLE

The Unesco heritage award winning Bao'an Temple (p65) is hard to beat as a place to start your study of traditional temple art and architecture.

➡ To begin, stand before the Front Hall (basically a colonnaded entrance portico with five doors) and observe the sweeping swallowtail ridgeline, elaborate rooftop decoration (*jiǎnniàn* figurines), and row of cochin pottery figures nestled snugly between the roof's double eaves.

➡ Then note the stone lions, octagonal dragon pillars, rectangular pillars, and side dragon and tiger panels. These all welcome visitors and protect against demons. They are also among the oldest parts of the temple. The dragon columns, for example, were carved in 1804.

➡ Above the lions look for carved wood panels between the posts. See the Western-style balcony on the left panel? When Bao'an was renovated in 1917 during the Japanese-era, two teams (one from China, one from Taiwan) were given one half of the temple each to complete: the left side was given to the Taiwanese and features more innovations and touches of modernity

➡ The interior of the Front Hall serves as a worship area, with long kneelers and tables piled high with offerings and flowers. In other temples this worship area may be further in toward the Main Hall.

➡ Next, step into the open stone courtyard (this area is covered in many temples). Note the large incense burner (made in 1918) and bell and drum towers on the sides. These towers are Japanese influences and are now widely found in other temples.

➡ The Main Hall is another double-eaved structure with stunning rooftop decoration, hanging flower pots in differing styles, and carved pillars. On the far left eave, look up for a Western figure with an umbrella and dog. Also note the different *dǒugǒng* styling on the left and right (the left is shaped like the character 人 *(rén)*, meaning people). A long panel of cochin figurines represents the Eight Immortals Crossing the Sea.

➡ Inside the Main Hall (where the resident god always resides) check out the gorgeous roof truss. This is an example of traditional *san tong wu gua*, or three beams and five melon posts. Also lock on either side for the astonishing ceramic green dragon and tiger reliefs (created by master cochin artist Hong Kunfu in 1917), and the celebrated wood statues of the 36 celestial guardians (carved between 1827 and 1833).

➡ Inside the Main Hall look for lacquered tables piled high with offerings. As with most temples, the shrine at the back is elaborately carved and features multiple statues of the resident god (the smallest inside the glass is the oldest). Note the pillars in here are rounded. In pillar hierarchy, round is best, octagonal second-best, and rectangular third.

➡ The exterior of the Main Hall is covered in masterful paintings completed by Pan Lishui in 1973. The back shows the legendary ghost queller Zhong Kui welcoming his sister home.

➡ Like most larger temples, Bao'an features a rear hall (note the single eave) with shrines to various deities. Check out the delicate bird and flower pillars (made in 1918) and the exorcism room to the far right.

BRANCH TEMPLES & THE DIVINE POWER OF THE MOTHER

New temples are almost always established as a branch (or daughter) of a larger and more famous mother temple. This involves a rather fascinating process called *fēnxiāng* (分香, spirit division).

In this practice, representatives from the newly built temple go to the elder one to obtain incense ash or statues. By doing so they bring back a little of the *líng* (靈, divine efficacy) of the original temple deity to their own humble house of worship.

Periodically representatives from the daughter temple must return to the mother to renew or add power to the *líng* of their statue. At the mother temple they once again scoop out incense ash to place in the incense burner of their own temple and also pass their statue through the smoke of the mother temple's incense burner. The process is usually accompanied by a large parade.

Cochin pottery is found under eaves, on lintels or on the rooftop.

Examples are Chenghuang Temple in Chiayi, Confucius Temple in Taipei, Zhenxing Temple in Jiali, Ciji Temple in Xuejia, and Cochin Ceramic Museum in Chiayi.

Woodcarving

Woodcarving is usually found on cross beams, brackets, hanging pillars (often carved in the shape of flower pots), doors, window lattice and screen walls. Its basic function is decorative, though many parts are integral to the temple structure. Many temple god statues are also carved from wood and are exquisite pieces of art.

Examples are Bao'an Temple in Taipei, Yinshan Temple in Tamsui, Matsu Temple in Makung, and Longshan Temple in Lukang.

Painting

Painting is mainly applied to wood beams and walls. Though decorative, painting also helps to preserve wood, and is said to drive away evil, bless and inspire good deeds. Common motifs include stories from literature and history.

Probably the most distinctive paintings at any temple are the guardians on the doors to the Front Hall. Examples are Xiahai City God and Bao'an Temples in Taipei, and Matsu and Dongyue Temples in Tainan.

Stone Carving

Before the 20th century most stone came from China, and was often used as ballast in the rough ship ride over. Later locally sourced Guanyin stone became the preferred choice, though today cheaper Chinese imports are often used.

Stone is most commonly used for courtyard surfaces, stairs and doorposts, dragon columns and other pillars, lion statues, and relief wall panels showing scenes from history and literature.

Examples are Lukang's Longshan Temple, Tzushr Temple in Sansia, and Chaotian Temple.

Temples Today

Temples are fragile structures and prone to weathering, and subject to outright destruction by fire, flooding, earthquakes, typhoons, landslides, wars, occupations and indifference. Nearly every temple in Taiwan has been restored at least once since 1945, in many cases radically re-altering the original style.

In fact, most temples you see in Taiwan today will not have a traditional southern style at all. Since the 1960s the trend has been to build

Temple Etiquette

In general, temples welcome visitors.

You can take pictures but be courteous.

Don't go past gated altar areas.

Enter via the right door of a temple and exit via the left. The main door is reserved for the resident god.

Remove your hat and don't smoke.

Some Buddhist temples might ask you to remove your shoes.

In every temple look for animals in the paintings, carvings and ceramic figures. The dragon, phoenix, tortoise and qilin are known as the 'four Spiritual beasts'. The tiger, leopard, lion and elephant are also important symbols in both Buddhism and Taoism.

in the so-called northern palace style. Such temples are squat and broad, with a flat roof ridgeline and a flat interior ceiling. Decorations tend to be repetitive and are often prefabricated in China. The change resulted from political reasons (to please the Nationalist government), insecurity among Taiwanese regarding the worth of their southern heritage, and cost-cutting measures.

The Dying Masters

Taiwan has a serious problem ahead with the lack of fresh blood moving into the traditional decorative-arts field. The last survey of *jiǎnniàn* masters in 2004, for example, showed that only 37 remained. A combination of low prestige, long hours and low pay has made traditional craftwork unattractive to younger Taiwanese. One master woodcarver we met from Pingdong even said he refused to pass his skills on to his children, not wanting them to get stuck in a dead-end career.

The Arts of Taiwan

Taiwan has a rich and varied art scene covering familiar Western genres such as painting, film, dance, ceramics and literature. Local arts are either wholly indigenous or evolved from Chinese genres, carried over by waves of immigration.

The most visited museum in Taiwan is the National Palace Museum in Taipei. As outstanding as this is, it's important to realise that nothing in the collection was made by a Taiwanese, or for a Taiwanese. By all means visit (it's a world-class museum), but just don't think it tells you much, if anything, about local art and culture.

The Yingge Ceramics Museum covers not just the history of pottery and ceramics in Taiwan, but also showcases the current leading masters and their efforts to keep expanding the boundaries of their art.

Visual Arts

Modern Art

Western styles of painting were introduced to Taiwan by the Japanese. Ishikawa Kinichiro (1871–1945), now considered the father of modern Taiwanese art, taught local painters to work the tropical landscapes of Taiwan in a French impressionistic style. Ishikawa's students included Li Mei-shu (1902–83) who is best known for his work overseeing the reconstruction of Sansia's masterful Tzushi Temple.

During the 1970s a strong nativist movement, sometimes referred to as 'Taiwan Consciousness', began to develop. Artists found inspiration in Taiwanese folk traditions and the arts and crafts of indigenous tribes. The sculptor Ju Ming (born 1938), whose stone and woodwork can be seen in his personal Juming Museum on the north coast, is the most well-known artist from this period.

The opening of the Taipei Fine Arts Museum and the ending of martial law were two of the most significant events in the 1980s. For the first time, artists could actively criticise the political system without suffering consequences. And they had a public venue to do so.

Since then alternative art spaces have blossomed and Taiwan's participation on the international stage has been well established. Artists regularly exhibit at top venues such as the Venice Biennale, and work in multimedia as much as traditional forms.

Indigenous Arts & Crafts

The indigenous people of Taiwan have their own distinct art traditions, many of which are alive and well these days.

Woodcarving

The Tao of Lanyu Island are famous for their handmade canoes, built without nails or glue. The striking canoes have carved relief designs embellished with human and sun motifs painted in white, red and black.

The Paiwan and Rukai also excel at woodcarving, and building homes and utensils that feature elaborate carvings of humans, snakes and fantastical creatures. Along the east coast the Amis use driftwood for sculptures of humans and animals and fantastic abstract pieces. You can check out part of the scene at the Dulan Sugar Factory (p188).

The first Taiwanese artist to study in Japan was Huang Tu-shui (1895–1930) whose relief masterwork called 'Water Buffalo' can be seen in Taipei's Zhongshan Hall.

Dance & Music

Vocal music is one way aborigines preserve their history and legends, passing down songs from one generation to the next. This music has become popular in recent years and music stores in Taiwan's larger cities carry recordings.

Aboriginal dances, accompanied by singing and musical instruments, are usually centred on festivals, which may celebrate coming-of-age rituals, harvests or hunting skills. These days, it's relatively easy to watch a genuine performance of traditional dance in the summer along the east coast.

The Atayal and Seediq are well known for their weaving which uses hand-planted ramie. The bright 'traditional' colours were actually introduced in the 1920s.

Though rarely performed now, the Bunun *Pasibutbut,* a song with a complex eight-part harmony, was once considered impossible for a 'primitive' hunter gatherer society to have created.

Music

In addition to aboriginal song, Taiwan has a long and rich tradition of classical instrumental music such as Nanguan (southern pipes) and Beiguan, which originated in Fujian province (the ancestral home to most Taiwanese).

Folk music includes Hakka *shan ge* (山歌, mountain songs), and the Holo music of the Hengchun Peninsula (very southern Taiwan) in which singers are accompanied by the *yuèqín* (月琴, moon lute). In the hit Taiwanese movie *Cape No 7,* the character of Old Mao plays the *yuèqín.*

Taiwanese pop music goes back decades. One of the most popular singers in the 1970s was silky voiced Teresa Teng (1953–95) whose grave in Jinbaoshan Cemetary (just up from the Juming Museum) is still visited by adoring fans to this day. Perhaps even more well known in the Chinese-speaking world is A-mei (阿妹, Ā Mèi; born 1972), a singer-songwriter from Taiwan's Puyuma tribe. Younger stars include Jay Chou and Joline, both huge idols in China.

Since the late 1990s, Taiwan has developed a vibrant indie, hip hop, folk and underground scene, with some bands, like metal Chthonic becoming near household names. Popular music festivals such as Spring Scream (p276) and Hohaiyan Rock Festival (p144) continue to introduce new bands to a wide audience.

Performance Arts

Taiwanese Opera

The various styles of folk opera commonly seen in Taiwan have their origin in Fujian and Guangdong provinces, though over the centuries they have been completely localised to the point where they are now recognised as distinct art forms. Initially performed on auspicious occasions such as weddings, birthdays and temple festivals, folk opera later developed into a more public art form, drawing larger audiences. By the 1940s opera was the most popular folk entertainment in Taiwan and remains well-received to this day.

Learn more about native aboriginal arts and crafts at Wulai Atayal Museum, Shung Ye Museum of Formosan Aborigines in Taipei, and Ketagalan Culture Centre in Beitou.

Taiwanese opera is complimented by a wide range of musical instruments, including drums, gongs, flutes, lutes and two- and three-stringed mandolins. Common opera styles include Nanguan Xi Opera and Gezai Xi (sometimes just called Taiwanese opera), which evolved out of a ballad tradition that involved musical accompaniment. It's the most folksy and down-to-earth form of opera, making use of folk stories and sayings and, of course, the Hokkien language. The occasional martial arts display is a result of a merger of Beijing Opera and Taiwanese Opera troupes in the 1920s.

Dance

Modern dance in Taiwan has its roots in the 1940s, when it was introduced by the Japanese. In the 1960s and '70s a number of outstanding dancers, trained abroad or influenced by American dancers who had toured Taiwan, began to form their own troupes and schools, some of which remain influential today.

The most highly regarded is the Cloud Gate Dance Theatre of Taiwan (p99), founded in the early 1970s by Lin Hwai-min. Lin was a student under Martha Graham and upon his return to Taiwan in 1973 desired to combine modern dance techniques with Chinese opera.

Lin's first works were based on stories and legends from Chinese classical literature. Soon, however, Lin decided to try to explore Taiwanese identity in his work. *Legacy,* one of Lin's most important works, tells the story of the first Taiwanese settlers. Later works are more abstract and meditative as Lin explored Tibetan, Indian and Indonesian influences. No matter what, Cloud Gate performances are breathtaking in their colour and movement.

It's common to see free performances of opera held on stages outside local temples. Check out Bao'an Temple, Xiahai City God Temple and also Dadaocheng Theatre.

Cinema

Taiwanese cinema began in 1901 with Japanese-made documentaries and feature films. Many of these show the progress of Taiwan under colonial rule and were clearly meant for a Japanese audience.

In the 1960s the Nationalist government created the Central Motion Picture Corporation (CMP) and a genuine movie industry took off. During the 1960s and '70s, audiences were treated to a deluge of romantic melodramas and martial arts epics.

In the 1980s a New Wave movement began as directors like Hou Hsiao-hsien broke away from escapism to depict the gritty reality of Taiwan life. Hou's most successful film, *City of Sadness* (1989), follows the lives of a Taiwanese family living through the KMT takeover of Taiwan and the 2-28 Incident. This movie was the first to break the silence around 2-28 and won the Golden Lion award at the 1989 Venice Film Festival.

Emerging a little later in the Second New Wave was Ang Lee, Taiwan's most famous director, known for his mega-hits *Crouching Tiger, Hidden Dragon* (2000) and *Brokeback Mountain* (2005). Ang joined Hollywood in the mid-'90s but he continues to work with and support the local industry in Taiwan.

Piracy and competition from Hong Kong and Hollywood films sent the Taiwanese film industry into near collapse by the late '90s. With the release of Wei Te-sheng's *Cape No 7* (2008), a romantic comedy that became a box office smash, audiences and critics began to feel re-newed hope for the industry. Wei's *Seediq Bale* (2011), an epic about an aboriginal revolt against the Japanese, as well as Doze Niu's *Monga* (2010), about gangsters in Taipei in the 1980s, and Tien-Lun Yeh *Night Market Hero* (2011), are keeping the dream alive.

Taiwan has a rich puppetry tradition in marionette (string), glove, rod and shadow styles. Check out the Lin Liu-Hsin Puppet Theatre Museum in Taipei.

Literature

Although Taiwanese writers have produced a significant body of literature, including novels, short stories and poems, most works have not been translated into English. Much modern writing has focused on the harsh realities of Taiwan's history and present-day social issues. One of the most controversial novels for its time, translated into English, is Pai Hsien-yung's *Crystal Boys* (1983), a novel about Taiwan's gay scene.

To learn more about Taiwanese literature check out the National Museum of Taiwanese Literature in Tainan.

The Landscape of Taiwan

At merely six million years of age, the gorgeous island of Taiwan is a bouncy child pumping with vigour and potential compared to the 4.6 billion years that planet earth has clocked up.

At 3805m, Siouguluan Mountain not only represents the apex of the Central Mountain Range, but it's also sitting on the busiest tectonic collision zone in the whole of Taiwan. At present it's rising by approximately 0.5cm a year. Expect more spouting to come.

Taiwan lies 165km off the coast of mainland China, separated by the Taiwan Strait. The area of the island is 36,000 sq km (roughly the size of the Netherlands), 394km in length and 144km wide at its widest point. The territory of the country includes 15 offshore islands; the most important are the Penghu Archipelago, the islands of Matsu and Kinmen in the Taiwan Strait, and, off the east coast, Green Island and Lanyu.

The Beauty

Visitors to Taiwan and the surrounding islands can experience a stunningly broad variety of landscapes, from rugged mountains in the centre of the main island (there's even snow in winter at higher altitudes) to low-lying wetlands teeming with wildlife on the western coast, rice paddies and farmland in the south, and lonely windswept beaches punctuated with basalt rock formations on the outer islands. The east coast, with its towering seaside cliffs and rocky volcanic coastline, is utterly spectacular. The Central Cross-Island Highway and the Southern Cross-Island Highway link the island from east to west, cutting through spectacular mountain scenery.

However, Taiwan's colourful – and wild – topography means that the majority of the country's 23 million people are forced to live on the small expanses of plains to the west of the Central Mountain Range, and this is where agriculture and industry concentrate.

Mountains

Mountains are the most dominant feature of Taiwan. The island is divided in half by the Central Mountain Range, a series of jagged peaks that stretch for 170km from Su-ao in the northeast to Eluanbi at the southern tip. Gorges, precipitous valleys and lush forests characterise this very rugged ridge of high mountains.

Running diagonally down the right half of the island like a sash are the country's four other mountain ranges. The East Coast Mountain Range runs down the east coast of Taiwan from the mouth of the Hualien River in the north to Taitung County in the south. The Xueshan Range lies to the northwest of the Central Mountain Range. Xueshan, the main peak, is 3886m high.

Flanking the Central Mountain Range to the southwest is the Yushan Range, home to the eponymous Yushan (Jade Mountain). At 3952m, Yushan is Taiwan's pinnacle and one of the tallest mountains

NATURAL DISASTERS: EARTHQUAKES, TYPHOONS & LANDSLIDES

Taiwan is in a singular geological and climatic setting. It is highly susceptible to earthquakes and typhoons, while heavy rainfalls exacerbate the risk of landslides.

Earthquakes

Geologically Taiwan is on one of the most complex and active tectonic collision zones on earth. Sitting atop the ever-colliding (albeit slowly colliding) Eurasian and Philippine plates has given Taiwan the beautiful mountains, scenic gorges and amazing hot springs that keep people coming back. Alas, these same geological forces also put the island smack dab in earthquake central, meaning that nary a week goes by without some form of noticeable seismic activity. Most of these quakes are small tremors, only noticed by folks living in the upper storeys of buildings as a gentle, peculiar rocking sensation. Others can be far more nerve-wracking to locals and visitors alike.

One quake on the southern coast in late 2006 caused only a few casualties, but severed several underground cables, disrupting telephone and internet service across Asia. On 4 March 2010 an earthquake measuring 6.4 on the Richter scale with an epicentre 362km south of Taiwan's southernmost city caused buildings to tremble as far north as Taipei, knocking out power and rail service for a short time and causing several injuries. The most devastating earthquake to hit Taiwan is remembered locally simply as '9-21' after the date it occurred, 21 September 1999. Measuring 7.3 on the Richter scale, the earthquake collapsed buildings and killed thousands. Damage caused by the 9-21 earthquake – especially the dramatic collapse of buildings in commercial and residential neighbourhoods – led to the passage of laws requiring that new buildings be designed to withstand future earthquakes of high magnitude.

Typhoons

Common during the summer months in the western Pacific area and the China seas, typhoons are tropical cyclones that form when warm moist air meets low pressure conditions. Taiwan experiences yearly tropical storms, some of which reach typhoon level. Having better infrastructure than many of its neighbours, Taiwan tends to weather most typhoons fairly well, with the majority resulting in flooding, property damage, delays and headaches – but little loss of life. In August 2009, however, Taiwan found itself in the direct path of Typhoon Morakot. The island was unable to cope with the massive rainfall brought by the typhoon (it delivered over a long weekend what in the UK would be about three years' worth of rain) which, combined with winds of up to 150km/h, triggered heavy flooding and landslides, especially in the southern counties of Pingtung, Chiayi and Kaohsiung. Nearly 600 people were killed in the disaster.

Although there has been no official consensus on precisely why Morakot was so devastating, many who study local climate and land-use issues in Taiwan factor in poor land management, excessive draining of aquifers and wetlands, and climate change in general as being partially responsible.

Landslides

According to Dave Petley, one of the world's top landslide specialists, Taiwan is the 'landslide capital of the world' because of the high rates of tectonic uplift, weak rocks, steep slopes, frequent earthquakes and extreme rainfall events. But while Taiwan has almost every type of landslide, the number of known ancient rock avalanches remains surprisingly low given the prevailing conditions.

A fact of life for people living in Taiwan, natural disasters are also something that travellers need to take into account when planning their trip. Aside from the obvious dangers that may arise from being in the vicinity while one is occurring, landslides, typhoons and earthquakes have the potential to actually alter the landscape, rendering once-scenic areas unreachable and roads impassable. Sections of the Central Cross-Island Highway that once stretched across the middle of the island from Taichung to Hualien remain closed to visitors, while large sections of the Southern Cross Hwy are still impassable after being altered beyond recognition by Typhoon Morakot in 2009.

in northeast Asia. The Alishan Range sits west, separated by the Kaoping River valley.

Rivers & Plains

Legendary Japanese engineer Yoichi Hatta (1886–1942) still commands hero status in Taiwan today thanks to the major contributions he made to hydraulic engineering in the country.

According to the Taiwanese government's Council of Agriculture, the country boasts 118 rivers, all originating in the mountains, and it thus appears rather well watered. Despite that considerable number, most of Taiwan's rivers follow short, steep and rapid courses down into the ocean, which causes flooding during typhoon season. During the dry season, however, the river beds are exposed and the reservoirs alone are unable to supply adequate water to the population. An extensive network of canals, ditches and weirs has therefore evolved over time to manage and channel this elusive river flow for irrigation.

The country's longest river is the 186km Zhuoshui, which starts in Nantou County and flows through the counties of Changhua, Yunlin and Chiayi, and serves as the symbolic dividing line between northern and southern Taiwan. It is also the most heavily tapped for hydroelectricity. The Tanshui, which runs through Taipei, is the only navigable stream. Other rivers include the Kaoping, Tsengwen, Tachia and Tatu.

Located in the foothills of the Central Mountain Range, Sun Moon Lake is the largest body of freshwater in Taiwan and is one of the country's top tourist destinations.

Fertile plains and basins make up most of western Taiwan, which is criss-crossed with many small rivers that empty into the sea and has the most suitable land for agriculture. Over on the east coast, however, even plains are in short supply. Outside the three cities of Ilan, Hualien and Taitung, the area is among the most sparsely populated on the island.

Wetlands

Taiwan is home to 100 wetlands that have been officially declared 'nationally important', with estuaries being the most common form. There are large wetland concentrations in the southwest and southeast of the island; Tsengwen Estuary and Sihcao Wetland, both in Tainan, are classified 'international class' wetlands.

Besides providing a valuable ecosystem that supports a multitude of life-forms including insects, amphibians and fish, Taiwan's wetlands are a precious gift to vast populations of migratory birds. These enamoured, annual visitors stop in Taiwan when migrating from northern areas such as Siberia, Manchuria, Korea and Japan for southern wintering sites in, for instance, the Philippines and Indonesia.

If you drive along Lanyang River in the dry season, you'll be greeted by a giant cabbage patch instead of flowing waters. To find the impressive, curious sight, follow the highway through the Xueshan and Yushan Mountain Ranges up to Wuling Farm.

Environmental Issues

When Chiang Kai-shek's Nationalist troops were driven off the mainland, they brought more than just millions of Chinese people fleeing communism with them: they also brought capital, much of which was used to transform a primarily agrarian society into a major industrial powerhouse. Taiwan became wealthy, quickly, but it also became toxic, with urban air quality ranking among the world's worst, and serious pollution in most of its waterways. Indeed, Taiwan's 'economic miracle' came at a serious price, and pollution, urban sprawl and industrial waste have all taken a heavy toll on the island.

Things have improved markedly over the last decade. Environmental laws, once largely ignored by industry and individuals alike, are now enforced far more rigorously across the board, and the results have been tangible (the Danshui and Keelung Rivers in Taipei, for example, once horribly befouled, are significantly cleaner in sections).

Rice fields in eastern Taiwan

Urban air quality is noticeably better, thanks to a combination of improved public transport, more stringent clean-air laws, and a switch to unleaded petrol.

The Taiwanese collective unconscious has changed as well: so much of the new 'Taiwanese identity' is tied in with having a clean and green homeland that people are tending to take environmental protection far more seriously.

Lest we paint too rosy a picture, it's possible to counter any perceived step forward with another step back towards the bad old days.

One of the bigger issues belying the image that the Taiwan government hopes to project as an environmentally conscious democracy is that of land expropriation – that is, the legal removal of farmers from privately owned lands. Critics said that a December 2011 revision of the Land Expropriation Act had only served to reinforce the interests of development, which is very loosely defined to cover anything from military construction to projects approved by the Executive, over farmers' rights.

Government and industrial proponents of expropriation point to the issue of common good, saying that transforming farmland into industrial areas creates jobs, reducing the country's climbing unemployment rate. However, opponents say that the main beneficiaries are a conglomerate of large corporations and real-estate developers.

Although Taiwan's High Speed Rail (HSR) has been touted for making travel around the island even more convenient, many feel that placement of the stations – in the far outskirts of Taiwan's westernmost cities as opposed to in the city centres themselves – has actually promoted both increased traffic and urban sprawl.

A lack of energy resources means that Taiwan is highly reliant on imports to meet its energy needs. However, the country has a poor record in the use of renewable energy: it is a major exporter of solar panels but there's almost no domestic use. Against this context, the KMT-led government's nuclear power policy is unlikely to be reversed anytime soon.

And of course, the ongoing issue of decaying barrels of nuclear waste buried on the aboriginal island of Lanyu has also yet to be resolved to anybody's satisfaction.

Taiwan's environmental issues are a global concern as well. Despite its diminutive size, Taiwan is a major CO_2 producer. A 2009 study contended that the 4130-megawatt coal-burning Taichung power station was the biggest CO_2 emitter on the planet, with yearly CO_2 emissions from the one plant alone roughly equal to the emissions of Switzerland. To date, it remains one of the most polluting coal power plants globally.

So while it's fair to say that Taiwan has made great strides on the environmental front, it's clear that more remains to be done.

Taiwan Wildlife Guide

To most of the world Taiwan is best known as one of the Asian Tigers, an economic powerhouse critical to the world's IT supply chains. Decades earlier it had a reputation (now overtaken by China) as a manufacturer of cheap toys and electronics. But going back even earlier, Taiwan was not just the 'beautiful island' but also the kingdom of the butterfly and an endemic species wonderland where one could find the most astonishing variety of native plants and animals.

Is there anything left of this old world? Plenty. Taiwan is in fact 60% forested, with about 20% (and growing) of the land officially protected as national park or forest reserve. One of the absolute highlights of any trip to Ilha Formosa involves getting to know the flora and fauna, much of which you can't find anywhere else on earth.

Taiwan lies across the Tropic of Cancer and most fact books record its climate as subtropical. But with an extremely mountainous terrain (it's almost 4000m high in the centre), Taiwan's climate can range from subtropical to subarctic, and its vegetation zones can range from coastal to montane to alpine. It's been said that a journey 4km up to the 'roof' of Taiwan reproduces a trip of many thousands of kilometres north from Taiwan to the Russian steppes.

There are no comprehensive English books on Taiwan's wildlife, but the visitor information centres at the country's national parks sell a wide range of individual books and DVDs that cover butterflies, birds, mammals, reptiles and more.

Plants

Taiwan has 4000 to 5000 plant species, with an estimated 26% found nowhere else. Travellers will be most interested in the forest zones, which is a good thing because Taiwan has plenty of forest cover.

Foothills (Tropical Zone): 0–500m

Most of Taiwan's original tropical forests have long been cleared to make room for tea fields, orchards, and plantations of Japanese cedar, camphor and various bamboos. Intact lowland forests still exist along the east and in parts of Kenting National Park. In other areas you will find dense second-growth forests.

Submontane (Subtropical Zone): 300–1500m

It's in these broadleaf forests that most people get their first taste of just how unspoiled and luxuriant Taiwan's forests can be. It's a jungle-like environment teeming with birds, insects, snakes and so many ferns that you often can't count the number of species in one patch. Though ferns can grow as high as trees (giving forests a distinct 'Lost World' feel), common larger plant species include camphor, *Machilus,* crepe myrtle, maple tree, gums and cedar.

You can see submontane plants in Nanao, the Pingxi Branch Rail Line, the Walami Trail and Wulai.

Montane (Temperate Zone): 1600–3100m

The montane forests vary greatly because the elevation changes mean there are warm temperate and cool temperate zones. You might start your journey in a mixed broadleaf forest that soon turns to evergreen

Taiwan's Birds

Birding in Taiwan (www.birdingintaiwan.com)

Birdlife International (www.birdlife.org/regional/asia)

Wild Bird Society of Taipei (p77)

Birds of East Asia by Mark Brazil

oaks. At higher elevations conifers such as Taiwan red cypress, Taiwania, alder, hemlock and pine start to predominate. In areas that have been disturbed by landslide or fire you often get large tracts of Taiwan red pine. When their needles fall, the forest floor becomes almost ruby in colour.

Between 2500m and 3100m in elevation a natural pine-hemlock zone runs down the centre of Taiwan. This is one of the most pristine parts of the country (logging never went this high) and many trees are hundreds and even thousands of years old. A good part of any hike to the high mountains will be spent in this zone.

You can see montane plants along the Alishan Forest Train (p217), Forestry Road 200 (p211), and the hiking trails in Yushan National Park and Snow Mountain.

Subalpine (Cold Temperate Zone): 2800–3700m

You might think that this high-altitude zone is inaccessible unless you hike in, but you can actually reach sections of it by road. Taiwan's highest pass sits at 3275m on Hwy 14, just before Hehuanshan (Hohuanshan) Forest Recreation Area. The rolling meadows of Yushan cane (a type of

STOPPING TO SMELL THE FLOWERS

Taiwan is not hurting for beautiful flowers to appreciate. The blooming period is long and you can usually see something year-round. Here are a few scented petals to watch out for, besides the sublime day lilies.

Flamegold tree Appropriately named native tree with large yellow and red blooms in autumn. It grows in lowland forests, and it's widely planted on city streets as it does well in polluted air.

Youtong The large white flowers of the youtong tree bloom all over the north in April. Around the Sanxia Interchange on Fwy 3, entire mountainsides go near-white in good years.

Rhododendron & azalea Native species bloom from low to high altitudes from April to June.

Formosa lily One of the tallest of lilies, with long trumpet-like flowers. Blooms wild all over Taiwan twice a year in spring and autumn.

Orchid There are many wild species but large farms around Tainan and Pingtung also grow these delightful flowers. Taiwan is, in fact, the world's largest orchid exporter.

Lotus Baihe in Tainan County has a two-month-long summer festival devoted to this flower.

Cherry blossom Cherry trees bloom in great numbers in February and March in Yangmingshan, Wulai and Alishan Forest Recreation Area.

Calla lily These beautiful long-stemmed white lilies bloom in large fields in Yangmingshan in spring. There's even a festival for them.

Plum blossom The national flower (at least for the Kuomintang) blooms in February in orchards all over the island at midaltitudes. Intoxicating scent.

Butterfly ginger A hopeless romantic, the white flower of the native butterfly ginger gives off its strongest scent at night. Blooms from spring to autumn all over the island.

Awn grass (silvergrass) A tall swaying grass, with light, airy blooms. Its blooming signals the end of autumn in the north. The Caoling Historic Trail is one of the best places to see entire hillsides covered in it.

Alpine flowers Taiwan has dozens of petite flowers that splash a bit of colour above the treeline all summer long.

Robert Kelly, Coordinating Author

dwarf bamboo) that you can see from the roadside stand as one of the most beautiful natural sights on the island.

Less accessible are forests of tall straight Taiwan fir and juniper (a tree-line species). To see these you will need to put on your boots and strap on a knapsack.

You can see subalpine plants in the Hehuanshan Forest Recreation Area (p238), Snow Mountain, Tatajia and Wuling Pass.

For a closer look at the variety of snakes in Taiwan, check out Snakes of Taiwan (www.snakesoftaiwan.com).

Alpine (Subarctic Zone): 3500m plus

If you manage to climb your way to this elevation you'll be above the tree line. The zone is divided into a lower scrub zone and an upper herb zone where tiny patches of vegetation cling to the exposed rocks. It's a chilly place even in summer but the amazing views are worth every effort to get here.

You can see alpine plants on the peaks of Snow Mountain and Yushan National Park.

Animals

Mammals

There are about 70 species of mammals in Taiwan, and about 70% of those are endemic. Once over-hunted and threatened by development, species like the Formosan macaque, wild boar, martin, civet, sambar deer, and the delightful and diminutive barking deer (Reeves' muntjac) have made great comebacks and are relatively easy to spot in national parks and forest reserves. Sika deer, which once roamed the grasslands of the west from Kenting to Yangmingshan, have been reintroduced to Kenting National Park and are doing well. Head out at night in submontane forests with a high-powered torch (flashlight) if you want to catch Taiwan's flying squirrels in action.

Though tropical at lower elevations, Taiwan lacks large species of mammals such as elephants, rhinos and tigers. Taiwan's biggest cat the spotted cloud leopard, is almost certainly extinct, while the Formosan black bear is numbered at fewer than 1000. Your chances of seeing one of these creatures are pretty slim. In 15 years of hiking the wilds of Taiwan we have seen only one.

You can see mammals in Chihpen Forest Recreation Area, Jiaming Lake National Trail, Kenting National Park, Nanao, Sheipa National Park and Yushan National Park.

Birds

With its great range of habitats, Taiwan is an ideal place for birds, and birdwatchers. Over 500 species have been recorded here: 150 are considered resident species, 69 are endemic subspecies, and 15 are endemic species (though some authorities say there are 24, or more). It's an impressive list and compares very well with larger countries in the region such as Japan.

Bird conservation has been a great success over the past two decades, and it's therefore easy to spot endemics like the comical blue magpie, or multicoloured Muller's Barbet even in the hills surrounding Taipei. For one of the world's truly great shows, however, check out the raptor migration over Kenting National Park. Once threatened by over-hunting, bird numbers have tripled in the past decade. Several years back, over 50,000 raptors passed over the park in a single day.

You can see birds in Aowanda Forest Recreation Area, Dasyueshan Forest Recreation Area, Kenting National Park, Kinmen, Tatajia, Wulai and Yangmingshan National Park.

Taiwan's Wildlife Highlights

- *Super-high rate of species endemism*
- *Huge variety of flora and fauna within a small area*
- *Easy access to wild areas*
- *Fascinating yearly migrations of birds and butterflies*

Butterflies

In the 1950s and '60s Taiwan's butterflies were netted and bagged for export in the tens of millions (per year!). Remarkably, only three species became extinct, though numbers plummeted for decades. These days top butterfly areas are well protected, and these delightful creatures can be seen everywhere year-round.

Taiwan has over 400 species of butterflies, of which about 60 are endemic. Some standouts include the Blue Admirals, Red-base Jezebels and Magellan's Iridescent Birdwing, which has one of the largest wingspans in the world.

Prominent sites include Yangmingshan National Park's Datunshan, where chestnut tigers swarm in late spring; the overwintering purple butterfly valleys in the south; Fuyuan Forest Recreational Area; and the Yellow Butterfly Valley (p264) outside Meinong. You can also see butterflies in Linnei, Maolin and Tatajia.

ON WINGS OF GOSSAMER

Butterfly migration is fairly common the world over, but Taiwan's purple crow migration can hold its own. Each year in the autumn, as the weather cools, bands of shimmering purples (four species of Euploea, also known as milkweed butterflies) leave their mountain homes in north and central Taiwan and begin to gather in larger and larger bands as they fly south. By November they have travelled several hundred kilometres, and in a series of 12 to 15 warm, sheltered valleys in the Dawu Mountain Range, 10 to 15 million of them settle in for the winter.

This mass overwintering is not common. In fact, Taiwan is one of only two places in the world where it happens: the other is in the Monarch Butterfly Valleys of Mexico. The most famous overwintering site in Taiwan is in Maolin Recreation Area, but according to experts this is actually the least populated valley. It simply had the advantage of being the first to be discovered and written about.

The discovery happened in 1971 when an amateur entomologist was invited into Maolin by local Rukai aboriginals. Though not aware of just how significant the find was, the entomologist (and others) continued to study the valley. By the mid-1980s it was obvious that a north–south migration route existed, though it wasn't until 2005 that the 400km route along the west could be roughly mapped out. Since then a second migration path along the east coast and a connecting path joining the two have also been discovered.

The northern migration usually begins around March, and, astonishingly, it involves many of the same individuals who flew down in the autumn (purples have been found to live up to nine months). Some good places to spot the spring migration are Linnei, Dawu (in Taitung County), Pingtung County Rd 199, Taichung's Metropolitan Park, Baguashan, and coastal areas of Jhunan (Miaoli County) where the purples stop to breed. In May and June large numbers of purples appear to take a mysterious detour and are blown back south over the high mountain pass at Tatajia.

If you're curious as to just how the migration occurs in the first place, the answer is relatively simple: seasonal winds. In the autumn they come strong out of Mongolia and China, while in the spring they blow up from the Philippines. Without them the purples would be unlikely to move such great distances and this would mean their death when the temperatures drop during northern winters.

From spring until autumn, purple butterflies are easily spotted all over Taiwan. So give a nod to these brave wayfarers when you encounter them in a park or mountain trail. They may have come a long way.

For a mostly accurate look at the discovery of the western migratory route check out *The Butterfly Code*, a Discovery Channel DVD.

Sika deer

Other Wildlife

Taiwan has a host of reptiles including a wide variety of beautiful but deadly snakes. Lizards, frogs and a long list of insects including stag beetles, cicadas and stick insects can be found anywhere where there's a bit of undisturbed land.

Marine life (whales and dolphins, as well as corals and tropical fish) is abundant on the offshore islands and the east coast where the rich Kuroshio Current passes. You can see corals in Little Liuchiu, Green Island, Lanyu, Penghu and Kenting National Park. Many species of river fish are also making a good comeback, though sports fishermen are sadly too quick to catch (and not release) fry.

Conservation

Today, conservation projects all over Taiwan are restoring mangroves and wetlands, replanting forests and protecting the most vulnerable species. A 10-year moratorium on river fishing has succeeded in restocking streams, while a 2013 ban on the destructive practice of gill-net fishing in Little Liuchiu should protect the corals and the 200 endangered green sea turtles inhabiting the coasts.

Furthermore, hundreds of small community projects are bringing back balance to urban neighbourhoods; even in Taipei the sound of song birds and the flittering of butterfly wings is now common stuff. There are also vast areas now inaccessible to the public because of the closing of old forestry roads (a deliberate policy). In 2012 Pingtung County Government declared the section of coastline along Alangyi Old Trail to be a nature reserve, and the construction of a controversial highway was halted – a victory for the wildlife and ecosystem of the coast (there are 49 protected species, including the endangered sea turtles).

Taiwan has many relic species that survived the last ice age. One of the more intriguing is the Formosan landlocked salmon, which never leaves the mountain streams in which it was born.

THE NATIONAL BIODIVERSITY RESEARCH PROMOTION PROJECT

In 2009 a seven-year study by the Biodiversity Research Centre of Academia Sinica reported that Taiwan had 50,164 native species in eight kingdoms, 55 phyla, 126 classes, 610 orders and 2900 families. To cut to the chase, this means that Taiwan, with only 0.025% of the world's land mass, holds 2.5% of the world's species. It's a rate of endemism 100 times the world average.

The study, the first since British diplomat and naturalist Robert Swinhoe completed his own in the late 19th century, was a revelation – to put it mildly. Altogether, it was found that 70% of Taiwan's mammals, 17% of its birds, 26% of its plants and 60% of its insects are endemic species.

What accounts for such a high rate of bio-density? It's Taiwan's long isolation from the mainland, as well as a geographic environment that harbours a variety of ecosystems in a small area. About the only ecosystem that Taiwan is missing, scholars have noted, is a desert.

However, it's not all good news. The oceans and rivers are still treated as dumping grounds by industry and overdevelopment is rampant (constrained in many cases only by the extreme terrain). At press time, the Miramar Resort Village construction project on Taitung County's Shanyuan Beach is set to go ahead even though it's been ruled invalid more than once by the Supreme Administrative Court. Campaigners worry that the case would open the door to other development projects along the eastern coastline and cause further long-term damage to the environment.

Survival Guide

Directory A–Z

Accommodation

Taiwan provides the full range of lodgings, from basic hostels to world-class resorts, though it's at the midrange level, especially at guesthouses, that you will get the best quality for money. Air-con is standard and no key deposit is required, but you'll need your passport or ID to check in. Note that quality can really vary at the same price range. Outside of popular areas in summer, on holidays and weekends there is usually no need to prebook rooms.

Accommodation is generally priced per room (or number of beds per room) and not per guest. What is called a 'single' room in other countries (one single bed) is rare; a 'single' in Taiwanese hotel lingo usually means a room with one double-sized bed, suitable for a couple. 'Double' generally means a double bed but could also mean a twin (for example, two beds per room). In general, use the term *dān rén fáng* (單人房) to mean a room for one. Use *shuāng rén fáng* (雙人房) to mean a double or twin: emphasise *yī dà chuáng* (一大床) to mean one large bed for two; *liǎng chuáng* (兩床) to mean two beds.

A suite is generally called a *tàofáng* (套房; a room with a separate living area). In the countryside many hotels and homestays have rooms called *tōngpù* (東埔); these have no beds but offer thick quilts and floor mats. Usually you must book the whole room but if it's not busy you can often have the room to yourself and just pay for a single person.

Summer, Chinese New Year and Saturday nights are high season. Winter months are also high season for hot-spring hotels. Discounts of 10% to 50% off the rack rate are the norm even in high season except for a few hotels (mostly strictly budget) that always charge the same price. Sometimes you must ask, but mostly discounts are given automatically (often they are written on the hotel's price list). For resort discounts try midweek and for business hotel discounts try the weekends.

Making Reservations

You can reserve by phone or internet (which often gives better rates) but unless you go through a booking site you will likely need to use Chinese. When reserving homestays you may be asked to wire a deposit.

Camping

Camping is generally safe and inexpensive, and hot showers (may be limited to the evenings) and toilets are standard. It is best to bring a free-standing tent, as many sites have raised wooden platforms. You can pick up a cheap tent in Taiwan for NT$1000. Along the east coast you can set up a tent on pretty much any beach, but it can get very hot if you aren't under the shade. Public campgrounds tend to have the best facilities.

Homestays & B&Bs

Mínsù (民宿; homestays) offer travellers a way to meet local people as well as fellow travellers. There has been an explosion of new homestays in the past few years, and most are well run and offer good accommodation at a fair price. In fact, many are far superior to hotels and often offer locally cooked meals. Signs for homestays are everywhere and you can usually just drop in without reservations on weekdays (when rates are often substantially discounted).

If you have a Youth Travel Card (www.youthtravel.tw), you sometimes get a discount rate at homestays.

BOOK YOUR STAY ONLINE

For more accommodation reviews by Lonely Planet authors, check out www.lonelyplanet.com/taiwan/hotels. You'll find independent reviews, as well as recommendations on the best places to stay. Best of all, you can book online.

Hostels

A basic dorm bed starts at NT$400 to NT$500, though the better places charge NT$600 to NT$800 per night. Private rooms are usually tiny and start at NT$800. You can often arrange weekly or monthly rates. Taiwanese hostels affiliated with **Hostelling International** (http://taiwan.yh.org.tw) or the **Youth Travel Card** (www.youthtravel.tw) program offer discounts for cardholders. Many affiliates are hotels, not hostels, and offer a limited number of twin rooms (two beds) for sharing.

Almost all genuine hostels are technically illegal, though there is nothing dodgy about them (bizarre regulations, such as the need to have a parking lot, prevent them from getting licences). Hostels generally have laundry, simple cooking facilities, computers, ADSL or wi-fi and a room for socialising.

Hotels

Budget hotels in the NT$600 to NT$1000 range give you threadbare accommodation with cheap furniture, private bathroom, TV and phone. No English will be spoken. Quality varies greatly from NT$1000 to NT$1600. Above NT$1400 rooms are usually good enough that you wouldn't feel embarrassed putting family up there.

In the midrange (NT$1600 to NT$4000), you're likely to find a fancy lobby, one or more restaurants on-site, ADSL, wi-fi, plasma TVs, and a laundry room with free DIY washer and dryer. Private bathrooms include shower (or bathtub with shower). Decor can range from a little dated to very slick. Unless you're looking for a luxury experience, most travellers will feel comfortable here. In the big cities usually at least one staff member speaks some English.

The big cities abound with international-standard, top-end hotels. Typical amenities include business centres, English-speaking staff, concierge services, and a spa or fitness centre.

Rental Accommodation

English-language newspapers carry rental listings, usually luxury accommodation catering to expats on expense accounts. For upscale or even good m drange apartments it's useful to hire an agent; check the newspapers. The usual agent fee is about half a month's rent. You can also look around the area in which you want to live and ask building guards or at real estate offices. For mid- to low-range accommodation by area and price in Taipei check out **Tsui Mama** (www.tmm.org.tw) and websites catering to the foreign community.

Basic studio apartments (with no kitchen) in Taipei cost around NT$5000 to NT$10,000 per month. Small three-bedroom apartments start at NT$15,000 to NT$20,000 – in good downtown neighbourhoods rent is at least double this. You'll find the best value in suburbs such as Muzha, Xindian, Neihu and Guandu. Outside of Taipei, even in the cities, rent is cheap. Decent three-bedroom apartments start at NT$8000. Negotiations are usually possible everywhere.

Temple & Church Stays

Many cyclists stay at small temples and Catholic churches, though you'll need to speak Chinese if you want to do this. A small donation is appropriate. For proper rooms for pilgrims and visitors, try Shitoushan or Foguangshan.

SLEEPING PRICE RANGES

The following price ranges refer to a double room with bathroom.

$ less than NT$1600

$$ NT$1600-4000

$$$ more than NT$4000

Children

The Taiwanese are very welcoming, and doubly so when it comes to children. If you're travelling with kids, they will probably attract a lot of positive attention. Strangers may want to touch or handle your babies. Some use a sling to help minimise contact as they perform daily business. You can also tell people your child has a cold. If you can't speak Chinese a little sign language will do.

You're not likely to find high chairs or booster seats for kids at lower-end restaurants, but you may well find them at more expensive places. Stands and outdoor markets tend to be very informal. Upper-end restaurants may have set menus for families or even kids. You can generally find Western baby formula and baby foods at supermarkets.

The Parenting forum on **Taiwanease** (www.taiwanease.com) is a very helpful resource. The **Community Services Centre** (www.communitycenter.org.tw) in Taipei has information for families relocating to Taiwan.

Lonely Planet's *Travel with Children* prepares you for the joys and pitfalls of travelling with the little ones.

Convenience Stores

Convenience stores are ubiquitous and handy for fresh daily foods, fruit and drinks (especially cheap fresh coffee). Services include bill payment (such as phone, gas, electricity), fax, copy and printing services, and ticket purchases (such as local fights, High Speed Rail, concerts). Staff are usually willing to help unless they are very busy. 7-Elevens also offer cheap shipping of goods across Taiwan to other outlets and many online purchases can be paid for and picked up at a convenience store nearest to you. Most stores have ATMs that accept international bankcards.

Customs Regulations

Up to US$10,000 in foreign currency (and NT$60,000) may be brought into the country but there is a limit on goods (clothes, furniture, dried goods) brought in from China. Drug trafficking is punishable by death.

Passengers who are 20 years and older can import the following duty free:

- 200 cigarettes, 25 cigars or 450g of tobacco
- one bottle of liquor (up to 1L)
- goods valued at up to NT$20,000 (not including personal effects)

Discount Cards

Student discounts are available for public transport, museums, parks, some movie tickets and performances at public theatres. Foreign student cards are not likely to be accepted; however, foreigners studying Chinese can get student cards from their school.

Children's discounts are available and based on height (rules vary from 90cm to 150cm) or age (usually under 12). Foreign children are usually eligible for this discount.

Seniors 65 years and older are usually given the same discounts as children. Seniors over 70 often get in free. Foreign seniors are usually eligible for this discount.

Government-issued **Youth Travel Cards** (www.youthtravel.tw) are available to visitors between 15 and 30 years old for discounts on admission tickets, accommodations, transportation, food and shopping. You can pick up a Youth Travel Card at the airport or train visitor centres.

Electricity

Taiwan has the same electrical standard as the US and Canada: 110V, 60Hz AC. Electrical sockets have two vertical slots. If you bring appliances from Europe, Australia or Southeast Asia, you'll need an adaptor or transformer.

Embassies & Consulates

Only a handful of countries and the Holy See have full diplomatic relations with Taiwan. It's likely that your country is represented not by an embassy but by a trade office or cultural institute.

Overseas, Taiwan is represented by consular, information and trade offices. Both Taiwanese legations abroad and foreign legations in Taiwan serve the same functions as embassies or consulates would elsewhere: services to their own nationals, visa processing, trade promotion and cultural programs.

For a complete list visit the **Ministry of Foreign Affairs** (www.mofa.gov.tw) site.

Gay & Lesbian Travellers

Taiwan's official stance towards gays and lesbians is among the most progressive in Asia. There is no sodomy law to penalise homosexuality; in 2002 the military lifted its ban on homosexuals and the Chinese-speaking world's best **Gay Pride Parade** (www.twpride.org) has been held in Taipei every year since 1997. Taiwanese gays and lesbians have made great strides towards openness and equality, particularly since the end of martial law. In Taiwan's family-oriented society, however, where the propagation of children is considered a duty, there is still a stigma attached to homosexuality for many.

Taipei is an open, vibrant city for gay and lesbian visitors, and has gained a reputation as *the* place for gay nightlife in Asia. Other cities in Taiwan offer far less, if any, gay nightlife.

Useful resources include www.utopia-asia.com/tipstaiw.htm and http://twpride.org.

EMBASSIES & CONSULATES

FOREIGN MISSION	CONTACT	ADDRESS (IN TAIPEI)
Australia (Australia Office)	www.australia.org.tw	The President International Tower, 27th & 28th fl, 9-11 Song Gao Rd
Canada (Canadian Trade Office in Taipei)	www.canada.org.tw	Hua-Hsin Building, 6th fl, 1 Song Zhi Rd
France (French Institute; Institut Français de Taipei)	www.fi-taipei.org	10th fl, 205 Dunhua N Rd
Germany (German Trade Office)	www.taiwan.ahk.de	19th fl, 333, Keelung Rd, Sec 1
Ireland (Institute for Trade & Investment of Ireland)	02-2552 6101	7fl, 41 Nanjing W Rd
Japan (Interchange Association)	www.koryu.or.jp	Ching Cheng St
Netherlands (Netherlands Trade & Investment Office)	www.ntio.org.tw	5th fl, 133 Minsheng E Rd, Sec 3
New Zealand (New Zealand Commerce & Industry Office)	www.nzcio.com	9th fl, 1 Songzhi Rd
South Africa (Liaison Office of South Africa)	www.southafrica.org.tw	Suite 1301, 13th fl, 205 Dunhua N Rd
South Korea (Korean Mission in Taipei)	http://taiwan.mofat.go.kr	Room 1506, 15th fl, 333 Keelung Rd, Sec 1
Thailand (Thailand Trade & Economic Office)	www.tteo.org.tw	12th fl, 168 Song Jiang Rd
UK (British Trade & Cultural Office)	02-8758 2088	26th fl, 9-11 Song Gao Rd
USA (American Institute in Taiwan)	www.ait.org.tw	7 Lane 134, Xinyi Rd, Sec 3

Health

Before You Go

In Taiwan it may be difficult to find some newer drugs, particularly the latest antidepressants, blood-pressure medications and contraceptive pills. If you take any regular medication bring double.

REQUIRED VACCINATIONS

Proof of Yellow Fever vaccination is required if entering Taiwan within six days of visiting an infected country. If you are travelling to Taiwan from Africa or South America check with a travel-medicine clinic whether you need the vaccine.

RECOMMENDED VACCINATIONS

If you plan to travel from Taiwan to a country with a typhoid problem you should get the vaccination elsewhere as Taiwan does not have typhoid vaccinations.

Check **MD Travel Health** (www.mdtravelhealth.com) and with your local travel health clinic about recommended vaccinations for travellers to Taiwan.

WEBSITES

Centers for Disease Control & Prevention (www.cdc.gov) Good general information.

Lonely Planet (www.lonelyplanet.com) A good place to visit for starters.

MD Travel Health (www.mdtravelhealth.com) Provides complete travel-health recommendations for every country including Taiwan. Revised daily.

World Health Organization (www.who.int/ith) Publishes a superb book called *International Travel and Health*, revised annually and available free online. There is no information on Taiwan, however.

In Taiwan

AVAILABILITY & COST OF HEALTH CARE

Taiwan is a developed country with excellent universal medical coverage. Most medical care is cheaper than in Western countries. Many doctors are trained in Western countries and speak at least some English.

In rural areas the quality of health care is not as high but Taiwan is small and you should be able to get to a good hospital in a few hours.

INFECTIOUS DISEASES

Dengue Fever This mosquito-borne disease causes sporadic problems in Taiwan in both cities and rural areas (mostly urban areas). Prevention is by avoiding mosquito bites – there is no vaccine. Mosquitoes that

EATING PRICE RANGES

The following food price ranges generally refer to the cost of a meal rather than a single dish (unless a single dish is what is usually ordered, such as beef noodles).

$ less than NT$180

$$ NT$180–500

$$$ more than NT$500

carry dengue bite day and night. Symptoms include high fever, severe headache and body ache (previously dengue was known as 'break-bone fever').

Hepatitis A & B All travellers to Taiwan should be vaccinated against hepatitis A and B.

Japanese B Encephalitis Potentially fatal viral disease transmitted by mosquitoes, but rare in travellers. Transmission season runs June to October. Vaccination is recommended for travellers spending more than one month outside of cities.

Rabies Taiwan had its first rabies outbreak in 60 years in 2013. At the time of writing it was limited to a small number of ferret-badgers and house shrews.

ENVIRONMENTAL HAZARDS

Air pollution Air pollution, particularly vehicle pollution, is a problem in all urban areas, including many smaller cities. Avoid downtown during busy hours. Air is much better in the early morning, at night and after rain. Much of the west coast, however, is also affected by Taiwan's many coal-fired plants.

Insect bites & stings Insects are not a major issue in Taiwan, though there are some insect-borne diseases present such as scrub typhus and dengue fever.

Ticks Ticks can be contracted from walking in rural areas, and are commonly found behind the ears, on the belly and in armpits. If you have had a tick bite and experience symptoms such as a rash at the site of the bite or elsewhere, or fever or muscle aches, see a doctor.

WOMEN'S HEALTH

In most developed areas of Taiwan, supplies of sanitary products are readily available.

Birth-control options may be limited so bring supplies of your own contraception.

Taiwan's heat and humidity can contribute to thrush.

TRADITIONAL & FOLK MEDICINE

Traditional Chinese Medicine (TCM) remains very popular in Taiwan. TCM views the human body as an energy system in which the basic substances of *chi (qì;* vital energy), *jing* (essence), blood (the body's nourishing fluids) and body fluids (other organic fluids) function. The concept of Yin and Yang is fundamental to the system. Disharmony between Yin and Yang or within the basic substances may be a result of internal causes (emotions), external causes (climatic conditions) or miscellaneous causes (work, exercise, sex etc). Treatment modalities include acupuncture, massage, herbs, dietary modification and *qijong* (the skill of attracting positive energy) and aim to bring these elements back into balance. These therapies are particularly useful for treating chronic diseases and are gaining interest and respect in the Western medical system. Conditions that can be particularly suitable for traditional methods include chronic fatigue, arthritis, irritable bowel syndrome and some chronic skin conditions.

Be aware that 'natural' doesn't always mean 'safe', and there can be drug interactions between herbal medicines and Western medicines. If you are using both systems, inform both practitioners what the other has prescribed.

Insurance

A travel-insurance policy to cover theft, loss and medical problems is a good idea. There are a wide variety of policies available, so check the small print.

Some policies specifically exclude 'dangerous activities', which can include scuba diving, motorcycling and even trekking. A locally acquired motorcycle licence is not valid under some policies. Some policies pay doctors or hospitals directly rather than you having to pay on the spot and claim later. If you have to claim later, make sure you keep all documentation. You may be asked to call (reverse charges) a centre in your home country where an immediate assessment of your problem is made. Check whether the policy covers ambulances or an emergency flight home.

Travel insurance is available at www.lonelyplanet.com/travel_services. Buy, extend and claim online anytime, even on the road.

Internet Access

Taiwan is internet-savvy with the majority owning personal computers, laptops and smart phones. In urban areas wi-fi is widely accessible in cafes, restaurants, libraries, on Mass Rapid Transit (MRT), at visitor information centres and many museums, either for free or with a pay-for-time card (*wúxiàn wǎng kǎ*). **Wifly** (www.wifly.com.tw) offers 10,000 hot spots in Taiwan. One-day/one-month cards cost NT$100/500. Purchase cards online or at 7-Elevens, which are also Wifly hot spots.

Many, if not most, hotels, even budget ones, as well as homestays offer free wi-fi or broadband. Computers with internet access can be found at libraries, visitor information centres and internet cafes. The latter are not as common as they used to be, though most towns and cities do have them. Ask for a *wǎngbā* (網吧).

This book denotes internet access, whether broadband cable or a business centre, with the icon @. Wi-fi access is denoted with the icon ᯤ.

Travellers in Taipei can register for the **Taipei Free** (www.tpe-free.taipei.gov.tw/tpe) wi-fi program, which offers thousands of hot spots across the city. Registration also allows use of i-Taiwan (for wi-fi in government offices, museums and so on).

Language Courses

Chinese-language programs are widely available at universities and private cram schools. Most offer classes for two to four hours a day, five days a week, as well as private classes for as many hours as you like. Costs vary from NT$400 to NT$500 for a private one-hour class and up to US$1000 a month at a top university program.

At the time of writing, to obtain a study visa you had to enrol at a school approved by the **Ministry of Education** (http://english.moe.gov.tw/mp.asp?mp=1) for at least 15 hours a week. Some of the better-known programs include **ICLP** (http://iclp.ntu.edu.tw) at National Taiwan University and the **Mandarin Training Program** (www.mtc.ntnu.edu.tw/mtcweb) at National Taiwan Normal University. Both universities are in Taipei but there are programs around the country.

A decent private school, if you are looking for a less rigorous program, is **Taipei Language Institute** (www.tli.com.tw).

You normally apply for a program in your own country. Once accepted, apply for a multi-entry extendable visitor visa at a local trade office or ROC mission. You must start classes within the first month upon arrival and after four months of good standing apply for a resident visa at the **Bureau of Consular Affairs** (www.boca.gov.tw). After receiving your visa apply for an ARC (Alien Resident Card) at the **National Immigration Agency** (www.immigration.gov.tw), formerly the Foreign Affairs Police. Remember to renew your ARC each year. Note that your school may not do much to help you through the process.

Having a resident visa without an ARC is the same as not having one at all. You need an ARC to stay legally in Taiwan on your resident visa.

Legal Matters

Taiwan's legal system is under heavy criticism these days because of erratic judgements, political bias in arrests and sentencing, and willingness to try frivolous cases. In general, Taiwanese try to settle disputes out of court and both police and prosecutors encourage this even for violent crimes such as assault. In general, it is best to avoid trouble which in many cases means backing down even when you are in the right.

Smuggling drugs can carry the death penalty: possession can also get you arrested. If caught working illegally, you'll get a fine, a visa suspension and an order to leave the country. You may not ever be allowed back.

Knowingly transmitting HIV to another person is punishable by up to seven years in prison. This law also allows for mandatory testing of members of high-risk groups, namely sexual partners of HIV carriers and intravenous drug users, as well as foreigners who come to work certain jobs and require an ARC. Adultery is also a crime.

Libel and slander are criminal offenses in Taiwan and in recent years it has become very common for people to be prosecuted for insults, which can include telling someone to f-off, or even simply giving them the middle finger. While you won't go to jail over this, you may be required to publically apologise and pay compensation. Control your temper in public.

If you're detained or arrested, contact your country's legation in Taiwan or the **Legal Aid Foundation** (www.laf.org.tw/en/index.php). You have the right to remain silent and to request an attorney (your legation can provide a list of English-speaking attorneys), although authorities are under no obligation to provide an attorney. You also have the right to refuse to sign any document. In most cases, a suspect can't be detained for more than 24 hours without a warrant from a judge – notable exceptions are those with visa violations.

Legal ages:

- Voting: 20
- Driving: 18
- Military conscription: 18, but most do it after their university studies
- Consumption of alcohol: 18
- Consensual sex (heterosexual or homosexual): 16. Travellers should note that they can be prosecuted under the law of their home country regarding age of consent, even when abroad.

Maps

In most places in Taiwan your Lonely Planet guidebook map will be sufficient. Full city and county maps are available at tourist offices and are useful as they often

PRACTICALITIES

English Newspapers

Taipei Times (www.taipeitimes.com)

China Post (www.chinapost.com.tw)

Taiwan Today (http://taiwantoday.tw)

Magazines

Taiwan Panorama (formerly Sinorama; www.sinorama.com.tw) An intelligent look at Taiwanese language and culture, sports, finance, history, travel and more.

Commonwealth Magazine (http://english.cw.com.tw) Highly informative on business, cross-Strait and social issues.

Travel in Taiwan (www.tit.com.tw) An excellent resource for all things cultural and touristy, with calendars of events and colourful coverage.

Radio & TV

- International Community Radio Taipei (ICRT) broadcasts nationwide in English 24 hours a day at 100MHz (FM) with a mix of music, news and information.
- Taiwan has five major free broadcast networks: CTS, CTV and TTV, FTV and PTS with shows in Chinese, including dubbed foreign shows.
- Cable TV is available cheaply throughout Taiwan, with some English movie channels (HBO, AXN), news channels (CNN, CNBC), Japanese stations such as NHK and the like. Buddhist groups such as Tzuchi also have their own channels, as do the Hakka and Taiwan's aboriginals.

Weights & Measures

Taiwan uses the metric system alongside ancient Chinese weights and measures. For example, apartment floor space is measured by *píng* (approximately 4 sq metres), fruit and vegetables are likely to be sold by the catty (*jīn*, 600g), and teas and herbal medicines are sold by the tael (*liǎng*, 37.5g).

Smoking

Smoking is common but not allowed in public facilities, public transport, restaurants or hotels. This prohibition is almost always followed.

list additional places. For driving, the four-part collection of bilingual maps called *Taiwan Tourist Map* is usually sufficient. Pick it up at any visitor information centre. Otherwise, the best road map (in Chinese) is the two-volume *Formosa Complete Road Atlas* by Sunriver Press. A compass can be useful if you're going to be travelling on country roads.

Money

Taiwan's currency is the New Taiwanese Dollar (NT$). Bills come in denominations of NT$100, NT$200, NT$500, NT$1000 and NT$2000. Coins come in units of NT$1, NT$5, NT$10, NT$20 (rare) and NT$50. Taiwan uses the local currency exclusively.

ATMs

ATMs are widely available at banks and convenience stores. 7-Elevens are on the Plus or Cirrus network and have English-language options. ATMs at banks are also on the Plus and Cirrus networks, and are sometimes on Accel, Interlink and Star networks.

Cash

If you have foreign cash to exchange, the most widely accepted currency is US dollars.

Credit Cards

Credit cards are widely accepted – cheap budget hotels, however, won't take them. If rooms cost more than NT$1000 a night, the hotel usually accepts credit cards but most homestays do not accept them. Small stalls or night-market food joints never take credit cards. Most midrange to top-end restaurants do, but always check before you decide to eat.

Moneychangers

Private moneychangers do not proliferate in Taiwan. Hotels will change money for guests, but banks are the most common option.

Tipping

Tipping is not customary in restaurants or taxis (but is still appreciated). It is usual to tip the porter at better hotels (NT$100 is considered courteous). Many foreigners tip at better bars and clubs so staff may expect this. Note that the 10% service charge added to bills at many restaurants is not a tip to be shared with the staff.

Travellers Cheques

As with cash, it is best if your travellers cheques are in US dollars. Not widely accepted.

Opening Hours

Standard hours are as follows.

Banks 9am–3.30pm Mon-Fri

Convenience stores 24hr

Department stores 11am–9.30pm

Government offices 8.30am–5.30pm

Museums 9am–5pm Tue–Sun

Night markets 6pm–midnight

Offices 9am–5pm Mon–Fri

Post offices 8am–5pm Mon–Fri; larger offices may open till 9pm and have limited hours on weekends.

Restaurants 11.30am–2pm and 5–9pm

Shops 10am–9pm

Supermarkets to at least 8pm, sometimes 24hr

Photography

➡ In general, people in Taiwan are fine with you photographing them.

➡ On Kinmen and Matsu Islands be careful photographing airports or military sites.

➡ On Lanyu ask permission before photographing anything.

➡ For photography tips check out Lonely Planet's *Travel Photography*.

Public Holidays

Founding Day/New Year's Day 1 January

Chinese Lunar New Year January or February, usually four to nine days

Peace Memorial Day 2-28 Day; 28 February

Tomb Sweeping Day 5 April

Labour Day 1 May

Typhoon holidays possible from May to October

Dragon Boat Festival 5th day of the 5th lunar month; usually in June

Moon Festival 5th day of the 8th lunar month; usually September

National Day 10 October

Safe Travel

Taiwan is affected by frequent natural disasters, such as earthquakes, typhoons, floods and landslides. Avoid going out during typhoons and avoid mountainous areas after earthquakes, typhoons or heavy rains.

Urban streets are very safe, for both men and women, and while pickpocketing occasionally happens, muggings or violent assaults are almost unheard of. If you forget a bag somewhere, chances are very good it will still be there when you go back.

Bars and clubs are generally safe but especially outside Taipei it's best to get a recommendation. In some areas we specifically avoid listing clubs and bars for this reason.

If you feel trouble is brewing get away before it escalates. And avoid making people lose face. When people become violent in Taiwan, they go to extremes and it is common to call a dozen friends to help in a fight even against a single opponent.

Telephone

The country code for Taiwan is ☎886. Taiwan's telephone carrier for domestic and international calls is **Chunghwa Telecom** (www.cht.com.tw). For information on rates and services, visit the website.

Area Codes

Do not dial the area code when calling within an area code. Area codes are listed under town headings throughout this book.

The number of digits in telephone numbers varies with the locality: from eight in Taipei to five in the remote Matsu Islands.

Domestic Calls

Local calls (all Taiwan is local as of 2012 though you still use area codes between counties) cost NT$1.6 every three minutes. Calls to mobile phones (beginning with 09XX) cost NT$0.06 to NT$0.09 per second depending on the provider and the time of day. General phone rates are discounted from 10pm to 8am Monday

GOVERNMENT TRAVEL ADVICE

The following government websites offer travel advisories and information on current hot spots:

Australian Department of Foreign Affairs (www.smarttraveller.gov.au)

British Foreign Office (www.gov.uk/foreign-travel-advice)

Canadian Department of Foreign Affairs (www.dfait-maeci.gc.ca)

US State Department (http://travel.state.gov)

TAP WATER

- Drinkable in Taipei without treatment but still best to filter.
- Filtered hot and cold water from dispensers is available in every hotel, guesthouse, visitor information centre and 7-Eleven so it's handy to bring your own bottle. Otherwise purchase bottled.
- Ice is usually fine at restaurants.
- Shaved ice (with fruit) is usually fine but take a look at the shop.

to Friday, from noon on Saturday and all day Sunday.

Fax

Most hotels offer expensive fax services, so almost everyone uses 7-Eleven stores, which transmit local black-and-white faxes for NT$15 per page and international faxes for NT$85 per page.

Mobile Phones

In Taiwan, mobile phones are called *dàgēdà, shǒujī* or just 'cell phone'. Numbers start with the prefix 09XX, followed by six digits. When calling within an area code, you have to use the area code. A Taipei call would look like this: 02-XXXX XXXX. Most foreign mobile phones can use local sim cards with prepaid plans, which you can purchase at airport arrival terminals (the average plan per day is NT$100) and top up at telecom outlets or 7-Elevens. You can also rent mobile phones (per day NT$100, deposit NT$6000) at the airport. If you have an ARC you can apply for a mobile phone in Taiwan. The main carriers are Chunghwa Telecom and **FarEastone** (www.fareastone.com.tw).

Public Phones & Phonecards

You can buy domestic IC cards (NT$200) at convenience stores to use on public phones.

For overseas calls, internet phone services such as **Skype** (www.skype.com) are best. To dial out directly from a landline or mobile, dial 009 or 002 before the country code and number. Chunghwa Telecom's E-call cards (which can be used with mobile phones, and landlines) are sold in denominations of NT$200, NT$300 and NT$520 and give users up to a 30% discount on standard rates. Note that the quality of connection can be somewhat low. Cards can be purchased at Chunghwa Telecom locations and 7-Elevens. To use, dial the access number on the back of the card and then follow the instructions (an English option is available).

Time

Taiwan is eight hours ahead of GMT on the same time zone as Beijing, Hong Kong, Singapore and Perth. When it is noon in Taiwan, it is 2pm in Sydney, 1pm in Japan, 4am in London, 11pm the previous day in New York and 8pm the previous day in Los Angeles. Taiwan does not observe daylight-saving time. A 24-hour clock is used for train schedules.

Toilets

Free public toilets are widely available in parks, transport stations, public offices, museums, temples and rest areas. They are usually squat toilets, except for stalls for people with disabilities, and are usually clean but probably won't have toilet paper. Restaurants and cafes usually have their own bathroom facilities, and Western-style toilets are standard in apartments and hotels. It is handy to know the characters for men (男, *nán*) and women (女, *nǚ*). Many places ask you not to flush toilet paper but to put it in the wastebasket beside the toilet. Most cleaners are women and can enter the men's areas at any time.

Tourist Information

Visitor information centres are present in most city train stations, High Speed Rail (HSR) stations, popular scenic areas and airports. English- and Japanese-language brochures, maps, and train and bus schedules will usually be available.

Visitor centres in Taipei and other big cities usually have English- and, sometimes, Japanese-speaking staff. Often staff are poorly trained, however, so when in doubt, trust your guidebook and the word of other travellers and hostel/guesthouse owners.

Welcome to Taiwan (www.taiwan.net.tw) is the official site of the Taiwan Tourism Bureau, and the **Tourism hotline** (☎0800-011 765) is a 24-hour service in English, Japanese and Chinese which is generally very useful.

Much of Taiwan is organised under National Scenic Areas. Their visitor centres can be hit or miss depending on the staff but their websites are informative:

Alishan National Scenic Area (www.ali-nsa.net)

East Coast National Scenic Area (www.eastcoast-nsa.gov.tw)

East Rift Valley National Scenic Area (www.erv-nsa.gov.tw)

Maolin National Scenic Area (www.maolin-nsa.gov.tw)

Matsu National Scenic Area (www.matsu-nsa.gov.tw/)

North Coast & Guanyinshan National Scenic Area (www.northguan-nsa.gov.tw)

Northeast & Yilan Coast National Scenic Area (www.necoast-nsa.gov.tw)

Penghu National Scenic Area (www.penghu-nsa.gov.tw)

Sun Moon Lake National Scenic Area (www.sunmoonlake.gov.tw)

Tri-Mountain National Scenic Area (www.trimt-nsa.gov.tw)

These websites, while not aimed at tourists, are helpful:

Forumosa.com (www.forumosa.com)

Taiwanease (www.taiwanease.com)

Information for Foreigners (http://iff.immigration.gov.tw)

TEALIT (www.tealit.com)

Travellers with Disabilities

While seats and parking for people with disabilities are respected, in general Taiwan is not a very disabled-friendly environment. Street footpaths are uneven, kerbs are steep, and public transport, other than the MRT and HSR, is not equipped with wheelchair access. Taipei and other cities are slowly modernising facilities. **Eden Social Welfare Foundation** (http://engweb.eden.org.tw) provides advice and assistance for travellers with disabilities.

Visas

At the time of writing, citizens of many countries could enter Taiwan without a visa. The period granted cannot be extended under any circumstances. All travellers need a passport that is valid for six months and an onward ticket with confirmed seat reservation. Countries permitted 90-day stays are Austria, Belgium, Bulgaria, Canada, Croatia, Cyprus, Czech Republic, Denmark, Estonia, Finland, France, Germany, Greece, Hungary, Iceland, Ireland, Israel, Italy, Japan, Republic of Korea, Latvia, Liechtenstein, Lithuania, Luxembourg, Malta, Monaco, the Netherlands, New Zealand, Norway, Poland, Portugal, Romania, Slovakia, Slovenia, Spain, Sweden, Switzerland, the UK and the US.

Thirty-day stays apply to citizens of Australia, Malaysia and Singapore.

Those coming to Taiwan to study, work or visit relatives for an extended period of time should apply at an overseas mission of the ROC for a visitor visa, which is good for 60 to 90 days. Visas can be extended up to six months under certain circumstances on the **National Immigration Agency** (www.immigration.gov.tv) website. If you're planning to stay longer than six months, the law requires you to have an ARC. See the **Bureau of Consular Affairs** (www.boca.gov.tw) website for more information.

Volunteering

Animal groups need volunteers to work in shelters, walk dogs, participate in fundraisers and also foster dogs and cats (something you can do even if you are in Taiwan for a short time). Contact **Taiwan Animal SOS** (www.facebook.com/taiwananimalsos) and **Taiwan SPCA** (台灣防止虐待動物協會; www.spca.org.tw).

You can volunteer at an organic farm through **WWOOF** (www.wwooftaiwan.com).

Women Travellers

Taiwan (and especially Taipei) is a safe place to travel, but women should take normal precautions at night and in uncrowded areas. Apart from the usual attention given to foreign travellers, women travellers should not expect any special attention. If you have to take a taxi home alone at night, call for one as this will be recorded. For additional safety let the driver see a friend write down the taxi licence-plate number. If the driver can also see that you have a mobile phone, trouble is less likely.

Women travelling to Taiwan for business should dress modestly and conservatively (as should men). Drinking and smoking are a part of Taiwanese business culture, but Taiwanese women tend to smoke and drink less than Taiwanese men (though this is changing among the younger generation).

Work

To work legally in Taiwan you generally need to enter on a visitor visa, have your company apply for a work permit, apply for a resident visa after you receive your work permit, and apply for an ARC after receiving your resident visa. You can apply for a visitor visa at any overseas Taiwan trade office or foreign mission. Your company applies for your work permit from the **Council of Labour Affairs** (www.cla.gov.tw). You can apply for a resident visa through the **Bureau of Consular Affairs** (BOCA; www.boca.gov.tw). An ARC can be applied for at any office of the **National Immigration Agency** (www.immigration.gov.tw). For short-term employment rules see the BOCA website or visit your local Taiwan trade office or overseas mission.

Job listings can be found at **104 Job Bank** (www.104.com.tw) and **TEALIT** (www.tealit.com).

Teaching English is not what it once was and there are fewer and fewer openings. Salaries have not risen in 15 years. Jobs are listed on TEALIT, **Taiwanease** (www.taiwanease.com), **Dave's ESL Cafe** (www.eslcafe.com) and plenty of other websites. If you have a teaching degree you can apply to work in a government-run school (http://fetit.eng.ntnu.edu.tw).

Transport

GETTING THERE & AWAY

Entering the Country

Immigration procedures are smooth and hassle free. Most guards speak some English.

Passport

There aren't any countries whose stamps in your passport will cause a problem at immigration.

Air

Airports & Airlines

INTERNATIONAL AIRPORTS

Taiwan Taoyuan International Airport (www.taoyuan-airport.com) The main international airport is in Dayuan, 40km (40 minutes) west of central Taipei. Formerly known as Chiang Kai-shek International Airport.

Taichung Airport (www.tca.gov.tw) In Taichung, for domestic flights to the outer islands, Hualien, and to China, Hong Kong and Vietnam.

Siaogang Airport (www.kia.gov.tw) In Kaohsiung, Siaogang Airport has domestic flights to Hualien and the outer islands, as well as direct flights to China, Hong Kong and other Asian destinations.

Taipei Songshan Airport (Songshan Airport; www.tsa.gov.tw) Located in Taipei County, this airport handles domestic flights to Hualien, Taitung, and the outer islands; internationally it has direct flights to China, Japan and Korea.

NATIONAL AIRLINES

Taiwan has two major international airlines. Eva Air started operation in 1991 and has had no fatalities to date. China Airlines was somewhat infamous for its safety record in the 1990s. Incidents since the turn of the century have been few. Officials credit this to new training practices (with pilots training at US flight schools) and a new corporate culture.

China Airlines (www.china-airlines.com)

Eva Air (www.evaair.com)

TICKETS

Most people book flights through a local travel agent, online at www.eztravel.com.tw, or through worldwide sites such as www.expedia.com. If flying to the outer islands, book directly with the airline by phone, via their website, or at 7-Eleven ibon kiosks.

For flights within Asia the best options are to book directly with low-cost carriers such as **AirAsia** (www.airasia.com), **Scoot** (www.flyscoot.com) and **Peach** (www.flypeach.com).

For general good deals check **ezTravel** (www.eztravel.com.tw), **Expedia** (www.expedia.com) and **Govolo** (www.govolo.com).

CLIMATE CHANGE & TRAVEL

Every form of transport that relies on carbon-based fuel generates CO_2, the main cause of human-induced climate change. Modern travel is dependent on aeroplanes, which might use less fuel per kilometre per person than most cars but travel much greater distances. The altitude at which aircraft emit gases (including CO_2) and particles also contributes to their climate change impact. Many websites offer 'carbon calculators' that allow people to estimate the carbon emissions generated by their journey and, for those who wish to do so, to offset the impact of the greenhouse gases emitted with contributions to portfolios of climate-friendly initiatives throughout the world. Lonely Planet offsets the carbon footprint of all staff and author travel.

Sea

There are daily ferries from/to Xiamen (Fujian province, China) and Kinmen Island, as well as Matsu Island to Fuzhou (Fujian province, China). There are also weekly fast ferries with **Cosco Taiwan** (www.coscotw.com.tw) from Taichung, Keelung and Kaohsiung to Xiamen, Fujian province, China. Service between Taipei Habour to China may also commence in 2014. If travelling from Taiwan to China you must have your Chinese visa prepared.

GETTING AROUND

Taiwan has an excellent transport system but it is important to note that travel directly *across* the island is very limited.

Air

Airlines in Taiwan

Because of the High Speed Rail (HSR) there are very few domestic flights except to the outer islands and east coast cities.

Daily Air Corporation (☎07-801 4711; www.dailyair.com.tw) Mostly flies to outer islands from Kaohsiung (to Penghu) or Taitung (to Green Island and Lanyu).

Mandarin Airlines (☎02-2717 1230; www.mandarin-airlines.com) Flies to Hualien, Kaohsiung, Kinmen, Penghu, Taichung, Taipei and Taitung.

TransAsia Airways (☎02-2972 4599; www.tna.com.tw) Flies to Taipei, Taichung, Hualien, Penghu, Kaohsiung and Kinmen.

Uni Air (☎07-801 0189; www.uniair.com.tw) Flies to Chiayi, Kaohsiung, Kinmen, Penghu, Matsu, Taichung, Tainan, Taipei and Taitung.

Bicycle

Bicycle rentals are common in tourist areas. Bikes can be shipped by regular train one day in advance, and can be carried with you in a bag on the high-speed trains and all slow local trains. You'll have no problems bringing bicycles into the country. See the Taiwan Outdoors chapter for more information.

Boat

There are regular predictable ferry routes to Penghu, Lanyu and Green Island (and between Lanyu and Green Island as well) in summer, and to Little Liuchiu Island year-round. Sailings to Green Island, Lanyu and Matsu are subject to weather conditions, however. Expect cancellations in bad weather and winter schedules to change frequently.

In the summer of 2013, ferry service began from Suao to Hualien, but it was uncertain if it would continue.

Bus

Buses are generally safe, reliable and cheap, and comfortable for a Western-sized frame. Some companies offer very large, cosy airplane-style reclining seats. Reservations are advisable on weekends and holidays.

Intercity Buses

There's an extensive network from Taipei to Kenting National Park and across the north as far as Yilan. Service from the west coast to the east coast is limited to a few buses a day from Taichung across to Hualien and Kaohsiung to Taitung. Service is also limited within the east area (from Hualien to Taitung).

On the west coast there are very frequent departures (some 24-hour operations), with midweek and late-evening discounts. Other than Kamalan Bus, all companies serve the same west-coast routes. The main transit points are Taipei, Taichung, Tainan and Kaohsiung.

INTERCITY BUS COMPANIES

Aloha Bus (☎0800-043 168; www.aloha168.com.tw)

Kamalan Bus (☎03-956 6198; www.kamalan.com.tw) To Yilan and Lodong from Taipei.

Kuo Kuang Bus Company (國光客運, Guóguāng kèyùn; ☎0800-010 138; www.kingbus.com.tw)

UBus (Map p209; ☎0800-241 560; www.ubus.com.tw)

Rural Buses

The network is wide, but there are few daily departures except to major tourist destinations (such as Sun Moon Lake). In most cases you are better off taking the Tourism Shuttle Buses.

Tourism Shuttle Buses

An excellent system of small shuttle buses with well-planned routes that connect major and minor tourist sites and destinations. The buses usually leave hourly on weekdays and half-hourly on weekends. Use your EasyCard for discounted rates. See www.taiwantrip.com.tw for information on timetables, fares and routes in English.

Car & Scooter

Your own vehicle is handy on the east coast and mountain areas, and throughout this guide we've noted where this applies. In general, your motorised renting options will be a car or a scooter.

Driving in Taiwan

By the standards of many countries, driving in Taiwan can be chaotic and dangerous. Accidents are common and almost always the result of carelessness compounded by poor judgement and a 'me first' mentality. Always

BUS TRIPS FROM TAIPEI

The following sample trips are from Taipei with Kuo Kuang Motor Transport.

DESTINATION	FARE (NT$)	DURATION (HR)
Kaohsiung	530	5
Sun Moon Lake	460	3½
Taichung	260	4½
Tainan	360	4½

be alert for approaching cars driving in your lane (especially when going around blind corners).

You're not advised to drive in cities or medium-sized towns until familiar with conditions. On freeways and expressways, on the east coast, and in rural and mountainous areas, it's usually relatively safe to drive, especially midweek. Highway 11 on the east coast can be dangerous on weekends.

FUEL & SPARE PARTS

Petrol stations and garages are widely available for parts and repairs for scooters and cars. Check out www.forumosa.com for a thread on reliable and trustworthy mechanics.

ROAD CONDITIONS

Roads are generally in good shape, though washouts are common in mountain areas, and roads are often closed. Be cautious when driving in such areas during or after heavy rains.

Freeways and expressways are in excellent shape. There are tolls (per toll NT$40) on freeways which you can pay with prebought tickets or cash if your vehicle is not set up for electronic payment. If paying with cash use the cash payment toll booths. Using other booths may result in a fine.

Most road signage is bilingual.

ROAD RULES

- Taiwanese drive on the right-hand side of the road.
- Right turns on red lights are illegal.
- Mobile phone usage is prohibited (even texting at red lights).
- Drivers and all passengers must wear seatbelts, and children under the age of four (and 18kg) must be secured in safety seats (though rarely done and rarely enforced).
- In general, only speeding, drunk driving, and turning-on-red-light violations are enforced.
- See the **Information for Foreigners** (http://iff.immigration.gov.tw) website for more.

Driving Licence

INTERNATIONAL DRIVER'S PERMIT (IDP)

This is valid in Taiwan for up to 30 days. With an ARC (Alien Resident Certificate) you can apply to have your permit validated at a local Motor Vehicles Office. This simple procedure validates the IDP for up to one year.

LOCAL DRIVER'S LICENCE

Driver's licences are issued by county, and if you have an ARC you can apply. Tests include a written and driving section – both parts are challenging for their sheer absurdity (such as the infamous backwards 'S' test and questions that refer to national pride). For an example of a test, see the **Taipei Motor Vehicle Office** (http://tmvso.thb.gov.tw/) website.

RECIPROCAL LICENCE AGREEMENTS

If your country has a reciprocal agreement with Taiwan, you may be able to obtain a Taiwanese licence just by showing your home licence and passport.

Check the websites of the Taipei Motor Vehicle Office or Information for Foreigners.

Vehicle Hire

CAR HIRE

Day rates start at NT$2400, with multiday and long-term discounts available.

All airports, and most High Speed Rail stations, have car-rental agencies (or free delivery).

Car Plus (☎0800-222 568; www.car-plus.com.tw) Good reputation with island-wide offices.

Easy Rent (☎0800-024 550; www.easyrent.com.tw) Island-wide locations including downtown Taipei, major airports and High Speed Rail stations. Can usually handle email enquiries in English.

INSURANCE

Third-party liability insurance and comprehensive insurance, with a NT$10,000 deduction for damages is included in rental costs. In the case of theft or loss, renters are charged 10% of the value of the car.

SCOOTER HIRE

On average, hire costs NT$300 to NT$600 per day. Some places will allow you to rent with an International Driver's Permit, while others require a local scooter licence.

The following areas only require an International Driver's Permit (though this could change): Hualien, Ruisui, Kenting, Chiayi, Sun Moon Lake, Tainan, Jiaoxi, Nanzhuang and Kaohsiung, and the offshore islands (best on these latter places to ask your homestay or hotel to arrange a scooter).

Hitching

Hitching is never entirely safe in any country in the world, and we don't recommend it.

Travellers who do decide to hitch should understand that they are taking a small but potentially serious risk. If you do choose to hitch you will be safer if you travel in pairs and let someone know where you are planning to go.

At times, such as getting to or from a mountain trail-head, hitching may be your only option if you don't have a vehicle. Taiwanese are usually more than happy to give you a lift. Money is almost never asked for.

Local Transport

Bus

Outside of Taipei and Kaohsiung, buses are the only public transport option in the big cities. Most city buses have signs in English at the front and many have LED displays inside announcing the next stop.

You can usually find bus-schedule information at the visitor information centre in town (often located inside the train station). In smaller towns and cities it's easier just to walk than to bother with sporadic bus services.

FARES

Fares vary by city. For example, a single zone fare in Taipei is NT$15, while in Kaohsiung it's NT$12. The cost of travelling in two zones is double the price of a one-zone fare.

Sometimes you pay when you get on and sometimes when you get off. If you cross a zone, you pay when you get on and again when you get off. As a general rule, follow the passengers ahead of you or look for the characters 上 or 下 on the screen to the left of the driver. The character 上 (up) means pay when you get on; 下 (down) means pay when you get off. If you make a mistake the driver will let you know.

Mass Rapid Transit

Taipei's and Kaohsiung's Mass Rapid Transit (MRT) metro systems are clean, safe, convenient and reliable. All signs and ticket machines are in English. English signs around stations indicate which exit to take to nearby sights. Posters indicate bus transfer routes.

Check out the stations' websites, which both feature excellent maps of areas around each station.

Kaohsiung MRT (www.krtco.com.tw; fares NT$20-60; ⏲6am-midnight) Two lines, 37 stations, 42.7km of track. Connects with the international and domestic airports. On average trains leave every four to eight minutes.

Taipei MRT (www.trtc.com.tw; fares NT$20-65; ⏲6am-midnight) Ten lines, 102 stations and 112.8km of track. New lines in the works. Connects with Taipei (Songshan) Airport and hopefully will connect with Taoyuan International Airport by 2015. On average trains leave every three to eight minutes.

ROAD DISTANCES (KM)

	Chiayi	Hsinchu	Hualien	Ilan	Kaohsiung	Keelung	Kenting	Taichung	Tainan	Taipei	Taitung
Hsinchu	169										
Hualien	339	240									
Ilan	270	101	139								
Kaohsiung	103	272	337	373							
Keelung	264	95	185	46	367						
Kenting	203	372	306	473	100	467					
Taichung	86	83	253	184	189	178	289				
Tainan	63	232	373	333	40	327	140	149			
Taipei	239	70	170	31	342	25	442	153	302		
Taitung	272	407	167	306	170	352	132	348	210	337	
Taoyuan	215	46	194	55	318	49	418	129	278	24	361

Taxi

HOTLINES & LANGUAGE SERVICES

In Taipei call the taxi hotline at 0800-055 850 (wait for the message and press 2; on a mobile phone call 55850). Call 02-2799 7997 for English drivers. In Kaohsiung call 0800-087 778 or 07-315 6666. If you have safety concerns call for a cab as all calls are recorded and saved for one month.

WITHIN LARGE CITIES

Taxis are everywhere. In Taipei a ride will cost you NT$70 for the first 1.25 km and then NT$5 for every 250 meters. From 11pm to 6am fares are surcharged at an additional NT$20. Surcharges may also apply for things such as luggage and reserving a cab (as opposed to hailing one). Two days prior to the Chinese New Year's Eve until the end of the holidays, the nighttime rate applies to all rides plus an extra NT$20. For night-time travelling during Chinese New Year holidays, there is an extra NT$40 charge.

OUTSIDE LARGE CITIES

Drivers will either use meters or ask for a flat rate (the smaller the town the more likely the latter). Taxis are not that abundant, so it's a good idea to get your hotel to call first, and then to keep the driver's number for subsequent rides.

Tours

Green Island Adventures (www.greenislandadventures.com) Diving and scuba tours to islands and the mainland.

InMotion Asia (www.inmotionasia.com) Small-group cycling trips around Taiwan, with an emphasis on mountain-biking tours.

Taiwan Ecotours (www.taiwanecotours.com) Foreign-run company offering day and multiday ecotours with an emphasis on birding.

Taiwan Tour Bus (www.taiwantourbus.com.tw) Organised by the tourism bureau with easy-to-understand half- and full-day itineraries. Buses depart from train stations, airports and major hotels.

Tribe Asia (www.tribe-asia.com) For custom and packaged tours to aboriginal areas in Taiwan. The website is also an outlet for aboriginal crafts and books on aboriginal regions of Taiwan.

Whose Travel (www.whosetravel.com) Reliable foreign- and Taiwanese-run travel agency that organises tickets, tours and discount accommodation.

Train

Taiwan Railway Administration (TRA; www.railway.gov.tw) has an extensive system running up the east and west coasts. There are no services into the Central Mountains, except tourism branch lines.

In the coming years expect travel times to speed up, especially on the east coast as lines become electrified and straightened, new tunnels are added and more tilting trains are brought into operation.

Trains are comfortable, clean, safe and reliable, with few delays. Reserved seating is available, and food and snacks are served on trains. All major cities are connected by train. For fares and timetables, see the TRA website.

Classes

Chu-kuang (莒光, Jǔguāng) & **Fu-hsing** (復興, Fùxīng) Slower than Tze-chiang class, with less legroom. The fare is about 20% to 40% cheaper than Tze-chiang.

SAMPLE TRAIN FARES

FROM	TO	FARE (NT$; TZE-CHIANG/CHU-KUANG CLASS)	DURATION (HR; TZE-CHIANG/CHU-KUANG CLASS)
Hualien	Taitung	345/266	2½/3½
Kaohsiung	Taitung	362/279	2½/3½
Taipei	Hualien	440/340	2½/3½
Taipei	Kaohsiung	843/650	5-7
Taipei	Taichung	375/289	2-3

Local Train (區間車, Qūjiānchē) Cheap and stops at all stations; more like commuter trains, no reserved seating.

Taroko Express (太魯閣號, Tàilǔgé Hào) Special tilting trains that travel from Taipei to Hualien in two hours.

Tze-chiang (自強, Zìqiáng) The fastest and most comfortable class.

Reservations & Fares

For fast trains, especially on weekends or holidays, it is advisable to buy tickets up to two weeks in advance. You can book online (in English) or at 7-Eleven ibon kiosks (in Chinese only). You'll need your passport number to book online. Within two days of booking, you must collect tickets (and pay for them) at any train station.

Tourism Branch Lines

Several small branch lines are maintained for tourist purposes: Alishan (217), Jiji (p233) and Pingxi (p129).

Visitor Information Centres

Most cities have visitor centres with English-speaking staff, inside or just outside the train station. The centres are usually open from 9am to 6pm and have local bus, food and accommodation information.

High Speed Rail

Taiwan High Speed Rail (HSR, THSR; www.thsrc.com.tw) started operations in 2007. There is one 345km track between Taipei and Kaohsiung. So far eight stations have opened (Taipei, Banciao, Taoyuan, Hsinchu, Taichung, Chiayi, Tainan and Zuoying). More are expected to open in the coming years. The HSR has a perfect safety record.

Trains offer airplane-like comfort. Reserved seating is available. Food is available (though smelly foods such as stinky tofu are prohibited).

For timetables and fares, see the HSR website. In general, there are three trains per hour. All stations have visitor information centres with English-speaking staff to help with bus transfers, hotel bookings and car rentals.

Most stations are 30 to 40 minutes from downtown areas. Free (or inexpensive) and frequent shuttle buses or commuter trains connect HSR stations and downtown areas.

Classes

There are two classes: standard and business. Business fares are about 50% higher than the price of standard, and offer larger seats and 110V electrical outlets.

Reservations & Fares

On weekends or holidays, it's advisable to buy tickets in advance (up to 28 days). You can buy tickets at stations, online and at 7-Eleven stores. There are small discounts for unreserved seating areas and 10% to 35% discounts when booking eight to 28 days in advance. Tickets for seniors, children and people with disabilities are half the standard fare.

Language

The official language of Taiwan is referred to in the west as Mandarin Chinese. The Chinese call it Pǔtōnghuà (common speech) and in Taiwan it is known as Guóyǔ (the national language). Taiwanese, often called a 'dialect' of Mandarin, is in fact a separate language and the two are not mutually intelligible. Today at least half the population speaks Taiwanese at home, especially in the south and in rural areas. However, travellers to Taiwan can get by without using any Taiwanese, as virtually all young and middle-aged people speak Mandarin. Hakka, another Chinese language, is spoken in some areas, and Taiwan's aboriginal tribes have their own languages, which belong to a separate language family from Chinese.

WRITING

Chinese is often referred to as a language of pictographs. Many of the basic Chinese characters are in fact highly stylised pictures of what they represent, but most (around 90%) are compounds of a 'meaning' element and a 'sound' element. It is estimated that a well-educated, contemporary Chinese person might use between 6000 and 8000 characters. To read a Chinese newspaper you will need to know 2000 to 3000 characters, but 1200 to 1500 would be enough to get the gist.

Theoretically, all Chinese dialects share the same written system. In practice, however, Taiwan doesn't use the system of 'simplified' characters like China does. Instead, Taiwan has retained the use of traditional characters, which are also found in Hong Kong.

WANT MORE?

For in-depth language information and handy phrases, check out Lonely Planet's *Mandarin Phrasebook*. You'll find it at **shop.lonelyplanet.com**, or you can buy Lonely Planet's iPhone phrasebooks at the Apple App Store.

PINYIN & PRONUNCIATION

In 1958 the Chinese adopted a system of writing their language using the Roman alphabet, known as Pinyin. Travellers to Taiwan are unlikely to encounter much Pinyin other than for names of people, places and streets. The new signs tend to be in one of two different systems: Hanyu Pinyin, which is used in China (and has become the international standard for Mandarin), and Tongyong Pinyin, a home-grown alternative created in the late 1990s. Although the central government has declared Tongyong Pinyin to be Taiwan's official Romanisation system for both Hakka and Mandarin (but not for Taiwanese), it left local governments free to make their own choices. Taipei has selected to use Hanyu Pinyin and has applied the system consistently, but in most of the country progress towards standardisation in any form of Pinyin is slow.

In this chapter we've provided Hanyu Pinyin alonside the Mandarin script.

Vowels

a	as in 'father'
ai	as in 'aisle'
ao	as the 'ow' in 'cow'
e	as in 'her', with no 'r' sound
ei	as in 'weigh'
i	as the 'ee' in 'meet' (or like a light 'r' as in 'Grrr!' after c, ch, r, s, sh, z or zh)
ian	as the word 'yen'
ie	as the English word 'yeah'
o	as in 'or', with no 'r' sound
ou	as the 'oa' in 'boat'
u	as in 'flute'
ui	as the word 'way'
uo	like a 'w' followed by 'o'
yu/ü	like 'ee' with lips pursed

Consonants

c	as the 'ts' in 'bits'
ch	as in 'chop', but with the tongue curled up and back
h	as in 'hay', but articulated from farther back in the throat
q	as the 'ch' in 'cheese'
r	as the 's' in 'pleasure'
sh	as in 'ship', but with the tongue curled up and back
x	as in 'ship'
z	as the 'dz' in 'suds'
zh	as the 'j' in 'judge' but with the tongue curled up and back

The only consonants that occur at the end of a syllable are n, ng and r.

In Pinyin, apostrophes are occasionally used to separate syllables in order to prevent ambiguity, eg the word píng'ān can be written with an apostrophe after the 'g' to prevent it being pronounced as pín'gān.

Tones

Chinese is a language with a large number of words with the same pronunciation but a different meaning. What distinguishes these words is their 'tonal' quality – the raising and the lowering of pitch on certain syllables. Mandarin employs four tones – high, rising, falling-rising and falling, plus a fifth 'neutral' tone that you can all but ignore. Tones are important for distinguishing meaning of words – eg the word ma can have four different meanings according to tone, as shown below.

Tones are indicated in Pinyin by the following accent marks on vowels:

high tone	mā (mother)
rising tone	má (hemp, numb)
falling-rising tone	mǎ (horse)
falling tone	mà (scold, swear)

BASICS

When asking a question it is polite to start with qǐng wèn – literally, 'may I ask?'.

Hello.	您好.	Nín hǎo.
Goodbye.	再見.	Zàijiàn.
Yes.	是.	Shì.
No.	不是.	Bùshì.
Please.	請.	Qǐng.
Thank you.	謝謝.	Xièxie.
You're welcome.	不客氣.	Bùkèqì.
Excuse me, ...	請問, ...	Qǐng wèn, ...

What's your name?
請問您貴姓? Qǐngwèn nín guìxìng?

My name is ...
我姓 ... Wǒ xìng ...

Do you speak English?
你會講英文嗎? Nǐ huì jiǎng yīngwén ma?

I don't understand.
我聽不懂. Wǒ tīngbùdǒng.

ACCOMMODATION

I'm looking for a ...	我要找 ...	Wǒ yào zhǎo ...
campsite	露營區	lùyíngqū
guesthouse	賓館	bīnguǎn
hotel	旅館	lǚguǎn
youth hostel	旅社	lǚshè

Do you have a room available?
你們有房間嗎? Nǐmen yǒu fángjiān ma?

Where is the bathroom?
浴室在哪裡? Yùshì zài nǎlǐ?

I'd like (a) ...	我想要 ...	Wǒ xiǎng yào ...
double room	一間 雙人房	yījiān shuāngrénfáng
single room	一間 單人房	yījiān dānrénfáng
to share a dorm	住宿舍	zhù sùshè

How much is it ...?	... 多少 錢?	... duōshǎo qián?
per night	一個 晚上	Yīge wǎnshàng
per person	每個人	Měigerén

DIRECTIONS

Where is (the) ...?
... 在哪裡? ... zài nǎlǐ?

What is the address?
地址在哪裡? Dìzhǐ zài nǎlǐ?

Could you write the address, please?
能不能請你把地址寫下來? Néngbùnéng qǐng nǐ bǎ dìzhǐ xiě xiàlái?

Could you show me (on the map)?
你能不能(在地圖上)指給我看? Nǐ néng bùnéng (zài dìtú shàng) zhǐ gěi wǒ kàn?

Go straight ahead.
一直走. Yīzhí zǒu.

at the next corner
在下一個轉角 zài xià yīge zhuǎnjiǎo

at the traffic lights
在紅綠燈 zài hónglǜdēng

SIGNS

入口	Entrance
出口	Exit
詢問處	Information
開	Open
關	Closed
禁止	Prohibited
廁所	Toilets
男	Men
女	Women

behind	後面	hòumiàn
far	遠	yuǎn
in front of	前面	qiánmiàn
near	近	jìn
opposite	對面	duìmiàn
Turn left.	左轉.	Zuǒ zhuǎn.
Turn right.	右轉.	Yòu zhuǎn.

EATING & DRINKING

I'm vegetarian.
我吃素. Wǒ chī sù.

I don't want MSG.
我不要味精. Wǒ bú yào wèijīng.

Not too spicy.
不要太辣. Bú yào tài là.

Let's eat.
吃飯. Chī fàn.

Cheers!
乾杯! Gānbēi!

KEY WORDS

bill (check)	買單/結帳	mǎidān/jiézhàng
chopsticks	筷子	kuàizi
cold	冰的	bīngde
fork	叉子	chāzi
hot	熱的	rède
knife	刀子	dāozi
menu	菜單	càidān
set meal (no menu)	套餐	tàocān
spoon	調羹/湯匙	tiáogēng/tāngchí

TAIWANESE DISHES

clear oyster soup with ginger	蚵仔湯	kézǎi tāng
coffin cakes	棺材板	guāncái bǎn
congealed pig's blood	豬血糕	zhū xiě gāo
oyster omelette	蚵仔煎	ô-á-chian
stinky tofu	臭豆腐	chòu dòufu
tea egg	茶葉蛋	cháyè dàn
turnip cake	蘿蔔糕	luóbuó gāo

BREAD, BUNS & DUMPLINGS

baked layered flatbread	燒餅	shāobing
boiled dumplings	水餃	shuǐjiǎo
pot stickers/ pan-grilled dumplings	鍋貼	guōtiē
steamed buns	饅頭	mántou
steamed meat buns & meat sauce	小籠湯包	xiǎo lóng tāng bāo
steamed vegetable buns	素菜包子	sùcài bāozi

SOUP

clam & turnip soup	蛤蠣湯	gě lì tāng
cuttlefish potage	魷魚羹	yóu yú gēng
hot and sour soup	酸辣湯	suānlà tāng
soup	湯	tāng
Taiwanese meatball soup	貢丸湯	gòng wán tāng
wonton soup	餛飩湯	húntún tāng

NOODLE DISHES

bean & mince-meat noodles	炸醬麵	zhájiàng miàn
fried noodles with pork	肉絲炒麵	ròusī chǎomiàn
fried noodles with vegetables	蔬菜炒麵	shūcai chǎomiàn
noodles (not in soup)	乾麵	gān miàn
noodles (in soup)	湯麵	tāngmiàn
sesame-paste noodles	麻醬麵	májiàng miàn
soupy beef noodles	牛肉麵	niúròu miàn
soupy noodles with chicken	雞絲湯麵	jīsī tāngmiàn
wonton with noodles	餛飩麵	húntún miàn

RICE DISHES

fried rice with chicken	雞肉炒飯	jīròu chǎofàn
fried rice with egg	蛋炒飯	dàn chǎofàn
fried rice with vegetables	蔬菜炒飯	shūcài chǎofàn
steamed white rice	白飯	báifàn
sticky rice	筒仔米糕	tǒngzǎi mǐgāo
watery rice porridge (congee)	稀飯/粥	xīfàn/zhōu

PORK DISHES

deep-fried pork chop with rice	炸排骨飯	zhà páigǔ fàn
deep-fried pork-mince buns	肉圓	ròu yuán
diced pork with soy sauce	醬爆肉丁	jiàngbào ròudīng
pork mince in soy sauce with rice	魯肉飯	lǔròu fàn
sweet and sour pork	咕嚕肉	gūlū ròu

BEEF DISHES

beef braised in soy sauce	紅燒牛肉	hóngshāo niúròu
beef steak platter	鐵板牛肉	tiěbǎn niúròu
beef with rice	牛肉飯	niúròu fàn

POULTRY DISHES

diced chicken braised in soy sauce	紅燒雞塊	hóngshāo jīkuài
diced chicken in oyster sauce	蠔油雞塊	háoyóu jīkuài
sweet and sour chicken	糖醋雞丁	tángcù jīdīng
congealed duck blood	鴨血糕	yāxiě gāo
duck with rice	鴨肉飯	yāròu fàn

SEAFOOD DISHES

clams	蛤蠣	gélì
crab	螃蟹	pángxiè
diced shrimp with peanuts	宮爆蝦仁	gōngbào xiārén
fish braised in soy sauce	紅燒魚	hóngshāo yú
lobster	龍蝦	lóngxiā
octopus	章魚	zhāngyú
squid	魷魚	yóuyú

QUESTION WORDS

How?	怎麼?	Zěnme?
What?	什麼?	Shénme?
When?	什麼時候?	Shénme shíhòu?
Where?	在哪裡?	Zài nǎlǐ?
Which?	哪個?	Nǎge?
Who?	誰?	Shéi?

VEGETABLE & TOFU DISHES

clay pot tofu	砂鍋豆腐	shāguō dòufu
omelette with pickled radishes	菜脯蛋	càifǔ dàn
smoked tofu	滷水豆腐	lǔshǔi dòufu
sweet and sour lotus root cakes	糖蓮藕	táng liánǒu
tofu	豆腐	dòufu

DRINKS

beer	啤酒	píjiǔ
black tea	紅茶	hóng chá
coconut juice	椰子汁	yēzi zhī
coffee	咖啡	kāfēi
green tea	綠茶	lǜ chá
Kaoliang liquor	高梁酒	gāoliáng jiǔ
jasmine tea	茉莉花茶	mòlìhuā chá
milk	牛奶	niúnǎi
milk tea with tapioca balls	珍珠奶茶	zhēnzhū nǎi chá
mineral water	礦泉水	kuàngquán shuǐ
oolong tea	烏龍茶	wūlóng chá
orange juice	柳丁汁	liǔdīng zhī
red wine	紅葡萄酒	hóng pútao jiǔ
rice wine	米酒	mǐjiǔ
soft drink	汽水	qìshuǐ
soybean milk	豆漿	dòujiāng
tea	茶	chá
water	水	shuǐ
white wine	白葡萄酒	bái pútao jiǔ

EMERGENCIES

Help!	救命啊!	Jiùmìng a!
I'm lost.	我迷路了.	Wǒ mílùle.
Leave me alone!	別煩我!	Bié fán wǒ!

Call ...!	請叫 ...!	Qǐng jiào ...!
a doctor	醫生	yīshēng
the police	警察	jǐngchá

There's been an accident.
發生意外了. Fāshēng yìwài le.

NUMBERS

1	一	yī
2	二, 兩	èr, liăng
3	三	sān
4	四	sì
5	五	wŭ
6	六	liù
7	七	qī
8	八	bā
9	九	jiŭ
10	十	shí
20	二十	èrshí
30	三十	sānshí
40	四十	sìshí
50	五十	wŭshí
60	六十	liùshí
70	七十	qīshí
80	八十	bāshí
90	九十	jiŭshí
100	一百	yībăi
1000	一千	yìqiān

I'm ill.
我生病了. Wŏ shēngbìngle.

It hurts here.
這裡痛. Zhèlĭ tòng.

I'm allergic to (antibiotics).
我對(抗生素)過敏. Wŏ duì (kàngshēngsù) guòmĭn.

SHOPPING & SERVICES

I'd like to buy ...
我想買 ... Wŏ xiăng măi ...

I'm just looking.
我只是看看. Wŏ zhĭshì kànkan.

Can I see it?
能看看嗎? Néng kànkàn ma?

I don't like it.
我不喜歡. Wŏ bù xĭhuān.

How much is it?
多少錢? Duōshăo qián?

That's too expensive.
太貴了. Tài guìle.

Is there anything cheaper?
有便宜一點的嗎? Yŏu piányí yīdiăn de ma?

Do you accept credit cards?
收不收信用卡? Shōu bùshōu xìnyòngkă?

Where can I get online?
我在哪裡可以上網? Wŏ zài nălĭ kěyĭ shàngwăng?

I'm looking for ...	我在找 ...	Wă zài zhăo ...
an ATM	自動櫃員機/提款機	zìdòng guìyuánjī/tíkuănjī
the post office	郵局	yóujú
the tourist office	觀光局	guānguāngjú

TIME & DATES

What's the time?	幾點?	Jĭ diăn?
... hour	... 點	... diăn
... minute	... 分	... fēn
in the morning	早上	zăoshàng
in the afternoon	下午	xiàwŭ
in the evening	晚上	wănshàng
yesterday	昨天	zuótiān
today	今天	jīntiān
tomorrow	明天	míngtiān

Monday	星期一	Xīngqíyī
Tuesday	星期二	Xīngqí'èr
Wednesday	星期三	Xīngqísān
Thursday	星期四	Xīngqísì
Friday	星期五	Xīngqíwŭ
Saturday	星期六	Xīngqíliù
Sunday	星期天	Xīngqítiān

January	一月	Yīyuè
February	二月	Èryuè
March	三月	Sānyuè
April	四月	Sìyuè
May	五月	Wŭyuè
June	六月	Liùyuè
July	七月	Qīyuè
August	八月	Bāyuè
September	九月	Jiŭyuè
October	十月	Shíyuè
November	十一月	Shíyīyuè
December	十二月	Shí'èryuè

TRANSPORT

PUBLIC TRANSPORT

What time does the ... leave/arrive?	...幾點開/到?	... jĭdiăn kāi/dào?
boat	船	chuán
city bus	公車	gōngchē

intercity bus	客運	kèyùn
minibus	小型公車	xiǎoxíng gōngchē
plane	飛機	fēijī
train	火車	huǒchē

I'd like a ... ticket.	我要一張...票.	Wǒ yào yìzhāng ... piào
one-way	單程	dānchéng
platform	月台票	yuètái piào
return	來回	láihuí

I want to go to ...
我要去 ... Wǒ yào qù ...

The train has been delayed/cancelled.
火車(晚點了/取消了). Huǒchē (wǎndiǎn le/qǔxiāo le).

When's the ... bus?	... 班車什麼時候來?	... bānchē shénme shíhòu lái?
first	頭	tóu
last	末	mò
next	下	xià

airport	機場	jīchǎng
left-luggage room	寄放處	jìfàng chù
long-distance bus station	客運站	kèyùn zhàn
platform number	月台號碼	yuètái hàomǎ
subway (underground)	捷運	jíeyùn
subway station	捷運站	jíeyùn zhàn
ticket office	售票處	shòupiào chù
timetable	時刻表	shíkèbiǎo
train station	火車站	huǒchē zhàn

DRIVING & CYCLING

I'd like to hire a ...	我要租一輛 ...	Wǒ yào zū yíliàng ...
bicycle	腳踏車	jiǎotàchē
car	汽車	qìchē
motorcycle	摩托車	mótuōchē

diesel	柴油	cháiyóu
petrol	汽油	qìyóu

Does this road lead to ...?
這條路到 ... 嗎? Zhè tiáo lù dào ... ma?

Where's the next service station?
下一個加油站在哪裡? Xià yíge jiāyóuzhàn zài nǎlǐ?

Can I park here?
這裡可以停車嗎? Zhèlǐ kěyǐ tíngchē ma?

How long can I park here?
這裡可以停多久? Zhèlǐ kěyǐ tíng duōjiǔ?

I need a mechanic.
我需要汽車維修員. Wǒ xūyào qìchē wéixiūyuán.

The car has broken down (at ...).
車子 (在⋯) 拋錨了. Chēzi (zài ...) pāomáo le.

I have a flat tyre.
輪胎破了. Lúntāi pòle.

I've run out of petrol.
没有汽油了. Méiyǒu qìyóu le.

GLOSSARY

aborigines *(yuánzhùmín)* – the original residents of Taiwan, of which there are currently 14 recognised tribes; believed to be the ancestors of all Austronesian people

Amis – Taiwan's largest aboriginal tribe; lives on the coastal plains of eastern Taiwan

ARC – Alien Resident Certificate; foreign visitors must apply for one if planning to stay for long-term work or study

Atayal – Taiwan's second-largest aboriginal tribe; lives in mountainous regions of the north

Bao chung – type of oolong tea grown around Pinglin

Běnshěngrén – Taiwanese people whose ancestors came to Taiwan prior to 1949

Bunun – Taiwan's third-largest aboriginal tribe; lives in Central Mountains

chá – tea, especially Chinese tea

Chu-kuang *(Jǔguāng)* – 2nd-class regular train

cochin pottery (also *koji*) – colourful decorative art for temples

congee – rice porridge

cūn – village

dàgēdà (literally 'big-brother-big') – mobile phone

dǒugǒng – special bracketing system for Chinese architecture

DPP – Democratic Progressive Party; Taiwan's first opposition party

fēnxiāng – spirit division, or the process by which branch temples are founded

Forest Recreation Area – similar to a state or provincial park in the West

Fujianese – people originally from Fujian province in China who migrated to Taiwan; the Taiwanese dialect is derived from that of southern Fujian

Fu-hsing *(fùxīng)* – 2nd-class regular train

gǎng – harbour/port

gōng – Taoist temple

Hakka – nomadic subset of the Han Chinese, the Hakka were among the first Chinese to settle in Taiwan; many prominent Taiwanese are also Hakka people

Hanyu Pinyin – system of Romanisation used in mainland China; though there is some crossover, most signs in Taiwan outside Taipei use the *Tongyong Pinyin* or *Wade-Giles* systems

HSR – High Speed Rail, Taiwan's 'bullet train'

Ilha Formosa – the name Portuguese sailors gave Taiwan, meaning 'beautiful island'

jiǎnniàn – mosaic-like temple decoration

jiǎotàchē zhuānyòng dào – bike path

jié – festival

jiē – street

Kaoliang – sorghum liquor; made in Matsu and Kinmen

KMRT – Kaohsiung's MRT system

KMT – Kuomintang; Nationalist Party of the Republic of China

líng – divine efficaciousness; a god's power to grant wishes

Lu Tung Pin – one of the eight immortals of classical Chinese mythology; couples avoid his temples as he likes to break up happy lovers

Matsu *(Māzǔ)* – Goddess of the Sea, the most popular deity in Taiwan; also the name of one of the Taiwan Strait Islands

miào – general word for temple

Minnan – used to refer to the language, people, architecture etc of southern China (especially Fujian)

mínsù – B&B, homestay

mountain permit – special permit you pick up from local police stations to allow you to enter restricted mountainous areas

MRT – Mass Rapid Transit; Taipei's underground railway system

National Trail System – a system of hiking trails running over the entire island

One China – the idea that mainland China and Taiwan are both part of one country: People's Republic of China

oolong (also *wulong*) – semi-fermented tea

opera (Taiwanese) – also known as Beijing or Chinese opera, an art form that has been an important part of Chinese culture for more than 900 years

Oriental Beauty – heavily fermented tea, first grown in Taiwan

Paiwan – small aboriginal tribe; lives south of Pingtung

PFP (People First Party); offshoot of *KMT* started by James Soong

PRC – People's Republic of China

pùbù – waterfall

Puyuma – small aboriginal tribe; lives on Taiwan's southeast coast

qiáo – bridge

qū – district/area

ROC – Republic of China; covered all of China before the *PRC* was established

Rukai – small aboriginal tribe; lives on Taiwan's southeast coast

Saisiyat – very small aboriginal tribe; lives in mountains of Miaoli County

Sakizaya – very small aboriginal tribe; lives around Hualien

Sediq – small aboriginal tribe; lives in Nantou

sēnlín – forest

shān – mountain

sì – Buddhist temple

Sinicism – Chinese method or customs

suòxī – river tracing; sport that involves walking up rivers with the aid of nonslip shoes

taichi – slow-motion martial art

Taipeiers – people from Taipei

Taroko – a sub-branch of the aboriginal Atayal tribe, recognised in 2004

Thao – very small aboriginal tribe; lives around Sun Moon Lake

Three Small Links – the opening of cross-Strait trade between China and Taiwan's offshore islands

Tieguanyin (Iron Goddess of Compassion) – type of oolong tea

tongpu – a type of multi-person room with no beds, just blankets and floor mats

Tongyong Pinyin – system of Romanisation used in parts of Taiwan

Truku – small aboriginal Atayal tribe; lives around Hualien

Tsou – small aboriginal tribe; lives around Kaohsiung

Tze-Chiang (*Zìqiáng*) – the fastest and most comfortable regular train

VAT – Value-Added Tax

Wade-Giles – a Romanisation system for Chinese words; widely used until the introduction of *Hanyu Pinyin*

Wàishěngrén – Taiwanese who emigrated from mainland China following the *KMT* defeat in the Chinese civil war

Wang Yeh – a Tang-dynasty scholar, said to watch over the waters of southern China; worshipped all over the south

wēnquán – hot spring

White Terror – a large-scale campaign started by the *KMT* to purge the island of political activists during the 1950s; one of the grimmest times in Taiwan's martial-law period

xiàng – lane

Yami – A small aboriginal tribe inhabiting Lanyu Island

yèshì – night market

zhàn – station

Behind the Scenes

SEND US YOUR FEEDBACK

We love to hear from travellers – your comments keep us on our toes and help make our books better. Our well-travelled team reads every word on what you loved or loathed about this book. Although we cannot reply individually to postal submissions, we always guarantee that your feedback goes straight to the appropriate authors, in time for the next edition. Each person who sends us information is thanked in the next edition – the most useful submissions are rewarded with a selection of digital PDF chapters.

Visit **lonelyplanet.com/contact** to submit your updates and suggestions or to ask for help. Our award-winning website also features inspirational travel stories, news and discussions.

Note: We may edit, reproduce and incorporate your comments in Lonely Planet products such as guidebooks, websites and digital products, so let us know if you don't want your comments reproduced or your name acknowledged. For a copy of our privacy policy visit lonelyplanet.com/privacy.

OUR READERS

Many thanks to the travellers who used the last edition and wrote to us with helpful hints, useful advice and interesting anecdotes:

Anders Abrahamsson, Hanna Abrahamsson, Katarina Abrahamsson, Ludovic Boulicaut, Peter Calingaert, Haw-Bin Chai, Chi Ming Chen, Gene Chiang, Peter Cudmore, Faye Duns, Saskia Fikke, Justin Fisch, Gavin Fisher, Olivia Floros, George Fogh, Susan Forte, John Fotheringham, Erik Futtrup, Damien Le Gal, Stanislaw Gasik, Martin Hellwagner, Eddie Joseph, Robert Kisler, A Schuurman-Kleijberg, Stephen Lerman, Jaime Melanson, Jenny Moon, Allan Moon, Noel Nicholls, Vanessa Nolan, Jan Novak, John Pasley, Art Poirier, David Prentice, Susanne Schick, Pietro Schisler, Kai Schmitz, E Schuurman, Wanda Serkowska, Jorieke Sluiter, Johan Smeets, Francine Guerrette-Smith, Rachel Snyder, Estela Teng, S Thomson. Ulbe Tolner, Yen-Ping Tsao, Nerissa Wong-VanHaren, Catherine Waters, Esther Wong, Chien-Hao Wu, Yang Ye, Tim Yu

AUTHOR THANKS

Robert Kelly

This book is dedicated first to Tania Simonetti, the loving anchor of my life. A big hi to Ping and the Bear, faithful companions to the end. Here's to Will Ryan, who kept my back straight and healthy through the endless days of writing. Chris Nelson, thanks for all the dinners, buddy! To my partners at TEA, here's to great things in the future. And finally, thanks to Richard Foster for coming through at the end as I knew he would.

Chung Wah Chow

Robert Kelly and Kathleen Munnelly gave me expert advice and extended deadlines, for which I am extremely grateful. A big bucket of thanks goes out to my dear friend Chang Yun Chih – your help makes this book possible. Huge thanks also to mountaineering gurus Li Chia San and Lee Yu Ching, for your invaluable tips and insights. Fellow travellers Griet Dierckxsens and Andre de Bree: I enjoyed your great company. Very special thanks are reserved, as always, for Haider Kikabhoy.

ACKNOWLEDGMENTS

Climate map data adapted from Peel MC, Finlayson BL & McMahon TA (2007) 'Updated World Map of the Köppen-Geiger Climate Classification', Hydrology and Earth System Sciences, 11, 1633¬44.

Taipei metro system map © 2013 Taipei Rapid Transit Corporation.

Cover photograph: Taipei's skyline, including Taipei 101, Marc Dozier/Alamy.

THIS BOOK

This 9th edition of Lonely Planet's *Taiwan* guidebook was researched and written by Robert Kelly and Chung Wah Chow. The previous two editions were written by Robert Kelly and Joshua Samuel Brown. This guidebook was commissioned in Lonely Planet's Oakland office, and produced by the following:

Commissioning Editor Kathleen Munnelly

Coordinating Editors Gabrielle Innes, Luna Soo

Senior Cartographers Diana Von Holdt, Julie Sheridan

Book Designer Lauren Egan

Managing Editors Martine Power, Angela Tinson

Senior Editor Catherine Naghten

Assisting Editors Janice Bird, Adrienne Costanzo, Ali Lemer, Jenna Myers

Assisting Cartographers Mick Garrett, Eve Kelly, Alison Lyall

Cover Research Naomi Parker

Language Content Branislava Vladisavljevic

Thanks to Anita Banh, Sasha Baskett, Ryan Evans, Samantha Forge, Larissa Frost, Genesys India, Jouve India, Indra Kilfoyle, Katherine Marsh, Wayne Murphy, Trent Paton, Phillip Tang, John Taufa, Gerard Walker, Juan Winata

Index

Map Pages **000**
Photo Pages **000**

Map Pages **000**
Photo Pages **000**

Map Pages **000**
Photo Pages **000**

Map Pages **000**
Photo Pages **000**

Map Legend

Sights
- Beach
- Buddhist
- Castle
- Christian
- Hindu
- Islamic
- Jewish
- Monument
- Museum/Gallery
- Ruin
- Winery/Vineyard
- Zoo
- Other Sight

Activities, Courses & Tours
- Diving/Snorkelling
- Canoeing/Kayaking
- Skiing
- Surfing
- Swimming/Pool
- Walking
- Windsurfing
- Other Activity/Course/Tour

Sleeping
- Sleeping
- Camping

Eating
- Eating

Drinking
- Drinking
- Cafe

Entertainment
- Entertainment

Shopping
- Shopping

Information
- Bank
- Embassy/Consulate
- Hospital/Medical
- Internet
- Police
- Post Office
- Telephone
- Toilet
- Tourist Information
- Other Information

Transport
- Airport
- Border Crossing
- Bus
- Cable Car/Funicular
- Cycling
- Ferry
- Monorail
- Parking
- Petrol Station
- Taxi
- Train/Railway
- Tram
- Underground Train Station
- Other Transport

Routes
- Tollway
- Freeway
- Primary
- Secondary
- Tertiary
- Lane
- Unsealed Road
- Plaza/Mall
- Steps
- Tunnel
- Pedestrian Overpass
- Walking Tour
- Walking Tour Detour
- Path

Geographic
- Hut/Shelter
- Lighthouse
- Lookout
- Mountain/Volcano
- Oasis
- Park
- Pass
- Picnic Area
- Waterfall

Population
- Capital (National)
- Capital (State/Province)
- City/Large Town
- Town/Village

Boundaries
- International
- State/Province
- Disputed
- Regional/Suburb
- Marine Park
- Cliff
- Wall

Hydrography
- River, Creek
- Intermittent River
- Swamp/Mangrove
- Reef
- Canal
- Water
- Dry/Salt/Intermittent Lake
- Glacier

Areas
- Beach/Desert
- Cemetery (Christian)
- Cemetery (Other)
- Park/Forest
- Sportsground
- Sight (Building)
- Top Sight (Building)

OUR STORY

A beat-up old car, a few dollars in the pocket and a sense of adventure. In 1972 that's all Tony and Maureen Wheeler needed for the trip of a lifetime – across Europe and Asia overland to Australia. It took several months, and at the end – broke but inspired – they sat at their kitchen table writing and stapling together their first travel guide, *Across Asia on the Cheap*. Within a week they'd sold 1500 copies. Lonely Planet was born.

Today, Lonely Planet has offices in Melbourne, London and Oakland, with more than 600 staff and writers. We share Tony's belief that 'a great guidebook should do three things: inform, educate and amuse'.

OUR WRITERS

Robert Kelly

Coordinating Author; Taipei, Northern Taiwan, Taroko National Park & the East Coast Robert Kelly has been living in Taiwan continuously since 1996 and to say this place is now home would be quite the understatement. This permanent resident has helmed the *Taiwan* guidebook three times now (his ninth title for Lonely Planet), and has written about the Beautiful Isle, and other topics, for publishers such as the BBC, Wall Street Journal and The South China Morning Post. An avid hiker, cyclist and road-trip enthusiast, there are precious few places on this island he hasn't been (and even fewer he wouldn't go back to in a second). Robert is currently writing the script for a documentary on Taiwan's outstanding but little-known temple arts.

Chung Wah Chow

Yushan National Park & Western Taiwan, Southern Taiwan, Taiwan's Islands From her base in Hong Kong, Chung Wah can't help but be repeatedly lured back to Taiwan, where she spends part of every year revelling in its wonderful landscape and culture. Researching this book provided her with the opportunity to join many colourful, only-in-Taiwan festivities and hop over to some of the country's most beautiful islands. Chung Wah has previously co-authored other Lonely Planet titles, including ones on China and Hong Kong.

Chung Wah also wrote the Eat & Drink Like a Local, Religion in Taiwan, The Landscape of Taiwan and Taiwan Wildlife Guide chapters.

Read more about Chung Wah Chow at:
lonelyplanet.com/members/cwchow

Published by Lonely Planet Publications Pty Ltd
ABN 36 005 607 983
9th edition – Mar 2014
ISBN 978 1 74220 135 1

10 9 8 7 6 5 4 3 2
Printed in Singapore